An Introduction to Theory of Computation

Mitsunori Ogihara

An Introduction to Theory of Computation

An Algorithmic Exploration

 Springer

Mitsunori Ogihara
University of Miami
Coral Gables, FL, USA

ISBN 978-3-031-84739-4   ISBN 978-3-031-84740-0   (eBook)
https://doi.org/10.1007/978-3-031-84740-0

This Springer imprint is published by the registered company Springer Nature Switzerland AG
The registered company address is: Gewerbestrasse 11, 6330 Cham, Switzerland

If disposing of this product, please recycle the paper.

To my family

Preface

I conceived the idea of writing this book in 2018 when I taught an undergraduate Theory of Computation course at the University of Miami. I used a popular textbook for the course, but felt that incorporating results not appearing in the book could make the learning experience more interesting. That feeling prompted me to start writing this book, but it took me several years to complete it. Since the number of pages in a textbook cannot be too large, the amount of materials I could add to the book was limited. A short list of the materials not appearing as frequently in undergraduate theory textbooks is as follows:

- The Myhill-Nerode Theorem and its use for proving non-regularity of languages (Chap. 3)
- Constructing Chomsky Normal Form grammars with a quadratic size increase (Chap. 4)
- Constructing Greibach Normal Form grammars (Chap. 4)
- An inherently ambiguous language and a proof of its inherent ambiguity (Chap. 4)
- Ogden's and Pumping Lemmas for context-free languages using pushdown automata as the computation model (Chap. 5)
- The undecidability of the Context-Free Language's totality problem (Chap. 8)
- The undecidability of the inherent ambiguity problem (Chap. 8)
- The two-tape time-efficient simulation by Hennie and Stearns (Chap. 9)
- Time-constructibility (Chap. 9)
- Separations of deterministic time complexity classes based on the Time Hierarchy Theorems (Chap. 9)
- The Space Hierarchy Theorem (Chap. 10)
- Ladner's Theorem, which shows that if $P \neq NP$, then there is a language that is neither NP-complete nor polynomial-time decidable (Chap. 12)
- The membership of Bounded Probabilistic Polynomial Time in the Polynomial Hierarchy (Chap. 13) and in P/poly (Chap. 14)
- The Isolation Lemma (Chap. 14)
- $NL \subseteq UL/poly$ (Chap. 14)

Some of the proofs presented in this book are long or complex. I have attached a proof overview to each lemma and theorem that is complex or long. A reader may choose to read an overview before reading its accompanying full proof.

Additionally, an appendix of this book has a list of major results that are grouped according to their types. A reader may consult with the appendix to know where to find results.

I hope the reader will find studying with this book to be interesting. If you have comments and corrections, please feel free to reach out to me.

I would like to thank the Springer team for granting me the opportunity to publish this book, as well as technical help with resolving issues in LaTeX formatting.

I would like to thank Ashwin Lall, Ryan Lin, Kevin Ma, Hawken Rives, Burt Rosenberg, and Melanie Xia for their helpful comments. My biggest thanks go to Ellen Ogihara, who proofread the entire book and provided valuable suggestions to me. Finally, this project was supported in part by the National Science Foundation Award NSF-CNS-2310807.

Coral Gables, FL, USA   Mitsunori Ogihara
2025

Contents

Part I   Preparation

1   Mathematics and Computer Science Basics 3
1.1   Sets 3
    1.1.1   Set Operations 4
1.2   Boolean Algebra 5
    1.2.1   Implication and Equivalence 6
    1.2.2   Predicates 7
    1.2.3   Truth Assignments and Quantifications 8
1.3   Functions 8
    1.3.1   Big-O Notation 9
1.4   Languages 9
    1.4.1   Alphabets and Strings 10
    1.4.2   Languages and Their Classes 10
1.5   Graphs and Trees 11
    1.5.1   Directed Graphs 11
    1.5.2   Reachability 12
    1.5.3   Undirected Graphs 13
    1.5.4   Trees 14
1.6   Proof Methods 15
1.7   Algorithmic Concepts 17

Part II   Formal Language Theory and Automata

2   The Regular Languages 23
2.1   The Finite Automaton (DFA) Model 23
    2.1.1   The Definition 24
    2.1.2   Example DFAs 26
2.2   The Nondeterministic Finite Automaton (NFA) Model 30
    2.2.1   The Definition 30
    2.2.2   Converting NFAs to DFAs 34

        2.2.3   Constructing Regular Languages from Other
                  Regular Languages..   40
  2.3   Regular Expressions   44
        2.3.1   The Definition..   44
        2.3.2   Equivalence Between Regular Expressions and NFAs ...   45
        2.3.3   Visualizing the Construction   50
  References..   56

3   Non-regularity   57
  3.1   Minimizing the State Number.....................................   57
        3.1.1   A Motivation   57
        3.1.2   Distinguishable State-Pairs   57
  3.2   The Myhill-Nerode Theorem   62
  3.3   Proving Non-regularity...   64
        3.3.1   Proving Non-regularity Using the
                  Myhill-Nerode Theorem....................................   64
        3.3.2   Proving Non-regularity Using the Pumping
                  Lemma for Regular Languages...........................   65
        3.3.3   Proving Non-regularity Using Closure Properties........   68
  References..   72

4   The Context-Free Languages...   73
  4.1   The Context-Free Grammar (CFG)   73
        4.1.1   The Definition..   73
        4.1.2   Examples of CFGs   74
        4.1.3   Production Trees   77
        4.1.4   Leftmost and Rightmost Productions   78
        4.1.5   Closure Properties of CFLs..............................   79
  4.2   Normal Forms of CFGs   80
        4.2.1   The Chomsky Normal Form (CNF) Grammars   80
        4.2.2   Normalizing CFGs to CNF Grammars...................   82
        4.2.3   The Greibach Normal Form (GNF) Grammars..........   87
  References..   93

5   The Pushdown Automaton Model   95
  5.1   The Pushdown Automaton (PDA) Model   95
        5.1.1   The Definition..   95
        5.1.2   Examples of PDAs   97
  5.2   Equivalence Between CFLs and PDAs 101
  5.3   The Deterministic Pushdown Automaton (DPDA) Model 108
  5.4   Proving Non-context-Freeness 111
        5.4.1   The Pumping Lemma for CFLs 111
        5.4.2   Inherent Ambiguity of CFLs 114
        5.4.3   Non-context-Free Languages............................. 117
        5.4.4   Ogden's Lemma... 118

5.4.5 Proving Ogden's Lemma by Analyzing a PDA's
Behavior 121
References.. 131

Part III Undecidability and Turing Machines

6 The Turing Machines 135
6.1 The Turing Machine (TM) Model 135
6.1.1 The Definition 135
6.1.2 Examples of TMs 138
6.1.3 Instantaneous Descriptions 141
6.1.4 Fundamental Subroutines................................. 145
6.2 The Multi-tape TM Model 149
6.2.1 The Definition 149
6.2.2 Examples of Multi-tape TMs............................. 150
6.2.3 Simulating Multi-tape TMs Using Single-Tape TMs 152
6.3 The Nondeterministic Turing Machine (NTM) Model 157
6.4 Alternate Definitions of RE 162
6.4.1 Enumerators 162
6.4.2 Witness Schemes... 164
6.5 Computing Functions Using TMs and the Church-Turing
Thesis.. 165
References.. 169

7 Decidable Languages 171
7.1 The Universal TM Model 171
7.1.1 Encoding Schemes 171
7.1.2 Fundamental Problems 172
7.1.3 Using Universal TMs 174
7.2 Decidable Fundamental Problems 175
7.2.1 Decidable Problems About Regular Languages 175
7.2.2 Decidable Problems About CFLs 181
References.. 184

8 Undecidable Languages 185
8.1 The Halting Problem 185
8.1.1 Proving Impossibility Using Diagonalization 185
8.1.2 The Halting Problem....................................... 187
8.1.3 Some Variants of the Halting Problem 188
8.2 Many-One Reductions and Rice's Theorem....................... 188
8.2.1 Many-One Reductions 189
8.2.2 Rice's Theorem 190
8.3 Undecidable Problems About CFLs 191
8.3.1 The Totality Problem About CFLs 191

        8.3.2   Undecidable Problems About DCFLs   193
    8.4   Post's Correspondence Problem (PCP)   195
        8.4.1   The Definitions of PCP and MPCP   195
        8.4.2   The Undecidability of MPCP............................   196
        8.4.3   The Undecidability of PCP   202
    8.5   Beyond RE   203
    References...   210

**Part IV   Computational Complexity and Resource-Bounded
             Turing Machine Computation**

9   The Time Complexity   215
    9.1   The Time Complexity Measure   215
    9.2   Time-Efficient Simulations of Multi-tape TMs   220
        9.2.1   Simulating with One Tape   220
        9.2.2   Simulating with Two Tapes..............................   221
    9.3   The Time Hierarchy Theorems   230
    9.4   The Nondeterministic Time Complexity   233
    9.5   Fundamental Time Complexity Classes   234
    9.6   Examples of Time Complexity Classifications   236
        9.6.1   The DFA State Minimization Problem....................   236
        9.6.2   The Problem of Converting an NFA to a Regular
                 Expression   238
        9.6.3   The CFL Membership Problem   239
    References...   243

10   The Space Complexity   245
    10.1   The Space Complexity Measure   245
    10.2   Savitch's Theorem   248
    10.3   Fundamental Space Complexity Classes   250
    10.4   The Reachability Problem...   252
    10.5   Examples of Space Complexity Classifications   257
    References...   261

11   The Theory of NP-Completeness   263
    11.1   The Polynomial-Time Many-One Reducibility   263
        11.1.1   The Definition...   263
        11.1.2   The Definition of NP-Complete Languages   265
        11.1.3   A Canonical NP-Complete Language....................   266
        11.1.4   Polynomial-Time Witness Schemes......................   267
    11.2   The Satisfiability Problem (SAT)   268
        11.2.1   The NP-Completeness of SAT   268
        11.2.2   NP-Complete Variants of SAT   270
        11.2.3   Some Complete Problems for coNP   273
    11.3   Fundamental NP-Complete Problems   274
        11.3.1   The Clique Problem.......................................   274

	11.3.2	The Vertex Cover Problem	276
	11.3.3	The 3-Coloring Problem	279
	11.3.4	The Hamilton Path Problem	280
	11.3.5	NP-Completes Problems About Integers	284
	11.3.6	NP-Complete Problems About Matching and Set Partitioning	287
	11.3.7	More Examples of NP-Complete Problems	289
	References		293

12 Beyond NP-Completeness 295

12.1	The Complexity of Finding a Witness	295
12.2	The Polynomial-Time Turing Reducibility	298
	12.2.1	The Problem of Finding the Least Satisfying Assignment	299
12.3	The Polynomial Hierarchy (PH)	303
	12.3.1	The Definition	303
	12.3.2	Logical Characterizations of PH	304
12.4	Between P and NP-Complete	309
	12.4.1	Two Enumerations of TMs	310
	12.4.2	T's Program	311
	12.4.3	T's Running Time	312
	12.4.4	t's Range and Its Non-decreasing Property	312
	12.4.5	t's Unboundedness	313
	12.4.6	The Final Touch	313
12.5	PSPACE-Complete Problems	314
	12.5.1	Quantified Boolean Formulas (QBF)	314
	12.5.2	Games and Winning Strategies	316
	12.5.3	The Geography Game	317
	References		322

Part V   Advanced Topics in Computational Complexity Theory

13 The Probabilistic Polynomial-Time Classes 325

13.1	The Probabilistic Turing Machine Model	325
	13.1.1	The Definition	325
13.2	Primality Testing Algorithms	328
	13.2.1	Number Theory Basics	328
	13.2.2	The Miller-Rabin Test	334
	13.2.3	The Polynomial Zero-Testing Problem	340
13.3	Relations Between BPP and PH	341
13.4	The Class PP	343
	References		345

14 Circuit Complexity and Unambiguity 347

| 14.1 | The Circuit Computation Models | 347 |
| | 14.1.1 | The Boolean Circuit Model | 347 |

14.1.2 Relations Between Boolean Circuit-Based
Classes and TM-Based Classes............................ 350
14.1.3 The Arithmetic Circuit Model............................ 352
14.2 The Class P/poly 352
14.3 Unambiguous Accepting Computation Paths of NTMs 355
References... 361

A A List of Major Results 363
A.1 Characterizations of Language Classes............................ 363
A.2 Relations Between Language Classes 364
A.3 Closure Properties of Language Classes........................... 365
A.4 Non-closure Properties of Language Classes...................... 366
A.5 Classifications of Specific Languages 366
A.6 Polynomial-Time Many-One and Witness Reductions 368
A.7 Pumping Lemmas 369
A.8 Normalization and Behavior of Computing Objects 369
A.9 Time and Space Constructibility 370
A.10 Number and Probability Theories.................................. 371

Index.. 373

List of Figures

Fig. 1.1   The fundamental set operations... 5
Fig. 1.2   An example of a directed graph 11
Fig. 1.3   An acyclic graph... 12
Fig. 1.4   A connected component.. 13
Fig. 1.5   An undirected graph 14
Fig. 1.6   A tree.. 15
Fig. 1.7   The pigeon-hole principle.. 16
Fig. 2.1   The "turning game" solution.. 24
Fig. 2.2   A finite automaton for the "turning game" 24
Fig. 2.3   The operation of an NFA 31
Fig. 2.4   The two DFAs: M and M' 42
Fig. 2.5   The construction of an NFA accepting L^* 42
Fig. 2.6   The construction of an NFA accepting $L \cup L'$ 43
Fig. 2.7   The construction of an NFA for LL' 43
Fig. 2.8   A mystery NFA with three states 48
Fig. 2.9   The mystery NFA after adding self-loops 49
Fig. 2.10   Incorporating an intermediate point 51
Fig. 2.11   An NFA with three states 51
Fig. 2.12   Initialization for the conversion................................... 52
Fig. 2.13   Applying the label-replacement procedure with q_2 as the
intermediate point 52
Fig. 2.14   Applying the label-replacement procedure with q_3 as the
intermediate point 52
Fig. 2.15   Applying the label-replacement procedure with q_4 as the
intermediate point 52
Fig. 3.1   The input for the state-minimization algorithm 61
Fig. 3.2   The finite automaton after state-minimization 61
Fig. 3.3   The idea behind the Pumping Lemma................................... 67
Fig. 4.1   A production tree 78
Fig. 5.1   A typical drawing of a PDA 96
Fig. 5.2   The computation path for $aaabbb$................................... 98

Fig. 5.3   The computation path for *abbba* 100
Fig. 5.4   The modifications for the initial and final states 104
Fig. 5.5   The modification for the pop-then-push operations................. 104
Fig. 5.6   The node selection for Lemma 5.1 112
Fig. 5.7   The decomposition of w 113
Fig. 5.8   The production tree involving $A \overset{G,*}{\Rightarrow} x_1 A x_2$ 115
Fig. 5.9   The pumping on $a^p b^p c^p$ 117
Fig. 5.10   The node selection for Ogden's Lemma............................ 120
Fig. 5.11   The partition of the input into $V_0, \dots, V_m$ 123
Fig. 5.12   Two examples of a segment's internal structure 123
Fig. 5.13   Pumping structure discovery Case 1................................ 125
Fig. 5.14   Pumping structure discovery Subcase 2a........................... 127
Fig. 5.15   Pumping structure discovery Subcase 2b 129
Fig. 6.1   A TM with a one-way infinite tape 136
Fig. 6.2   A diagram for $\{a^n b^n a^n \mid n \geq 0\}$ 140
Fig. 6.3   Handling the first triple 141
Fig. 6.4   Handling the second triple 142
Fig. 6.5   Handling the last triple 143
Fig. 6.6   Processing of the first triple with a state as the leading
              symbol 144
Fig. 6.7   A diagram for the palindromes over $\{1, 2\}$ 146
Fig. 6.8   Processing of 1221221 146
Fig. 6.9   A two-tape TM 150
Fig. 6.10   The ID sequence of the TM accepting *aabbaa* 151
Fig. 6.11   An example of double-character encoding 153
Fig. 6.12   An example of double-track encoding 153
Fig. 6.13   The mechanism for reducing the number of branches to 2 159
Fig. 6.14   A 3-tape simulation of an NTM 160
Fig. 7.1   The six tapes after extracting information from the input 176
Fig. 8.1   TOTAL$_{\text{CFG}}$ and NONTOTAL$_{\text{CFG}}$ 191
Fig. 8.2   The arithmetical hierarchy 204
Fig. 9.1   The block encoding 217
Fig. 9.2   The traversal of blocks. 219
Fig. 9.3   Implementing a two-way infinite tape 222
Fig. 9.4   Two tapes with two tracks each................................... 223
Fig. 9.5   One pair of tracks, and the color and marking tracks.
              The section corresponding to Cells -8 through Cell 12
              is shown 224
Fig. 9.6   The coloring procedure 225
Fig. 9.7   The two cases of the push operation............................... 227
Fig. 9.8   The two cases of the pull operation............................... 228
Fig. 9.9   Inclusions among the standard time complexity classes............. 236
Fig. 10.1   An offline TM with two work tapes 246

Fig. 10.2   Inclusions among the standard time and space
             complexity classes 251
Fig. 11.1   A Hamilton path 264
Fig. 11.2   A Hamilton cycle 264
Fig. 11.3   A reduction to the Hamilton Cycle Problem 265
Fig. 11.4   Cliques. 274
Fig. 11.5   An example of a graph constructed for reducing 3SAT to
             CLIQUE 276
Fig. 11.6   A graph and one of its vertex covers................................ 277
Fig. 11.7   A vertex cover instance.. 278
Fig. 11.8   The local connection surrounding a triangle 279
Fig. 11.9   A 3-coloring instance.. 280
Fig. 11.10   The Hamilton path gadget and its three Hamilton-path
             traversals 282
Fig. 11.11   Conversion to HAMPATH from VERTEXCOVER. 283
Fig. 11.12   A Subset Sum instance. 285
Fig. 11.13   The variable assignment triples for 3DM............................ 288
Fig. 11.14   The clause triples for 3DM.. 289
Fig. 12.1   The polynomial hierarchy. 304
Fig. 12.2   The variable selection gadget in the reduction to
             GEOGRAPHY 318
Fig. 12.3   The construction for reducing TQBF to GEOGRAPHY 319
Fig. 14.1   A four-input Boolean circuit 348

List of Algorithms

1.1   A greedy algorithm for reachability 18
2.1   An algorithm for computing an equivalent pseudo-NFA................... 36
2.2   An algorithm for computing a DFA from a pseudo-NFA 37
2.3   A greedy algorithm for constructing a DFA from an NFA............... 37
3.1   A greedy algorithm for finding all distinguishable pairs 60
3.2   An algorithm for finding all maximal equivalence groups 60
4.1   A CNF-construction algorithm (part 1) 84
4.2   A CNF-construction algorithm (part 2) 85
4.3   A CNF-construction algorithm (part 3) 86
4.4   An algorithm for converting a CNF to a GNF 89
6.1   A TM algorithm for $\{a^n b^n a^n \mid n \geq 0\}$ 139
6.2   A TM algorithm for the palindrome over $\{1, 2\}$ 144
6.3   An enumerator for A 163
7.1   A universal TM algorithm for T_D 174
8.1   A TM F for L_{self}, with E as a subroutine for ACCEPT$_{\text{TM}}$................ 187
8.2   A TM that recognizes NONTOTAL$_{\text{CFG}}$................................ 192
9.1   A TM that decides the diagonal language 231
9.2   A TM encoding test 232
9.3   A TM that decides the minimum number of states 237
9.4   An algorithm for CFL membership test.................................... 240
10.1 A TM that decides the space diagonal language 247
10.2 The enumeration algorithm.. 255
10.3 The reachability testing algorithm 255
10.4 The extended reachability testing algorithm.............................. 256
10.5 An extended counting.. 256
10.6 A non-reachability testing algorithm...................................... 257
10.7 A logarithmic-space validity test of a TM encoding 259
11.1 A TM that recognizes CLIQUE 275
11.2 A TM that recognizes VERTEXCOVER 277
11.3 A TM that recognizes HAMPATH 281
12.1 An algorithm for finding a satisfying assignment using an oracle 296

12.2   Finding a solution to the subset sum problem 297
12.3   Recursive algorithm for FORMULAGAME 317
12.4   Recursive algorithm for GEOGRAPHY 320
13.1   A recursive method for computing $\gcd(m, n)$ 329
13.2   An algorithm for primitive random number generation 336
13.3   A binary exponentiation algorithm 336
13.4   A probabilistic primality testing 337

Symbols, Acronyms, and Class Names

$\aleph_1$	Aleph One
$\aleph_0$	Aleph Zero
$\Delta_k, \Sigma_k, \Pi_k$	Arithmetical Hierarchy Classes
$\emptyset$	Empty Set
ϵ	Empty String
$\lceil \cdot \rceil$	Function, Ceiling
$dom(\cdot)$	Function, Domain of
$\lfloor \cdot \rfloor$	Function, Floor
$range(\cdot)$	Function, Range of
$O(\cdot)$	Function Relation, Big-O
$\Omega(\cdot)$	Function Relation, Big-Omega
$o(\cdot)$	Function Relation, Little-O
$\omega(\cdot)$	Function Relation, Little-Omega
$\Theta(\cdot)$	Function Relation, Theta
$\overset{G}{\Longrightarrow}$	Grammar's Production, Single Step
$\overset{G,*}{\Longrightarrow}$	Grammar's Production, Multiple Steps
$\rightarrow$	Grammar's Production Rule
$[\cdot]$	Integer Congruence Class
$*$	Language Operation, Kleene-Star
$+$	Language Operation, Kleene-Plus
$\wedge$	Logical Operation, And
$\neg$	Logical Operation, Negation
$\vee$	Logical Operation, Or
$\Delta_k^p, \Sigma_k^p, \Pi_k^p$	Polynomial Time Hierarchy Classes
$\forall^\infty$	Quantifier, Almost-All
$\exists$	Quantifier, Existential
$\forall$	Quantifier, Universal
$\leq_m$	Reducibility, Many-One
$\leq_T^p$	Reducibility, Polynomial-Time Turing
$\leq_{\mathrm{wit}}^p$	Reducibility, Polynomial-Time Witness-Preserving

$\leq_{ctt}^{p}$	Reducibility, Polynomial-Time Conjunctive Truth-Table
$\leq_{dtt}^{p}$	Reducibility, Polynomial-Time Disjunctive Truth-Table
$\leq_{m}^{p}$	Reducibility, Polynomial-Time Many-One
$\leq_{T}^{p}$	Reducibility, Polynomial-Time Turing
$\leq_{wit}^{p}$	Reducibility, Polynomial-Time Witness
$\leq_{wit}$	Reducibility, Witness
$\Longleftrightarrow$	Relation, Equivalence
$\rightarrow$	Relation, Implication
$\equiv$	Relation, Equivalent
$\Vert \cdots \Vert$	Set Cardinality
$\{\cdots\}$	Set Specification
$\in$	Set Membership, Is a Member of
$\ni$	Set Membership, Contains
$\mathbb{Z}$	Set of Integers
$\mathbb{N}$	Set of Natural Numbers
$\mathbb{Q}$	Set of Rational Numbers
$\mathbb{R}$	Set of Real Numbers
^{c}	Set Operation, Complement
$\overline{}$	Set Operation, Complement
$\setminus$	Set Operation, Difference
$\cap$	Set Operation, Intersection
$P(\cdot)$	Set Operation, Power Set
$\triangle$	Set Operation, Symmetric Difference
$\cup$	Set Operation, Union
$\subset$	Set Relation, Proper Subset
$\supset$	Set Relation, Proper Superset
$\subseteq$	Set Relation, Subset
$\supseteq$	Set Relation, Superset
Σ_ϵ	Σ Augmented with ϵ
Σ^*	All Strings over Σ
Σ^n	All Strings over Σ Having a Length of n
$\Sigma^{\leq n}$	All Strings over Σ Having a Length of $\leq n$
$\Sigma^{<n}$	All Strings over Σ Having a Length of $< n$
$\sqcup$	Symbol, Blank
$\vdash$	Symbol, Left-End Marker
$\dashv$	Symbol, Right-End Marker
AC	Polylogarithmic-Depth, Polynomial-Size Unbounded-Fan-In Circuits
BPP	Bounded-Error Probabilistic Polynomial Time
CFG	Context-Free Grammar
CFL	Context-Free Language
CNF	Chomsky Normal Form
CNF	Conjunctive Normal Form
CNFSAT	Conjunctive Normal Form Satisfiability

DCFL	Deterministic Context-Free Languages
DFA	Deterministic Finite Automaton
DNF	Disjunctive Normal Form
DPDA	Deterministic Pushdown Automaton
DTM	Deterministic Turing Machine
EXPSPACE	Exponential Space
EXPTIME	Exponential Time
FA	Finite Automaton
GCD	Greatest Common Divisor
GNF	Greibach Normal Form
ID	Instantaneous Description
L	Logspace
LCM	Least Common Multiple
NC	Polylogarithmic-Depth, Polynomial-Size Bounded-Fan-In Circuits
NEXPSPACE	Nondeterministic Exponential Space
NEXPTIME	Nondeterministic Exponential Time
NFA	Nondeterministic Finite Automaton
NL	Nondeterministic Logspace
NP	Nondeterministic Polynomial Time
NPSPACE	Nondeterministic Polynomial Space
NTM	Nondeterministic Turing Machine
P	Polynomial Time
P/log	P with Logarithmic Advice
P/poly	P with Polynomial Advice
PDA	Pushdown Automaton
PH	Polynomial Hierarchy
PNF	Prenex Normal Form
PP	Probabilistic Polynomial Time
PSAPCE	Polynomial Space
PTM	Probabilistic Turing Machine
R	Regular Languages
RE	Recursively Enumerable Languages
REC	Recursive Languages
REG	Regular Languages
RP	Random Polynomial Time
SAC	Polylogarithmic-Depth, Polynomial-Size Semi-Unbounded-Fan-In Circuits
TM	Turing Machine
UL	Unambiguous Logspace
ZPP	Zero-Error Probabilistic Polynomial Time

Part I
Preparation

Chapter 1
Mathematics and Computer Science Basics

1.1 Sets

The first topic is set theory.

A **set** consists of its **members** (or **elements**). We use $\in$ and $\ni$ to denote the **set membership** relation. We write $x \in S$ and $S \ni x$ to mean that the element x belongs to the set S. $\emptyset$, called the **empty set**, is a special set with no elements.

There are two ways to specify sets. One is to list the members, like "the set consisting of 1, 2, 3, 4, and 5." The other is to describe the requirement that a prospective element must satisfy to belong to the set, like "the set of all integers between 1 and 5." We encompass the list and description with curly brackets ($\{$ and $\}$) to denote mathematical sets. When listing, we write:

$$\{\text{the list of elements}\}.$$

If listing all the elements is impossible or impractical, ellipses are used, like:

$$\{1, 2, \ldots, 99, 100\} \text{ and } \{\ldots, -4, -2, 0, 2, 4, 6 \ldots\}.$$

For specifying these two sets by their membership requirements, we write:

$$\{x \mid x \text{ is an integer and } 1 \leq x \leq 100\} \text{ and } \{x \mid x \text{ is an even integer}\}.$$

Let A and B be sets. If every element of A belongs to B, we say that A is a **subset** of B and B is a **superset** of A. We denote the relations with $A \subseteq B$ and $B \supseteq A$, respectively. If $A \subseteq B$ and $A \neq B$, we say that A is a **proper subset** of B and B is a **proper superset** of A and denote the relation with $A \subset B$ and $B \supset A$.

For example, let $A = \{4, 5, 7\}$, $B = \{4, 7\}$, and $C = \{8, 10\}$. Then, $4 \in A$, $4 \in B$, and $4 \notin C$. Also, A is a proper superset of B, B is a proper subset of A, and A is neither a subset nor a superset of C. We can denote these relations with $A \supset B$, $B \subset A$, $A \not\subseteq C$, and $A \not\supseteq C$.

© The Editor(s) (if applicable) and The Author(s), under exclusive license to
Springer Nature Switzerland AG 2025
M. Ogihara, *An Introduction to Theory of Computation*,
https://doi.org/10.1007/978-3-031-84740-0_1

The **cardinality** (or the **size**) of a set is its number of elements. For a set S, we write $\|S\|$ to indicate the number of elements in S. For example, $\|\emptyset\| = 0$ and $\|\{1, 2, 4, 8\}\| = 4$. If the number of elements in S is finite, we say that S's cardinality is **finite** and S is a **finite set**. Otherwise, we say that S's cardinality is **infinite** and S is an **infinite set**. We often write $\|S\| < \infty$ and $\|S\| = \infty$ to mean that S is finite and S is infinite, respectively.

We will frequently use the following infinite sets of numbers:

- $\mathbb{N}$ is the set of all **natural numbers** $\{1, 2, 3, \ldots\}$.
- $\mathbb{Z}$ is the set of all **integers**, $\{\ldots, -3, -2, -1, 0, 1, 2, 3, \ldots\}$.
- $\mathbb{Q}$ is the set of all **rational numbers** $\mathbb{Q}$.
- $\mathbb{R}$ is the set of all **real numbers**.

For the last two, by attaching the superscript $+$ ($\mathbb{Q}^+$ and $\mathbb{R}^+$), we denote that their subsets consist solely of positive members. As we will see later in Chap. 8, there are two types of infinite cardinality, $\aleph_0$ and $\aleph_1$. The first three sets above have the cardinality $\aleph_0$, and the last set has the cardinality $\aleph_1$.

1.1.1   Set Operations

There are operations for constructing sets from other sets.

The **power set** of a set S is the set consisting of all subsets of S, including the empty set and S itself. We write 2^S or $\mathcal{P}(S)$ to denote the power set of S. If $S = \emptyset$, the power set of S is the set consisting of just one set, $\emptyset$; that is, $\{\emptyset\}$.

The **intersection** (or the **meet**) of sets A and B is the set consisting of all the elements in both A and B. The **union** (or the **join**) of sets A and B is the set consisting of all the elements in either A or B. We write $A \cap B$ to denote the intersection of A and B, and $A \cup B$ for the union of A and B. The sets A and B are **disjoint** if their intersection is empty. When A and B are disjoint, we may write $A + B$ instead of $A \cup B$.

For two sets A and B, the **set difference** of A from B is the set consisting of all elements appearing in A but not in B. We write $A \setminus B$ to denote the set difference of A from B. The **symmetric difference** between sets A and B is the union of the two set differences, $A \setminus B$ and $B \setminus A$. In other words, the symmetric difference between A and B is the set of all elements that appear in only one of the two sets. Alternatively, it is the difference between the union of the two sets and the intersection of the two sets. We denote the symmetric difference of A and B with $A \triangle B$.

Often, a set A is presented with a **universe** from which its members are drawn. When the universe is known, we write $\overline{A}$ or A^c to mean the **complement** of A; that is, the set of all elements in the universe that are not elements of A. Note that $\overline{\overline{A}} = A$ for all sets A. Figure 1.1 demonstrates the intersection, union, and complement vconcepts.

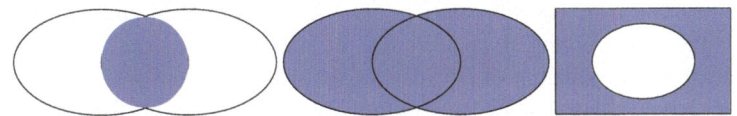

Fig. 1.1 The fundamental set operations: intersection (left), union (center), and complement (right)

Here are some examples. Let $A = \{4, 5, 7\}$, $B = \{4, 7, 8\}$, and $C = \{8, 10\}$. Then $A \cap B = \{4, 7\}$, $A \cup B = \{4, 5, 7, 8\}$, $A \cap C = \emptyset$, and $B \cap C = \{8\}$. Thus, A and C are disjoint. Additionally, $A \setminus B = \{5\}$, and $B \setminus A = \{8\}$, and so $A \triangle B = \{5, 8\}$.

De Morgan's Laws relate the union and the intersection in light of the complement operation. De Morgan's Laws state that for all sets A and B, which are subsets of a universe U,

$$\overline{A \cup B} = \overline{A} \cap \overline{B} \text{ and } \overline{A \cap B} = \overline{A} \cup \overline{B}.$$

The **Cartesian product** of sets A and B is the set of pairs $\{(a, b) \mid a \in A \text{ and } b \in B\}$. We write $A \times B$ as the Cartesian product of A and B. For example, if $A = \{1, 2, 3\}$ and $B = \{5, 6\}$, the Cartesian product $A \times B$ is $\{(1, 5), (1, 6), (2, 5), (2, 6), (3, 5), (3, 6)\}$. The concept of Cartesian products extends to a collection of more than two sets. For sets $A_1, \ldots, A_k, k \geq 2$, the Cartesian product of $A_1, \ldots, A_k$ is the set $\{(a_1, \ldots, a_k) \mid a_1 \in A_1, \ldots, a_k \in A_k\}$.

1.2 Boolean Algebra

Next, we go over Boolean algebra.

Boolean algebra is an algebraic system built on two constant Boolean values (*true* and *false*), variables representing a value, and Boolean algebraic operations. The value pair (*true*, *false*) is often identified with (T, F) and $(1, 0)$. The two fundamental values complement one another. We say that *true* is *false*'s **negation** and *false* is *true*'s negation. We attach the symbol $\neg$ in front or draw a line on top to indicate the negation. Thus, $\neg x$ and $\overline{x}$ similarly represent the negation of x. Note that a double negation is an identity operation.

This logic has two other operations: **conjunction** and **disjunction**.

A conjunction is an operation that takes two or more Boolean values and produces a new value representing if all the values are *true*. An expression representing the conjunction of Boolean values lists the values with the symbol $\wedge$ between each neighboring pair. For example, $x \wedge y \wedge z$ represents the conjunction of x, y, and z. We can draw elements from Boolean values and compute their conjunction. If S is a set of Boolean values, we write $\wedge_{x \in S} x$ to mean the conjunction of all values in S. We often call the conjunction the **logical AND**.

A disjunction is an operation that takes two or more Boolean values and produces a new value representing if at least one of the values is *true*. An expression representing the disjunction of Boolean values lists the values with the symbol $\vee$ between each neighboring pair. For example, $x \vee y \vee z$ represents the disjunction of x, y, and z. As with conjunction, we can write $\vee_{x \in S}$ to indicate the disjunction of the (Boolean) values in the set S. We often call the disjunction the **logical OR**.

To the right is a table for the value of $x \wedge y$ on all four possible combinations of values for x and y. Here, we use T and F for *true* and *false*, respectively.

x	y	$x \wedge y$
T	T	T
T	F	F
F	T	F
F	F	F

We can construct a Boolean formula using constants, variables, and Boolean operations. A variable can appear in a Boolean formula as a **literal**. For each variable x, a literal has two forms, x and $\overline{x}$. The former is a **positive literal**, whose value equals the value of x. The latter is a **negative literal**, whose value equals the x's negative value. The evaluation of a Boolean formula follows rules similar to that of mathematical formulas, where $\neg$, $\wedge$, and $\vee$ correspond to $-$, $*$, and $+$, respectively. Using parentheses changes the priorities, so we process the leftmost, inner-most pair of parentheses first.

Both conjunctions and disjunctions are **commutative**. In other words, for all Boolean formulas x and y, $x \wedge y = y \wedge x$, and $x \vee y = y \vee x$. The two operations are also **associative**. In other words, for all Boolean formulas x, y, and z, $x \wedge (y \wedge z) = (x \wedge y) \wedge z$ and $x \vee (y \vee z) = (x \vee y) \vee z$. Because of this associativity, we can unite a series of Boolean objects with the same binary operation without parentheses.

Both conjunctions and disjunctions also follow the **distributive laws**. For all x, y, and z, $x \wedge (y \vee z) = (x \wedge y) \vee (x \wedge z)$, and $x \vee (y \wedge z) = (x \vee y) \wedge (x \vee z)$.

De Morgan's Laws we reviewed in the set section apply to Boolean logic as well. For all Boolean expressions X and Y, $\overline{X \cup Y} = \overline{X} \cap \overline{Y}$, and $\overline{X \cap Y} = \overline{X} \cup \overline{Y}$.

1.2.1 Implication and Equivalence

From the three fundamental Boolean logic operations, we can build relations. Because of De Morgan's Laws, it is sufficient to have either negation and conjunction or negation and disjunction to express all Boolean logic. Two critical operations are **implication**: $x \to y$, and **equivalence**: $x \equiv y$. The implication $x \to y$ means, "wherever x is true, y is true," and the equivalence $x \equiv y$ means, "x and y have the same values." The implication $x \to y$ is equivalent to $\overline{x} \vee y$. The equivalence $x \equiv y$ is equivalent to $(x \to y) \wedge (y \to x)$ and thus equivalent to $(\overline{x} \vee y) \wedge (\overline{y} \vee x)$.

The **contrapositive** (or **contraposition**) of an implication $x \rightarrow y$ is $\overline{y} \rightarrow \overline{x}$. The contrapositive has the same value as the original. We can derive that the two are equal to each other using the following transformations:

$$(x \rightarrow y) \equiv (\overline{x} \vee y) \equiv (y \vee \overline{x}) \equiv (\overline{\overline{y}} \vee \overline{x}) \equiv (\overline{y} \rightarrow \overline{x}).$$

In addition to De Morgan's Laws, distributive laws, removal of double negations, and replacement of implications with disjunctions, we can use the following rules for simplifying formulas:

- $x \wedge x$ equals x; $x \vee x$ equals x.
- $x \wedge \neg x$ equals *false*; $x \vee \neg x$ equals *true*.
- $x \wedge$ *false* equals *false*; $x \vee$ *false* equals x.
- $x \wedge$ *true* equals x; $x \vee$ *true* equals *true*.

1.2.2 Predicates

Here, we define predicates.

A **predicate** is an expression involving variables such that the expression receives a truth value (i.e., *true* or *false*) when all the variables in the expression receive a value. A set of permissible values is associated with each variable in the predicate. This set of permissible values is called the variable's **domain**.

We may classify predicates based on its variables' domains, like integer predicates, real number predicates, and Boolean predicates. We also classify predicates based on the number of its variables. We call a predicate with only one variable a **unary predicate**, one with two variables a **binary predicate**, one with three variables a **ternary predicate**, and so on. Generally, for a positive integer k, a **k-ary** predicate is one with k variables. For example, $P(x) = [x * x - 3x + 2 > 0]$ is a unary predicate with x as its variable. The domain of the variable x must admit multiplication, addition, and subtraction. The value of the predicate is *true* for $x > 2$ and for $x < -1$. The predicate $Q(x, y) = [x * y = 1]$ is a binary predicate whose variables x and y must be in a domain that admits multiplication.

We often use the term **binary relation** as a synonym for the term "binary predicate." Let $Q(x, y)$ be a binary predicate such that the domain of x and y is D. The binary relation representing Q is the relationship between two elements x and y in D such that $Q(x, y) = true$. We write xRy to mean that the relation representing Q exists between x and y. The pair (x, y) for which xRy holds is:

$$\{(x, y) \mid x, y \in D \wedge Q(x, y) = true\}.$$

This set is a subset of the Cartesian product $D \times D$.

There are three essential properties of binary predicates. Let $Q(x, y)$ be a binary predicate. We say that Q is **reflexive** if $Q(x, x)$ is *true* for all choices of x. We say that Q is **symmetric** if for all choices for x and y, $Q(x, y) = Q(y, x)$. We say that

Q is **transitive** if for all x, y, and z, $Q(x, y) \land Q(y, z)$ implies $Q(x, z)$. If R is reflexive, symmetric, and transitive, it is an **equivalence**.

A distinguished type of predicates is the **tautology**. A predicate is a tautology if its value is *true* regardless of the value assignments to the variables. For example, the binary predicate $[x \geq y \lor x \leq y]$ with $x, y \in \mathbb{R}$ is a tautology because regardless of the choices of the values for x and y in $\mathbb{R}$, either $x \geq y$ or $x \leq y$.

1.2.3 Truth Assignments and Quantifications

Given a Boolean formula with some variables, we can **assign** values to the variables and evaluate the formula with those assigned values. The combination of the values assigned to the variables is a **truth assignment**. Let P be a Boolean formula built on some variables $x_1, \ldots, x_n$. Given a truth assignment α for P, we write $P(\alpha)$ to denote the result of evaluation P with the truth assignment. We say that α satisfies P if $P(\alpha) = true$. We say that P is **satisfiable** if some truth assignment satisfies P, **unsatisfiable** if no truth assignments satisfy P, and a tautology if every truth assignment satisfies P.

It is possible to **quantify** variables in a predicate. We frequently use the **existential quantifier** $\exists$ and the **universal quantifier** $\forall$.

For a predicate $P(x)$, $(\exists x)P(x)$ means "for some choice for x, the value of $P(x)$ is true," and $(\forall x)P(x)$ means "for all choices for x, the value of $P(x)$ is true." Without using the quantifiers attached to x, the two predicates are expressed as follows:

$$(\exists x)P(x) \text{ is equivalent to } P(true) \lor P(false), \text{ and}$$

$$(\forall x)P(x) \text{ is equivalent to } P(true) \land P(false).$$

Because a quantification considers the two possible assignments to the variable to which it is attached, you cannot assign a value to the variable externally.

Let $P(x_1, \ldots, x_m)$ be a formula free of quantifiers. We say that P is satisfiable if $(\exists x_1, \ldots, x_m)[P(x_1, \ldots, x_m) = true]$ and P is unsatisfiable if $(\forall x_1, \ldots, x_m)[P(x_1, \ldots, x_m) = false]$. In addition, we say that P is a tautology if $(\forall x_1, \ldots, x_m)[P(x_1, \ldots, x_m) = true]$.

1.3 Functions

Here, we go over some important concepts about functions.

Let D and R be two nonempty sets. A **function** f from D to R associates with a value in R to each element of D. We also use the word **mapping** in place of "function." We write

$$f : D \rightarrow R$$

to mean that f is a function from D to R. For an element $x \in D$, the value of f at x has the notation $f(x)$. We refer to D and R as the **domain** and **range** of f, respectively. We write $dom(f)$ and $range(f)$ to refer to them.

If there may be some x for which $f(x)$ is undefined, we say that f is a **partial function**. If there is no x for which $f(x)$ is undefined, we say that f is a **total function**. We usually omit the word "total." We say that f is a **one-to-one function** if for all x and $x' \in D$, $f(x) \neq f(x')$. We say that f is an **onto function** if, for all $y \in R$, there is at least $x \in D$ such that $f(x) = y$. We say that f is a **bijection** if f is both a one-to-one and an onto function. If f is a bijection, we use f^{-1} to mean the **inverse function** of f, i.e., the function that maps each $y \in R$ to the unique (because of f being a bijection) $x \in D$ such that $f(x) = y$. The inverse function f^{-1} is a bijection. While $f(x)$ represents the value with which f associates x, for a set $S \subset D$, $f(S) = \{f(x) \mid x \in S\}$. When f is an onto function, we can express the property as $f(D) = R$.

Let $P(n)$ be a predicate where n's domain is $\mathbb{N}$. We say that $P(n)$ holds **for all but finitely many n** if there exists an integer n_0 such that for all $n \geq n_0$, $P(n)$ is *true*. We write

$$(\forall^\infty n)[P(n)]$$

to express this property.

1.3.1 Big-O Notation

We use the "big-O" notation to compare the speed of growth of functions from $\mathbb{N}$ to $\mathbb{R}$. Let $f(n)$ and $g(n)$ be functions whose domain is $\mathbb{N}$ and range is $\mathbb{R}^+$. We define the big-O relations between them as follows:

1. We write $f(n) = O(g(n))$ if there exists a constant $c > 0$ and an integer n_0 such that for all but finitely many n, $f(n) \leq cg(n)$.
2. We write $f(n) = \Omega(g(n))$ if there exists a constant $c > 0$ and an integer n_0 such that for all but finitely many n, $f(n) \geq cg(n)$.
3. We write $f(n) = o(g(n))$ such that $\lim_{n \to \infty} f(n)/g(n) = 0$, i.e., for all $c > 0$, there exists an integer n_0 such that for all $n \geq n_0$, $f(n) \leq cg(n)$.
4. We write $f(n) = \omega(g(n))$ such that $\lim_{n \to \infty} f(n)/g(n) = \infty$, i.e., for all constants $c > 0$, there exists an integer n_0 such that for all integers $n \geq n_0$, $f(n) \geq cg(n)$.
5. We write $f(n) = \Theta(g(n))$ if $f(n) = O(g(n))$ and $f(n) = \Omega(g(n))$.

1.4 Languages

Here, we define the components for defining language classes.

1.4.1 Alphabets and Strings

Let us begin with alphabets and strings.

An essential component of a language is the string, which is an assembly of characters from the alphabet. An **alphabet** is any nonempty finite set. An element of an alphabet is a **symbol**. Typically, we use an uppercase Greek letter to represent an alphabet and other types of letters (e.g., the English alphabet and the lowercase Greek letters) to represent a symbol in an alphabet.

A **string** (or **word**) over an alphabet is a sequence whose elements are from the alphabet. We specify a word by putting the elements within the sequence from left to right. We often refer to each symbol occurrence in a string as a **character**. In other words, each string is a sequence of characters, with each character representing a symbol in the alphabet. For example, if a string w is a sequence $[a, b, a, b, c]$, we write $ababc$ to specify the sequence. The string w's alphabet is a finite set of symbols whose members include a, b, and c.

For a string w, $|w|$ denotes the length of w. Note that the single vertical line differs from the double vertical line we use for cardinality. The symbol ϵ denotes an **empty string** (or **empty word**) whose length is 0. Let Σ be an alphabet and n be a non-negative integer. For a non-negative integer n, Σ^n represents the set of all strings over Σ with a length equal to n. We define $\Sigma^{<n}$ to be the set of all strings over Σ, whose length is less than n, and $\Sigma^{\leq n}$ to be the set of all strings over Σ, whose length is at most n. Furthermore, Σ^* is the set of all strings over Σ; that is, $\Sigma^* = \cup_{n \geq 0} \Sigma^n$. Similarly, Σ^+ is the set of all nonempty strings over Σ; that is, $\Sigma^+ = \cup_{n \geq 1} \Sigma^n$.

For two strings u and v, $u \cdot v$ is the **concatenation** of u and v; that is, the string we can create by appending v after u. We often omit the period in the middle and write uv. For example, if $u = abcab$ and $v = cccbbb$, $uv = abcabcccbbb$. If u is empty, then uv and vu are identical to v. If w is the concatenation of u and v, i.e., uv, then u is a **prefix** of w, and v is a **suffix** of w. If $w = uv$ and $u \neq \epsilon$, then v is a **proper suffix** of w. Similarly, if $w = uv$ and $v \neq \epsilon$, then u is a **proper prefix** of w. A **substring** (or **subword**) of a string w is any string we can construct from w by removing a (possibly empty) prefix and a (possible empty) suffix. In other words, v is a substring of w if, and only if, strings x and y (possibly empty) exist, such as $w = xvy$. A **proper substring** (or **proper subword**) is a substring that is not equal to the original. For example, if $w = bbaaba$, then the substrings of w are ϵ, $a, b, aa, ab, ba, bb, aab, aba, baa, bba, aaba, baab, bbaa, baaba, bbaab$, and $bbaaba$. Among these, $\epsilon, b, bb, bba, bbaa, bbab$, and $bbaba$ are prefixes, and ϵ, a, $ba, aba, aaba, baaba$, and $bbaaba$ are suffixes.

1.4.2 Languages and Their Classes

Here, we go over the general concepts about languages.

A **language** over an alphabet Σ is any subset of Σ^*. If A is a language over an alphabet Σ, then its complement is $\Sigma^* - A$. For example, if the language A is the set of all strings over $\{a, b\}$ containing at least one a, its complement is the set $\{b\}^*$.

For languages $A_1, \ldots, A_m, m \geq 1$, $A_1 \cdots A_m = \{a_1 \cdots a_m \mid a_1 \in A_1, \ldots, a_m \in A_m\}$. For a language A, $A^* = \{\epsilon\} \cup \{a_1 \cdots a_m \mid m \geq 1$ and $a_1, \ldots, a_m \in A\}$. In other words, $A^* = \{\epsilon\} \cup A \cup AA \cup AAA \cup AAAA \cup \cdots$. We call A^* the **Kleene-star** (or simply the **star**) of A. Additionally, we write A^+ for AA^*. We call A^+ the **Kleene-plus** of A. We define $(\emptyset)^*$ to be ϵ, not $\emptyset$.

A **language class** (or simply, **class**) is a collection of languages. The **complementary class** of a class, C, consists of the complements of the languages in C. We use co-C to denote the complementary class of C.

1.5   Graphs and Trees

Here, we review graphs and trees.

1.5.1   Directed Graphs

We start with the definition of directed graphs.

A **directed graph** (or **digraph**) G is a pair (V, A), where V is a finite set and $A \subseteq V \times V$. The elements of V are the **vertices** (or **nodes**) of the graph G, and the elements of A are the **[directed] edges** (or the **arcs**) of G. Let $e = (u, v)$ be a directed edge. We call the endpoint u as the **source vertex** (or the **source node**) of e and the endpoint v as the **destination vertex** (or the **destination node**) of e. Furthermore, e is an **incoming edge** to v and an **outgoing edge** from u. We often use a directed graph to represent a binary relation between a set of finite objects, with A encoding the relation. Figure 1.2 shows an example of a directed graph.

Fig. 1.2 An example of a directed graph. The circles are vertices, and the arrows are edges

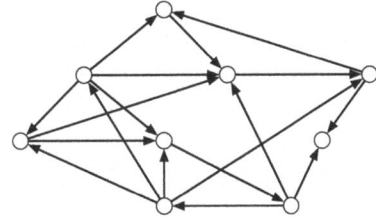

1.5.2 Reachability

Let $G = (V, A)$ be a directed graph. A **path** in G from a vertex u to a vertex v is a series of vertices $\pi = [u_1, \ldots, u_m]$, $m \geq 1$, such that:

- $u_1 = u$.
- $u_m = v$.
- for all i such that $1 \leq i \leq m - 1$, $(u_i, u_{i+1}) \in A$.

We call the two endpoints of the path u and v the **source** and **destination** of the path, respectively, or the **start** and **end** of the path. We say that v is **reachable** from u in G if G has a path from u to v. The length of a path $[u_1, \ldots, u_m]$ is $m - 1$.

If the source and the destination are identical, we call this a **cycle**. A cycle is **simple** if no vertices appear twice other than its start and end vertices. A directed graph is **acyclic** (or **cycle-free**) if it contains no cycles (see Exercises 1.10 and 1.11). Each acyclic graph has at least one vertex without incoming edges and at least one vertex without outgoing edges. These vertices are called **source vertices** and **sink vertices**, respectively. Figure 1.3 shows an example of an acyclic directed graph.

Since the edges are between two vertices, we often use a matrix to represent a graph. Let $G = (V, A)$ be a directed graph. Let $n = \|V\|$. Let $u_1, \ldots, u_n$ be an enumeration of G's vertices. We define the matrix M representing G to be an $n \times n$ matrix with elements m_{ij}, $1 \leq i, j \leq n$, such that for all i and j between 1 and n,

$$m_j = 1 \text{ if there is a directed edge from } u_i \text{ to } u_j, \text{ and 0 otherwise.}$$

We call the matrix the **adjacency matrix** of G (based on the ordering of the vertices).

Once we have established a matrix representation of a directed graph G, we can compute the reachability for all pairs of vertices using matrix multiplication. Let $G = (V, A)$ be a directed graph and M be the adjacency matrix of G. Let n be the number of vertices in G. Let I be the identity matrix of size n, the $n \times n$ matrix with 1 at all diagonal positions, and 0 elsewhere. For each k such that $1 \leq k \leq n$, define M_k to be the k-th power of M where the arithmetic is Boolean, with the value of 1 representing *true*, the value of 0 representing *false*, the multiplication representing the conjunction, and the addition representing the disjunction. In other words, the matrix product calculation treats the entries as integers but reduces any integer greater than 1 to 1. Then for each k such that $1 \leq k \leq n$, and for each pair

Fig. 1.3 An acyclic graph. The squares are the source vertices (at the upper-left and lower-right corners). The stars are the sink vertices (at the upper-right and lower-left corners)

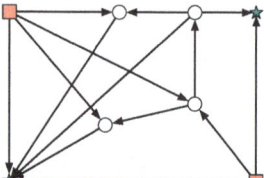

$(i, j), 1 \leq i, j \leq n$, the (i, j)-th element of M_k is 1 if, and only if, there is a path from u_i to u_j with at most k edges (see Exercise 1.13).

A graph $G' = (V', A')$ is a **subgraph** of another graph $G = (V, A)$ if $V' \subseteq V$ and $A' \subseteq A$. If G' is a subgraph of G and G' is different from G, then G' is a **proper subgraph** of G.

Let $G = (V, A)$ be a directed graph. For $V' \subseteq V$, the vertex-induced subgraph of G concerning V' is the directed graph $G' = (V', A')$ such that $A' = \{(x, y) \mid x \in V, y \in V, \text{ and } (x, y) \in A\}$. Let $A' \subseteq A$. The edge-induced subgraph of G concerning A' is the directed graph $G' = (V', A')$ such that $V' = \{x \mid x \text{ is an end-point of some edge in } A'\}$.

A **strongly connected component** of a directed graph $G = (V, A)$ is a set $S \subseteq V$ such that in the subgraph of G induced by S, every pair of nodes (u, v) is connected in both directions. A **maximally strongly connected component** of a directed graph $G = (V, A)$ is a strongly connected component of G with the property that no proper superset of S is a strongly connected component of G. Figure 1.4 shows connected components of a graph. There are two ways to derive a subgraph: **vertex-induced subgraphs** and **edge-induced subgraphs**.

1.5.3   Undirected Graphs

Here, we go over the definitions of undirected graphs.

An **undirected graph** (or simply a **graph**) is a pair $G = (V, E)$ such that $E \subseteq V \times V$ and for all x and y, $(x, y) \in E$ if, and only if, $(y, x) \in E$. In other words, an undirected graph is a directed graph where the arcs are symmetric. When drawing an undirected graph, we collapse the arcs in opposite directions between each pair of vertices into a single line with no arrowheads.

Let $G = (V, E)$ be an undirected graph. For each $(x, y) \in E$, we say that x is **adjacent** to y and y is adjacent to x. We define subgraphs, vertex-induced subgraphs, and edge-induced subgraphs in the same manner as we did for directed graphs. We define paths similarly, but note that each edge on a path has no direction.

While **self-loops** are permissible edges in directed graphs, in undirected graphs, the lack of direction in undirected graphs makes the existence of self-loops pointless. We, therefore, assume that there are no self-loops in undirected graphs. Figure 1.5 shows an undirected graph.

Fig. 1.4 A connected component. The highlighted edges and vertices form fully connected components. Two components appear here

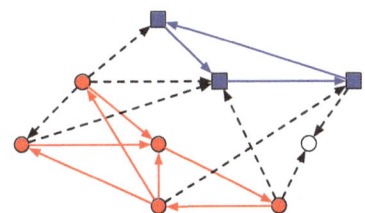

Fig. 1.5 An undirected graph

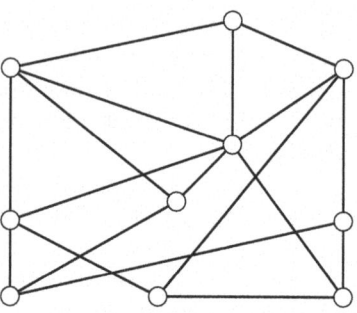

In an undirected graph, if there is a path from a vertex u to v, there is a path from v to u. This symmetry occurs because edges have no direction. Therefore, the definition of connected components in undirected graphs is different from the definition of connected components in directed graphs.

A **clique** (or **complete graph**) is a graph in which every pair of vertices has an edge between them. For an integer $k \geq 1$, a **k-clique** is a clique having k vertices.

1.5.4   Trees

Here, we go over the definitions of trees.

A **tree** is a fully connected undirected graph without loops. Choosing one vertex as its **root** provides an orientation of each edge for specifying a cycle-free path from the root to each vertex. Such straight paths are unique. Thus, we can classify the vertices in a tree based on the length of the path to the root:

- There is only one vertex at distance 0 from the root, which is the root itself.
- For each $i \geq 1$, a vertex is **at a distance i from the root** if the shortest path from the root to the vertex has length i. The shortest path is necessarily cycle-free.

   Put differently, a vertex is at a distance i from the root if it does not have a distance of $< i$ and is adjacent to another vertex whose distance from the root is $i - 1$.

The **depth** of a vertex in a rooted tree (i.e., a tree with a designated root) is the length of the shortest path from the root. Given a rooted tree, a vertex's **parent** appears immediately before the vertex on the shortest path from the root. A **leaf** of a rooted tree is a vertex without children in this hierarchical structure. The **height** of a tree is the length of the longest path from its root to any leaf. A **binary tree** is a rooted tree in which every non-leaf has at most two children. A **forest** is a collection of trees.

Figure 1.6 shows an example of a tree.

Fig. 1.6 A tree. The numbers represent the depth of the path

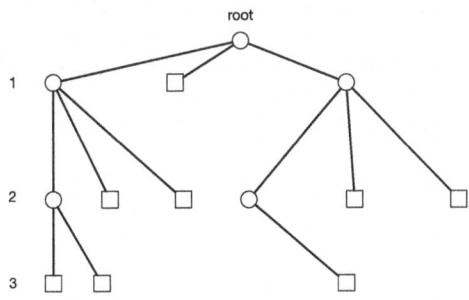

1.6 Proof Methods

This section covers proof methods.

In **proof by inference**, we start from a set of facts and assumptions and apply logical inference to conclude. A simple example of this is an inference of this form:

if $S \subset T$ and x is an element of S, then x is an element of T.

A way to show that a statement "for every x, $P(x)$ holds" is to find an x for which $P(x)$ does not hold. A x that contradicts the statement is a **counterexample**. For example, the statement "for all odd prime numbers n, $n^2 + 4$ is a prime number" is false. While $3^2 + 4 = 13$, $5^2 + 4 = 29$, and $7^7 + 4 = 53$ are all prime numbers, $11^2 + 4 = 125 = 5^3$ is not a prime number. Thus, $n = 11$ serves as a counterexample.

Proof by contradiction is a method for showing that a statement is *true* by demonstrating that the assumption that the statement is false leads to a contradiction of that belief. In other words, we prove that a statement S is true by showing that $\overline{S} \rightarrow$ *false*, whose contrapositive is *true* $\rightarrow S$. Since *true* holds with no assumption, we know that S is *true*.

A well-known example of this proof method is "$\sqrt{2}$ is not a rational number." The proof goes as follows:

1. By contradiction, assume $\sqrt{2}$ is a rational number.
2. If $\sqrt{2}$ is rational, there exist two strictly positive integers m and n such that $\sqrt{2} = \frac{m}{n}$.
3. We can assume that m and n are relatively prime to each other, i.e., the greatest common divisor of m and n is 1.
4. From the above, we can assume that m or n is an odd number.
5. By taking the square of each side of the equality, we get $2 = \frac{m^2}{n^2}$. By moving terms, we have $2n^2 = m^2$.
6. Since 2 appears on the left-hand side of the equation, m is even. Let $m = 2p$ for some integer p.

7. By substituting $2p$ for m, we get $2n^2 = 4p^2$. By dividing both sides by 2, we get $n^2 = 2p^2$.
8. Using the same argument, we have $n = 2q$ for some integer q.
9. Thus, both m and n are divisible by 2, which contradicts Step 4. Hence, $\sqrt{2}$ cannot be rational.

Another example of proof by contradiction is the **pigeon-hole principle**. The principle, in the standard form, states that if m and n are positive integers and $m > n$, then labeling m elements with one of the n labels produces a pair of elements having the same labels. The proof of the principle is as follows:

• Suppose we have already assigned a label to some n elements. Our claim holds if we have already assigned an identical label to two elements. Otherwise, the n elements have used up all the n labels, so we must assign an already-used label to one of the remaining elements.

An extended version of this principle is the following:

• For all integers $k \geq 1$, if there are $m > kn$ elements to label, we must label a group of $k + 1$ elements identically.

The extended version's proof follows the same argument as the standard version. Figure 1.7 illustrates this principle.

Proof by induction is a method for proving a statement $P(n)$ for all integers in a possibly infinite series of integers $\{m_i\}_{i \geq 1}$. Initially, the proof shows that $P(n)$ holds for some initial values $n = m_1, \ldots, n = m_k$ for some $k \geq 1$ (the **base case(s)**). Then, it shows that for all $\ell \geq k$, if $P(n)$ holds for $n = m_1, \ldots, n = m_\ell$, then it holds for $n = m_{\ell+1}$ (the **induction step**).

An example of proof by induction is:

$$(\forall n \geq 1) \left[\sum_{i=1}^{n} i = \frac{n(n+1)}{2} \right].$$

Fig. 1.7 The pigeon-hole principle. There are four pigeons and three holes. One hole gets two pigeons

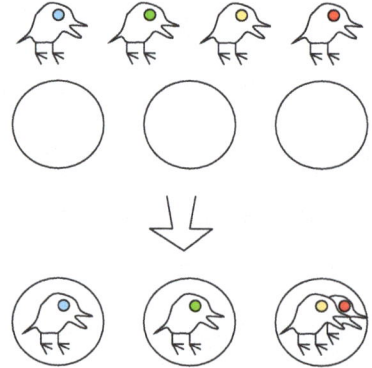

We can prove this property as follows:

- The base case of our induction proof is $n = 1$. If $n = 1$, the left-hand side of the equation is equal to $\sum_{i=1}^{1} i = 1$, and the right-hand side is equal to $\frac{1 \cdot 2}{2} = 1$. Thus, the equality holds.
- For the induction step, suppose $k \geq 1$, and the equality holds for all values of n that are at most k. Specifically, we have

$$\sum_{i=1}^{k} i = \frac{k(k+1)}{2} .$$

Then,

$$\begin{aligned}
\sum_{i=1}^{k+1} i &= k+1+\sum_{i=1}^{k} i \\
&= k+1+\frac{k(k+1)}{2} \\
&= \frac{2(k+1)+k(k+1)}{2} \\
&= \frac{(k+1)(k+2)}{2} ,
\end{aligned}$$

and so the equality holds for $k + 1$. This means that for all integers $k \geq 1$, if the equality holds for $n = k$, then the equality holds for $n = k+1$. Since the equality holds for $n = 1$, we have the equality holds for all values of $n \geq 1$.

1.7 Algorithmic Concepts

Here, we review some algorithm concepts.

Exhaustive search refers to a search strategy in which we generate all candidates for an answer with some (usually simple) procedure and then check each candidate to see if it satisfies our search criteria.

A well-known problem where exhaustive search is used to solve is the **reachability problem**. This is the problem of testing, given G, u, and w as input such that G is a directed graph and u and w are vertices of G if G has a path from u to w. We can solve the problem using an exhaustive search as follows:

Let $G = (V, A)$ with $\|V\| = n$. Let numbers $1, \ldots, n$ represent the vertices. We can solve the problem using the following exhaustive search: we generate all nonempty sequences having lengths n with entries from $\{1, \ldots, n\}$, say $[i_1, \ldots, i_n]$, and testing whether a prefix of the sequence represents a path from u and w in the following sense:

- for some $k \geq 1$, $i_1 = u$, $i_k = w$, and for all j such that $1 \leq j \leq k - 1$, there is a directed edge from i_j to i_{j+1}.

The beauty of this exhaustive approach is simplicity. The search, however, may generate several invalid sequences, such as those that do not start with u or contain w.

A **greedy algorithm** is a search algorithm where we build a solution through repeated scanning of building blocks. Using Algorithm 1.1, we can solve the reachability problem by building the set S of all vertices reachable from u.

An **inductive algorithm** finds the solution to a problem by gradual construction. There, we start from a solution to a simple subproblem. We then extend the solution to a larger subproblem. By repeating the extension, the subproblem becomes the whole problem, and we obtain the answer.

Algorithm 1.1 A greedy algorithm for reachability

```
 1: procedure GREEDY-REACHABILITY(G, u, w)
 2:     G = (V, A) is a directed graph; u, w ∈ V;
 3:     initialize S ← {u};
 4:     repeat
 5:         for each y ∈ V − S do
 6:             if some x ∈ S exists such that (x, y) ∈ A then
 7:                 S ← S ∪ {y};
 8:             end if
 9:         end for
10:     until no additions occur during the for loop
11:     if w ∈ S then
12:         assert w is reachable from u;
13:     else
14:         assert w is not reachable from u;
15:     end if
16: end procedure
```

Exercises

1.1 Let $A = \{a, b, c\}$ and $B = \{a, d, f\}$. State the elements of the following sets: $A \cup B$, $A \cap B$, $A \setminus B$, $B \setminus A$, and $A \triangle B$.

1.2 State the power set of $A = \{a, b, c\}$.

1.3 List the elements of $\{a, b\} \times \{c, d\}$.

1.4 Let $\phi(x, y, z) = (x \vee y) \wedge (\neg x \vee z)$. State the value ϕ for each possible truth assignment.

1.5 For each of the following properties P, prove or disprove whether P is symmetric, reflexive, or transitive.

1. $P(x, y) = x < y$ where the domain of x and y is $\mathbb{R}$.
   Hint: $x < y$ is equivalent to "there exists some strictly positive d such that $y - x = d$."

2. $P(x, y) = |x - y| \leq 5$ where the domain of x and y is $\mathbb{R}$.
3. $P(S, T) = \|S \cap T\| = 1$, where S and T are sets.
4. $P(G, H)$ is G is a subgraph of H, where both G and H are undirected graphs.
5. $P(X, Y)$ is the predicate $X \cap Y = \emptyset$, where X and Y are sets.

1.6 Let $\Sigma = \{a, b\}$ be an alphabet. List the elements of $\Sigma^{\leq 3}$.

1.7 Let $S = \{1\}$. State the elements of $\mathcal{P}(S)$, $\mathcal{P}(\mathcal{P}(S))$, and $\mathcal{P}(\mathcal{P}(\mathcal{P}(S)))$.

1.8 Use proof by induction to show for all $n \geq 1$ that $\sum_{i=1}^{n} i^2 = \frac{n(n+1)(2n+1)}{6}$.

1.9 Using the pigeon-hole principle, prove that for all $n \geq 2$, if π is a path in an n-vertex graph (or directed graph) and has length $geqn$, then π contains a cycle.

1.10 Prove that if C is a non-simple cycle in a directed graph $G = (V, A)$, $C = [u_1, \ldots, u_m]$ contains at least one simple cycle.

1.11 Prove that if P is a non-simple path from u_1 to u_m ($u_1 \neq u_m$) in a directed graph $G = (V, A)$, we can obtain a simple path from u_1 to u_m by repeatedly removing simple cycles in P.

1.12 Use the property from Exercise 1.10 to prove that if a directed graph is fully connected, every pair of vertices (u, v) has a simple cycle containing both u and v.

1.13 Prove the property on Page 13, i.e., for each k such that $1 \leq k \leq n$, the k-th power of the adjacency matrix of a directed graph represents the reachability with at most k edges.

1.14 Prove that for all $n \geq 2$, all undirected graphs with n vertices and n edges have a cycle whose length is ≥ 2.

Part II
Formal Language Theory and Automata

Chapter 2
The Regular Languages

2.1 The Finite Automaton (DFA) Model

Here, we introduce the finite automaton model and study its computational power for recognizing languages.

Imagine the following "turning game":

- A friend blindfolds you and stands you facing North.
- The friend then gives you a series of commands. You have yet to learn how long the series will be.
- Each command you receive is one of "right face," "left face," and "about face." You respond to the three types of commands by turning 90° to your right, turning 90° to your left, and turning 180°.
- At some point, the friend informs you that the commands are complete. At the end, the friend asks you to state which direction (North, East, South, or West) you are facing.
- You win if you state the correct answer to the question.

Let's simplify the problem by changing the goal to the following: you need to identify if you are facing **east at the end**.

How do you tackle the game? A simple solution to the problem is as follows:

You let the numbers 0, 1, 2, and 3 represent the cardinal directions (North, East, South, and West, respectively) and use the numbers to memorize the direction you are facing. The initial direction is North, so the number you memorize is 0. When you receive a command, you update your direction by adding an integer from 1, 2, and 3 and then reducing to an integer between 0 and 3 by subtracting four if the value after addition is greater than or equal to 4. The quantity to add is 1, 2, and 3 if the command is "right face," "about face," and "left face," respectively. After the command sequence, you have only to examine the value you have. If the number is 1, the direction is the east; otherwise, it isn't.

M. Ogihara, *An Introduction to Theory of Computation*, https://doi.org/10.1007/978-3-031-84740-0_2

Fig. 2.1 The "turning game" solution. The letters 'a', 'r,' and 'l' respectively represent the commands "about face," "right face," and "left face." Each circle has a label representing the direction and the number representing it

Fig. 2.2 A finite automaton for the "turning game"

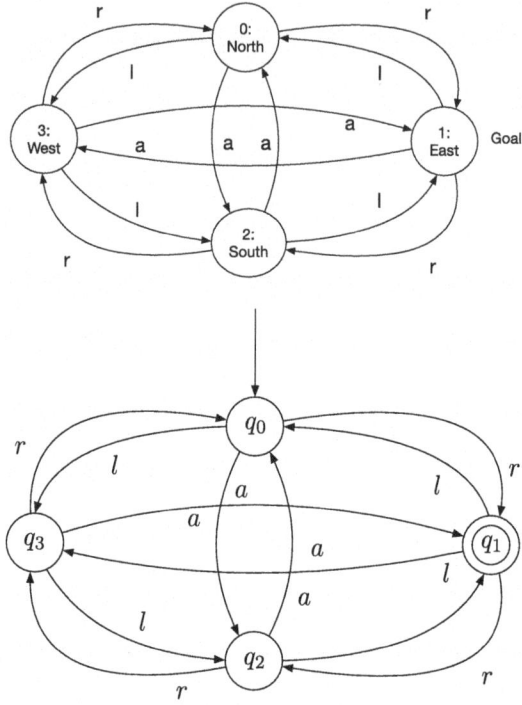

Figure 2.1 shows a diagram representing this idea.

Let us build a new diagram by removing the North, East, South, and West annotations, replacing the "Start" marking with an arrow pointing to it, replacing the "End" marking with an interior concentric circle, and replacing the direction number x with q_x for $x = 0, 1, 2, 3$. The resulting diagram, Fig. 2.2, is the finite automaton produced from this strategy.

2.1.1   The Definition

A formal definition of the finite automaton model is as follows:

Definition 2.1 A **(deterministic) finite automaton (DFA or FA)** is a quintuple $(Q, \Sigma, \delta, q_0, F)$ where Q and Σ are finite sets, δ is a function from $Q \times \Sigma$ to Q, $q_0 \in Q$, and F is a nonempty subset of Q. We call the five components the state set, the alphabet, the transition function, the initial state, and the final states, respectively.

The transition $\delta(p, a) = q$ means if the present state is p and the input character is a, then the next state is q.

We define the computation of a DFA using the transition function. Given an input $w = w_1 \cdots w_m$, the DFA processes the characters $w_1, \ldots, w_m$ in the order they appear. M initializes its state with q_0. Then, for $i = 1, \ldots, m$, M processes w_i and updates its state by using the value of δ given the present state and the symbol w_i as the input. The DFA M accepts if it arrives one of the final states after processing the input.

We use the following mathematical formulation to express this idea.

Definition 2.2 Let $M = (Q, \Sigma, \delta, q_0, F)$ be a DFA. For all states $p \in Q$, define $\delta(p, \epsilon) = p$, and for all states $p \in Q$, for all integers $m \geq 1$, and for all $w_1, \ldots, w_m \in \Sigma$, define

$$\delta(p, w_1 \cdots w_m) = \delta(\delta(\cdots \delta(\delta(p, w_1), w_2), \cdots, w_{m-1}), w_m).$$

It is possible to redefine the formula using a state series $[p_0, \ldots, p_m]$ to define $\delta(p, w_1 \cdots w_m)$ as follows:

- $p_0 = p$.
- For each i such that $1 \leq i \leq m$, $p_i = \delta(p_{i-1}, w_i)$.
- $\delta(p, w_1 \cdots w_m) = p_m$.

We now define the notion of acceptance.

Definition 2.3 Let $M = (Q, \Sigma, \delta, q_0, F)$ be a DFA and let $w \in \Sigma^*$. We say that M **accepts** w if $\delta(q_0, w) \in F$.

We can state the DFA for the "turning game" as $M = (Q, \Sigma, \delta, q_0, F)$, where $Q = \{q_0, q_1, q_2, q_3\}$, $\Sigma = \{a, r, l\}$, $q_0 = 0$, $F = \{q_1\}$, and δ has the following transition table:

State	a	r	l
q_0	q_2	q_1	q_3
q_1	q_3	q_2	q_0
q_2	q_0	q_3	q_1
q_3	q_1	q_0	q_2

Here are two examples of the moves that the "turning game" DFA makes.

- If the input is $alrlar$, the resulting state-sequence is

$$[q_0, q_2, q_1, q_2, q_1, q_3, q_0].$$

This implies $\delta(q_0, alrlar) = q_0$. The DFA thus does not accept the input.
- If the input is $aaalllrr$, the resulting state-sequence is

$$[q_0, q_2, q_0, q_2, q_1, q_0, q_3, q_0, q_1].$$

This implies $\delta(0, aaalllrr) = 1$. The DFA thus accepts the input.

We can use a drawing like Fig. 2.2 for presenting a DFA using the following general rules:

- Use a circle to represent a state.
- Connect states p and q with an arrow going from p to q if a symbol produces a change from p to q.
- Label each arrow with a list of all the symbols that produce the change with a comma in between.
- Draw a special arrow pointing to the initial state.
- For each final state, double the circle.

We now define the regular languages.

Definition 2.4 Let $L \subseteq \Sigma^*$ be a language. Let $M = (Q, \Sigma, \delta, q_0, F)$ be a DFA. We say that M **accepts** L if for all $w \in \Sigma^*$, M accepts w if, and only if, $w \in L$. We write $L(M)$ to represent the language M accepts.

Definition 2.5 We say that a language is **regular** if a DFA accepts it. We use REG to represent the class of all regular languages.

2.1.2 Example DFAs

Let us look at some DFA examples.

Example 2.1 Let $A = \{w \mid w \in \{0, 1\}^*$ and w has an odd number of 0s$\}$. We need just two states, q_0 and q_1, where q_0 is the initial state and q_1 is the final state. The transition function and the transition diagram are as follows:

State	0	1
q_0	q_0	q_1
q_1	q_1	q_0

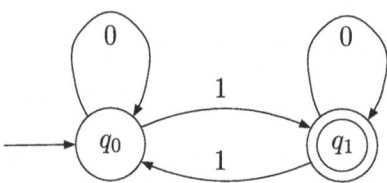

Let us examine the behavior of the DFA with a couple of input strings.

- On input 001101, the DFA in state q_0 follows the state sequence $[q_0, q_0, q_0, q_1, q_0, q_0, q_1]$ upon encountering the characters 0, 0, 1, 1, 0, and 1. The last state of the sequence is q_1, so the DFA accepts the input.
- On input 10101010, the DFA starts in state q_0 and follows the state sequence $[q_0, q_1, q_1, q_0, q_0, q_1, q_1, q_0]$ upon encountering the characters 1, 0, 1, 0, 1, 0, 1, and 0. The last state of the sequence is q_0, so the DFA accepts the input.

Example 2.2 Let $B = \{w \mid w \in \{a, b\}^*$ and w has abb as a suffix$\}$. We need four states, q_0, q_1, q_2, and q_3, where q_0 is the initial state and q_3 is the only final state. The transition function and the transition diagram are as follows:

State	a	b
q_0	q_1	q_0
q_1	q_1	q_2
q_2	q_1	q_3
q_3	q_1	q_0

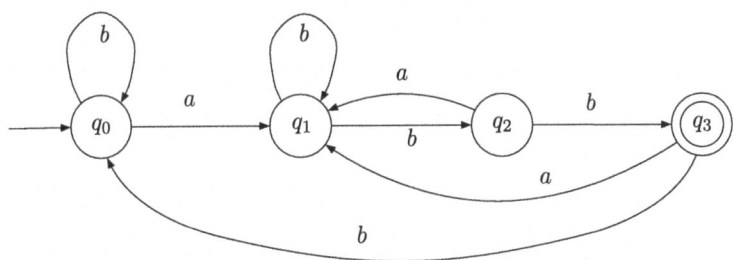

The states have the following meanings:

- q_1 represents the situations where the input has a at the end.
- q_2 represents the situations where the input has ab at the end.
- q_3 represents the situations where the input has abb at the end.
- q_0 represents all other situations.

The automaton's action is as follows:

- When the DFA receives an a, it transitions to q_1 regardless of where it is.
- When the DFA receives a b, it transitions from q_1 to q_2, q_2 to q_3, and q_3 to q_0; if it is in state q_0, it remains there.

Let us examine the behavior of the DFA with a couple of examples:

- On input aab, starting from q_0, the DFA follows the state sequence $[q_0, q_1, q_1, q_2]$. Thus, the DFA does not accept w.
- On input $aabbbabb$, starting from q_0, the DFA follows the state sequence $[q_0, q_1, q_1, q_2, q_3, q_0, q_1, q_2, q_3]$ arriving at q_3, The DFA thus accepts w.

Example 2.3 Let $C = \{w \mid w \in \{a, b\}^*$ and w contains an a somewhere and then a b some place after the $a\}$. Let w be an arbitrary member of C. Then w must be $xaybz$, where $x, y, z \in \{a, b\}^*$. It is possible to choose x and y so that x has no as and y has no bs. (We prove this property in Exercise 2.1.) In other words, we may choose x to consist only of b and y to consist only of a. This observation leads to the following transition function, for which we need only three states, q_0, q_1, and q_2, where q_0 is the initial state and q_2 is the only final state. We derive the transition function and the transition diagram as follows:

State	a	b
q_0	q_1	q_0
q_1	q_1	q_2
q_2	q_2	q_2

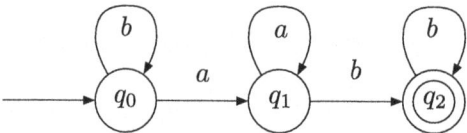

Let us examine the behavior of the DFA with a couple of examples:

- On input $w = bbaabbabbb$, the DFA follows the state sequence $[q_0, q_0, q_0, q_1, q_1, q_2, q_2, q_2, q_2, q_2, q_2]$. Thus, the automaton accepts w.
- On input $w = baa$, the DFA follows the state sequence $[q_0, q_0, q_1, q_1]$. Thus, the automaton does not accept w.

Example 2.4 Let $D = \{w \mid w \in \{a, b\}^*$ and contains aa or bb as a substring$\}$. We can construct a DFA for D with four states: q_0, q_1, q_2, and q_3. We designate q_0 as the initial state in which the DFA has yet to read any character. We also designate q_3 as the final state in which it has found that the input contains aa or bb, whichever comes first. Once arriving at q_3, the DFA will remain in q_3. The states q_1 and q_3 are intermediate states. The state q_1 represents the state where the DFA has just seen one a, and the character preceding the a, if any, is a b. The state q_2 represents the state where the DFA has just seen one b, and the character preceding the b, if any, is an a. In state q_1, if the character is an a, the DFA has found an occurrence of aa, so it advances to the state q_3. Otherwise, the character is a b. Since the previous character is an a (because the state is q_1), the DFA advances to q_2. Similarly, in state q_2, if the character is a b, the DFA has found an occurrence of bb, so it advances to the state q_3. Otherwise, it advances to q_1. In state q_0, the DFA advances to q_1 if the character is an a and to q_2 if the character is a b. The transition function and the transition diagram are as follows:

State	a	b
q_0	q_1	q_2
q_1	q_3	q_2
q_2	q_1	q_3
q_3	q_3	q_3

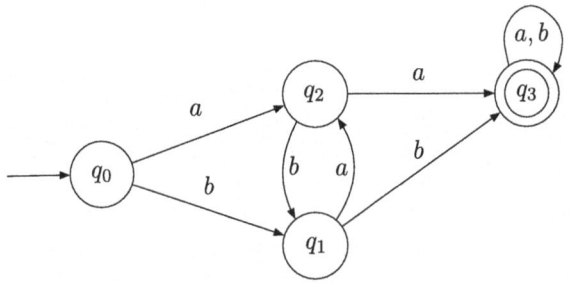

Let us examine the behavior of the DFA using two examples:

- Let $w = ababb$. The state sequence that the DFA follows is $[q_0, q_1, q_2, q_1, q_2, q_3]$. Thus, the DFA accepts w.
- Let $w = bababa$. The DFA follows the state sequence $[q_0, q_2, q_1, q_2, q_1, q_2, q_1]$. Thus, the DFA does not accept w.

Example 2.5 Let $E = \{w \mid w \in \{a, b\}^*$ and w contains neither aa nor bb as a substring$\}$. The language is complementary to the language D from the previous example. We can use the same DFA for D but treat $q_0, q_1,$ and q_2 as final states instead of q_3.

State	a	b
q_0	q_1	q_2
q_1	q_3	q_2
q_2	q_1	q_3
q_3	q_3	q_3

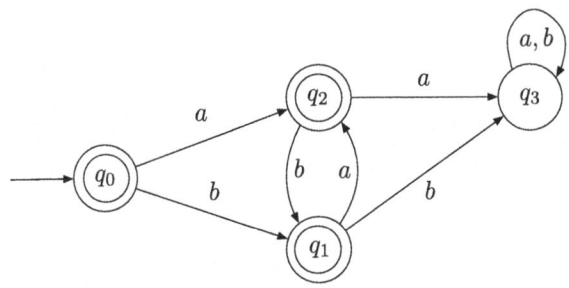

2.2 The Nondeterministic Finite Automaton (NFA) Model

Here, we study a variant of the DFA model called the **nondeterministic finite automaton (NFA)** model.

2.2.1 The Definition

Let us begin with the definition of the NFA model.

The term "nondeterministic" refers to the property that the state-symbol combinations may have any number of choices for the next state, and the automaton may choose any available state. In addition, the automaton may not need to read a character to make a state transition.

There are two factors that distinguish NFAs from DFAs. First, by adding the empty string ϵ to the alphabet, we can change the states without consuming an input character. Second, by expanding the range of the transition function from one state to any number of states, we give the finite automata choices for which state it transitions to. We call the transitions with ϵ **ϵ-transitions** or **ϵ-moves**.

Intuitively, how does an NFA operate? In the "deterministic" case we discussed earlier, a DFA followed whatever its transition function instructed at each state and each character it read. The deterministic cad has no ambiguity in how to operate.

In the case of an NFA, however, the automaton may see multiple possibilities for potential actions to take. This means that the automaton may use nondeterministic decisions to compute. Additionally, the automaton may keep running unless it finds no available transitions.

The automaton's action is basically as follows:

1. **Checking the end of input**. The automaton checks if there is any character remaining in the input. If there is no remaining character, the automaton advances to (2); otherwise, it advances to (4).
2. **Checking the availability of ϵ-transitions at the end of input**. If an ϵ-transition is available, the automaton advances to (3); otherwise, it advances to (4).
3. **Selecting the use/not-use of ϵ-transitions at the end of input**. The automaton chooses whether or not to use an ϵ-transition. If it chooses to use one, the automaton advances to (6); otherwise, it advances to (4).
4. **Accepting/not-accepting at the end of input**. If the state is final, the automaton accepts; otherwise, it halts without accepting.
5. **Checking the availability of transitions**. The automaton checks if there is a possible move. If a transition is possible, the automaton advances to (6); otherwise, it halts without accepting.
6. **Selecting a transition and executing it**. The automaton selects one transition and executes it.

Figure 2.3 shows how an NFA operates.

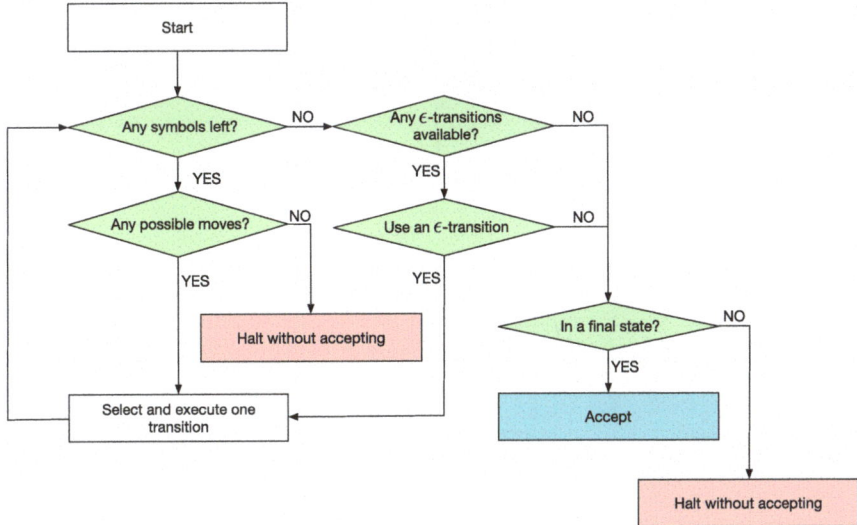

Fig. 2.3 The operation of an NFA

The mathematical representation of an NFA is a quintuple $(Q, \Sigma, \delta, q_0, F)$. The presentation looks similar to a DFA but uses a different type of function for δ. First, we incorporate the ϵ-transitions by changing the domain of the transition function to $\Sigma \cup \{\epsilon\}$, in which we use Σ_ϵ for notation. Second, we incorporate the diversity of possible transitions on a symbol by changing the range of the transition function δ to 2^Q, which is the power set of Q.

Definition 2.6 Let $M = (Q, \Sigma, \delta, q_0, F)$ be an NFA. Let $w \in \Sigma^*$. The automaton M **accepts** w if it selects its transitions to complete reading all the input characters and then arrive at a final state.

In a more mathematical expression, M accepts w if, and only if, there exists a sequence of states $\pi = [q_1, \ldots, q_m]$ and a sequence of symbols $\lambda = [\ell_1, \ldots, \ell_m]$ from Σ_ϵ that satisfy the following conditions:

- $q_m \in F$.
- For all i such that $1 \leq i \leq m$, $q_i \in \delta(q_{i-1}, \ell_i)$.
- The string $\ell_1 \cdots \ell_m$ is constructible from w by inserting ϵ.

Definition 2.7 For an NFA M, we write $L(M)$ to represent the language M accepts; that is, the set of all $w \in \Sigma^*$ such that M on w accepts.

Next, we give examples of NFAs.

Example 2.6 Let F be the set of all strings w in $\{a, b\}^*$ that satisfy:

(a) $w = \epsilon$.
(b) w ends with aa.
(c) w ends with bb.

We can design a five-state NFA that accepts F. The state set is $\{q_0, \ldots, q_4\}$, the initial state is q_0, and the final state set is $\{q_0, q_4\}$. The transition table and the transition diagram of the NFA are as follows:

State	a	b	ϵ
q_0			q_1
q_1	q_1, q_2	q_1, q_3	
q_2	q_4		
q_3		q_4	
q_4			

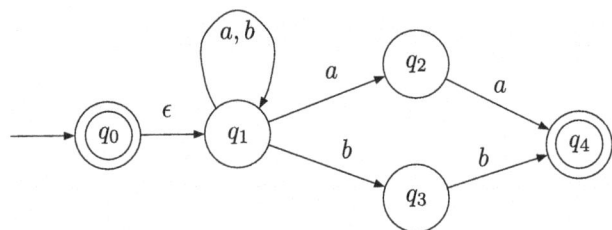

The intuition behind this program is the following:

- The initial state is q_0, which is also a final state. The NFA may move to q_1 or remain in q_0. If the input is ϵ and the automaton remains in q_0, the automaton accepts the input. If the input is ϵ and the automaton moves to q_1, the computation ends with accepting the input. If the input is not ϵ, the automaton can use the ϵ-transition to move to q_1.
- In q_1, the automaton consumes an indeterminate number of characters using the self-loop and can move to q_2 on an a and q_3 on a b. The automaton halts without accepting if the input ends before moving to q_2 or q_3.
- In q_2, if the character is an a, the automaton advances to q_4; otherwise, it halts without accepting. In addition, if no more characters exist, the automaton stops without accepting.
- In q_3, if the character is a b, the automaton advances to q_4; otherwise, it halts without accepting. In addition, if no more characters exist, the automaton stops without accepting.
- In q_4, if any character remains, the automaton halts without accepting. Otherwise, since q_4 is a final state, the automaton accepts.

An intuitive description of the NFA is as follows:

At the start, if the input is ϵ, the automaton accepts. Otherwise, the automaton advances to a state that consumes an indefinite number of input characters. In addition, in the same state, on seeing an a, the automaton may advance to a final state where it anticipates reading one more character before the end of input, and the last character is an a. Alternatively, on seeing a b in the same state, the automaton may advance to the same final state as in the case of a, where it anticipates reading one more character before the end of input, and the last character is an b.

If the automaton's choices fail to meet its anticipation, it halts without accepting. However, if the input is a non-ϵ member of F, the automaton can make choices so that it arrives at the final state q_4.

The nonmembers of F are a, b, and those ending with either ab or ba. If the input is not a language member, the automaton cannot arrive at q_4.

We can construct a DFA that accepts the language with five states. The number of states is the same, as shown next, but the automaton needs three final states instead of two.

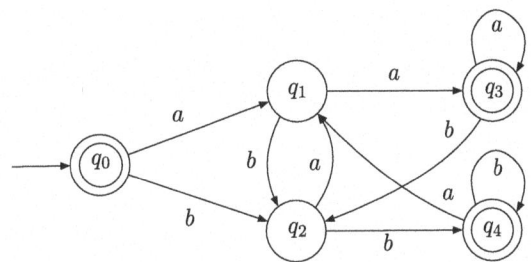

Example 2.7 Let G be the set $\{abc, abcabc, abcabcabc, \ldots\}$: i.e., any number of repetitions of abc, excluding ϵ. We can build an NFA for G with four states: q_0, q_1, q_2, and q_3, where q_0 is the initial state and q_3 is the final state. The transitions among these states are as follows:

State	a	b	c
q_0	q_1		
q_1		q_2	
q_2			q_3
q_3	q_1		

Next is the diagram of the NFA.

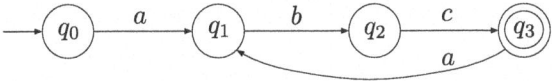

We can design a deterministic version of the language, as shown next. The deterministic version looks more complex.

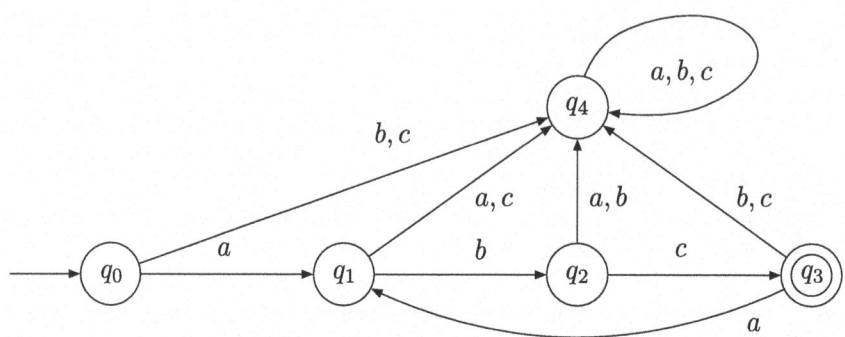

The principal idea in the design of the nondeterministic version is as follows:

We first construct a DFA that anticipates receiving a cycle of abc. The construction uses a non-final sink state. Once the automaton gets to the sink state, it will loop at that state until the end of the input. We then get rid of the transition to the sink state.

2.2.2   Converting NFAs to DFAs

The condition for acceptance of an NFA is existential; it accepts its input if, and only if, nondeterministic selections of actions at each computation point take it to a final state. The existential nature gives us the impression that NFA can accept languages that deterministic ones cannot. Surprisingly, the NFA model is only as powerful as the DFA model. Below, we will show that the quest for a series of selections by NFAs is something that DFAs can simulate as well.

Before formally presenting how such simulations are possible, we make a simple but important observation about the behavior of an NFAs. An NFA may nondeterministically choose to follow a series of ϵ-transitions before and after consuming an input character. The automaton may be able to follow ϵ-transitions indefinitely if we can form a loop using ϵ-transitions only. This may raise a concern that the automaton may not stop. However, according to Exercise 1.11, if there is a loop on a path, we can create a loop-free path without changing its start and end points. Furthermore, according to Exercise 1.9, each loop-free path has no more nodes than there are states. These properties imply that we can assume that the number of successive ϵ-transitions shall be strictly less than the number of states (the path length is the number of nodes minus 1).

Proposition 2.1 *Suppose an NFA M has k states. If M can transition from one state to another on ϵ-transitions only, it can do so in at most $k-1$ steps. Thus, if M accepts an input having a length of n, it can arrive at a final state in $\leq n + (k-1)(n+1) = kn + k - 1$ steps.*

The proposition means we can answer if an NFA M accepts an input w by examining all its computations with a length of $k|w| + k - 1$.

2.2.2.1 The Pseudo-Nondeterministic Finite Automaton (Pseudo-NFA) Model

Proposition 2.1 states that whether or not a k-state NFA accepts its n-character input can be determined by examining all its computation paths having a length of $\leq kn + k - 1$. We can shorten the search depth to $|w|$ using some precomputation. Let $M = (Q, \Sigma, \delta, q_0, F)$ be an NFA and $k = \|Q\|$. Let us pick an enumeration, $p_1, \ldots, p_k$, of M's state so that $q_0 = p_1$. We think of the directed graph derived from the state diagram of M by keeping only ϵ-transitions. The graph's adjacency matrix, T_ϵ, is $k \times k$ and given as follows:

For all i and j, the (i, j) entry of T_ϵ is 1 if $i = j$ or $p_j \in \delta(p_i, \epsilon)$; the entry is 0 otherwise.

Similarly, we define T_a for each symbol a:

For all i and j, the (i, j) entry of T_a is 1 if $p_j \in \delta(p_i, \epsilon)$; the entry is 0 otherwise.

Note that the diagonal entries of T_a may or may not be 1.

For each $\ell \geq 1$, $(T_\epsilon)^\ell$ represents the ϵ-transitions-only reachability in ℓ steps. Let $\hat{T}_\epsilon = (T_\epsilon)^{k-1}$. Then, for all i and j, the (i, j) entry of $\hat{T}_\epsilon$ is 1 if, and only if, p_j is reachable from p_i by following any number of ϵ-transitions.

Using $\hat{T}_\epsilon$ and $T_a, a \in \Sigma$, we can construct a pseudo-NFA $\hat{M} = (Q, \Sigma, \hat{\delta}, \theta, F)$, where $\hat{\delta}$ is an updated transition without ϵ-transitions and $q_0 \in I \subseteq Q$. The pseudo-NFA $\hat{M}$ starts from a state nondeterministically chosen from θ, uses $\hat{\delta}$ to process the input, and accepts when it finishes in a final state. The set θ consists of all states that M can reach from $q_0(= p_1)$ with ϵ-transitions. The set θ can be obtained from $\hat{T}_\epsilon$. It is the set of states represented by the indices where the entry is 1 in the first row of $\hat{T}_\epsilon$.

For each $q \in Q$ and $a \in \Sigma$, $\hat{\delta}(q, a)$ is the set of all states M can reach from q by following some ϵ-transitions, a directed edge labeled by a, and some ϵ-transitions. The transition function $\hat{\delta}$ on a symbol a is given by:

$$\hat{T}_a = \hat{T}_\epsilon T_a \hat{T}_\epsilon.$$

Here, for all i and j, $p_j \in \hat{\delta}(p_i, a)$ if, and only if, the (i, j) entry of the matrix product is 1. Because of the incorporation of ϵ-transitions in $\hat{\delta}$, no separate ϵ-transitions are needed in $\hat{\delta}$, and $\hat{M}$ accepts the same language as M. Algorithm 2.1 presents the algorithm for computing the pseudo-NFA. The running time of the algorithm is $O(k^3(\|\Sigma\| + \log k))$ (see Exercise 2.21).

Algorithm 2.1 An algorithm for computing an equivalent pseudo-NFA

1: **procedure** PSEUDO-NFA-CONVERSION(M)
2:     receive an NFA $M = (Q, \Sigma, \delta, q_0, F)$;
3:     enumerate the states of Q as $p_1, \ldots, p_k$ where $q_0 = p_1$;
4:     construct a $k \times k$ 0/1 matrix T_ϵ as follows:
5:     for all i and j, the (i, j) entry of T_ϵ is 1 if $i = j$ or $p_j \in \delta(p_i, \epsilon)$; it is 0 otherwise;
6:     $\hat{T}_\epsilon \leftarrow (T_\epsilon)^{k-1}$;
7:     **for** each $a \in \Sigma$ **do**
8:         construct a $k \times k$ 0/1 matrix T_a: for all i and j, the (i, j) entry is $1 \Leftrightarrow p_j \in \delta(p_i, a)$;
9:         $\hat{T}_a \leftarrow B T_a B$;
10:    **end for**
11:    $\theta \leftarrow$ the set the first row of B represents;
12:    **for** each i such that $1 \le i \le k$ **do**
13:        **for** each $a \in \Sigma$ **do**
14:            $\hat{\delta}(p_i, a) \leftarrow$ the set the i-th row of $\hat{T}_a$ represents;
15:        **end for**
16:    **end for**
17:    return $(Q, \Sigma, \hat{\delta}, \theta, F)$;
18: **end procedure**

2.2.2.2   Converting NFAs to DFAs

We now use $\hat{M}$ to construct a DFA $N = (Q', \Sigma, \delta', q_0', F')$ for $L(M)$. The state set $Q' = 2^Q$, i.e., the set of all combinations of states in Q. The transition function takes each state combination to another on each symbol. The initial state q_0' is θ; i.e., the set of all possible initial states of $\hat{M}$. The final state set F' is $\{S \mid S \cap F \ne \emptyset\}$; i.e., the set of all combinations containing some element of F. The transition function δ' is determined from $\hat{\delta}$: for each $S \in 2^Q$ and each $a \in \Sigma$,

$$\delta'(S, a) = \cup_{p_i \in S} \hat{\delta}(p_i, a).$$

If v is the vector representing S, $\delta'(S, a)$ can be calculated as the set representing $v\hat{T}_a$.

Since $\hat{M}$ accepts the same language as $L(M)$ and is without ϵ-transitions, N captures the exhaustive search for an accepting computation of $\hat{M}$. Thus, N is a DFA accepting $L(M)$.

Hence, we have proven the following theorem:

Theorem 2.1 *NFAs accept only regular languages.*

2.2.2.3   A Greedy Conversion Algorithm

In the proof of Theorem 2.1, the DFA we derived from the NFA with k states has 2^k states. Some of the states may be unreachable from the initial state. Such states are irrelevant, and we can safely remove them. While we can eliminate them after

---

Algorithm 2.2 An algorithm for computing a DFA from a pseudo-NFA

1: **procedure** PSEUDO-NFA-TO-DFA($\hat{M}$)
2:     receive a pseudo-NFA $M = (Q, \Sigma, \hat{\delta}, \theta, F)$ along with $\hat{T}_a$ for all $a \in \Sigma$;
3:     $Q' \leftarrow 2^Q$;
4:     $q'_0 \leftarrow \theta$;
5:     $F' \leftarrow \{S \mid S \cap F \neq \emptyset\}$;
6:     **for** each $S \in 2^Q$ **do**
7:         **for** $a \in \Sigma$ **do**
8:             $v \leftarrow$ the vector representing S;
9:             $u \leftarrow v\hat{T}_a$;
10:            $S' \leftarrow$ the set representing u;
11:            $\delta'(S, a) \leftarrow S'$;
12:        **end for**
13:    **end for**
14:    return $(Q', \Sigma, \delta', q'_0, F')$;
15: **end procedure**

---

completing the construction, we can construct the deterministic one dynamically so that we never consider the unreachable states, as shown in Algorithm 2.3.

An alternate, dynamic approach would be to combine the construction of the transition function and the exclusion of unreachable states, as follows:

Algorithm 2.3 A greedy algorithm for constructing a DFA from an NFA

1: **procedure** GREEDY-DFA-CONSTRUCTION(M)
2:     receive $M = (Q, \Sigma, \delta, q_0, F)$ is an NFA;
3:     construct a pseudo-NFA $\hat{M} = (Q, \Sigma, \hat{\delta}, \theta, F)$ along with $\hat{T}_a$ for each $a \in \Sigma$;
4:     initialize a set $Q' \leftarrow \{\theta\}$;
5:     initialize a queue $R \leftarrow \langle \theta \rangle$;
6:     **while** $R \neq \emptyset$ **do**
7:         dequeue the first element s from the queue R;
8:         **for** each $a \in \Sigma$ **do**
9:             $t \leftarrow \delta'(s, a)$;
10:            record $\delta'(s, a) = t$;
11:            **if** $t \notin Q'$ **then**
12:                $Q' \leftarrow Q' \cup \{t\}$;
13:                add t to the queue R;
14:            **end if**
15:        **end for**
16:    **end while**
17:    return $(Q', \Sigma, \delta', \theta, F)$;
18: **end procedure**

In this algorithm, we will examine, for each state combination that emerges during exploration, which combinations are reachable from the first combination by reading a symbol. Each time a new combination emerges, we will add it to a list of state combinations. The exploration begins with the combination of all states reachable from the initial state by following any number, including 0, of

ϵ-transitions. There is no guarantee that this meager construction can reduce the number of states from 2^k to a smaller value. We can only guarantee that any combination unreachable from the initial combination is not part of the DFA.

Example 2.8 Let A be the language of all nonempty strings in $\{a, b\}^*$ starting with an a and ending with a b in which neither symbol repeats more than twice. The members of the language A include ab, abb, aab, $aabb$, $abab$, $abbaab$, etc. The nonmembers of the language include a, b, $aaabb$, $abbb$, baa, aba, etc. We design the following NFA that accepts A. The final state is q_4. The automaton repeats a four-step cycle of [either ϵ or a, a, either ϵ or b, b] with the last position being the final state.

State	a	b	ϵ
q_0	q_1		q_1
q_1	q_2		
q_2		q_3	q_3
q_3			q_4
q_4	q_1		q_1

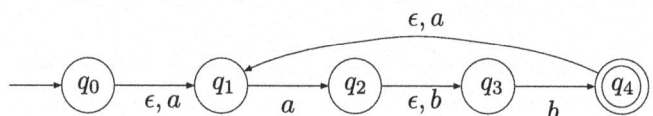

In this order, we assign indices $1, \ldots, 5$ to the five states $q_0, \ldots, q_4$. We obtain the matrices T_ϵ, T_a, and T_b as follows:

$$T_\epsilon = \begin{pmatrix} 1 & 1 & 0 & 0 & 0 \\ 0 & 1 & 0 & 0 & 0 \\ 0 & 0 & 1 & 1 & 0 \\ 0 & 0 & 0 & 1 & 0 \\ 0 & 1 & 0 & 0 & 1 \end{pmatrix}, T_a = \begin{pmatrix} 0 & 1 & 0 & 0 & 0 \\ 0 & 0 & 1 & 0 & 0 \\ 0 & 0 & 0 & 0 & 0 \\ 0 & 0 & 0 & 0 & 0 \\ 0 & 1 & 0 & 0 & 0 \end{pmatrix}, T_b = \begin{pmatrix} 0 & 0 & 0 & 0 & 0 \\ 0 & 0 & 0 & 0 & 0 \\ 0 & 0 & 0 & 1 & 0 \\ 0 & 0 & 0 & 0 & 1 \\ 0 & 0 & 0 & 0 & 0 \end{pmatrix}.$$

We have $\hat{T}_\epsilon = T_\epsilon$. By combining $\hat{T}_\epsilon$ and T_a and T_b, we get $\hat{T}_a$ and $\hat{T}_b$:

$$\hat{T}_a = \begin{pmatrix} 0 & 1 & 1 & 1 & 0 \\ 0 & 0 & 1 & 1 & 0 \\ 0 & 0 & 0 & 0 & 0 \\ 0 & 0 & 0 & 0 & 0 \\ 0 & 1 & 1 & 1 & 0 \end{pmatrix}, \hat{T}_b = \begin{pmatrix} 0 & 0 & 0 & 0 & 0 \\ 0 & 0 & 0 & 0 & 0 \\ 0 & 1 & 0 & 1 & 1 \\ 0 & 1 & 0 & 0 & 1 \\ 0 & 0 & 0 & 0 & 0 \end{pmatrix}.$$

The initial state θ is $\{q_0, q_1\}$. Any state combination containing q_4 is a final state. We then obtain a DFA from the NFA using Algorithm 2.3 as follows:

1. We initialize the set Q' as $\{\{q_0, q_1\}\}$ and the queue R as $[\{q_0, q_1\}]$.
2. We remove the first element $\{q_0, q_1\}$ of R as s. Receiving an a in s results in the state set $\{q_1, q_2, q_3\}$. Receiving a b in s results in the state set $\emptyset$ because it has nowhere to go. Both $\{q_1, q_2, q_3\}$ and $\emptyset$ are new combinations. We add both to Q' and R. Q' becomes $\{\{q_0, q_1\}, \{q_1, q_2, q_3\}, \emptyset\}$, and R becomes $[\{q_1, q_2, q_3\}, \emptyset]$.
3. We remove the first element $\{q_1, q_2, q_3\}$ of R as s. Receiving an a in s results in the state set $\{q_2, q_3\}$. Receiving a b in s results in the state set $\{q_1, q_3, q_4\}$. Both $\{q_2, q_3\}$ and $\{q_1, q_3, q_4\}$ are new combinations. We add both to Q' and R. Q' becomes $\{\{q_0, q_1\}, \{q_1, q_2, q_3\}, \emptyset, \{q_2, q_3\}, \{q_1, q_3, q_4\}\}$, and R becomes $[\emptyset, \{q_2, q_3\}, \{q_1, q_3, q_4\}]$.
4. We remove the first element $\emptyset$ from R as s. Receiving an a or a b results in $\emptyset$. We have already seen $\emptyset$, so there is no update on Q' or R.
5. We remove the first element $\{q_2, q_3\}$ from R as s. Receiving an a in s results in the state set $\emptyset$. Receiving a b in s results in the state set $\{q_1, q_3, q_4\}$. Both combinations are already in Q', so neither Q' nor R receives an update.
6. We remove the first element $\{q_1, q_3, q_4\}$ from R as s. Receiving an a in s results in the state set $\{q_1, q_2, q_3\}$. Receiving a b in s results in the state set $\{q_1, q_4\}$. We already have $\{q_1, q_2, q_3\}$ in Q', so we add only $\{q_1, q_4\}$ to both Q' and R. The set Q' becomes

$$\{\{q_0, q_1\}, \{q_1, q_2, q_3\}, \emptyset, \{q_2, q_3\}, \{q_1, q_3, q_4\}, \{q_1, q_4\}\},$$

and R becomes $[\{q_1, q_4\}]$.
7. We remove the first element $\{q_1, q_4\}$ from R as s. Receiving an a in s results in the state set $\{q_1, q_2, q_3\}$. Receiving a b in s results in the state set $\emptyset$. We have seen both, so there are no new additions to Q' or R.
8. The queue R has become empty. Thus, we have completed the exploration. Let us refer to the six state sets in Q' by $r_0, \ldots, r_5$ in the order we have discovered them; i.e.,

$$r_0 = \{q_0, q_1\},$$
$$r_1 = \{q_1, q_2, q_3\},$$
$$r_2 = \emptyset,$$
$$r_3 = \{q_2, q_3\},$$
$$r_4 = \{q_1, q_3, q_4\}, \text{ and}$$
$$r_5 = \{q_1, q_4\}.$$

The final states of the DFA are those that have q_4; they are r_4 and r_5. We obtain the following DFA based on the analysis we have just done.

State	a	b
r_0	r_1	r_2
r_1	r_3	r_4
r_2	r_2	r_2
r_3	r_2	r_4
r_4	r_1	r_5
r_5	r_1	r_2

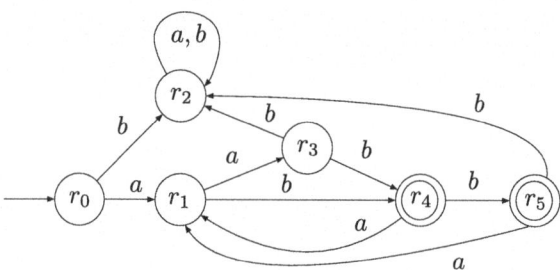

2.2.3   Constructing Regular Languages from Other Regular Languages

Here, we consider composing regular languages into new languages and examine if the new languages remain regular.

Let χ be an operation for creating a language from some languages. Depending on the number of languages χ requires for its production, we call it a **unary** operation, **binary** operation, **ternary** operation, and so on. We think of applying χ to all languages in a class C to generate a new one, C'; that is, C' collects all you can produce by applying χ to some members of C. We ask whether or not C' is the same as C. If it is, we say that C is **closed under** χ. We also say that χ is a **closure property** of C.

The operations we already know are complementation, union, intersection, concatenation, and Kleene-star. Of these, the first and the last are unary operations. The other three may take two or more operands. An operation involving more than two languages can be represented by a sequence of binary operations. Thus, we need only consider the binary version.

The previous section (Sect. 2.2.2) shows that NFAs are computationally equivalent to DFAs. This equivalence is a powerful tool with which we can show that the class of regular languages is **closed under all Boolean operations and the Kleene-star**.

Theorem 2.2 *The class of regular languages is closed under complement, union, intersection, concatenation, and Kleene-star.*

Proof Overview

We previously showed the equivalence between the deterministic and NFA models. We prove this theorem using that equivalence.

- To prove the closure property under complement, we switch the roles between final and non-final states in the DFA at hand.
- To prove the closure property under union, we construct an NFA that, at the start, selects the execution between two DFAs.
- Then, using the DeMorgan Laws, we prove the closure property under intersection.
- To prove the closure property under concatenation, we construct an NFA that executes the first DFA, nondeterministically switches from the first to the second when it is in any final state, and then accepts when it finishes reading the input in any final state of the second.
- To prove the closure property under the Kleene-star, we construct an NFA with a new initial state from which makes an ϵ-transition to the initial state of the DFA at hand. The automaton can return to the additional state with an ϵ-transition from each final state. Adding the new initial to the final states makes the nondeterministic one accept the Kleene-star.
- To prove the closure property under the Kleene-plus, we connect the given DFA to the NFA for the Kleene-star.

Proof Let L and L' be arbitrary regular languages. Let $M = (Q, \Sigma, \delta, q_0, F)$ and $M' = (Q', \Sigma, \delta', q_0', F')$ be DFAs accepting L and L', respectively. We may assume $Q \cap Q' = \emptyset$. Let the two diagrams representing the computation of M and M' be as in Fig. 2.4.

[**Complement**] We define N as the DFA $(Q, \Sigma, \delta, q_0, Q - F)$; that is, the same automaton as M but the final states are the non-final states of M'. It is easy to see that for all $w \in \Sigma^*$, M on w arrives at a final state if, and only if, N on w arrives at a non-final state. Thus, N accepts the complement of L. This proves that the class of regular languages is closed under complement.

[**Kleene-Star**] We construct, from M, an NFA N by adding a new initial state p_0. p_0 also becomes a unique final state. Additionally, we add an ϵ-transition from p_0 to q_0 and an ϵ-transition from each state in F to p_0 (see Fig. 2.5). Adding p_0 as the initial and a final state allows N to accept ϵ. The ϵ-transition from p_0 to q_0 allows N to commence the computation of M from q_0' without reading any character. The ϵ-transition from each member of F to p_0, along with the ϵ-transition from p_0 to q_0, allows N to restart the computation of M from any final state of M. Thus, for all strings w of the form $w_1 \cdots w_m$ such that $w_1, \ldots, w_m \in L$, N can accept w. This means that $L^* \subseteq L(N)$.

Fig. 2.4 The two DFAs: M
and M'

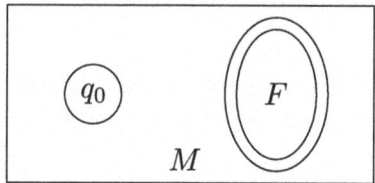

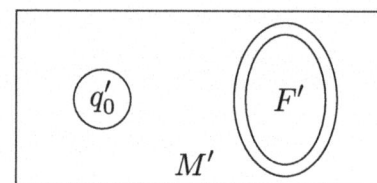

Fig. 2.5 The construction of
an NFA accepting L^*

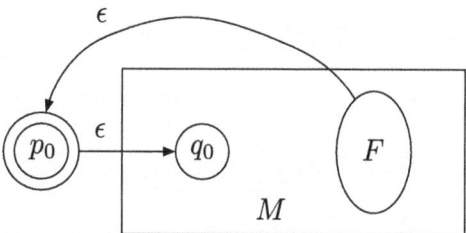

Conversely, let w be a string that N accepts. We take an arbitrary state sequence π that N follows when it accepts w. We divide π into sub-sequences wherever p_0 appears and eliminate p_0 from the sub-sequences. Let $\pi_1, \ldots, \pi_k$ be the sub-sequences. Let $w_1, \ldots, w_k$ be the substring of w that N processes with the sub-sequences, respectively. We have the following properties:

- Since π is a state sequence when N accepts, π begins and ends with p_0. Thus,

$$\pi = p_0 \pi_1 p_0 \cdots p_0 \pi_k p_0.$$

- An ϵ-transition to q_0 is the only one transition from p_0. Every transition to p_0 is an ϵ-transition from a state in F. Thus,

$$w = \epsilon w_1 \epsilon \cdots \epsilon w_k \epsilon.$$

In addition, for each j such that $1 \leq j \leq k$, $w_j \in L(M)$.

Hence, $L(N) = L(M)^*$. Figure 2.5 shows this construction.

[**Union**] We construct an NFA N from M and M'. The state set of N is $Q \cup Q' \cup \{p_0\}$, where p_0 is a new initial state. The final state set of N is $F \cup F'$. We preserve all the transitions of M and M' and add two new transitions: an ϵ-transition from p_0 to q_0 and another from p_0 to q_0'. The automaton N operates by selecting between M and

Fig. 2.6 The construction of
an NFA accepting $L \cup L'$

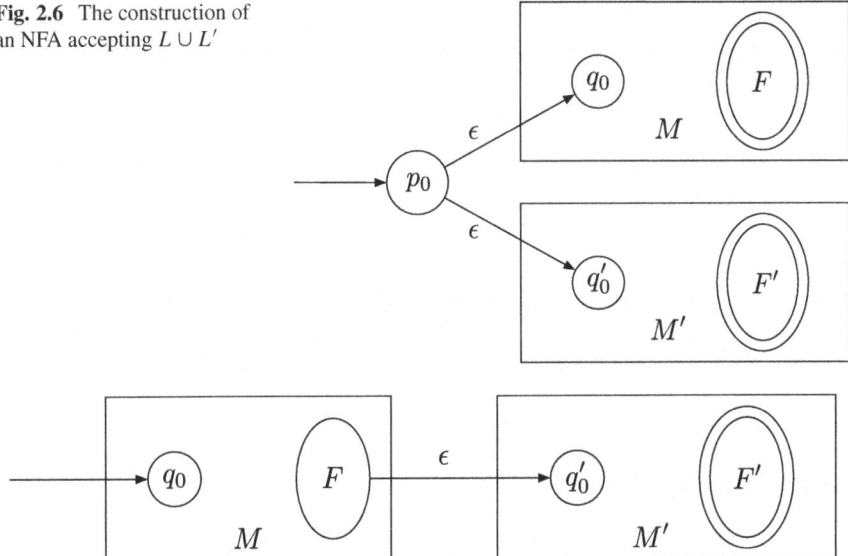

Fig. 2.7 The construction of an NFA for LL'

M' without consuming an input character and then executes the DFA it has chosen. The automaton N accepts if, and only if, the DFA it has chosen to execute accepts the input. Thus, $L(N) = L(M) \cup L(M')$.

Figure 2.6 shows this construction.

[Intersection] We note that for all languages L and L', $L \cap L' = \overline{\overline{L} \cup \overline{L'}}$. Because the regular languages are closed under union and complement, $L \cap L'$ is regular if both L and L' are regular. Direct construction of a DFA that accepts $L \cap L'$ uses the state set $R = Q \times Q'$, the Cartesian product of the two-state sets. The initial state is (q_0, q_0'), and the final state set is $F \times F'$. The transition function ξ maps each $((q, q'), a)$ to $(\delta(a), \delta'(a))$; that is, ξ applies δ to the first component and δ' to the second component of the state pair (q, q').

[Concatenation] We construct an NFA N from M and M'. The state set of N is $Q \cup Q'$. The initial state is q_0. The final state set is F'. The transition function of N is the join of the transition functions of M and M'; if the state is in Q, N uses δ, and if the state is in Q', N uses δ'. We also add an ϵ-transition from each final state in F to q_0' (see Fig. 2.7). We show that $L(N) = LL'$ as follows:

Suppose $w \in LL'$ so that $w = w_1 w_2$ with $w_1 \in L$ and $w_2 \in L'$. Then, N can process w_1. When N arrives at a final state of M at the end of w_1, it jumps to q_0', processes the remainder of the input, and accepts. Thus, $w \in L(N)$.

Conversely, suppose that $L(N)$ accepts the input w. It must be the case that after reading some characters of w, N transitions to q_0'. Let w_1 be the string that N processes before jumping to q_0', and let w_2 be the remainder. We see that w_1 takes N from q_0 to a state in F using the transition function of M and w_2 takes

N from q_0' to a state in F' using the transition function of M'. Thus, $w_1 \in L$ and $w_2 \in L$'. This means that $w \in LL'$. Hence, $L(N) = LL'$.

The proof of the theorem is now complete.   □

2.3   Regular Expressions

While we define regular languages using DFAs and NFAs, there is an alternate way of defining regular languages, which is by using regular expressions. In this section, we define regular expressions and show that their expressive power is equal to that of DFAs and NFAs.

2.3.1   The Definition

Let us begin with the definition of regular expressions.

A **regular expression** is a method for expressing a language using a pattern that every language member must satisfy, but none of its nonmembers satisfy. A specification of a regular expression may use an alphabet, symbols from the alphabet, ϵ, $\emptyset$, (), $\cup$, $*$, and $+$. For a regular expression E, we write $L(E)$ to indicate the language E represents.

The regular expression construction uses the following inductive definition:

Base expressions

- $\emptyset$ represents the empty set.
- ϵ represents the empty string.
- For each $a \in \Sigma$, a represents the string a.
- Σ represents the single-letter word whose unique letter is from Σ.

Induction

- For each regular expression E, (E) represents E.
- For each regular expression E, E^* represents $L(E)^*$.
- For each regular expression E, E^+ represents $L(E)^+$.
- For all $m \geq 2$ and regular expressions $E_1, E_2, \ldots, E_m$, $E_1 E_2 \cdots E_m$ represents $L(E_1) L(E_1) \cdots L(E_m)$.
- For all $m \geq 2$ and regular expressions $E_1, E_2, \ldots, E_m$, $E_1 \cup E_2 \cup \cdots \cup E_m$ represents $L(E_1) \cup L(E_2) \cup \cdots \cup L(E_m)$.

Example 2.9 The language of all strings in $\{a, b, c\}^*$ that contain at least one of aa, bb, and cc has a regular expression:

$$(a \cup b \cup c)^* (aa \cup bb \cup cc)(a \cup b \cup c)^*.$$

Using Σ for $\{a, b, c\}$, we have an alternate expression:

$$\Sigma^*(aa \cup bb \cup cc)\Sigma^*.$$

Example 2.10 The language of all strings in $\{a, b\}^*$ that are either empty or ending with one of aa and bb has a regular expression:

$$\epsilon \cup (a, b)^*(aa \cup bb).$$

2.3.2 Equivalence Between Regular Expressions and NFAs

We now see the equivalence between regular expressions and NFAs by proving the following theorem.

Theorem 2.3 *A language is regular if, and only if, it has a regular expression.*

Proof Overview

The proof consists of two parts. Part One shows how to build an equivalent NFA from any regular expression. The proof is inductive and matches the inductive construction of regular expressions. Each symbol in the alphabet, including ϵ, has a two-state NFA accepting it. The induction operations for constructing regular expressions are concatenation, union, Kleene-star, and Kleene-plus. Theorem 2.2 shows that an NFA can execute these operations. Thus, every regular expression has a matching NFA, representing a regular language.

Part Two shows how to construct a regular expression from an arbitrary NFA. The construction is complex. Given a DFA with states $q_1, \ldots, q_n$, using t as a parameter, we construct a regular expression corresponding to the path from each state to another, where only states among $q_1, \ldots, q_t$ are usable as intermediate nodes. To build the expressions, we increase the value of t from 0 (no intermediate nodes) to n.

Proof **[Every Regular Expression Defines a Regular Language]** By definition, every expression in the base case has a DFA that accepts it. For the inductive step, the permissible operations are union, concatenation, Kleene-star, and Kleene-plus. These are closure properties of regular languages. Since the base case defines regular languages and the inductive step uses regular language closure operations, regular expressions generate only regular languages.

[Every Regular Language Is Expressible as a Regular Expression] Let L be an arbitrary regular language and M_0 be an arbitrary NFA that accepts L. We modify the automaton by adding an ϵ-transition to each state. Let $M = (Q, \Sigma, \delta, q_1, F)$ be the automaton we have just constructed, where $Q = \{q_1, \ldots, q_n\}$.

For all i, j, and k such that $1 \leq i \leq n$, $1 \leq j \leq n$, and $0 \leq k \leq n$, let $W_{i,j,k}$ be the set of all strings w, with the following properties:

- $\delta(q_i, w) = q_j$.
- Let $w = w_1 \cdots w_m$ and let $[p_0, \ldots, p_m]$ be the state sequence that M follows while processing w starting at state q_i. Here, $p_0 = q_i$ and $p_m = q_j$. Then, for all ℓ such that $1 \leq \ell \leq m - 1$, there is some $t \leq k$ such that $p_i = q_t$. In other words, the index of any state that M visits after leaving q_i and arriving at q_j while processing w is at most k.

Below, for each combination of i, j, and k, we will construct a regular expression $E_{i,j,k}$. The construction is by way of induction on k. We will then show for all i, j, and k that $L(E_{i,j,k}) = W_{i,j,k}$. Since for all integers i and j between 1 and n, $W_{i,j,n}$ has no restriction on the states between q_i and q_j, we have for all j such that $1 \leq j \leq n$ that $W_{1,j,n}$ is the set of all input that takes M to q_j. Then, L is $\cup_{j:q_j \in F} W_{1,j,n}$. The regular expression for L is the union of all $E_{1,j,n}$ such as $q_j \in F$.

The regular expressions are as follows:

- $(k = 0)$ For all i and j between 1 and n, $E_{i,j,0}$ is a list of all $a \in \Sigma$ such that $\delta(q_i, a) = q_j$ joined with the symbol $\cup$.
- $(k \geq 1)$ For all i and j between 1 and n, we define

$$E_{i,j,k} = E_{i,j,k-1} \cup E_{i,k,k-1}(E_{k,k,k-1})^* E_{k,j,k-1}.$$

Because $E_{i,j,k-1}$ appears in the definition of $E_{i,j,k}$ as an element of the union, we have, for all i and j,

$$L(E_{i,j,0}) \subseteq L(E_{i,j,1}) \subseteq \cdots \subseteq L(E_{i,j,n}).$$

In addition, we know that the following holds by definition:

$$W_{i,j,0} \subseteq W_{i,j,1} \subseteq \cdots \subseteq W_{i,j,n}.$$

We now claim that $L(E_{i,j,k}) = W_{i,j,k}$ for all i, j, k by induction on k.

The base case is where $k = 0$. Let $1 \leq i \leq n$ and $1 \leq j \leq n$. By definition, $W_{i,j,0}$ is the set of all strings that takes M from state q_i to q_j without going through any state between the two endpoints. This means that $W_{i,j,0} = \{a \mid a \in \Sigma_\epsilon$ and $\delta(q_i, a) = q_j\}$. The definition of $E_{i,j,0}$ is precisely this. Thus, the claim holds for $k = 0$.

For the induction step, let $1 \leq k \leq n$ and suppose that the claim holds for all smaller values of k; i.e., for all k' such that $0 \leq k' \leq k - 1$, $L(E_{i,j,k'}) = W_{i,j,k'}$ holds for all i and j. Pick any i and j. We will show that every element of $L(E_{i,j,k})$ is in $W_{i,j,k}$ and every element of $W_{i,j,k}$ is in $L(E_{i,j,k})$.

First, let w be an arbitrary word in $L(E_{i,j,k})$. Then w matches either $E_{i,j,k-1}$ or $E_{i,k,k-1}(E_{k,k,k-1})^* E_{k,j,k-1}$. Suppose w matches $E_{i,j,k-1}$. Then, by our induction hypothesis, we have w in

$$L(E_{i,j,k-1}) = W_{i,j,k-1} \subseteq W_{i,j,k}$$

so $w \in W_{i,j,k}$. Suppose w does not match the expression $E_{i,j,k-1}$. Then w must match the expression $E_{i,k,k-1}(E_{k,k,k-1})^* E_{k,j,k-1}$. By our induction hypothesis, the three regular expression components represent $W_{i,k,k-1}$, $W_{k,k,k-1}^*$, and $W_{k,j,k-1}$, respectively. Of the three, $W_{i,k,k-1}$ requires that the state sequence starts at q_i and ends at q_k, $W_{k,k,k-1}$ starts at q_k and ends at q_k, and $W_{k,j,k-1}$ starts at q_k and ends at q_j. Therefore, we can "join" the three state sequences. Here, by "joining," we connect two sequences by identifying the last element of the first sequence and the first element of the second sequence. In other words, the "join" of two sequences $[a, \ldots, b, c]$ and $[c, d, \ldots, e]$ is $[a, \ldots, b, c, d, \ldots, e]$. The joint sequence starts in q_i and ends in q_j In addition, k is the largest value of h such that q_h appears in the sequence between the first and last elements of the sequence. Thus, in this case, $w \in W_{i,j,k}$, too.

Conversely, let w be an arbitrary member of $W_{i,j,k}$. Let $\Pi = [p_1, \ldots, p_m]$ be an arbitrary state sequence that M may follow while processing w starting at q_i and ending at q_j, where $p_1 = q_i$ and $p_m = q_j$. Such a sequence may not be unique because we have inserted an ϵ-labeled self-loop to each state. Let T be the set of all indices ℓ between 2 and $m-1$ such that $p_\ell = q_k$. Let $t_1, \ldots, t_d$ be an enumeration of the indices in T in increasing order. This means that for all $\ell \in \{2, \ldots, m-1\} - T$, $p_\ell = q_h$ such that $h \leq k - 1$. Using T, we construct the following sequences from Π:

$$\pi_0 = [p_1, \ldots, p_{t_1}],$$
$$\pi_1 = [p_{t_1}, \ldots, p_{t_2}],$$
$$\pi_2 = [p_{t_2}, \ldots, p_{t_3}],$$
$$\cdots$$
$$\pi_{d-1} = [p_{t_{d-1}}, \ldots, p_{t_d}],$$
$$\pi_d = [p_{t_d}, \ldots, p_m].$$

Using the "join" operation from the previous paragraph, the joint sequence of $\pi_0, \ldots, \pi_d$ is Π. Noting that a state sequence of M having length a $\ell \geq 1$ can process strings having a length $\ell - 1$ only, we can decompose w into substrings $u_0, \ldots, u_d$ such that $w = u_0 \cdots u_d$, and for each h, $0 \leq h \leq d$, M can process u_h using the sequence π_d. Since we have exhausted all the occurrences of q_k between p_2 and p_{m-1} and Π is a state sequence for a member in $W_{i,j,k}$, we know that the following properties hold:

- $u_0 \in W_{i,k,k-1}$.
- $u_1, \ldots, u_{d-1} \in W_{k,k,k-1}$.
- $u_d \in W_{k,j,k-1}$.

From our induction hypothesis, the Ws appearing on the right-hand side are equivalent to the regular languages corresponding to the same triple indices, as follows:

- $L(E_{i,k,k-1}) = W_{i,k,k-1}$.
- $L(E_{k,k,k-1}) = W_{k,k,k-1}$.
- $L(E_{k,j,k-1})$.

Thus, we have:

- $u_0 \in L(E_{i,k,k-1})$.
- $u_1, \ldots, u_{d-1} \in L(E_{k,k,k-1})$.
- $u_d \in L(E_{k,j,k-1})$.

Since $w = u_0 \cdots u_d$, $w \in L(E_{i,k,k-1})L(E_{k,k,k-1})^*L(E_{k,j,k-1})$. This means

$$w \in L(E_{i,k,k-1}(E_{k,k,k-1})^* E_{k,j,k-1}).$$

The regular expression on the right-hand side is the second component for $E_{i,j,k}$. Thus, $w \in L(E_{i,j,k})$.

From the two membership paragraphs, we get that $W_{i,j,k} = L(E_{i,j,k})$, and so the claim holds for k. Hence, we have the equality $W_{i,j,k} = L(E_{i,j,k})$ for all i, j, k, and complete the proof for the induction step.

This proves the theorem.   □

Let us see one example of applying the algorithm from Theorem 2.3 to generate an equivalent regular expression from an NFA.

Example 2.11 Consider the NFA shown in Fig. 2.8. By inspecting the diagram, we see that the language the NFA accepts has a regular expression $(abc)^*(\epsilon \cup a)$.

We first modify the automaton with the addition of ϵ-loops, as shown in Fig. 2.9. The enumeration of the states we use is p_1, p_2, p_3.

The construction of the regular expressions proceeds as follows:

- First, we obtain the regular expressions for $k = 0$.

Fig. 2.8 A mystery NFA
with three states

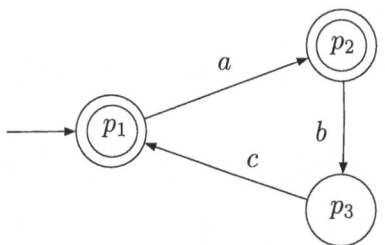

Fig. 2.9 The mystery NFA
after adding self-loops

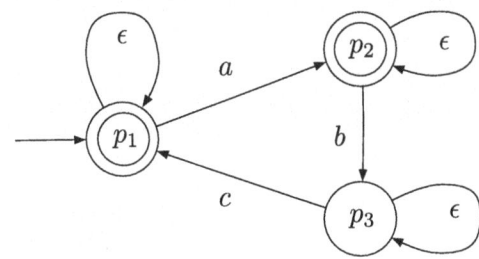

From	To p_1	p_2	p_3
p_1	ϵ	a	$\emptyset$
p_2	$\emptyset$	ϵ	b
p_3	c	$\emptyset$	ϵ

- For $k = 1$, we make p_1 available. The expression changes in the pair (p_3, p_2) as a result of combining (p_3, p_1) and (p_1, p_2).

From	To p_1	p_2	p_3
p_1	ϵ	a	$\emptyset$
p_2	$\emptyset$	ϵ	b
p_3	c	ca	ϵ

- For $k = 2$, changes occur in (p_1, p_3) as a result of combining (p_1, p_2) and (p_2, p_3) and in (p_3, p_3) as a result of combining (p_3, p_2) and (p_2, p_3).

From	To p_1	p_2	p_3
p_1	ϵ	a	$\emptyset \cup ab$
p_2	$\emptyset$	ϵ	b
p_3	c	ca	$\epsilon \cup cab$

- For $k = 3$, changes occur in all the pairs.

From	To p_1	p_2	p_3
p_1	$\epsilon \cup ab(cab)^*c$	$a \cup ab(cba)^*ca$	$(\emptyset \cup ab)(cab)^*$
p_2	$b(cab)^*c$	$\epsilon \cup b(cba)^*ca$	$b(cab)^*$
p_3	$(cab)^*c$	$(cba)^*ca$	$(cab)^*(\epsilon \cup cab)$

We can manually simplify the expressions as follows:

	To		
From	p_1	p_2	p_3
p_1	$(abc)^*$	$(abc)^*a$	$(abc)^*ab$
p_2	$(bca)^*bc$	$(bca)^*$	$(bca)^*b$
p_3	$(cab)^*c$	$(cab)^*ca$	$(caab^*$

- The expression for the language is now the union of the expressions for (p_1, p_1) and (p_1, p_2). The union $(abc)^* \cup (abc)^*a$. Since $(abc)^* = (abc)^*\epsilon$, we can rewrite the union as $(abc)^*(\epsilon \cup a)$.

2.3.3 Visualizing the Construction

While the construction algorithm in the proof runs correctly, and its correctness is easy to establish using induction, the algorithm's workings are somewhat complex to visualize. If we focus on finding a regular expression for the language, we can visually capture the algorithm.

Let L be a regular language and M_0 be a finite automaton (deterministic or nondeterministic) that accepts L. We add two designated states. One is a new initial state with an ϵ-transition to M_0's initial state. The other is a new final state with an ϵ-transition to each of M_0's final state. The new final state is the only final state in the new automaton. Like before, we add an ϵ-loop to each state from M_0. Let $M = (Q, \Sigma, \delta, q_1, \{q_n\})$ be the NFA we have thus constructed, where q_1 and q_n are the states we have added.

Our visualization starts with a drawing of M, where for each pair (i, j) such that there is an arrow from q_i to q_j, we replace its label with $E_{i,j,0}$. Then, for each k such that $1 \leq k \leq n$, and for all i and j, we replace the label of the arc from q_i to q_j with $E_{i,j,k}$ if the arc exists; if there is no arc from q_i to q_j and $E_{i,j,k}$ is no longer $\emptyset$, we draw a new arc from q_i and q_j with label $E_{i,j,k}$. After completing the revision concerning k, we erase q_k from the drawing if $2 \leq k \leq n - 1$ because q_k is no longer relevant to $E_{1,n,n}$. We present this idea in Fig. 2.10.

Here is a demonstration of the visualization. Suppose we have an NFA as appearing in Fig. 2.11.

We start with an NFA with additional initial and final states, as in Fig. 2.12. To prepare for the conversion, we add q_1 and q_2 as the initial and final states, respectively. Additionally, we rename p_1, p_2, and p_3 as q_2, q_3, and q_4, respectively. Furthermore, we add a self-loop labeled with ϵ to q_2, q_3, and q_4.

We then apply the label-replacement procedure three times in succession. The first application uses q_2 as the intermediate vertex, the second uses q_3, and the last uses q_4. The results of the three applications are shown in Figs. 2.13, 2.14, and 2.15, respectively.

Fig. 2.10 The step for incorporating an intermediate point q_k and eliminating the intermediate point from the diagram afterward. The top panel shows before short-circuiting. The bottom panel shows after short-circuiting. The dashed arrows show those that we can remove after this step

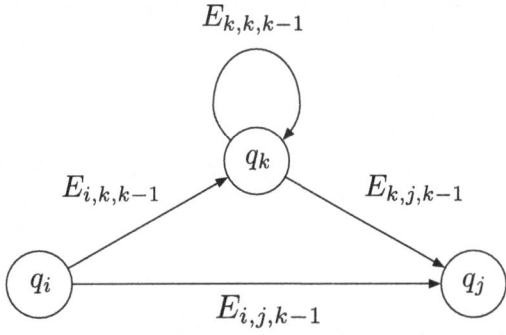

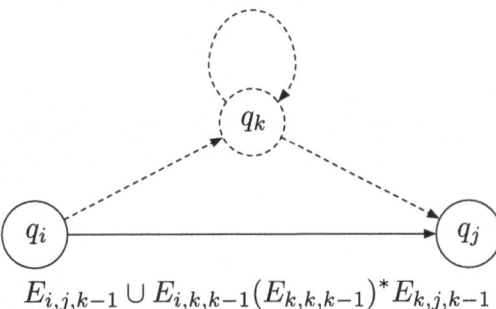

$$E_{i,j,k-1} \cup E_{i,k,k-1}(E_{k,k,k-1})^* E_{k,j,k-1}$$

Fig. 2.11 An NFA with three states

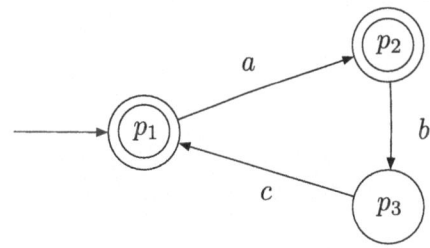

Corollary 2.1 summarizes the equivalence relations we have seen.

Corollary 2.1 *The following are all the same:*

- *DFAs*
- *NFAs*
- *Regular expressions*

Exercises

2.1 Example 2.3 states that for an arbitrary member w of C, w's decomposition $xaybz$ can be such that x is free of a and y is free of b. Prove that such a decomposition is indeed possible.

2.2 Construct a DFA that accepts $\{w \mid w \in \{a, b\}^*$ such that $|w|$ is a multiple of 3$\}$.

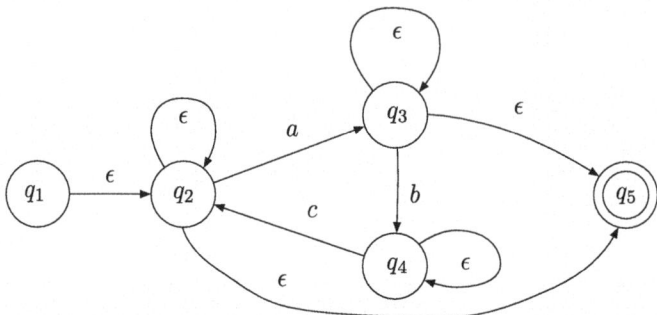

Fig. 2.12 Initialization for the conversion. q_1 and q_5 have been added as the initial and final states. p_1, p_2, and p_3 have been renamed as q_2, q_3, and q_4, respectively. A self-loop labeled with ϵ has been added to q_2, q_3, and q_4

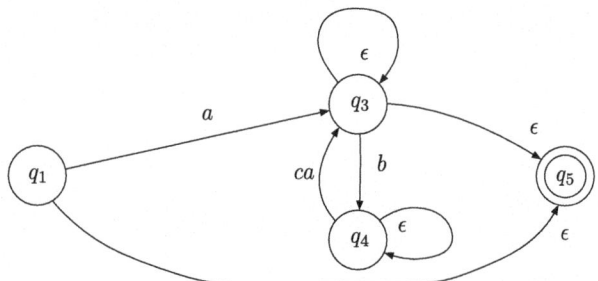

Fig. 2.13 Applying the label-replacement procedure with q_2 as the intermediate point

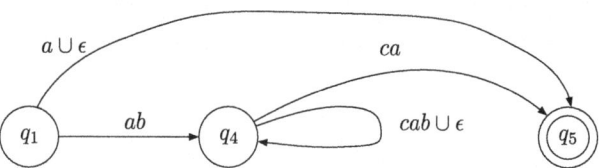

Fig. 2.14 Applying the label-replacement procedure with q_3 as the intermediate point

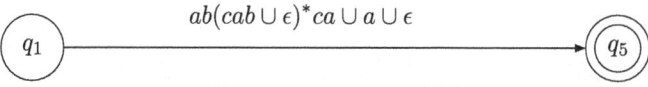

Fig. 2.15 Applying the label-replacement procedure with q_4 as the intermediate point. The label on the remaining arrow is the final form of the regular expression

2.3 Construct a DFA that accepts $\{w \mid w \in \{a, b\}^*$ such that w does not contain aaa or $bbb\}$.

2.4 Construct a DFA that accepts the set of all strings in $\{a, b\}^*$ with an odd number of as and an odd number of bs.

2.5 Construct a DFA that accepts the complement of $C = \{w \mid w \in \{a, b\}^*$ such that w contains an a and then a b someplace later$\}$.

2.6 For each of the following languages over $\{a, b\}$, give a DFA accepting it, a DFA for its star, and then a DFA that accepts the complement of its star.

1. $\{ab, ba\}$.
2. $\{a, ab, abb, abbb, \ldots\}$.
3. $\{a, ab, abb, abbb, \ldots\} \cup \{b, ba, baa, baaa, \ldots\}$.

2.7 Construct a two-state NFA for the complement of $\{a, ab, abb, abbb, \ldots\}^*$.

2.8 Let L be a regular language and let $M = (Q, \Sigma, \delta, q_0, F)$ be a DFA that accepts L. Let Σ' be an alphabet that includes Σ. Show that L is a language over the alphabet Σ', and build, from M, a DFA for L as a language over Σ'.

2.9 In many programming languages, literal character sequences take the form of "X," where X is a sequence in which each occurrence of " has a pair of \s: one \ in front and one \ elsewhere. For example, "\\\"a" is a syntactically correct literal expression, while ""\\\" is not. Assuming that a programming language employs an alphabet consisting of ", \, 0, 1, and -, design a five-state DFA for deciding the language of syntactically correct literal character sequences.

2.10 In the United States, the expression of a currency amount combines the dollar part with the cent part, using a period in between. A comma appears before every power of a thousand in the dollar part. In the cent part, the expression is exactly two digits, with a 0 before any amount less than 10. For example, "two billion seventeen million nine hundred three thousands five hundred sixty-four dollars and eight cents" has the expression $2, 017, 903, 564.08$, while "four dollars and fifty cents" has the expression 4.50. Also, "zero dollars and one cent" has the expression 0.01. Design a DFA for accepting valid currency expressions in the United States.

2.11 Modify the proof in Theorem 2.2 (of the closure of the regular languages under the Kleene-star) to show that the class of regular languages is closed under the Kleene-plus; that is, for all regular languages L, L^+ is regular.

2.12 Design a three-state NFA for the language $(abc)^*$, which is the language of all strings that are some repetitions of abc.

2.13 Construct an NFA that accepts the complement of $\{w \mid w \in \{a, b\}^*$ such that w contains an a and then someplace later has a $b\}$.

2.14 Construct a three-state NFA that accepts $L((aa)^* \cup (bb)^*)$.

2.15 Let $\Sigma = \{0, 1\}$. Construct a DFA that accepts $L(\Sigma^*(01 \cup 10)\Sigma^*)$. Also, construct a DFA for the language's complement.

2.16 Construct a DFA that accepts $L(0^+10^+)$.

2.17 Design a three-state NFA for the language $a^*b^*c^*$.

2.18 Let $\Sigma = \{a, b\}$. Let M be an NFA $(Q, \Sigma, \delta, q_0, F)$ where $Q = \{q_0, q_1\}$, $F = \{q_1\}$, and δ's transition table is as follows:

State	a	b	ϵ
q_0	q_0	q_1	–
q_1	–	q_1	X

Suppose we have the following four choices for the cell X corresponding to (q_1, ϵ): $\{q_1\}$, $\{q_0\}$, $\{q_0, q_1\}$, and $\emptyset$. For each of the four choices, state the language M accepts.

2.19 Let $M = (Q, \Sigma, \delta, q_0, F)$ be a DFA accepting a language L. Build an NFA N from M, which accepts any string constructed from a member of L by replacing exactly one character with a different character.

2.20 Let Σ be an alphabet of size ≥ 2. Let $\oplus$ be a binary operation on Σ that produces a symbol from each pair of elements in Σ. For all $w \in \Sigma^+$, define $\oplus(w)$ inductively as follows:

- If $w = a$ for some Σ (i.e., $|w| = 1$), $\oplus(w) = a$.
- If $w = xa$ where $x \in \Sigma^+$ and $a \in \Sigma$, $\oplus(w) = \oplus(\oplus(x), a)$.

Define $L(\oplus, a)$ as the set of all strings $w \in \Sigma^+$ such that $\oplus(w) = a$. Show that $L(\oplus, a)$ is regular.

2.21 Show that the running time of Algorithm 2.1 is $O(k^3(\|\Sigma\| + \log k))$, where $k = \|Q\|$.

2.22 Give a recursive algorithm to search for an accepting computation of a pseudo-NFA whose recursion depth is the length of the input.

2.23 Use the NFA conversion algorithm (Algorithm 2.2) to convert each of the following NFAs into a DFA:

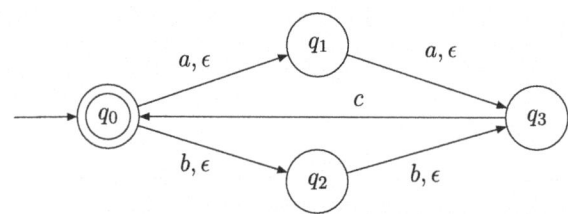

1.

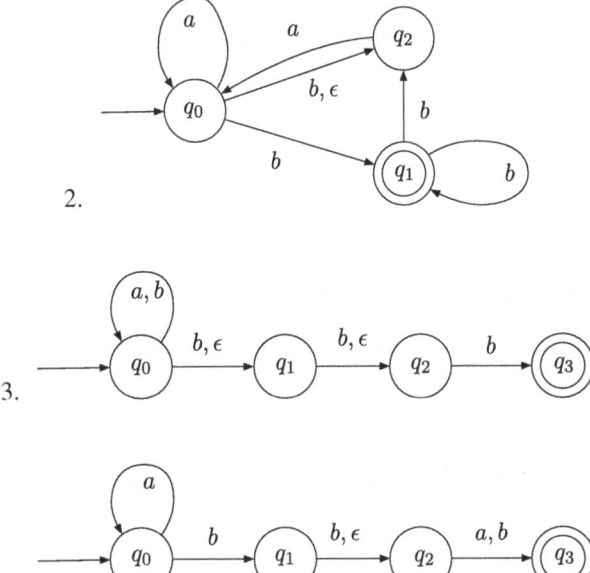

2.

3.

4.

2.24 Let L be an arbitrary nonempty language over $\{0\}$. Show that L^* is the union of a finite set and $\{(0^p)^k \mid k \geq t\}$ for some positive integers p and t.

Hint: Think of the set $N = \{n \mid 0^n \in L\}$. Then $L^* = \{0^n \mid n$ is 0 or the sum of integers in $N\}$.

2.25 Suppose M is a DFA accepting ϵ and at least one other string and the initial state is the only final state of M. Then for some nonempty w, $L(M)$ includes w^*.

2.26 A **synchronizing sequence** of a DFA $M = (Q, \Sigma, \delta, q_0, F)$ is a string that forces M to transition from any state to the same state. In other words, a synchronizing sequence is a string w such that for some state h, $\delta(q, w) = h$ for all $q \in Q$. If a DFA has a synchronizing sequence, it is **synchronizable**. Give a synchronizable DFA for $L((01)^*)$.

2.27 Following the previous question, show that no DFAs for $\{w \in \{0, 1\} \mid w$ has an odd number of 0s$\}$ are synchronizable.

2.28 Let $M = (Q, \Sigma, \delta, q_0, F)$ be a synchronizable DFA with n states. Show that for each state-pair (p, q) such that $p \neq q$, a sequence w exists such that $\delta(p, w) = \delta(q, w)$ and $|w| \leq n(n - 1)/2$.

Hint: Use the pigeon-hole principle.

Bibliographic Notes and Further Reading

The finite automaton model originates from McCulloch and Pitts [5]. The model also appears in the papers by Mealy [6], Moore [7], and Huffman [2]. The NFA model is due to Rabin and Scott [8]. The pseudo-NFAs with multiple initial states and the conversion to FAs are by Rabin and Scott as well [8]. As mentioned at the beginning of the chapter, DFAs and NFAs have many applications. Well-known examples are the Knuth-Morris-Pratt (KMP) algorithm [3], a bibliographic search algorithm by Aho and Corasick [1], and the lexical analyzer Lex [4].

References

1. A.V. Aho, M.J. Corasick, Efficient string matching: an aid to bibliographic search. Commun. ACM **18**(6), 333–340 (1975)
2. D.A. Huffman, The synthesis of sequential switching circuits. J. Franklin Inst. **257**(3–4), 161–190, 275–303 (1954)
3. D.E. Knuth, J.H. Morris, V.R. Pratt, Fast pattern matching in strings. SIAM J. Comput. **6**(2), 323–350 (1977)
4. M.E. Lesk, E. Schmidt, *Lex: A Lexical Analyzer Generator*, vol. 39 (Bell Laboratories, Murray Hill, 1975)
5. W.S. McCulloch, W.A. Pitts, A logical calculus of the ideas immanent in nervous activity. B. Math. Biophys. **5**, 115–133 (1943)
6. G.H. Mealy, A method for synthesizing sequential circuits. Bell. Syst. Tech. J. **34**(5), 1045–1079 (1955)
7. E.F. Moore, Gedanken experiments on sequential machines, in *Automata Studies* (Princeton University Press, Princeton, 1956), pp. 129–153
8. M.O. Rabin, D. Scott, Finite automata and their decision problems. IBM Res. J. **3**(2), 115–125 (1959)

Chapter 3
Non-regularity

3.1 Minimizing the State Number

This section studies the problem of minimizing a given DFA's state number. The minimization process involves identifying groups of states with the same roles as the other members.

3.1.1 A Motivation

When two distinct DFAs accept the same languages, can we say which is better? A famous principle for model comparison is **Occam's Razor**, which states that we must avoid unnecessary duplications. According to the principle, if one model is smaller, the smaller model is better. How should we compare the sizes of two finite automata? We can use the size of the transition function as a measurement. Since the size of the alphabet is equal between the automata, we can use the number of states as the measurement.

Now that we have determined that the number of states is our measurement for size, we can ask if a DFA has a smaller equivalent automaton. The **state minimization problem** asks to find the smallest equivalent DFA.

3.1.2 Distinguishable State-Pairs

The key with the state minimization problem is distinguishability. A distinguishable pair of states consists of two states having different outcomes when processing the remainder of an input.

Let L be a regular language and let $M = (Q, \Sigma, \delta, q_0, F)$ be a DFA that accepts L. We can assume that every state in Q is reachable from q_0; otherwise, we erase from Q all the states unreachable from q_0 and then return to the minimization question. We solve the minimization problem by inquiring, for each pair of states (p, q), if they are functionally different from each other (i.e., if there is a string that leads M from p to a final state and leads M from q to a non-final state). We call such a pair **distinguishable**.

Here is a formal definition of distinguishability.

Definition 3.1 Let $M = (Q, \Sigma, \delta, q_0, F)$ be a DFA. A state pair (p, q) of M is **distinguishable** if there is some $w \in \Sigma^*$ such that exactly one of $\delta(p, w)$ and $\delta(q, w)$ is in F (and thus, the other is in $Q - F$). Otherwise, (p, q) is **indistinguishable**.

We can view both distinguishability and indistinguishability as binary relations between states.

Proposition 3.1 *The distinguishability has the following properties.*

1. *Distinguishability is symmetric; i.e., a state pair (p, q) of a DFA M is distinguishable if, and only if, (q, p) is distinguishable.*
2. *Indistinguishability is an equivalence.*
3. *Distinguishability admits the following inductive definition:*
   For each state pair (p, q),

   - *[Base Case] if either (p, q) or (q, p) is in $F \times (Q - F)$, the pair is distinguishable;*
   - *[Induction Step] if there is a known distinguishable pair (s, t) and there is a symbol $a \in \Sigma$ such that $\delta(p, a) = s$ and $\delta(q, a) = t$, (p, q) is distinguishable.*

Proof Let $M = (Q, \Sigma, \delta, q_0, F)$ be a DFA. As we did for proving the closure property of regular languages under intersection (Theorem 2.2), we extend δ to a transition function that takes a pair of states in $Q \times Q$ and a string in Σ^*. The extended version of the transition function is given as follows:

$$\delta((p, q), w) = (\delta(p, w), \delta(q, w)).$$

Here, $p, q \in Q$ and $w \in \Sigma^*$.

With this extended version of δ, we have a new definition for distinguishable pairs as follows:

A state pair (p, q) is distinguishable if there is some $w \in \Sigma^*$ such that

$$\delta((p, q), w) \in (F \times (Q - F)) \cup ((Q - F) \times F).$$

The first property we prove is the symmetry of distinguishability. To prove this property, we see that $\delta((p, q), w) \in (F \times (Q - F)) \cup ((Q - F) \times F)$ if, and only if, $\delta((q, p), w) \in (F \times (Q - F)) \cup ((Q - F) \times F)$. Thus, the relation is symmetric.

The second property we prove is the statement that indistinguishability is an equivalence relation. To prove this property, we rephrase indistinguishability as follows:

A state pair (p, q) is indistinguishable if, and only if, for all $w \in \Sigma^*$,

$$\delta((p, q), w) \in (F \times F) \cup ((Q - F) \times (Q - F)).$$

The symmetry of the relation is apparent because each of the two Cartesian products has two sets on either side. The reflexivity is easy to show because if $q = p$, the two components of $\delta(p, q, w)$ are identical. For the transitivity, suppose both (p, q) and (q, r) are indistinguishable. Let $w \in \Sigma^*$ be an arbitrary string. Suppose $\delta(p, w) \in F$. Then $\delta(q, w) \in F$ because (p, q) is indistinguishable. Then $\delta(r, w) \in F$ because (q, r) is indistinguishable. Because $\delta(p, w) \in F$ and $\delta(r, w) \in F$, we know (p, r) is indistinguishable. The same argument holds when $\delta(p, w) \in Q - F$. The relation is reflexive, symmetric, and transitive, so it is an equivalence.

We will prove the last property as follows:

Suppose (p, q) is distinguishable. There is some $w \in \Sigma^*$ such that $\delta((p, q), w) \in F \times (Q - F) \cup (Q - F) \times F$. Select one such w. If $w = \epsilon$, (p, q) satisfies the base case of the inductive definition as appearing in the proposition statement. If $w \neq \epsilon$, let $w_1, \ldots, w_m$ be the symbols of w, where $m = |w|$. Let $(s_0, t_0) = (p, q)$ and for each i such that $1 \leq i \leq m$, let $(s_i, t_i) = \delta(s_{i-1}, t_{i-1}, w_i)$, so $\delta((p, q), w) = (s_m, t_m)$. The pair (s_m, t_m) has just one element in F because of the indistinguishability definition, so (s_m, t_m) satisfies the base case. Then working backward in index i, from m down to 0, we know that $\delta((s_{i-1}, t_{i-1}), w_i)$ is a distinguishable pair, and thus (s_{i-1}, t_{i-1}) is distinguishable according to the induction case. The last pair in the sequence is (p, q), therefore satisfying the inductive definition.

Conversely, suppose that a pair (p, q) is indistinguishable according to the inductive definition. If the pair satisfies the base case, then $w = \epsilon$ in the original definition. Otherwise, there is a series of additions to the set of indistinguishable pairs, culminating in the addition of (p, q). Suppose the smallest number of additions at (p, q) is $m \geq 1$. Let $(b_0, c_0), (b_1, c_1), \ldots, (b_m, c_m)$ be the series of additions where $(b_m, c_m) = (p, q)$. The first pair (b_0, c_0) is a pair in the base case. For each i such that $1 \leq i \leq m$, there is a symbol a_i such that $\delta((b_i, c_i), a_i) = (b_{i-1}, c_{i-1})$. Let $a = a_m a_{m-1} \cdots a_1$. Then, $\delta(b_m, a) = b_0$ and $\delta(c_m, a) = c_0$. Since (b_0, c_0) is a base-case distinguishable pair, (b_0, c_0) satisfies the requirement for a distinguishable pair.

This proves the proposition.   □

The inductive definition from Proposition 3.1 gives Algorithms 3.1 and 3.2. Since indistinguishability is an equivalence relation, we can partition the states into equivalence classes, where each equivalence class is the largest group of pairwise indistinguishable states. We use a greedy algorithm to compute a collection of all maximally large equivalence classes concerning indistinguishability. The sets X appearing in the algorithm are all such maximally large equivalence classes, and the set H is the collection.

Algorithm 3.1 A greedy algorithm for finding all distinguishable pairs

```
 1: procedure INDISTINGUISHABLE-PAIRS(M)
 2:     M = (Q, Σ, δ, q₀, F) is a DFA;
 3:     D ← F × (Q − F) ∪ (Q − F) × F;              ▷ the distinguishable pairs
 4:     I ← (Q × Q) − D;                            ▷ the indistinguishable pairs
 5:     while true do
 6:         S ← {(p, q) ∈ I | (∃a ∈ Σ)(δ(p, a), δ(q, a)) ∈ D};
 7:         if S = ∅ then
 8:             terminate the loop;
 9:         else
10:             D ← D + S;
11:             I ← I − S;
12:         end if
13:     end while
14:     report D as the set of all distinguishable pairs;
15:     report I as the set of all indistinguishable pairs;
16: end procedure
```

Line 2: $M = (Q, \Sigma, \delta, q_0, F)$ is a DFA;
Line 3: $D \leftarrow F \times (Q - F) \cup (Q - F) \times F$;
Line 4: $I \leftarrow (Q \times Q) - D$;
Line 6: $S \leftarrow \{(p, q) \in I \mid (\exists a \in \Sigma)(\delta(p, a), \delta(q, a)) \in D\}$;
Line 7: if $S = \emptyset$ then
Line 10: $D \leftarrow D + S$;
Line 11: $I \leftarrow I - S$;

Algorithm 3.2 An algorithm for finding all maximally indistinguishable groups using Algorithm 3.1 that finds all indistinguishable pairs

```
 1: procedure MAXIMALLY INDISTINGUISHABLE-GROUP(Q, I)
 2:     Q is the set of states;
 3:     I is the set of indistinguishable pairs;
 4:     R ← Q;                                ▷ the states requiring processing
 5:     H ← ∅;              ▷ the collection of maximally indistinguishable states
 6:     while R ≠ ∅ do
 7:         select an arbitrary state p from R;
 8:         X ← {q | (p, q) ∈ I};
 9:         R ← R − X;
10:         H ← H ∪ {X};
11:     end while
12:     report H as the set of mutually indistinguishable groups;
13: end procedure
```

We construct a nondeterministic finite automaton (NFA) N from M by adding an ϵ-transition from each state p to every other state in the same equivalence class. The introduction of the ϵ-transitions allows transitions within each equivalence class. Due to the definition of indistinguishability, following ϵ-transitions does not change whether or not the automaton accepts the input. Let us construct a DFA M' from N

Fig. 3.1 The input for the
state-minimization algorithm

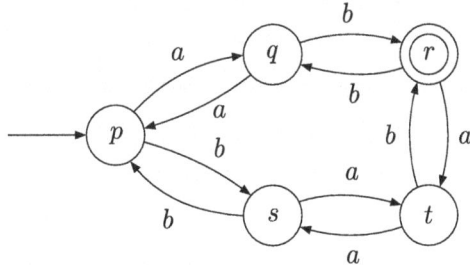

Table 3.1 The distinguishability results. The distinguishability is symmetric, so only the lower diagonal of the table is present. The letter i indicates that the pair is indistinguishable. The number 0 indicates that one pair element is in F and the other is in $Q - F$, so its distinguishability is in the base case. The number 1 indicates that the distinguishability is after the base case

p	i				
q	1	i			
r	0	0	i		
s	i	1	0	i	
t	1	i	0	1	i
	p	q	r	s	t

Fig. 3.2 The finite
automaton after application of
the state-minimization
algorithm

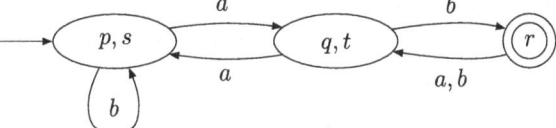

using Algorithm 2.3 for constructing a deterministic automaton from an NFA. The algorithm puts the members from each equivalence class together while keeping each distinguishable state pair separate. We see that the process collapses each equivalence class into a superstate. Because we have exhausted all distinguishable pairs, the DFA we have constructed is not reducible to a smaller DFA.

Example 3.1 Here is an example of applying the statement minimization algorithm. The input is a five-state finite automaton, as shown in Fig. 3.1.

By applying the algorithm, we get the following table showing the distinguishability and indistinguishability, as demonstrated in Table 3.1. Since the distinguishability and indistinguishability are symmetric, we present each pair only once. The combination of Row x and Column y represents the pair (x, y) (and so (y, x) as well). A 0 appearing on the table means the pair is distinguishable according to the base case. A 1 appearing on the table means the pair is distinguishable according to the induction step. An i indicates that the pair is indistinguishable.

We find that p and s are indistinguishable and that q and t are indistinguishable. We obtain the minimal DFA from the table in Fig. 3.2.

3.2   The Myhill-Nerode Theorem

In this section, we look at DFAs using equivalence classes.

Definition 3.2 Let Σ be an alphabet and L be a language over Σ. Let $u, v \in \Sigma^*$. We say that u and v are equivalent concerning L if for all strings $z \in \Sigma^*$, $uz \in L$ if, and only if, $vz \in L$. We write $u \equiv_L v$ to mean that u and v are equivalent concerning L.

We leave the proof of the following proposition to the reader.

Proposition 3.2 *For every language L, the relation $\equiv_L$ is an equivalence.*

We also have the following relatively simple properties about equivalence classes. We also leave the task of proving the next proposition to the reader.

Proposition 3.3 *Let L be an arbitrary language. We have the following:*

1. *For all equivalence classes S concerning L, either $S \subseteq L$ or $S \subseteq \overline{L}$.*
2. *For all equivalence classes S and T concerning L, if $S \cap T \neq \emptyset$, then either $S \subseteq T$ or $T \subseteq S$.*

We say that an equivalence class S concerning a language L is **maximal** if no other equivalence classes concerning L properly contain S.

Now, we can characterize regular languages using equivalence classes.

Theorem 3.1 (The Myhill-Nerode Theorem) *A language L is regular if, and only if, it has a finite number of maximal equivalence classes.*

Proof Overview

The theorem comes from the minimum DFA we obtain using the minimization algorithm. Every pair of states is distinguishable in the minimum DFA we construct. In other words, for each pair, a string leads the automaton to a final state from one and a non-final state from the other. Thus, the strings on which the automaton arrives at one state and those on which the automaton arrives at the other belong to different equivalence classes. Because of the construction, the equivalence classes are maximal.

Conversely, given a group of maximal equivalence classes, appending one specific symbol to every word in an equivalence class transforms the class into an equivalence class. Because of the maximality, the target equivalence class must be one of the maximal equivalence classes.

Proof Suppose L is a regular language. Let $M = (Q, \Sigma, \delta, q_0, F)$ be an arbitrary DFA for L. Suppose we have constructed a DFA $M^* = (Q^*, \Sigma, \delta^*, q_0^*, F^*)$ from M with the minimization algorithm in Sect. 3.1.2. For each state $q \in Q^*$, define $W(q)$ as the set of all strings that take M^* from its initial state to q. For each state

q and each pair (x, y) in $W(q)$, we have $x \equiv_L y$ because they take M^* to the same states. Also, for all states q and q' in Q^* such that $q \neq q'$, a string z takes M^* to acceptance from only one of q and q'. Otherwise, the algorithm would have found indistinguishable q and q'. This means the equivalence classes $W(q), q \in Q^*$ are maximal. Since M^* is a DFA, Q^* should be a finite set, so the number of maximal equivalence classes concerning $\equiv_L$ is finite.

Conversely, suppose $[C_1, C_2, \ldots, C_m]$ is an enumeration of all maximal equivalence classes of L. We claim that for all i such that $1 \leq i \leq m$, and for all $a \in \Sigma$, $C_i a \subseteq C_j$ for some j such that $1 \leq i \leq m$. We prove this claim by contradiction. Assume that the claim does not hold. Then we can select some i, some a, and some $u, v \in C_i$ such that ua and va belong to separate classes (say, C_j and C_k), where $j < k$. We select an arbitrary pair of C_j and C_k satisfying this condition. Let x and y be any members of C_j and C_k, respectively. Let w be an arbitrary member of Σ^*. Since C_i, C_j, and C_k are equivalence classes, we have:

$$uaw \in L \iff vaw \in L,$$

$$xw \in L \iff uaw \in L, \text{ and}$$

$$yw \in L \iff vaw \in L.$$

Thus,

$$xw \in L \iff yw \in L.$$

We have arbitrarily chosen x, y, and w, so the equivalence implies that $C_j \cup C_k$ is an equivalence class. If we remove C_k from the enumeration and add all its members to C_j, we obtain the following new enumeration:

$$[C_1, \ldots, C_{j_1}, C_j \cup C_k, C_{j+1}, \cdots, C_{k_1}, C_{k+1}, \ldots, C_m].$$

This new enumeration partitions Σ^* with just $m - 1$ equivalence classes. However, we assume that m is the number of maximal equivalence classes. So, we have a contradiction. Thus, the claim holds.

Now, we can build a DFA based on the equivalence classes. We introduce states $q_1, \ldots, q_m$ representing the membership in $C_1, \ldots, C_m$. Based on the above "unique index" observation, we can develop a transition function δ; for all i such that $1 \leq i \leq m$, and $a \in \Sigma$, $\delta(q_i, a) = q_j$ where j is such that for all $w \in C_i$, $wa \in C_j$. Let q_0 be q_i such that $\epsilon \in C_i$. Let F be the set of all q_i such that $C_i \subseteq L$. Since $C_1, \ldots, C_m$ are equivalence classes concerning L, either $C_i \subseteq L$ or $C_i \subseteq \Sigma^* - L$ (see Proposition 3.3). Thus, $M = (Q, \Sigma, \delta, q_0, F)$ is a DFA that accepts L. $\square$

3.3   Proving Non-regularity

There are languages for which proving regularity seems impossible. Can we prove
that a language is not regular? We can use the Myhill-Nerode Theorem to prove this
impossibility. Later in this section (Sect. 3.3.2), we show an alternate approach, "the
Pumping Lemma."

3.3.1   Proving Non-regularity Using the Myhill-Nerode
Theorem

Let us explore using the Myhill-Nerode Theorem to prove non-regularity.

The Myhill-Nerode theorem states that a language is regular if, and only if, the
number of maximal equivalence classes for the language is finite, where two strings
u and v are equivalent concerning a language L if for all strings w, $uw \in L$ if, and
only if, $vw \in L$.

From the definition of equivalence classes, we obtain the following property:

Proposition 3.4 *For all strings u and v, $u \not\equiv_L v$ if, and only if, a string w exists
such that $uw \in L$ and $vw \in \overline{L}$ or $uw \in \overline{L}$ and $vw \in L$.*

Based on this proposition, we immediately obtain a characterization of non-
regular languages in the form of a lemma. In the following lemma, the strings w_{ij}
serve as the prefix, witnessing that x_i and x_j belong to separate equivalence classes.

Lemma 3.1 *A language $L \subseteq \Sigma^*$ is non-regular if, and only if, there exists
$x_1, x_2, \ldots$ satisfying the following condition:*

(*)   *For all i and j such that $1 \leq i < j$, $x_i \not\equiv_L x_j$. In other words, for all i and j
      such that $1 \leq i < j$, there exists some w_{ij} such that $x_i w_{ij} \in L$ if, and only if,
      $x_j w_{ij} \notin L$.*

Using Lemma 3.1, we can use the following strategy for proving that a language
L is not regular:

- Define an infinite sequence $\{x_i\}_{i \geq 1}$.
- Define an infinite double-index sequence $\{w_{i,j}\}_{j > i \geq 1}$.
- Argue for all i and j such that $1 \leq i < j$, $x_i w_{ij} \in L$ if, and only if, $x_j w_{ij} \notin L$.

Finding the sequences x and w is cumbersome because of the double-indexing in
w. We thus slightly simplify the statement as follows:

Lemma 3.2 *A language $L \subseteq \Sigma^*$ is non-regular if there is a series of string pairs
$\{(x_i, w_i)\}_{i \geq 1}$ satisfying the following:*

- *Either for all $i \geq 1$, $x_i w_i \in L$ or for all $i \geq 1$, $x_i w_i \notin L$.*
- *For all i and j such that $j > i \geq 1$, either $x_i w_i \in L$ and $x_i w_j \notin L$ or $x_j w_j \in L$
  and $x_j w_i \notin L$.*

Proof Suppose a sequence of pairs exists that satisfy the conditions. Let $A = L$ if it is the case that for all $i \le 1$, $x_i w_i \in L$ and $A = \overline{L}$ otherwise. The maximal equivalence classes concerning L are the same as those concerning $\overline{L}$. For each $i \ge 1$, let E_i be the maximal equivalence class concerning A that contains x_i. Then, for all i and j such that $j > i \ge 1$, we have either

- $x_i w_j \notin A$ and $x_i w_i \in A$.
- $x_j w_i \notin A$ and $x_j w_j \in A$.

Either property implies that $E_i \ne E_j$. Thus, the classes $E_1, E_2, \dots$ are pairwise-different and maximal. Since the Myhill-Nerode Theorem states that the number of maximal equivalence classes is finite for any regular language, we know that L is not regular. $\qquad\qquad\qquad\qquad\qquad\qquad\qquad\qquad\qquad\qquad\qquad\qquad\qquad\qquad\square$

Using Lemma 3.2, we can show the following.

Example 3.2 The language $L = \{0^n 1^n \mid n \ge 1\}$ is not regular.
For each $i \ge 1$, let $x_i = 0^{i+1} 1$ and let $w_i = 1^i$. Let $A = L$. For all $i \ge 1$, we have:

- $x_i \notin A$.
- $x_i w_i \in A$.
- for all $j > i$, $x_i w_j = 0^{i+1} 1^{i+1} 1^{j-i}$ so $x_i w_j \notin A$.

Thus, by Lemma 3.2, $A(= L)$ is not regular.

Example 3.3 The language $L = \{0^{n^2} \mid n \ge 1\}$ is not regular.
For each $i \ge 1$, let $x_i = 0^{i^2+1}$ and let $w_i = 0^{2i}$. Let $A = L$. For all $i \ge 1$, we have:

- $x_i \notin A$ because $i^2 < i^2 + 1 < (i+1)^2$ so $i^2 + 1$ is not a perfect square.
- $x_i w_i \in A$ because $(i^2 + 1) + 2i = (i+1)^2$.
- for all integers i and j such that $j > i \ge 1$, $x_j w_i = 0^k$ such that $j^2 < k = j^2 + 1 + 2i < j^2 + 1 + 2j = (j+1)^2$ so k is not a perfect square, and thus, $x_j w_i$ is not in A.

Thus, by Lemma 3.2, $A(= L)$ is not regular.

3.3.2 Proving Non-regularity Using the Pumping Lemma for Regular Languages

An alternate method for proving non-regularity is using a Pumping Lemma for regular languages. In this section, we prove the lemma and learn how to use it to prove non-regularity.

3.3.2.1 The Pumping Lemma

Here, we state and prove the lemma.

Lemma 3.3 (The Pumping Lemma for Regular Languages) *Suppose a language L is regular. Then there exists an integer $p \geq 1$ such that for all strings $w \in L$ having a length of $\geq p$, w has a partition uvx satisfying the following conditions:*

1. $|v| \geq 1$.
2. $|uv| \leq p$.
3. *for all $i \geq 0$, $uv^i x \in L \iff w \in L$.*

We call the constant p the pumping constant *(or the* pumping length*) of L.*

Proof Let L be a regular language and $M = (Q, \Sigma, \delta, q_0, F)$ be a DFA that accepts L. Let $p = \|Q\|$. Let w, $|w| \geq p$, and $w = a_1 \cdots a_p b$ such that $a_1, \ldots, a_p \in \Sigma$ and $b \in \Sigma^*$. For each i such that $1 \leq i \leq p$, let $q_i = \delta(q_0, a_1 \cdots a_i)$ and $q' = \delta(q_0, w)$. The states $q_0, q_1, \ldots, q_p$ are from Q. By the pigeon-hole principle, a pair (q_s, q_t) exists such that $0 \leq s < t \leq p$ and $q_s = q_t$. Let $u = a_1 \cdots a_s$, $v = a_{s+1} \cdots a_t$, and $x = a_{t+1} \cdots a_p b$. Then $|uv| = t \leq p$, $|v| = t - s \geq 1$, and $uvx = w$. Because $q_s = q_t$, $\delta(q_s, v) = q_t$, and so, for all $i \geq 0$, $\delta(q_s, v^i) = q_s$. Also, because $q_s = q_t$ and $\delta(q_0, uv) = q_t$, $\delta(q_0, x) = \delta(q_0, uv^i x)$ for all $i \geq 0$. Thus, for all $i \geq 0$, $uv^i x \in L \iff w \in L$.

This proves the lemma.   □

Figure 3.3 shows the idea behind the Pumping Lemma.

Here, we state the exact contrapositive of the lemma.

- Let L be a language. Suppose that for all integers $p \geq 1$, there is a string $w \in L$ having a length of $\geq p$ satisfying the following property:

  (*)   For all decompositions of w as uvx satisfying $|uv| \leq p$ and $|v| \geq 1$, $uv^i x \notin L$ for some $i \geq 0$.

  Then, L is not regular.

We observe that every $|w|$ satisfying the condition for some p satisfies the condition for any smaller value of p. From this observation, we obtain the following slightly relaxed version of the contrapositive.

Lemma 3.4 *A language L is not regular if the following holds:*

For infinitely many p, there is a string w having a length of $\geq p$ such that for every partition uvx of w satisfying $|uv| \leq p$ and $|v| \geq 1$, $uv^i x \notin L$ and $w \in L$ or $uv^i x \in L$ and $w \notin L$.

We can extend the Pumping Lemma further by replacing the characters $a_1, \ldots, a_p$ appearing in the lemma's proof with nonempty strings.

Lemma 3.5 *Let $L \subseteq \Sigma^*$ be an arbitrary regular language. Then, there is a constant $p \geq 1$ with the following property:*

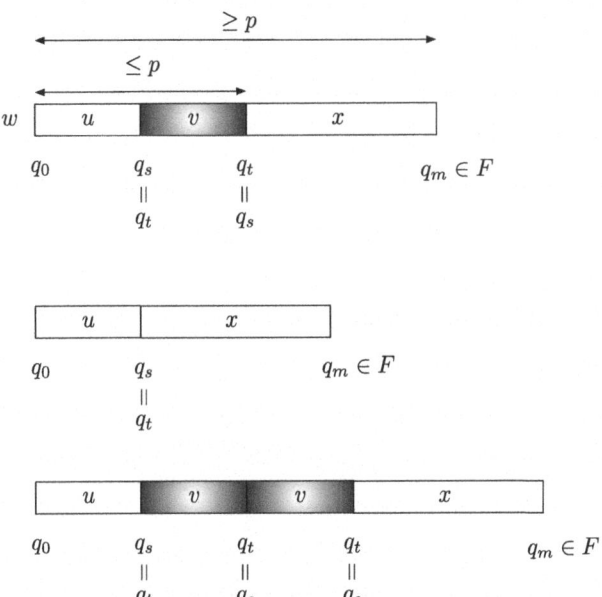

Fig. 3.3 The idea behind the Pumping Lemma. The top panel is a decomposition whose existence is guaranteed by the lemma. The middle panel is the string generated by removing v from w. The bottom panel is the string generated by inserting v

For all $a_1, \cdots a_p \in \Sigma^+$ and $b \in \Sigma^*$, there exist s and t such that $0 \le s < t \le p$ and for all $i \ge 0$,

$$a_1 \cdots a_s (a_{s+1} \cdots a_t)^i a_{t+1} \cdots a_p b \in L \iff a_1 \cdots a_p b \in L.$$

3.3.2.2 Proving Non-regularity Using the Pumping Lemma

Let us learn how to use the Pumping Lemma to prove non-regularity.

For a string w, let w^R denote its *reverse*, i.e., the string in which the characters of w appear in the reverse order. For example, if $w = abcccaabb$ then $w^R = bbaacccba$.

A string is a **palindrome** if $w = w^R$.

Example 3.4 Let Σ be an arbitrary alphabet having a size of ≥ 2. Let A be the set of all palindromes over Σ. Then A is not regular.

We use the contrapositive (Lemma 3.4) to prove that A is not regular.

We choose any two distinct symbols, α and β. Let p be an arbitrary positive integer. We select $\alpha^p \beta \alpha^p$ for the value of w. The string is a palindrome, and so is in A. Let $w = a_1 \cdots a_p b$, where $a_1 = \cdots = a_p = \alpha$ and $b = \beta \alpha^p$. Let c and d be integers such that $0 \le c < d \le p$. Then $u = \alpha^c$, $v = \alpha^{d-c}$, and $x = \alpha^{p-d} \beta \alpha^p$. We have $uv^0x(= ux) = \alpha^{p-d+c}\beta\alpha^p$. Since $d > c$, $uv^0x \notin A$, and so we have found an i such that

$$uv^ix \notin L \iff w \in L.$$

Thus, A is not regular.

We can view the non-regularity proof as the following "pumping game" you play against an adversary:

1. The adversary specifies the pumping constant p.
2. You specify w and $a_1, \ldots, a_p, b$ such that $w = a_1 \cdots a_p b$, where $a_1, \ldots, a_p$ are nonempty.
3. The adversary chooses c and d, $0 \le c < d \le p$, thereby breaking down w into uvx, where $u = a_1 \cdots a_c$, $v = a_{c+1} \cdots a_d$, and $w = a_d \cdots a_p b$.
4. You select the value of i from $\{0, 2, 3, \ldots\}$ and argue that $uv^ix \notin L$ in the case where $w \in L$ and $uv^ix \in L$ otherwise.

The language L is non-regular if, and only if, you have a winning strategy in the "pumping game." You can prove non-regularity by presenting a winning strategy.

In Example 3.2, we showed that the language $\{0^n1^n \mid n \ge 0\}$ is not regular using the Myhill-Nerode Theorem. Here, we prove the non-regularity using the Pumping Lemma.

Example 3.5 The language $B = \{0^n1^n \mid n \ge 0\}$ is not regular. Here is the winning strategy in the "pumping game" for B.

For any adversarial choice p, you select $w = 0^p1^p$ and set $a_1 = \cdots = a_p = 0$ and $b = 1^p$. The string $w \in B$. For any adversarial choice of c and d, you select $i = 0$. The string v is $a_{c+1} \cdots a_d = 0^{d-c}$, and so uv^0x is $0^{p-d+c}1^p$. Since $d-c > 0$, $ux \notin B$. Thus, B is not regular.

Example 3.6 The language $C = \{0^m1^n2^s \mid 0 \le m \le n \le s\}$ is not regular. Here is the winning strategy in the "pumping game" for C.

For any adversarial choice p, you select $w = 0^p1^p2^p$ and set $a_1 = \cdots = a_p = 0$ and $b = 1^p2^p$. The string $w \in C$. For any adversarial choice of c and d, you select $i = 2$. The string v is $a_{c+1} \cdots a_d = 0^{d-c}$, $uv^2x = 0^{p+d-c}1^p2^p$. Since the 0-part is longer than the 1-part, $uv^2x \notin C$, its membership differs from that of w. Thus, C is not regular.

3.3.3 Proving Non-regularity Using Closure Properties

If non-regularity proofs appear challenging to establish, we can use a closure property to convert the language to another and then prove that the new language is non-regular.

The principle idea is the following proposition.

Proposition 3.5 *Let A be a language. Let B be a language we construct from A with a series of operations under which the regular languages are closed. If B is not regular, then A is not regular.*

We leave the proof of the proposition to the reader (see Exercise 3.3).

We already know that REG (the class of all regular languages) is closed under complement, union, intersection, concatenation, and the Kleene-star.

Definition 3.3 Let a be a symbol and w be a string. By $\#_a(w)$, we denote the number of occurrences of a in w.

Example 3.7 Let $A = \{w \in \{a, b\}^* \mid \#_a(w) \neq \#_b(w)\}$. We show that A is not regular.

Let $B = L(a^*b^*)$. Then B is regular. Let $C = A \cap B$. If A is regular, then C is regular. Assume C is regular. Let p be the pumping constant for C. Let $w = a^p b^{p+p!}$. We obtain a partition $w = uvx$ by the lemma. Here, $|uv| \leq p, |v| \geq 1$, and for all $i \geq 0, uv^i x \in C$. Both u and v are in $\{a\}^*$. Since $|v| \leq p, |v|$ is a divisor of $p!$. Let $w' = uv^{1+p!/|v|}x$. Then $w' = a^{p+p!}b^{p+p!}$ and is not a member of C. Thus, C is not regular; thus, A is not.

Another approach is to use $D = \overline{A} \cap B$. Then $D = \{a^n b^n \mid n \geq 0\}$. If A is regular, then D is regular because the class of regular languages is closed under complement and intersection. Then, using the proof for Example 3.5 with a in place of 0 and b in place of 1, we get that D is not regular. Thus, A is not regular.

Exercises

3.1 Prove Proposition 3.2.

3.2 Prove Proposition 3.3.

3.3 Prove Proposition 3.5.

3.4 Prove that $\{w \in \{a, b, c\}^* \mid \#_a(w), \#_b(w),$ and $\#_c(w)$ are pairwise different$\}$ is not regular.

3.5 Using the Pumping Lemma, prove that $\{0^p \mid p$ is a prime number$\}$ is not regular.

3.6 Prove that $\{a^m b^n a^d \mid m + n = d\}$ is not regular.

3.7 Show that the class of regular languages is closed under reverse. In other words, show that for each regular language $L, L^R = \{w^R \mid w \in L\}$ is regular.

Hint: From a DFA accepting L, construct an NFA accepting L^R.

3.8 Let $\Sigma = \{a, b\}$. Define $A = \{w^k \mid w \in \Sigma^*$ and $k \geq 2\}$. Prove that A is not regular.

3.9 Let Σ and Γ be alphabets. Let f be a mapping from Σ^* to Γ^*. For each $L \subseteq \Sigma^*$, let $f(L) = \{f(w) \mid w \in L\}$. We say that f is **homomorphic** if for all x and y in $\Sigma^*, f(xy) = f(x)f(y)$. Answer the following questions:

1. Prove that if f is homomorphic, then $f(\epsilon) = \epsilon$.
2. Prove that if f is homomorphic, then for all $n \geq 1$ and $w = w_1 \cdots w_n$ such that $w_1, \ldots, w_n \in \Sigma$, $f(w) = f(w_1) \cdots f(w_n)$, i.e., the mapping $f(w)$ is the concatenation of the symbol-wise image.
3. Prove that the class of regular languages is closed under homomorphism, i.e., for all alphabets Σ and Γ, for all homomorphic function f from Σ^* to Γ^*, and for all regular languages $L \subseteq \Sigma^*$, $f(L)$ is regular.

   Hint: From a DFA accepting L and a homomorphic function f, construct an NFA that nondeterministically traverses the DFA and matches the transition image with the input.
4. Prove that the class of regular languages is closed under inverse homomorphism; i.e., for all alphabets Σ and Γ, for all homomorphic function f from Σ^* to Γ^*, and for all regular languages $A \subseteq \Gamma^*$, every language $L \subseteq \Sigma^*$ such that $f(L) = A$ is regular.

3.10 Use the Myhill-Nerode Theorem to prove that the language $\{0^m 1^n \mid m > n\}$ is not regular.

3.11 Use the Myhill-Nerode Theorem to prove that the language $L_{\text{prime}} = \{0^p \mid p$ is a prime number$\}$ is non-regular.

Hint: Show that the language members belong to different equivalence classes. Suppose $x = 0^p$ and $y = 0^q$ such that $p < q$ belong to different equivalence classes. Let $z = 0^{q-p}$. Argue that xz^i is in L_{prime} for all $i \geq 0$ and draw a contradiction.

3.12 Prove that the language $L_{\text{prime}} = \{0^p \mid p$ is a prime number$\}$ is non-regular in the following manner:

1. Let $L \subseteq \{0\}^*$ be a regular language. Suppose there exists some a and b such that $a < b$ and for all i between a and b,

$$0^i \in L \iff i \in \{a, b\}.$$

   Use the Myhill-Nerode Theorem and prove that for all i and j such that $a < i < j < b$, 0^i and 0^j belong to different equivalence classes for L.
2. It is known that the gap between a prime number and the next prime number is unbounded. In other words, for each integer B, a pair of consecutive prime numbers, (p, q), exists such that $q - p \geq B$. Prove that there exists an infinite sequence of triples $\{(a_i, b_i, g_i)\}_{i \geq 1}$ such that the sub-sequence $g_1, g_2, \ldots$ is length increasing and for all $i \geq 1$, a_i and b_i are consecutive prime numbers and $b_i - a_i = g_i$.
3. Combine (1) and (2) to show that the number of equivalence classes for L_{prime} is unbounded.

3.13 Define HALF(L) of a language L as the language $\{x \mid x$ for some y, $|y| = |x|$, $xy \in L\}$. Prove that HALF(L) is regular for each regular language.

3.14 Let $k \geq 2$ be a positive integer. As an extension of the previous problem, define $\text{PREFIX}_{1/k}(L)$ of a language L as the language $\{x \mid x$ for some $y, |y| = (k-1)|x|, xy \in L\}$. Prove that $\text{PREFIX}_{1/k}(L)$ is regular for each regular language.

3.15 For a language L, let $\text{CYCLE}(L)$ as $\{xy \mid yx \in L\}$. In other words, $\text{CYCLE}(L)$ is the language constructed from L by choosing an arbitrary string in L, choosing an arbitrary prefix of the string, and then moving the prefix to the end. For example, the CYCLE-operation produces $aabc$, $abca$, $bcaa$, and $caab$ from $aabc$. Show that the regular languages are closed under the CYCLE operation.

3.16 Prove Lemma 3.5.

3.17 For two languages A and B, define $\text{MINGLE}(A, B)$ as $\{a_1 b_1 \cdots a_m b_m \mid a_1, \ldots, a_m, b_1, \ldots, b_m$ are symbols, $a_1, \cdots, a_m \in A$, and $b_1, \ldots, b_m \in B\}$. Show that for all regular languages A and B, $\text{MINGLE}(A, B)$ is regular.

3.18 Let L be a regular language and ℓ be an integer. Show that $\{w \mid |w| \geq \ell$ and $w \in L\}$ is regular.

3.19 For a language L, define $\text{MID3}(L)$ as the language of strings w such that for some $x, y, |x| = |y| = |w|$, $xwy \in L$. Show that $\text{MID3}(L)$ is regular for each regular language L.

3.20 For a language L, define $\text{NOMID3}(L)$ as the language of strings xy such that for some $w, |x| = |y| = |w|$, $xwy \in L$. Show that the regular languages are not closed under NOMID3.

3.21 Show that if $L \in \{0\}^*$ is regular, $\text{NOMID3}(L)$ is regular.

3.22 Let Σ be an alphabet. For languages $A, B \subseteq \Sigma^*$, we define the **right-quotient** of A by B, denoted A/B, as

$$\{w \in \Sigma^* \mid (\exists x \in B)[wx \in A]\}.$$

In other words, the right-quotient of A by B is the set of all strings that can be turned into a member of A by appending a member of B. Prove that the class of regular languages is closed under the right-quotient operation.

3.23 Let Σ be an alphabet. For languages $A, B \subseteq \Sigma^*$, we define the **left-quotient** of A by B, denoted $A \setminus B$, as

$$\{w \in \Sigma^* \mid (\exists x \in B)[xw \in A]\}.$$

In other words, the left-quotient of A by B is the set of all strings that can be turned into a member of A by attaching after a member of B. Prove that the class of regular languages is closed under the left-quotient operation.

3.24 Let $P = \{0^k \mid k$ is not a power of 2$\}$. Prove that P is not regular.

Bibliographic Notes and Further Reading

Kleene [9, 10] considered the regular expression as a mathematical formulation of McCulloch and Pitt's nerve net (i.e., neural net) model [11]. In the above work, Kleene first proved the equivalence between the regular expressions and the nondeterministic finite automata. The equivalence proof that uses ϵ-transitions is created by McNaughton and Yamada [12] and Brzozowski [2, 3]. The Pumping Lemma is by Bar-Hillel, Perles, and Shamir [1]. The Myhill-Nerode Theorem (Theorem 3.1) is by Nerode [13] and Myhill [4]. The closure properties of regular languages are studied well in the literature. The closure properties under homomorphisms, inverse homomorphisms, and quotient are due to Ginsburg and Rose [6, 8] and Ginsburg and Spaniel [7].

Methods exist other than the Pumping Lemma and the Myhill-Nerode Theorem to prove non-regularity (see Gasarch's Survey [5]).

References

1. Y. Bar-Hillel, M. Perles, E. Shamir, On formal properties of simple phrase structure grammars. Sprachtypologie und Universalienforschung **14**, 143–172 (1961)
2. J.A. Brzozowski, A survey of regular expressions and their applications. IRE Trans. Electr. Comp. **EC-11**(3), 324–335 (1962)
3. J.A. Brzozowski, Derivatives of regular expressions. J ACM **11**(4), 481–494 (1964)
4. *Fundamental Concepts in the Theory of Systems*. ASTIA Document. Wright Air Development Center, Air Research and Development Command, United States Air Force (1957)
5. W. Gasarch, Open problems column. ACM SIGACT News **49**(1), 40–54 (2018)
6. S. Ginsburg, G.F. Rose, Operations which preserve definability in languages. J. ACM **10**(2), 175–195 (1963)
7. S. Ginsburg, E.H. Spanier, Bounded ALGOL-like languages. Trans. Am. Math. Soc. **113**(2), 333–368 (1964)
8. S. Gisburg, G.F. Rose, Preservation of languages by transducers. Inf. Control **9**(2), 153–176 (1966)
9. S.C. Kleene, Representation of events in nerve nets and finite automata. Research Memorandum RM-704, US Air Force Project Rand, 12 (1951)
10. S.C. Kleene, Representation of events in nerve nets and finite automata, in ed. by C.E. Shannon, J. McCarthy, *Automata Studies* (Princeton University Press, Princeton, 1956), pp. 3–41
11. W.S. McCulloch, W.A. Pitts, A logical calculus of the ideas immanent in nervous activity. B. Math. Biophys. **5**, 115–133 (1943)
12. R. McNaughton, H. Yamada, Regular expressions and state graphs for automata. IRE Trans. Electr. Comp. **EC-9**(1), 39–47 (1960)
13. A. Nerode, Linear automaton transformations. Proc. Am. Math. Soc. **9**(4), 541–544 (1958)

Chapter 4
The Context-Free Languages

4.1 The Context-Free Grammar (CFG)

This section introduces context-free grammar and presents some examples.

4.1.1 The Definition

Let us start with the definition of context-free grammars and context-free languages.

A **context-free grammar** (**CFG**) is an apparatus for producing language members through a series of simple substitutions. The substitution process starts with a string consisting solely of one specific symbol, which we call the start variable. The symbols that may appear in the string during the process consist of two groups. The first group is the collection of terminals, which do not permit substitutions. The second group is the collection of variables. Each variable is substitutable with a string consisting of terminals and variables. The variables have an arbitrary number of possible substitutions. The substitution procedure selects an arbitrary variable and applies an arbitrary replacement from the available replacements. The procedure is executed until the string becomes terminal-only. The language the grammar defines is the collection of all terminal-only strings that you can produce from the start variable.

Here is a formal definition of CFGs. A CFG is a quadruple $G = (V, \Sigma, R, S)$, where V is a nonempty set of **variables** (or **non-terminals**), Σ is a nonempty set of **terminals**, R is a nonempty set of **production rules** (or **derivation rules**) and is a subset of $V \times (V \cup \Sigma)^*$, and $S \in V$ is the **start variable**. You can substitute symbols with a sequence of variables and terminals. Each production rule specifies which symbol can be substituted with which sequence. You cannot substitute terminals. The terminals and the variables are disjoint. We write each production rule as $x \rightarrow$

w, where $x \in V$ and $w \in (V \cup \Sigma)^*$. For a production rule $r : x \to w$, $|w|$ is the **length** of r, and each character of w is a **component** of w.

The rule $x \to w$ signifies that any string $z \in (V \cup \Sigma)^*$ containing at least one occurrence of x is rewriteable into a string in which w replaces one arbitrary occurrence of x in z. More specifically, suppose $z \in (V \cup \Sigma)^*$ is equal to uxv such that $u, v \in (V \cup \Sigma)^*$ and $x \in V$, and $x \to w \in R$. Then, applying the rule to the x produces uwv. We say that G **produces** (or **derives**) uwv from z (according to G) and write $z \xrightarrow{G} uwv$. For strings z and $z' \in (V \cup \Sigma)^*$, we write $z \xrightarrow{G,*} z'$ to mean that G produces z' from z with multiple successive substitutions. In other words, there exist some $z_1, \ldots z_k \in (V \cup \Sigma)^*$ such that

$$z_1 \xrightarrow{G} z_2 \xrightarrow{G} G\, z_3 \cdots z_{k-1} \xrightarrow{G} z_k.$$

Here, $z = z_1$ and $z' = z_k$. We call the series $[z_1, \ldots, z_k]$ a **production sequence** (or a **derivation sequence**) of z' from z. For both $\xrightarrow{G}$ and $\xrightarrow{G,*}$, we omit G if the grammar G is evident from the context.

Definition 4.1 For a CFG $G = (V, \Sigma, R, S)$, $L(G)$ is the set of all $w \in \Sigma^*$ that we can derive from the start variable S. We say that G **produces** $L(G)$.

Definition 4.2 A language L is **context-free** if a CFG produces L.

Definition 4.3 **CFL** is the class of all context-free languages.

We often combine rules for substituting the same variables for presenting production rules using $|$ to enumerate the right-hand side of the production rules. If there are rules $A \to w_1, \ldots, A \to w_k$, we write:

$$A \to w_1 \mid \cdots \mid w_k.$$

4.1.2 Examples of CFGs

Let us see some examples of CFGs.

Example 4.1 Our first example is $A = \{a^n b^n \mid n \geq 0\}$. We can develop a grammar for A with just one variable, S, which also serves as the start variable. The empty string is a language member. We thus introduce the rule $S \to \epsilon$. We observe that a nonempty string w is a member of A if, and only if, $w = aw'b$ such that $w' \in A$. This observation gives a rule $S \to aSb$. These two rules are sufficient for generating A. Thus, our grammar is $G = (\{S\}, \{a, b\}, R, S)$ where $R = \{S \to \epsilon, S \to aSb\}$. Using $|$, we present the production rules as:

$$S \to \epsilon \mid aSb.$$

When considering a sequence of productions, the variable subject to production can be ambiguous. We can make this explicit by attaching a marker to it. We use underlines for the specification here. With this grammar, we obtain the following production sequences:

$$\underline{S} \Longrightarrow \epsilon,$$

$$\underline{S} \Longrightarrow a\underline{S}b \Longrightarrow ab,$$

$$\underline{S} \Longrightarrow a\underline{S}b \Longrightarrow aa\underline{S}bb \Longrightarrow aabb, \text{ and}$$

$$\underline{S} \Longrightarrow a\underline{S}b \Longrightarrow aa\underline{S}bb \Longrightarrow aaa\underline{S}bbb \Longrightarrow aaabbb.$$

With a slight change in the rules, we can construct a grammar for $\{a^n b^n \mid n \geq 1\}$ (see Exercise 4.3).

Example 4.2 Our next example is the language B of all palindromes over the alphabet $\{a, b\}$; that is, $B = \{w \mid w \in \{a, b\}^* \text{ and } w = w^R\}$, where w^R denotes the reverse of w.

We can produce the language using CFG with just one variable. The idea is that a string u, $|u| \geq 2$, is a palindrome if, and only if, $u = xwx$, where w is a palindrome and x is either a or b. From the observation, we obtain the rules:

$$S \rightarrow \epsilon \mid a \mid b \mid aSa \mid bSb.$$

With this grammar, we obtain the following production sequences:

$$\underline{S} \Longrightarrow \epsilon,$$

$$\underline{S} \Longrightarrow a,$$

$$\underline{S} \Longrightarrow b,$$

$$\underline{S} \Longrightarrow a\underline{S}a \Longrightarrow aa,$$

$$\underline{S} \Longrightarrow a\underline{S}a \Longrightarrow aaa,$$

$$\underline{S} \Longrightarrow b\underline{S}b \Longrightarrow aaa, \text{ and}$$

$$\underline{S} \Longrightarrow a\underline{S}a \Longrightarrow ab\underline{S}ba \Longrightarrow abba.$$

With a slight change in the rules, we can construct a grammar for the language of all nonempty palindromes and a grammar for the language of all nonempty even-length palindromes, etc. (see Exercise 4.4).

Example 4.3 Our next example is $\{a^i b^j c^k \mid a = j \text{ or } j = k\}$. The language is equal to

$$\{a^i b^i \mid i \geq 0\} \cdot \{c^j \mid j \geq 0\} \cup \{a^i \mid i \geq 0\} \cdot \{b^j c^j \mid j \geq 0\}.$$

Here, $\cdot$ is the concatenation.

Using this decomposition, we construct a grammar with five variables: S, A, C, T, and U.

- S is the start variable for selecting between two components, TC and AU.
- A is for producing any number of as.
- C is for producing any number of cs.
- T is for producing $\{a^i b^i \mid i \geq 0\}$.
- U is for producing $\{b^j c^j \mid j \geq 0\}$.

The rules are as follows:

$$S \rightarrow TC \mid AU,$$

$$C \rightarrow \epsilon \mid cC,$$

$$A \rightarrow \epsilon \mid aA,$$

$$T \rightarrow \epsilon \mid aTb, \text{ and}$$

$$U \rightarrow \epsilon \mid bUc.$$

Example 4.4 The last example is the language C of all strings over $\{a, b\}$ in which a occurs the same number of times as b. We can state the membership of a string in C using induction:

- A nonempty string w is in C if, and only if, either

  - $w = \alpha w' \beta$ such that α and β are opposite members of the alphabet and w' is a member of the language
  - $w = uv$ such that u and v are nonempty members of C

To see why the induction works, let $w = \alpha w' \beta$ be a nonempty member of the language with $\alpha, \beta \in \{a, b\}$. We consider two cases: $\alpha \neq \beta$ and $\alpha = \beta$. First, suppose $\alpha \neq \beta$. The two characters collectively contribute 1 to the number of as in w and 1 to bs in w. Since w is in C, w' must be in C.

Next, suppose $\alpha = \beta$. Suppose, further, $\alpha = a$. Let $w_0, \ldots, w_n$ be the prefixes of w in the increasing order of length, where $w_0 = \epsilon$ and $w_m = w$. For each i such that $0 \leq i \leq n$, let d_i be the difference in the occurrences between a and b in w_i. For all i such that $0 \leq i \leq n - 1$, $d_{i+1} - d_i$ is 1 if w's character at position $i + 1$ is a and -1 otherwise (i.e., the character is b). So, we have:

- Since w is a language member, we have $d_n = 0$.
- Since w's last symbol is a, $d_{n-1} = -1$.
- Since $w_0 = \epsilon$, $d_0 = 0$.
- Since $w_1 = a$, $d_1 = 1$.

Since d_1 is positive, d_{n-1} is negative, and the change from d_i to d_{i+1} is ± 1, an index j must exist between 2 and $n-2$ such that $d_j = 0$. Pick any such j. Then, w_j belongs to the language. This implies that w's suffix after s_j is a language member. Thus, $w = uv$, where both u and v are language members.

The proof for the case where $\alpha = \beta = b$ is the same, with the roles switched between a and b.

From the observation, we obtain a grammar with just one variable, S, with the rules:

$$S \to \epsilon \mid aSb \mid bSa \mid SS.$$

The last rule, $S \to SS$, has two occurrences of S. The double occurrences of S make it possible to split the production into two successive ones.

Here are some examples of producing members of the language.

$$\underline{S} \Longrightarrow S\underline{S} \Longrightarrow Sa\underline{S}b \Longrightarrow \underline{S}aSb \Longrightarrow baa\underline{S}b \Longrightarrow baab \text{ and}$$

$$\underline{S} \Longrightarrow S\underline{S} \Longrightarrow ba\underline{S} \Longrightarrow baS\underline{S} \Longrightarrow baSb\underline{S}a \Longrightarrow ba\underline{S}ba \Longrightarrow baba.$$

4.1.3 Production Trees

Let us explore the concept of production trees, which is a way to visualize the action of CFGs.

A **production tree** (or **derivation tree**) is an upside-down tree that presents derivation. Each node of a production tree has an element from $V \cup \Sigma \cup \{\epsilon\}$ as its label. A production tree has only one root. When drawing a production tree, we place its root at the top and leaves at the bottom. If the label of a node in a production tree is a variable, say x, the node may have children. The children come from one of the rules for substituting x, and the concatenation of the children's labels matches the right-hand side of the rule. If a production tree's root is labeled by A and the concatenation of its leaf labels is w, the tree corresponds to $A \Longrightarrow w$. A production tree is **complete** if the root's label is the start variable and no leaf has a variable as its label (i.e., the leaves have labels belonging to Σ_ϵ).

Figure 4.1 shows a complete production tree.

Note that if a production tree has X as its root and w as its leaf labels, the tree represents $X \Longrightarrow w$. We can view this production as a new production rule and add it to the grammar. This new rule is redundant and consistent with the grammar because it can be decomposed into a sequence of existing derivation rules. Thus, the addition preserves the grammar's language. This observation gives the following proposition.

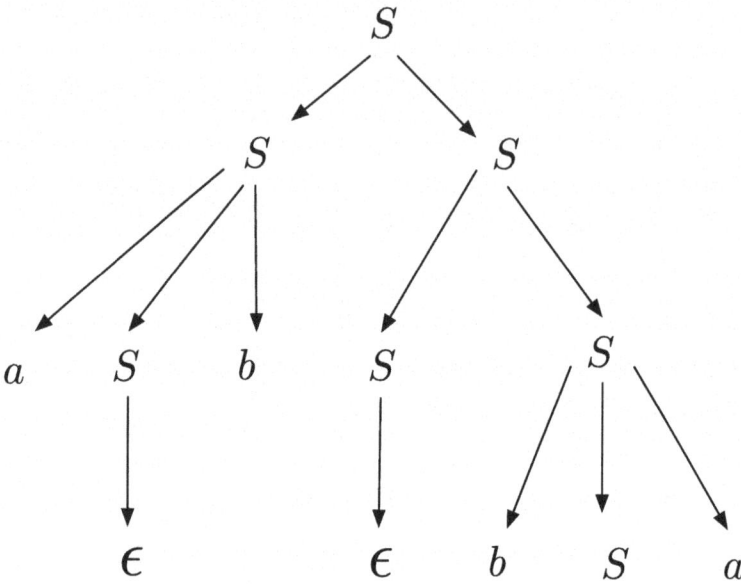

Fig. 4.1 A production tree according to the palindrome's grammar. The tree corresponds to the production of *abba*

Proposition 4.1 *Let G be a CFG and T be a production tree. Suppose we construct a grammar H by adding the rule corresponding to the production tree. Then* $L(G) = L(H)$.

4.1.4   Leftmost and Rightmost Productions

In this section, we explore leftmost and rightmost productions.

We sometimes observe that a CFG can produce some members through different sequences of productions. For example, *abba* in the language from Example 4.4 has at least two productions:

$$S \implies SS \implies abS \implies abba \text{ and } S \implies SS \implies Sba \implies abba.$$

We ask if we can define a preference order so that there is always a unique, most preferable production. In response to the question, we consider the **leftmost production**, which dictates that applying a production rule must be to the leftmost variable. Similarly, we define the **rightmost production**. For example, with our grammar for producing all strings having the same number of *a*s as *b*s, the following is a leftmost production:

$$S \implies \underline{S}S \implies ab\underline{S} \implies abba.$$

Definition 4.4 A CFG for a language is **unambiguous** if, for each language member, there is only one leftmost derivation sequence for the member. Otherwise, we call the grammar **ambiguous**.

Note that the grammar for the palindromes over $\{a, b\}$ from Example 4.2 is unambiguous because the variable S always appears once in the string the grammar produces.

Is every context-free language unambiguous? Can we construct an unambiguous grammar for each context-free language?

Definition 4.5 A CFL is **inherently ambiguous** if it lacks unambiguous CFG.

The question in the above is restated as: is there an inherently ambiguous CFL?

The answer to the question is positive; we will postpone this discussion to the next chapter.

4.1.5   Closure Properties of CFLs

In this section, we explore the closure properties of CFLs.

Proposition 4.2 CFL *is closed under union, concatenation, and the Kleene-star.*

Proof Let L_1 and L_2 be two CFLs. Let $G_1 = (V_1, \Sigma_1, R_1, S_1)$ and $G_2 = (V_2, \Sigma_2, R_2, S_2)$ be two CFGs for the two languages, where $L_1 = L(G_1)$ and $L_2 = L(G_2)$. We can assume that $V_1 \cap V_2 = \emptyset$ by renaming the variables. Define $V = V_1 \cup V_2 \cup \{S\}$. Here, S is a new variable, $\Sigma = \Sigma_1 \cup \Sigma_2$, and $R = R_1 \cup R_2 \cup \{S \rightarrow S_1, S \rightarrow S_2\}$, where $S \rightarrow S_1$ is a rule that turns S to S_1 and $S \rightarrow S_2$ is a rule that turns S to S_2. Now define $G = (V, \Sigma, R, S)$. Using one of the additional rules, we select one of G_1 and G_2 and then execute derivation according to the chosen grammar. Thus, G is the grammar for $L_1 \cup L_2$.

Define $R' = R_1 \cup R_2 \cup \{S \rightarrow S_1 S_2\}$, and define $G' = (V, \Sigma, R', S)$. With this new rule, the grammar produces $S_1 S_2$ from S. The two, S_1 and S_2, respectively produce members of L_1 and L_2. Thus, G' is a grammar for $L_1 L_2$.

Define $V'' = V_1 \cup \{S''\}$ where S'' is a new variable. Define $R'' = R_1 \cup \{S'' \rightarrow \epsilon, S'' \rightarrow S'' S_1\}$. Define $G'' = (V'', \Sigma_1, R'', S'')$. We can exclusively produce $(S_1)^*$ using the two new rules. Then, by applying independent derivations to the S_1' s, we can produce a member of $L(G_1)^*$. Thus, G'' is a grammar for $(L_1)^*$. $\square$

Theorem 4.1 CFL *is not closed under complement. It is also not closed under intersection.*

Proof Let $A = \{0^n 1^n 2^t \mid n, t \geq 0\}$ and $B = \{0^n 1^n 2^t \mid n, t \geq 0\}$. Let $L = A \cap B$. We saw in Example 5.7 that L is not context-free. Both A and B are context-free.

If the class of context-free languages were closed under intersection, L would be context-free. Thus, by contradiction, the class is not closed under intersection.

Note that the class is closed under union. Under the De Morgan laws, if the class were closed under complement, it would be closed under intersection. Thus, by contradiction, the class is not closed under complement.   □

4.2   Normal Forms of CFGs

Here, we study two normal forms of CFGs. Because of the form's flexibility, analyzing a CFG's behavior is challenging. The normal forms will help in this analysis.

4.2.1   The Chomsky Normal Form (CNF) Grammars

Let us start with the Chomsky Normal Form grammar.

The **Chomsky Normal Form (CNF)** is a regular form where each grammar consists of only three types of rules. A grammar $G = \{V, \Sigma, R, S\}$ is in the Chomsky Normal Form if R consists only of the following three types:

1. $S \to \epsilon$.
2. $X \to a$ for some $a \in \Sigma$.
3. $X \to YZ$, where $Y, Z \in V - \{S\}$.

Because of this restriction, the first type appears in the grammar only when $\epsilon \in L(G)$. The third type prohibits S from appearing on the right-hand side of any rule.

None of the CFGs we have seen so far are CNF grammars. As we see later, we can construct an equivalent Chomsky Normal Form grammar from every CFG.

Here is an equivalent CNF grammar for $A = \{a^n b^n \mid n \geq 0\}$. We construct a CNF grammar from the one in Example 4.1.2, where the rules are $S \to \epsilon \mid aSb$. The CNF grammar has five variables (S, A, B, X, and T) and has the following rules:

$$S \to \epsilon \mid AB \mid AX,$$

$$A \to a,$$

$$B \to b,$$

$$X \to TB, \text{ and}$$

$$T \to AB \mid AX.$$

The thought process for arriving at the grammar is as follows:

First, we introduce variables A and B for producing terminals a and b, respectively, and have no other roles. We replace each occurrence of a with A and each occurrence of b with B. Since S cannot appear on the right-hand side, we duplicate the rules for S with T on the right-hand side, like $S \rightarrow ATB \mid AB \mid \epsilon$ and $T \rightarrow ATB \mid AB$. We introduce a variable X and a rule $X \rightarrow TB$ and replace ATB with AX. The set of rules we obtain from these modifications is as follows:

$$S \rightarrow \epsilon,$$
$$S \rightarrow AX,$$
$$S \rightarrow AB,$$
$$X \rightarrow TB,$$
$$T \rightarrow AX,$$
$$T \rightarrow AB,$$
$$A \rightarrow a, \text{ and}$$
$$B \rightarrow b.$$

Here are examples of the production sequences with the grammar:

$$\underline{S} \Longrightarrow \epsilon,$$
$$\underline{S} \Longrightarrow \underline{A}B \Longrightarrow a\underline{B} \Longrightarrow ab, \text{ and}$$
$$\underline{S} \Longrightarrow \underline{A}X \Longrightarrow a\underline{X} \Longrightarrow a\underline{T}B \Longrightarrow a\underline{A}BB \Longrightarrow aa\underline{B} \Longrightarrow aab\underline{B} \Longrightarrow aabb.$$

The grammar is unambiguous. The nonempty strings that the grammar produces with leftmost production are one of the following patterns:

1. $a^i A B^{i+1}$,
2. $a^{i+1} X B^i$,
3. $a^{i+j+1} b^i B^{j+1}$,
4. $a^{i+1} T B^{i+1}$, and
5. $a^i A X B^{i+1}$.

Here, $i \geq j \geq 0$. Note the following properties:

- Applying $A \rightarrow a$ to (1) produces (3).
- Applying $X \rightarrow AB$ to (2) produces (1).
- Applying $X \rightarrow TB$ to (2) produces (4).
- Applying $B \rightarrow b$ to (3) produces (3).
- Applying $T \rightarrow AB$ to (3) produces (1).
- Applying $T \rightarrow AX$ to (3) produces (5).
- Applying $A \rightarrow a$ to (5) produces (3).

- Note that the number of occurrences of A or a equals the number of occurrences of B or b in all the patterns.

Thus, the grammar is unambiguous.

In a CNF grammar, applying a rule of the form $X \rightarrow YZ$ increases the length of any final (i.e., terminal-only) string by 1.

Proposition 4.3 *To produce a string having a length $n \geq 2$ with a CNF grammar, we must apply rules of the form $X \rightarrow YZ$ $n-1$ times and rules of the form $X \rightarrow a$ n times.*

This proposition plays a crucial role in our attempt to establish methods for showing languages to be non-context-free in Sect. 5.4.3.

4.2.2 Normalizing CFGs to CNF Grammars

Every CFG is convertible to a CNF grammar. The following theorem shows such a conversion is possible.

Theorem 4.2 *For every CFL, a CNF grammar produces the language.*

Before getting into the construction's details, let us define some terminology about production rules. The classifications are not exclusive.

- We call a length-0 rule an ϵ **rule**.
- A variable from which ϵ can be produced is a **nullable variable**.
- A rule having a length of ≥ 1 if a **terminal-only rule** if its right-hand side consists only of terminals, a **variable-only rule** if its right-hand side consists only of variables, and a **mixed rule** otherwise.
- A length-1 variable-only rule is a **unit rule**.
- A rule with a ≥ 3 length is a **long rule**.

Proof Overview

We convert an arbitrary CFG $G = (V, \Sigma, R, S)$ to an equivalent CNF grammar through the following steps:

1. For each terminal, we introduce a variable with a length-1 rule that produces the terminal, and we replace every occurrence of the terminal in the existing rules with the variable if the rule has a length of ≥ 2.
   The process eliminates all the mixed rules.
2. We introduce a new variable and duplicate each rule from the start variable to the new variable; after the duplication, we make the new variable the start variable.

(continued)

The process eliminates the start variable on the right-hand side of the rules.

3. We identify all nullable variables. If the new start variable is nullable, we record the information and introduce an ϵ rule from the start variable at the end.

4. We turn all long rules into a series of length-2 rules while duplicating each length-2 rule containing a nullable variable, with one of the nullable variables erased.

   We then eliminate all ϵ rules.

5. We identify all unit rules and their chains.

6. We short-circuit all unit rules to create length-2 rules and terminal-only rules.

   After that, we remove all unit rules.

7. If we found earlier that the grammar produces ϵ, we add an ϵ rule from the (new) start variable.

Proof Let $G = (V, \Sigma, R, S)$ be an arbitrary CFG. We will convert G to a CNF grammar through the seven steps in the overview.

Step 1: For each terminal $a \in \Sigma$, we introduce a variable X_a and a rule $X_a \to a$ and then, in every other rule, replace each occurrence of a with X_a. The process replaces a rule containing k terminals with a production consisting of a series of $k + 1$ rules. After the modification, no mixed rules exist in the grammar.

Step 2: We use a greedy algorithm to identify nullable variables. Let N be the variables found to be nullable. The initial members of N are those variables with ϵ rules. Let V be the present set of all variables. Let $W = V - N$. We repeat the following until no element is moved from W to N; if a variable $X \in W$ exists with a rule $X \to w, w \in N^*$, move X from W to N. After the addition, we record if $S \to \epsilon$.

Step 3: We introduce a new variable S_0, and for each rule, $S \to w$, add $S_0 \to w$.

Step 4: For each variable-only rule $A \to X_1 \cdots X_\ell$ such that $\ell \geq 2$, we apply the following:

- If $\ell = 2$ and X_1 is nullable, we add a new rule $A \to X_2$.
- If $\ell = 2$ and X_2 is nullable, we add a new rule $A \to X_1$.
- If $\ell \geq 3$, we add a new variable Y, replace the rule with $A \to X_1 Y$ and $Y \to X_2 \cdots X_\ell$. In addition, if X_1 is nullable, add another rule $A \to Y$.

After this process, we remove all ϵ rules.

Step 5: We find all existing unit rules and those induced by combining them. We initialize U as the set of all unit rules in the grammar. We then repeat the following: as long as rules $X \to Y$ and $Y \to Z$ exist in U such that $X \to Z$ is not in U and $X \neq Z$, add $X \to Z$ to U.

Step 6: For each unit rule $X \rightarrow Y$ in U and non-unit rule $Y \rightarrow w$, we add a rule $X \rightarrow w$.

Step 7: If $S_0 \rightarrow \epsilon$ is a required rule, add it to the grammar.

Algorithms 4.1 and 4.2 present a pseudocode of the conversion algorithm. □

Algorithm 4.1 An algorithm for converting a CFG to an equivalent CNF grammar (part 1)

```
 1: procedure CNF-CONVERSION-PART1(G = (V, Σ, R, S))              ▷ Step 1
 2:     for each a ∈ Σ do
 3:         add X_a to V;
 4:         add X_a → a to R;
 5:     end for
 6:     for each rule X → w, |w| ≥ 2 do
 7:         if w contains a terminal then
 8:             w′ → w with each a ∈ σ replaced with X_a;
 9:             replace X → w with X → w′;
10:         end if
11:     end for                                                    ▷ Step 2
12:     N ← {X | X has an ε rule};
13:     W ← V − N;
14:     while (∃X ∈ W)(∃X → w ∈ R_0)w ∈ N^+ do
15:         for each such X do
16:             add X to N;
17:         end for
18:     end while
19:     β ← S ∈ N;                                                 ▷ Step 3
20:     add S_0 to V;
21:     for each rule S → w do
22:         add S_0 → w to R;
23:     end for
24:     replace S with S_0;
25: end procedure
```

Example 4.5 Here is a demonstration of how the conversion algorithm works. Let G be a grammar for $\{(aa)^n(bb)^n \mid n \geq 0\}$. The rules are:

$$S \rightarrow \epsilon \mid aaSbb \mid \epsilon.$$

- In Step 1, we add variables X_a and X_b, add rules $X_a \rightarrow a$ and $X_b \rightarrow b$, and then change the rules for S to:

$$S \rightarrow \epsilon \mid X_a X_a S X_b X_b \mid \epsilon.$$

- Step 2 finds $N = \{S\}$ as the set of nullable variables. We record β as *true*.
- In Step 3, we introduce S_0 and the rules:

Algorithm 4.2 An algorithm for converting a CFG to an equivalent CNF grammar (part 2)

```
 1: procedure CNF-CONVERSION-PART2(G = (V, Σ, R, S))                    ▷ Step 4
 2:     R₁ ← ∅;
 3:     while R is not empty do
 4:         select one rule r : A → w in R;
 5:         if |w| ≥ 1 then
 6:             add r to R₁;
 7:             remove r to R;
 8:             if |w| = 2 then
 9:                 let w = X₁X₂;
10:                 add r to R₁;
11:                 if X₁ ∈ N then
12:                     add A → X₂ to R₁;
13:                 end if
14:                 if X₂ ∈ N then
15:                     add A → X₁ to R₁;
16:                 end if
17:             else
18:                 let w = X₁X₂ · · · Xₗ;
19:                 add a new variable Y;
20:                 add A → X₁Y to R₁;
21:                 add Y → X₂ · · · Xₗ to R;
22:                 if X₁ ∈ N then
23:                     add A → Y to R₁;
24:                 end if
25:             end if
26:         end if
27:     end while
28:     R ← R₁;
29: end procedure
```

$$S_0 \rightarrow \epsilon \mid X_a X_a S X_b X_b \mid \epsilon.$$

- In Step 4, we decompose long rules, possibly erasing occurrences of the nullable S. The new variables are Y_1 and Y_2, and the new rules are:

$$S \rightarrow X_a Y_1,$$

$$Y_1 \rightarrow X_a S X_b X_b,$$

$$Y_1 \rightarrow X_a Y_2,$$

$$Y_2 \rightarrow S X_b X_b,$$

$$Y_2 \rightarrow X_b X_b,$$

$$Y_2 \rightarrow S Y_3,$$

$$Y_2 \rightarrow Y_3,$$

$$Y_3 \rightarrow X_b X_b, \text{ and}$$

$$S_0 \rightarrow X_a Y_1.$$

Algorithm 4.3 An algorithm for converting a CFG to an equivalent CNF grammar (part 3)

```
 1: procedure CNF-CONVERSION-PART3(G = (V, Σ, R, S))              ▷ Step 5
 2:     U ← all the unit rules;
 3:     while true do
 4:         if ∃X, Y, Z ∈ V, X → Y ∈ R, Y → Z ∈ R, X → Z ∉ R, X ≠ Z then
 5:             add X → Z to U;
 6:         else
 7:             terminate the loop;
 8:         end if
 9:     end while                                                ▷ Step 6
10:     for each X → Y, Y → w ∈ R do
11:         if Y → w ∉ U then
12:             add a rule X → w;
13:         end if
14:     end for
15:     remove all rules in U from R;                            ▷ Step 7
16:     if β = true then
17:         add a rule S₀ → ε;
18:     end if
19:     return the grammar;
20: end procedure
```

Here, the second and fourth rules require further decompositions.

- In Step 5, we find all unit rules. There is only one unit rule: $Y_2 \to Y_3$.
- Step 6 combines unit and non-unit rules to produce $Y_2 \to X_3 X_3$.
- Finally, in Step 7, we add $S_0 \to \epsilon$.

The final set of rules is:

$$S_0 \to X_a Y_1,$$

$$X_a \to a,$$

$$X_b \to b,$$

$$S \to X_a Y_1,$$

$$Y_1 \to X_a Y_2,$$

$$Y_2 \to S Y_3,$$

$$Y_2 \to X_b X_b, \text{ and}$$

$$Y_3 \to X_b X_b.$$

4.2.3 The Greibach Normal Form (GNF) Grammars

CFLs have another normalized form, the **Greibach Normal Form (GNF)**. Intuitively, in a Greibach Normal Form grammar, terminals may appear only as the first symbol on the right-hand side of the rules.

Definition 4.6 A CFG $G = (V, \Sigma, R, S)$ not producing ϵ is a Greibach Normal Form (GNF) grammar if every rule is of the form $X \rightarrow aY$ for some $X \in V$, $a \in \Sigma$, and $Y \in V^*$.

If a GNF grammar G produces ϵ, S does not appear on the right-hand side of any rules, and G has a rule $S \rightarrow \epsilon$.

We can construct a Greibach Normal Form grammar from an arbitrary CFG not producing ϵ.

Theorem 4.3 *For every CFL not producing ϵ, a Greibach Normal Form grammar produces the language.*

Proof Let $G = (V, \Sigma, R, S)$ be a Chomsky Normal Form grammar for a language L. We fix some ordering of the variables, $A_1, \ldots, A_k$, where $A_k = S$. We may add new variables A_{k+1}, A_{k+2}, etc., during the conversion. The addition will be in this order, and it will be one variable at a time.

We classify the rules we handle into the following four types:

1. (Terminal-leading) $A \rightarrow aw$ where $a \in \Sigma$ and $w \in (\Sigma \cup V)^*$.
2. (Index-increasing) $A_i \rightarrow A_j w$ where $i < j$ and $w \in (\Sigma \cup V)^*$.
3. (Index-decreasing) $A_i \rightarrow A_j w$ where $i > j$ and $w \in (\Sigma \cup V)^*$.
4. (Index-preserving) $A_i \rightarrow A_i w$ where $w \in (\Sigma \cup V)^*$.

Our task is to convert the grammar so there are only terminal-leading rules. We accomplish this task in two phases. First, we eliminate all index-increasing and index-preserving rules. Then, we eliminate index-decreasing rules.

The elimination in the first phase occurs in the decreasing order of the index to the variables, starting with A_k and ending with A_1. For the base case, A_k is the variable. Since A_k is the start variable, and the start variable of a CNF grammar does not appear on the right-hand side of any production, A_k has no index-increasing or index-preserving rules. Thus, the requirement for A_k has already been met.

For the induction step, let $1 \le i \le k - 1$, and suppose that the requirement has been met for $A_{i+1}, \ldots, A_k$. Suppose A_i has an index-increasing rule $A_i \rightarrow A_j w$ such that $j > i$. We construct a new rule by combining $A_i \rightarrow A_j w$ and each rule of the form $A_j \rightarrow u$. We then replace $A_i \rightarrow A_j w$ with the new rules. The replacement may produce an index-increasing rule of the form $A_i \rightarrow A_p v$, but, due to our induction hypothesis, $p < j$. Thus, by repeatedly applying the replacement procedure to any index-increasing rule from A_i, all index-increasing rules from A_i can be eliminated.

After the elimination, suppose A_i has an index-preserving rule. If A_i has no index-increasing or terminal-leading rules, we cannot turn a string containing A_i to terminals, so we will remove all rules from A_i and those with A_i on the right-hand side. Let

$$A_i \rightarrow \alpha_1 \mid \cdots \mid \alpha_m$$

be an enumeration of all index-decreasing or terminal-leading rules from A_i. Additionally, let

$$A_i \rightarrow A_i\beta_1 \mid \cdots \mid A_i\beta_n$$

be an enumeration of all index-preserving rules from A_i. If we construct a string by combining these rules so that the right-hand side does not start with A_i, then the string must be in the form:

$$A_i \rightarrow \alpha_p \beta_{l_1} \cdots \beta_{l_q}$$

for some $q \geq 0$ and $l_1, \ldots, l_q$ between 1 and n. We introduce a new variable B (which receives the smallest available variable index) and replace the rules from A_i with the following rules:

$$A_i \rightarrow \alpha_1 \mid \cdots \mid \alpha_m \mid \alpha_1 B \mid \cdots \mid \alpha_m B \text{ and}$$
$$B \rightarrow \beta_1 \mid \cdots \mid \beta_n \mid \beta_1 B \mid \cdots \mid \beta_n B.$$

The rules from A_i free of B that we can produce from the new rules are exactly of the form:

$$A_i \rightarrow \alpha_p \beta_{l_1} \cdots \beta_{l_q}, q \geq 0.$$

After the replacement, A_i has no recursive rules. Also, since B has the highest index, each rule from B is index-decreasing or terminal-leading. This completes the induction step for A_i.

In the second phase, we eliminate all the index-decreasing rules, starting from A_1 and moving toward the variable with the highest index. The construction is inductive. The base case is A_1. Since A_1 has no preceding variable in the ordering, all its rules are terminal-leading. Thus, the requirement has already been met for A_1.

For the induction step, let $i \geq 2$ and suppose we have completed the construction for $A_1, \ldots, A_{i-1}$. Let $A_i \rightarrow A_j w$ be an arbitrary index-decreasing rule from A_i, where $j < i$. By our induction hypothesis, every rule from A_j is index-decreasing. We create new rules by replacing A_j in $A_i \rightarrow A_j w$ with each rule from A_j and substitute $A_i \rightarrow A_j w$ with the new rules. The new rules are terminal-leading. In this manner, we complete the construction for A_i.

Algorithm 4.4 presents the conversion algorithm.   □

Algorithm 4.4 An algorithm for converting a CNF to a GNF

```
 1: procedure GNF-CONVERSION(G)
 2:     receive a CNF grammar G = (V, Σ, R, S);
 3:     enumerate the variables of V as A_1, ..., A_k where S = A_k;
 4:     initialize the maximum index μ as k;
 5:     for i = k − 1, ..., 1 do
 6:         while R has an index-increasing rule from A_i do
 7:             select one rule r : A_i → A_j w;
 8:             find all rules from A_j : A_j → u_1 | ⋯ | u_s;
 9:             add A_i → u_1 w | ⋯ | u_s w;
10:             remove r from R;
11:         end while
12:         find all terminal-leadings from A_i : A_i → α_1 | ⋯ | α_m;
13:         find all index-preserving rules from A_i : A_i → A_i β_1 | ⋯ | β_n;
14:         if n ≥ 1 ∧ m = 0 then                    ▷ A_i cannot produce terminal-only strings
15:             for each rule r : A → w in R s.t. A = A_i or A_i appears in w do
16:                 remove r from R;
17:             end for
18:         else if n, m ≥ 1 then
19:             μ ← μ + 1; V ← V ∪ {A_μ};
20:             add A_i → α_1 A_μ | ⋯ | | α_m A_μ to R;
21:             add A_μ → β_1 | ⋯ | β_n to R;
22:             add A_μ → β_1 A_μ | ⋯ | β_n A_μ to R;
23:             remove all the index-preserving rules from A_i;
24:         end if
25:     end for
26:     for i = 1, ..., μ do
27:         for each rule r : A_i → A_j w ∈ R s.t. i > j do
28:             find all rules from A_j : A_j → u_1 | ⋯ | u_s;
29:             add A_i → u_1 w | ⋯ | u_s w to R
30:             remove r from R;
31:         end for
32:     end for
33: end procedure
```

Example 4.6 Here is an example of converting a CNF to a GNF. Let $G = (V, \Sigma, R, A_5)$ be a CNF grammar such that $V = \{A_1, \ldots, A_5\}$, $\Sigma = \{a, b\}$, and R consists of the following rules:

$$A_1 \rightarrow a,$$

$$A_2 \rightarrow b,$$

$$A_3 \rightarrow A_4 A_2 \mid b,$$

$$A_4 \rightarrow A_1 A_3, \text{ and}$$

$$A_5 \rightarrow A_1 A_3.$$

The grammar is for $\{a^n b^n \mid n \geq 1\}$. A_5's rule is index-decreasing; so is A_4's. A_3's first rule $A_3 \rightarrow A_4 A_2$ is index-increasing, so requires a replacement. We substitute the A_4 on the right-hand side with $A_1 A_3$ to create a new rule $A_3 \rightarrow A_1 A_3 A_2$. A_2 and A_1 have only a terminal-leading rule, so no change is necessary. We thus have:

$$A_1 \rightarrow a,$$
$$A_2 \rightarrow b,$$
$$A_3 \rightarrow A_1 A_3 A_2 \mid b,$$
$$A_4 \rightarrow A_1 A_3, \text{ and}$$
$$A_5 \rightarrow A_1 A_3.$$

Now, we turn all the rules into terminal-leading. No changes are needed for A_1 and A_2. We substitute the A_1 at the start of the remaining rules with a to get $A_3 \rightarrow a A_3 A_2$, $A_4 \rightarrow a A_3$, and $A_5 \rightarrow a A_3$. The final composition of the rules is:

$$A_1 \rightarrow a,$$
$$A_2 \rightarrow b,$$
$$A_3 \rightarrow a A_3 A_2 \mid b,$$
$$A_4 \rightarrow a A_3, \text{ and}$$
$$A_5 \rightarrow a A_3.$$

Exercises

4.1 Show that regular languages are already context-free using the following argument:

Let $M = (Q, \Sigma, \delta, q_0, F)$ be a DFA for some regular language L. For each pair of states $(p, q) \in Q \times F$, think of a variable $S_{p,q}$ representing all strings in Σ^* that take M from p to q. Let S be the start variable of the grammar you will construct. There shall be rules $S \rightarrow S_{q_0,q}$ for all $q \in F$. Present the rules for the remaining variables.

4.2 Give a CFG for $\{a^m b^n \mid m > 1 \text{ and } n \geq 1\}$.

4.3 Give a CFG for $\{a^n b^n \mid n \geq 1\}$.

4.4 Give a CFG for the nonempty palindromes over $\{a, b\}$.

4.5 Give a CFG for $\{a^m b^n c^m \mid m, n > 1\}$.

4.6 Using the grammar from the previous question, present a leftmost production tree for *aabcc* and *aabbcc*.

4.7 Give a CFG for the set of all strings over $\{0, 1\}$ containing the same number of 0s as 1s.

4.8 Give a CFG for the set of all strings over $\{0, 1\}$ containing strictly more 0s than 1s.

4.9 Give a CFG for the set of all strings over $\{0, 1\}$ containing unequal numbers of 0s and 1s.

4.10 The Dyck language D is the set of all strings over the alphabet $\{[,]\}$ such that for all w, $w \in D$ if, and only if, u has the same number of [s as]s and all prefixes of w has no less [s than]s. Prove that the Dyck language is context-free by constructing its CNF grammar.

4.11 Let $k \geq 1$. Let $[_j,]_j$ where $1 \leq j \leq k$ be k pairs of brackets. As an extension of the Dyck language from the previous question, define D_k as the set of strings $w \in \{[_1,]_1, \ldots, [_k,]_k\}^*$ such that for all i, the string constructed from w by erasing all characters except for $[_i,]_i$ is the member of the Dyck language with $[= [_i$ and $] =]_i$. Give a CFG for L.

4.12 Let A be a regular language. Define $L = \{xy^R \mid |x| = |y|$ and $xy \in A\}$. Show that L is context-free.

4.13 Let $k \geq 2$. Let $L_1, \ldots, L_k$ be CFLs not containing an ϵ. Suppose $G_1 = (V_1, \Sigma_1, R_1, S_1), \ldots, G_k = (V_k, \Sigma_k, R_k, S_k)$ are CNF grammars for $L_1, \ldots, L_k$, respectively. Define

$$((L_1 \cup \epsilon) \cdot \cdots \cdot (L_k \cup \epsilon)) - \{\epsilon\}.$$

In other words, L is the concatenation of some m strings from $L_1, \ldots, L_k$, where the m parts have increasing source indices, and $1 \leq m \leq k$. Show how to construct a CNF grammar for L using the existing CNF grammar for each source language.

4.14 Let Σ be an alphabet. Let $\$$ be a symbol not in Σ. Define $B = \{x\$y \mid |x| \neq |y|\}$. Show that B is context-free.

4.15 Let Σ be an alphabet. Let # and $\$$ be two symbols not in Σ. Define $C = \{\#w\$w^R\# \mid w \in \Sigma^*\}$ and $D = \{\#w\$y^R\# \mid w, y \in \Sigma^*$ and $y \neq w^R\}$. Show that both C and D are context-free.

4.16 Let Σ be an alphabet. Let $k \geq 1$ be an integer. Let Π be a nonempty subset of $\Sigma^k \times \Sigma^k$. Let # and $\$$ be two symbols not in Σ. Define $E = \{\#uxv\$wyu^R\# \mid u, v, w \in \Sigma^*,$ and $(x, y) \in \Pi\}$. Show that E is context-free.

4.17 Let Σ be an alphabet and let # be a symbol not in Σ. Let $F = \{\#w_1\#\cdots\#w_m\# \mid m$ is positive and even, and $|w_1| = \cdots = |w_m|\}$. Prove that $\overline{F}$ is context-free.

4.18 Let $A = \{w \mid w \in \{0, 1, 2\}^*$ and among the numbers of 0s, of 1s, and 2s, at least two of them have the same values$\}$. Show that A is context-free by providing its CFG.

4.19 Regarding the grammar you provided for the previous question, present the leftmost production trees for 0012110222 (0 and 1 appear three times each) and 2012012 (each symbol appears twice).

4.20 Define the size of a CFL as the sum of its number of rules and the total length of the right-hand side of the rules. Show that with our CNF conversion method, a grammar with a size of s becomes a CNF grammar with a size of $O(s^2 \log(s))$. You may assume that the individual elements of the alphabet and variables have a constant size.

4.21 A variable in a CFG is **useless** if the variable does not appear in any production from the start variable or does not produce a terminal-only string. Give an algorithm for finding all useless variables in an arbitrary CFG.

4.22 Show that the language $\{w \mid w \in \{0, 1\}^* \text{ and } w \text{ has twice as many 0s as 1s}\}$ is context-free by providing a CFG for the language.

4.23 Show that the class of context-free languages is closed under the reverse operation; i.e., for all context-free language L, L^R is context-free.

4.24 Let G_1 and G_2 be CNF grammars for two context-free languages, L_1 and L_2, respectively. Show how to construct CNF grammars for $L_1 L_2$ and $L_1 \cup L_2$ using G_1 and G_2.

4.25 Let G be a CNF grammar for a context-free language L. Let L' be the set of all prefixes of the members of L. State how to modify the grammar G into a grammar for L', where the grammar is like a CNF grammar, and the ϵ rule is available to any variable.

4.26 Prove that if every rule in a Greibach Normal Form grammar G has at most one variable on the right-hand side, then $L(G)$ is regular.

4.27 Show how to construct from an arbitrary DFA M, a Greibach Normal Form grammar for $L(M)$ where the right-hand side of each production is ϵ, a terminal, and a terminal followed by a variable.

4.28 In a CNF grammar, the rule's right-hand side, consisting solely of variables, has a length of 2. If we increase the required number of variables to exactly three, can we still convert an arbitrary CFL grammar to a normal-form grammar?

4.29 Let G be a CNF grammar (V, Σ, R, A_5), where $V = \{A_1, \ldots, A_5\}$, $\Sigma = \{0, 1, 2\}$ and R consists of the following rules:

$$A_1 \rightarrow 0,$$

$$A_2 \rightarrow 1,$$

$$A_3 \rightarrow A_4 A_2 \mid A_2 A_4,$$

$$A_4 \rightarrow A_1 A_3 \mid A_3 A_4 \mid 2, \text{ and}$$

$$A_5 \rightarrow A_4 A_4.$$

Convert G to a GNF grammar using the conversion algorithm from Sect. 4.2.3.

4.30 Let $G = (V, \Sigma, R, S)$ be a CNF grammar with $V = \{A_1, \ldots, A_m\}$ such that for all i between 1 and m, no variables having an index $\leq i$ appear in production rules for A_i. Prove that such a grammar necessarily produces a finite language.

Bibliographic Notes and Further Reading

The context-free languages are by Chomsky [2, 3]. The Chomsky Normal Form is from [3]. The Greibach Normal Form is by Greibach [8]. The CNF construction algorithm is by Rosenkrantz [11]. Rosenkrantz [11] also presents alternate normal forms derived from CNF. The ambiguity of CFGs was first mentioned in Cantor [1], Chomsky and Schützenberger [4], Floyd [5], and Greibach [7]. The inherent ambiguity was first studied in Ginsburg and Ullian [6], Gross [9], and Parikh [10].

References

1. D.G. Cantor, On the ambiguity problem of Backus systems. J. ACM **9**(4), 477–479 (1962)
2. N. Chomsky, Three models for the description of language. IRE Trans. Inform. Theory **2**(3), 113–124 (1956)
3. N. Chomsky, On certain formal properties of grammars. Inform. Control **2**(2), 137–167 (1959)
4. N. Chomsky, M.P. Schützenberger, The algebraic theory of context-free languages, in *Studies in Logic and the Foundations of Mathematics*, vol. 26 (Elsevier, 1959), pp. 118–161
5. R.W. Floyd, On ambiguity in phrase structure languages. Commun. ACM **5**(10), 526,534 (1962)
6. S. Ginsburg, J. Ullian, Ambiguity in context free languages. J. ACM **13**(1), 62–89 (1966)
7. S.A. Greibach, The undecidability of the ambiguity problem for minimal linear grammars. Inform. Control **6**(2), 119–125 (1963)
8. S.A. Greibach, A new normal-form theorem for context-free phrase structure grammars. J. ACM **12**(1), 42–52 (1965)
9. M. Gross, Inherent ambiguity of minimal linear grammars. Inform. Control **7**(3), 366–368 (1964)
10. R.J. Parikh, On context-free languages. J. ACM **13**(4), 570–581 (1966)
11. D.J. Rosenkrantz, Matrix equations and normal forms for context-free grammars. J. ACM **14**(3), 501–507 (1967)

Chapter 5
The Pushdown Automaton Model

5.1 The Pushdown Automaton (PDA) Model

First, we introduce the pushdown automaton computation model. We then show its equivalence to CFLs.

5.1.1 The Definition

Let us begin by defining the model. A **pushdown automaton (PDA)** is an NFA with an additional storage device, the **stack**.

A pushdown automaton's stack is similar to the stack (last-in, first-out) data structures but lacks the native testing of emptiness. A PDA uses a symbol indicating the stack's bottom to compensate for that lack. The symbol is referred to as an initial symbol (or bottom symbol). A PDA is expected to place the symbol at the computation's start and refrain from using the symbol at other stack positions. The designation of the initial symbol may or may not be part of the PDA's definition. In one step, like NFAs, the PDA reads at most one input symbol in the stream and removes the last symbol from the stack. We call the removal operation "popping." Depending on the input symbol, the stack symbol, and the state, the PDA nondeterministically decides its next state and the string to append to the stack. We call the append operation "pushing."

Formally, a PDA is a seven-tuple $(Q, \Sigma, \Gamma, \delta, q_0, \bot, F)$. The components of the tuple have the following roles:

- Q is the **set of states**.
- Σ is the **input alphabet**.
- Γ is the **stack alphabet**.

© The Editor(s) (if applicable) and The Author(s), under exclusive license to
Springer Nature Switzerland AG 2025
M. Ogihara, *An Introduction to Theory of Computation*,
https://doi.org/10.1007/978-3-031-84740-0_5

- δ is the **transition function** and is a mapping from $Q \times \Sigma_\epsilon \times \Gamma_\epsilon$ to $\mathcal{P}(Q \times \Gamma^*)$, i.e., the power set of $Q \times \Gamma_\epsilon$. Here, $\Sigma_\epsilon = \Sigma \cup \{\epsilon\}$.
- $q_0 \in Q$ is the **initial state**.
- $\perp \in \Gamma$ is the **initial symbol** (or **bottom symbol**).
- $F \subset Q$ is the **final state set**.

The move $(r, x) \in \delta(q, a, b)$ with $q, r \in Q$, $a \in \Sigma_\epsilon$, $b \in \Gamma_\epsilon$, and $x \in \Gamma^*$ means:

- If the PDA is in q, reads a in the input, and pops b from the stack, it pushes x onto the stack and enters r.

A PDA is nondeterministic because of the following nature of its computation:

(a) A PDA can choose between reading the input character (when available) and not reading it.
(b) A PDA can choose between popping the stack's top symbol (when available) and not popping it.
(c) Multiple choices (or no choices) may exist for each combination of state, input symbol, and stack symbol.

We often use a drawing as in Fig. 5.1 for graphical presentations of PDAs.

There are multiple variants of PDAs depending on the way they operate on the stack and when they choose to accept.

- **The Stack Initialization**

  – A PDA's computation may start with an empty stack.
  – A PDA's computation may start with a single initial symbol in its stack.

- **The Initial Symbol**

  – A PDA has a fixed initial symbol.
  – A PDA has no fixed initial symbol.

- **The Popping Operation**

  – A PDA must pop from its stack at each step. If popping is required, a PDA must start its computation with its initial symbol in its stack. Additionally, a PDA stops computing when the stack becomes empty because it cannot execute a popping operation.
  – A PDA may choose not to pop from its stack at any step.

Fig. 5.1 A typical drawing of a PDA. The vertical cells represent the stack. The stack contents are $\perp a B A$ from the bottom to the top

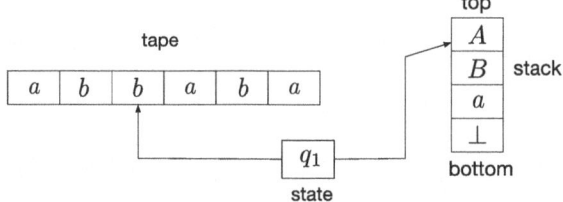

- **The Pushing Operation**
  - If popping is required, a PDA needs to push more than one character.
  - If popping is not required, a PDA may be restricted to push one character at a time.

  The Acceptance Condition
  - The PDA accepts when it enters a final state after reading its entire input.
  - The PDA accepts when it enters a final state after reading its entire input and emptying its stack. The PDA accepts when the state becomes final and the stack becomes empty.

These variants are all equivalent. In this section, we consider the model in which:

- A PDA starts its computation with the initial symbol in the stack and
- It accepts its input by entering a final state after reading the entire input and emptying its stack.

For a PDA, we combine the state, the remaining input characters, and the stack content from bottom to top to present its **instantaneous description (ID)**. In one step, if the PDA reads from the input, we remove the first character of the remaining input. In one step, if the PDA pops from the stack, we remove the string's first character representing the stack content. Similarly, if the PDA pushes onto the stack, we insert the symbol as the string's first character. The initial ID of the PDA with w as its input is $(q_0, w, \perp)$ since the computation starts with the empty stack. An accepting ID of the automaton is (p, ϵ, α) with $p \in F$ for any $\alpha \in \Gamma^*$, since the requirements for acceptance are an empty input and an arrival at a final state.

Definition 5.1 A PDA M accepts its input w if the ID of M on input w reaches one of its accepting IDs starting from its initial ID. We denote the language that M accepts (i.e., $\{w \mid M$ on x accepts$\}$) by $L(M)$.

5.1.2 Examples of PDAs

Here, we show that some non-regular languages we previously saw have PDAs to accept them.

Example 5.1 The example here is $\{a^n b^n \mid n \geq 0\}$. Anticipating that the input matches the regular expression $a^* b^*$, our PDA puts the leading as onto the stack. When the input switches to b, the PDA starts popping from the stack for each b appearing in the input. If the input is a language member, the stack becomes empty at the same time the input becomes empty; otherwise, the matching process prematurely ends with either input characters remaining or the stack remaining nonempty.

We can program this idea using only three states, q_0, q_1, and q_2, where q_0 is the initial state and q_2 is the final state. The stack alphabet is $\{\perp, a\}$. There are only three combinations of state and symbols for which we have nonempty values for the transition function:

$$\delta(q_0, a, \perp) = \{(q_0, a\perp)\},$$

$$\delta(q_0, a, a) = \{(q_0, aa)\},$$

$$\delta(q_0, b, a) = \{(q_1, \epsilon)\},$$

$$\delta(q_1, b, a) = \{(q_1, \epsilon)\}, \text{ and}$$

$$\delta(q_1, \epsilon, \perp) = \{(q_2, \epsilon)\}.$$

The first action is to start creating as in the stack. The second action is to continue creating as in the stack. The third action is to switch to matching a and b upon seeing the first b. The fourth action is to continue matching a and b. The last action is to remove the initial symbol and enter the final state for termination.

We show how the PDA may accept $aaabbb$ using the changes in its ID:

$$(q_0, aaabbb, \perp) \rightarrow (q_0, aabbb, \perp a) \rightarrow (q_0, abbb, \perp aa)$$

$$\rightarrow (q_0, bbb, \perp aaa) \rightarrow (q_1, bb, \perp aa) \rightarrow (q_1, b, \perp a)$$

$$\rightarrow (q_1, \epsilon, \perp) \rightarrow (q_2, \epsilon, \epsilon).$$

Here, the symbol $\rightarrow$ represents a change in a single step. Figure 5.2 shows the PDA's possible choices. The computation starts from the middle top ID, and the successful computation ends at the bottom right ID. A possible computation path with $abbb$ as the input is as follows:

$$(q_0, abbb, \perp) \rightarrow (q_0, bbb, \perp a) \rightarrow (q_1, bb, \perp).$$

Fig. 5.2 The computation path for $\{a^n b^n \mid n \geq 0\}$ on input $aaabbb$

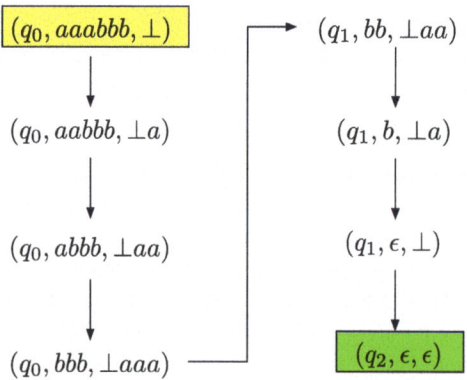

At this point, there is nothing for the automaton to do, so the automaton halts without accepting the input.

Example 5.2 In this example, we consider the language of palindromes over the alphabet $\{a, b\}$. Our PDA has two states, the initial q_0 and the final q_1. In q_0, the automaton builds a prefix that the PDA reverse-matches:

1. If the stack symbol is the initial symbol, the PDA may enter q_1 without pushing onto the stack.
2. If the stack symbol is the initial symbol, the PDA may push the symbol after the initial symbol and stay in q_0.
3. If the stack symbol is not the initial symbol, the PDA may add it to the stack and stay in q_0.
4. If the stack symbol is not the initial symbol, the PDA may add it to the stack and enter q_1.
5. If the stack symbol is not the initial symbol, the PDA may enter q_2 without adding the input character to the stack.

In q_1, the automaton reads an input character and pops a character from the stack. When no input character remains, the stack has only the initial symbol, and the state is q_1; the PDA may then remove the initial symbol.

Here is the transition function, where $x \in \{a, b\}$ and y is an arbitrary symbol in $\{a, b\}$:

$$(q_0, \epsilon, \perp) = \{(q_1, \epsilon)\},$$

$$(q_0, x, \perp) = \{(q_0, \perp x), (q_1, \epsilon)\},$$

$$(q_0, x, y) = \{(q_0, yx), (q_1, x), (q_1, yx)\},$$

$$(q_1, x, x) = \{(q_1, \epsilon)\}, \text{ and}$$

$$(q_1, \epsilon, \perp) = \{(q_2, \epsilon)\}.$$

With this program, a PDA finds the input *abbba* to be a member as follows:

$$(q_0, abbba, \perp) \rightarrow (q_0, bbba, \perp a) \rightarrow (q_0, bba, \perp ab)$$

$$\rightarrow (q_1, ba, \perp ab) \rightarrow (q_1, a, \perp a) \rightarrow (q_1, \epsilon, \perp) \rightarrow (q_2, \epsilon, \epsilon).$$

With this program, a PDA finds the input *abba* to be a member as follows:

$$(q_0, abba, \perp) \rightarrow (q_0, bba, \perp a) \rightarrow (q_1, ba, \perp ab)$$

$$\rightarrow (q_1, a, \perp a) \rightarrow (q_1, \epsilon, \perp) \rightarrow (q_1, \epsilon, \epsilon).$$

An example of how the PDA works appears in Fig. 5.3.

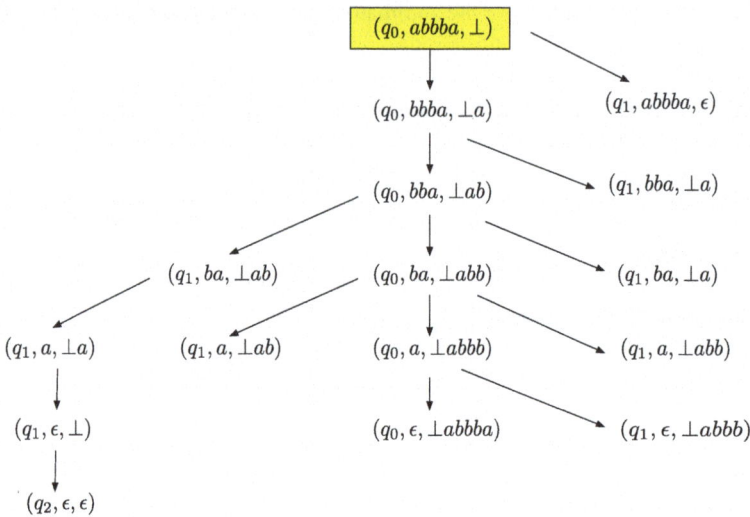

Fig. 5.3 The computation path of our PDA for the palindrome over $\{a, b\}$ on input $abbba$

Example 5.3 Our last example is the language of all strings over $\{a, b\}$ where a occurs the same number of times as b. Our program uses two states, q_0 and q_1, where q_0 is the initial state and q_1 is the final state. The stack alphabet is $\{\bot, a, b\}$, where $\bot$ represents the bottom of the stack. Our PDA scans the input and computes the running difference in the number of occurrences between as and bs using the symbols in excess. The stack content is $\bot a^k$ when the difference is positive k (i.e., more as than bs and the difference is k) and $\bot b^k$ when the difference is $-k$ (i.e., there are more bs than as and the difference is k). The stack content is $\bot$ exactly when there is no difference. The PDA may pop $\bot$ without reading the input and enter q_0. The state q_1 has no action. The following shows the transition function of the PDA, where x is a symbol in $\{a, b\}$ and y is the opposite symbol of a.

$$\delta(q_0, x, \bot) = \{(q_0, \bot x)\},$$

$$\delta(q_0, x, x) = \{(q_0, xx)\},$$

$$\delta(q_0, x, y) = \{(q_0, \epsilon)\}, \text{ and}$$

$$\delta(q_0, \epsilon, \bot) = \{(q_1, \epsilon)\}.$$

For the list, the transition function offers exactly one value for each triple of a state, an input symbol, and a stack symbol.

5.2 Equivalence Between CFLs and PDAs

This section proves that PDAs's computational power is equivalent to the expressive power of context-free grammars.

Theorem 5.1 *Each context-free language has a PDA accepting it.*

> **Proof Overview**
> From a CNF grammar of an arbitrary context-free language, we develop a PDA that executes leftmost production while comparing the input character each time it applies some single-terminal rule.

Proof Let L be an arbitrary context-free language. Let $G = (V, \Sigma, R, S)$ be a CNF grammar for L. We construct a PDA, $M = (Q, \Sigma, \Gamma, \delta, q_0, \bot, F)$, that executes leftmost production accoording to G, as follows:

- The stack alphabet of M, Γ, is $V \cup \{\bot\}$.
- The state set of M, Q, is $\{q_0, q_1, q_2\}$, where q_0 is the initial state and q_2 is a unique final state.
- In state q_0, two possible actions exist. First, the PDA replaces the $\bot$ with the string $\bot S$ without reading the input. Second, in the case where $\epsilon \in L(G)$, the PDA may enter q_2 after popping the $\bot$, without reading the input. Mathematically, these actions can be expressed as:

$$\delta(q_0, \epsilon, \bot) = \{(q_1, \bot S), (q_2, \epsilon)\}.$$

- In state q_1, the PDA has three types of actions:

  1. The PDA may try to match the character it pops from the stack and the input character it reads. Suppose the character from the stack is A and the input is a. The PDA continues in state q_1 if a rule $A \to a$ exists in G without pushing; the PDA has no action to perform otherwise.
  2. The PDA may choose to pop a character from the stack and push two characters onto the stack. Suppose the character from the stack is A and there is a rule $A \to BC$, where B and C are variables. The PDA pushes C and then B and remains in q_1.
  3. The PDA may pop a character from the stack and, if the character is $\bot$, enter q_2.

These possible actions are represented as the following values in the transition function.

1. For all $A \in V$ and $a \in \Sigma$ such that $A \rightarrow a$ is a production rule of G, $(q_1, \epsilon) \in \delta(q_1, a, A)$.
2. For all A, B, and C in V such that $A \rightarrow BC$ is a production rule of G, $(q_1, CB) \in \delta(q_1, \epsilon, A)$.
3. $(q_2, \epsilon) \in \delta(q_1, \epsilon, \bot)$.

The transitions of the first type correspond to using a rule that replaces a variable with a terminal. The transitions of the second type correspond to using a rule that replaces a variable with some two variables, including itself. The transition of the last type terminates the computation. Thus, the computation that M executes corresponds to the leftmost production.

Since all the transitions in q_1 demand popping from the stack, once it becomes empty, M terminates its computation. For a PDA to accept the input, it must consume the input completely and empty the stack. This requirement means that there are just two possibilities for M to accept: (1) directly entering from q_0 to q_2 without a push and (2) popping the bottom of the stack and reading the last character of the input at the same time. From these observations, the strings M accepts completely match those that G produces using leftmost production.

The proof is now complete.   □

Theorem 5.2 *For each PDA, there is a context-free grammar that produces the language it accepts.*

Proof Overview
From an arbitrary PDA $M = (Q, \Sigma, \Gamma, \delta, q_0, \bot, F)$, we develop a context-free grammar. A key idea here is the introduction of the variable $H_{p,q}$ for each $p, q \in Q$. From the variable $H_{p,q}$, the grammar derives all strings in Σ^* that M can process while transitioning from state p to q in the following stack-height preserving manner; the stack height at the start and the stack height at the end are equal, and during the process, the stack height never goes below the starting height. We also introduce variables $U_{p,q,c}$, where $c \in \Gamma$, for deriving all input symbols that M can process in one step by making a state transition from p to q and pushing an a onto the stack. We also introduce variables $D_{p,q,c}$, where $c \in \Gamma$, for deriving all input symbols that M can process in one step by making a state transition from p to q and popping an a from the stack. Finally, we introduce variables $S_{p,q}$ for deriving all the symbols M can process in one step while transitioning from p and q without touching the stack. We can build recursive relations on the three variable sets.

Proof Let $M = (Q, \Sigma, \Gamma, \delta, q_0, \bot, F)$ be an arbitrary PDA. We modify M as follows:

- We add a new initial state. The PDA starts with an empty stack. In the new initial state, the PDA pushes $\bot$ onto the stack without popping from the stack or reading the input.
- After the new initial step, for each $m \geq 0$, we stretch each pushing action of m characters onto the stack into a series of m steps after the pop step. In each of the m subsequent steps, the PDA pushes one character onto the stack without reading the input. In the last of the m steps, the PDA changes its state to the target state.
- We introduce a new final state, p_f. From each state in F, there is a transition to the new state without reading the input and without touching the stack. We make the new state a unique final state. In the state p_f, M pops as long as the stack is nonempty, i.e., $\delta(p_f, \epsilon, X) = \{(p_f, \epsilon)\}$ for all $X \in \Gamma$.

A concrete description of the modifications is as follows:

- We add a new state p_0 with the unique action $\delta(p_0, \epsilon, \epsilon) = \{(q_0, \bot)\}$.
- We add a new final state p_f with the action $\delta(q_f, \epsilon, X) = \{(p_f, \epsilon)\}$ for all $X \in \Gamma$.
- We set F to $\{p_f\}$.
- For each transition $(r, y_1 \cdots y_m) \in \delta(q, a, x)$ such that $m \geq 1$ and $x, y_1, \ldots, y_m \in \Gamma$, we assign a unique index k and introduce states $p_{k,1}, \ldots, p_{k,m}$, change the transition for $\delta(q, a, a)$ to $\{(p_{k,1}, \epsilon)\}$, and then introduce:

$$\delta(p_{k,1}, \epsilon, \epsilon) = \{(p_{k,2}, y_1)\},$$
$$\delta(p_{k,2}, \epsilon, \epsilon) = \{(p_{k,3}, y_2)\},$$
$$\cdots$$
$$\delta(p_{k,m-2}, \epsilon, \epsilon) = \{(p_{k,m-1}, y_m - 2)\},$$
$$\delta(p_{k,m-1}, \epsilon, \epsilon) = \{(p_{k,m}, y_m - 1)\}, \text{ and}$$
$$\delta(p_{k,m}, \epsilon, \epsilon) = \{(r, y_m)\}.$$

Figure 5.4 illustrates the modifications to the initial and final states.

Figure 5.5 illustrates the stretching of a step involving pop and push.

Suppose we have modified M so that it satisfies the two requirements. By "stack-preserving computation from p to q," we refer to the action of M as follows:

- M begins its computation in state p with stack height $h \geq 0$ and arrives in state q with stack height h.
- During the computation, the stack height is always greater than or equal to h.

For each pair, $(p, q) \in Q \times Q$, let $W(p, q)$ denote the set of all character sequences M processes in any stack-preserving computation from p to q. Since the

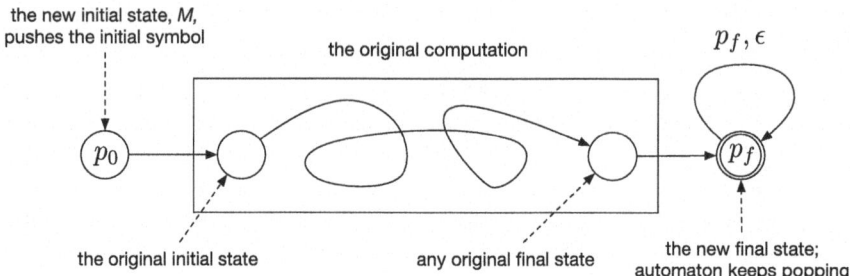

Fig. 5.4 The modifications for the initial and final states. The middle section in the rectangle represents the computation corresponding to the original behavior of M

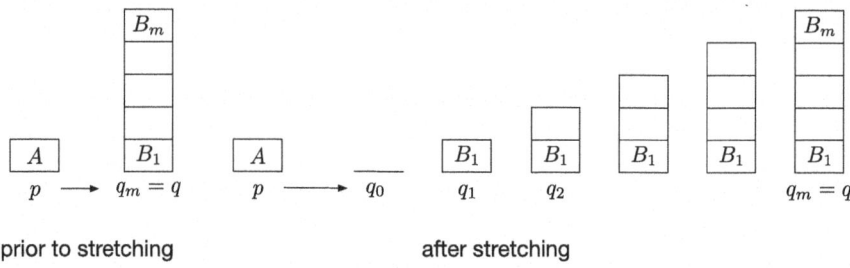

prior to stretching   after stretching

Fig. 5.5 The modification for the pop-then-push operations. The first action is popping only. Then, a series of pushes builds the result one character at a time. The final step is for transitioning to the target state

computation of M starts with the empty stack and M must empty its stack before accepting, we have

$$L(M) = W(p_0, p_f).$$

For each pair, $(p, q) \in Q \times Q$, we introduce a variable in the grammar $H_{p,q}$.

We introduce two variable groups, $U_{p,q,c}$ and $D_{p,q,c}$, for each $(p, q, c) \in Q \times Q \times \Gamma$. Both $U_{p,q,c}$ and $D_{p,q,c}$ produce subsets of Σ_ϵ.

- The production rules from $U_{p,q,c}$ take the form $U_{p,q,c} \to a$, where a is a symbol in Σ_ϵ such that $\delta(p, a, \epsilon)$ includes (q, c); i.e., the PDA may transition from p to q when it reads a in the input and, as a result, pushes c onto the stack.
- The production rules from $D_{p,q,c}$ take the form $D_{p,q,c} \to a$, where a is a symbol in Σ_ϵ such that $\delta(p, a, c)$ includes (q, ϵ); i.e., the PDA may transition from p to q when it reads a in the input and pops c from the stack.

We also add a variable group $S_{p,q}$ for each $(p, q) \in Q \times Q$.

- The production rules from $S_{p,q}$ take the form $S_{p,q} \rightarrow a$, where a is a symbol in Σ_ϵ such that $\delta(p, a, \epsilon)$ includes (q, ϵ); i.e., the PDA may transition from p to q when it reads a in the input with no action on the stack. If $p = q$, the rules include $S_{p,p} \rightarrow \epsilon$.

For $H_{p,q}$, we have the following possibilities:

- The transition from p to q occurs in one step, i.e., $H_{p,q} \rightarrow S_{p,q}$.
- After departing p, the PDA returns to the same stack height and then reaches q, i.e., $H_{p,q} \rightarrow H_{p,r} H_{r,q}$ for some $r \in Q$.
- In p, the PDA enters some state r while raising the height by 1 to $h + 1$ by pushing some c onto the stack, maintains the minimum height $h + 1$, arrives in some state s with $h + 1$ as the height, and then enters q by popping c from the stack, i.e., $H_{p,q} \rightarrow U_{p,r,c} H_{r,s} D_{s,q,c}$ for some $r, s \in Q$ and $c \in \Gamma$.

Some variables in the S, U, and D groups may be without rules to apply. By definition, a CFG may contain variables without rules, so keeping such variables does not prevent the grammar from being context-free. However, if we want to clean up the grammar by eliminating them, we can eliminate all rules in which such variables appear on the right hand and then eliminate such variables.

We now show that the grammar produces the language that the PDA accepts. For each variable X, let $L(X)$ denote the set of all strings in Σ^* the grammar can produce starting from X. Since $L(M) = W(p_0, p_f)$, we can establish our goal by showing, for all $p, q \in Q$, $L(H_{p,q}) = W(p, q)$. We show this equality by proving that the following inclusions hold true for all $p, q \in Q$:

1. $L(H_{p,q}) \subseteq W(p, q)$; i.e., for each full production tree with $H_{p,q}$ as the root, a computation of M in $W(p, q)$ corresponds to the tree.
2. $W(p, q) \subseteq L(H_{p,q})$; i.e., for each computation of M in $W(p, q)$, a full production tree corresponds to the computation.

□

First, we prove the following:

Proposition 5.1 $L(H_{p,q}) \subseteq W(p, q)$.

Proof We prove the claim by induction on the production tree's height, h. Let T be a full production tree with $H_{p,q}$ as the root. Let w be the string T produces. Let h be the height of T. Since H variables lack production rules that produce terminals, $h \geq 2$. Thus, the base case is $h = 2$. If the root has some H variable as a child, the tree's height is ≥ 3. Thus, the root has no H variable as a child. The lack of H as a child leaves only one possibility: $H_{p,q} \rightarrow S_{p,q} \rightarrow a$ where $a \in \Sigma_\epsilon$. The production $S_{p,q} \rightarrow a$ corresponds to the transition $\delta(p, a, \epsilon) \ni (q, \epsilon)$, which is reading a and transitioning from p to q without touching the stack. Since M does not touch the stack, the stack remains the same, which implies that $a \in W_{p,q}$. Thus, the claim holds for the base case.

For the induction step, let $h \geq 3$ and suppose that the claim holds for all smaller values of h. If the root has only one child, the child must be $S_{p,q}$, but then the tree's height is 2, which contradicts our assumption. Thus, the children must be one of the following:

- $H_{p,r}, H_{r,q}$ from left to right for some $r \in Q$
- $U_{p,r,c}, H_{r,s}, D_{s,q,c}$ from left to right for $r, s \in Q$ and $c \in \Gamma$.

For the first case, both children have a height of $\leq h - 1$. By our induction hypothesis, the subtrees produce strings in $W(p, r)$ and $W(r, q)$, respectively. Since M preserves the height, $W(p, r)W(r, q)$ is a member of $W(p, q)$. For the second case, the middle subtree has height h. The subtree produces a $W(r, s)$ string by our induction hypothesis. The flanking children $U_{p,r,c}$ and $D_{s,r,c}$ must produce a terminal each. The left increases the height by 1, and the right decreases the height by 1. Overall, the tree corresponds to some computation that preserves the height. Thus, the claim holds for h.   □

Next, we prove the inclusion in the opposite direction.

Proposition 5.2 $L(H_{p,q}) \supseteq W(p, q)$.   □

Proof We prove this by induction on the number of steps M makes. Let w be a member of $W(p, q)$. Let π be stack preserving computation from p and q that processes w. Let t be the number of steps in π. We prove $w \in L(H_{p,q})$ by induction on t.

For the base case, let $t = 0$. Since the computation has 0 steps, it must be the case that $w = \epsilon$ and $p = q$. We have $w \in L(H_{p,p})$ because of the rule $H_{p,p} \rightarrow S_{p,p} \rightarrow \epsilon$. Thus, the claim holds for the base case.

For the induction step, let $t \geq 1$. Assume that the claim holds for all smaller values of t. Suppose M increases the stack height at the beginning of π and decreases the height at the end of π. Let r be the state M enters in the first step, and let c be the symbol it pushes. Let s be the state from which M enters q at the last step. M must pop c from the stack at the last step. Let α be the input character that M processes in the first step, and let β be the input character that M processes in the last step. Let u be the input characters that M processes in between. Because of the assumptions we have made, we can apply the rule $H_{p,q} \rightarrow U_{p,r,c}H_{r,s}D_{s,q,c} \rightarrow \alpha H_{r,s}D_{s,q,c} \rightarrow \alpha H_{r,s}\beta$. The path π without its first and last steps starts in r, ends in s, and has length $t - 2$. By our induction hypothesis, this means that $L(H_{r,s})$ includes u. Thus, $L(H_{p,q})$ includes $w = \alpha u \beta$.

On the other hand, suppose that during π, the stack height returns to the same value as the start before it reaches the end. We split π into two parts, π_1 and π_2, where π_1 is the computation until the first return to the same stack height and π_2 is the remainder. Let r be the state that M reaches when it completes π_1. Let u be the input characters that M processes during π_1 and v be the input characters that M processes during π_2. Since both π_1 and π_2 are nonempty, their lengths are smaller than t. By our induction hypothesis, this means that $u \in L(H_{p,r})$ and $v \in L(H_{r,q})$.

Since the rule $H_{p,q} \to H_{p,r} H_{r,q}$ is available for all combinations of p, q, and r, we know that $L(A_{p,q})$ contains $w = uv$. Thus, the property holds for t.

Hence, the claim holds for all values of t, and so, $L(A_{pq}) \supseteq H(p, q)$. $\qquad\square$

We have proven both claims and therefore, the theorem holds.

Example 5.4 Let us examine the following PDA for $\{a^n b^n \mid n \geq 1\}$.

$$\delta(q_0, \epsilon, \epsilon) = \{(q_3, \epsilon), (q_1, \bot)\},$$
$$\delta(q_1, a, \epsilon) = \{(q_1, a)\},$$
$$\delta(q_1, b, a) = \{(q_2, \epsilon)\},$$
$$\delta(q_2, b, a) = \{(q_2, \epsilon)\}, \text{ and}$$
$$\delta(q_2, \epsilon, \bot) = \{(q_3, \epsilon)\}.$$

Here, q_0 is the initial state for pushing the initial symbol, and q_3 is the final state.

We simplify the notation in the variable names by using the subscripts $0, \ldots, 3$ instead of $q_0, \ldots, q_3$, respectively. There are $4 \times 4 = 16$ state combinations and 3 stack symbols ($\bot$, a, and ϵ). Since there are four variable groups (H, S, U, and D), the number of possible variables in the grammar is $16 \times 3 \times 4 = 192$. However, most of the variables are irrelevant. We need only the following variables and rules:

$$H_{0,3} \to S_{0,3},$$
$$S_{0,3} \to \epsilon,$$
$$H_{0,3} \to U_{0,1,\bot} H_{1,2} D_{2,3,\bot},$$
$$H_{1,2} \to U_{1,1,a} H_{1,2} D_{2,2,a},$$
$$H_{1,2} \to S_{1,2},$$
$$S_{1,2} \to \epsilon,$$
$$U_{0,1,\bot} \to \epsilon,$$
$$D_{2,3,\bot} \to \epsilon,$$
$$U_{1,1,a} \to a, \text{ and}$$
$$D_{2,2,a} \to b.$$

Since PDAs and context-free languages are equivalent in their power, we can prove the proposition with PDAs instead. We leave the reader to prove the proposition using PDAs (see Exercise 5.8).

Theorem 5.3 *The class of context-free languages is closed under intersection with regular languages.*

Proof Overview
From an arbitrary pair of PDA and DFA, we can construct a new PDA that
concurrently simulates the two automata and accepts when both do. The state
set of the new PDA is the Cartesian product of the states of the PDA and DFA.
The new PDA's transition function processes each input symbol individually
for the PDA and the DFA; the state for the DFA is unchanged if the input
symbol is ϵ. The final state set of the new PDA is the Cartesian product of the
final state sets of the PDA and the DFA.

Proof Let Σ be an alphabet. Let L_1 be a context-free language over the
alphabet Σ. Let L_2 be a regular language over the alphabet Σ. Let $M_1 =
(Q_1, \Sigma, \Gamma, \delta_1, q_1, \perp, F_1)$ be a PDA that accepts L_1. Let $M_2 = (Q_2, \Sigma, \delta_2, q_2, F_2)$
be a finite automaton that accepts L_2. Our goal is to show that $L_1 \cap L_2$ is context-
free. We accomplish this goal by designing a PDA that accepts the intersection.
    Define $Q = Q_1 \times Q_2$, $q_0 = (q_1, q_2)$, and $F = F_1 \times F_2$. Define the transition
function δ as follows:

- For all $\alpha \in \Sigma$, $p_1, r_1 \in Q_1$, $p_2, r_2 \in Q_2$, and $b, c \in \Gamma_\epsilon$, if (r_1, c) is one of the
  values of $\delta_1(p_1, \alpha, b)$ and $r_2 = \delta_2(p_2, \alpha)$, then $(r_1 \times r_2, c)$ is one of the values
  of $\delta(p_1 \times p_2, \alpha, b)$.
- For all $p_1, r_1 \in Q_1$, $p_2 \in Q_2$, and $b, c \in \Gamma_\epsilon$, if (r_1, c) is one of the values of
  $\delta_1(p_1, \epsilon, b)$, then $(r_1 \times p_2, c)$ is one of the values of $\delta(p_1 \times p_2, \alpha, b)$.

The former means that the new PDA processes α as M_1 and M_2 at the same time,
and the latter means that the new PDA processes α as M_1. However, since the input
character is ϵ, it will not change the state on the M_2 side.
    The new PDA is $(Q, \Sigma, \Gamma, \delta, q_0, \perp, F)$. The PDA accepts if, and only if, it
finishes reading the input with the product state in F and the empty stack. Thus,
the new PDA accepts its input if, and only if, both M_1 and M_2 do.   □

5.3   The Deterministic Pushdown Automaton (DPDA) Model

We know NFAs are as equally powerful as DFAs. Can we show a similar result for
PDAs? In other words, if we define a deterministic PDA model, will the model be
as powerful as the PDA model? We study this question in the following section.

Definition 5.2 A **deterministic pushdown automaton (DPDA)** is a pushdown
automaton $(Q, \Sigma, \Gamma, \delta, q_0, \perp, F)$ with the following properties:

- For all $q \in Q, a \in \Sigma_\epsilon$, and $x \in \Gamma$, $\delta(q, a, b)$ has at most one element, i.e., either
  no move at all or exactly one move.

- For all $q \in Q$ and $x \in \Gamma$, if $\delta(q, a, b)$ is nonempty for some $a \in \Sigma$, then $\delta(q, \epsilon, b)$ is empty; i.e., if the pushdown automaton can process an input symbol with this combination, then it cannot process ϵ.

The two properties guarantee that each ID of the pushdown automaton has no more than one possible next ID.

Definition 5.3 A language is **deterministically context-free** if a DPDA accepts it. DCFL is the set of all deterministically context-free languages.

For a DPDA, we remove the set notation $\{\}$ from the values of its transition function. Specifically, if $\delta(q, a, b) = \{(r, c)\}$, we write $\delta(q, a, b) = (r, s)$; we still write $\delta(q, a, b) = \emptyset$ if the function does not have values at (q, a, b).

Example 5.5 The PDA from Example 5.1 (for the language $\{a^n b^n \mid n \geq 0\}$) does not appear to be deterministic. However, the language is deterministic, as an extra b is attached at the end of each member. The new language is $\{a^n b^{n+1} \mid n \geq 0\}$.

The PDA for the revised version is as follows:

$$\delta(q_0, a, \perp) = (q_0, \perp a),$$
$$\delta(q_0, b, \perp) = (q_2, \perp),$$
$$\delta(q_0, a, a) = (q_0, aa),$$
$$\delta(q_0, b, a) = (q_1, \epsilon),$$
$$\delta(q_1, b, a) = (q_1, \epsilon), \text{ and}$$
$$\delta(q_1, b, \perp) = (q_2, \perp).$$

The initial state is q_0, and the final is q_2.

Example 5.6 If the input must be nonempty, the language $\{a^n b^n \mid n \geq 1\}$ is deterministic. We introduce an additional stack symbol $\perp_a$. The symbol combines $\perp$ and a into one. The PDA M for the revised version is as follows:

$$\delta(q_0, a, \perp) = (q_0, \perp_a),$$
$$\delta(q_0, a, \perp_a) = (q_0, \perp_a),$$
$$\delta(q_0, a, a) = (q_0, aa),$$
$$\delta(q_1, b, a) = (q_1, \epsilon), \text{ and}$$
$$\delta(q_1, b, \perp_a) = (q_2, \perp).$$

The initial state is q_0, and the final is q_2. The accepting ID is $(q_2, \epsilon, \perp)$. The automaton can enter q_2 if the input has a prefix $a^n b^n$ for some $n \geq 1$. If there is some character after the prefix, there is no action to perform for the pushdown automaton. This means the input with an extra character is not in $L(M)$.

Theorem 5.4 *The class of deterministic context-free languages is closed under complement.*

Proof Overview
We modify an arbitrary DPDA so that it will read its entire input and arrive at a non-final state with an empty stack. Then, we can make the DPDA accept the language's complement by switching between the final and non-final states.

Proof Let $M = (Q, \Sigma, \Gamma, \delta, q_0, \perp, F)$ be a DPDA that accepts some language L. We apply a series of modifications to M. First, we introduce a new initial symbol $\perp'$, a new initial state q_0', and a new non-final sink state q_s. We then add the following transitions:

- $\delta(q_0', \epsilon, \perp') = (q_0, \perp'\perp)$.
- $\delta(q, a, \perp') = (q_s, \perp')$ for each $q \in Q$ and $a \in \Sigma$.
- $\delta(q_s, a, X) = (q_s, X)$ for each $a \in \Sigma$.
- $\delta(q, a, X) = (q_s, X)$ for each $q \in Q$ and $a \in \Sigma$ such that $\delta(q, a, X) = \emptyset$ for all $a \in \Sigma_\epsilon$.

These modifications ensure the following:

(a) The pushdown automaton now preserves the new initial symbol $\perp'$ at the bottom of the stack.
(b) If the original pushdown automaton pops everything above $\perp'$ with part of the input remaining, the new automaton continues reading the input until the end.
(c) If the pushdown automaton enters q_s, it will keep reading the input without changing the stack content.
(d) If the pushdown automaton enters a state and sees a stack symbol with no possible moves regardless of the input symbol, it enters q_s.

Next, we ensure the computation never enters an infinite loop so it finishes reading the input. An infinite loop occurs with a chain of ϵ moves that don't decrease the stack height below the height at the start, bringing the state and the stack symbol back to the original combination. Let $m_0 = \|Q\|\|\Gamma\|$ where Q and Γ are the original states and the stack symbols, respectively. A minimal loop is one without repetition. Every minimal loop has a length of $\leq m_0$. We can find all minimal loops using an exhaustive search. For each pair $(p_0, X_0) \in Q \times X$, we try executing ϵ moves from $\delta(p_0, \epsilon, X_0)$ and check if the execution does not pop below the X at the start and if (p_0, X_0) returns. Put differently, each sequence we search for satisfies the following properties:

- The sequence has the form $\delta(p_0, \epsilon, X_0) = (p_1, Y_1), \ldots, \delta(p_{m-1}, \epsilon, X_{m-1}) = (p_m, Y_m)$.
- $p_0 = p_m$.
- We define $w_0, \ldots, w_m$ by

- $w_0 = X_0$.
- For each $i \geq 1$, w_i is the concatenation of w_{i-1} without the last character followed by Y_i.

Then,

- None of $w_0, \ldots, w_m$ are empty.
- The last character of Y_m is equal to X_0.
- For all i such that $1 \leq i \leq m - 1$, either $p_i \neq p_0$ or X_0 is not equal to the last character of w_i.

Because of the last property, we can apply the pigeon-hole principle, so $m \leq m_0 = \|Q\| \times \|\Gamma\|$. After finding all minimal infinite loops, we replace $\delta(p_i, \epsilon, X_i) = (p_{i+1}, Y_{i+1})$ with $\delta(p, \epsilon, X) = (q_s, X)$ for all i such that $0 \leq i \leq m - 1$.

The elimination of infinite loops forces every computation to read the entire input without changing the language the pushdown automaton accepts. The pushdown automaton remains deterministic.

We now swap the roles between the final and non-final states. The resulting pushdown automaton accepts the complement of $L(M)$.   □

Since CFL is not closed under complement (Theorem 5.6) and $\{a^n b^n \mid n \geq 0\}$ is deterministic context-free and is non-regular, we have the following result.

Corollary 5.1 REG $\subset$ DCFL $\subset$ CFL.

5.4 Proving Non-context-Freeness

In this section, we study how to prove languages are not context-free.

5.4.1 The Pumping Lemma for CFLs

We previously used the Pumping Lemma to prove the existence of non-regular languages. A similar result exists for context-free languages, but its statement is more complicated.

Lemma 5.1 (The Pumping Lemma for Context-Free Languages) *Let L be an arbitrary context-free language. A constant $p > 0$ exists such that for all $w \in L$, $|w| \geq p$, there is a decomposition $w = uvxyz$ with the following properties:*

1. *$|vxy| \leq p$.*
2. *$|vy| \geq 1$.*
3. *For all $i \geq 0$, $uv^i x y^i z \in L$.*

Proof Overview
The proof contains two critical ideas. A long, straight path in a production tree has two nodes whose labels are identical. If a production tree of a CNF grammar produces a long enough string, then the tree has a long, straight path.

Proof Let L be a context-free language. Let $G = (V, \Sigma, R, S)$ be a CNF grammar for L. Let n be the number of variables in V. Let $p = 2^n$. Let $w = w_1 \cdots w_m$ be L's member having a length of $m \geq p$. Let T be a full production tree for w. For each node h in T, let $\lambda(h)$ denote the number of leaves in the subtree rooted at T.

Let g_0 be the root of T. We construct a straight path $g_0, g_1, \ldots, g_k$ in T where the node g_k has a unique child. Since G is a CNF grammar, the node g_k is the parent of a leaf. To construct the path, we repeat the following process until the new node has a unique child.

- Suppose we have selected $g_0, \ldots, g_\ell$, where g_ℓ has two children (because G is a CNF grammar). We compare the two children of g_ℓ using the number of leaves. We select the child with the larger number of leaves as $g_{\ell+1}$. We break a tie arbitrarily.

Let $[g_0, \ldots, g_k]$ be the path. For all ℓ such that $0 \leq \ell \leq k - 1$, $\lambda(g_{\ell+1}) \geq \lambda(g_\ell)/2$. Since $\lambda(g_k) = 1$ and $\lambda(g_0) = \|J\| \geq p = 2^n$, $k \geq n$. Figure 5.6 shows our selections for the sequence $[g_0, \ldots, g_k]$.

Fig. 5.6 The node selection for Lemma 5.1. The square nodes are the ones on the chosen path. The chosen nodes have at least the same number of leaves as their siblings

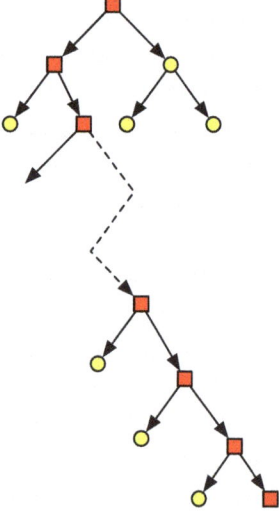

Let $X_0, \ldots, X_k$ be the sequence of variables that appear as the labels of $g_0, \ldots, g_k$. Since n is the number of variables and $k \geq n$, by the pigeon-hole principle, there are two indices, c and d, such that $0 \leq c < d \leq n$ such that $X_c = X_d$. Since selecting c and d is possible whenever $k \geq n$, we can choose c and d so that $k - n \leq c < d \leq k$. Then, we have:

$$1 \leq \lambda(g_d) < \lambda(g_c) \leq 2^n.$$

Let x be the word the subtree rooted at $g[_d$ produces. The subtree rooted at g_c produces the string vxy since g_d is a descendant of g_c. In other words, v appears to the left of x, and y appears to the right of x. The tree T produces the string $uvxyz$, where u is to the left of vxy, and z is to the right of vxy in the production tree. Since the labels of g_c and g_d are equal, substituting the subtree rooted at g_c with the subtree rooted at g_d produces a valid full production tree. Also, substituting the subtree rooted at g_d with the subtree rooted at g_c produces a valid production tree. The former produces the word uxz, and the latter, $uvvxyyz$. In addition, the latter contains g_d and g_c with g_d as a descendant of g_c; the same substitution, i.e., the substitution of g_d with g_c, works again. This substitution gives a new tree, which produces $uvvvxyyyz$. By repeating this substitution, we obtain strings $uv^i xy^i z$. Here, $i = 0$ produces uxz. Figure 5.7 shows the relations among the five components.

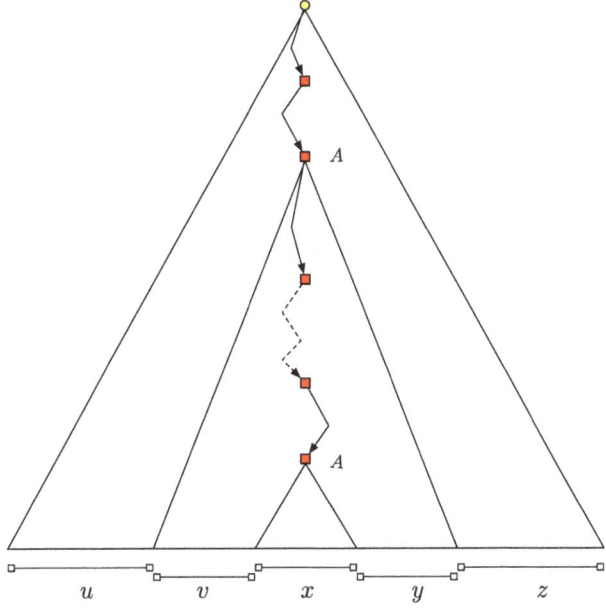

Fig. 5.7 The decomposition of w as the lemma states. The node label A is common between the node that produces vxy and the one that produces x

Since $\lambda(g_c) \leq 2^n$, $|vxy| \leq 2^n$. In addition, $|vy|$ is $\lambda(g_c) - \lambda(g_d)$. According to the way we construct $g_0, \ldots, g_s$, the difference is strictly positive. We have thus proven the lemma. $\square$

5.4.2   Inherent Ambiguity of CFLs

In Sect. 4.1.4, we asked if every context-free language has an unambiguous grammar. We prove here that there is an inherently ambiguous language. The proof uses ideas reminiscent of the Pumping Lemma.

Theorem 5.5 *The following language is inherently ambiguous:*

$$L = \{a^n b^n c^m d^m \mid n, m \geq 1\} \cup \{a^n b^m c^m d^n \mid n, m \geq 1\}.$$

Proof Overview
We apply some normalization to an arbitrary grammar for L. We then extract two separate grammars from the normalized grammar, where one will be responsible for the first component of the union where $n \neq m$ and the other will be responsible for the second component of the union where $n \neq m$. The two grammars have only the start symbol in common. We then show that for some n, both grammars generate $a^n b^n c^n d^n$. This implies that the word has two leftmost production trees. Thus, L is inherently ambiguous.

Proof Let $L_1 = \{a^n b^n c^m d^m \mid n, m \geq 1\}$ and $L_2 = \{a^n b^m c^m d^n \mid n, m \geq 1\}$. Let G be an arbitrary grammar for L. We first apply some procedures from the CNF conversion (see Sect. 4.2.2 and Exercise 4.21) to remove all useless variables and eliminate both ϵ and unit rules. Additionally, we ensure that S does not appear on the right-hand side of the production rules. We then check if the grammar has a variable $X \neq S$ such that X never reappears in any production tree rooted at X. We can eliminate all such variables X by replacing each occurrence of X on the right-hand side of any rule with one of the rules from X, as we did in eliminating unit rules in the conversion algorithm to CNF. (This idea is reminiscent of the elimination of ϵ and unit rules.) More specifically, if X is such a variable and $Y \rightarrow w$ is a production rule containing an occurrence of X, we independently replace each occurrence of X with each rule $X \rightarrow z$. If w has k occurrences of X and X has d rules, we create d^k rules. We then replace $Y \rightarrow w$ with the d^k rules.

These modifications preserve the ambiguity; i.e., the original G is ambiguous if, and only if, the modified G is ambiguous.

After completing the modifications, every variable $A \in V - \{S\}$ has a production of the form $A \overset{G,*}{\Rightarrow} x_1 A x_2$ such that x_1 and x_2 consist only of terminals, and either x_1 or x_2 is nonempty. Since there are no useless variables, a production tree rooted at

Fig. 5.8 The production tree involving $A \overset{G,*}{\Rightarrow} x_1 A x_2$. The top A can be substituted with the bottom A and vice versa

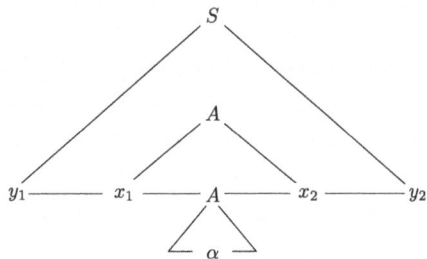

S produces a string containing A, and a production tree rooted at A can produce a terminal-only string. Then, using the same idea as the Pumping Lemma, we have:

$$\text{some } y_1 \text{ and } y_2 \in \Sigma^* \text{ exist such that for all } k \geq 0, \; y_1(x_1)^k \alpha (x_2)^k y_2 \in L.$$

Figure 5.8 shows this idea.

We find the following properties of x_1 and x_2:

1. Neither x_1 nor x_2 are empty.
2. Neither x_1 nor x_2 have two different symbols. Specifically,

   a. If $x_1 = a^t$ for some $t \geq 1$, then $x_2 = b^t$ or d^t.
   b. If $x_1 = b^t$ for some $t \geq 1$, then $x_2 = c^t$.
   c. If $x_1 = c^t$ for some $t \geq 1$, then $x_2 = c^t$.
   d. $x_1 \in d^*$.

Thus, the variables A other than S are exactly one of the following types:

- $A \overset{G,*}{\Rightarrow} a^k A b^k$ for some k.
- $A \overset{G,*}{\Rightarrow} a^k A d^k$ for some k.
- $A \overset{G,*}{\Rightarrow} b^k A c^k$ for some k.
- $A \overset{G,*}{\Rightarrow} c^k A d^k$ for some k.

Otherwise, we can combine two distinct types of a single variable to create a new $x_1 A x_2$ such that either x_1 or x_2 has two different symbols. Let us partition the variables into four groups according to the four properties. Let X_{ab}, X_{ad}, X_{bc}, and X_{cd} be the groups, respectively. We see that the following are the only possible rules in G.

- For L_1:

  - $S \to a^n u_1 b^n c^m v_1 d^m$ for some $n, m \geq 0$, $u_1 \in X_{ab} \cup \{\epsilon\}$, and $u_2 \in X_{cd} \cup \{\epsilon\}$, where if $u_1 = \epsilon$, then $n \geq 1$, and if $u_2 = \epsilon$, then $m \geq 1$.
  - $x_{ab} \to a^n u b^n$ for some $n \geq 0$, $x_{ab} \in X_{ab}$, and $u \in X_{ab} \cup \{\epsilon\}$, where if $u = \epsilon$, then $n \geq 1$.
  - $x_{cd} \to c^m u d^m$ for some $m \geq 0$, $x_{cd} \in X_{cd}$, and $u \in X_{cd} \cup \{\epsilon\}$, where if $u = \epsilon$, then $m \geq 1$.

- For L_2:
    - $u \rightarrow a^n v d^n$ for some $n \geq 1$, $u \in S \cup X_{ad}$, and $v \in X_{ad}$.
    - $u \rightarrow a^n b^m v c^m d^n$ for some $n, m \geq 1$, $u \in S \cup X_{ad}$, and $v \in X_{bc} \cup \{\epsilon\}$.
    - $u \rightarrow b^m v c^m$ for some $m \geq 1$ and $u \in X_{bc} \cup \{\epsilon\}$.

We construct a grammar G_1 using the first group of rules and a grammar G_2 using the second group. The variable set of G_1 is $\{S\} \cup X_{ab} \cup X_{cd}$, and the variable set of G_2 is $\{S\} \cup X_{ad} \cup X_{bc}$. S is the only variable in common. Let $S \rightarrow \alpha_1, \ldots, S \rightarrow \alpha_r$ be an enumeration of the rules from S in G_1. For each (n, m) such that $n \neq m$, $a^n b^n c^m d^m$ is produced from one of $\alpha_1, \ldots, \alpha_s$. Because of the types of available rules in G_1, we can show that for each i, if $a^n b^n c^m d^m$ and $a^s b^s c^t d^t$ can be produced from α, so are $a^n b^n c^t d^t$ and $a^s b^s c^m d^m$. Thus, for each i, sets of integers N_i and M_i exist such that:

$$\{(n, m) \mid \alpha_i \overset{G_*}{\Rightarrow} a^n b^n c^m d^m, n \neq m\} = N_i \times M_i.$$

Because G_1 is responsible for $a^n b^n c^m d^m$ such that $n \neq m$, we have:

$$(N_1 \times M_1) \cup \cdots \cup (N_r \times M_r) \supseteq \{(n, m) \mid n, m \geq 1, n \neq m\}.$$

We argue that this union includes all but finitely many (n, n), $n \geq 1$. In other words, G_1 produces all but finitely many $a^n b^n c^n d^n$, $n \geq 1$.

Assume, by way of contradiction, that $N_1 \times M_1 \cup \cdots \cup N_r \times M_r$ misses (n, n) for infinitely many n. For each i such that $1 \leq i \leq r$, let

$$Q_i = \{n \mid (n, n) \notin (N_i \times M_i) \cup \cdots \cup (N_r \times M_r)\}.$$

We know $Q_1 \subseteq Q_2 \subseteq \cdots \subseteq Q_r$. By our assumption, Q_1 is infinite. For each $q \in Q_1$, N_1 does not have q, or M_1 does not. Since Q_1 is infinite, either $Q_1 \setminus N_1$ or $Q_1 \setminus M_1$ is infinite. We select $Q_1 \setminus N_1$ if it is infinite and $Q_1 \setminus M_1$ otherwise. We call the chosen set J_1. Then, $J_1 \subseteq Q_1 \subseteq Q_2$ and J_1 is infinite. Since J_1 is infinite, either $J_1 \setminus N_2$ or $J_1 \setminus M_2$ is infinite. We select $J_1 \setminus N_2$ if it infinite one and $J_1 \setminus M_2$ otherwise. We call the chosen set J_2. Then, $J_2 \subseteq Q_2 \subseteq Q_3$ and J_2 is infinite. By repeating this process for $i = 3, \ldots, r$, we obtain J_r. We have:

$$J_r \subseteq J_{r-1} \subseteq \cdots \subseteq J_1 \subseteq Q_1 \subseteq Q_2 \subseteq \cdots \subseteq Q_r.$$

Thus, J_r is missing entirely from N_i or M_i for each i. This means that for each pair $(n, m) \in J_r \times J_r$, (n, m) does not appear in $N_1 \times M_1 \cup \cdots \cup N_r \times M_r$. This contradicts that $L(G_1) \supseteq L_1$. Thus, $L(G_1)$ misses only a finite number of $a^n b^n c^n d^n$.

We can apply the same argument to G_2 to show that $L(G_2)$ misses only a finite number of $a^n b^n c^n d^n$. This implies G_1 and G_2 generate $a^n b^n c^n d^n$ for infinitely many n. Since the two grammars have only S in common, and S never appears on the right-hand side of the rules, every such $a^n b^n c^n d^n$ has two different leftmost productions, one from G_1 and the other from G_2. Thus, L is inherently ambiguous.

This proves the theorem.   □

5.4.3 Non-context-Free Languages

Using the lemmas from Sect. 5.4.1, we can prove languages to be non-context-free. As our first example, consider $\{a^n b^n c^n \mid n \geq 0\}$.

Example 5.7 $L = \{a^n b^n c^n \mid n \geq 0\}$ is not context-free.

Assume, on the contrary, that L is context-free. Let p be the constant for the language according to the Pumping Lemma (Lemma 5.1). Let $w = a^p b^p c^p$. According to the lemma, we can decompose w as $uvxyz$ such that $|vxy| \leq p$, $|vy| \geq 1$, and for all $i \geq 0$, $uv^i xy^i z$ is the member of L. Let $w' = uxz$. By our supposition, w' must be a member of the language. Since $|vxy| \leq p$, vxy is either part of $a^p b^p$ or part of $b^p c^p$. Suppose the former is the case. Since $|vy| \geq 1$, the number of as appearing in w' is less than p, or the number of bs appearing in w' is less than p. However, since vxy is part of $a^p b^p$, the number of cs in w' is p. Thus, w' cannot be a language member, a contradiction. Similarly, we draw a contradiction if uvy is part of $b^p c^p$. Thus, L is not context-free.

An alternative proof looks at the distance between the last a and the first c. Since the language members have three parts of equal length, the inflatable parts, (v, y), must collectively contain the same number of as as bs and cs. However, the distance between the last a and the first c is p, and the length of vxy is at most p. So, a, b, and c do not appear together in vy. Figure 5.9 presents how we visualize the limitation of covering with vxy of the input string $a^p b^p c^p$.

Since the class of context-free languages is closed under concatenation, we obtain the following:

Theorem 5.6 *The class of context-free languages is not closed under intersection. It is not closed under complement either.*

Proof Let $L_1 = \{a^n b^n \mid n \geq 0\}$, $L_2 = \{b^n c^n \mid n \geq 0\}$, $L_3 = \{c^n \mid n \geq 0\}$, and $L_4 = \{a^n \mid n \geq 0\}$. All four languages are context-free (actually, L_3 and L_4 are regular). Because the class of context-free languages is closed under concatenation (Proposition 4.2), we know that $L_1 L_3$ and $L_4 L_2$ are context-free.

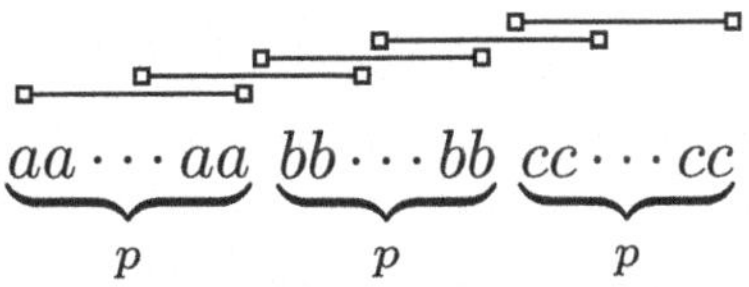

Fig. 5.9 The pumping on $a^p b^p c^p$. The lines represent the longest stretches that vxy can cover

$$\underbrace{aa \cdots aa}_{p} \; \underbrace{bb \cdots bb}_{p} \; \underbrace{cc \cdots cc}_{p}$$

The two concatenations are $\{a^n b^n c^m \mid m, n \geq 0\}$ and $\{a^m b^n c^n \mid m, n \geq 0\}$; the intersection of the two is $\{a^n b^n c^n \mid n \geq 0\}$. This intersection is not context-free. Thus, the class of context-free languages does not have the closure property under intersection.

By DeMorgan's Laws, we can express the intersection of two languages, A and B, using complement and union as:

$$\overline{\overline{A} \cup \overline{B}}.$$

Thus, the class of context-free languages does not have the closure property under complement.   □

5.4.4   Ogden's Lemma

A more flexible version of the Pumping Lemma is called **Ogden's Lemma**. We mark some characters of a given string from the rest. We then pretend the unmarked characters do not exist and obtain a decomposition of the input.

Below is the lemma.

Lemma 5.2 (Ogden's Lemma) *For each context-free language L, there is a constant $p \geq 1$ with the following property:*

- *For all $w \in L$, $|w| \geq p$, and for all selections of $\geq p$ positions, w is decomposable as $uvxyz$ such that:*

    1. *x covers at least one marked position.*
    2. *vxy covers at most p marked positions.*
    3. *Both u and v cover at least one marked position, or both y and z cover at least one marked position.*
    4. *For all $i \geq 0$, $uv^i xy^i z$ is a member of L.*

There is a simpler version of Ogden's Lemma, which immediately follows from the first version.

Lemma 5.3 (A Simpler Version of Ogden's Lemma) *For each context-free language L, there is a constant $p \geq 1$ with the following property:*

- *For all $w \in L$, $|w| \geq p$, and for all selections of $\geq p$ positions, w is decomposable as $uvxyz$ such that:*

    1. *vxy covers at most p marked positions.*
    2. *uv covers at least one marked position.*
    3. *For all $i \geq 0$, $uv^i xy^i z$ is a member of L.*

Proof Overview

Given a CNF grammar $G = (\Sigma, V, R, S)$, we choose $p = 2^{4\|V\|}$. Given w with its $\geq p$ marked positions, we examine a production tree of w and select a straight path by always selecting the branch covering more marked positions than the opposite branch. The path length is $\geq 4\|V\| + 1$. We look at the last $4\|V\| + 1$ nodes. For some variable A, five nodes exist labeled with A, where the marked positions are split between their children. Three of the five choose their left branch, or three choose their right branch. From such a triple, we can produce the desired decomposition.

Proof Let $G = (V, \Sigma, S, R)$ be a CNF grammar. Let $t = \|V\|$ and $p = 2^{4t}$. Let $w \in L$ and $|w| = n \geq p$. Let $J \subseteq \{1, \ldots, n\}$ be a set that specifies the chosen positions. Let $\|J\| = m \geq p$. Let T be an arbitrary production tree of w. Because G is a CNF grammar, T is fully binary, except the parent of each leaf has only one child. Each leaf of T is labeled with a terminal, and every non-leaf of T is labeled with a variable. For each node e of T, let $\mu(e)$ be the number of marked positions appearing at the leaf level of the subtree rooted at e. The μ value of the root is $\|J\| = m$, and for every non-leaf, its μ value is the sum of its children's μ values. We construct a straight path from the tree's root by selecting, at each non-leaf node, the branch with a larger μ value than the opposite branch. Here, a tie can be broken arbitrarily. Let $P = [u_0, \ldots, u_k]$ be the downward path. Let $M = [\mu_0, \ldots, \mu_k]$ be the sequence $\mu(u_0), \ldots, \mu(u_k)$. M is non-increasing with $\mu_0 = m$ and $\mu_k = 1$. Also, for each i such that $\mu_i > \mu_{i+1}$, $\mu_i \leq 2\mu_{i+1}$ (equivalently, $\mu_{i+1} \geq \mu_i/2$). Since $m \geq p = 2^{4t}$, $\mu_i > \mu_{i+1}$ holds for at least $4t = \lceil \log(p) \rceil$ values of i. We select the last $4t$ indices i satisfying $\mu_i > \mu_{i+1}$ and the first i such that $\mu_i = 1$. Let $\hat{P} = [v_0, \ldots, v_{4t}]$ be the node sequence derived from the chosen indices in the order they appear on P. Let $\hat{M} = [v_0, \ldots, \mu_{4t}]$ be $\hat{P}$'s accompanying μ sequence. We have the following properties of $\hat{M}$:

- $v_{4t} = 1$.
- For all i such that $0 \leq i \leq 4t$, $v_{i+1} < v_i \leq 2v_{i+1}$.
- $v_0 \leq 2^{4t} = p \leq m$.

The branch selections at these nodes are either left or right. Let S_L be the nodes where the branch is the left one plus v_{4t}. Let S_R be the nodes where the branch is the right one plus v_{4t}. The intersection of S_L and S_R is $\{v_{4t}\}$. So, $\|S_L\| \geq 2t + 1$ or $\|S_R\| \geq 2t + 1$. Figure 5.10 shows the path construction.

Suppose the former is the case. Since $t = \|V\|$, the pigeon-hole principle states that some three nodes in S_L have an identical label. Let $\alpha, \beta,$ and γ be the three nodes in order of appearance in the path $\hat{P}$. Let A be the label of the three nodes. Among the three, α and β split the value of μ and choose the left branch. Let $u, v, x, y,$ and z be as follows:

Fig. 5.10 The node selection
for Ogden's Lemma. The
triangles are those children
who receive no marked
leaves. Their siblings inherit
all the marked leaves from
their parents. The squares are
those where the two children
split marked leaves. The
squares become elements of
the sequence

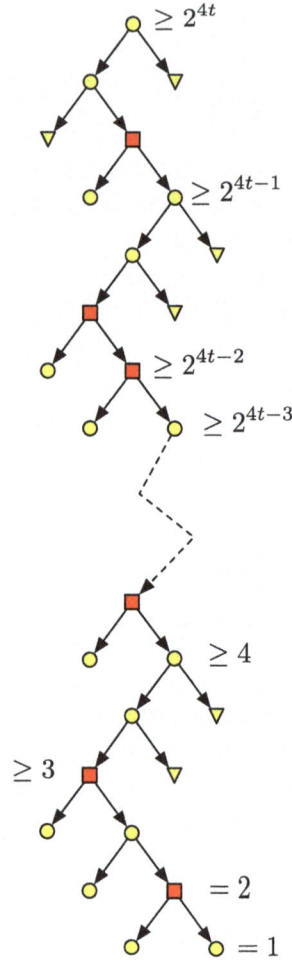

- u is the terminal string to the left of β.
- v is the terminal string appearing to the left of γ in the subtree rooted at β.
- x is the terminal string in the subtree rooted at γ.
- y is the terminal string appearing to the right of γ in the subtree rooted at β.
- z is the terminal string to the right of β.

Since the three nodes have the same label, we can replace the subtree rooted at β
with a copy of the subtree rooted at γ, or vice versa, to produce a production tree
that produces a string in L. Thus, for all $i \geq 0$, $uv^i xy^i z \in L$. Since the right child
of α and the right child of β receive some marked positions, y and z cover at least
one marked position. In addition, x covers $\mu(\gamma) \geq 1$ marked positions. Similarly,
vxy covers $\mu(\beta) \leq p$ marked positions.

For the proof for $\|S_R\| \geq 2^t + 1$, we switch the roles between the left and right branches. This proves the lemma.   □

When the Pumping Lemma does not help prove that a language is not context-free, we can use Ogden's Lemma.

Example 5.8 Let a, b, and c be symbols. $L = \{a^i b^k c^k \mid i \neq j, i \neq k,$ and $j \neq k\}$ is not context-free.

Assume, by way of contradiction, that L is context-free. Let p be the constant from the simpler version of Ogden's Lemma. Let $w = a^p b^{p+p!} c^{p+2p!}$ be a chosen member of L. We select the positions $1, \ldots, p$ and apply the lemma. We obtain a decomposition $w = uvxyz$ such that vy has at least one a and for all $i \geq 0$, $uv^i x y^i z \in L$. If v or y has different symbols, $uvvxyyz$ has ba or cb as a string, which is not a member. Thus, v and y have only one symbol. Specifically, $v \in a^+$. We have the following three possibilities:

- If $vy \in a^+$, let $\ell = |vy|$ and choose $i = p!/\ell + 1$. Then, $uv^i x y^i z = a^{p+p!} b^{p+p!} c^{p+2p!}$. This does not belong to L, so we have a contradiction.
- If $v \in a^+$ and $y \in b^+$, let $\ell = |v|$ and choose $i = 2p!/\ell + 1$. Then, $uv^i x y^i z = a^{p+2p!} b^{p+p!+(i-1)|y|} c^{p+2p!}$. This does not belong to L, so we have a contradiction.
- If $v \in a^+$ and $y \in c^+$, let $\ell = |v|$ and choose $i = p!/\ell + 1$. Then, $uv^i x y^i z = a^{p+p!} b^{p+p!} c^{p+2p!+(i-1)|y|}$. This does not belong to L, so we have a contradiction.

In all three cases, we can produce a nonmember from a member. Thus, L is not context-free.

5.4.5 Proving Ogden's Lemma by Analyzing a PDA's Behavior

This section presents an alternate proof of Ogden's Lemma, which analyzes PDAs.

Suppose we want to compute the pumping constant of Ogden's Lemma from a PDA. Assuming that the PDA empties its stack before accepting, we can convert the PDA to a CFL grammar, convert the grammar to a CNF grammar, and then obtain the constant from the number of variables in the CNF grammar. This approach works as long as the PDA is nondeterministic because we can modify it to empty the stack before accepting. The stack-emptying property is not necessarily applicable to DPDAs. Thus, this raises the question of whether or not Ogden's Lemma can be proven by analyzing the PDA's behavior, which may not empty its stack. The answer to this question is positive, as we shall see next.

Proof Let L be a context-free language. Let $M = (Q, \Sigma, \Gamma, q_0, \delta, \bot, F)$ be a pushdown automaton, possibly deterministic, that accepts L. Without loss of generality, we may assume the following:

- M starts with $\perp$ in the stack and one ϵ-move.
- For each $q \in Q$, $a \in \Sigma_\epsilon$, and $b \in \Gamma$, every element (q', x) in $\delta(q, a, b)$ satisfies that $x = \epsilon$ or bc for some $c \in \Gamma$. In other words, M removes the top symbol and decreases the stack height by 1; alternatively, M adds a new symbol after pushing the top symbol back to the stack, which increases the stack height by 1.

We define the following size parameters:

$$\Delta = 4\|Q\|\|\Gamma\| + 1,$$
$$\Pi = 12\|Q\|^2\|\Gamma\| + 1,$$
$$\Theta = \Delta + \Pi,$$
$$\hat{p}_i = \Delta^{\Theta+1-i} \text{ for all } i \text{ such that } 0 \le i \le \Theta, \text{ and}$$
$$p = \hat{p}_0 = \Delta^{\Theta+1}.$$

Let w be a string in $L(M)$ such that $|w| \ge p$. Suppose M has an n-step computation path π to accept w and a set J of $m \ge p$ positions have been designated. For any step j such that $1 \le j \le n$, let us use the following notation:

- ID(j) is the instantaneous description (ID) at steps j.
- char(j) is the input M processes at step j.
- stack(j) is the stack string of M at step j.
- top(j) is the stack string of M at step j.
- state(j) is the stack string of M at step j.
- height(j) is the stack height of M at step j.

We note that at $n - |w|$ places, input$_t = \epsilon$ and

$$w = \text{char}(1) \cdots \text{char}(n).$$

We partition π into $m + 1$ segments $V_0, \dots, V_m$.

- V_0 is the computation before processing the first marked position.
- V_m is the computation from step m that processes the last marked position to the last step.
- For each j such that $1 \le j \le m - 1$, V_j is the computation from the step M processes the j-th marked position and the step immediately before M processes the $(j + 1)$-th marked position.

By definition,

(*)   for all $j \ge 1$, V_j processes exactly one marked position, and the processing occurs at the first step of V_j.

Figure 5.11 shows the partition into $V_0, \dots, V_m$. Our decomposition $w = uvxyz$ relies on the changes in the stack height in each segment. The stack height in a segment, V_k, starts with a value, reaches the maximum within the segment, and

Fig. 5.11 The partition of the input into $V_0, \ldots, V_m$. The highlighted rectangles represent the individual marked positions

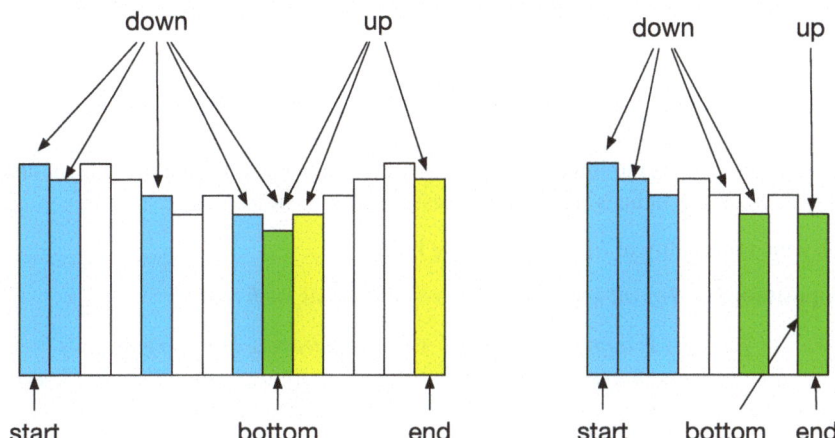

Fig. 5.12 Two examples of a segment's internal structure. In the left panel, there is only one step number at which the bottom height is achieved, and the two sequences have a length of > 1. In the right panel, the bottom height is achieved at two places, and the upward sequence has only one element

ends at some value. The minimum height may be equal to the start value and the end value. Also, the minimum may appear multiple times in the segment. For each k such that $0 \leq k \leq m$, we formalize the change (see Fig. 5.12) as follows:

- We denote the minimum height in V_k by bot_k, the starting height by $start_k$, and the ending height by end_k.
- $down_k$ is the sequence of the positions where the stack height moves from the starting value to bot_k. The sequence specifies the first positions where the height value becomes $start_k, start_k - 1, \ldots, bot_k + 1$, and bot_k occur, respectively. These positions exist because M cannot remove more than one top symbol in one step and $start_k \geq bot_k$ by the minimality of bot_k as the height. The length of $down_k$ is thus $start_k - bot_k + 1$.
- up_k is the sequence of the positions where the stack height moves from bot_k to the ending value. The sequence specifies the last positions where the height value becomes $bot_k, bot_k + 1, \ldots, end_k - 1, end_k$, respectively. These positions exist because M can push only one symbol in one step and $bot_k \leq end_k$ because of the minimality of bot_k. The length of up_k is thus $end_k - bot_k + 1$.

We construct a finite sequence of segment blocks that shrink in size, where the index to the sequence starts from 0. By "block" we mean that it is a set of segments having consecutive indices, like $\{V_j \mid a \leq j \leq b\}$ for some $a, b, 0 \leq a < b \leq p$. We represent a block using its corresponding index interval $[a, b]$. We let $I_k = [\ell_k, r_k]$ denote the index interval at k. We also let $\hat{I}_k$ denote the open interval corresponding to I_k; that is, $[\ell_k + 1, r_k - 1]$. The initial interval I_0 is $[0, p]$; i.e., $\ell_0 = 0$ and $r_0 = p$. In addition, $\hat{I}_0 = [1, p - 1]$. We also define a height sequence $h_0, h_1, \ldots$ corresponding to $I_0, I_1, \ldots$, and the value of h_0 is 0. For each $k \geq 1$, we define

$$h_k = \min\{bot_j \mid j \in \hat{I}_{k-1}\} \text{ and } H_k = \{j \mid j \in \hat{I}_{k-1} \text{ and } bot_k = h_k\}.$$

In other words, h_k is the lowest height across the segments with indices in $\hat{I}_{k-1}$, and H_k is the segment indices where the lowest height is achieved.   □

By the minimality of h_k, the following holds:

Proposition 5.3 *For all $k \geq 1$, a string $s \in \Gamma^{h_k}$ exists such that:*

1. *For all $j \in \hat{I}_k$, s is a prefix of all stack strings appearing in the segment V_j.*
2. *For all $j \in H_k$, s appears as the stack string in V_j at the position the last element of $down_j$ specifies and at the position the first element of up_j specifies.*

Additionally, we have:

Proposition 5.4 *For each $k \geq 1$, let ξ_k be the smallest index in H_k and v_k be the last element of $down_{\xi_k}$. If $bot_{\ell_{k-1}} < h_k$ and $\xi_k \geq \ell_{k-1}+2$, then $end_{\ell_{k-1}} \geq h_k$, so $up_{\ell_{k-1}}$ contains a position at which the stack string is equal to s from Proposition 5.3 Part 1.*

The claim holds due to the following argument:

Assume, on the contrary, $end_{\ell_{k-1}} \leq h_k - 1$. Since the amount of change in the stack height is ± 1, $start_{\ell_{k-1}+1} \leq h_k$. Then, $bot_{\ell_{k-1}+1} \leq h_k$, and so, $\ell_{k-1} + 1$ should belong to H_k. However, the smallest element in H_k is $\geq \ell_{k-1} + 2$. This is a contradiction. Thus, the stack height reaches h_k in $up_{\ell_{k-1}+1}$. Let s' be the stack string where the height becomes h_k. After this point, the stack height returns to h_k for the first time at v_k, so $s' = s$.

After constructing h_k and H_k, we consider two major cases.

5.4.5.1   (Case 1) $\|H_k\| \geq 4\|Q\| + 1$

For each segment index j in H_k, we select the first position at which bot_j occurs and make it represent the block V_j. Put differently, the position is the last element in the position sequence $down_j$. Let $f_1, \ldots, f_t$ be the positions, where $t = \|H_k\|$. Let s be the stack prefix from Proposition 5.3. Since $\|H_k\| \geq 4\|Q\| + 1$, by the pigeon-hole principle, there are five distinct indices a, b, c, d, e such that $1 \leq a < b < c < d < e \leq t$ and $state(f_a) = state(f_b) = state(f_c) = state(f_d) = state(f_e)$. We select an arbitrary quintuple. The five members satisfy the following:

$$\mathrm{ID}(f_a) = \mathrm{ID}(f_b) = \mathrm{ID}(f_c) = \mathrm{ID}(f_d) = \mathrm{ID}(f_e).$$

Let

$$u_0 = \mathrm{char}(f_a) \cdots \mathrm{char}(f_c - 1) \text{ and } v = \mathrm{char}(f_c) \cdots \mathrm{char}(f_e - 1).$$

Because $a < b < c$, u_0 fully covers the segments $V_{a+1}, \ldots, V_{c-1}$: in particular, V_b. In addition, because $c < d < e$, v fully covers the segments $V_{c+1}, \ldots, V_{e-1}$: in particular, V_d. Thus, u_0 and v contain at least one marked position.

We terminate the construction. We decompose w into uvz, where u is w's prefix preceding v and z is w's suffix after v. Here, u_0 is now part of u. Let $x = y = \epsilon$. Then, $w = uvwyz$, and for all $i \geq 2$, $uv^i x y^i z = uv^i x$; because the IDs before and after proceeding of v are equal, M accepts this string.

Additionally, since the stack has s as a prefix between f_a and f_c, it is safe to remove v without changing the outcome. This means that M accepts uz, which is equal to uzy. Thus, for all $i \geq 0$, M accepts $uv^i x y^i z$.

Because u contains u_0, the number of marked positions is at least one in u. Additionally, because we have been dealing with $V_1, \ldots, V_p$, there are only p marked positions, and so the number of marked positions in vxy is at most p. The decompostion therefore satisifies the requirements.

Figure 5.13 shows the discovery of pumping structure in this case.

5.4.5.2 (Case 2) $\|H_k\| \leq 4\|Q\|$

Let $d = \|H_k\|$ and $\alpha_1, \ldots, \alpha_d$ be the indices in H_k in the increasing order. We consider $d + 1$ index intervals with overlapping endpoints.

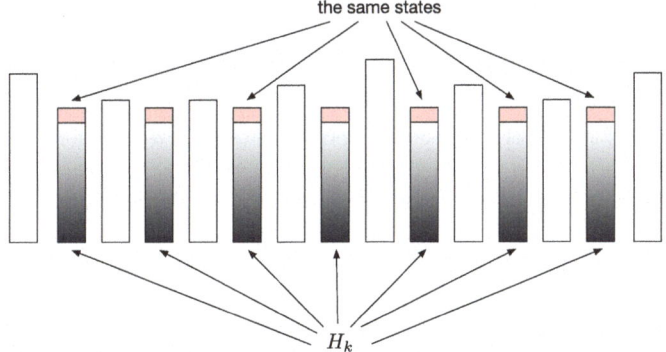

Fig. 5.13 Pumping structure discovery Case 1. Each tall box represents the stack in a block at its bottom positions. The stack strings with solid-colored top rectangles are identical. The stack strings in other boxes are taller. By the pigeon-hole principle, among the stack strings with solid-colored top rectangles exist two with the same states

$$[\ell_{k-1}, \alpha_1], [\alpha_1, \alpha_2], \ldots, [\alpha_{d-1}, \alpha_d], [\alpha_d, r_{k-1}].$$

From these intervals, we select the largest one as I_k. There are $d + 1$ candidate intervals, every pair of neighboring candidates share one segment, and $d \leq 2\|Q\|$. Thus, we have

$$\|I_k\| \geq \frac{\|I_{k-1}\| + d}{d + 1} > \frac{\|I_{k-1}\|}{d + 1} \geq \frac{\|I_{k-1}\|}{2\|Q\| + 1}.$$

Since $p = (2\|Q\| + 1)^{\Theta+1}$, by induction on k, we have

$$\|I_k\| \geq (2\|Q\| + 1)^{\Theta+1-k} = p_k.$$

Because of the way we constructed h_ks and H_ks, we have the following:

Proposition 5.5 *For all $k \geq 1$, $h_k > h_{k-1}$.*   □

We consider the following situations:

5.4.5.3   (Subcase 2a) $k = \Delta$, We Have Kept Choosing the Last Block Index p as the Right End of the Interval At Each Step (i.e., $r_0 = \cdots = r_\Delta = p$), and $h_\Delta \leq bot_p$

For each j such that $1 \leq j \leq \Delta$, we designate the first element of up_j in the segment V_{ℓ_j} as f_j and $s_j = \text{stack}(f_j)$. Since the right end of the index interval has been p, we have chosen the last candidate interval at each step. Thus,

$$\ell_1 < \ell_2 < \cdots < \ell_\Delta.$$

By Proposition 5.3, we have:

(*) For each j such that $1 \leq j \leq \Delta$, s_j is a prefix of the stack string at all positions between f_j and f_Δ.

Since $\Delta = 4\|Q\|\|\Gamma\| + 1$, there are five positions (a, b, c, d, e) among $f_1, \ldots, f_\Delta$, such that $a < b < c < d < e$, $\text{state}(a) = \text{state}(b) = \text{state}(c) = \text{state}(d) = \text{state}(e)$ and $\text{top}(a) = \text{top}(b) = \text{top}(c) = \text{top}(d) = \text{top}(e)$. As with Case 1, let

$$u_0 = \text{char}(a) \cdots \text{char}(c - 1) \text{ and } v = \text{char}(c) \cdots \text{char}(e - 1).$$

We terminate the construction. We take the same form of decomposition as with Case 1; $w = uvzxy$, where u is w's prefix before v, z is w's suffix after v, and $x = y = \epsilon$. Since $h_\Delta \leq bot_p$, s_Δ remains as a prefix of the stack for all positions after f_Δ. Thus, we can freely remove v or add multiples of v to produce the same outcome. For all $i \geq 0$, M on $uv^i xy^i z$ accepts. Figure 5.14 presents this case.

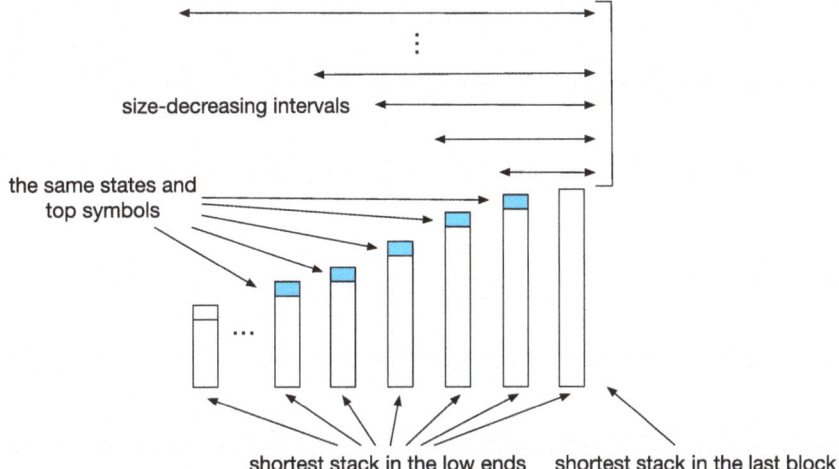

size-decreasing intervals

the same states and
top symbols

shortest stack in the low ends   shortest stack in the last block

Fig. 5.14 Pumping structure discovery Subcase 2a. The high end of the interval is always V_p in the interval sequence, and the bottom height of V_p is greater than the bottom height of the low ends. The high end of the intervals is always the last block. The low end of the intervals constantly moves to the right. By the pigeon-hole principle, two highlighted stack strings have the same top symbols and are in the same states

5.4.5.4 (Subcase 2b) $k = \Theta = \Delta + \Pi$

Let $J = \{\Delta + 1, \ldots, I_{\Delta+\Pi}\}$, that is, the values for k in the last Π steps. Our construction ensures the following properties hold for all $k \in J$:

1. Because the intervals are proper sub-intervals of their predecessors, either $\ell_k \geq \ell_{k-1} + 1$ or $r_k \leq r_{k-1} - 1$.
2. By Proposition 5.5, $h_k > h_{k-1}$.
3. Because $bot_0 = bot_{\ell_0} = 1$, $bot_{\ell_k} \leq h_k$, and because Subcase 2a did not occur at step Δ, $bot_{r_k} \leq h_k$.
4. By (3) and Propositions 5.3 and 5.4, a position in up_{ℓ_k} exists where the stack height is h_k, and a position in $down_{r_k}$ exists where the stack height is h_k.

   Let these positions be f_k and g_k, respectively.

We have

$$f_{\Delta+1} < \cdots < f_{\Delta+\Pi} < g_{\Delta+\Pi} < \cdots < g_{\Delta+1}.$$

Since $\Pi = 12\|Q\|^2\|\Gamma\| + 1$, the pigeon-hole principle states that there exists a combination of $q, r \in Q$ and $\beta \in \Gamma$ such that for ≥ 13 values of k, the state at f_k is q, the top symbol at f_k is β, and the state at g_k is r. We select one combination of q, r, and β and, in the combination, thirteen k values to form a set T. Due to 1, for all k and k' in T such that $k < k'$, either f_k comes from one of the preceding segments of $f_{k'}$ or $g_{k'}$ comes from one of the preceding segments of g_k. Then, seven indices $k_1, \ldots, k_7$ exist such that either $f_{k_1}, \ldots, f_{k_7}$ are from different segments or $g_{k_7}, \ldots, g_{k_1}$ are from different segments. Suppose the former is the case. Let

$$u_0 = \text{char}(f_{k_1}) \cdots \text{char}(f_{k_3}),$$

$$v = \text{char}(f_{k_3}) \cdots \text{char}(f_{k_5}),$$

$$x_1 = \text{char}(f_{k_5}) \cdots \text{char}(f_{k_7}),$$

$$x_2 = \text{char}(f_{k_7}) \cdots \text{char}(g_{k_5}),$$

$$x = x_1 x_2, \text{ and}$$

$$y = \text{char}(g_{k_5}) \cdots \text{char}(g_{k_3}).$$

Let u be w's prefix before v, which contains u_0, and z be w's suffix after y. We have:

- v raises the stack height from h_{k_3} to h_{k_5}, brings the state from the one at f_{k_3} to the same one, then places the same stack symbol as the top symbol at f_{k_3}.
- x brings the height to the same level as f_{k_5} and brings the state to q.
- y lowers the stack height from h_{k_5} to h_{k_3} and brings the state back to q.
- u contains V_{k_2}, so covers at least one marked position.
- v contains V_{k_4}, so covers at least one marked position.
- x contains V_{k_6}, so covers at least one marked position.

Thus, M accepts uxz and for all $i \geq 2$, $uv^i xy^i z$. The number of marked positions in vy is at least one. The number is at most p because y ends before the last point of $down_p$. We have thus found a desired decomposition. Figure 5.15 presents this case.

5.4.5.5   (Subcase 2c) Neither Subcase 2a Nor Subcase 2b Holds

We proceed to the next value of k.

This is the end of the construction. Case 1, Subcase 2a, and Subcase 2b collectively cover all possible situations. We have now proven the lemma.   □

Exercises

5.1 Show that the language $\{0^s 1^t \mid s > t > 0\}$ is context-free by designing a pushdown automaton accepting it.

5.2 Show that the language $\{0^n 1^m 2^m \mid n, m \geq 0\}$ is context-free by designing a pushdown automaton accepting it.

5.3 Show that the language $\{0^n 1^n 2^m \mid n, m \geq 0\}$ is context-free by designing a pushdown automaton accepting it.

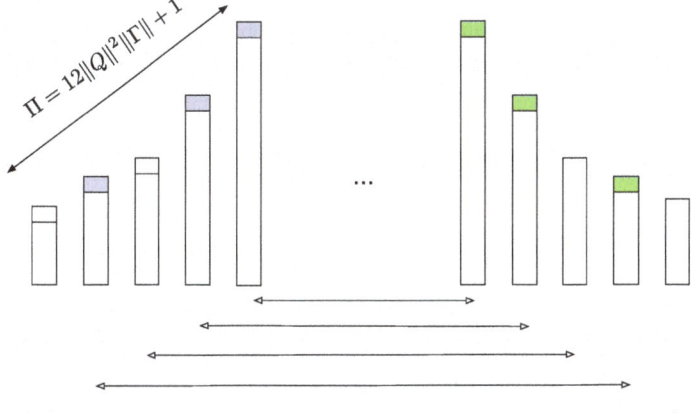

Fig. 5.15 Pumping structure discovery Subcase 2b. The intervals in decreasing sizes offer sections that are simultaneously repeatable. The arrows at the bottom indicate the intervals. The tall rectangles are stack strings, and the top rectangles are the top symbols of the stack. The states are equal on the solid-colored rectangles on the right-hand side. Among the solid-colored bars on the left-hand side, the states and the top symbols are identical

5.4 Show that the language $\{w \mid w \in \{0, 1\}^* \text{ and } w \text{ has twice as many 0s as 1s}\}$ is context-free by giving its pushdown automaton.

5.5 Let M be a PDA. Suppose M may not empty its stack before accepting. Show that M can be modified so that it empties its stack before accepting.

5.6 Let M be a PDA. Show that M can be modified so that M decreases or increases its stack height by 1 at each step.

5.7 Prove that the normalization from the previous question (i.e., the stack height increases by 1 or decreases by 1) applies to DPDA as well.

5.8 Prove Proposition 4.2 using a PDA.

5.9 Show that $\{0^n 1^n 2^m \mid n, m \geq 1\}$ is a deterministic context-free language by designing a DPDA accepting it.

5.10 Show that for each $k \geq 1$, $\{0^{n+k} 1^n \mid n \geq 1\}$ is a deterministic context-free language by designing a DPDA accepting it.

5.11 A homomorphism f from an alphabet Σ to another alphabet Θ is prefix-free if for all $a, b \in \Sigma$ such that $a \neq b$, $f(a)$ is not a prefix or $f(b)$ and $f(b)$ is not a prefix of $f(a)$. Prove that for all deterministic context-free languages $L \subseteq \Sigma^*$ and prefix-free homomorphisms f from Σ to Θ, $f(L) \subseteq \Theta^*$ is a deterministic context-free language.

5.12 Define prefix-free homomorphisms as in the last question. For each language L and for each prefix-free homomorphism f, define $f^{-1}(L) = \{w \mid f(w) \in L\}$. Prove that for all deterministic context-free languages $L \subseteq \Theta^*$ and prefix-free homomorphisms f from Σ to Θ, $f^{-1}(L) \subseteq \Theta^*$ is a deterministic context-free language.

5.13 Show that for each PDA, there is an equivalent PDA with a binary stack alphabet.

5.14 Using the Pumping Lemma, prove that $\{a^n b^n a^n \mid n \geq 0\}$ is not context-free.

5.15 Using Ogden's Lemma (the simpler version), prove that $\{a^i b^j c^k \mid j = \max\{i, k\}\}$ is not context-free.

5.16 Using Ogden's Lemma (the simpler version), prove that $\{a^i b^j c^k \mid j < \min\{i, k\}\}$ is not context-free.

5.17 Using Ogden's Lemma (the simpler version), prove that $\{a^i b^j c^k \mid i = j \neq k\}$ is not context-free.

5.18 By simulating PDAs, show that the class of context-free languages is closed under the prefix operation; i.e., for all context-free languages L, the language $\{w \mid w$ is a prefix of some member of $L\}$ is context-free as well.

5.19 Show that the class of context-free languages is closed under the proper prefix operation; i.e., for all context-free language L, $\{w \mid w$ is a proper prefix of some member of $L\}$ is context-free as well.

5.20 Use either the Pumping Lemma for context-free languages or Ogden's Lemma to prove $\{a^n b^n a^n b^n \mid n \geq 1\}$ is not context-free.

5.21 For a language L, $\mathrm{NoMID3}(L)$ is $\{xy \mid |x| = |y|$ and for some w, $|w| = |x|$, $xwy \in L\}$. Show that the context-free languages are not closed under the $\mathrm{NoMID3}$ operation.

  Hint: Use $\{a^n b^n c^m a^p b^p \mid n, m, p \geq 1\}$ is context-free.

5.22 Let M be a pushdown automaton that empties its stack whenever it accepts. Construct a pushdown automaton N from M that reverses the action to accept $L(M)^R$.

5.23 Let L_1 and L_2 be two languages in Σ^*. The **marked concatenation** of L_1 and L_2 is $\{u\$v \mid u \in L_1$ and $v \in L_2\}$, where $\$ \notin \Sigma$. Show that DCFL is closed under marked concatenation.

5.24 Let $A = \{a^n b^n \mid n \geq 1\}$, $B = \{a^n b^{2n+1} \mid n \geq 1\}$, $C = A \cup B$, and $D = \{a^n b^n c d^n \mid n \geq 1\}$. Show that $C \in$ DCFL implies $D \in$ CFL, so DCFL is not closed under union.

5.25 Based on the previous result, prove that DCFL is not closed under intersection.

Bibliographic Notes and Further Reading

The pushdown automaton model was first studied by Oettinger [7] and Schützen-berger [10]. The equivalence between CFLs and PDAs is by Chomsky [3] and Evey [4]. The Pumping Lemma for context-free languages is by Bar-Hillel, Perles, and Shamir [1]. Ogden's Lemma is by Ogden [8]. Ogden proved results called intercalation theorems, which extend the Pumping Lemma for more powerful computation models [9]. The exposition of Ogden's Lemma was adopted from [9]. Boasson [2] showed pumping lemmas for various models. Bar-Hillel, Perles, and Shamir [1] showed various closure properties of CFLs. DPDA is by Haines [6] and Ginsburg and Greibach [5].

References

1. Y. Bar-Hillel, M. Perles, E. Shamir, On formal properties of simple phrase structure grammars. Sprachtypologie und Universalienforschung **14**, 143–172 (1961)
2. L. Boasson, Two iteration theorems for some families of languages. J. Comput. Syst. Sci. **7**(6), 583–596 (1973)
3. N. Chomsky, Context-free grammars and pushdown storage. MIT Res. Lab. Electron. Quart. Prog. Rep. **65**, 187–194 (1962)
4. R.J. Evey, Application of pushdown-store machines, in *Proceedings of the November 12–14, 1963, Fall Joint Computer Conference* (1963), pp. 215–227
5. S. Ginsburg, S.A. Greibach, Deterministic context free languages. Inform Control **9**, 620–648 (1966)
6. L.G. Haines, *Generation and recognition of formal languages*. PhD thesis, Massachusetts Institute of Technology, 1965
7. A.G. Oettinger, *Automatic Syntactic Analysis and the Pushdown Store* (American Mathematical Society, 1961)
8. W.F. Ogden, A helpful result for proving inherent ambiguity. Math. Syst. Theory **2**(3), 191–194 (1968)
9. W.F. Ogden, Intercalation theorems for stack languages, in *Proceedings of the First Annual ACM Symposium on Theory of Computing* (1969), pp. 31–42
10. M.P. Schützenberger, On context-free languages and push-down automata. Inform. Control **6**, 246–264 (1963)

Part III
Undecidability and Turing Machines

Chapter 6
The Turing Machines

6.1 The Turing Machine (TM) Model

In this chapter, we study the Turing machine computation model. The model resembles the finite automaton model but is more complex.

6.1.1 The Definition

Here is the definition of the model.

A **Turing machine (TM)** operates in discrete time and has three components:

- **Tape**: The tape of a TM is a sequence of **cells**. Each cell holds a symbol from the TM's **tape alphabet**. The cells have unique sequential **indices** (or **positions**). The range of cell indices may be infinite or finite. The finite-index model is the Linear Bounded Automaton model (we will study this model in Chap. 7). When the range is unlimited, the minimum is 1 or undefined. In the former case, the tape is **one-way infinite**; in the latter case, the tape is **two-way infinite**. We will consider mainly one-way infinite tapes in this book.
- **Head**: The head is an apparatus for a TM utilized to access the tape's content. At each computation step, a TM has access to exactly one cell through its head. A TM can read the symbol written in the cell and store a symbol in the same cell. To prepare for the next step, a TM may move the head to a neighbor of the cell on which the head is located; alternatively, it may keep the head in the same cell. The move decreasing the cell index by 1 is a **left move**, and the move increasing the cell index by 1 is a **right move**, If a TM tries to move its head in a direction where no additional cell is available, the head remains in the same position. We call this phenomenon a **bounceback**.

Fig. 6.1 A TM with a
one-way infinite tape

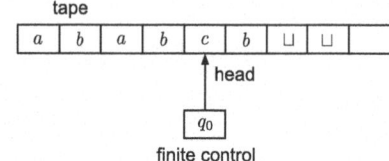

- **Finite control**: The finite control is where a TM determines its action. Like automata, a TM holds a state from its finite **state set** in its finite control. A TM determines which symbol it will write, to which direction it will move its head, and to which state it will transition. This determination is based on the present state and the symbol stored in the cell on which the head is located.

Figure 6.1 is a typical drawing of a TM, where the TM has a one-way infinite tape.

A TM commences and terminates its computation as follows:

At the start of computation, the tape of a TM holds its input in the cells starting from index 1, its head is on Cell 1, and its state is the **initial state**, denoted as q_0. The cells not occupied by the input hold a special "blank" symbol, which we denote with $\sqcup$. If the input is ϵ, the head reads $\sqcup$ at the start of the computation. Otherwise, the head reads some symbol not equal to $\sqcup$. Thus, a TM can tell if the input is ϵ when it starts computing.

Once the computation commences, a TM uses its finite control to determine and execute its action. The computation terminates when the state becomes one of two special states, q_{acc} and q_{rej}. We call these states the **accepting state** and **rejecting state**, respectively. We say that the machine **accepts** when it enters q_{acc} and **rejects** when it enters q_{rej}.

6.1.1.1 The Mathematical Definition

Formally, a TM is an eight-tuple $(Q, \Gamma, \sqcup, \Sigma, \delta, q_0, q_{acc}, q_{rej})$, whose components are as follows:

- Q is the state set.
- Γ is the tape alphabet.
- $\sqcup$ is the blank symbol.
- Σ is the **input alphabet** and is a subset of $\Sigma \subseteq (\Gamma - \{\sqcup\})$.
- $\delta : Q \times \Gamma \to Q \times \Gamma \times D$ is the **transition function**, where $D = \{L, R, -\}$. The elements L, R, and $-$ represent the left head move, the right head move, and the stationary head move, respectively.

  We define the transitions in states q_{acc} and q_{rej} as $\delta(q_{acc}, a) = (q_{acc}, a, -)$ and $\delta(q_{rej}, a) = (q_{rej}, a, -)$ for all $a \in \Gamma$.
- $q_0 \in Q$ is the initial state.
- $q_{acc} \in Q$ is the accepting state.
- $q_{rej} \in Q, q_{rej} \neq q_{acc}$ is the rejecting state.

The computation by a TM on an input has three possible outcomes:

- The TM accepts the input.
- The TM rejects the input.
- The TM runs forever.

6.1.1.2 Recognition and Decision

Here, we define the concepts of recognition and decision by TMs.

Definition 6.1 Let $M = (Q, \Gamma, \sqcup, \Sigma, \delta, q_0, q_{acc}, q_{rej})$ be a TM.

1. The language that M **recognizes** is:

$$\{w \mid w \in \Sigma^* \text{ and } M \text{ on } w \text{ accepts}\}.$$

We denote the language by $L(M)$.
2. The language that M **co-recognizes** is:

$$\{w \mid w \in \Sigma^* \text{ and } M \text{ on } w \text{ does not accept}\}.$$

3. If M halts on all inputs, we say M **decides** $L(M)$ (Table 6.1).

We then define the following language classes:

Definition 6.2 A language is **recursive** or **decidable** if a TM decides the language. A language is **co-recursive** or **co-decidable** if a TM decides its complement.

Definition 6.3 If a TM accepts the language, a language is **recursively enumerable**.
If a TM accepts its complement, a language is **co-recursively enumerable**.

By swapping the roles between q_{acc} and q_{rej}, we obtain the following proposition:

Proposition 6.1 *A language A is recursive if, and only if, its complement, $\overline{A}$, is recursive.*

Table 6.1 The terminology we use in describing languages that TMs characterize according to their behavior

Class	Terminology	Outcome on members	Outcome on non-members
Recursively enumerable	Recognition	Accept	Reject or run forever
Co-recursively enumerable	Co-recognition	Reject or run forever	Accept
Decidable	Decision	Accept	Reject
Co-decidable	Co-decision	Reject	Accept

Definition 6.4 R, RE, and coRE, respectively, denote the classes of all languages that are decidable, recursively enumerable, and co-recursively enumerable.

6.1.2 Examples of TMs

Let us explore some examples of TMs.

The first TM example decides $L = \{a^n b^n a^n \mid n \geq 0\}$. From Exercise 5.14, we know that L is not context-free. Let $w \in \{a, b\}^*$ be an arbitrary input. As mentioned earlier, a TM can tell at the start if $w = \epsilon$. We thus design a TM, M, to accept ϵ. If $w \neq \epsilon$, M repeatedly "finds and erases" the leftmost a, the leftmost b appearing after the a, and the rightmost a appearing after the b. More specifically, while executing the search for the three characters, M "erases" the triple by turning the three characters into $\sqcup$, x, and $\sqcup$, respectively. When no more triple is found, if the tape has no a or b, M learns that the input was a member of L, so enters q_{acc}. Otherwise, M enters q_{rej}.

In other words, M turns some leading as into $\sqcup$s, an equal number of trailing as into $\sqcup$s, and the same number of leading bs into x. After erasing k triples, the tape holds a string with the following form:

$$\underbrace{\sqcup \cdots \sqcup}_{k} a \cdots a \underbrace{x \cdots x}_{k} b \cdots bza \cdots a \underbrace{\sqcup \cdots \sqcup}_{k} \sqcup \cdots .$$

Here, z is some string in $\{a, b\}^*$. After successfully finding and erasing a trio, M's next target for erasure consists of three characters as follows:

1. First, the character immediately to the right of the leading $\sqcup$s must be found. This character is a or x. For the search to continue, the character must be a.
2. Next, the character to the right of the run of xs must be found. This character is b or $\sqcup$. For the search to continue, the character must be b.
3. Finally, the character immediately to the left of the trailing $\sqcup$s must be found. This character is a, b, or $\sqcup$. For the search to complete, the character must be a.

If the character does not have a match in (2) or (3), that indicates that the search failed, so the TM rejects the input. If the character does not match in (1), the TM checks if the tape content matches $\sqcup^+ x^+ \sqcup^+$.

Algorithm 6.1 shows the algorithm for M. As stated earlier, by requiring the middle to be the leftmost b after the first a, we plan to change the input of the form $a^i b^j a^k$ with positive i, j, and k into:

$$\sqcup a^{i-1} x b^{j-1} a^{k-1} \sqcup .$$

If i, j, and k are all ≥ 2, we change the tape content further into:

$$\sqcup \sqcup a^{i-2} x x b^{j-2} a^{k-2} \sqcup \sqcup.$$

Algorithm 6.1 A TM algorithm for $\{a^n b^n a^n \mid n \geq 0\}$

1: **procedure** TESTING-FOR-$a^n b^n a^n(w)$
2:     the computation begins with the head on the input's leftmost character;
3:     **if** the character is ⊔ **then**
4:         accept;
5:     **end if**
6:     **while** *true* **do**
7:         search to the right for an a, a b, or a ⊔;   ▷ the initial check
8:         **if** the character at the head position is ⊔ **then**
9:             enter q_{acc};
10:        **else if** the character is b **then**
11:            enter q_{rej};
12:        **else if** the character is x **then**
13:            scan to the right to locate a non-x;
14:            **if** the character is ⊔ **then**
15:                enter q_{acc};
16:            **else**
17:                enter q_{rej};
18:            **end if**
19:        **else**   ▷ the character is a
20:            replace the a with ⊔;
21:            scan to the right to locate a b or a ⊔;
22:            **if** the character is ⊔ **then**
23:                enter q_{rej};
24:            **end if**
25:            replace the b with an x;
26:            scan to the right for a ⊔;
27:            move the head to the left neighbor of the ⊔;
28:            **if** the character is not a **then**
29:                enter q_{rej};
30:            **end if**
31:            replace the a with ⊔;
32:            scan to the right for a ⊔;
33:            move to the right neighbor of the ⊔;
34:        **end if**
35:    **end while**
36: **end procedure**

In general, if i, j, and k are $\geq m$, after m rounds, we change w to:

$$\sqcup^m \, a^{i-m} x^m b^{j-m} a^{k-m} \, \sqcup^m \, .$$

If $i = j = k = m$, then w will become $\sqcup^m x^m \sqcup^m$.

Figure 6.2 shows the program as a diagram. The letters a and r appearing in the circles represent acceptance and rejection, respectively. The arrows represent transitions between states. A label of the form $Y/Z, D$ on an arrow specifies that the transition occurs when the symbol is Y and that the machine writes Z and moves the head to the direction of D.

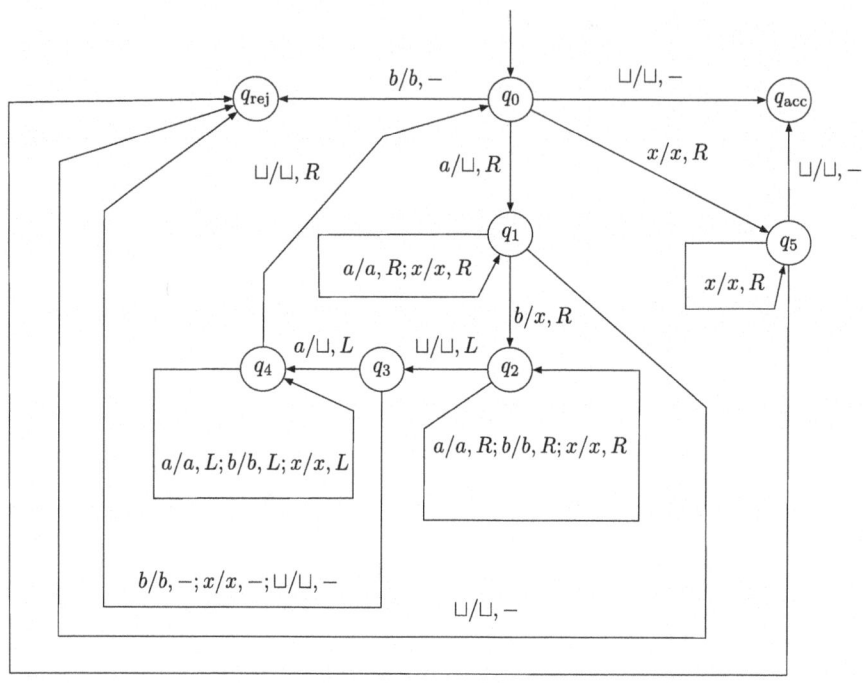

Fig. 6.2 A diagram for a TM that accepts $\{a^n b^n a^n \mid n \geq 0\}$

Table 6.2 The transition table of the TM for $\{a^n b^n a^n\}$

State	Symbol			
	a	b	x	$\sqcup$
q_0	$(q_1, \sqcup, R)$	$(q_{\text{rej}}, b, -)$	(q_5, x, R)	$(q_{\text{acc}}, \sqcup, -)$
q_1	(q_1, a, R)	(q_2, x, R)	(q_1, x, R)	$(q_{\text{rej}}, \sqcup, -)$
q_2	$(q_2, a, -)$	$(q_2, b, -)$	$(q_2, x, R)^{\dagger}$	$(q_3, \sqcup, L)$
q_3	$(q_4, \sqcup, L)$	$(q_{\text{rej}}, b, -)$	$(q_{\text{rej}}, x, -)$	$(q_{\text{rej}}, \sqcup, -)^{\dagger}$
q_4	(q_4, a, L)	(q_4, b, L)	(q_4, x, L)	$(q_0, \sqcup, R)$
q_5	$(q_{\text{rej}}, a, -)$	$(q_{\text{rej}}, b, -)$	(q_5, x, R)	$(q_{\text{acc}}, \sqcup, -)$

We encode the algorithm into a transition function δ. We represent Step i with q_i for all i between 1 and 6. The computation halts when the state becomes q_{acc} or q_{rej}. The transition function δ is in Table 6.2. In the table, the rows are the states, the columns are the symbols, and the entries are the values of the transition function. The $\dagger$ symbol indicates the transitions that never occur. This table suggests $\Sigma = \{a, b\}$, $Q = \{q_0, \ldots, q_5, q_{\text{acc}}, q_{\text{rej}}\}$, $\Gamma = \{a, b, X, \sqcup\}$, and q_0 as the initial state.

Figures 6.3, 6.4, and 6.5 present how the program runs on $a^3 b^3 c^3$ as a series of diagrams representing the tape, the head position, and the state, respectively. The order of the diagrams is row-wise.

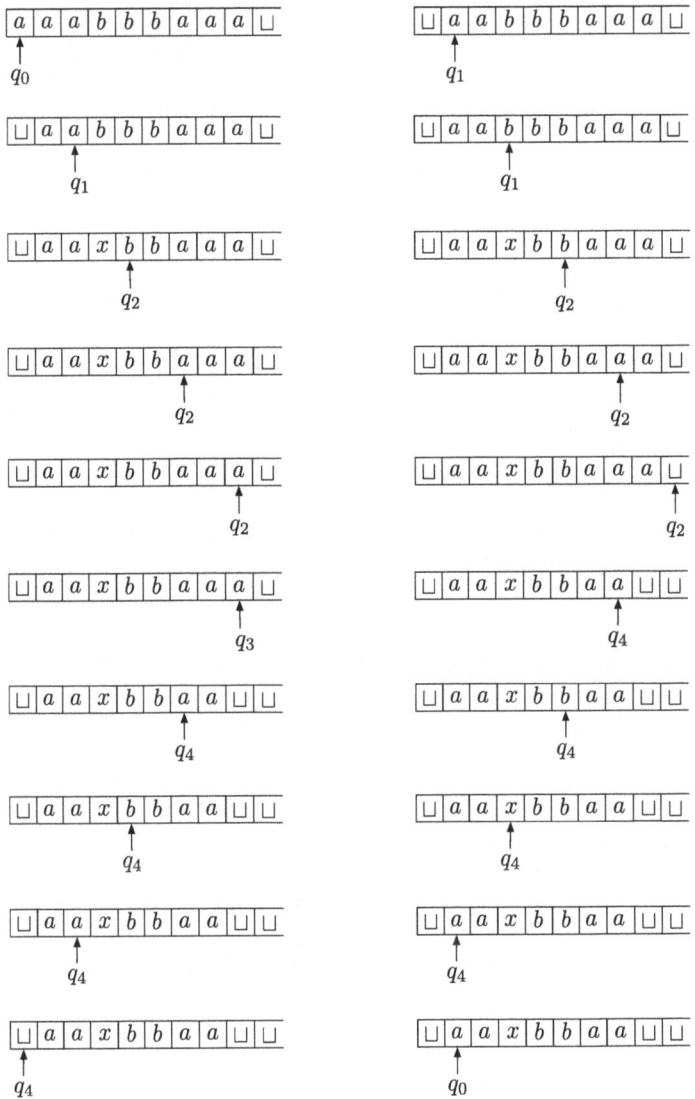

Fig. 6.3 Handling the first triple and searching for the next triple

6.1.3 Instantaneous Descriptions

Here, we define a TM's instantaneous descriptions.

We use the term **configuration** to refer to the status of a TM at a step of its computation. The configuration comprises of the state, the tape's content, and the head's position. A pictorial representation like Fig. 6.1 can present a configuration. However, encoding the configuration as a character sequence is much

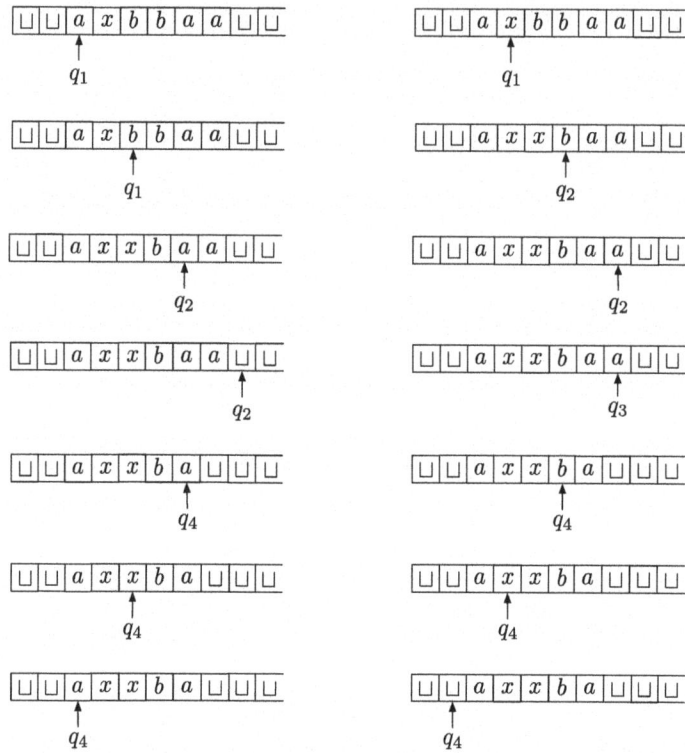

Fig. 6.4 Handling the second triple

more convenient than a pictorial representation for treating it mathematically. We call such an encoding **instantaneous description (ID)**.

There are multiple ways to encode configurations into ID.

Consider a configuration where the tape holds $aabbcaabb \sqcup \sqcup \cdots$, the head is on the c, and the state is q_3. By treating q_3 as a symbol not part of the tape alphabet, we encode the ID as the string:

$$aabbq_3caabb \sqcup^k .$$

The encoding format assumes that the state-representing symbol appears immediately to the left of the symbol at the position of the head. Therefore, an ID must match the regular expression $(\Gamma)^* Q \Gamma^+$. We truncate the infinite stretch of blank appearing in the tape to a finite string but do not restrict its length after truncation. In other words, we do not demand that the IDs be as short as possible. Thus, for each configuration, there exist infinitely many strings representing it because if w is an ID, then so is $w\sqcup$.

Sometimes, we use an alternate representation in which the state-representing symbol appears at the beginning, and a symbol with a marking indicates the location

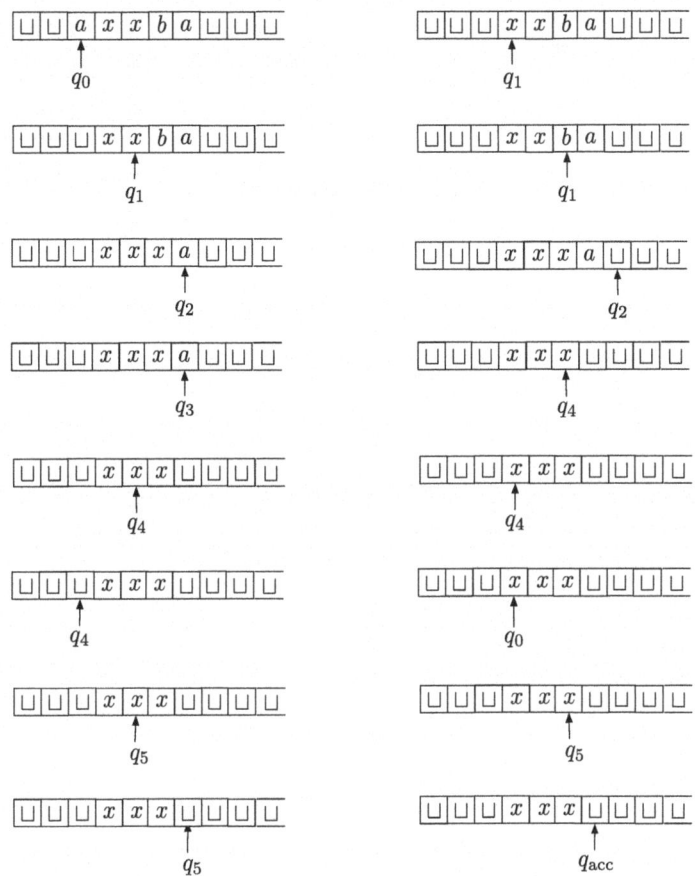

Fig. 6.5 Handling the last triple and then checking if no a or b is remaining

of the head. For a TM whose tape alphabet is Γ, we consider its marked version $\tilde{\Gamma}$, whose letters are those from Γ with a squiggle. If the state set of the machine is Q, then the IDs with a state-representing symbol match the regular expression $\Gamma^* Q \Gamma^+$, and those without it match $Q\Gamma^* \tilde{\Gamma}\Gamma$. Figure 6.6 shows changes in the ID with this alternate representation.

We present a TM for the palindromes over $\{1, 2\}$. Let L denote the language. The basis of the program is the following recursive definition for L:

- Let w be a string over $\{1, 2\}$. If $|w| \leq 1$, $w \in L$. Otherwise, $w \in L$ if and only if $w = cyc$ for some $c \in \{1, 2\}$ and $y \in L$.

Imagine checking to see if the tape content is in the form $\sqcup^* cyc\sqcup^*$ for some $c \in \{1, 2\}$ and $y \in \{1, 2\}^*$ and, if so, replacing each c to $\sqcup$. Imagine, also, repeating the check and replacements until the tape content reduces to $\sqcup^* (a \cup b \cup \epsilon)\sqcup^*$. For example, we make a series of reductions of an input string 1221221 to generate:

Fig. 6.6 Processing of the first triple with a state as the leading symbol

$q_0\ \tilde{a}\ a\ a\ b\ b\ b\ a\ a\ a\ \sqcup \Rightarrow q_1\ \sqcup\ \tilde{a}\ a\ b\ b\ b\ a\ a\ a\ \sqcup$

$\Rightarrow q_1\ \sqcup\ a\ \tilde{a}\ b\ b\ b\ a\ a\ a\ \sqcup \Rightarrow q_1\ \sqcup\ a\ a\ \tilde{b}\ b\ b\ a\ a\ a\ \sqcup$

$\Rightarrow q_2\ \sqcup\ a\ a\ x\ \tilde{b}\ b\ a\ a\ a\ \sqcup \Rightarrow q_2\ \sqcup\ a\ a\ x\ b\ b\ a\ a\ a\ \sqcup$

$\Rightarrow q_2\ \sqcup\ a\ a\ x\ b\ b\ \tilde{a}\ a\ a\ \sqcup \Rightarrow q_2\ \sqcup\ a\ a\ x\ b\ \tilde{b}\ a\ a\ a\ \sqcup$

$\Rightarrow q_2\ \sqcup\ a\ a\ x\ b\ b\ a\ a\ \tilde{a}\ \sqcup \Rightarrow q_3\ \sqcup\ a\ a\ x\ b\ b\ a\ a\ a\ \tilde{\sqcup}$

$\Rightarrow q_3\ \sqcup\ a\ a\ x\ b\ b\ a\ a\ \tilde{a}\ \sqcup \Rightarrow q_4\ \sqcup\ a\ a\ x\ b\ b\ a\ \tilde{a}\ \sqcup\ \sqcup$

$\Rightarrow q_4\ \sqcup\ a\ a\ x\ b\ b\ \tilde{a}\ a\ \sqcup\ \sqcup \Rightarrow q_4\ \sqcup\ a\ a\ x\ b\ \tilde{b}\ a\ a\ \sqcup\ \sqcup$

$\Rightarrow q_4\ \sqcup\ a\ a\ x\ b\ b\ a\ a\ \sqcup\ \sqcup \Rightarrow q_4\ \sqcup\ a\ a\ \tilde{x}\ b\ b\ a\ a\ \sqcup\ \sqcup$

$\Rightarrow q_4\ \sqcup\ a\ \tilde{a}\ x\ b\ b\ a\ a\ \sqcup\ \sqcup \Rightarrow q_4\ \sqcup\ \tilde{a}\ a\ x\ b\ b\ a\ a\ \sqcup\ \sqcup$

$\Rightarrow q_4\ \tilde{\sqcup}\ a\ a\ x\ b\ b\ a\ a\ \sqcup\ \sqcup \Rightarrow q_0\ \sqcup\ \tilde{a}\ a\ x\ b\ b\ a\ a\ \sqcup\ \sqcup$

$\sqcup$	2	2	1	2	2	$\sqcup$	$\Rightarrow$
$\sqcup$	$\sqcup$	2	1	2	$\sqcup$	$\sqcup$	$\Rightarrow$
$\sqcup$	$\sqcup$	$\sqcup$	1	$\sqcup$	$\sqcup$	$\sqcup$	$\Rightarrow$
$\sqcup$	$\sqcup$	$\sqcup$	1	$\sqcup$	$\sqcup$	$\sqcup$	.

The last element in this series has only one non-$\sqcup$, which is the 1 in the middle. An examination of this last ID reveals that the input was a palindrome.

Algorithm 6.2 is the program demonstrating this.

Algorithm 6.2 A TM algorithm for the palindrome over $\{1, 2\}$

```
 1: procedure PALINDROME-TES(w)
 2:     receive input w ∈ {0, 1};
 3:     while true do
 4:         if the cell has ⊔ then
 5:             enter q_acc;
 6:         else
 7:             c ← the symbol in the cell;
 8:             write ⊔ in the cell;
 9:             scan to the right for ⊔;
10:             move the head to the left neighbor;
11:             if the cell has ⊔ then
12:                 enter q_acc;
13:             else if the cell has a symbol different from c then
14:                 enter q_rej;
15:             else
16:                 the cell has c;
17:                 write ⊔ in the cell;
18:                 scan to the left for ⊔;
19:                 move the head to the right neighbor;
20:             end if
21:         end if
22:     end while
23: end procedure
```

We can implement the algorithm using states q_0, q_1, q_2, q_3, q_4, and q_5, where q_0 is the initial state. The states play the following roles:

- In q_0, the TM examines the leftmost character yet to turn into ⊔. The TM proceeds to q_{acc} if no character must turn into ⊔; otherwise, the TM has identified a 1 or a 2 as the leftmost character to turn that into ⊔. If the character is 1, the TM proceeds to q_1 after changing the character to ⊔. If the character is 2, the TM proceeds to q_2 instead after changing the character to ⊔. The TM memorizes the erased character by choosing between q_1 and q_2.
- In q_1, the TM scans to the right, looking for ⊔. After finding one, the TM moves the head to the left neighbor of the ⊔ and enters q_3.
- In q_2, the TM scans to the right, looking for ⊔. After finding one, the TM moves the head to the left neighbor of the ⊔ and enters q_4.
- In q_3, if the character is ⊔, it indicates that the character the TM has erased was the middle character in an odd-length palindrome, so the TM enters q_{acc} immediately. If the character is 2, it is a mismatch with the character the TM has erased, so the TM enters q_{rej} immediately. If the character is 1, it matches the character the TM has erased, so the TM changes the character to ⊔ and enters q_5.
- Similarly, in q_4, if the character is ⊔, it indicates that the character the TM has erased was the middle character in an odd-length palindrome, so the TM enters q_{acc} immediately. If the character is 1, it is a mismatch with the character the TM has erased, so the TM enters q_{rej} immediately. If the character is 2, it matches the character the TM has erased, so the TM changes the character to ⊔ and enters q_5.
- In q_5, the TM moves the head to the left, looking for ⊔. Upon finding one, the machine moves the head to the right neighbor of the ⊔ and enters q_0.

Here is the TM's transition table.

States	Symbols		
	1	2	⊔
q_0	$(q_1, ⊔, R)$	$(q_2, ⊔, R)$	$(q_{acc}, ⊔, -)$
q_1	$(q_1, 1, R)$	$(q_1, 2, R)$	$(q_3, ⊔, L)$
q_2	$(q_2, 1, R)$	$(q_2, 2, R)$	$(q_4, ⊔, L)$
q_3	$(q_5, ⊔, L)$	$(q_{rej}, 2, -)$	$(q_{acc}, ⊔, -)$
q_4	$(q_{rej}, 1, -)$	$(q_5, ⊔, L)$	$(q_{acc}, ⊔, -)$
q_5	$(q_5, 1, L)$	$(q_5, 2, L)$	$(q_0, ⊔, R)$

Figure 6.7 is the transition diagram of the TM.
Figure 6.8 shows how the machine accepts an input of 1221221.

6.1.4 Fundamental Subroutines

Designing TM programs is challenging because of two features of the TM model. One is that the tape access is sequential, and the other is that the cell index is unknown. We respond to this challenge by adding special symbols, like the initial/bottom symbol for PDA.

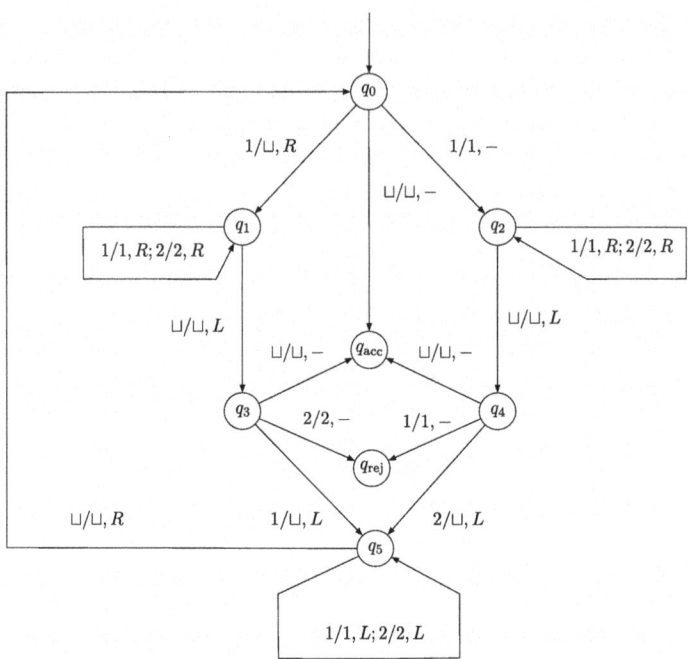

Fig. 6.7 A diagram for the palindromes over $\{1, 2\}$

$$
\begin{aligned}
&q_0\ 1\ 2\ 2\ \ 1\ \ 2\ 2\ 1\ \sqcup\ \sqcup\ \Rightarrow\ \sqcup\ q_1\ 2\ 2\ 1\ 2\ 2\ 1\ \sqcup\ \sqcup\\
\Rightarrow\ &\sqcup\ \sqcup\ \sqcup\ 2\ q_1\ \ 2\ \ 1\ 2\ 2\ 1\ \sqcup\ \Rightarrow\ \sqcup\ 2\ 2\ q_1\ 1\ 2\ 2\ 1\ \sqcup\ \sqcup\\
\Rightarrow\ &\sqcup\ \sqcup\ \sqcup\ 2\ 2\ \ 1\ \ q_1\ 2\ 2\ 1\ \sqcup\ \Rightarrow\ \sqcup\ 2\ 2\ 1\ 2\ q_1\ 2\ 1\ \sqcup\ \sqcup\\
\Rightarrow\ &\sqcup\ \sqcup\ \sqcup\ 2\ 2\ \ 1\ \ 2\ 2\ q_1\ 1\ \sqcup\ \Rightarrow\ \sqcup\ 2\ 2\ 1\ 2\ 2\ 1\ q_1\ \sqcup\ \sqcup\\
\Rightarrow\ &\sqcup\ \sqcup\ \sqcup\ 2\ 2\ \ 1\ \ 2\ 2\ q_3\ 1\ \sqcup\ \Rightarrow\ \sqcup\ 2\ 2\ 1\ 2\ q_5\ 2\ \sqcup\ \sqcup\ \sqcup\\
\Rightarrow\ &\sqcup\ \sqcup\ \sqcup\ 2\ 2\ \ 1\ \ q_5\ 2\ 2\ \sqcup\ \sqcup\ \Rightarrow\ \sqcup\ 2\ 2\ q_5\ 1\ 2\ 2\ \sqcup\ \sqcup\ \sqcup\\
\Rightarrow\ &\sqcup\ \sqcup\ \sqcup\ 2\ q_5\ \ 2\ \ 1\ 2\ 2\ \sqcup\ \sqcup\ \Rightarrow\ \sqcup\ q_5\ 2\ 2\ 1\ 2\ 2\ \sqcup\ \sqcup\ \sqcup\\
\Rightarrow\ &\sqcup\ q_5\ \sqcup\ 2\ \ 2\ \ 1\ 2\ 2\ \sqcup\ \sqcup\ \Rightarrow\ \sqcup\ q_0\ 2\ 2\ 1\ 2\ 2\ \sqcup\ \sqcup\ \sqcup\\
\Rightarrow\ &\sqcup\ \sqcup\ \sqcup\ \sqcup\ q_2\ \ 2\ \ 1\ 2\ 2\ \sqcup\ \sqcup\ \Rightarrow\ \sqcup\ \sqcup\ 2\ q_2\ 1\ 2\ 2\ \sqcup\ \sqcup\ \sqcup\\
\Rightarrow\ &\sqcup\ \sqcup\ \sqcup\ \sqcup\ 2\ \ 1\ \ q_2\ 2\ 2\ \sqcup\ \sqcup\ \Rightarrow\ \sqcup\ \sqcup\ 2\ 1\ 2\ q_2\ 2\ \sqcup\ \sqcup\ \sqcup\\
\Rightarrow\ &\sqcup\ \sqcup\ \sqcup\ \sqcup\ 2\ \ 1\ \ 2\ 2\ q_2\ \sqcup\ \sqcup\ \Rightarrow\ \sqcup\ \sqcup\ 2\ 1\ 2\ q_4\ 2\ \sqcup\ \sqcup\ \sqcup\\
\Rightarrow\ &\sqcup\ \sqcup\ \sqcup\ \sqcup\ 2\ \ 1\ \ q_5\ 2\ \sqcup\ \sqcup\ \sqcup\ \Rightarrow\ \sqcup\ \sqcup\ 2\ q_5\ 1\ 2\ \sqcup\ \sqcup\ \sqcup\ \sqcup\\
\Rightarrow\ &\sqcup\ \sqcup\ \sqcup\ \sqcup\ q_5\ \ 2\ \ 1\ 2\ \sqcup\ \sqcup\ \sqcup\ \Rightarrow\ \sqcup\ q_5\ \sqcup\ 2\ 1\ 2\ \sqcup\ \sqcup\ \sqcup\ \sqcup\\
\Rightarrow\ &\sqcup\ \sqcup\ \sqcup\ \sqcup\ q_0\ \ 2\ \ 1\ 2\ \sqcup\ \sqcup\ \sqcup\ \Rightarrow\ \sqcup\ \sqcup\ \sqcup\ q_2\ 1\ 2\ \sqcup\ \sqcup\ \sqcup\ \sqcup\\
\Rightarrow\ &\sqcup\ \sqcup\ \sqcup\ \sqcup\ \sqcup\ \ 1\ \ q_2\ 2\ \sqcup\ \sqcup\ \sqcup\ \Rightarrow\ \sqcup\ \sqcup\ \sqcup\ 1\ 2\ q_2\ \sqcup\ \sqcup\ \sqcup\ \sqcup\\
\Rightarrow\ &\sqcup\ \sqcup\ \sqcup\ \sqcup\ \sqcup\ \ 1\ \ q_4\ 2\ \sqcup\ \sqcup\ \sqcup\ \Rightarrow\ \sqcup\ \sqcup\ \sqcup\ q_5\ 1\ \sqcup\ \sqcup\ \sqcup\ \sqcup\ \sqcup\\
\Rightarrow\ &\sqcup\ \sqcup\ \sqcup\ \sqcup\ q_5\ \ \sqcup\ \ 1\ \sqcup\ \sqcup\ \sqcup\ \sqcup\ \Rightarrow\ \sqcup\ \sqcup\ \sqcup\ q_0\ 1\ \sqcup\ \sqcup\ \sqcup\ \sqcup\ \sqcup\\
\Rightarrow\ &\sqcup\ \sqcup\ \sqcup\ \sqcup\ \sqcup\ \ \sqcup\ \ q_1\ \sqcup\ \sqcup\ \sqcup\ \sqcup\ \Rightarrow\ \sqcup\ \sqcup\ \sqcup\ q_3\ \sqcup\ \sqcup\ \sqcup\ \sqcup\ \sqcup\ \sqcup\\
\Rightarrow\ &\sqcup\ \sqcup\ \sqcup\ \sqcup\ q_{acc}\ \sqcup\ \sqcup\ \sqcup\ \sqcup\ \sqcup\ .
\end{aligned}
$$

Fig. 6.8 Processing of 1221221

6.1.4.1 Restoring the Input

We can modify the program for $\{a^n b^n a^n \mid n \geq 0\}$ so that the TM changes the input back to the original after making its accept/reject decision. The main idea is to use three symbols ($\tilde{a}$, a', and a'') for erasing as. The TM uses these new symbols and behaves as follows:

1. As before, the machine immediately accepts or rejects if the symbol it sees at the start is ⊔ or b, respectively.
2. The erasure process goes as follows:

    (a) The TM erases the as in the first segment with a', not ⊔, except it uses $\tilde{a}$ instead for the very first a,
    (b) The TM erases the as in the third segment with a'', not ⊔.
    (c) The TM erases bs with x as before.
    (d) The search to the right for ⊔ will become a search for a''.
    (e) The search to the left for ⊔ will become a search for a'.

3. When the TM is about to accept or reject, it executes the following restoration process:

    (a) The TM enters non-halting states p_A and p_R instead of q_{acc} and q_{rej}, respectively.
    (b) In p_A and p_R, the TM moves the head to the right in search of ⊔.
    (c) When ⊔ is found, the TM enters p'_A from p_A and p'_R from p_R. It then begins to move the head to the left.
    (d) While moving the head to the left, the TM replaces a's and a''s with a and xs with b.
    (e) When it arrives at $\tilde{a}$, the TM writes a and enters q_{acc} from p'_A and q_{rej} from p'_R.

These changes altogether give the following property to the machine:

- When the machine accepts or rejects, the input returns to the original, and the head is on the leftmost cell.

The reader is encouraged to write a code for the input-restoring version (see Exercise 6.3).

Next, we will study two fundamental operations of inserting a string at a location on the tape and deleting a section of input.

6.1.4.2 Insertion

Suppose a TM, whose state set is Q and whose alphabet is Γ, has the task of changing the tape contents by inserting one character at the head's present position. In terms of ID, the TM must turn its present ID upw to $us\alpha w$, where $s, t \in Q$, $\alpha \in \Gamma$, $u \in \Gamma^*$, and $w \in (\Gamma - \{⊔\})^* ⊔$. The change is easy if $w = ⊔$; the TM writes α, keeps the head at the present location, and enters s. Otherwise, the TM can accomplish this task as follows:

- Add a state $i_{a,s}$ for each $a \in \Gamma$.
- Add a symbol $\tilde{\alpha}$.

The TM's program is as follows:

1. At the start, let a be the symbol appearing in the cell on which the head is located.
2. The TM writes $\tilde{a}$, moves the head to the next cell, and enters $i_{a,s}$.
3. In the next phase, if the state is $i_{a,s}$ and the cell has b, the TM writes a, moves the head to the right neighbor, and enters $i_{b,s}$. The TM will remain in the phase until it enters $i_{\sqcup,s}$.
4. In $i_{\sqcup,s}$, the TM scans to the left for $\tilde{a}$ without changing the cell's content.
5. When it reaches $\tilde{\alpha}$, the TM writes α, keeps the head in the same position, and enters s.

Here is an example of how the insertion algorithm works. Suppose a TM's present ID is $aapbbcd\sqcup$ with $p \in Q$, and the TM needs to insert an e between aa and bb and enter q. Using the state-in format, we see the program execution as follows:

	a	a	p	b	b	c	d	$\sqcup$	$\Rightarrow$	a	a	$\tilde{e}$	$i_{b,s}$	b	c	d	$\sqcup$
$\Rightarrow$	a	a	$\tilde{e}$	b	$i_{b,s}$	c	d	$\sqcup$	$\Rightarrow$	a	a	$\tilde{e}$	b	b	$i_{c,s}$	d	$\sqcup$
$\Rightarrow$	a	a	$\tilde{e}$	b	b	c	$i_{d,s}$	$\sqcup$	$\Rightarrow$	a	a	$\tilde{e}$	b	b	c	d	$i_{\sqcup,s}$
$\Rightarrow$	a	a	$\tilde{e}$	b	b	c	$i_{\sqcup,s}$	d	$\Rightarrow$	a	a	$\tilde{e}$	b	b	$i_{\sqcup,s}$	c	d
$\Rightarrow$	a	a	$\tilde{e}$	b	$i_{\sqcup,s}$	b	c	d	$\Rightarrow$	a	a	$\tilde{e}$	$i_{\sqcup,s}$	b	b	c	d
$\Rightarrow$	a	a	$i_{\sqcup,s}$	$\tilde{e}$	b	b	c	d	$\Rightarrow$	a	a	s	e	b	b	c	d	.

A TM can insert a constant number of characters using the above algorithm in sequence.

6.1.4.3   Deletion

Suppose a TM whose state set is Q and alphabet is Γ has the task of changing the tape contents by deleting the character at the present position of the head. More specifically, the machine must turn its present ID upw to $us\alpha w$, where $s, t \in Q$, $\alpha \in \Gamma$, and $u, w \in \Gamma^*$.

The machine can accomplish this task with the following additional symbols and states:

- A state $d_{a,s}$ for each $a \in \Gamma$ (including $\sqcup$),
- A symbol $\tilde{\alpha}$
- A state r_s

The action of the machine is as follows:

1. Let us say w begins with some $a \in \Gamma$. In one step, the machine writes $\tilde{a}$, moves the head to the right neighbor, and enters r_s.
2. The present state is r_s. The machine searches for $\sqcup$ to the right. Upon encountering one, the machine preserves the $\sqcup$, moves the head to the left neighbor, and enters $d_{\sqcup,s}$.
3. The present state is $d_{a,s}$ for some $a \in \Gamma$. If what the machine reads is some b for some $b \in \Gamma$, the machine writes a, moves the head to the left neighbor, and enters $d_{b,s}$. If the machine reads $\tilde{b}$ for some $b \in \Gamma$ (b may equal a), the machine writes a and enters s without moving the head.

Here is an example of how the deletion algorithm works. Suppose a TM has $cbabcc \sqcup \sqcup \cdots$ on its tape and needs to remove the a and enter s. Suppose the present state is p and the head is on the cell holding the a. The program runs as follows:

	c	b	p	a	b	c	c	$\sqcup$	$\Rightarrow$	c	b	$\tilde{a}$	r_s	b	c	c	$\sqcup$
$\Rightarrow$	c	b	$\tilde{a}$	b	r_s	c	c	$\sqcup$	$\Rightarrow$	c	b	$\tilde{a}$	b	c	r_s	c	$\sqcup$
$\Rightarrow$	c	b	$\tilde{a}$	b	c	c	r_s	$\sqcup$	$\Rightarrow$	c	b	$\tilde{a}$	b	c	$d_{\sqcup,s}$	c	$\sqcup$
$\Rightarrow$	c	b	$\tilde{a}$	b	$d_{c,s}$	c	$\sqcup$	$\sqcup$	$\Rightarrow$	c	b	$\tilde{a}$	$d_{c,s}$	b	c	$\sqcup$	$\sqcup$
$\Rightarrow$	c	b	$d_{b,s}$	$\tilde{a}$	c	c	$\sqcup$	$\sqcup$	$\Rightarrow$	c	b	s	b	c	c	$\sqcup$	$\sqcup$.

6.2 The Multi-tape TM Model

We can extend the previous TM model to one with multiple tapes.

6.2.1 The Definition

Multi-tape TMs (see Fig. 6.9) have one or more tapes besides the input tape. Multi-tape TMs access their tapes with independently moving heads; i.e., the head's movement on a tape can differ from the other heads' movement. We call a TM having k tapes a **k-tape TM**. The TM model we previously studied is thus a **single-tape TM**. We assign numbers 1 through k to the tapes of a k-tape TM. At the computation's start, Tape 1 has the input like the tape of a single-tape TM, and the other tapes are all blank, with the head on the first cell at the computation's start.

A multi-tape TM executes its computation in the following manner. At each computation step, a multi-tape TM decides its action depending on the present state and the symbols it reads through its heads. Like single-tape TMs, the action consists of writing on the cells through the heads, moving the heads, and updating the state. A k-tape TM's transition function maps from $Q \times \Sigma^k$ to $Q \times (\Sigma \times D)^k$, where $D = \{L, -, R\}$. We often refer to one-tape TMs as **single-tape TMs**.

Fig. 6.9 A two-tape TM

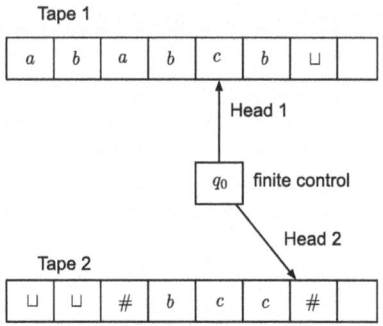

A multi-tape TM variant is the **offline TM**. Tape 1 of an offline TM is ready-only and holds the input. Since a TM cannot detect the left end of the tape without placing a marking, the input tape has marks immediately on the left and right of the input. These marks are special symbols that the machine must not write anywhere else. The other tapes permit reading and writing. We use the offline TM model to assess the amount of storage a TM must use.

6.2.2   Examples of Multi-tape TMs

Here, we present TM algorithms that take advantage of the availability of multiple tapes.

Conceiving algorithms for TMs is often easy when additional tapes are available. Let us examine $\{a^n b^n a^n \mid n \geq 0\}$ from the previous section. A two-tape TM may use the following algorithm for deciding the language:

- If the input is ϵ, accept.
- If the input starts with a b, reject.
- Copy the prefix of the input consisting of a to Tape 2.
- Accept if the remainder of the input matches $b^+ a^+$ such that the b-portion and the a-portion have the same lengths as the copy on Tape 2; reject otherwise.

More specifically, we envision using the following algorithm, where c_1 represents the symbol Head 1 is seeing and c_2 represents the symbol Head 2 is seeing:

1. **Initial Check**   If $c_1 = \sqcup$, accept; if $c_1 = b$, reject; if $c_1 = a$, write an x on Tape 2 as the end marker, move Head 2 to the right neighbor, and proceed to the next step.
2. **Copying the leading as**   If $c_1 = a$, write a on Tape 2 and move both heads to the right neighbor; if $c_1 = \sqcup$, reject; if $c_1 = b$, move Head 2 to the left neighbor without moving Head 1 and proceed to the next step.
3. **Matching the copied as and the following bs**   If $c_1 = b$ and $c_2 = a$, move Head 1 to the left neighbor and Head 2 to the right neighbor; if $c_1 = \sqcup$, reject; if $c_1 = b$ and $c_2 = x$, reject; if $c_1 = a$ and $c_2 = x$, move Head 2 to the right neighbor without moving Head 1 and proceed to the next step.

Table 6.3 The transition table of a two-tape TM that decides $\{a^n b^n a^n \mid n \geq 0\}$. The symbol combinations that do not appear on the table are impossible. The empty cells are impossible symbol pairs

	q_0	q_1	q_2	q_3
$(⊔, ⊔)$	$(q_{acc}, ⊔, -, ⊔, -)$	$(q_{rej}, ⊔, -, ⊔, -)$		$(q_{acc}, ⊔, -, ⊔, -)$
$(a, ⊔)$	$(q_1, a, -, x, R)$	(q_1, a, R, a, R)		$(q_{rej}, a, -, ⊔, -)$
$(b, ⊔)$	$(q_{rej}, b, -, ⊔, -)$	$(q_2, b, -, ⊔, R)$		
(b, a)			(q_2, b, L, a, L)	
(a, x)			$(q_3, a, -, x, R)$	
(a, b)				(q_3, a, R, b, R)
(a, a)			$(q_{rej}, a, -, a, -)$	
(b, x)			$(q_{rej}, b, -, x, -)$	
$(⊔, a)$			$(q_{rej}, ⊔, -, a, -)$	

Fig. 6.10 The ID sequence
of the TM accepting *aabbaa*

$$
\begin{array}{ll}
q_0 & \tilde{a}\ \tilde{⊔}\ a\ ⊔\ b\ ⊔\ b\ ⊔\ a\ ⊔\ a\ ⊔ \\
q_1 & \tilde{a}\ x\ a\ \tilde{⊔}\ b\ ⊔\ b\ ⊔\ a\ ⊔\ a\ ⊔ \\
q_1 & a\ x\ \tilde{a}\ a\ b\ \tilde{⊔}\ b\ ⊔\ a\ ⊔\ a\ ⊔ \\
q_1 & a\ x\ a\ a\ \tilde{b}\ a\ b\ \tilde{⊔}\ a\ ⊔\ a\ ⊔ \\
q_2 & a\ x\ a\ a\ \tilde{b}\ \tilde{a}\ b\ ⊔\ a\ ⊔\ a\ ⊔ \\
q_2 & a\ x\ a\ \tilde{a}\ b\ a\ b\ \tilde{⊔}\ a\ ⊔\ a\ ⊔ \\
q_2 & a\ \tilde{x}\ a\ a\ b\ a\ b\ ⊔\ \tilde{a}\ ⊔\ a\ ⊔ \\
q_3 & a\ x\ a\ \tilde{a}\ b\ a\ b\ ⊔\ \tilde{a}\ ⊔\ a\ ⊔ \\
q_3 & a\ x\ a\ a\ b\ \tilde{a}\ b\ ⊔\ a\ ⊔\ \tilde{a}\ ⊔ \\
q_3 & a\ x\ a\ a\ b\ a\ b\ \tilde{⊔}\ a\ ⊔\ \tilde{a}\ ⊔\ \tilde{⊔}\ ⊔ \\
q_{acc} & a\ x\ a\ a\ b\ a\ b\ \tilde{⊔}\ a\ ⊔\ \tilde{a}\ ⊔\ \tilde{⊔}\ ⊔ \\
\end{array}
$$

4. **Matching the copied *as* and the trailing *as*** If $c_1 = c_2 = a$, move both heads to the right neighbor; if exactly one of c_1 and c_2 is a, reject; if $c_1 = c_2 = ⊔$, accept.

We can implement the algorithm using four non-halting states (q_0, q_1, q_2, and q_3) in addition to q_{acc} and q_{rej}. The initial state is q_0. We transpose the transition Table 6.3 so that the columns represent the states and the rows represent the symbol pairs.

For multi-tape TMs, we similarly define configurations and IDs like that for single-tape TMs. Since the heads of multi-tape TMs move independently, the positions of the heads may differ among the heads. Thus, we use IDs by placing a state-representing symbol at the start.

Figure 6.10 shows an ID sequence of the two-tape TM defined for the input *aabbaa*.

6.2.3 Simulating Multi-tape TMs Using Single-Tape TMs

Although the availability of multiple tapes enriches the algorithm design strategies, single-tape TMs can do whatever multi-tape TMs can do. We delve into this on a technical level by proving the following theorem.

Theorem 6.1 *A language is decidable if, and only if, a multi-tape TM decides the language.*

Proof Overview
A single-tape TM can simulate a multi-tape TM by storing an ID of a multi-tape TM on its sole tape. The format of the single-tape encoding can be one connecting the tape contents with a delimiter in between (horizontal concatenation) or one grouping the tape cells at the same cell indices together (vertical slicing). We use the latter in this proof. After converting the input to an initial ID, the machine keeps updating the string by following the instructions of the multi-tape machine until the ID becomes either accepting or rejecting. At this point, the single-tape machine accepts or rejects the input.

Proof Let $k \geq 2$. Let $M = (Q, \Gamma, \sqcup, \Sigma, \delta, q_0, q_{acc}, q_{rej})$ be a k-tape TM. We aim to design a single-tape TM, S, that simulates M.

We encode the IDs of M using a format in which the state-representing symbol appears at the start. Since there is no limit on the size of the alphabet, we introduce a set of symbols representing $(\Gamma \cup \tilde{\Gamma})^k$. Each k-tuple encodes the k symbols appearing in the cells with the same cell number.

The TM S's input tape alphabet equals M's. The tape alphabet of S is the union of Γ, Q, and $(\Gamma \cup \tilde{\Gamma})^k$. The squiggle version of the alphabet indicates the existence of the head on the cell. Using this extended alphabet, the first five steps of the two-tape program with input *aabbaa* have the series of single-tape encodings as shown in Fig. 6.11.

We now return to the simulation.

An alternate view of the encoding using multiple symbols appearing in the same cells uses tape tracks. A reader familiar with cassette tapes may know that the tapes are horizontally divided into four tracks, representing the left and right audio channels of Side A and Side B. The components are vertically represented in this representation, and the elements at the same component positions are viewed as tracks. The previous presentation thus can be presented using tracks as shown in Fig. 6.12

We now return to the simulation.

We use θ to represent the transition function of S. In this simulation, S first addresses any case where the input is empty. We can assume that S knows whether

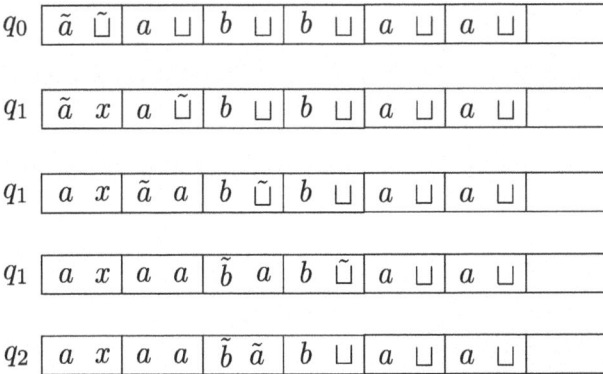

Fig. 6.11 An example of double-character encoding. Two symbols appearing in one box are a double-character encoding

Fig. 6.12 An example of double-track encoding. Two symbols aligned vertically are at the same cell positions

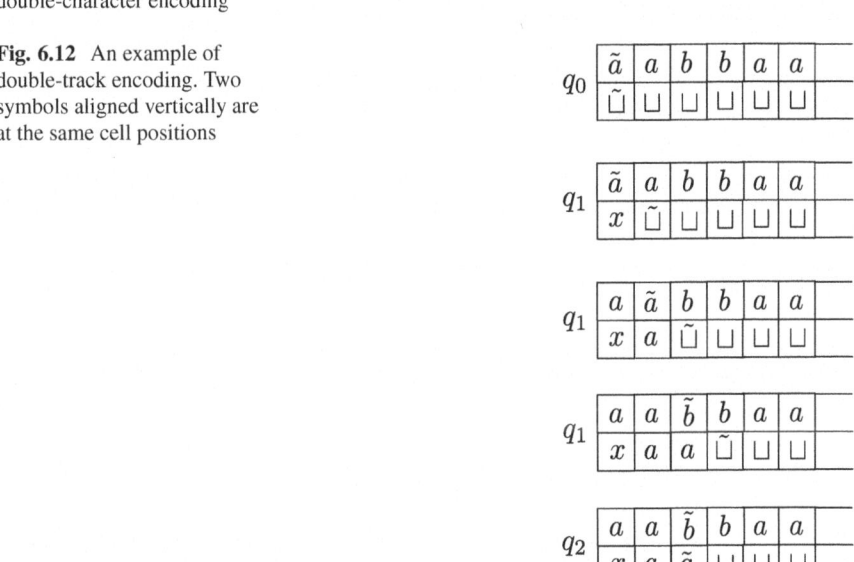

or not $\epsilon \in L(M)$. In the first step, if S sees the character is $\sqcup$, S accepts or rejects accordingly. Otherwise, S executes the following simulation program.

The machine S prepares for simulation by converting the input to a k-tuple form with a leading state-representing symbol. If the input is $x_1 \cdots x_m$, where $m \geq 1$ and $x_1, \ldots, x_m \in \Gamma$, then S converts it to:

$$q_0 \quad \tilde{x}_1 \tilde{\sqcup}^{k-1} \quad x_2 \sqcup^{k-1} \quad \cdots \quad x_m \sqcup^{k-1}.$$

We can adapt the insertion algorithm from the previous section for the conversion (see Exercise 6.12).

The simulation's main idea is to scan the tape to identify which k symbols M is presently seeing through its heads.

A straightforward method for the discovery task is to make k round-trips of the tape content. At the j-th round, the goal of the round-trip is to discover the symbol on the j-th tape. Scanning the head from the left end to the cell index where any head has ever reached reveals the symbol as the j-th component, which has a squiggle in the k-tuple encoding. There is exactly one such tuple, so the scan successfully finds the symbol. While making the k round-trips, S can record M's state as part of its state. More specifically, S's state can combine the following:

- An indication that S is in the discovery mode
- The value of the trip number j
- The direction (left or right) in which S is moving the head
- The symbols S has discovered (the number of symbols is $j - 1$ for a forward scan and j otherwise)

We imagine that this information is accumulated in the state. The number of possible combinations is fixed and independent of the input length. To initialize a round-trip, S moves the head to the left until it encounters a cell holding a state of M.

Once the k symbols have been identified, S can decide how the tape should be updated, as well as the state of M in the next step. Then, using another set of k round-trips, S can update the content of its tape.

Now, let us get into the details of the simulation. The simulation uses six steps as follows:

1. For $j = 1, \ldots, k$, move the head to the right to locate the cell containing a k-tuple whose j-th component has a squiggle. Upon finding the cell, memorize the j-th component, and move the head back to the leftmost cell (i.e., the cell containing a state-representing symbol).

   After completing the discovery, determine the instruction M is about to perform. Accept if M has reached q_{acc} and reject if it has reached q_{rej}. Otherwise, rewrite the state-representing symbol.

2. If M does not halt, move the head to Cell 2. If a squiggle appears on some tape and the head on the tape must move to the left, the head's actual move is stationary because of the bounceback. The machine S revises the head's move to stationary. Move the head to Cell 1.

3. For each $j = k, \ldots, 1$, scan to the right, looking for a cell whose j-th component has a squiggle. Then:

   (a) Rewrite the j-th component according to the action M is to take.
   (b) If the head movement is to the right, remove the marking and reattach it to the right neighbor. If the right neighbor is not in a k-tuple form, change it to a k-tuple form (it must be "all $\sqcup$") before adding the mark.
   (c) If the head movement is to the left, remove the marking on the j-th component and reattach to the left neighbor.
   (d) Move the head back to the leftmost cell.

We now describe the implementations of this algorithm.   □

6.2.3.1   Discovering the Symbols

This step uses states of the form:

$$q_{\text{find}}(a_1, \ldots, a_{j-1}, ?), 1 \leq j \leq k, a_1, \ldots, a_j \in \Gamma$$

and

$$q_{\text{found}}(a_1, \ldots, a_j), 1 \leq j \leq k, a_1, \ldots, a_j \in \Gamma.$$

For each j, the former type is used to find the cell with a squiggle on the j-th component. In the state $q_{\text{find}}(a_1, \ldots, a_{j-1}, ?)$, S moves the head to the right. Upon encountering a cell with a squiggle on the j-th component, S switches to the latter type with the symbol on the j-th component, say, a_j, replacing the state name's j-th component. The new state is thus $q_{\text{found}}(a_1, \ldots, a_{j-1}, a_j)$. In the state, S moves the head to the left until it returns to Cell 1. Upon returning to Cell 1, if $j < k$, the state switches to $q_{\text{find}}(a_1, \ldots, a_j, ?)$. If $j = k$, S examines M's state, say, p, in Cell 1 and determines the action of M given by:

$$\delta(p, a_1, \ldots, a_k) = (p', b_1, \ldots, b_k, e_1, \ldots, e_k).$$

Here, $p' \in Q, b_1, \ldots, b_k \in \Gamma$, and $e_1, \ldots, e_k \in D$. The determination is by entering a state. The state is q_{acc} if $p' = q_{\text{acc}}$ and q_{rej} if $p' = q_{\text{rej}}$. Otherwise, S writes p' in Cell 1 and enters the state:

$$r_1(b_1, e_1, \ldots, b_k, e_k).$$

6.2.3.2   Determining What to Update

If the state is $r_1(b_1, e_1, \ldots, b_k, e_k)$, S moves to the right neighbor (Cell 2) and changes the state to $r_2(b_1, e_1, \ldots, b_k, e_k)$. If the state is $r_2(b_1, e_1, \ldots, b_k, e_k)$, S scans the symbol in Cell 2, returns to Cell 1, and changes the state to:

$$q_{\text{write}}(b_1, e'_1, \ldots, b_k, e'_k).$$

Here, for all j, $e'_j = e_j$, if either the squiggle is absent on the j-th component of k-tuple symbol in Cell 2 or $e_j = L$; otherwise, $e'_j = -$. Replacing e_j with e'_j incorporates the bounceback on Tape j.

6.2.3.3   Executing the Updates

The machine uses three groups of states:

1. $q_{\text{write}}(b_1, e_1, \ldots, b_j, e_j)$
2. $q_{\text{write}+}(b_1, e_1, \ldots, b_j, e_j)$
3. $q_{\text{written}}(b_1, e_1, \ldots, b_j, e_j)$

Here, $1 \leq j \leq k, r \in Q, b_1, \ldots, b_j \in \Gamma$, and $e_1, \ldots, e_j \in D$. The first group is for scanning to the right for the cell with the squiggle on the j-th component. Upon finding the cell, the machine changes the j-th component to b_j without squiggle. In addition, the machine moves the head to the right neighbor if $e_j = R$ and to the left neighbor if $e_j = L$. Then the machine enters $q_{\text{write}+}(b_1, e_1, \ldots, b_j, e_j)$. In $q_{\text{write}+}(b_1, e_1, \ldots, b_j, e_j)$, the machine adds squiggle to the j-th component and enters $q_{\text{written}}(b_1, e_1, \ldots, b_j, e_j)$, in which the machine moves the head to the leftmost position. Returning the head to the leftmost position completes the round for j, so the machine switches to the next round, $j - 1$. Upon entering $q_{\text{written}}()$, S changes its state to $q_{\text{find}}(?)$ and commences the simulation of the next step of M. The simulation requires k round-trips in Step 1 and Step 3 for each step of M. □

If the multi-tape TM has reached the farthest position d, each round-trip may require as many as $2d$ steps. With k tapes to examine individually, each procedure may require as many as $2kd$ steps. It is possible to compress the k trips into one by discovering the symbols the heads see in the increasing order of their position. We leave the detail of the algorithm to the reader (see Exercise 6.12), but the alternate procedures require $\leq 2d$ steps for discovery and $\leq 2d + 2k$ steps for rewriting.

The proof above applies to recognizers.

Theorem 6.2 *A language is recursively enumerable if, and only if, a multi-tape TM recognizes the language.*

6.2.3.4   R Is the Intersection of RE and coRE

Here, we study the relations between R and RE.

The multi-tape TM model offers an essential characterization of R.

Theorem 6.3 $R = RE \cap \text{coRE}$; *that is, a language is recursive if, and only if, it is both recursively enumerable and co-recursively enumerable.*

Proof Overview
A two-tape TM can simulate two single-tape TMs concurrently. If the two machines recognize complementary languages, the concurrent two-tape simulation finds which of the two machines accepts the input. The two-tape machine can then decide whether or not it should accept the input.

Proof Let $A \subseteq \Sigma^*$ be a recursive language. Then, by Proposition 6.1, $\overline{A}$ is recursive. Since a recursive language is already recursively enumerable, we know that A and $\overline{A}$ are recursively enumerable. Thus, $R \subseteq RE \cap coRE$.

Conversely, suppose that a language A is recursively enumerable and co-recursively enumerable. Let $M = (Q, \Gamma, \sqcup, \Sigma, \delta, q_0, q_{acc}, q_{rej})$ be a recognizer for A. Let $M' = (Q', \Gamma', \sqcup, \Sigma, \delta', q_0', q_{acc}, q_{rej})$ be a recognizer for $\overline{A}$. Then, for all inputs x,

- If $x \in A$, then M_1 on x accepts and M_2 on x does not accept.
- If $x \notin A$, then M_1 on x does not accept and M_2 on x accepts.

We construct a two-tape TM N for A. On all inputs x, N simulates M_1 on input x using Tape 1 and M_2 on x using Tape 2 concurrently. The TM N prepares its concurrent simulations using the following algorithm:

1. If the head on Tape 1 sees $\sqcup$ at the start, the input is ϵ. The TM N accepts or rejects depending on whether or not ϵ is a member of A.
2. Otherwise, N creates a copy of the input on Tape 2. After that, N moves each head to Cell 1 (see Exercise 6.10).
3. The TM N concurrently simulates M_1 with Tape 1 and M_2 with Tape 2, one step at a time. The transition function, θ, during the simulation, uses the Cartesian product $Q_1 \times Q_2$ as the states:

$$\theta((q, q'), a, a') = ((p, p'), b, d, b', d').$$

Here, $a \in \Gamma, a' \in \Gamma'$, $\delta(q, a) = (p, b, d)$, and $\delta'(q', a') = (p', b', d')$. There are two exceptions; if $p = q_{acc}$ or $p' = q_{rej}$, use q_{acc} in place of (p, p'), and if $p = q_{rej}$ or $p' = q_{acc}$, use q_{rej} in place of (p, p').

As discussed earlier, exactly one of the two simulations enters q_{acc}, so N accepts all members of A and rejects all members of $\overline{A}$. Thus, N decides A.   □

6.3 The Nondeterministic Turing Machine (NTM) Model

We stipulate that the transition function of a TM does not necessarily have exactly one value for all state-symbol combinations. This stipulation gives rise to the **nondeterministic Turing machine (NTM)** model. In contrast with NTMs, we call the TM model we have studied in the previous sections **deterministic Turing machines (DTMs)**.

A mathematical definition of an NTM uses the same kind of tuples as the DTM, i.e., the definition uses an eight-tuple $(Q, \Gamma, \sqcup, \Sigma, \delta, q_0, q_{acc}, q_{rej})$. Here, δ is a mapping from $Q \times \Gamma$ to the power set of $Q \times \Gamma \times D$, where $D = \{L, R, -\}$. An NTM may abort its computation if there is no action to perform in the transition function. NTMs offer no guarantee of condensed outcomes. On one halting computation path, the machine may enter q_{acc}, while on another path, the machine may enter q_{rej}. NTMs also may produce computation paths that run forever.

We say that an NTM **accepts** an input x if it enters q_{acc} for some computation path with x as the input.

Definition 6.5 An NTM M **recognizes** a language if for all inputs, x, the following properties hold:

- If x is in the language, M accepts x on some computation path.
- If x is not in the language, M does not accept x on any computation path.

We introduce an NTM with a guarantee of **halting**.

Definition 6.6 A halting NTM halts on all inputs regardless of its action choices.

Definition 6.7 An NTM M **decides** a language if M is a halting machine and recognizes the language.

The single-tape simulation technique for DTMs can be applied to NTMs.

Theorem 6.4 *For each multi-tape NTM N, a single-tape NTM S recognizes the same language as N. Furthermore, if N is a decider, S is a decider.*

Like the finite automaton models, the availability of nondeterministic choices does not increase the fundamental computation power of TMs.

Theorem 6.5 *A language is recursively enumerable if, and only if, an NTM recognizes it. Furthermore, a language is recursive if, and only if, an NTM decides it.*

Proof Overview
Since each DTM is a special NTM, every language a DTM decides is decidable by an NTM, and every language a DRM recognizes is recognizable by an NTM. Thus, our task is to show that every language an NTM decides is decidable by a DTM and every language an NTM recognizes is recognizable by a DTM. The single-tape simulation method from the proof of Theorem 6.1 also applies to NTMs, so we consider simulating single-tape NTMs with multi-tape DTMs. Specifically, we show that for each single-tape NTM N, a three-tape DTM can simulate S. We construct S so that for each input x, S's simulation has the following outcome:

- If N accepts x, S finds an accepting computation of N on x in a finite time and accepts x.
- If N does not accept x, S does not accept.
- If N is a halting machine, S rejects x.

(continued)

The three-tape simulator tries all computation paths whose lengths are no more than ℓ, with ℓ increasing from 1 to higher numbers. Since S examines N's computation paths exhaustively, if N accepts, S eventually finds an accepting computation path when ℓ is large enough.

Proof All DTMs are NTMs, by definition. Thus, each recursively enumerable language has an NTM recognizer, and each recursive language has an NTM decider.

For the other inclusions, we show that NTMs can be simulated by DTMs. Let $N = (Q, \Gamma, \sqcup, \Sigma, \delta, q_0, q_{acc}, q_{rej})$ be an arbitrary single-tape NTM. We modify N so its transition function has at most two possible values for each state-symbol combination.

- If $\delta(q, a)$ has $m \geq 3$ values $(r_1, b_1, d_1), \ldots, (r_m, b_m, d_m)$, we add $m - 2$ intermediate states, say $p_1, p_2, \ldots, p_{m-2}$, and a series of transitions:

  - $\delta(q, a)$ has two values, (r_1, b_1, d_1) and $(p_1, a, -)$.
  - For each i such that $1 \leq i \leq m - 3$, $\delta(p_i, a)$ has two values, $(r_{i+1}, b_{i+1}, d_{i+1})$ and $(p_{i+1}, a, -)$.
  - $\delta(p_{m-2}, a)$ has two values, $(r_{m-1}, b_{m-1}, d_{m-1})$ and (r_m, b_m, d_m).

Figure 6.13 shows the result of such a conversion. The modification preserves the overall acceptance behavior. The original version of N accepts if, and only if, the modified version accepts.

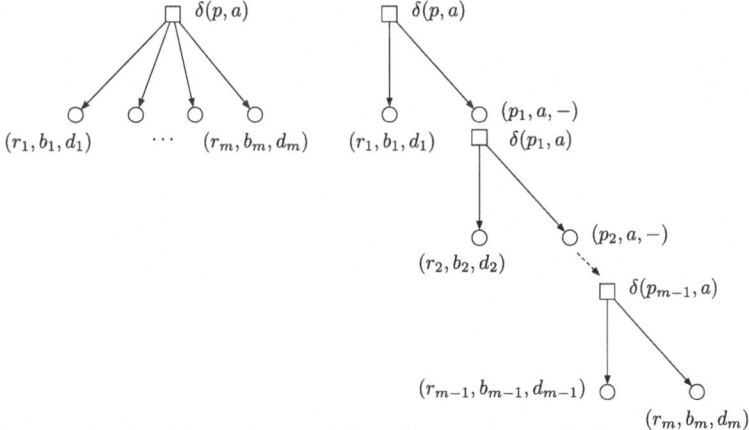

Fig. 6.13 The mechanism for reducing the number of branches to 2. The boxes represent the input to the transition function, and the circles represent the elements and values of the transition function

Fig. 6.14 Simulating an
NTM deterministically using
three tapes. The top three
lines show the tape contents
at the start of computation.
The bottom three lines show
the tape contents immediately
after preparation

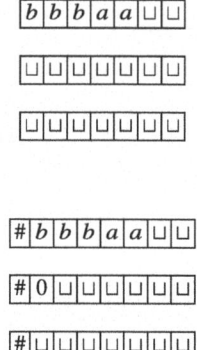

The role of the three tapes is as follows:

- On Tape 1, S preserves the input.
- On Tape 2, S generates computation paths.
- On Tape 3, S simulates N's tape.

Let x be an arbitrary input to M. The string x also appears on S's Tape 1 at the start.

The machine S prepares for its simulation by inserting a left-end marker, #, on all three tapes, and then appends 0 on the second tape (see Fig. 6.14). We can adapt the character insertion algorithm from Sect. 6.1.1 for this purpose.

The string appearing on Tape 2 after the marker is a binary representation encoding the branches to follow. Since the transition function of N has at most two possible values for each state-symbol combination, the i-th character after the marking represents which of the two branches S must follow. The interpretation is 0 for the first choice and 1 for the second. The machine S follows the computation of N using the branch sequence as a guide. S simulates N for no more steps than there are bits in the guide.

When S finishes its simulation on the present path, it rewrites the encoding into the next path. The machine accomplishes this updating by changing the leftmost 0 or the leftmost ⊔, whichever comes first, to 1 while changing each 1 it encounters during the search to 0. The paths generated in this manner will be:

#0, #1, #00, #10, #01, #11, #000, #100, #010, #110, #001, #101, #011, #111, ...

We can view these as the downward paths on an infinite complete binary tree and think of S as executing a breadth-first search on the tree.

Now, let us see the details of the deterministic simulation.

Before each simulation, Tape 3 has #⊔ · · · ⊔ as its content. The machine S copies x on Tape 1 to Tape 3 after the #. Then, S commences the simulation of N in the following manner:

- Tape 3 serves as the tape of N.
- If Head 3 sees a # as the result of moving the head to the left, it means N has experienced a bounceback. Thus, S moves the head to Cell 2 before executing the next step of N.
- During the simulation, S marks the farthest cell reached on Tape 3 using a marker, such as a squiggle. If the head is about to go beyond the marker, S removes it and attaches it to whatever appears in the right neighbor (the cell must hold ⊔).
- Let p be the present state of N and let a be the symbol appearing on Tape 3. The simulation of one step of N is as follows:

    - If $\delta(p, a)$ has no value, S aborts the simulation because there is no action to perform.
    - If $\delta(p, a)$ is not empty and the symbol that Head 3 sees is ⊔, S aborts the simulation because the path on Tape 3 is not long enough.
    - If $\delta(p, a)$ has only one value and the symbol that Head 3 sees is not ⊔, S advances with $\delta(p, a)$.
    - If $\delta(p, a)$ has two values and the symbol that Head 3 sees is 0, S advances with the first value.
    - If $\delta(p, a)$ has two values and the symbol that Head 3 sees is 1, S advances with the second value.
    - If the state of N has become q_{acc}, S accepts immediately.
    - If the state of N has become q_{rej}, S moves on to the next path.

- Before proceeding to the next path on the list, S moves the heads on Tapes 1 and 2 back to the leftmost position and clears all the cells it has touched during the simulation. For the erasure, S moves Head 3 to the marking for the farthest position and then brings it back to the leftmost position while writing ⊔ in each cell.
- After the erasure, S updates the computation path on Tape 2.

If $x \in L(N)$, at least one computation path exists along which N on x accepts. Since S generates all possible computations, S eventually finds that N on x accepts and thus accepts. Otherwise, N on x never accepts. Thus, S accepts the same language as M.   □

In the case where M is a halting machine, for every input $x \notin A$, there exists an integer ℓ such that all computation paths having length ℓ lead M to rejection without abortion. The machine S checks the "all rejection" property during its simulation and rejects x if that happens. We explore modifying the action of S in detail as an exercise (see Exercise 6.14).

Theorem 6.6 *A language is decidable if, and only if, an NTM decides the language.*

6.4   Alternate Definitions of RE

This section explores two alternate ways to define recursively enumerable languages. One is by using enumerators, and the other is by using witness schemes.

6.4.1   *Enumerators*

The name "recursively enumerable" comes from the fact that each language in the class has a method for producing all members.

A language A's **enumerator** is a multi-tape TM that writes a list of all members of A on one tape, where each member appears exactly once on the list. More specifically, an enumerator E operates as follows:

- The input is irrelevant to the action of E.
- If A is infinite, E runs forever.
- One tape of E is an "output tape." An output tape is write-only in that (a) the transition function of E ignores that the output tape sees, and (b) the output tape's head does not move to the left.
- When E discovers a new member of A, E appends # and the latest member to the output tape. The list thus takes the form of:

$$\#x_1\#x_2\#x_3\# \cdots .$$

We show that all recursively enumerable languages have enumerators. Then, we show that all languages with enumerators are recursively enumerable.

Theorem 6.7 *A language is recursively enumerable if, and only if, it has an enumerator.*

Proof Overview
Let M be an arbitrary deterministic single-tape TM. We use a five-tape DTM and simulate M. The simulator runs with a round number $\ell = 1, 2, 3$, etc. In the round ℓ, the simulator examines each string whose length is $\leq \ell$ by simulating at most ℓ steps of M's program. Each time the simulator finds that M accepts an input (say, x), the simulator checks whether or not x is already on the list; if not, the simulator adds x to the list. The five tapes are for ℓ, input, M's simulation, output, and output's copy, respectively.

Proof Let $A \subseteq \Sigma^*$ be recursively enumerable. Let M be a single-tape TM that accepts A. Our enumerator, E, has four tapes. A high-level description of E's algorithm is Algorithm 6.3.

Algorithm 6.3 An enumerator for A

1: **procedure** ENUMERATOR-FOR-A
2:   initialize the output as the empty string;
3:   **for** $\ell \leftarrow 1, 2, 3, \ldots$ **do**
4:     **for** $w \in \Sigma^{\leq \ell}$ **do**
5:       simulate M on w for at most ℓ steps;
6:       **if** M accepts w **then**
7:         **if** w does not appear on the output **then**
8:           append #w to the list;
9:           add w to λ;
10:         **end if**
11:       **end if**
12:     **end for**
13:   **end for**
14: **end procedure**

The algorithm's four-tape implementation is as follows:

- Tape 1 is for specifying the value of ℓ.
- Tape 2 generates the members of $\Sigma^{\leq \ell}$.
- Tape 3 is where E runs simulations of M.
- Tape 4 is the output of E: i.e., #w_1#w_2#$\cdots$ that E finds as members of $L(M)$. There is no left move of the head on Tape 4.
- Tape 5 is an exact copy of Tape 4.

The simulation goes as follows:

- The simulator E moves Head 1 to Cell 2. The simulator E moves Head 2 to Cell 2. The simulator E copies the input from Tape 2 to Tape 3.
- The simulator E executes M using Tape 3 as its tape. During the simulation, it records the rightmost place Head 3 has visited using a squiggle. At each step, E moves Head 1 to the right neighbor. The simulation ends when Head 1 sees ⊔ or M's state becomes q_{acc} or q_{rej}.

  - If Head 1 arrives at a cell showing ⊔, E aborts the simulation for the present input.
  - If M's state becomes q_{rej}, E moves to the next simulation.
  - If M's state becomes q_{acc}, E compares the input with the strings appearing on Tape 5.

    · The simulator E moves Head 2 to Cell 1 and compares the content to the right of # with each member appearing in Tape 5.
    · It compares each string after # with the input in Tape 2, character by character.

· If there is no match (different symbols or either string longer than the other), E moves to the following comparison by moving Head 2 to Cell 1.

· If there is a match, E has already identified the input as a member, so it moves to the next simulation. Otherwise, E appends # and the input to Tapes 4 and 5.

– In all cases, the preparation for the next simulation is as follows:

· Move all the heads to Cell 1.

· On Tape 2, E scans to the right from # and locates a cell holding a symbol not equal to a_c. If the symbol is a_d such that $d < c$, change it to a_{d+1}; otherwise, change it to a_1. During the scan, change each a_c to a_1. Also, when Head 2 moves to the right neighbor, E moves Head 1 to the right neighbor.

· After updating is complete, if Head 1 sees ⊔, the content of Tape 2 must be #$a_1 \cdots a_1$. The simulator E changes the ⊔ to 0, indicating that the simulation for round ℓ is over.

Let w be an arbitrary member of A. Let t_0 be an integer such that M on w enters q_{acc} at step τ. Let t_1 be the larger of $|w|$ and t_0. Then E simulates M on w for all $\ell \geq |w|$ and finds that M on w accepts for all $\ell \geq t_1$. Specifically, the latter occurs when $\ell = t_1$ for the first time, so E adds w to the output. This completes the proof that every recursively enumerable language has an enumerator.

Conversely, suppose a language A has an enumerator E. Let D be a TM that, on input x, runs E, compares x with each new member on the list that E produces, and accepts if there is a match. Because E is an enumerator if x is a member of A, E eventually adds x to the list, although D does not necessarily know when. On the other hand, if x is not a member of A, E never produces x on the list, so D never accepts x. Thus, D accepts A.   □

An enumerator may not make its enumeration in lexicographic order. For example, if M accepts 00 in eight steps, 0001 in six steps, 1100 in six steps, and all other members in more than eight steps, then the output E generates starts with

$$\#1100\#0001\#00\# \cdots .$$

Furthermore, if an enumerator produces its output strings in the lexicographic order, then A is recursive. We prove this in Exercise 6.11.

6.4.2   Witness Schemes

Another characterization of RE is by way of witness languages.

Let L be recursively enumerable. Let M be a TM that recognizes L. Define A as the language of all pairs $\langle x, C_1 \# \cdots \# C_m \rangle$ such that $C_1, \ldots, C_m$ are IDs of M, C_1 is the initial ID of M on x, C_m is an accepting ID, and for all i such that $1 \leq i \leq m - 1$, C_{i+1} is the next ID of C_i }. The language A is decidable, and for all x:

$$x \in L \iff (\exists y)[\langle x, y \rangle \in A].$$

In this formulation, A is a **recursive witness language** for L, and any y satisfying the right-hand side of the equivalence is a **witness** for $x \in L$ concerning A. Based on the membership condition, we can show that L is in RE (see Exercise 6.30).

Thus, we have:

Theorem 6.8 *A language L is in RE if, and only if, L has a recursive witness language.*

6.5   Computing Functions Using TMs and the Church-Turing Thesis

We define TMs that compute functions by extending the idea from Theorem 6.7. A TM that computes a function is a **transducer**, while a TM that decides a language is a **decider**. A transducer accepts all inputs; its output is the tape's content when it halts, ignoring the trailing $\sqcup$.

Definition 6.8 Let Σ and Γ be alphabets. Let f be a function from Σ^* to Γ^*. We say that f is computable if a TM M is a transducer such that for all $x \in \Sigma^*$, the output of M on input x is $f(x)$.

Although transductions appear more complex than decisions, we can build transductions from decisions. Let f be a function from Σ^* to Γ^*. Let # be a symbol not in $\Sigma \cup \Gamma$. Let 0 be another symbol.

Define:
$$A_f = \{x \# 0^k \# a \mid x \in \Sigma^*, k \geq 1, a \in \Gamma, \text{ and the } k\text{'s character of } f(x) \text{ is } a\}.$$

Proposition 6.2 *The function f is computable if, and only if, A_f is decidable.*

We leave the proof of the proposition to the reader.

We can encode an arbitrarily long list of arbitrary large integers using just one tape of a TM and process it dynamically with insertion, deletion, indexing, and search as permissible operations (see Exercise 6.18). The ability to mimic a dynamic list empowers TMs to simulate an arbitrary computer code. The observation emboldens us to hypothesize that TMs can compute everything that is computable; we call this idea the **Church-Turing thesis**.

Conjecture 6.1 A function on natural numbers is computable with an algorithm if, and only if, it is computable by a TM.

A computing system that can compute something a TM cannot is unknown. However, researchers have shown that the TM model is as powerful as all known programming languages, and the bit size of each dataset and the number of variables are unlimited.

Exercises

6.1 Give a single-tape TM program for the following languages:

1. $\{w \in \{a, b\}^+ \mid w$ has the same number of as as bs$\}$.
2. $\{w \in \{a, b\}^+ \mid |w|$ is even and w is not a palindrome$\}$.
3. $\{w\#w \mid w \in \{a, b\}^+\}$.
4. $\{a^i b^j c^k \mid 0 < i < j < k\}$.
5. $\{a^n b^n c^n \mid n \geq 0\}$.

6.2 The program for $\{a^n b^n a^n \mid n \geq 0\}$ we reviewed had six states other than q_{acc} and q_{rej}. We can reduce the number of states from six to five by changing the order of finding a triple to the leftmost a, the rightmost a, and the rightmost b in between. Give a TM that accommodates this modification.

6.3 It is possible to generalize the idea of input preservation by introducing an auxiliary tape alphabet $\Gamma \times \Gamma$ and its squiggled version in addition to Γ. Here, $(a, b) \in \Gamma \times \Gamma$ represents that the cell had a originally, which now is replaced with b. Each element $(\tilde{a}, \tilde{b})$ in the squiggled version is for use in Cell 1.

Describe how a TM can use the Cartesian-product alphabets and recover the input.

6.4 Suppose a two-tape TM has a string $\#a$ on Tape 1 and $\#b$ on Tape 2, where both a and b are binary. Write a code for this machine to compare a and b for equality. You may assume the following: (a) At the start, the heads are on the cells that contain $\#$. (b) At the end of the comparison, the TM enters q_{acc} if $a = b$ and q_{rej} otherwise.

6.5 Suppose a two-tape TM has $\#xz$ on Tape 1 and $\#y$ on Tape 2, where $x, y, z \in \{0, 1\}^*$. Write a code for this machine to insert y between x and z in the following manner:

(a)   At the start, the head of Tape 1 is on the cell immediately to the right of x. Also, the head of Tape 2 is on the cell immediately to the right of y.
(b)   The machine appends $\#z$ after y on Tape 2 while erasing z on Tape 1.
(c)   Copy yz (without the $\#$ between y and z) after $\#x$ on Tape 1.
(d)   Remove $\#z$ from Tape 2.
(e)   Move the heads to $\#$ and enter q_{acc}.

6.6 Suppose a three-tape TM has $\#0^a$ on Tape 1, $\#0^b$ on Tape 2, and $\#$ on Tape 3, where the heads are initially on their respective $\#$s. Write a program for the TM to append 0^{a+b} after the $\#$ on Tape 3, move the heads back to their $\#$s, and enter q_{acc}.

6.7 Suppose a three-tape TM has $\#0^a$ on Tape 1, $\#0^b$ on Tape 2, and $\#$ on Tape 3, where the heads are initially on their respective $\#$s. Write a program for the TM to append 0^{ab} after the $\#$ on Tape 3, move the heads back to their $\#$s, and enter q_{acc}.

6.8 Write a program for a two-tape TM that receives a binary number $n \geq 1$ on Tape 1 and produces #0^n on Tape 2. Here, n is the integer the input represents. The machine must terminate its computation by entering q_{acc} with Head 2 on the #. Note that the integer that a binary number $b_1 \cdots b_m$ represents is

$$((\cdots((b_1 * 2 + b_2) * 2 + b_3) \cdots) * 2 + b_{m-1}) * 2 + b_m.$$

We can execute "times 2 then plus b" as follows:

- Presently Tape 2 has #0^k for some $k \geq 1$.
- There is an additional bit b indicating the #0^k must turn into #0^{2k+b}.
- Turn each 0 on Tape 2 to 2, starting from the leftmost one, and for each 0, append a 1 at the end.
- After this, the tape contains #$2^k 1^k$. Append one 1 if $b = 1$.
- Move Head 2 back to # while turning each 1 and each 2 to 0.

6.9 Prove Proposition 6.1.

6.10 Write a program for a two-tape TM that copies the input from Tape 1 to Tape 2. After copying, the machine moves the heads to the leftmost positions and enters a state r.

6.11 Prove that if there exists an enumerator for a language A that produces the members of A in the lexigraphic order, then there is a TM that decides A.

6.12 In the proof of Theorem 6.1, the simulation S made k round-trips to find the symbols that the k heads are seeing. It is possible to combine the k round-trips into one by changing the states S uses for discovery so that they record for which tapes S has found the symbol the head is scanning. Provide details for S to execute this discovery.

6.13 Continuing the previous question, describe how S can execute all its actions during k round-trips in just one round-trip.

6.14 Complete the proof of Theorem 6.5 by showing that a DTM can check to see if the present path length covers all possible computation paths of the NTM N.

6.15 Prove Proposition 6.2.

6.16 A two-tape NTM can simulate an arbitrary PDA using the second tape as the stack. Describe how a two-tape NTM can execute such a simulation.

6.17 Think of a PDA with two stacks such that the input appears in the second stack from top to bottom with a special symbol $ appearing at the last symbol of the input as the bottom sign. Show that such a "two-stack PDA" can simulate an arbitrary single-tape TM.

6.18 Describe how to implement a dynamic list of non-negative integers on a multi-tape TM, where an element n on the list takes the encoding 0^n, a symbol # appears at the start of the list, and \$ appears between elements. The operations that the list needs to accommodate are:

- Insertion of an element 0^n at the k-th position on the list, where 0^k is the string that specifies k
- Deletion of an element at the k-th position, where 0^k is the string that specifies k
- Obtaining the element at the k-th position, where 0^k is the string that specifies k
- Obtaining the length, ℓ, of the list as 0^ℓ
- Returning the position of the first occurrence of 0^n

6.19 Show that we can augment each TM M so that at the time of termination, the tape cells hold the blank on each tape, and all the heads are in their leftmost positions.

6.20 Let L be an arbitrary language and α be an arbitrary symbol. Define $L' = \{\alpha w \mid w \in L\}$. Show that L is decidable if, and only if, L' is decidable. In addition, prove that L is recognizable if, and only if, L' is recognizable.

6.21 Prove that R is closed under union, intersection, and complement.

6.22 Prove that R is closed under Kleene-star.

6.23 Prove that RE is closed under union and intersection.

6.24 Prove that RE is closed under Kleene-star.

6.25 The **marked union** of languages A and B is $\{0w \mid w \in A\} \cup \{1w \mid w \in B\}$. We write $A \oplus B$ as the marked union of A and B. We say that a language class C has the closure property under marked union if for all $A, B \in C$, $A \oplus B$ is in C. Prove that the class of recursively enumerable languages has the closure properties under marked union.

6.26 Prove that the class of recursive languages has the closure properties under marked union.

6.27 Describe how a TM with a one-way-infinite tape can simulate another with a two-way-infinite tape.

6.28 Recall that if a TM attempts to move its head to the left when the head is on the leftmost cell, the head does not move. Let M be a single-tape TM that may attempt to make such a move. Answer how this impossible attempt can be avoided by introducing new symbols and modifying M's transition function without changing the language that M recognizes.

6.29 Let M be a single-tape TM whose possible head moves are L, $-$, and R. Answer how another single-tape TM N whose possible head moves are L and R only can simulate M without slowdonw; for all t, N can simulate t steps of M in at most t steps.

6.30 Show that if a language is characterized as the set of all x such that for some y, $\langle x, y \rangle \in A$, where A is recursive, then the language is recursively enumerable.

6.31 Show that if L has a recursive witness scheme as in the previous question and a recursive function exists that computes an upper bound on the length of a witness, then L is recursive.

Bibliographic Notes and Further Reading

Turing introduced the TM in his 1936 paper [8]. In the same year, Church [1], Kleene [4], and Post [6] published their papers proposing models as equally powerful as the TM model. Their papers are available in a compendium by Davis [3] along with their historical importance. The Church-Turing thesis and other equivalent models for the recursively enumerable can be found in Davis [2], Kleene [5], and Rogers [7].

References

1. A. Church, An unsolvable problem of elementary number theory. Am. J. Math. **58**, 345–363 (1936)
2. M. Davis, *Computability and Undecidability* (McGraw-Hill, New York, 1958)
3. M. Davis, *The Undecidable* (Raven Press, New York, 1965)
4. S.C. Kleene, General recursive functions of natural numbers. Math. Ann. **112**, 727–742 (1936)
5. S.C. Kleene, *Introduction to Mathematics* (D. van Nostrand, Princeton, 1952)
6. E.L. Post, Finite combinatory process-formulation, I. J. Symbol Logic **1**, 103–105 (1936)
7. H. Rogers, Jr., *Theory of Recursive Functions and Effective Computability*. (The MIT Press, Cambridge, 1987)
8. A.M. Turing, On computable numbers, with an application to the Entscheidungsproblem. J. Math. **58**(345–363), 5 (1936)

Chapter 7
Decidable Languages

7.1 The Universal TM Model

Here, we will explore the concept of encoding computing devices.

7.1.1 Encoding Schemes

First, we study the properties of TMs and other computing models by defining languages whose members are computing models for which certain conditions hold. This necessitates a scheme for encoding individual computing devices as strings without ambiguity. The previous chapters described devices and their inputs using symbols, mathematical notation, diagrams, and plain text. While we can make those descriptions as accurate as possible, they are complex and can be redundant. Can we simplify those descriptions while maintaining their accuracy?

The answer to this question is positive. Let us derive some simple encoding schemes. A crucial observation necessary here is that the references we make to device components are only abstract. We know that language classes are closed under one-to-one character replacements. Let Σ and Σ' be arbitrary alphabets of equal size. Let h be an arbitrary bijection from Σ to Σ'. Then, h acts as a homomorphism from the languages over Σ to the languages over Σ'. Let L be an arbitrary language over Σ. Let $L' = h(L)$. For all language classes C, $L \in C$ if, and only if, $L' \in C$.

The preservation of class membership under a bijection between alphabets reveals that to study complexity, we need to know how the symbols in the alphabet are related. A similar universality exists in variables within context-free grammars and stack alphabets in PDAs. Thus, we can treat automata and grammars as lists of indices where the indices appear in a specific order.

For example, the following list adequately describes an NFA $(Q, \Sigma, \delta, q_0, F)$:

1. The cardinality of $\|Q\|$
2. The index of q_0 in Q
3. The cardinality of F
4. A list of indices of the states in F
5. The size of Σ_ϵ
6. ϵ's index in Σ_ϵ
7. A list of triples (i.e., the state in the present step, the symbol, and the state in the next step) representing the elements of δ

Here, the indices can be represented as tally strings in $\{0\}^*$; i.e., 0^k represents k as an index. In addition, these indices should be separated with a delimiter in between, and we will use a tally string in $\{1\}^*$, e.g., 1. While a single type of delimiter may be sufficient for encoding NFAs, using multiple delimiters may make extracting information easier.

Suppose the NFA is $Q = \{p_1, p_2\}$, $\Sigma = \{a_1, a_2\}$, $q_0 = p_1$, and $F = \{p_2\}$ and δ comprises of

$$(p_1, a_1) = \{p_2\}, (p_1, \epsilon) = \{p_2\}, \text{and} (p_2, a_2) = \{p_2\}.$$

Then, the encoding can be:

00 111 0 111 0 111 00 111 000 111 010100 11 01000100 11 00100100.

Here, we use three different delimiters: 111 for the top level, 11 between the transition function's triples, and 1 for separating three elements in triples.

If necessary, we can turn these binary encodings into unary encodings. For example, we can use 0^m to encode the binary string whose lexicographic order is m.

We will use these encodings in our studies without specifying the formats used. From now on, we assume an encoding scheme for each computing object type and use $\langle X \rangle$ to represent the encoding. We can connect multiple encodings using a punctuation mark that does not appear in the individual parts. We use $\langle X_1, \ldots, X_k \rangle$ to represent an encoding of objects $X_1, \ldots, X_k$ in such a manner. We call this the **semantic encoding** function.

7.1.2 Fundamental Problems

Now that we have our encoding scheme, we can study how difficult it is to determine the properties of computing devices and the languages they define. We assign the task of determining the properties to TMs. TMs of this sort are similar to those we have seen previously. However, they are expected to (a) receive an encoding as input, (b) validate the encoding while extracting the components of the device(s), (c) analyze the extracted device(s), and (d) simulate the device(s). Such TMs can simulate all TMs. These are called **universal Turing machines ("universal TMs")**.

While the choices of the problems to study may be broad, we have a strong interest in the following fundamental questions:

- **Acceptance** Is a string x a member of a language A?
- **Emptiness** Does a language A have any members?
- **Infiniteness** Does a language A have infinitely many members?
- **Totality** Does a language A include all possible members?
- **Equality** Is a language A equal to another language B?
- **Containment** Is a language A a subset of another language B?

Which language classes shall we consider for these questions? The language classes we have seen are REG, CFL, DCFL, R, and RE. For R, there is no obvious way to specify TMs that are deciders. We thus exclude R and consider only the four remaining classes: REG, CFL, DCFL, and RE. As for REG, we know regular expressions, FAs, and NFAs are equivalent through conversion algorithms. Similarly, for CFL, we know that CFGs, normal-form CFGs, and PDAs are equivalent through conversion algorithms. Thus, we can use any alternative to specify these language classes.

Since we have six types of problems, the total number of fundamental questions we will examine is twenty-four. We combine a property type T and a class type D and write T_D to specify the problem. For example, $\text{ACCEPT}_{\text{REG}}$ is:

- The language of all combinations $\langle M, w \rangle$ such that M is a regular language and $w \in L(M)$

We will identify which of the 24 problems are decidable and, if they do not appear decidable, prove that they are undecidable.

Table 7.1 shows each problem's decidability property.

Table 7.1 The decidability table. The columns are computing devices representing language classes. Cells D and U indicate the decidable and undecidable problems, respectively. Underneath the D/U indicator is the place where the proof appears. The * indicates that the proof is not provided in the book

Type	FA	DPDA	PDA	TM
Acceptance	D	D	D	U
	Theorem 7.1	Corollary 7.3	Theorem 7.7	Theorem 8.2
Emptiness	D	D	D	U
	Theorem 7.2	Corollary 7.3	Exercise 7.9	Corollary 8.2
Infiniteness	D	D	D	U
	Theorem 7.3	Corollary 7.3	Exercise 7.11	Corollary 8.2
Totality	D	D	U	U
	Theorem 7.4	Corollary 7.3	Theorem 8.5	Corollary 8.2
Containment	D	U	U	U
	Theorem 7.5	Theorem 8.7	Corollary 8.5	Corollary 8.3
Equality	D	D*	U	U
	Theorem 7.6	Theorem 7.8	Corollary 8.4	Corollary 8.3

In addition to the twenty-four questions, we study the following question about TMs:

- **The Halting Problem**: Does a TM halt on all inputs?

We show that this problem is undecidable in Theorem 8.3.

7.1.3   Using Universal TMs

The universal TM model mentioned earlier is a primary tool for the classification process.

A universal TM operates similarly to the simulators from Chap. 6. However, the simulations here are more complex than the previous ones because the universal TM simulators need to decode the language objects appearing as part of the input. The size of the objects, e.g., the size of the alphabet, has no limits. Thus, the simulators need to deal with objects of an arbitrary size. To clarify this requirement, consider a problem type T and an object type D. Our universal TM has a fixed number of tapes and receives a binary (or unary) string that could encode an instance. The format of the encoding depends on T and D. A basic algorithm, which appears in Algorithm 7.1, is for the universal TM to test the membership of its input in the language T_D. We may expect that for each combination of T and D, the number of

---

Algorithm 7.1 A universal TM algorithm for T_D

1: **procedure** MEMBERSHIP-FOR-$T_D(w)$
2:     w is an input;
3:     check the validity of input as an encoding;
4:     **if** w is invalid **then**
5:         accept or reject according to the definition of T_D;
6:     **else**
7:         prepare for a simulation by extracting components from w;
8:         simulate to test the membership property;
9:         **if** the simulation is complete **then**
10:             accept reject according to the definition;
11:         **end if**
12:     **end if**
13: **end procedure**

---

components separated by 111 in any valid input is a constant. We can give a fixed number of tapes to our universal TM solving T_D for extracting the components embedded in the input and checking the validity. After successfully verifying the input, our universal TM does some work to check the property T.

7.2   Decidable Fundamental Problems

Here, we present some decidable problems.

7.2.1   Decidable Problems About Regular Languages

We first present decidable problems about regular languages.

7.2.1.1   Acceptance

The accepting problem about regular languages is decidable.

Theorem 7.1 *The following language is decidable:*

$$\text{ACCEPT}_{\text{FA}} = \{\langle M, w \rangle \mid M \text{ is a DFA accepting } w\}.$$

Proof We will develop a multi-tape universal TM, U, that decides the language
$\text{ACCEPT}_{\text{FA}}$. We assume that the input alphabet of U is in binary. Let x be an input
U. U operates as follows:

First, U checks the validity of the input. While confirming the validity, U extracts
the DFA and its associated input from x. Let us call the DFA M and the input w.
U can use its tapes to store the components of M. If the validity checking fails, U
rejects x immediately.

Next, U simulates M and an input w, which will terminate in a finite number of
steps. Then, U accepts x if M accepts w in the simulation and rejects x otherwise.

Next are more details about the action of U.

U extracts the following information about M, according to its expected
encoding scheme:

1. The cardinality of the state set
2. The cardinality of the alphabet
3. The transition table as a list of triples, where the components of each triple are
   separated by 1 and the triples are separated by 11
4. The index of the initial state
5. The list of final states with 1 in between
6. The input w as a sequence of numbers separated by 1

U writes these numbers as tallies of 0 (as they appear in the input w). U may write
these six components on six separate tapes. In addition, U may write the components
with a left-end mark (e.g., #) in front for convenience.

The validity checks U conducts are the following:

- The transition table must be a series of triples in the format mentioned previously. In each triple, the first and third components must be between 1 and the state set's cardinality, and the second component must be between 1 and the alphabet's cardinality. In addition, for each combination of a state number and a symbol number, a unique triple must exist whose first component matches the state number and whose second component matches the symbol number.
- The initial state must be between 1 and the state set's cardinality.
- Each final state must be between 1 and the state set's cardinality.
- Each element of the input w must be between 1 and the alphabet's cardinality.

Figure 7.1 presents the contents of the six tapes that U extracts from the input.

Let $(Q, \Sigma, \delta, q_0, F)$ be the DFA M. After confirming the validity, U operates as follows:

1. U will use yet another tape to record M's state during simulation. U initializes the value with the initial state number.
2. U reads the index of each symbol in w. For each symbol index, U compares the present state and symbol numbers with the first two components of all the triples in the transition information. A unique match must exist because the $\langle M, w \rangle$ passed the validity test. U extracts the third component from the triple and updates M's state with the third component.
3. Upon processing all the input symbols, U compares M's state with each final state. If a match exists, U accepts x; otherwise, it rejects x.

Comparing two numbers appearing in separate tapes is relatively easy for U since the numbers are tallies. U can compare them by moving the heads on the two tapes in one direction, starting from one end of the tally, aiming for the other end, and checking if the heads will simultaneously arrive at any symbol other than 0.

We see that U can execute all its work in a finite amount of steps. Thus, U decides ACCEPT$_{FA}$.   □

Fig. 7.1 The six tapes after extracting information from the input

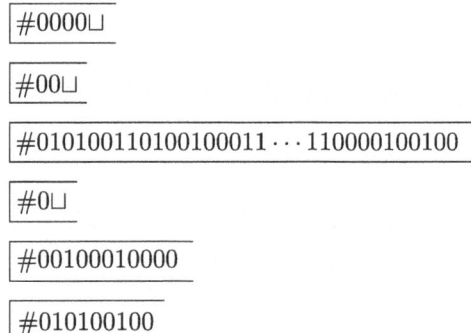

7.2.1.2 Emptiness

Like the acceptance problem, the emptiness problem is decidable.

Theorem 7.2 *The following language is decidable:*

$$\text{EMPTY}_{\text{FA}} = \{\langle M \rangle \mid M \text{ is a DFA that accepts no input}\}.$$

Proof Overview
Unlike the acceptance problem, the emptiness problem does not specify an input. We can consider simulating the DFA on each possible input to determine if a given DFA accepts any input. This question is complementary to the emptiness question. The input can be generated one after another in lexicographic order. If the DFA accepts any input, we know the emptiness question is negative. However, the simulation will never stop if the DFA accepts no input. Thus, the strategy puts the emptiness problem in coRE but not necessarily in R. Is there a way to terminate the simulation when the DFA does not accept input? Indeed, there is a strategy for termination. According to the Pumping Lemma, if an m-state DFA accepts a string w having a length $\geq m$, the removal of the y-part of the xyz decomposition produces a string the DFA agrees with that is shorter than w. Thus, the examination of input in lexicographic order can be terminated when we discover that no strings having a length $<m$ are accepted.

Proof We develop a universal TM, U, that decides the language. As with the proof of Theorem 7.1, the initial action of U is to validate its input x as an encoding of a DFA and extract the information from that input. As with the previous proof, U rejects x if U finds that x is invalid.

Assuming that x is valid, U advances to testing emptiness. Let M be the DFA and n be the cardinality of M's state set.

We then use the following proposition in the emptiness test:

Proposition 7.1 *A DFA with n states accepts a nonempty set if, and only if, it accepts a string having a length $<n$.*   □

Proof Let M be an arbitrary DFA and n be the number of states of M. Suppose M accepts no input. Then, M accepts no input with a length $<n$.

Conversely, suppose M accepts at least one string. If there is one having a length $<n$, we are done. So, think of a string $u = u_1 \cdots u_k$ that M accepts, whose length $k \geq n$. Here, $u_1, \ldots, u_k$ are from M's alphabet. Then, we can use the Pumping Lemma for regular languages (Lemma 3.3) to obtain xyz as a decomposition of u, where $|y| \geq 1$ and M accepts xz. If $|xz| < n$, we have identified a string M accepts whose length is less than n. Otherwise, we can re-apply the Pumping Lemma to xz to construct another shorter member.

We can repeat the decomposition-then-removal procedure until we find a string M accepts whose length is $<n$. Thus, the proposition holds.   □

We can now use Proposition 7.1 to test the "emptiness." In this test, U generates all inputs for M having a length less than n in lexicographic order. U can use the algorithm for the acceptance problem to test if M accepts any prospective members.

The generation of prospective members can follow an idea reminiscent of the path generation for deterministically simulating NTMs (Theorem 6.4) as follows:

For a prospective member whose symbol indices are $j_1, \ldots, j_t$, its representation for simulation is

$$\#0^{j_1} 10^{j_2} 1 \cdots 10^{j_t} \sqcup \cdots .$$

- If $j_t < n$, the next candidate is the same as the current one, expect that j_t becomes $j_t + 1$. U accomplishes this by replacing the leftmost $\sqcup$ with 0.
- If $j_t = n$ and there is some k such that $j_k < n$, U finds the largest such k, inserts 0 after 0^{j_k}, and reduces each of $j_{k+1}, \cdots, j_t$ to 1.
- If $j_1 = \cdots = j_t = m$ and $t < m - 1$, U turns each of $j_1, \cdots, j_t$ into 1 and appends 10.
- If $j_1 = \cdots j_t = m$ and $t = m - 1$, U terminates the simulation.

This completes the description of U's algorithm.

An alternate proof of the theorem uses reachability; a DFA accepts some input if, and only if, one of its final states is reachable from the initial state by following its transition function (see Exercise 7.1).

7.2.1.3 Infiniteness

The infiniteness problem about regular languages is decidable.

Theorem 7.3 *The following language is decidable:*
  INFINITE$_{FA} = \{\langle M \rangle \mid M$ *is a DFA and accepts infinitely many inputs*$\}$.

Proof Using the Pumping Lemma, we can show that if an n-state DFA accepts a string with a reappearing state, we can construct, from that string, a member having a length between n and $2n$ by pumping. Based on this observation, consider a universal TM that extracts a DFA from the input and tests whether or not the DFA accepts a string whose length is in the interval $[n, 2n]$. The universal TM exhaustively examines all the strings in the length range. The universal TM accepts if the encoding is valid, and the DFA accepts at least one such input. Then the machine witnesses that INFINITE$_{FA}$.   □

7.2.1.4 Totality

The totality problem about regular languages is decidable.

Theorem 7.4 *The following language is decidable:*
$$\text{TOTAL}_{FA} = \{\langle M \rangle \mid M \text{ is a DFA and accepts all inputs}\}.$$

Proof Let $M = (Q, \Sigma, \delta, q_0, F)$ be a DFA. Construct M' from M by substituting its final state set F with $Q - F$. Then, M accepts Σ^* if, and only if, M' accepts $\emptyset$. From Theorem 7.2, we already know that the emptiness problem is decidable. Let U_0 be a universal TM that decides EMPTY_{FA}. Define a new machine U from U_0 as follows:

After executing the initial check on the code, if the input is a valid DFA encoding, U replaces the list of final states with the states that do not appear on the list. Then, U enters the post-verification part of U_0. Finally, U accepts if U_0 accepts and rejects if U_0 rejects.

This program halts on all inputs and correctly decides the totality problem. □

7.2.1.5 Containment

The containment problem about regular languages is decidable.

Theorem 7.5 *The following language is decidable:*
$$\text{SUBSET}_{FA} = \{\langle M, N \rangle \mid M \text{ and } N \text{ are finite automata and } L(M) \subseteq L(N)\}.$$

Proof Think of a universal TM that, on input w, behaves as follows:

1. Attempt to decompose the input into the five components (the states, the alphabet, the transition function, the initial state, and the final states) of M and the five components of N. If the attempt is not successful, reject it immediately.
2. Check if the five components are valid for representing finite automata and if the alphabet size is the same for both. If the check fails, reject the input immediately.
3. Construct a new DFA for $L(M) \cap \overline{L(N)}$. If $M = (Q, \Sigma, \delta, q_0, F)$ and $N = (Q', \Sigma, \delta', q_0', F')$, then the new DFA, $H = (R, \Sigma, \theta, p_0, G)$, has the following components:

   - $R = Q \times Q'$.
   - $\theta((q, q'), a) = (\delta(q, a), \delta(q', a))$ for all $a \in \Sigma$.
   - $p_0 = (q_0, q_0')$.
   - $G = F \times (Q' - F')$.

   Let $k = \|Q\|$ and $k' = \|Q'\|$. Since the states require sequential numbering, the universal TM combines the index i for a state in Q and the index j for a state in Q' into $(i - 1)k' + j$.

4. The universal TM then conducts the emptiness test. The universal TM carries out this test by checking to see if H accepts any string having a length less than $\|R\|$. If H accepts any such string, $L(H) \neq \emptyset$; otherwise, $L(H) = \emptyset$.
5. The universal TM accepts the input if H accepts $\emptyset$ and rejects the input otherwise.

The universal TM halts on all inputs. Also, for all inputs that encode some two finite automata, M and N, the universal TM accepts if, and only if, $L(M) \cap \overline{L(N)} = \emptyset$, which is equivalent to $L(M) \subseteq L(N)$.

This proves the theorem.   □

7.2.1.6   Equality

The equality problem is also decidable for regular languages.

Theorem 7.6 *The following language is decidable:*
   $\text{EQUAL}_{FA} = \{\langle M, N\rangle \mid M \text{ and } N \text{ are finite automata and } L(M) = L(N)\}.$

Proof A language A equals a language B if, and only if, $A \triangle B = \emptyset$. So, given DFAs M and N, the question as to whether or not $L(M) = L(N)$ can be answered as follows:

We construct a DFA for accepting the symmetric difference between $L(M)$ and $L(N)$; we then check if the DFA accepts the empty set. This proves the theorem.   □

7.2.1.7   Decidable Problems About NFAs and Regular Expressions

As mentioned earlier, we can also specify the six fundamental problems from Sect. 7.1.2 using NFAs. A slight difference, if any, is that the validation of a transition table is less strict. The requirement that the transition table must contain an entry for each combination of a state number and a symbol number does not apply to NFAs.

From the above observation, we obtain the following result:

Corollary 7.1 ACCEPT_{NFA}, EMPTY_{NFA}, EQUAL_{NFA}, TOTAL_{NFA}, *and* SUBSET_{NFA} *are decidable.*

Similarly, we can develop a strategy for converting an arbitrary regular expression to a DFA.

Corollary 7.2 ACCEPT_{REX}, EMPTY_{REX}, EQUAL_{REX}, TOTAL_{REX}, *and* SUBSET_{REX} *are decidable.*

7.2.2 Decidable Problems About CFLs

As we discussed earlier in this chapter, CFGs, CNF grammars, and PDAs are equivalent using the conversion algorithms. Thus, we can study the problems with CFLs using any of these three models.

Theorem 7.7 ACCEPT$_{CFG}$ *is decidable.*

Proof We will develop a universal TM for the language, we will call the machine U.

Suppose we want to decide if a binary string x belongs to ACCEPT$_{CFG}$. As with decision problems for regular languages, the first thing U does is check the validity of x as a CFG encoding. The components U extracts are:

1. The number of variables in the grammar
2. The number of terminals in the grammar
3. The production rules of the grammar
4. The index of the start variable
5. The input string as a sequence of indices

The scheme requires a distinction between variable indices and terminal indices. For example, the distinction can be achieved by assigning a variable index d to 0^{2d} and a terminal index d to 0^{2d-1}, where the length of the former tally is an even number; in contrast, the length of the latter tally is an odd number. We can then assume the following:

- The rules are separated by 111.
- The left-hand side and the right-hand side of each rule are separated by 11.
- The elements on the right-hand side of each rule are separated by 1.

Suppose the validation is successful. Let n be the length of w. U can convert the grammar G to its equivalent CNF grammar H by executing the conversion algorithm from Sect. 4.2.2. Then, U can enumerate all possible leftmost production trees that use $n-1$ rules whose form is $A \rightarrow BC$ and n rules whose form is $A \rightarrow a$. If any of the leftmost productions generates w, $w \in L(G)$; otherwise, $w \notin L(G)$.

The number of leftmost productions U examines is finite, so U decides ACCEPT$_{CFG}$.   □

Exercises 7.9 and 7.11 are about the decidability of the emptiness and infiniteness problems for context-free languages.

Since DPDAs are PDAs, decidable problems for context-free languages are decidable for DCFLs. Additionally, since the class of DCFLs is closed under complement, the totality problem for DCFLs is decidable.

Corollary 7.3 ACCEPT$_{DPDA}$, EMPTY$_{DPDA}$, TOTAL$_{DPDA}$, *and* INFINITE$_{DPDA}$ *are decidable.*

The decidability of the DCFL equivalence problem remained unsolved until it was positively resolved at the end of the twentieth century. The proof is very long, so we only state the result.

Theorem 7.8 EQUAL$_{\text{DPDA}}$ *is decidable.*

The decidability contrasts with the equality problem about PDAs, which is undecidable (see Corollary 8.4).

Exercises

7.1 Let $M = (Q, \Sigma, \delta, q_0, F)$ be a DFA. Let $G = (Q, A)$ be a directed graph such that

$$A = \{(p, q) \mid \delta(p, a) = q \text{ for some } a \in \Sigma\}.$$

Prove that M accepts at least one input if G has a directed path from q_0 to some $p \in F$. Then use the result to show that EMPTY$_{\text{FA}}$ is decidable.

7.2 Let M be a DFA with n states. Based on the Pumping Lemma, prove that M accepts infinitely many inputs if, and only if, it accepts a string with a length between n and $2n$.

7.3 The general strategy for universal TMs appearing in Sect. 7.2.1.7 states that the universal TM must check the validity of the input components. Describe the conditions the components must satisfy to be valid, assuming that the components are the number of states, the size of the alphabet, the transition function, the initial state, the final states, and the input.

7.4 Building off the previous problem, describe the conditions the components must satisfy to be a valid encoding of a regular expression appearing as a string.

7.5 Show that the following language is decidable:

$\{\langle M \rangle \mid M$ is a single-tape TM and makes a left move regardless of its input$\}$.

Hint: We can modify M so that it makes no stationary moves, construct a DFA accepting all inputs on which M makes a left move (M keeps reading input until it makes a left move), and test if the DFA accepts all inputs.

7.6 Show that the problem of deciding if an NFA has an equivalent DFA with no more than a specified number of states is decidable.

7.7 Show that the following language is decidable:

$\{\langle G \rangle \mid G$ is a CFG and has a variable A such that A does not appear on the

right-hand side on any production starting from the start variable$\}$.

7.8 Show that the following language is decidable:

$\{\langle E, k \rangle \mid E$ is a regular expression, k is a positive integer, and there exists a DFA

with at most k states that accept $L(E)\}$.

7.9 Show that EMPTY$_{\text{CFG}}$ is decidable.

7.10 Show that the following language is decidable:
$\{\langle G, k \rangle \mid G$ is a CFG, k is an integer, and $L(G)$ has a string whose length is $k\}$.

7.11 Show that INFINITE$_{\text{CFG}}$ is decidable.

7.12 Show that the following language is decidable:
$$\{\langle P \rangle \mid P \text{ is a deterministic PDA}\}.$$

7.13 Show that the following language is decidable:
$$\{\langle G \rangle \mid G \text{ is a CNF grammar}\}.$$

7.14 Show that the following language is decidable:
$$\{\langle G \rangle \mid G \text{ is a GNF grammar}\}.$$

7.15 Show that the following language is decidable:

$\{\langle G, w \rangle \mid G$ is a CNF grammar and G has a unique leftmost production tree that

produces $w\}$.

7.16 A **linear bounded automaton** is a single-tape TM such that the input appears between left-end and right-end markers and the head does not move out of the region between end markers. Prove that linear bounded automata recognize only decidable languages.

7.17 Show that the following language is decidable:
$\{\langle A, B \rangle \mid A$ and B are DFAs, $L(A) \cap L(B) = \emptyset$, and $L(A) \cup L(B) = \Sigma^*\}$.

7.18 Let $L \subseteq \Sigma^*$. Show that $L^* = \Sigma^*$ if, and only if, $\Sigma \subseteq L$.

7.19 Based on the previous question, prove that the problem of testing if a CFL L satisfies $L^* = \Sigma^*$ is decidable, where L is given by its CNF grammar.

7.20 Prove that $\{\langle M \rangle \mid M$ is a PDA and accepts $\epsilon\}$ is decidable.

Bibliographic Notes and Further Reading
The concept of universal TMs is by Turing [5]. The decidability of the equivalence problem of DPDA is by Sénizergues [3]; the proof is complex. A less complex proof is given by Stirling [4]. CFL's decidability is by Cocke and Schwartz [1] but first appeared in Younger [6] and Kasami [2].

References

1. J. Cocke, J.T. Schwartz, Programming languages and their compilers: Preliminary notes. Technical Report (2nd revised ed.), CIMS, New York University (1970)
2. T. Kasami, An efficient recognition and syntax-analysis algorithm for context-free languages. Coordinated Science Laboratory Report no R-257 (1966)
3. G. Sénizergues, $L(A) = L(B)$? decidability results from complete formal systems. Theor. Comput. Sci. **251**(1–2), 1–166 (2001)
4. C. Stirling, Decidability of DPDA equivalence. Theor. Comput. Sci. **255**(1–2), 1–31 (2001)
5. A.M. Turing, On computable numbers, with an application to the Entscheidungsproblem. J. Math. **58**(345–363), 5 (1936)
6. D.H. Younger, Recognition and parsing of context-free languages in time n^3. Inf. Control **10**(2), 189–208 (1967)

Chapter 8
Undecidable Languages

8.1 The Halting Problem

In this section, we present some fundamental results about undecidable problems.

8.1.1 Proving Impossibility Using Diagonalization

We begin with the diagonalization technique, which takes an enumeration of all the members in an infinite set and creates something different from each one.

An infinite set S is **countable** if there is a sequence $s_1, s_2, s_3, \ldots$ such that $S = \{s_1, s_2, s_3, \ldots\}$. This definition of countability permits the reappearance of the same value in the sequence. If necessary, this reappearance can be eliminated by selecting a sub-sequence $\{s_i \mid i = 1 \text{ or } i \geq 2 \text{ and } s_i \neq s_j \text{ for all } j \text{ such that } 1 \leq j \leq n - 1\}$.

Examples of countable sets are $\mathbb{N}$, $\mathbb{Z}$, and $\mathbb{Q}$. The set of real numbers, $\mathbb{R}$, is different from the three and is uncountable using the following **diagonal argument**:

Proposition 8.1 $\mathbb{R}$ *is uncountable.*

Proof Assume, by way of contradiction, that $\mathbb{R}$ is countable. Then, there is an enumeration, $s_1, s_2, s_3, \ldots$, such that $\mathbb{R} = \{s_1, s_2, s_3, \ldots\}$. We define a new real number t such that $0 < t < 1$ as follows:

- For all $j \geq 1$, if s_j's digit in the j-th place after the decimal point is d, the t's digit in the same place is equal to the remainder of $d + 1$ divided by 10.

For example, if $s_1 = 7.9\underline{8}0123\ldots$, $s_2 = -123.4\underline{4}3$, $s_3 = 3.00\underline{7}89$, $s_4 = 5.555\underline{5}$, $s_5 = 5.1470\underline{1}4\ldots$, etc., then $t = 0.05862\ldots$ A mathematical expression for t is:

© The Editor(s) (if applicable) and The Author(s), under exclusive license to
Springer Nature Switzerland AG 2025
M. Ogihara, *An Introduction to Theory of Computation*,
https://doi.org/10.1007/978-3-031-84740-0_8

$$\sum_{i \geq 1} ((\lfloor s_i * 10^i \rfloor) \bmod 10)/10^i.$$

This number t is real. Then, owing to the assumption that $\mathbb{R}$ is countable, there is an index j such that $t = s_j$. Let us pick one such j. However, because of the construction, t and s_j have different digits in the j-th place after the decimal point. This is a contradiction. Thus, $\mathbb{R}$ is not countable.   □

Since $\aleph_0$ and $\aleph_1$ are the cardinalities of $\mathbb{N}$ and $\mathbb{R}$ respectively, the diagonalization result implies that $\aleph_0 \neq \aleph_1$.

Now, we apply the diagonalization argument to languages. Let $M_1, M_2, \ldots$ be an enumeration of single-tape TMs given as follows:

For each $i \geq 1$, if the i-th nonempty binary string passes the encoding test according to the encoding scheme from Sect. 7.1.1, then M_i is the TM that the binary string encodes; otherwise, it is a TM accepting no inputs with $\{0\}$ as its input alphabet. For every language $A \in \mathrm{RE}$, there is an index i such that $L(M_i) = A$.

Definition 8.1 Define $L_{diag} = \{0^i \mid M_i$ does not accept 0^i, where 0 is the first symbol of the unary encoding of some TM D, and D does not accept $0^m\}$.

As we will prove in Exercise 8.4, $L_{diag} \in \mathrm{coRE}$. However, $L_{diag} \notin \mathrm{RE}$. Assume, on the contrary, that $L_{diag} \in \mathrm{RE}$. Then, there is an index i such that M_i recognizes L_{diag}. We observe the following:

- Suppose M_i accepts 0^i. Then, due to the definition of L_{diag}, $0^i \notin L_{diag}$, which implies that M_i does not accept 0^i.
- Suppose M_i does not accept 0^i. Then, due to the definition of L_{diag}, $0^i \in L_{diag}$, which implies that M_i accepts 0^i.

Therefore, we have a contradiction.

We have thus proven the following:

Theorem 8.1 $L_{diag} \in (\mathrm{coRE} \setminus \mathrm{RE})$.

Let us define L_{self} as the complementary language of L_{diag} as follows:

Definition 8.2 Define $L_{self} = \{\langle D \rangle \mid D$ accepts $\langle D \rangle\}$.

Since $L_{diag} \in \mathrm{coRE} \setminus \mathrm{RE}$, we have:

Corollary 8.1 $L_{self} \in \mathrm{RE} \setminus \mathrm{coRE}$.

We leave the proof of the result to the reader (Exercise 8.5).

Using L_{self}, we can show the following language is not decidable.

Definition 8.3 Define $\mathrm{ACCEPT_{TM}} = \{\langle G, w \rangle \mid G$ is a DTM, w is an input to G, and G on w accepts$\}$.

Theorem 8.2 $\mathrm{ACCEPT_{TM}}$ *is undecidable. More specifically,* $\mathrm{ACCEPT_{TM}}$ *is recursively enumerable but not recursive.*

We leave to the reader the task of proving that $\text{ACCEPT}_{\text{TM}}$ is in RE (Exercise 8.6). We show that $\text{ACCEPT}_{\text{TM}} \notin \text{coRE}$ by contradiction.

By way of contradiction, assume that $\text{ACCEPT}_{\text{TM}}$ is in coRE. Since we already know that $\text{ACCEPT}_{\text{TM}} \in \text{RE}$, we have $\text{ACCEPT}_{\text{TM}} \in \text{R}$. Let E be a TM that decides $\text{ACCEPT}_{\text{TM}}$. Using E as a subroutine, we can construct a three-tape TM that decides L_{self}. We present its algorithm in Algorithm 8.1.

Algorithm 8.1 A TM F for L_{self}, with E as a subroutine for $\text{ACCEPT}_{\text{TM}}$

```
 1: procedure TURING-MACHINE-FOR-Lself(w)
 2:     receive a unary input x = 0^k;
 3:     if |x| = 0 then
 4:         reject x;
 5:     else
 6:         on Tape 2, construct the k-th nonempty binary string;
 7:         check if the string encodes some TM;
 8:         if the encoding is invalid then
 9:             reject x;
10:         else
11:             extract the machine M that x encodes;
12:             on Tape 3, construct the encoding ⟨M, x⟩;
13:             simulate E assuming that Tape 3 is E's only tape;
14:             if E accepts then
15:                 accept x;
16:             else
17:                 reject x;
18:             end if
19:         end if
20:     end if
21: end procedure
```

By our assumption, E decides $\text{ACCEPT}_{\text{TM}}$, so F halts on all inputs. Then, for all inputs x, M on x accepts if, and only if, E accepts x. This implies that L_{self} is decidable, which is a contradiction. Thus, $\text{ACCEPT}_{\text{TM}}$ is undecidable.

8.1.2 The Halting Problem

The next undecidable problem is the **Halting Problem**. The Halting Problem asks if a given TM halts on all inputs.

Definition 8.4 Define $\text{HALT}_{\text{TM}} = \{\langle M \rangle \mid M \text{ is a TM that halts on all inputs}\}$.

Theorem 8.3 HALT_{TM} *is undecidable.*

Proof We can prove the theorem by contradiction. Assume, on the contrary, that HALT_{TM} is decidable. Let E be a TM that decides HALT_{TM}. We construct the following TM, F, from E.

1. Receive a binary string x.
2. Test if x is an encoding of the form $\langle M, w \rangle$ such that M is a TM and w is an input to M.
3. If x does not pass the test, reject x.
4. Construct $\langle N \rangle$, where N is a TM that, on each input y, behaves as follows:

   a. N tests if $y = w$.
   b. If $y \neq w$, N accepts y.
   c. If $y = w$, N moves the head to the leftmost cell and simulates M.
   d. If M accepts, N accepts; if M rejects, N enters an infinite loop.

5. Run E on $\langle N \rangle$.
6. If E accepts, accept w; otherwise, reject w.

N is specific to M and w; it has w as part of its code and compares w with its input y, character by character.

Since E halts on all inputs, F halts on all inputs as well. In addition, N accepts all inputs if M accepts w and runs forever on all inputs otherwise. Thus, N halts on all inputs if, and only if, M on w accepts. Since we assume that E decides HALT_{TM}, we have a program that decides $\text{ACCEPT}_{\text{TM}}$, which is a contradiction. □

8.1.3   Some Variants of the Halting Problem

Since the TM from the proof of Theorem 8.3 accepts either all inputs or no inputs, we obtain the following result:

Corollary 8.2 EMPTY_{TM}, $\text{INFINITE}_{\text{TM}}$, and TOTAL_{TM} are undecidable.

Since both TMs accepting no inputs and TMs accepting all inputs can be constructed, we have the following result:

Corollary 8.3 $\text{SUBSET}_{\text{TM}}$ and EQUAL_{TM} are undecidable.

8.2   Many-One Reductions and Rice's Theorem

Here, we study two general techniques for proving undecidability. One technique is the many-one reduction, which, instance by instance, transforms a decision problem into another. The other technique is Rice's Theorem, which states that all nontrivial properties of TMs are undecidable.

8.2.1   Many-One Reductions

We begin with the use of many-one reductions.

We have seen undecidability proofs that take the form: "If X were decidable, then a problem Y that is already known to be undecidable would be decidable, and so X must be undecidable." We study this type of argument here, where every input about one language can be translated into some input about another problem.

Definition 8.5 Let $A \subseteq \Sigma^*$ and $B \subseteq \Gamma^*$ be two languages, where Σ and Γ are two (possibly equal) alphabets. We say that A is **many-one reducible** to B if there is a computable function f from Σ^* to Γ^* such that for all $x \in \Sigma^*$, $x \in A$ if, and only if, $f(x) \in B$.

We write $A \leq_m B$ to denote that A is many-one reducible to B.

The many-one reducibility is a tool for finding upper and lower bounds to the difficulty of problems.

Proposition 8.2 *If $A \leq_m B$ and B is recursive, then A is recursive. Conversely, if A is not recursive and $A \leq_m B$, B is not recursive.*

Proof Suppose $A \leq_m B$. Then, a reduction, f, exists from A to B. Let R be a TM that computes f.

Suppose B is recursive. We select a TM M that decides B. We may assume that M is a single-table TM.

Let N be a TM that for each input x executes the following algorithm:

1. Compute $f(x)$ using R, where a normal read/write tape plays the role of the output tape of R.
2. Simulate M assuming the tape that played the role of R's output tape is M's tape.
3. Accept x if M accepts; reject x otherwise.

Since R and M halt on all inputs, N halts on all inputs as well. Because of the translational property of many-one reductions, N accepts its input if, and only if, the input is a member of A. Thus, A is recursive. $\square$

The many-one reducibility is a relation between languages. It is reflexive and transitive but not symmetric.

Proposition 8.3 *The many-one reducibility is reflexive and transitive.*

Proposition 8.4 *The many-one reducibility is not symmetric.*

We leave the proofs of the above propositions to the reader.

Here is an example of using the many-one reducibility to show the undecidability of a language.

Example 8.1 Define $A = \{xx \mid x = \langle M \rangle$ for some TM M where M does not accept $x\}$. A is not recursive for the following reason:

Assume A is recursive. Then, there is a TM M that decides A. For all $x, x \in L_{self}$ if, and only if, $xx \in A$. Define f as the function that maps each x to xx. The function

f is computable by a TM that copies its input to the output tape twice. Then f is a many-one reduction from L_{self} to A. Since L_{self} is not recursive, we have $A \notin R$ by Proposition 8.2.

8.2.2   Rice's Theorem

Next, we show Rice's Theorem.

Rice's Theorem is a technique for proving the undecidability of properties of TMs.

Definition 8.6   Let Q be any property of recursively enumerable languages; i.e., for each recursively enumerable language L, L either satisfies the requirement for Q or it doesn't. We say that Q is **nontrivial** if there is a recursively enumerable language that has Q and there is another recursively enumerable language that does not have Q.

Theorem 8.4 (Rice's Theorem)   *Every nontrivial property of recursively enumerable languages is undecidable. More specifically, for each nontrivial property Q, $L_Q = \{\langle M \rangle \mid M \text{ is a TM, and } L(M) \text{ has the property } Q\}$ is undecidable.*

Proof Let Q be an arbitrary nontrivial property of recursively enumerable languages. Let A_1 be a recursively enumerable language with Q, and let A_2 be a recursively enumerable language without Q. Let M_1 and M_2 be TMs that recognize A_1 and A_2, respectively. We can assume that A_1 or A_2 is $\emptyset$.

Suppose $A_2 = \emptyset$. Let Σ be an alphabet such that $A_1 \subseteq \Sigma^*$. Let M_0 be a TM that runs forever on every input. Then $L(M_0) = \emptyset$. We may assume that M_0's input alphabet is Σ. Let f be the function that maps each w as follows:

1. If $w \neq \langle M, x \rangle$ such that M is a TM and x is an input to M, $f(w) = \langle M_0 \rangle$.
2. Otherwise, $f(w) = \langle N \rangle$, where on each input $y \in \Sigma^*$, N behaves as follows:

   - N simulates M on x.
   - N simulates M_1 on y if M accepts x.
   - N simulates M_0 on y otherwise.

Let T be a TM such that $f(w) = \langle T \rangle$. If $w = \langle M, x \rangle$ such that M accepts x, $L(T) = A_1$ so $L(T)$ has Q; otherwise, $L(T) = \emptyset$ so $L(T)$ does not have Q. Thus, $\text{ACCEPT}_{TM} \leq_m L_Q$. Since ACCEPT_{TM} is undecidable (Proposition 8.2), L_Q is undecidable.

The proof where $\emptyset$ has the property Q is similar. We leave the proof to the reader (see Exercise 8.11).   □

8.3 Undecidable Problems About CFLs

In this section, we prove the undecidability of some problems concerning CFLs.

8.3.1 The Totality Problem About CFLs

The totality problem is the opposite of the emptiness problem. In the case of regular languages, both the emptiness and totality problems are decidable. In the previous chapter, we saw that the membership and emptiness problems about context-free languages are decidable. We show here the totality of context-free languages is an undecidable problem.

Theorem 8.5 TOTAL$_{\text{CFG}}$ *is undecidable.*

We can say something more specific about the problem. Let NONTOTAL$_{\text{CFG}}$ be TOTAL$_{\text{CFG}}$'s complementary problem (i.e., the problem of deciding if a context-free language has a nonmember).

Theorem 8.6 TOTAL$_{\text{CFG}} \in$ coRE \ RE, *and* NONTOTAL$_{\text{CFG}} \in$ RE \ coRE.

Figure 8.1 shows the classification of the two decision problems.

NONTOTAL$_{\text{CFG}} \in$ RE comes from ACCEPT$_{\text{CFG}}$ being decidable (Theorem 7.7). For proving that $L(G) \neq \Sigma^*$, we try checking $w \in L(G)$ for all w in lexicographic order using a recursive algorithm. Each membership testing halts. If $L(G) \neq \Sigma^*$, we eventually encounter the smallest nonmember, w, of $L(G)$ in lexicographic order. Upon encountering such w, we accept. Algorithm 8.2 shows the algorithm.

Let's turn to the proof of Theorem 8.5.

Proof To prove the undecidability of TOTAL$_{\text{CFG}}$, we translate the acceptance problem of TMs to NONTOTAL$_{\text{CFG}}$. We can capture the translation as a many-one reduction, f, from ACCEPT$_{\text{TM}}$ to NONTOTAL$_{\text{CFG}}$. In other words, for an arbitrary binary string x, $x \in$ ACCEPT$_{\text{TM}}$ if, and only if, $f(x) \in$ NONTOTAL$_{\text{CFG}}$.

The computation of $f(x)$ begins by checking the validity of x as an encoding of some machine, say M, and an input, w, to it. If x fails the test, x is a nonmember of ACCEPT$_{\text{TM}}$, so we set the value of $f(x)$ to some nonmember of NONTOTAL$_{\text{CFG}}$. The trivial nonmember can be the empty string because an empty string cannot

Fig. 8.1 TOTAL$_{\text{CFG}}$ and NONTOTAL$_{\text{CFG}}$

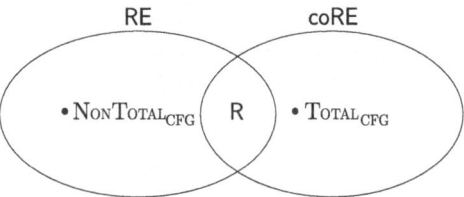

Algorithm 8.2 A TM that recognizes NONTOTAL$_{\mathrm{CFG}}$

1: **procedure** TM-FOR-NONTOTAL$_{\mathrm{CFG}}(w)$
2:    check the validity of w as an encoding of a context-free grammar;
3:    **if** w is valid **then**
4:        extract the grammar $G = (V, \Sigma, R, S)$ from w;
5:    **else**
6:        reject w;
7:    **end if**
8:    convert G to a CNF grammar $G' = (V'\Sigma, R', S')$;
9:    **for** $\ell \leftarrow 0, 1, 2, \ldots$ **do**
10:       **for** each $u \in \Sigma^\ell$ **do**
11:           **for** each sequences s of $2\ell - 1$ production rules **do**
12:               **if** s represents a leftmost derivation producing u **then**
13:                   terminate the loop generating s;
14:               **end if**
15:           **end for**
16:           **if** no s produces u **then**
17:               accept w;
18:           **end if**
19:       **end for**
20:   **end for**
21: **end procedure**

---

encode any grammar. On the other hand, if x passes the test, $f(x)$ is a CFG $G = (V, \Sigma, R, S)$ such that M accepts w if, and only if, G's production omits some string in Σ^*.

The construction of the grammar goes as follows:

Let $M = (Q, \Sigma.\Gamma, \delta, q_0, q_{\mathrm{acc}}, q_{\mathrm{rej}})$ be an arbitrary single-tape TM. Let # and \$ be two symbols not in Γ. Let $\Theta = \Sigma \cup Q$ and $\zeta = \Theta \cup \{\#, \$\}$. We define the language $Z_{M,x} \subseteq \zeta^*$ as the set of all strings of the form

$$\#C_1 \$ D_1 \# C_2 \$ D_2 \# \cdots \# C_m \$ D_m \#$$

satisfying the following conditions:

1. $C_1, \ldots, C_m$ and $D_1, \ldots, D_m$ are in $\Gamma^* Q \Gamma^*$.
2. For all i such that $1 \le i \le m$, $D_i = C_i^R$.
3. $|C_1| = |D_1| = \cdots = |C_m| = |D_m|$.
4. C_1 is the initial ID of M on input x (with an arbitrary number of trailing ⊔s).
5. C_m is an accepting ID of M: i.e., in $\Gamma^* q_{\mathrm{acc}} \Gamma^*$ (with an arbitrary number of trailing ⊔s).
6. For all i such that $1 \le i \le m - 1$, C_{i+1} is M's ID immediately after C_i (with an arbitrary number of trailing ⊔s).

For each $w \in Z_{M,x}$, the sub-sequence $C_1, \ldots, C_m$ appearing in it represents the accepting computation of M of x. Thus,

$$M \text{ accepts } x \text{ if, and only if, } Z_{M,x} \neq \emptyset.$$

By taking the complement of each side, we have:

$$M \text{ does not accept } x \text{ if, and only if, } \overline{Z_{M,x}} = \zeta^*.$$

We can thus test the membership $\langle M, x \rangle$ in ACCEPT$_{\text{TM}}$ using the totality of $\overline{Z_{M,x}}$. The membership conditions for $w \in \overline{Z_{M,x}}$ are as follows:

1. $w \notin (\#\Gamma^* Q\Gamma^* \$\Gamma^* Q\Gamma^*)^* \#$.
2. w contains a substring $\#u\$v\#$ such that $u, v \in \Theta^*$ and $v \neq u^R$.
3. w contains a substring $\#u\$v\#$ such that $u, v \in \Theta^*$ and $|u| \neq |v|$ or a substring $\$u\#v\$$ such that $u, v \in \Theta^*$ and $|u| \neq |v|$.
4. w has a prefix $\#u\$$ such that u is in Θ^* and does not match the regular expression $q_0 x \sqcup^*$.
5. w has a suffix $\$u\#$ such that u is in Θ^* and does not match the regular expression $\Gamma^* q_{\text{acc}} \Gamma^*$.
6. w has a substring $\$u\#v\$$ such that u and v are in Θ^* and v is not M's ID immediately after u^R.

Among these conditions, (1), (4), and (5) are each testable with a DFA, and thus context-free. The remaining conditions are also context-free, according to Exercises 4.14 and 4.15 Since the class CFL is closed under union, the $\overline{Z_{M,x}}$ is context-free.

This proves the theorem. □

We obtain the following corollaries from Theorem 8.5.

Corollary 8.4 EQUAL$_{\text{CFG}}$ *is undecidable.*

Proof Consider the following function f:

Let x be an arbitrary binary string. If x is not encoding a CFG, $f(x)$ is a fixed nonmember of EQUAL$_{\text{CFG}}$. Otherwise, $f(x) = \langle G', G \rangle$, where G' is a grammar that produces Θ^* and Θ is G's terminal set. For the latter case, $L(G) = \Theta^*$ if, and only if, $L(G') = L(G)$. Thus, f is a many-one reduction from TOTAL$_{\text{CFG}}$ to EQUAL$_{\text{CFG}}$.

This completes the proof. □

The function f from the proof is also a many-one reduction from TOTAL$_{\text{CFG}}$ to SUBSET$_{\text{CFG}}$.

Corollary 8.5 SUBSET$_{\text{CFG}}$ *is undecidable.*

The proof is left to the reader (see Exercise 8.3).

8.3.2 Undecidable Problems About DCFLs

Here, we prove two undecidability results about DCFLs.

Theorem 8.7 SUBSET$_{\text{DPDA}}$ *is undecidable.*

Proof Overview
We use the palindrome-like language $Z_{M,x}$ from Sect. 8.3.1. We slightly modify $Z_{M,x}$ so that the last # is replaced with another symbol, $\tilde{\#}$, to mark the end. We show that the language is the intersection of two DCFL languages. Since DCFL is closed under complement, we can complement one of the two languages. The complemented language includes the other language if, and only if, the modified version of $Z_{M,x}$ is empty.

Proof We use the language $Z_{M,x}$ from Sect. 8.3.1. We assume here that M does not attempt a left move when the head is on the leftmost cell, and so does not experience a bounceback. We define $Z'_{M,x}$ as $Z_{M,x}$ with the last # replaced with a new symbol, $\tilde{\#}$. Let $\Theta = Q \cup \Gamma$ and $\zeta' = \Theta \cup \{\#, \$, \tilde{\#}\}$. We decompose $Z'_{M,x}$ as the intersection of the following two languages, R_1 and R_2.

- R_1 is the set of all strings of the form

$$\#C_1\$D_1\#C_2\$D_2\#\cdots\#C_m\$D_m\tilde{\#}$$

  such that:

  - $m \geq 2$.
  - $C_1, \cdots, C_m \in \Gamma^*Q\Gamma^*$.
  - For all i such that $1 \leq i \leq m$, $D_i = C_i^R$.

- R_2 is the set of all strings of the form

$$\#C_1\$D_1\#C_2\$D_2\#\cdots\#C_m\$D_m\tilde{\#}$$

  such that:

  - $m \geq 2$.
  - $C_1, \cdots, C_m \in \Gamma^*Q\Gamma^*$.
  - C_1 matches the regular expression $q_1x\sqcup^*$.
  - D_m matches the regular expression $\Gamma^*q_{\text{acc}}\Gamma^*$.
  - For all i such that $1 \leq i \leq m-1$, C_{i+1} is the ID resulting from executing M's action on $(D_i)^R$.

Combining all the requirements for R_1 and R_2 is equivalent to the conditions for $Z'_{M,x}$, so $Z'_{M,x} = R_1 \cap R_2$.

R_1 is a series of palindromes such that each component is in a regular language with a marker between palindromes, a marker at the halfway point of each palindrome, and $\tilde{\#}$ as the end marker; thus, it is in DCFL (see Exercise 8.16). R_2 has a structure similar to R_1 with $\#C_1$ added as a prefix and $D_m\tilde{\#}$ as a suffix. In addition, although the string $D_i\#C_{i+1}$ is similar to a palindrome, it is not a palindrome. We can also show that R_2 is a DCFL (see Exercise 8.17).

Now, let $R_3 = \overline{R_2}$. Since the class of DCFLs is closed under complement, R_3 is a DCFL. If $Z'_{M,x} = \emptyset$, $R_1 \cap R_2 = \emptyset$, so $R_1 \subseteq R_3$. If $Z'_{M,x} \neq \emptyset$, each member of $R_1 \cap R_2 = Z'_{M,x}$ is in R_1 but not in R_3, so $R_1 \nsubseteq R_3$. Thus, $x \in L(M)$ if, and only if, $R_1 \nsubseteq R_3$.

Since we can construct R_1 and R_3 from the description of M and x, we can reduce the acceptance question to the DCFL inclusion problem. $\qquad\square$

8.4 Post's Correspondence Problem (PCP)

A well-known undecidable problem is Post's Correspondence Problem. Using the concept of accepting ID sequences, we define Post's Correspondence Problem as a puzzle-like problem. In this section, we show that Post's Correspondence Problem is undecidable.

8.4.1 The Definitions of PCP and MPCP

Here, we define the problem.

Let Σ be an alphabet. An instance of **Post's Correspondence Problem** over Σ is a collection, P, of string pairs, $(t_1, b_1), \ldots, (t_k, b_k)$, for some $k \geq 1$, such that $t_1, \ldots, t_k, b_1, \ldots, b_k \in \Sigma^*$. We call each pair a **domino tile**. In addition, for a domino tile (t, b), we call t the **top portion** and b the **bottom portion**. Let $s = [p_1, \ldots, p_m]$ be a sequence whose elements are from P. The **top string** of s is the concatenation of all its top portions. The **bottom string** of s is the concatenation of all its bottom portions. The sequence s is a **match** (or a **complete match**) if its top string is identical to its bottom string. The sequence s is a **partial match** if either the top string is a proper prefix of the bottom string or the bottom string is a proper prefix of the top string. In the former, we call the part of the top string extending beyond the bottom string the **top protrusion**. In the latter, we call the part of the bottom string extending beyond the top string the **bottom protrusion**. The problem asks whether or not P has a nonempty sequence with a match. We call a sequence that has a match a **solution**.

Here is an example. Suppose that the following four domino tiles are the elements of an instance of Post's Correspondence Problem:

$$p_1 = (aaa, a), \ p_2 = (b, aaaabc), \ p_3 = (cdd, d), \ p_4 = (e, de),$$

or, with the stacked presentations

$$p_1 = \begin{bmatrix} aaa \\ a \end{bmatrix}, p_2 = \begin{bmatrix} b \\ aaaabc \end{bmatrix}, p_3 = \begin{bmatrix} cdd \\ d \end{bmatrix}, p_4 = \begin{bmatrix} e \\ de \end{bmatrix}.$$

There is a solution $[p_1, p_1, p_2, p_3, p_4]$, whose top and bottom strings are equal to $aaaaaabcdde$. The sequences $[p_1]$, $[p_1, p_1]$, $[p_1, p_1, p_2]$, and $[p_1, p_1, p_2, p_3]$ produce partial matches:

$$\begin{bmatrix} aaa \\ a \end{bmatrix}, \begin{bmatrix} aaaaaa \\ aa \end{bmatrix}, \begin{bmatrix} aaaaaab \\ aaaaaabc \end{bmatrix}, \text{ and } \begin{bmatrix} aaaaaabcdd \\ aaaaaabcd \end{bmatrix},$$

with a top protrusion aa, a top protrusion $aaaa$, a bottom protrusion c, and a top protrusion d, respectively.

For each instance of PCP, we encode the symbols of its alphabet in binary so that they are identical in length. A domino tile's top and bottom portions are the concatenations of the binary representations. Then, using the forward slash as a separator between the top and bottom of each domino tile, and the comma as a separator between the domino tiles, we obtain an encoding of the instance with a four-letter alphabet. Then, representing the four letters with two bits, we obtain a complete binary encoding of the instance.

We now define the language of Post's Correspondence Problem.

Definition 8.7 Define PCP = $\{\langle P \rangle \mid P$ is an instance of Post's Correspondence Problem and P has a solution$\}$.

We define a variant of PCP, which we call the **Marked Post's Correspondence Problem (MPCP)**. Each instance of MPCP designates one tile as the start tile; every match must begin with the start title.

Definition 8.8 Define MPCP = $\{\langle P \rangle \mid P$ is an instance of the Marked Post's Correspondence Problem, and P has a solution$\}$.

8.4.2 The Undecidability of MPCP

In this section, we prove the undecidability of MPCP.

Theorem 8.8 MPCP *is undecidable.*

8.4.2.1 An Accepting ID Sequence

We adapt the concept of accepting ID sequences from the proof of Theorem 8.5.

Let $M = (Q, \Gamma \sqcup, \Sigma, \delta, q_0, q_{acc}, q_{rej})$ be an arbitrary single-tape TM. Let $L = L(M)$. We may assume the following:

- M has just one accepting ID; the head is on the leftmost cell, the tape has ⊔ everywhere, and the state is q_{acc}.
- M never attempts to move the head on the leftmost cell to the left neighbor.

If M does not meet the requirements, we will augment the transition function of M with the addition of new states and symbols in the following manner:

- M marks the leftmost cell. M will keep the mark throughout its computation. It will not mark other cells with the same marker.
- M places a different mark on all other cells it visits. The mark will be removed just before the input is accepted.
- For cleaning, M scans the head to the right, looking for a ⊔ without any mark. Upon finding the unmarked ⊔, M starts scanning to the left, looking for the left end of the tape (the left end was marked at the first step of computation). While looking for the left end, M writes ⊔ in every cell it visits. Upon arriving at the leftmost cell, M writes ⊔ in the cell and then enters q_{acc}.

Let # be a symbol not in $\Gamma \cup Q$. Let $w \in \Sigma^*$ be an input to M. We will construct a set of domino tiles P and designate one tile as the start domino tile. Let $\pi = \#C_1\#\cdots\#C_m\#$, where $C_1, \ldots, C_m \in L(\Gamma^* Q\Gamma^*)$. We say that π is an accepting ID sequence of M on w if the following conditions are met:

- $C_1, \ldots, C_m$ are IDs.
- For each i between 1 and $m - 1$, C_i's next ID is C_{i+1}.
- C_1 is the initial ID of M on input w: $q_0 w$.
- C_m is the unique accepting ID of M: q_{acc}.

Then, M on w accepts if, and only if, an accepting ID sequence of M on w exists.

8.4.2.2   Designing Domino Tiles

Here, we describe the design of the domino tiles for MPCP.
  The domino tiles are as follows:

1. **The Start Domino Tile** The designated start domino tile is

$$\begin{bmatrix} \#q_0 w\# \\ \# \end{bmatrix}.$$

  The start domino tile creates $q_0 w\#$ as the top protrusion. The protrusion encodes the initial ID of M on w.

2. **The Computation Domino Tiles** We introduce domino tiles for transforming the top protrusion representing a non-accepting ID of M to one representing the next step.

a. For each $x \in \Gamma \cup \{\#\}$, we introduce a domino tile, $\begin{bmatrix} x \\ x \end{bmatrix}$, that clears one letter in the protrusion and appends the same domino tile on the top.

b. We also introduce a domino tile $\begin{bmatrix} \sqcup\# \\ \# \end{bmatrix}$, whose role is to extend the top protrusion by transforming the last # to $\sqcup\#$, thereby inserting $\sqcup$ at the end.

c. For all $(p, a) \in (Q - \{q_{\mathrm{acc}}, q_{\mathrm{rej}}\}) \times \Gamma$ such that the move of the head is R, we introduce

$$\begin{bmatrix} bq \\ pa \end{bmatrix},$$

where $\delta(p, a) = (q, b, R)$.

d. For all $(p, a) \in (Q - \{q_{\mathrm{acc}}, q_{\mathrm{rej}}\}) \times \Gamma$ such that the move of the head is $-$, we introduce

$$\begin{bmatrix} qb \\ pa \end{bmatrix},$$

where $\delta(p, a) = (q, b, -)$.

e. For all $(p, a) \in (Q - \{q_{\mathrm{acc}}, q_{\mathrm{rej}}\}) \times \Gamma$ such that the move of the head is L and for all $c \in \Gamma$, we introduce

$$\begin{bmatrix} qcb \\ cpa \end{bmatrix}.$$

3. **The Clean-up Domino Tile** We introduce domino tiles for transforming the top protrusion (representing an accepting ID of M) into a protrusion shorter by one character. In addition to $\begin{bmatrix} \sqcup \\ \sqcup \end{bmatrix}$ from the above, we also introduce

$$\begin{bmatrix} \# \\ \sqcup\# \end{bmatrix}.$$

4. **The Final Domino Tile** We introduce one domino tile to clear the top protrusion of $q_{\mathrm{acc}}\#$, which is $\begin{bmatrix} \epsilon \\ q_{\mathrm{acc}}\# \end{bmatrix}$.

8.4.2.3 The Correctness

We now prove the correctness of the construction for MPCP.

Let P denote the instance we have just described. We show that P has a solution if, and only if, M accepts w.

First, suppose M on w accepts. Suppose a sequence of domino tiles, s, has the top and bottom strings in the following form with C as an ID:

$$\begin{bmatrix} \#W\#C\# \\ \#W\# \end{bmatrix}.$$

Here, $C\#$ is the top protrusion and C is an ID. We must attach a series of domino tiles whose bottom part matches the top protrusion. The protrusion $C\#$ contains exactly one symbol representing a state (say q), and the symbol immediately following the state-representing symbol is a tape symbol (say q). If this state-representing symbol is not q_{acc}, the piece that we select for matching the pattern qa in the top protrusion must be the one that represents M's transition $\delta(q, a)$. Thus, if q is not q_{acc}, in the new top protrusion we have part representing the local change that occurs by executing the transition $\delta(q, a)$. If this state-representing symbol is q_{acc}, we must use $\begin{bmatrix} q_{acc} \\ q_{acc} \end{bmatrix}$ instead. Using these domino tiles to clear the protrusions necessitates using domino tiles without state-representing symbols. Unless $C = q_{acc}$, the available domino tiles are for clearing one character and appending the same character, except for clearing $\#$ and appending $\sqcup\#$ or clearing $\sqcup\#$ and appending $\#$. Except for the final domino, every domino tile in which $\#$ appears has the property that $\#$ appears as the last character on the top and as the last character on the bottom. This means that matching the $\#$ at the end of the top protrusion $C\#$ appends $\#$ at the end of the next protrusion. Thus, an extension of the partial match is:

$$\begin{bmatrix} \#W\#C\#D\# \\ \#W\#C\# \end{bmatrix}.$$

Here, D satisfies one of the following two properties:

- D is a string representing M's ID immediately after the ID that C represents.
- $D = q_{acc}v$ and $C = q_{acc}v\sqcup$ for $v \in \Gamma^*$.

Since the start domino tile has the initial ID of M on w and the final domino tile is the only domino tile with a state only on the bottom portion, we conclude that M on w accepts if, and only if, there is a sequence beginning with the start domino tile producing a complete match as follows:

$$\begin{bmatrix} \#C_1\#C_2\#\cdots\#C_k\#\cdots\#C_{k+\ell}\#q_{acc}\# \\ \#C_1\#C_2\#\cdots\#C_k\#\cdots\#C_{k+\ell}\#q_{acc}\# \end{bmatrix}.$$

Here, k and ℓ are non-negative. Additionally, the following three properties hold:

- For all i such that $2 \leq i \leq k$, C_k represents M's ID immediately after the ID that C_{k-1} represents.
- C_k is an accepting ID and is equal to $q_{acc}\sqcup^{\ell+1}$.
- For all j such that $1 \leq j \leq \ell$, $C_{k+\ell}$ is $q_{acc}\sqcup^{\ell+1-k}$.

The proof of the theorem is now complete.

Example 8.2 Here is an example. Suppose $D = R$. In addition, suppose v is nonempty and $v_1 \ldots v_r$ with $v_1, \ldots, v_s \in \Gamma$. We use

$$\begin{bmatrix} u_1 \\ u_1 \end{bmatrix}, \ldots, \begin{bmatrix} u_r \\ u_r \end{bmatrix}, \begin{bmatrix} c \\ c \end{bmatrix}, \begin{bmatrix} a'p' \\ pa \end{bmatrix}, \begin{bmatrix} v_1 \\ v_1 \end{bmatrix}, \ldots, \begin{bmatrix} v_s \\ v_s \end{bmatrix}, \begin{bmatrix} \# \\ \# \end{bmatrix}.$$

Then, we can extend the partial match to

$$\begin{bmatrix} \#C_1\#C_2\# \cdots \#C_{k-1}\#ucpav\#uca'p'v\# \\ \#C_1\#C_2\# \cdots \#C_{k-1}\#ucpav\# \end{bmatrix}.$$

The new protrusion is $uca'p'v\#$, representing C_k. If v is empty, we use

$$\begin{bmatrix} u_1 \\ u_1 \end{bmatrix}, \ldots, \begin{bmatrix} u_r \\ u_r \end{bmatrix}, \begin{bmatrix} c \\ c \end{bmatrix}, \begin{bmatrix} a'p' \\ pa \end{bmatrix}, \text{ and then } \begin{bmatrix} \sqcup\# \\ \# \end{bmatrix}.$$

The partial match becomes

$$\begin{bmatrix} \#C_1\#C_2\# \cdots \#C_{k-1}\#ucpa\#uca'p' \sqcup \# \\ \#C_1\#C_2\# \cdots \#C_{k-1}\#ucpa\# \end{bmatrix}.$$

We have omitted the empty v from the expression. The string $uca'p'\sqcup$ represents M's ID immediately after the ID $ucpa$. In the case where $D = R$, pa becomes bq, and the domino sequence becomes

$$\begin{bmatrix} \#C_1\#C_2\# \cdots \#C_{k-1}\#ucpav\#ucbqv\# \\ \#C_1\#C_2\# \cdots \#C_{k-1}\#ucpav\# \end{bmatrix}.$$

The protrusion represents M's ID immediately after the ID that C_{k-1} represents.

When v is empty, when attaching a # on the bottom, we need to insert at least one $\sqcup$ after q. This is because the extension domino tile needs a symbol from Γ to the right of a symbol from Q on the bottom side and appending a # after q on the top makes using any such domino tiles impossible. So, in this case, we use

$$\begin{bmatrix} \sqcup\# \\ \# \end{bmatrix}$$

instead of

$$\begin{bmatrix} \# \\ \# \end{bmatrix}.$$

The new partial match is

$$\left[\begin{array}{l} \#C_1\#C_2\#\cdots\#C_{k-1}\#ucpa\#ucbq \sqcup \# \\ \#C_1\#C_2\#\cdots\#C_{k-1}\#ucpa\# \end{array} \right].$$

We have removed the empty v from both sides.

Suppose $D = -$. We use

$$\left[\begin{array}{l} u_1 \\ u_1 \end{array} \right], \ldots, \left[\begin{array}{l} u_r \\ u_r \end{array} \right], \left[\begin{array}{l} c \\ c \end{array} \right], \left[\begin{array}{l} p'a' \\ pa \end{array} \right], \left[\begin{array}{l} v_1 \\ v_1 \end{array} \right], \ldots, \left[\begin{array}{l} v_s \\ v_s \end{array} \right], \text{ and then } \left[\begin{array}{l} \# \\ \# \end{array} \right].$$

This extends the partial match to

$$\left[\begin{array}{l} \#C_1\#C_2\#\cdots\#C_{k-1}\#ucpav\#ucp'a'v\# \\ \#C_1\#C_2\#\cdots\#C_{k-1}\#ucpav\# \end{array} \right].$$

The new protrusion is $ucp'a'v\#$, representing M's ID immediately after $ucpav$.

Suppose $D = L$ and $c \neq \epsilon$. We use

$$\left[\begin{array}{l} u_1 \\ u_1 \end{array} \right], \ldots, \left[\begin{array}{l} u_r \\ u_r \end{array} \right], \left[\begin{array}{l} p'ca' \\ cpa \end{array} \right], \left[\begin{array}{l} v_1 \\ v_1 \end{array} \right], \ldots, \left[\begin{array}{l} v_s \\ v_s \end{array} \right], \text{ and then } \left[\begin{array}{l} \# \\ \# \end{array} \right].$$

This extends the partial match to

$$\left[\begin{array}{l} \#C_1\#C_2\#\cdots\#C_{k-1}\#ucpav\#up'ca'v\# \\ \#C_1\#C_2\#\cdots\#C_{k-1}\#ucpav\# \end{array} \right].$$

The new protrusion is $up'ca'v\#$, representing M's ID immediately after $ucpav$.

Suppose $D = L$ and $u = c = \epsilon$. Since we are assuming that M does not move the head to the left on the leftmost cell, this situation never occurs.

Since the start domino tile has a string representing the initial ID and a # as its protrusion, the above observation informs us that we can extend the partial match of the start domino tile to a string representing an accepting ID with a #, if M on w accepts.

Once the protrusion becomes an accepting ID, we can start shrinking the protrusion. Suppose the partial match is

$$\left[\begin{array}{l} \#C_1\#C_2\#\cdots\#C_k\#ucq_{\text{acc}}v\# \\ \#C_1\#C_2\#\cdots\#C_k\# \end{array} \right]$$

with $u, v \in \Gamma^*$ and $c \in \Gamma$. Suppose $u = u_1 \ldots u_r$ and $v = v_1 \ldots v_s$. We use the sequence

$$\left[\begin{array}{l} u_1 \\ u_1 \end{array} \right], \ldots, \left[\begin{array}{l} u_r \\ u_r \end{array} \right], \left[\begin{array}{l} q_{\text{acc}} \\ cq_{\text{acc}} \end{array} \right], \left[\begin{array}{l} v_1 \\ v_1 \end{array} \right], \ldots, \left[\begin{array}{l} v_s \\ v_s \end{array} \right], \left[\begin{array}{l} \# \\ \# \end{array} \right].$$

This extends the partial match to

$$\begin{bmatrix} \#C_1\#C_2\#\cdots\#C_k\#ucq_{\mathrm{acc}}v\#uq_{\mathrm{acc}}v\# \\ \#C_1\#C_2\#\cdots\#C_k\#ucq_{\mathrm{acc}}v\# \end{bmatrix}.$$

We thus decrease the length of the protrusion by one.

Similarly, when the partial match is

$$\begin{bmatrix} \#C_1\#C_2\#\cdots\#C_k\#uq_{\mathrm{acc}}cv\# \\ \#C_1\#C_2\#\cdots\#C_k\# \end{bmatrix}$$

with $u \in \Gamma^*$, $v \in \Gamma^+$, and $c \in \Gamma$. Suppose $u = u_1 \ldots u_r$ and $v = v_1 \ldots v_s$. We extend the partial match using the sequence

$$\begin{bmatrix} u_1 \\ u_1 \end{bmatrix}, \ldots, \begin{bmatrix} u_r \\ u_r \end{bmatrix}, \begin{bmatrix} q_{\mathrm{acc}} \\ cq_{\mathrm{acc}} \end{bmatrix}, \begin{bmatrix} v_1 \\ v_1 \end{bmatrix}, \ldots, \begin{bmatrix} v_s \\ v_s \end{bmatrix}, \begin{bmatrix} \# \\ \# \end{bmatrix}.$$

This extends the partial match to

$$\begin{bmatrix} \#C_1\#C_2\#\cdots\#C_k\#ucq_{\mathrm{acc}}v\#uq_{\mathrm{acc}}v\# \\ \#C_1\#C_2\#\cdots\#C_k\#ucq_{\mathrm{acc}}v\# \end{bmatrix}.$$

Thus, we decrease the length of the protrusion by one character.

Using the two length-reduction processes, the protrusion becomes $q_{\mathrm{acc}}\#$, which we can clear with the domino tile

$$\begin{bmatrix} \epsilon \\ q_{\mathrm{acc}}\# \end{bmatrix}.$$

8.4.3   The Undecidability of PCP

We now prove the undecidability of the PCP problem.

Theorem 8.9 PCP *is undecidable.*

We will modify the construction in the previous proof to show that PCP is undecidable. Let $*$ be a new symbol not in $\Gamma \cup Q \cup \{\#\}$. Construct from the above instance, P, of Post's Correspondence Problem, a new instance, P^*, with the following modifications:

- For each domino tile, insert a $*$ after each symbol for its top string and before each symbol for its bottom string.
- Insert a $*$ before the first symbol of the top string of the start domino tile.
- Insert a $*$ after the last symbol of the bottom string of each closing domino tile.

The last two additional modifications enforce the starting of a match with the new start domino tile and the ending of a match with the new final domino tile. Since the insertion of $*$ is between symbols, once we have fixed the first and the final domino tiles, the construction of a match will proceed as before.

We have thus proven Theorem 8.8.

8.5 Beyond RE

Here, we study the realm beyond the recursively enumerable and the co-recursively enumerable.

We have learned that there are languages in RE \ coRE and coRE \ RE. Do RE and coRE jointly cover all the languages? Certainly not. Some languages are neither RE nor coRE. We can construct a language outside RE $\cup$ coRE by taking the union of a language not in RE and one not in coRE. Define:

$$L = \{0w \mid w \in \text{ACCEPT}_{\text{TM}}\} \cup \{1w \mid w \in \overline{\text{ACCEPT}_{\text{TM}}}\}.$$

We can construct a many-one reduction from $\text{ACCEPT}_{\text{TM}}$ to L because for all w, $w \in \text{ACCEPT}_{\text{TM}}$ if, and only if, $0w \in L$. Similarly, we can construct a many-one reduction from $\overline{\text{ACCEPT}_{\text{TM}}}$ to L because for all w, $w \in \overline{\text{ACCEPT}_{\text{TM}}}$ if, and only if, $1w \in L$. Since $\text{ACCEPT}_{\text{TM}}$ is in RE \ coRE and $\overline{\text{ACCEPT}_{\text{TM}}}$ is in coRE \ RE, L is thus neither coRE nor RE.

We can systematically construct language classes that are increasing in difficulty. We will use the **oracle Turing machine (oracle TM)** model for this purpose. An oracle TM has a mechanism for executing an external black-box subroutine that can answer the membership question of some language. The calls to the subroutine are through an **oracle tape**, which is different from the input tape. Like the output tape, the query tape is write-only (see Sect. 6.4). The transition function of an oracle TM is independent of the symbol appearing in the cell that the head on the oracle tape is seeing, and does not move the head on the query tape to the left.

An oracle TM calls the subroutine by entering a query state. This special state is q_{query}. Upon entering q_{query}, the subroutine checks the membership of the query string (ignoring the infinitely long suffix of the blank character). The subroutine reports the result of its membership checking by setting the state of the oracle TM. If the query is a member, the subroutine sets the state to q_{yes}; otherwise, it sets to q_{no}. After processing the query, the subroutine erases all non-blank characters appearing on the query tape and moves the head on the query tape to the leftmost position.

An oracle TM does not control the language that appears as its subroutine (oracle), but its program may expect a specific language as the oracle. We design an oracle TM assuming that a specific language plays the role of the oracle. This means that the program's decisions may be incorrect if a wrong language is used as the oracle.

Definition 8.9 We say that an oracle TM M accepts a language L with O as its oracle if for all x,

- If $x \in L$, M on input x with O as its oracle accepts
- If $x \notin L$, M on input x with O as its oracle rejects

We define the concepts of recognition and co-recognition similarly.

We define the **arithmetical hierarchy** $\{\Delta_k, \Sigma_k, \Pi_k\}_{k \geq 0}$ as follows.

Definition 8.10 Define $\Delta_0 = \Sigma_0 = \Pi_0 = R$, and for all $k \geq 1$, define Δ_k, Σ_k, and Π_k as follows:

- Δ_k is the collection of all languages L some oracle TM decides with some language in Σ_{k-1} as the oracle.
- Σ_k is the collection of all languages L some oracle TM recognizes with some language in Σ_{k-1} as the oracle.
- Π_k is the collection of all languages L some oracle TM co-recognizes with some language in Σ_{k-1} as the oracle.

Figure 8.2 shows the relations among the first three levels of the arithmetical hierarchy.

Here are some known examples of languages in the arithmetical hierarchy at levels greater than 1.

- $\{\langle M, N \rangle \mid M$ and N are TMs and they recognize the same languages$\}$ is in $\Pi_2 - (\Sigma_1 \cup \Pi_1)$.
- $\{\langle M \rangle \mid M$ is a TM and does not halt on at least one input$\}$ is in $\Sigma_2 - (\Sigma_1 \cup \Pi_1)$.
- $\{\langle M \rangle \mid M$ is a TM and $L(M)$ is recursive$\}$ is in $\Sigma_3 - (\Sigma_2 \cup \Pi_2)$.

Theorem 8.10

1. $\Delta_1 = R$, $\Sigma_1 = RE$, and $\Pi_1 = \text{coRE}$.

Fig. 8.2 The arithmetical hierarchy. The classes that appear higher contain the classes that appear lower

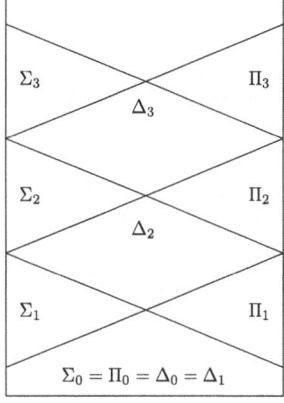

2. *Each class C in the arithmetical hierarchy has closure properties under union,
   intersection, and marked union.*
3. *For all k, $\Delta_k = \Sigma_k \cap \Pi_k$.*

Proof

(1) Let M be an oracle TM that recognizes L and uses a language A as its oracle.
Suppose A is in Σ_0. Since $\Sigma_0 = R$ by definition, a single-tape TM N decides A.
We assume that N has a property that, before accepting or rejecting, writes the
blank in all cells holding non-blank symbols and moves the head to the leftmost
cell (see Exercise 6.19).

We combine M's and A's programs and construct a TM, T, that recognizes
L. The tape alphabet of T is the unions of those of M and N. The input tape
alphabet of T is the unions of those of M and N. In constructing the latter
union, we can assume that the two machines have the same blank symbol. The
number of tapes of T is the same as that of M. The roles of the tapes are the
same between the two machines, except that we will treat the query tape of M
as a regular tape.

On each input x, the machine T executes the code for M with the following
modifications:

- While simulating M, T keeps track of the position of the head on the "query
  tape," which is a regular tape.
- When M is about to enter q_{query}, T moves the head on the "query tape" to
  its leftmost position. Then, T executes the program of N, assuming that the
  "query tape" is the tape of N. Since N is a single-tape machine, during the
  simulation of N, T does not touch other tapes.
- Since N is a decider, the simulation of N ends in q_{acc} or q_{rej} eventually. If
  the simulation ends in q_{acc}, T changes its state to q_{yes}, and if the simulation
  ends in q_{rej}, T changes its state to q_{no}. Then, T returns to the simulation of
  M.
- When the simulation of N takes T to either q_{acc} or q_{rej} of M, T accepts or
  rejects accordingly.

Since T substitutes queries with simulations of N, we can treat q_{yes} and q_{no} of
T as regular states. We can think of T as a non-oracle TM with this treatment.

For an arbitrary query M makes, if the query string is a member of A, the
simulation takes T to q_{acc} of N, and so T goes back to the simulation of M
in q_{yes}; otherwise, the state that T arrives at is q_{rej}, and so T goes back in q_{no}.
Thus, we conclude that T on x would behave like M on x, with A as the oracle.
Therefore, T recognizes the same language as M with A as the oracle; that is,
L.

Using the same argument as the above, we can show that Π_1 equals coRE
and Δ_1 equals R.

(2) The proof uses an induction on the level, k, of the hierarchy. For $k = 0$, the three
classes are each equal to R. From Exercises 6.21 and 6.25, we know that R has
the closure properties in question. For $k \geq 1$, assume that we have already

established the closure properties for all levels $< k$. Let L_1 and L_2 be two languages in Σ_k. Let M_1 and M_2 be, respectively, the machines that recognize L_1 and L_2 with oracles A_1 and A_2 in Σ_{k-1}. Let $A_0 = A_1 \oplus A_2$. By our induction hypothesis, $A_0 \in \Sigma_{k-1}$. Let M_1' be a TM that operates as if it were M_1 but would insert a 0 at the beginning of each query string M_1 would produce. The machine M_1' recognizes L_1 with oracle A_0. Let M_2' be a TM that operates as if it were M_2 but would insert a 1 at the beginning of each query string M_2 would produce. The machine M_2' recognizes L_2 with oracle A_0. Now, by following the solution to Exercise 6.23, we can show that a TM recognizes $L_1 \cup L_2$ with A_0 as the oracle and that another one recognizes $L_1 \oplus L_2$ with A_0 as the oracle. These machines witness that the two new languages are in Σ_k. The proofs for Π_k and Δ_k are similar, so we skip them.

(3) For $k = 0$, since $\Delta_0 = \Sigma_0 = \Pi_0 = R$ by definition, we have $\Delta_0 = \Sigma_0 \cap \Pi_0$. For $k = 1$, since $\Delta_1 = R$, $\Sigma_1 = RE$, and $\Pi_0 = coRE$, we have $\Delta_1 = \Sigma_1 \cap \Pi_1$. For $k \geq 2$, let $L_1 \in \Sigma_k$ and $L_2 \in \Pi_k$. There is an oracle TM M_1 and a language $A_1 \in \Sigma_{k-1}$ such that M_1 recognizes L_1 with A_1 as the oracle. There is an oracle TM M_2 and a language $A_2 \in \Sigma_{k-1}$ such that M_2 co-recognizes L_2 with A_2 as the oracle. Let $A_0 = A_1 \oplus A_1$. The language A_0 is in Σ_{k-1}.

By following the argument from (2), we can obtain oracle TMs M_1' and M_2' such that M_1' recognizes L_1 with A_0 as the oracle and M_2' co-recognizes L_2 with A_0 as the oracle. We can assume that both M_1' and M_2' have only two tapes, each using the second tape as the query tape.

Think of an oracle TM, M_0, that, like the machine from the proof of Theorem 6.3, attempts to simulate M_1' and M_2' concurrently. The machine M_0 has six tapes, where the fifth is the query tape and the sixth is for bit counting. M_0 uses its first two tapes for simulating M_1' and the next two tapes for simulating M_2'. As with the previous part of the proof, we will treat the query tapes of M_1' and M_2' as regular tapes.

The first action of M_0 is to copy the input from Tape 1 to Tape 3.

Next, M_0 simulates M_1' and M_2' on their respective tapes (the first, second, third, and fourth). The simulations will be one step and one machine at a time. When it is about to simulate a step of M_1, M_0 writes 1 on Tape 6 and keeps the head at the same position. Similarly, when it is about to simulate a step of M_2, M_0 writes 2 on Tape 6 and keeps the head at the same position.

When M_1' enters q_{query}, M_0 does the following:

a. Copy the contents of Tape 2 to Tape 5 with 0 in front.
b. Clear Tape 2 and move the head on Tape 2 to the leftmost position.
c. Enter q_{query}.

Similarly, when M_2' enters q_{query}, M_0 does the following:

a. Copy the contents of Tape 4 to Tape 5 with 0 in front.
b. Clear Tape 4 and move the head on Tape 4 to the leftmost position.
c. Enter q_{query}.

Upon returning from querying, the state is either q_{yes} or q_{no}. To identify the machine whose query it has executed, M_0 examines the cell on Tape 6. If the cell holds 1, then M_0 assumes that the state of M_1' has changed to q_{yes} or q_{no} accordingly. If the cell holds 2, then M_0 assumes that the state of M_2' has changed to q_{yes} or q_{no} accordingly.

After simulating one step action of M_1', if the state of M_1' becomes q_{acc}, then T accepts; after simulating one step action of M_2', if the state of M_2' becomes q_{acc}, then T rejects.

For all oracles X, the above program of T correctly simulates M_1' and M_2' with oracle X. By our assumption, for each input w, if the oracle is A_0, either M_1' on x accepts or M_2' accepts (we cannot necessarily guarantee the property if the oracle is not equal to A_0). Thus, for each input x, T on x either accepts or rejects, and the decision T makes is correct for L.

This proves the theorem.

$\square$

The inclusions are proper.

Theorem 8.11

1. *For all $k \geq 1$, Σ_k and Π_k are incomparable; that is, $\Delta_k \subset \Sigma_k \not\subseteq \Pi_k$ and $\Delta_k \subset \Pi_k \not\subseteq \Sigma_k$.*
2. *For all $k \geq 2$, $\Delta_k \supset \Sigma_{k-1} \cup \Pi_{k-1}$.*

Proof We use an argument similar to Sect. 8.1.1 to show that neither Σ_k nor Π_k include one another.

For (1), we prove the separations by induction on k. The first two properties of the theorem hold for $k = 1$ because $\Sigma_1 = $ RE, $\Pi_1 = $ coRE, and $\Delta_1 = $ R. For the induction step, let $k = 2$ and suppose that the theorem's properties hold for all smaller values of k.

We use the unary TM encoding from Sect. 7.1.1. We define D to be the set of all strings w of the form $0^{d_k} 10^{d_{k-1}} 1 \cdots 10^{d_1}$ such that

- $0^{d_{k-1}}, \ldots, 0^{d_1}$ are valid encodings of deterministic oracle TMs.
- 0^{d_k} is a valid encoding of a deterministic TM.
- Under the following formulation, $w \notin A_k$:

  - $M_k, \ldots, M_1$ are the machines that $0^{d_k}, \ldots, 0^{d_1}$ represent, respectively.
  - A_1 is the language that M_1 recognizes.
  - For $i = 2, \ldots, k$, A_i is the language that M_i recognizes with A_{i-1} as the oracle.

The language D is in Π_k. We can show the membership of D in Π_k using the following series of mechanical languages, $B_1, \ldots, B_k$, where for each i such that $1 \leq i \leq k$, B_i is the set of all y of the form

$$0^m 10^{d_k} 10^{d_{k-1}} 1 \cdots 10^{d_1}$$

such that 0^m encodes some input y to M_i and $y \in A_i$, where the definitions of M_i and A_i are the same as those for D. We can see that $B_1 \in \Sigma_1, B_2 \in \Sigma_2, \ldots, B_k \in \Sigma_k$. Since $B_{k-1} \in \Sigma_{k-1}$, we know that $D \in \Pi_k$. Assume D in Σ_k. Then, there is a series of TMs $N_k, \ldots, N_1$ witnessing the membership of D in Σ_k in the language definitions of $A_k, \ldots, A_1$. We define $w = 0^{d_k} 10^{d_{k-1}} 1 \cdots 10^{d_1}$ where the unary strings encoding $N_k, \ldots, N_1$. Then we know N_k accepts w with A_{k-1} as the oracle if, and only if, N_k does not take w with A_{k-1} as the oracle; this is a contradiction. Thus, $D \notin \Sigma_k$, and so, $\Pi_k \nsubseteq \Sigma_k$. Using the compliment of D, we get that $\Sigma_k \nsubseteq \Pi_k$. Hence, for all k, Σ_k and Π_k are incompatible. The incompatibility also implies that $\Delta_k \subset \Sigma_k$ and $\Delta_k \subset \Pi_k$.

For (2), let $k \geq 1$. Let $C_k = \{A \oplus B \mid A \in \Sigma_k \text{ and } B \in \Pi_k\}$. The class C_k is a subclass of Δ_{k+1} (see Problem 8.15). The class C_k cannot be a subset of Σ_k because the inclusion implies $\Pi_k \subseteq \Sigma_k$. For much the same reason, $C_k \nsubseteq \Pi_k$. Thus, $\Delta_{k+1} \supset \Sigma_k \cup \Pi_k$.   □

Exercises

8.1 Show that $\mathbb{Z}$ is countable.

8.2 Show that $\mathbb{Q}$ is countable.

Hint: You can develop an enumeration in the following manner:

First, we enumerate all pairs of integers, (m, n), such that $m, n \geq 1$. We use a nondecreasing sequence of values d representing $m + n$. The initial value of d is 2. For each value d, we start the enumeration with the pair $(1, d - 1)$ and increase the value of the first component one by one. In other words, the enumeration for d is $(1, d - 1), (2, d - 2), \ldots, (d - 2, 2), (d - 1, 1)$. After enumerating all pairs having the same value of d, we move on to the next value, $d + 1$.

We view each pair (m, n) as the representation of the rational number equal to m/n. For all pairs (m, n) and all positive integers g, (mg, ng) represents the same rational number as (m, n). We can design the enumeration so that we include exactly one pair from the pairs representing the same rational numbers; that way, we can avoid duplications.

We can then extend this enumeration so that it covers 0 and all negative rational numbers.

8.3 Prove Corollary 8.5.

8.4 Prove that $L_{diag} \in$ coRE.

8.5 Prove Corollary 8.1.

8.6 Prove that ACCEPT$_{TM}$ is recursively enumerable.

8.7 Prove Proposition 8.3.

8.8 Prove that the problem of deciding, given three CFGs, G_1, G_2, and G_3, whether or not $L(G_1) = L(G_2) \cup L(G_2)$, is undecidable.

8.9 Prove that the equality problem between a CFL and a DFA is undecidable, where the CFL is given by a CFG.

8.10 Prove Proposition 8.4.

8.11 Prove Rice's Theorem when the empty set has the property Q.

8.12 Using Rice's Theorem, prove that the following language is undecidable:

$$\{\langle M \rangle \mid M \text{ is a single-tape TM and } L(M) is regular\}.$$

8.13 Using Rice's Theorem, prove that the following language is undecidable:

$$\{\langle M \rangle \mid M \text{ is a single-tape TM and } L(M) \text{ is finite}\}.$$

8.14 Using Rice's Theorem, prove that the following language is undecidable:

$$\{\langle M \rangle \mid M \text{ is a single-tape TM and } L(M) is empty\}.$$

8.15 Let $k \geq 1$. Let $C_k = \{0A \cup 1B \mid A \in \Sigma_k \text{ and } B \in \Pi_k\}$. Show that C_k is in Δ_{k+1}.

8.16 Prove that R_1 in the proof of Theorem 8.7 is DCFL.

8.17 Prove that R_2 in the proof of Theorem 8.7 is DCFL.

8.18 Prove Corollary 8.3.

8.19 Prove that PCP is decidable if the strings in the domino pieces are over a single-letter alphabet.

8.20 Prove that PCP is undecidable if the strings in the domino pieces are over a two-letter alphabet.

8.21 We can prove that the ambiguity of CFLs is undecidable by constructing a many-one reduction from PCP to it. Let $I = \langle (t_1, b_1), \ldots, (t_k, b_k) \rangle$ be an instance for PCP where each pair is a tile. We define a grammar G as follows:

- The symbols appearing in the tiles are terminals.
- There are k additional terminals $d_1, \ldots, d_k$.
- There are three variables: S, T, and B.
- The rules of the grammar are as follows:

$$S \rightarrow T \mid B,$$
$$T \rightarrow d_1 T t_1^R \mid \cdots \mid d_k T t_k^R \mid \epsilon, \text{ and}$$
$$B \rightarrow d_1 B b_1^R \mid \cdots \mid d_k B t_k^R \mid \epsilon.$$

Prove that this grammar is ambiguous if, and only if, I has a match, so PCP is many-one reducible to the ambiguity problem.

8.22 Rice's Theorem makes it possible to state the undecidability of any nontrivial property of the language a TM accepts. One such property is context-freeness. It is not difficult to argue that not all languages TMs accept are context-free, but can you provide a concrete example? In other words, can you construct a reduction from ACCEPT$_{\text{TM}}$ such that the TM language generated from an instance of ACCEPT$_{\text{TM}}$ is context-free if, and only if, the instance is a positive member?

8.23 Consider the problem of testing if a CFL is properly contained in another CFL, where their respective grammars give both CFLs. Show that the problem is undecidable.

8.24 Show that the problem of deciding whether or not two RE languages are incomparable (i.e., neither contain the other) is undecidable, where TMs give the two languages.

8.25 Show that the problem of deciding whether or not two RE languages have exactly one member in common is undecidable, where TMs give the two languages.

8.26 Show that the problem of deciding if a CFL has an equivalent grammar with no more than a given number of variables is undecidable.

8.27 We say that a variable of a CFG is equivalent to another variable in the CFG if the variables produce the same sets of terminal-only strings. Show that the problem of deciding if two variables in a CFG are equivalent is undecidable.

Bibliographic Notes and Further Reading
The diagonal argument for showing that $\mathbb{R}$ is not countable is by Cantor [3]. The diagonal language is by Turing [9]. Post's Correspondence Problem and its marked version are by Post [6]. The undecidability of problems about context-free languages is from Bar-Hillel, Perles, and Shamir [1], Ginsburg and Rose [4], and Hartmanis [5]. The undecidability of unambiguity is by Cantor [2]. Rice's Theorem is by Rice [7, 8].

References

1. Y. Bar-Hillel, M. Perles, E. Shamir, On formal properties of simple phrase structure grammars. Sprachtypologie und Universalienforschung **14**, 143–172 (1961)
2. D.G. Cantor, On the ambiguity problem of Backus systems. J. ACM **9**(4), 477–479 (1962)
3. G. Cantor, Über eine elementare frage der mannigfaltigkeitslehre. *Jahresbericht der Deutschen Mathematiker-Vereinigung*, vol. 1 (1891)
4. S. Ginsburg, G.F. Rose, Operations which preserve definability in languages. J. ACM **10**(2), 175–195 (1963)
5. J. Hartmanis, Context-free languages and Turing machine computations, in *Proceedings of Symposia in Applied Mathematics*, vol. 19 (American Mathematical Society, Providence, 1967), pp. 42–51
6. E.L. Post, Finite combinatory process-formulation, I. J. Symbol Logic **1**, 103–105 (1936)
7. H.G. Rice, Classes of recursively enumerable sets and their decision problems. Trans. Am. Math. Soc. **74**(2), 358–366 (1953)

8. H.G. Rice, On completely recursively enumerable classes and their key arrays. J. Symbol Logic
   21(3), 304–308 (1956)
9. A.M. Turing, On computable numbers, with an application to the Entscheidungsproblem. J.
   Math. **58**(345–363), 5 (1936)

Part IV
Computational Complexity
and Resource-Bounded Turing Machine
Computation

Chapter 9
The Time Complexity

9.1 The Time Complexity Measure

Computational complexity theory studies computational problems regarding how much resources are necessary to solve them. Two types of resources are of concern: **time** and **space**. In this chapter, we study the time complexity measure. The next chapter will deal with the space complexity measure.

Definition 9.1 Let M be a TM that halts on all inputs. We define $time_M(x)$ as the function that maps each input x to the number of steps M on x executes before halting.

Definition 9.2 Let $f(n)$ be a function from $\mathbb{N}$ to itself. We say that $f(n)$ is a **time-bounding function** if $f(n)$ is non-decreasing and for all n, $f(n) \geq n + 1$.

This definition of time-bounding functions incorporates the following two anticipated properties about how TMs behave:

- TMs must read their entire input before accepting or rejecting. (TMs need a minimum of $n + 1$ steps to arrive at the cell that immediately follows the input.)
- TMs may operate for a longer time on a longer input.

Definition 9.3 Let $f(n)$ be a time-bounding function and M be a TM. We say that M is $f(n)$ **time-bounded** if for all but finitely many n, $time_M(x) \leq f(n)$ holds for all inputs x having length n.

Definition 9.4 Let $f(n)$ be a time-bounding function. Let L be a decidable language. We say that L has **time complexity** $f(n)$ if an $f(n)$ time-bounded TM decides L.

We sometimes refer to this time complexity notion as the **worst-case complexity** in the following sense:

- A TM deciding L faster than M may exist. Still, in the worst-case scenario, $f(n)$ is sufficient for solving L's decision problem.

We use multi-tape TMs to define complexity classes.

Definition 9.5   For a time-bounding function $f(n)$, we define:

$$\text{DTIME}[f(n)] = \{L \mid \text{ there exists a } f(n) \text{ time-bounded TM deciding } L\}.$$

The following theorem shows that reducing the time bound to its constant fraction does not change the DTIME classes.

Theorem 9.1 (The Linear Speed-Up Theorem)   *Let $f(n)$ be a time-bounding function. Then, for all constants $d > 1$, $\text{DTIME}[f(n)] \subseteq \text{DTIME}[n + f(n)/d]$.*

Proof Overview
A crucial idea behind the proof is compressing the tapes via combining multiple symbols into one symbol. Given a k-tape TM M that decides a language, we construct a $k+1$-tape TM whose alphabet can encode h symbols of M into just one symbol. Here, h is an integer parameter whose value we can select. The $k + 1$-tape TM constructs, from its input, an alternate input. The alternate input combines h symbols and then simulates M. The new machine simulates d steps of M in just six steps. If M is to run for $f(n)$ steps on an input having a length of n, the machine will run for approximately $n + (f(n) + n) * 8/h$ steps. By choosing a value significant enough for h, the computation time can be reduced by any constant factor.

Proof   Let L be a language in $\text{DTIME}[f(n)]$, where $f(n)$ is a time-bounding function. Let $M = (Q, \Sigma, \Gamma, \delta, q_0, q_{\text{acc}}, q_{\text{rej}})$ be a TM that decides L in time $f(n)$. Let k be the number of M's tapes. Let $d > 1$ be an arbitrary constant. Let $h \geq 8d$ be an arbitrary integer.

We will develop a simulator of M having $k + 1$ tapes. We call the simulator N. N's Tape 1 is exclusively for receiving M's input. N uses the remaining k tapes for running M's program.

Let $\tilde{\Gamma} = \{\tilde{a} \mid a \in \Gamma\}$. Each symbol $\tilde{a}$ in $\tilde{\Gamma}$ indicates that the symbol is a and the head of M is on the cell that holds the a. Let Π be the collection of all h-tuples, $(a_1, \ldots, a_h)$, from Γ. In addition, let Π' be the collection of all h-tuples $(a_1, \ldots, a_h)$ from $\Gamma \cup \tilde{\Gamma}$ such that exactly one of $a_1, \ldots, a_h$ is from $\tilde{\Gamma}$. Let $\vdash$ be a symbol representing the left end of the tape. We will identify the $(\sqcup, \ldots, \sqcup)$ in Π with $\sqcup$ in Γ.

We group the cells on each tape of M into blocks of consecutive h cells; i.e., for all $i \geq 1$, the i-th block consists of the cells at positions $(i-1)h + 1, \ldots, ih$. Each symbol of Π can encode the content of a block, including the case in which the head is on one of the cells. For example, if $a, b, c \in \Gamma$ and $h = 4$, a tuple-sequence

$$(abcc)(bbbb)(cac\tilde{a})(baba)$$

corresponds to the 16-symbol character sequence:

$$abccbbbbcac\tilde{a}baba.$$

The $\tilde{a}$ indicates that the head is on M's 12th cell. We refer to a block that contains the head position as the "center" block. We refer to the block immediately to the left of the center block as the "left guard" and the block immediately to the right of the center block as the "right guard." Figure 9.1 shows this encoding idea.

Let x be the input and $n = |x|$.

N prepares its simulation by developing a block-wise representation of the input. First, N writes $\vdash$ on Cell 1 of Tape 2 in one step. In the same step, N writes an h-symbol tuple $\tilde{\sqcup}\sqcup^{h-1}$ on Cell 1 of Tapes 2 through $k + 1$. The h-tuple represents the situation in which the h cells are all blank, and the head is on the leftmost cell of the h cells.

Next, N reads Tape 1 from the left end to the first appearance of $\sqcup$. While reading, N collects the symbols appearing in each block of h cells and writes their h-symbol representation on Tape 2. In addition, N adds the squiggle to the first element of the first h-symbol representation. The number of h-symbol representations N creates is $\lceil n/h \rceil$ symbols. If the length of the input is not a multiple of h, the last block contains some $\sqcup$. Upon encountering the first $\sqcup$, N knows it has reached the end of the input and can stop scanning it. Upon completing this conversion, N moves Head 2 back to Cell 2, where a squiggle appears.

The preparation is now complete.

Now that Tapes 2 through $k + 1$ have representations that combine h cells into one, N can simulate the action of M for h steps in just six steps via the following manner:

1. At the beginning of the six-step simulation cycle, N knows the present state of M. In addition, on each tape (Tapes 2 through $k + 1$), the head is on a cell that indicates the head position of M of its corresponding tape; i.e., one of the h symbols appearing in the cell is from $\tilde{\Gamma}$.

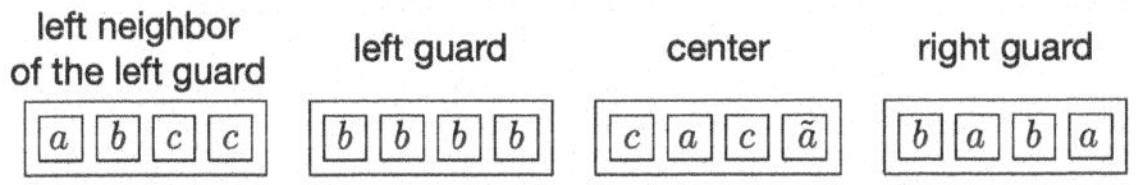

Fig. 9.1 The block encoding and its traversal. The size of the blocks is four in the diagram

2. Using three steps, N moves each head to the left guard, back to the center, and then to the right guard. The three-step move brings each head to the position of its right guard and reveals the $3h$ symbols appearing, where one of the middle h symbols holds the squiggle.
3. Since the cycle began with the knowledge of M's present state and M cannot move its heads more than h positions, N learns M's actions during the next h steps. The knowledge consists of the following:

   a. On each tape, N learns the contents of the $3h$ cells of M and the head position within the $3h$ cells. N can interpret them as three h-symbol representations to replace the present representations.
   b. N learns which of the three cells must move the head on each tape.
   c. N learns M's state after the h steps.

4. In the next three steps, N updates the contents of each tape and brings its head to the designated new position. Among the three cells, replacement is required for at most two, with the following possibilities:

   a. The head must move to the left guard. All three cells may require updating.
   b. The head must move to the center. All three cells may need updating.
   c. The head must move to the right guard. The left guard does not require updating.

   Given that updating starts with the head on the right guard, these cases are completed with the following corresponding head moves (the sequence of head positions resulting from the moves appears within the parentheses):

   a. $-, L, L$ (right guard, center, left guard)
   b. L, L, R (center, left guard, center)
   c. $L, R, -$ (center, right guard, right guard)

   Figure 9.2 presents how the head moves during the six-step action.
5. At the end of the sixth step, N updates M's state.
6. If the state becomes q_{acc} or q_{rej}, N accepts or rejects accordingly.

   Suppose the length of the input is n. The number of steps N uses for preparation is

$$1 + (n + 1) + (\lceil n/h \rceil - 1).$$

The first term is the time required for initializing Tapes 3 through $k + 1$, the second is for reading the input and creating the initial h-tuple encoding, and the third is for moving Head 2 to its starting position. The quantity is at most:

$$n + n/h + 2.$$

Fig. 9.2 The block encoding and its traversal. The size of the blocks is four in the diagram. The numbers $1, \ldots, 6$ represent the head positions after steps $1, \ldots, 6$, respectively. The circles indicate where the cell can be updated when executing the next step. (**a–c**) correspond to the cases that appear on p. 218

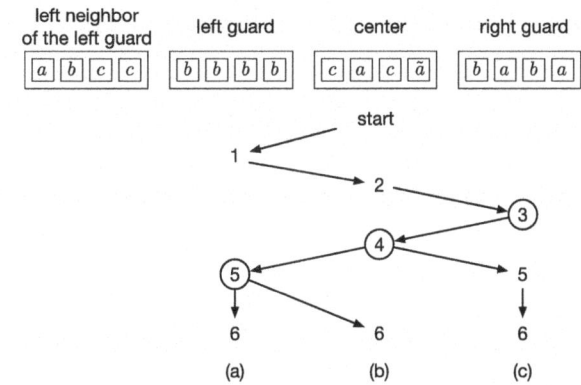

After the initialization, the time N spends on the simulation is:

$$6 \cdot \left\lceil \frac{f(n)}{h} \right\rceil \leq 6 \cdot \frac{f(n)}{h} + 6.$$

Combining the two, the running time of N is at most:

$$n + \frac{n}{h} + 2 + 6 \cdot \frac{f(n)}{h} + 6 \leq n + 7 \cdot \frac{f(n)}{h} + 8.$$

The last inequality holds because $f(n)$ is a time-bounding function, so $f(n) \geq n+1$. Since h is a constant, for all but finitely many n, $f(n)/h \geq 8$. Thus, for all but finitely many n, the running time is at most:

$$n + 8 \cdot \frac{f(n)}{h} = n + \frac{f(n)}{(h/8)}.$$

Since h is an integer greater than or equal to $8d$, $h/8 \geq d$, the running time is at most $n + f(n)/d$ for all but finitely many n. Thus, DTIME$[f(n)] \leq$ DTIME$[n + f(n)/d]$. This proves the theorem. $\qquad\square$

We obtain the following result from the theorem.

Corollary 9.1 *Suppose $f(n)$ satisfies $f(n) \geq (1 + \alpha)n$ for all but finitely many n, where α is a positive constant. Then, for all constants $c > 0$, DTIME$[f(n)] =$ DTIME$[cf(n)]$.*

We leave the proof to the reader (see Exercise 9.2).

9.2   Time-Efficient Simulations of Multi-tape TMs

An important issue to address when simulating time-bounded TMs is the time efficiency. In the proof of Theorem 9.1, the simulator N has $k + 1$ tapes when the original machine M has k tapes. Exercise 9.1 asks to reduce the number of tapes to k by reusing the input tape. If we limit the number of tapes of N to a fixed constant, some nontrivial amounts of "slowdown" appear. The simulations require $O(t(n)^2)$ steps when N has just one tape, but the multiplicative $t(n)$ factor will shrink to $\log(t(n))$ when N has two tapes. In this section, we prove these two simulation results.

9.2.1   Simulating with One Tape

First, we analyze the efficiency when the simulator has only one tape.

Theorem 9.2 (The Single-Tape Simulation Theorem)   *Let $t(n)$ be a time-bounding function. Let L be a language in* DTIME$[t(n)]$. *Then $L \in$ DTIME$[t(n)^2]$ by a single-tape TM.*

> **Proof Overview**
> We recall the proof of Theorem 6.1, where we showed that a two-tape TM can simulate a multi-tape TM. When the content of a multi-tape TM appears on one tape, determining the TM's action requires scanning the entire tape because the heads may be scattered in the region covered by the heads. After d steps, the cell indices that the heads have covered are between 1 and d. Simulating the action of the TM at step d thus requires $O(d)$ steps. Given that the TM has a time bound of $t(n)$, the simulation requires $O(t(n)^2)$ steps.

Proof   Let $k \geq 1$ be an integer. Let M be a k-tape TM that decides some language L. We construct an M's simulator N. Let $t(n)$ be a time-bounding function such that M runs in time $t(n)$. Let Γ be the tape alphabet of M. We combine the ideas from the proofs of Theorems 6.1 and 9.1 and expand the alphabet Γ by adding all k-tuples $(\Gamma \cup \tilde{\Gamma})^k$. Each k-tuple encodes the cells of M's tapes at the same cell index, along with k independent markers indicating the head position.

The initial preparation for the simulation requires rewriting the tape contents where the input appears in its k-tuple version, with an end marker appearing before the tape contents' encoding. Then, N conducts a step-by-step simulation of M, making k round trips on the tape to determine the action M is to perform and then k more round trips to rewrite the tape contents.

The length of the tape that a round trip covers at time ℓ is at most $2 + \max\{n, \ell\}$, where n is the length of the input. The quantity ℓ is at most $t(n)$ since M halts in at most $t(n)$ steps, and so one step of M requires at most $O(k \cdot t(n))$ steps. The initial conversion requires $O(n)$ steps. Since M halts in $t(n)$ steps, the total number of steps that N runs is at most $O(n) + O(t(n) \cdot k \cdot t(n)) = O(k \cdot t(n)^2)$. Since we can think of k as a constant, N decides L in time $O(t(n)^2)$.

This proves the theorem.   □

9.2.2   Simulating with Two Tapes

In the previous section, we saw that a single-tape TMs can simulate $t(n)$ time-bounded TMs in $O((t(n))^2)$ steps. While this quadratic time increase is unavoidable for single-tape simulation, adding one more tape reduces the time required for simulation to $O(t(n) \log(t(n)))$.

Theorem 9.3 *For all time-bounding functions and $L \in$ DTIME[$t(n)$], a two-tape TM decides L in time $O(t(n) \log(t(n)))$.*

Proof Overview
We assume that the simulator's Tape 1 is two-way infinite with two tracks (i.e., each cell can hold two symbols), and Tape 2 is one-way infinite. By doubling the number of tracks, the two-way infinite Tape 1 can be simulated with a one-way infinite tape; for all p, Cell p represents Cells $\pm p$.

The simulation's principle idea is to keep the character of the cell (on which the head is supposed to be) to Cell 0. To realize this arrangement, the tape is divided into blocks. When the first character of a block must move to Cell 0, the characters in the entire block move. Starting from Cell 0, the positive index cells are divided into blocks 0, 1, 2, 3, ... These blocks exponentially increase in size; their sizes are $2^0, 2^1, 2^2, 2^3, \ldots$. The same power-of-2 block-size allocation is applied to the region with negative indices.

During the simulation, the block having an index of i (or $-i$) covers 0, 2^i, or 2^{i+1} consecutive cells of the TM subject to simulation. This means that the characters travel from one block to another. The exponential increase in block sizes results in a running time of $O(t(n) \log(t(n)))$.

We devote the rest of this section to the proof of this theorem.

9.2.2.1   The Tape Organization

We first learn the tape organization of the two-tape simulator.

Let $k \geq 2$. Let $t(n)$ be a time-bounding function. Let M be a k-tape TM that runs in time $t(n)$. We will develop a two-tape simulator, S, of M. Tape 1 of S has

$2k + 2$ tracks (i.e., each cell has holds $2k + 2$ symbols); Tape 2 has three tracks. Of the $2k + 2$ tracks of Tape 1, S allocates *two* tracks to each tape of M. The remaining two tracks have particular roles; one provides block-wise coloring, and the other indicates the point closest to Cell 0 in each block. The markings appearing on the last two tracks will be commonly used among all the tape simulations. Tape 2 of S is a scratch area.

The head positions of Tape 1 are two-way infinite:

$$\ldots, -3, -2 - 1, 0, 1, 2, 3, \ldots.$$

As we examined in Exercise 6.27, we can implement two-way infinite tapes on one-way infinite ones by "folding" the tapes at position 0 (see Fig. 9.3). Folding a tape in half doubles the number of tracks. We understand that the actual coding of S uses the one-way infinite representation of two-way infinite tapes using $(2k+2) * 2 = 4k + 4$ tracks. The discussion here uses a two-way infinite tape.

The descriptions in the remainder of this section are for M's Tape 1. If $k \geq 2$, our simulator repeats the simulation for Tapes $2, 3, \ldots, k$.

The two tracks corresponding to each tape of M are the "lower" and the "upper" tracks. At each cell position, we refer to the upper- and lower-track combinations as "domino tiles." This view is reminiscent of Post's Correspondence Problem from Sect. 8.4. Each domino has an upper-track character and a lower-track character; these characters are from M's tape alphabet. We will introduce the symbol ⊔, which is different from the blank symbol of M. The new symbol is equivalent to the empty string ϵ, indicating that the character is empty. Let α and β be the characters of the lower and upper tracks in a domino, respectively. After each round of the simulation, the symbols satisfy the following conditions:

(R1) If $\alpha = ⊔$, then $\beta = ⊔$.
(R2) The domino represents $\alpha\beta$ as M's tape content.

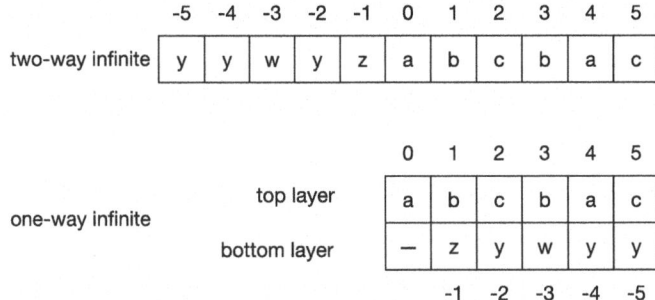

Fig. 9.3 Implementing a two-way infinite tape by a two-track, one-way infinite tape. Top panel: the contents of a two-way infinite tape requiring a one-way tape representation. Bottom panel: after folding, the bottom layer of the column at position 0 is empty. The numbers represent the cell positions in the two-way tape

We partition Tape 1 into blocks of consecutive cells, B_i, $i = 0, \pm 1, \pm 2$, etc. The block B_0 has just one cell and is at the cell position 0. The blocks with positive indices stretch to the right of B_0, with B_1 immediately to the right of B_0, B_2 immediately to the right of B_1, etc. The blocks with negative indices stretch to the left of B_0, with B_{-1} immediately to the left of B_0, B_{-2} immediately to the left of B_{-1}, etc.

The size of a block is the number of domino tiles in it. For each $p \geq 1$, the blocks B_p and B_{-p} have 2^{p-1} domino tiles. Therefore, the character-based capacity of B_p and B_{-p} is thus $2^{p-1} * 2 = 2^p$. The simulation maintains the following invariant holds for each block and each tape after simulating one step of M:

(R3) The occupancy condition of the cells is one of the following three:

   • All characters are ⊔.
   • None of the characters are ⊔.
   • All lower characters are non-⊔, and all upper characters are ⊔.

(R4) Combining (R3) with (R1), we have for all index p or $-p$:

   • **Empty** The upper and the lower characters in every domino tile are empty. The block represents ϵ.
   • **Packed** Both upper and lower characters are nonempty. The block represents a string of 2^p characters.
   • **Half-packed** Only the upper characters are empty. The block represents a string having 2^{p-1} characters.

Figure 9.4 shows the divisions into blocks representing two tapes of M. Figure 9.5 shows the coloring and marking tracks.

9.2.2.2 The Tape Coloring and Marking

Next, we describe the marking and coloring of the tape.

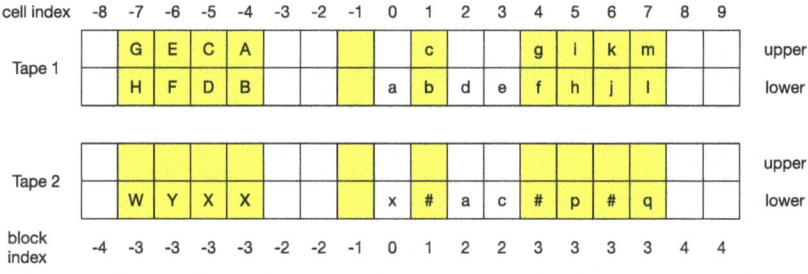

Fig. 9.4 Two tapes with two tracks each. The coloring rule is discussed in Sect. 9.2.2.2

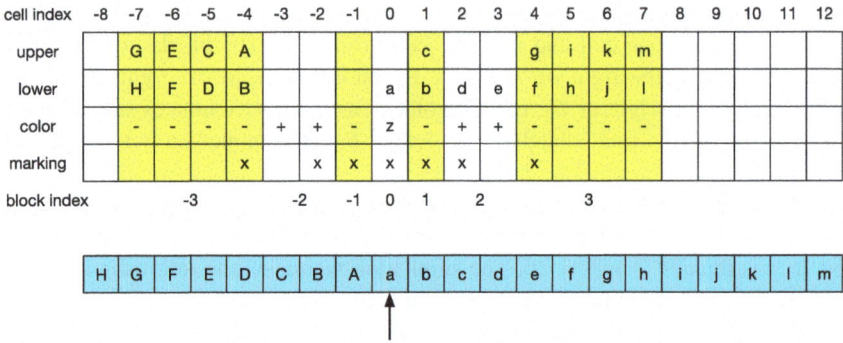

Fig. 9.5 One pair of tracks, and the color and marking tracks. The section corresponding to Cells − 8 through Cell 12 is shown

The color track contains one of three symbols: z, $+$, or $-$. The color symbols are fixed throughout the simulation. The color assignments are as follows:

(R5) The symbol z is exclusively for B_0. For other blocks, $+$ and $-$ appear in all the domino tiles in B_p with an even p and an odd p, respectively.

The marker track contains one of two symbols: x or ⊔. The marker x appears in the cell closest to Cell 0. The other cells have the marker ⊔.

When S visits a block, it scans the entire block. If the visit is for the first time, S assigns a value to the color and marker tracks. At the start of the computation, S places the color z on B_0 and the marker x on B_0. When S encounters a cell without color, it suspends its present task and assigns a color to the uncolored block in the following manner:

1. S can memorize the color of the cell it departs from when moving the head to the next cell; it can immediately determine the color γ of the uncolored block. If the color in its memory is z, then the color to assign is $-$; otherwise, it is the opposite of the color in memory. In addition, S places x as the marker.
2. S starts moving Head 1 to the left. For each cell with the previous color, S writes 1 on Tape 2 and moves Head 2 to the right. The process stops when Head 1 encounters the block marker x in the marker track. Let ℓ be the number of 1's S writes on Tape 2.
3. S erases the 1^ℓ on Tape 2 by moving the head straight back to the opposite end. For each move of Head 2, S writes γ on two color cells. The total number of cells S writes γ is 2ℓ.
4. S moves Head 1 back to the leftmost cell of the newly found block, where S sees the marker. The procedure is now complete.

Figure 9.6 shows the length of the 1s on Tape 2 and the color assignment of the new block. The duration of the procedure is as follows:

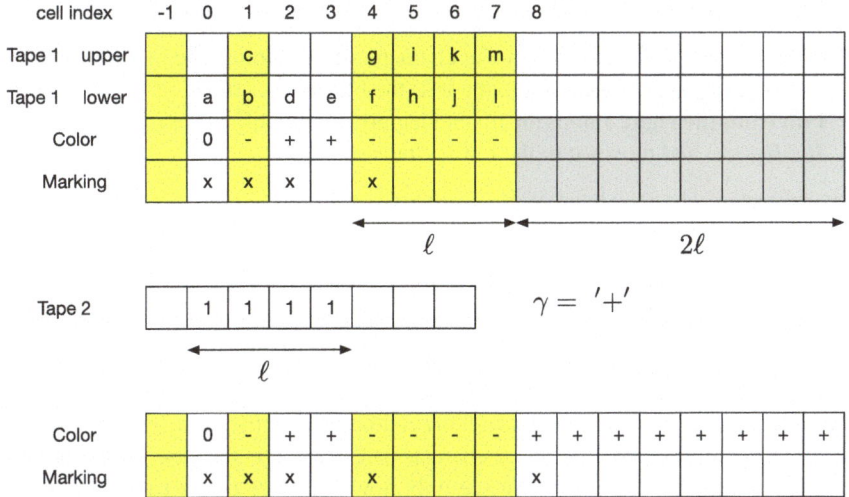

Fig. 9.6 The coloring procedure

- In the case of B_1, the duration is 2.
- In the case of B_p, $p \geq 2$, the duration is the sum of the following:

  - ℓ for writing 1^ℓ.
  - ℓ for moving Head 1 to the start of the new block.
  - 2ℓ for writing γ in the 2ℓ cells.
  - 2ℓ for moving Head 1 back to the first cell of B_p.

  The total is 6ℓ. This bound applies to B_1 also.

When the head movement is in the opposite direction, it is handled similarly by swapping the roles between left and right.

9.2.2.3 The Simulation Procedure

We are now ready to describe the simulation procedure.

S records M's tape contents using a dynamic procedure, in which S moves the tape contents so that the cell on which M's head is located will appear in B_0 for all tapes. S executes the procedure separately for the k tapes. The procedure demands that S uses multiple steps to simulate M's one step. After completing one step of M, each block is empty, half-empty, or packed. At the start of the computation, the input tape of S has only one track. The simulator treats a cell with some symbol a appearing in the single-track mode as having a in the lower track and the empty symbol in the upper track.

When the head of M must move to the right, S does the following:

- **Push to the left** S vacates the lower character of the domino tile in B_0 by moving the character appearing in B_0 to the left (the blocks $B_{-1}, B_{-2}, \ldots$).
- **Pull from the right** S finds the first nonempty domino tile to the right (the blocks $B_1, B_2, \ldots$) and moves it to the lower character of B_0.

By symmetry, when the head of M must move to the left, S does the following:

- **Push to the right** S vacates the lower character of the domino tile in B_0 by moving the character appearing there to the right (the blocks $B_1, B_2, \ldots$).
- **Pull from the left** S finds the first nonempty domino title to the left (the blocks $B_{-1}, B_{-2}, \ldots$) and moves it to the lower character of B_0.

The push-to-the-left action is symmetric to the push-to-the-right action, except that the upper character switches roles with the character track (because in every cell, the lower character precedes the upper character). The same is the case for the pulling actions. Noting the symmetry, we see only how S pushes to the right and how it pulls from the right.

9.2.2.4 Pushing Blocks to the Right

Suppose we must push the character in B_0 to the right. The algorithm that S executes is as follows:

1. S searches for any non-packed domino title to the right. While searching, S copies the contents (as domino titles) from Tape 1 to Tape 2. The upper and lower characters S encounters are nonempty during copying. Since Tape 2 has two tracks, S copies the characters domino-wise: i.e., upper to upper and lower to lower.
2. After arriving at a non-packed domino tile, if the domino tile is empty, S does the following:
   a. S continues scanning until the end of the block. The end is identifiable using the coloring and marking tracks. S keeps Head 2 at the same position.
   b. While moving Heads 1 and 2 to the left (back to the last packed block), S copies the two symbols in the domino tile appearing in Tape 2 to the lower track of Tape 1 and then clears the upper track of Tape 1. S counters Head 1's one move with Head 2's two moves.
   c. For some $q \geq 2$, the number of characters moved equals:

$$2^q + 2^{q-1} + \cdots + 4 + 2 = 2^{q+1} - 2.$$

   This means that the copying ends at B_2, with B_1 vacant. S moves the lower character of B_0 to B_1's lower character and clears B_1's upper character.

3. Otherwise, the non-packed block is half-packed. S does the following:

   a. S continues scanning until the end of the block and appends the contents of the lower track of the domino tiles by combining two symbols as a pair.
   b. While moving Heads 1 and 2 back to the left, S copies a pair of symbols from Tape 2 to Tape 1 as long as the head on Tape 1 is in the same non-packed block it has found.
   c. While moving Heads 1 and 2 back to the left, S copies the two symbols appearing in Tape 2 to the lower track of Tape 1 and clears the upper track for Tape 1. S counters Head 1's one move with Head 2's two moves.
   d. Like before, copying ends at B_2, with B_1 vacant. S moves the lower character of B_0 to B_1's lower track and clears B_1's upper character.

In both cases, S erases the contents of Tape 2 during the moving-back process.

Figure 9.7 shows the two cases of the push operation. Let us analyze the running time of the push operations. Head 1 moves straight to the right and then straight to the left. Let B_p be the block S finds to be non-packed. The movement to the right stops at the cell immediately to the right of B_p, which is at:

$$1 + 2 + \cdots + 2^{p-1} + 1 = 2^p.$$

Thus, the running time of the push operation is $2 \cdot 2^p$.

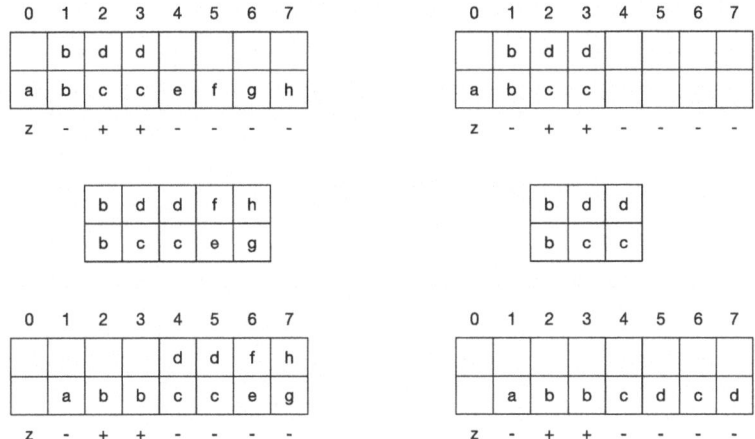

Fig. 9.7 The two cases of the push operation. Left panel: the case where the non-packed block is half-packed. Right panel: the case where the non-packed block is empty. The top represents the symbols in the two tracks before the push operation, and the bottom represents the symbols after the push operation. The middle part is the copy S creates on Tape 2

9.2.2.5 Pulling Blocks from the Right

We next explain the operation for pulling from the right. S executes the following:

1. S scans to the right for a nonempty block.
2. When a nonempty block is found, S continues scanning to the right and copies its contents to Tape 2.
3. If the nonempty block is packed, S moves Heads 1 and 2 to the left. While doing this, S spreads each symbol pair appearing on Tape 2 to the lower track over two cells on Tape 1. Also, while doing this, S erases the contents of Tape 2.
4. If the nonempty block is not packed, S moves Head 1 to the left while erasing the character appearing on the lower track while keeping Head 2 in the same position. Upon entering the previous block, S starts moving Tape 2 to the left and copies the contents on Tape 2 to Tape 1. During the execution, S erases the contents of Tape 2.

Figure 9.8 shows the two cases of the pull operation. Let us analyze the running time of the pull operations. Let B_p be the block S finds to be nonempty. The movement to the right stops at the cell immediately to the right of B_p, which is at position:

$$1 + 2 + \cdots + 2^{p-1} + 1 = 2^p.$$

Thus, the running time of the push operation is $2 \cdot 2^p$.

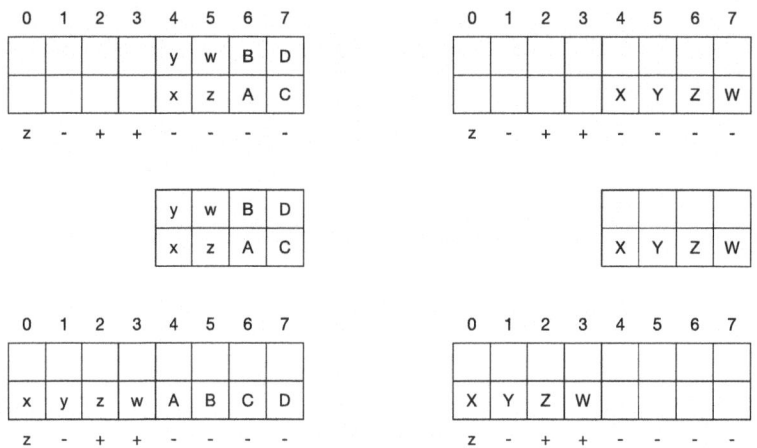

Fig. 9.8 The two cases of the pull operation. Left panel: the case where the nonempty block is packed. Right panel: the case where the nonempty block is half-packed. The top represents the symbols in the two tracks before the push operation, and the bottom represents the symbols after the push operation. The middle part is the copy S creates on Tape 2

9.2.2.6   An Analysis of the Running Time

Let us analyze the time it takes S to execute the simulation.

Let n be the length of the input. Let r_1 be the index of the farthest block S reaches to the right. Since the running time of M has $t(n)$ as an upper bound, $r_1 \leq \lceil \log(t(n)) \rceil$. Let $-r_2$ be the index in the opposite direction. We know $r_2 \leq \lceil \log(t(n)) \rceil$. Let $r_0 = \lceil \log(t(n)) \rceil$. The time that it takes for S to perform coloring is at most:

$$2 \sum_{p=1}^{r_0} (7 \cdot 2^{p-1}) \leq 14 \cdot 2^{r_0} \leq 14 \cdot 2^{1+\log(t(n))} = 28t(n).$$

The scaling factor of 2 applies here because we are looking at two directions.

The push or pull operation ending in B_p (or B_{-p}) leaves all the blocks between that and B_0 half-packed. The next time the same block receives modifications is when either

(A) all the half-packed blocks in between become packed, and another push occurs

or

(B) all the half-packed blocks in between become empty, and another pull occurs.

The number of steps necessary for S to run before either incident happens is the sum of the half-sizes of the blocks plus 1, which is:

$$(1 + 2 + \cdots + 2^{p-2}) + 1 = 2^{p-1}.$$

Since the running time of M is at most $t(n)$, the event that reaches B_p or B_{-p} occurs no more frequently than once in 2^p steps and requires $2 \cdot 2^p$ steps to complete. Thus, the largest p we need to consider is $\lceil \log(t(n)) \rceil = r_0$. Since each step involves one push operation and one pull operation, the contributions from the push and pull operations are:

$$\leq 2 \sum_{i=1}^{r_0} \left\lceil \frac{t(n)}{2^{p-1}} \right\rceil \cdot (2 \cdot 2^p)$$

$$= 2 \sum_{i=1}^{r_0} \frac{2t(n)}{2^{p-1}} \cdot (2 \cdot 2^p)$$

$$= 16 \sum_{i=1}^{r_0} t(n)$$

$$= 16t(n)r_0$$

$$\leq 16t(n)(1 + \log(t(n))).$$

This amount is for simulating one tape. S has k tapes to simulate. By combining the amount with the time for the coloring operation, the total running time of S is at most:

$$28t(n) + k \cdot 16t(n)(1 + \log(t(n)))$$
$$= 44t(n) + 16k \cdot t(n)\log(t(n))$$
$$= O(t(n)\log(t(n))).$$

Here, k is a constant. Therefore, the big O can include k. The analysis we have seen is an example of **amortized analysis**, which uses the idea that costly operations do not occur very often.

The proof of the theorem is now complete.

9.3   The Time Hierarchy Theorems

The simulation results from the previous section enable us to prove proper inclusions between time complexity classes. Proving proper inclusions about time complexity classes requires a "clock" that provides some steps allocated for simulation. A time-bounding function $f(n)$ can be turned into a clock if there is a TM that stops in steps $1^{f(n)}$ on each input 1^n, where 1 is an arbitrary symbol. Time-constructible functions are those we can turn into a clock.

Definition 9.6   A time-bounding function $f(n)$ is **time-constructible** if there is a multi-tape TM that, on all inputs x, stops in $1^{f(|x|)}$ steps.

Only some time-bounding functions are time-constructible. Showing time-constructibility is a cumbersome task. The following theorem helps in finding time-constructibility.

Theorem 9.4   *A time-bounding function $t(n)$ is time-constructible if, and only if, a TM that computes $1^{t(n)}$ from 1^n in $O(t(n))$ steps exists.*

We now use time-constructibility to show separations between time complexity classes.

Theorem 9.5   *Suppose $f(n)$ and $g(n)$ are time-bounding functions, $g(n)$ is time-constructible, and $g(n) = \omega(f(n)\log(f(n)))$. Then:*

$$\mathrm{DTIME}[f(n)] \subset \mathrm{DTIME}[g(n)].$$

> **Proof Overview**
>
> We construct a language of TM machine encodings with an arbitrary number of trailing 0s. The language's membership condition is that the machine does not accept the encoding as an input in $f(n)$ steps. Since $g(n)$ is time-constructible, a TM can count for $g(n)$ steps while simulating an arbitrary machine M. Using the two-tape simulation technique, simulating M for $f(n)$ steps is possible in $cf(n)\log(f(n))$ steps for some constant. Because of the ω-relation, the quantity $cf(n)\log(f(n))$ is less than $g(n)$ for all but finitely many n, and the simulator can make a decision opposite to M's decision.

Proof Let $f(n)$ and $g(n)$ be as appearing in the statement of Theorem 9.5. Let T be a TM witnessing that $g(n)$ is time-constructible.

Algorithm 9.1 A TM that decides the diagonal language

1: **procedure** DIAGONAL-LANGUAGE(w)
2:      w is a binary string;
3:      copy w to a separate tape;
4:      simulate T on w to generate $1^{g(|w|)}$;
5:      using $g(|w|)$ as the time limit, execute the following;
6:      **if** w does not have a suffix of the form 10^p for some $p \geq 1$ **then**
7:          reject w;
8:      **end if**
9:      check the validity of the machine portion of w;
10:     **if** the machine fails the test **then**
11:         reject w;
12:     **end if**
13:     extract M for simulation;
14:     simulate M on w;
15:     **if** M accepts **then**
16:         reject w;
17:     **else if** M rejects **then**
18:         accept w;
19:     **end if**
20:     **if** the execution reaches the time limit **then**
21:         accept w;
22:     **end if**
23: **end procedure**

Define D as the set of all strings w of the form $\langle M \rangle 10^{\ell}$ satisfying the following two conditions:

- M is a TM whose input alphabet has a size of ≥ 2.
- M on w does not accept w within $f(n)$ steps.

We assume that the encodings of the TMs follow the number-based scheme from Sect. 7.1.1. In the encoding, tallies of 1s serve as delimiters, where the length of the tally represents its meaning. We present the algorithm for N in Algorithm 9.1.

Algorithm 9.2 A TM encoding test

1: **procedure** POLYNOMIAL-TIME-ENCODING-TEST(x)
2:      x is a binary string;
3:      try to extract the number of tapes, k;
4:      try to extract the number of states, q;
5:      try to extract the tape alphabet size, s;
6:      try to extract the indices of the blank system, q_0, q_{acc}, and q_{rej};
7:      **if** the extraction fails **then**
8:          return *false*;
9:      **end if**
10:     extract the transition table;
11:     **if** the table is incomplete **then**
12:         return *false*;
13:     **end if**
14:     return *true*;
15: **end procedure**

We can use Algorithm 9.2 to test the validity of the encoding.

Let n be the length of the input w. The running time of N is then:

$$2n + O(g(n)) + g(n) = O(g(n)).$$

Since $g(n)$ is a time limit that applies to the entire computation, we assess the running time of Algorithm 9.2 as $O(r^2)$. By the linear speedup theorem, the language D is in DTIME[$g(n)$].

By contradiction, we show that D is not in DTIME[$f(n)$]. Assume M is a TM that decides D and has $f(n)$ as its time bound. Let w be an arbitrary input to N that contains the description of M. Let n be the length of w. Let r be the length of the description.

The encoding-checking consists of decoding the sizes of the input and tape alphabets, the size of the state set, and the transition table. Since the size information is unary, the decoding is possible in $O(r^2)$ steps. In the simulation of M on w, N can use the time-efficient simulation from Theorem 9.3. Since the alphabet size and the number of tapes of M are variable, N must use multiple cells to encode one character on one tape of M. Each element of the transition table has entries greater than or equal to the number of tapes. Also, the element size of the table is greater than or equal to the size of the alphabet. Thus, the number of bits necessary to encode one symbol on one M's tapes is at most r. Determining which action to perform requires matching the symbols and the state with the transition tape. The determination is thus possible in $O(r^2)$. The running time of simulation, without the time limit of $1^{g(n)}$, is:

$$O(r^2) + O(f(n)) + O((r^2)f(n)\log(f(n)))$$
$$= O((r^2)f(n)\log(f(n))).$$

Let c_0 be a constant such that the time requirement is at most $c_0 r^2 f(n) \log(f(n))$. Since we have fixed r and $g(n) = \omega(f(n)\log(f(n)))$, for all infinitely many n, $c_0 r^2 f(n) \log(f(n)) \leq g(n)$. Therefore, for infinitely many inputs w in which M appears, N produces the result contradicting M. Hence, M does not accept the language D. Thus, $D \notin \text{DTIME}[f(n)]$. ☐

The single-tape simulation technique (Theorem 9.2) produces a weaker version time hierarchy theorem.

Theorem 9.6 *Let $f(n)$ and $g(n)$ be time-constructible time-bounding functions such that $g(n) = \omega(f(n)^2)$. Then:*

$$\text{DTIME}[f(n)] \subset \text{DTIME}[g(n)].$$

For each rational number $\alpha > 1$, define n^α as representing $\lceil n^\alpha \rceil$. This function is time-constructible (see Exercise 9.3). 9.3 We thus obtain the following result.

Corollary 9.2 *For all rational constants c and d such that $c > d \geq 1$, $\text{DTIME}[n^d] \subset \text{DTIME}[n^c]$.*

9.4   The Nondeterministic Time Complexity

Next, we define nondeterministic analogs of the deterministic time complexity classes.

Definition 9.7 Let $f(n)$ be a time-bounding function. We say that a nondeterministic TM M is $f(n)$ **time-bounded** if, for all inputs x, M on x halts within $f(|x|)$ steps regardless of its nondeterministic choices.

Definition 9.8 Let $f(n)$ be a time-bounding function. Let L be a decidable language. We say that L has **nondeterministic time complexity** $f(n)$ if a nondeterministic TM is deciding L that is $f(n)$ time-bounded.

Definition 9.9 For a time-bounding function $f(n)$, we define $\text{NTIME}[f(n)]$ as the set of all languages that have nondeterministic time complexity $f(n)$.

The linear speedup theorem also holds for nondeterministic complexity.

Theorem 9.7 (The Nondeterministic Linear Speedup Theorem) *Let $f(n)$ be a time-bounding function. Then, for all constants $d > 1$:*

$$\text{NTIME}[f(n)] \subseteq \text{NTIME}\left[n + \frac{f(n)}{d}\right].$$

Corollary 9.3 *Suppose $f(n)$ satisfies $f(n) \geq (1 + \alpha)n$ for all but finitely many n, where α is a positive constant. Then, for all constants $c > 0$, $\text{NTIME}[f(n)] = \text{NTIME}[cf(n)]$.*

Since deterministic TMs are nondeterministic TMs without nondeterministic actions, the following proposition holds:

Proposition 9.1 *For all time-bounding functions $f(n)$:*

$$\text{DTIME}[f(n)] \subseteq \text{NTIME}[f(n)].$$

Using the deterministic simulation of NTMs (Theorem 6.5) for simulating time-bounded NTMs, we obtain the following theorem:

Theorem 9.8 (The Nondeterministic Time Hierarchy Theorem) *For all time-bounding functions $f(n)$:*

$$\text{NTIME}[f(n)] \subseteq \cup_{c \geq 1} \text{DTIME}[2^{cf(n)}].$$

9.5   Fundamental Time Complexity Classes

We now define the standard time complexity classes.

We group all polynomials. Since the time-bounding function requires that $f(n) \geq n + 1$, the time-bounding functions are upper bounds, and there are linear speedup theorems, we will consider only polynomials of the form $cn^c + c$ in defining the standard complexity classes.

Definition 9.10 P is the class of all decidable languages with some deterministic TM whose running time is $O(cn^c + c)$ for some integer c. In other words:

$$\text{P} = \cup_{c \geq 1} \text{DTIME}[cn^c + c].$$

By the second time hierarchy theorem (Theorem 9.5), we can show that there are hierarchies of time complexity classes inside P. For example, if $g(n)$ is a time-constructible polynomial and $f(n)\log(f(n)) = o(g(n))$, then $\text{DTIME}[f(n)] \subset \text{DTIME}[g(n)]$. While these hierarchies give partitions of P, we treat P as the class of all **tractable** problems.

Another important class is NP. This is the nondeterministic analog of P.

Definition 9.11 NP is the class of all decidable languages with some nondeterministic TM whose running time is $O(cn^c + c)$ for some integer c. In other words:

$$NP = \cup_{c \geq 1} NTIME[cn^c + c].$$

In addition, we also define coNP as the complementary class of NP.

Definition 9.12 coNP is the class of all languages whose complements are in NP. In other words:

$$coNP = \{A \mid \overline{A} \in NP\}.$$

An extension of the polynomials is the group of exponential functions: $2^{cn^c + c}$ for all $c \geq 1$.

Definition 9.13 EXPTIME is the class of all decidable languages with some deterministic TM whose running time is $O(2^{cn^c + c})$ for some integer c. In other words:

$$EXPTIME = \cup_{c \geq 1} DTIME[2^{cn^c + c}].$$

Definition 9.14 NEXPTIME is the class of all decidable languages with some nondeterministic TM whose running time is $O(2^{cn^c + c})$ for some integer c. In other words:

$$NEXPTIME = \cup_{c \geq 1} NTIME[2^{cn^c + c}].$$

Definition 9.15 coNEXPTIME is the class of all languages whose complements are in coNEXPTIME. In other words:

$$coNEXPTIME = \{A \mid \overline{A} \in NEXPTIME\}.$$

The following class inclusions hold:

Proposition 9.2 $P \subseteq NP \cap coNP \subseteq NP \cup coNP \subseteq EXPTIME \subseteq NEXPTIME \cap coNEXPTIME \subseteq NEXPTIME \cup coNEXPTIME$.

Figure 9.9 shows the relationship stated in Proposition 9.2.

By using either of the time hierarchy theorems (Theorems 9.5 and 9.6), we can prove that $P \subset EXPTIME$. From this separation, we immediately learn that P, NP, and coNP are proper subclasses of EXPTIME, NEXPTIME, and coNEXPTIME. Except for these separations, we do not know if any inclusion appearing in the sequence in Proposition 9.2 is proper. Specifically, whether or not $P = NP$ is a fundamental question in computational complexity theory. We refer to the problem as the **P vs. NP problem**.

Fig. 9.9 Inclusions among
the standard time complexity
classes

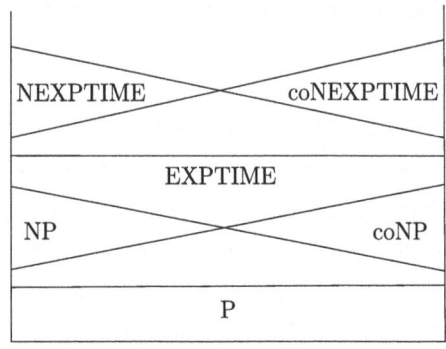

Table 9.1 The closure properties of the standard time complexity classes

Class	Intersection	Union	Concatenation	Complementation	Kleene-star
P	Y	Y	Y	Y	Y
NP	Y	Y	Y	?	Y
EXPTIME	Y	Y	Y	Y	Y
NEXPTIME	Y	Y	Y	?	Y

For most of the above classes, we know which closure properties they have.
Table 9.1 presents the list of the closure properties, where the question mark
represents that the field does not know whether or not the class has the property.

9.6   Examples of Time Complexity Classifications

We present example problems from the classes defined in the previous section.
   First, the validity tests of TM encodings are in P.

Proposition 9.3 *The language* $\{\langle M \rangle \mid M$ *is a TM*$\}$ *is in* P.

Using the same argument, we can show:

Proposition 9.4 *The language* $\{\langle M, w \rangle \mid M$ *is a TM, and* w *is an input to* $M\}$ *is in*
P.

The task of proving these propositions is left to the reader (see Exercises 9.10
and 9.11).

9.6.1   The DFA State Minimization Problem

We first show that the state minimization problem of DFA is in P.

Proposition 9.5 *The language* $\{\langle M, 0^k \rangle \mid M$ *is a DFA, and there is an equivalent DFA with* $\leq k$ *states*$\}$ *is in* P.

Proof After verifying the input's validity, we execute Algorithm 9.3 adapted from Sect. 3.1.

Algorithm 9.3 A TM that decides the minimum number of states

```
 1: procedure MINIMUM-NUMBER-OF-STATES(M, k)
 2:     M = (Q, Σ, δ, q₀, F) is a DFA, k is an integer;
 3:     Q = {p₁, . . . , pₛ};
 4:     instantiate an s × s table T;
 5:     store 0 in T[i, j] for all i and j between 1 and s;
 6:     for i ← 1, . . . s do
 7:         for j ← 1, . . . , s do
 8:             if pᵢ ∈ F ⟺ pⱼ ∉ F then
 9:                 store 1 in T[i, j];
10:             end if
11:         end for
12:     end for
13:     repeat
14:         f ← 0;
15:         for i ← 1, . . . , q do
16:             for j ← 1, . . . , q do
17:                 if T[i, j] = 0 then
18:                     for a ∈ Σ do
19:                         k ← such that pₖ = δ(pᵢ, a);
20:                         ℓ ← such that pₗ = δ(pⱼ, a);
21:                         if T[k, ℓ] = 1 then
22:                             store 1 in T[k, ℓ] and T[ℓ, k];
23:                             f ← 1;
24:                         end if
25:                     end for
26:                 end if
27:             end for
28:         end for
29:     until f ≠ 0
30:     J ← {j | 1 ≤ j ≤ s and for all ℓ such that 1 ≤ ℓ ≤ j − 1, T[ℓ, j] = 1};
31:     if j = k then
32:         accept (M, k);
33:     else
34:         reject (M, k);
35:     end if
36: end procedure
```

Let n be the length of the input. The sizes of Q and Σ are at most n, and so the size of T is at most n^2. The "repeat-until" loop at Line 7 appears to be the most time-consuming part. The algorithm executes its external loop at most n^2 times. The algorithm executes its internal double loop at most $n^2 \cdot n = n^3$ times. For each combination of i, j, and a, scanning the input is necessary to find the transition functions, which gives an $O(n)$ overhead. Thus, the algorithm's running time is $O(n^2 \cdot n^3 \cdot n) = O(n^6)$. Therefore, the language is in P.   □

Similarly, we can show that the following problems are in P.

Proposition 9.6 *The following problems are in* P.

- $N_{\text{rep}} = \{\langle M, 0^k \rangle \mid M \text{ is a DFA and the } k\text{-th state of } M \text{ is distinguishable from all states of } M \text{ with smaller indices}\}$.
- $N_{\text{final}} = \{\langle M, 0^k \rangle \mid M \text{ is a DFA and the } k\text{-th state of } M \text{ is distinguishable from all states of } M \text{ with smaller indices and is a final state}\}$.
- $N_{\text{trans}} = \{\langle M, 0^k, 0^\ell, 0^a \rangle \mid M \text{ is a finite automaton, the } k\text{-th and the } \ell \text{ states of } M \text{ are representative states, and on the } a\text{-th symbol, the states the } k\text{-th represents transition to the states the } \ell\text{-th represents}\}$.

9.6.2   The Problem of Converting an NFA to a Regular Expression

We now explore the time complexity of converting NFAs to regular expressions.

Suppose we apply the algorithm from the proof of Theorem 2.3 to generate a regular expression from an NFA. The expression we generate could be very long. Suppose N is an NFA from which we will generate a regular expression. Let m be the number of states of N. The graph we use in the generation has $m + 2$ nodes. Each arrow in the graph has a label of the form:

$$(a_1 \cup a_2 \cup a_p).$$

Here, $a_1, \ldots, a_p$ are from Σ_ϵ and Σ is the alphabet of N. Suppose $a_1, \ldots, a_p$ have unary representations and the other symbols in the expression; i.e., the parentheses, $\cup$, and * are single symbols. Then, the initial labels have a length of at most:

$$\left(\sum_{i=1}^{m+1} i \right) + m + 2 = \frac{m(m+1)}{2} + m + 2 = \frac{(m+1)^2}{2} + 1.$$

The last quantity in the equation is at least $\frac{(m+1)^2}{2}$ and at most $(m + 1)^2$.

Suppose the construction still needs to be completed (i.e., at least three nodes are remaining), and the maximum of the lengths of the labels is at most ℓ. The consolidation of a node x changes the label of the arrow (u, v) to:

$$(l_1 \cup l_2 l_3^* l_4).$$

Here, l_1, l_2, l_3, and l_4 are the labels on the arrows from u to v, from u to x, from x to x, and from x to v, respectively. Since each label before the consolidation has a length of $\leq \ell$, the new label has a length of $\leq 4\ell + 4$. For each i such that $0 \leq i \leq m$, let ℓ_i be the maximum length after the i-th conversion. Then we have the recurrence $\ell_i = 4\ell_{i-1} + 4$ and $\ell_0 \leq (m+1)^2$. The solution to the recurrence is $(\ell_i + 4/3) = 4(\ell_{i-1} + 4/3)$, so we have:

$$\ell_i = \ell_0 2^{2i} - \frac{4}{3}.$$

Specifically, for $i = m$, we have:

$$\ell_m = \ell_0 2^{2m} - \frac{4}{3} = \Theta(m^2 2^{2m}).$$

The value of m can be $\Theta(n)$ (where n represents the length of the encoding) if we restrict the size of the alphabet to be constant, so we have that the expression can be $\Theta(n^2 2^{\Theta(n)})$. Now, define the following languages:

- $R_{\text{length}} = \{\langle N, \ell \rangle \mid N$ is an NFA, and the expression we obtain from N has a length of at most ℓ, where ℓ is a binary integer$\}$.
- $R_{\text{symbol}} = \{\langle N, \ell, a \rangle \mid N$ is an NFA, ℓ is a binary integer, $a \in \{0, 1, (,), \cup, *\}$, the expression we obtain from N has a length of at least ℓ, and the ℓ-th symbol of the expression is $a\}$.

Proposition 9.7 R_{length} *and* R_{symbol} *are in* EXPTIME.

The proof is left to the reader (see Exercise 9.7).

9.6.3 The CFL Membership Problem

We show that each context-free language is in P.

Theorem 9.9 *Each context-free language belongs to* P.

Proof Overview
We use inductive programming. Let $G = (V, \Sigma, R, S)$ be a CNF formula and $w, |w| = m$, be an input whose membership in $L(G)$ we want to test. We compute the sets $T[i, j], 1 \leq i \leq j \leq n$, of all the variables that produce $w_i \cdots w_j$. $w \in L(G)$ if, and only if, $S \in T[1, n]$. Here, where $i = j$, $T[i, j]$ directly comes from the form $A \to a$ rules, where $a \in \Sigma$. In addition, where $i < j$, we think of applying a rule r in the form of $A \to BC$ such that $B \in T[i, \ell]$ and $C \in T[\ell + 1, j]$ for some ℓ between i and $j - 1$. We try all combinations of the rules r and ℓ and identify all qualifying variables A.

Proof Let L be a context-free language. Let $G = (V, \Sigma, R, S)$ be a CNF (Chomsky normal form) grammar for L. Let $w = w_1 \cdots w_n$, where $w_1, \ldots, w_n \in \Sigma$. For each pair of integers i and j such that $1 \leq i \leq j \leq m$, let $T[i, j]$ denote the set of all variables A such that $A \overset{G,*}{\Longrightarrow} w_i \cdots w_j$. We can compute the tables T using inductive programming as appears in Algorithm 9.4, and accept w if, and only if, $T[1, m]$ contains S. The algorithm uses the fact that each CNF grammar has only two forms of rules: $A \rightarrow a$ and $A \rightarrow BC$. In other words, $T[i, i]$ should consist solely of the variables that produce w_i in one step; for all i and j, $T[i, j]$ should consist of all variables A with a rule $A \rightarrow BC$ such that B produces $T[i, q]$ and C produces $T[q + 1, j]$ for some q such that $i \leq q \leq j - 1$. The algorithm's running time is cubic in n since there is a triple loop. The language L is thus $O(n^3)$. □

Algorithm 9.4 An algorithm for CFL membership test

1: **procedure** CFL-MEMBERSHIP(w)
2:     $G = (V, \Sigma, R, S)$ is a fixed CNF grammar;
3:     let $w = w_1 \cdots w_n$ be an input;
4:     **if** $n = 0$ **then**
5:         **if** $S \rightarrow \epsilon$ is in R **then**
6:             accept w;
7:         **else**
8:             reject w;
9:         **end if**
10:    **else**
11:        **for** $i \leftarrow 1, \ldots, n$ **do**
12:            $T[i, i] \leftarrow \{A \mid A \rightarrow w_i \in R\}$;
13:        **end for**
14:        **for** $\ell \leftarrow 2, \ldots, n$ **do**
15:            **for** $i \leftarrow 1, \ldots, n - \ell + 1$ **do**
16:                $T[i, i + \ell - 1] \leftarrow \emptyset$;
17:                **for** $k \leftarrow i, \ldots, n - \ell$ **do**
18:                    **if** a rule $A \rightarrow BC$ exists where $B \in T[i, k]$ and $C \in T[k + 1, i + \ell + 1]$ **then**
19:                        $T[i, j] \leftarrow T[i, j] \cup \{A\}$;
20:                    **end if**
21:                **end for**
22:            **end for**
23:        **end for**
24:        **if** $S \in T[1, n]$ **then**
25:            accept w;
26:        **else**
27:            reject w;
28:        **end if**
29:    **end if**
30: **end procedure**

Next, we consider the conversion algorithm from an arbitrary CFG to a CNF grammar that appears in the proof of Theorem 4.2. Recall that the algorithm processes a grammar $G = (V, \Sigma, R, S)$ as follows:

1. Eliminate mixed rules by introducing a variable for each terminal.
2. Introduce a new start variable.
3. Find all nullable variables using a greedy search algorithm.
4. Decompose long rules into rules with a length of at most 2 while independently choosing whether or not to include each nullable variable at each stage of decomposition.
5. Eliminate all ϵ rules.
6. Find all chains of unit rules using reachability.
7. Create new rules by combining all chains of unit rules and all non-unit rules.
8. Eliminate all unit rules.

As we observed in Exercise 4.20, the number of new variables and rules introduced in the conversion process is $O(m^2)$, where $m = |V| + |\Sigma| + |R|$. In addition, discovering nullable variables, decomposing long rules, finding unit-rule chains, and combining the chains and non-unit rules can be carried out in polynomial time. Thus, the entire construction can be done in polynomial time.

To translate the conversion problem into decision problems, the following languages can be used:

- $C_{\text{variables}} = \{\langle G, 0^k \rangle \mid G$ is a CFG, and the conversion program produces a rule with at most k variables$\}$.
- $C_{\text{terminal–rule}} = \{\langle G, 0^r 10^s \rangle \mid G$ is a CFG, and the converted CNF has a rule that produces the s-th terminal from the r-th variable$\}$.
- $C_{\text{split–rule}} = \{\langle G, 0^r 10^s 10^t \rangle \mid G$ is a CFG, and the converted CNF has a rule that turns the r-th variable into a concatenation of the s-th variable and the t-th variable$\}$.
- $C_{\text{start}} = \{\langle G, 0^r \rangle \mid G$ is a CFG, and the converted CNF's start variable has r as its index$\}$.

Proposition 9.8 $C_{\text{variables}}$, $C_{\text{terminal–rule}}$, $C_{\text{split–rule}}$, and C_{start} are in P.

Exercises
9.1 The simulator in the proof of Theorem 9.1 has one more tape than the original. Prove that it is possible to eliminate the need for one extra tape by reusing the input tape after reading the input.

9.2 Prove Corollary 9.1.

9.3 Show that for all rational constants $c > 1$, $\lceil cn^c + c \rceil$ is time-constructible.

9.4 Show that $\lceil n \log n \rceil$ is time-constructible.

9.5 Show that 2^n is a time-constructible function. *Hint*: In the proof of Theorem 6.4, we designed a method for generating all computation paths of an NTM with at most two branches at each computation step. We can modify the method so that for each $n \geq 1$, the method uses $2^n + c$ steps to generate all paths having length n.

9.6 Let $f(n)$ and $g(n)$ be time-constructible. Show that $f(n) + g(n)$ is time-constructible.

9.7 Let $f(n)$ and $g(n)$ be time-constructible. Show that $g(f(n))$ is time-constructible.

9.8 Let $f(n)$ and $g(n)$ be time-constructible. Show that $f(n) * g(n)$ is time-constructible.

9.9 Prove Theorem 9.8.

9.10 Prove Proposition 9.3.

9.11 Prove Proposition 9.4.

9.12 Prove Proposition 9.7.

9.13 In Theorem 9.9, we showed that each context-free language is in DTIME$[n^3]$. Show that each context-free language is in NTIME$[n]$.

9.14 In Theorem 9.9, we showed that each context-free language is in DTIME$[n^3]$. Consider $L = \{\langle G, w \rangle \mid G$ is a CNF grammar and $w \in L(G)\}$ is in P. Show that L is in DTIME$[n^7]$.

9.15 Show that the language $\{\langle M, w, \pi \rangle \mid M$ is a DPDA, w is an input to M, π is a series of transitions of M, and M accepts w along the path$\}$ is in P.
   Hint: The time complexity can be $O(n^2)$.

9.16 Define $T = \{\langle G, w, T \rangle \mid G$ is a CNF grammar, w is a string over the terminals of G, T is a labeled tree, and T is a valid tree producing $w\}$. Show that $T \in$ P.

9.17 Show that $\{\langle M, 1^t \rangle \mid M$ is a finite automaton and accepts a string having a length of $t\}$ belongs to NTIME$[n^2]$ by giving a nondeterministic TM for it.

9.18 Show that the language from the previous question is actually in DTIME$[n^3]$, noting that the symbols appearing can be arbitrarily chosen from the alphabet of M.

9.19 A **bipartite graph** is a graph with vertex sets U and V such that the edges of the graph are between U and V. Show that the problem of deciding if a graph is bipartite is in P.

9.20 Prove that NP is closed under the Kleene-star operation.

9.21 Prove that NP is closed under union.

9.22 Prove that NP is closed under intersection.

Bibliographic Notes and Further Reading
Hartmanis and Stearns [4] introduced the concept of time-bounded TM computation. Theorems 9.1 and 9.2 are from there. Grzegorzcyk [3] considered the number of steps required for TMs to compute function. Using polynomials as time bounds was suggested in Ritchie [7] and Cobham [1]. Using the polynomial time as the class of tractable problems is by Edmonds [2]. Theorem 9.4 about time-constructible

functions is by Kobayashi [6]. Theorem 9.3 is by Hennie and Stearns [5]. A more potent form of nondeterministic time hierarchy theorem is given by Seiferas, Fischer, and Meyer [8].

References

1. A. Cobham, The intrinsic computational difficulty of functions, in *Proceedings of the 1964 Congress for Logic, Methodology, and the Philosophy of Science* (North-Holland, Amsterdam, 1964), pp. 24–30
2. J. Edmonds, Paths, trees, and flowers. Can. J. Math. **17**, 449–467 (1965)
3. A. Grzegorczyk, Computable functionals. Fund. Math. **42**(19553), 168–202 (1955)
4. J. Hartmanis, R.E. Stearns, On the computational complexity of algorithms. T Am. Math. Soc. **117**, 285–306 (1965)
5. F.C. Hennie, R.E. Stearns, Two-tape simulation of multitape Turing machines. J. ACM **13**(4), 533–546 (1966)
6. K. Kobayashi, On proving time constructibility of functions. Theor. Comput. Sci. **35**, 215–225 (1985)
7. R.W. Ritchie, Classes of predictably computable functions. T Am. Math. Sci. **106**, 139–173 (1963)
8. J.I. Seiferas, M.J. Fischer, A.R. Meyer, Separating nondeterministic time complexity classes. J. ACM **25**(1), 146–167 (1978)

Chapter 10
The Space Complexity

10.1 The Space Complexity Measure

Let us begin with the definition of the space complexity measure.

The computation model for studying space complexity is the **offline Turing machine**, a variant of the multi-tape model (see Fig. 10.1). In an offline TM, the input appears on a read-only tape called the **input tape**.

Mathematically, the symbol the offline TM writes on its input tape is the same as the symbol it reads. Because it is read-only, the input tape on an offline TM holds the input between end markers. We often use ⊢ and ⊣ to represent the left and right markers. At the start of computation, the head on the input tape of an offline TM is on the cell immediately to the right of the left-end marker. If the input is an empty string, the head is on the right-end marker; otherwise, it is on the first character of the input. The other tapes permit reading and writing; we call these **work tapes**. We measure the space a TM uses with the number of distinct cells it accesses during computation, excluding read-only or write-only tapes.

Definition 10.1 Let $f(n)$ be a positive non-decreasing function from $\mathbb{N}$ to $\mathbb{N}$. A TM M is $f(n)$ **space-bounded** if for all inputs x, M on input x halts using no more than $f(|x|)$ cells on each work tape.

We require any space-bounding function to be positive and non-decreasing.

Definition 10.2 Any positive non-decreasing function from $\mathbb{N}$ to $\mathbb{N}$ is a **space-bounding function**.

Now, we define space complexity classes using space-bounding functions.

Definition 10.3 For a space-bounding function $f(n)$, we define:

$$\mathrm{DSPACE}[f(n)] = \{L \mid \text{there exists an } f(n) \text{ space-bounded TM deciding } L\}.$$

© The Editor(s) (if applicable) and The Author(s), under exclusive license to
Springer Nature Switzerland AG 2025
M. Ogihara, *An Introduction to Theory of Computation*,
https://doi.org/10.1007/978-3-031-84740-0_10

Fig. 10.1 An offline TM
with two work tapes

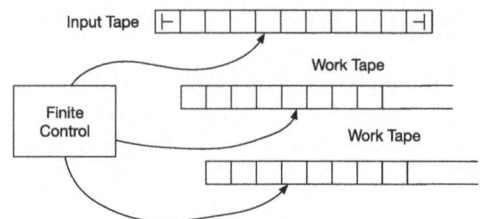

We can show the following space compression theorem by combining multiple symbols into one. We leave the proof to the reader.

Theorem 10.1 (The Space Compression Theorem) *For all space-bounding functions $f(n)$ and constants $c \geq 0$, DSPACE$[f(n)]$ = DSPACE$[cf(n)]$.*

Definition 10.4 A space-bounding function $f(n)$ is **space-constructible** if there is a multi-tape TM with space-bound $f(n)$ such that, for all inputs x, writes $1^{f(|x|)}$ on one tape and halts.

We can state a more stringent result about the definition of space-constructible functions.

Proposition 10.1 *If $f(n)$ is space-constructible, there is an offline TM with one work tape that produces $\vdash \sqcup^{f(n)-2} \dashv$ on its work tape and halts.*

We leave the task of proving the proposition to the reader.

Theorem 10.2 *Suppose $f(n)$ and $g(n)$ are space-bounding functions, $f(n) = \omega(g(n))$, and $g(n)$ is space-constructible. Then:*

$$\text{DSPACE}[f(n)] \subset \text{DSPACE}[g(n)].$$

Proof The proof follows the same idea as the time hierarchy theorem (Theorem 9.5). Suppose $f(n)$ and $g(n)$ are functions such that $g(n)$ is space-constructible and $f(n) = o(g(n))$ (in other words, $g(n) = \omega(f(n))$). Let S be a machine witnessing that $g(n)$ is space-constructible. We can assume that S has two work tapes and produces $1^{g(n)}$ on the second work tape. We define N as an offline TM with two work tapes executing Algorithm 10.1.

Algorithm 10.1 A TM that decides the space diagonal language
___
 1: **procedure** SPACE-DIAGONALIZATION(w)
 2:     simulate S on w to generate $1^{g(|w|)}$ on a work-tape;
 3:     mark all its work tapes with $\vdash 1^{g(|w|)-2} \dashv$;
 4:     check $w = \langle M, 0^{\ell} \rangle$, where M is a Turing machine;
 5:     **if** the check fails **then**
 6:         reject w;
 7:     **else**
 8:         simulate M on w while counting the number of steps;
 9:         **if** M accepts within $2^{g(|w|)}$ steps without using unmarked space **then**
10:             reject w;
11:         **else**
12:             accept w;
13:         **end if**
14:     **end if**
15: **end procedure**

Let $L = L(N)$. Then $L \in \text{DSPACE}[g(n)]$. We prove that $L \in \text{DSPACE}[g(n)] - \text{DSPACE}[f(n)]$ by contradiction. Assume $L \in \text{DSPACE}[f(n)]$. Then, an $f(n)$ space-bounded TM M accepts L. Let w be $\langle M, 0^{\ell} \rangle$ for some $\ell \geq 0$. Let $n = |w|$ and r be the portion length in M describing w. Suppose we give w to M and N. As we saw in the proof of the time hierarchy theorem, the need for simulating M raises the space requirement by a multiplicative factor of r^2. Since M is $f(n)$ space-bounded, the space requirement for N to simulate M on w is $r^2 f(n)$. If $r^2 f(n) > g(n)$, N on w may not finish simulating M on w. If $r^2 f(n) \leq g(n)$, N on w accepts w if, and only if, M on w does not accept. Since M is fixed, we can consider r as a constant and make ℓ arbitrarily large. Since $f(n) = o(g(n))$, for all but finitely many ℓ, $r^2 f(n) \leq g(n)$. We pick any such ℓ. Then, w witnesses that M does not decide L.

This proves the theorem. □

From the space hierarchy theorem, we can draw many separation results. The following two corollaries show examples of such results.

Corollary 10.1 *For all rational constants c and d such that $1 \leq c < d$,*

$$\text{DSPACE}[n^c] \subset \text{DSPACE}[n^d].$$

Corollary 10.2 *For all integer constants c and d such that $1 \leq c < d$,*

$$\text{DSPACE}[(\log n)^c] \subset \text{DSPACE}[(\log n)^c].$$

Here, $(\log n)^d = (\lceil \log n \rceil)^d$.

We now define nondeterministic analogs of the deterministic space complexity classes.

Definition 10.5 Let $f(n)$ be a space-bounding function. We say that an NTM M is $f(n)$ **space-bounded** if, for all inputs x, M on x halts without using more than $f(|x|)$ cells on any tape regardless of its nondeterministic choices.

Definition 10.6 Let $f(n)$ be a space-bounding function. Let L be a decidable language. We say that L has **nondeterministic space complexity** $f(n)$ if an NTM decides L that is $f(n)$ space-bounded.

Definition 10.7 For a space-bounding function $f(n)$, we define:

NSPACE$[f(n)] = \{L \mid$ there exists an $f(n)$ space-bounded NTM deciding $L\}$.

We now obtain the nondeterministic analog of the deterministic space compression theorem (Theorem 10.1) by applying the same proof.

Theorem 10.3 (The Nondeterministic Space Compression Theorem) *For all space-bounding functions $f(n)$ and constants $c \geq 0$:*

$$\text{NSPACE}[f(n)] = \text{NSPACE}[cf(n)].$$

10.2   Savitch's Theorem

Some major separation results in space complexity classes are derived from the following Savitch's theorem.

Theorem 10.4 (Savitch's Theorem) *For all space-constructible functions $f(n)$ such that $f(n) = \Omega(\log n)$, NSPACE$[f(n)] \subseteq$ DSPACE$[f(n)^2]$.*

Proof Overview
Given an $f(n)$ space-bounded NTM, we count the number of IDs, as with the proof for Theorem 10.2. The number of IDs on an input having a length of n is $O(2^{cf(n)})$ for some constant $c > 0$. We define a predicate that takes three variables. The first two variables are IDs (C and C'). The last one is an integer t. The predicate has a value of *true* if, and only if, C' is reachable from C in at most 2^t steps. For $t = 0$, the predicate can be evaluated deterministically in $f(n)$ space. We develop a recursive procedure for evaluating the predicate by exhaustively exploring all IDs as candidates for the halfway point.

Proof Let $f(n)$ be a space-constructible function. Suppose $f(n) = \Omega(\log n)$. Let L be a language in NSPACE$[f(n)]$. Let M be an NTM that decides L and is $f(n)$ space-bounded. We recall the proof of Theorem 6.1, where we showed that a two-tape TM can simulate a multi-tape TM. We treat the tapes of M in the same manner. In addition, since $f(n)$ is space-constructible, by using Proposition 10.1, M marks $f(n)$ cells on each work tape and, before accepting or rejecting, clears all the marked cells and then moves the heads to the leftmost positions. Because of this property, for each integer n, only one accepting ID exists for any input to M having a length of n.

Let Γ be the tape alphabet of M, and Q be the set of states of M. Let x be an input to M. Let $n = |x|$. Since we are examining one specific input for M, we can represent each ID of M on input x as a combination of the following components:

- The head position on the input tape, which is between 0 and $n + 1$ (assuming that the markers appear at positions 0 and $n + 1$)
- The head position on the work tape, which is between 1 and $f(n)$
- The state number, which is between $1, \ldots, \|Q\|$
- The tape contents $\|\Gamma\|^{f(n)}$

We encode each component in binary. This results in a binary encoding of each ID. The number of bits used in the binary-encoded ID is:

$$\lceil \log(n + 1) \rceil + \lceil \log(f(n)) \rceil + \lceil \|Q\| \rceil + f(n) \lceil \log \|\Gamma\| \rceil.$$

This total is $O(\log(n) + f(n))$. Since $f(n) = \Omega(\log(n))$, there is an integer constant c, independent of n, such that the ID has length at most $cf(n)$.

Note the following properties:

- Not all binary strings having a length of $cf(n)$ encode an ID of M on x.
- For an arbitrary two strings u and v that are valid encodings of M on input x, only $cf(n)$ space is necessary for testing whether or not one of the possible moves of M takes u to v in one step.
- For an arbitrary two strings u and v that are valid encodings of M on input x, only $cf(n)$ space is necessary for testing $u = v$.

For two binary strings having a length of $cf(n)$ and an integer t such that $0 \leq t \leq cf(n)$, we define $\rho(u, v, t)$ as the following predicate:

u and v are valid encodings of IDs of M on x, and v is reachable from u in at most 2^t steps by following the nondeterministic actions of M.

Let u_I be the initial ID of M on input x. Let u_A be the accepting ID of M on input x. Then, the following property holds:

$$M \text{ accepts } x \text{ if, and only if, } \rho(u_I, u_A, cf(n)) = true.$$

There is a recursive algorithm for testing $\rho(u, v, t)$ with a space requirement of $O(t f(n))$. The algorithm employs the following approach:

- If $t = 0$, test if $u = v$ or v results from u in one step.
- If $t \geq 1$, for each legitimate w, test:

$$\rho(u, w, t - 1) \wedge \rho(w, v, t - 1).$$

In other words, we search for a halfway point w between u and v; i.e., w is reachable from u in $\leq 2^{t-1}$ steps, and v is reachable from w in $\leq 2^{t-1}$ steps. We can implement this approach as a depth-first search algorithm. Executing the search requires remembering u, v, w, and t, as well as which side of the two terms is being evaluated.

The recursion depth of this depth-first search is $cf(n)$, and the information we need to remember at each level requires $\leq 3cf(n)$ bits. Thus, the algorithm requires $O(f(n)^2)$ space. One subtle point is that the value of t specifies "at most 2^t steps." We may encounter a situation for some u, v, and $t \geq 2$ such that $\rho(u, v, t)$ is *true* and (either $u = v$ or v is reachable from u in one step). In such a situation, the recursion will continue, but we can guarantee that if we keep choosing u (as the middle point w in the ensuing recursion), we will find that $\rho(u, v, t)$ is true.

This proves the theorem.   □

From Savitch's theorem, we obtain the following class separation result.

Theorem 10.5 (Nondeterministic Space Hierarchy Theorem) *For all space-bounding functions $f(n)$ and $g(n)$ such that $f(n) = \Omega(\log n)$ and $g(n) = \omega(f(n)^2)$, NSPACE$[f(n)] \subset$ NSPACE$[g(n)]$.*

10.3 Fundamental Space Complexity Classes

We now define the standard space complexity classes.

Definition 10.8 L is the class of all decidable languages with some TM that is $O(\log n)$ space-bounded.

Definition 10.9 NL is the class of all decidable languages with some TM that is $O(\log n)$ space-bounded.

Definition 10.10 coNL is the class of all languages whose complements are in NL. In other words, coNL $= \{A \mid \overline{A} \in$ NL$\}$.

Definition 10.11 PSPACE is the class of all languages that are decidable with some TM that is $O(cn^c + c)$ space-bounded for some $c \geq 1$; that is, PSPACE $= \cup_{c \geq 1}$DSPACE$[cn^c + c]$.

Definition 10.12 EXPSPACE is the class of all decidable languages with some TM that is $O(2^{cn^c+c})$ space-bounded for some $c \geq 1$; that is, EXPSPACE $= \cup_{c \geq 1}$DSPACE$[2^{cn^c+c}]$.

We know that the following relations hold (see Fig. 10.2).

Theorem 10.6 L $\subseteq$ NL $\subseteq$ P $\subseteq$ NP $\subseteq$ PSPACE $\subseteq$ EXPTIME $\subseteq$ NEXPTIME $\subseteq$ EXPSPACE.

Fig. 10.2 Inclusions among
the standard time and space
complexity classes

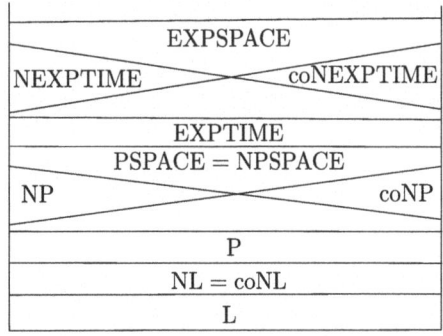

Proof L $\subseteq$ NL, P $\subseteq$ NP, and EXPTIME $\subseteq$ NEXPTIME are clear from the definition.

Suppose a language is in NTIME[$f(n)$] for some time-constructible function $f(n) = \omega(n)$ and an NTM M. As with the proof of Theorem 6.6, we can assume that M has at most two choices of actions at each computation step. Let T be a TM witnessing that $f(n)$ is time-constructible.

We can design a TM N that simulates M using an exhaustive search as follows:

- Using T, N obtains $1^{f(n)}$.
- N generates all binary strings having a length of $f(n)$ using one tape. Then, for each string it generates, N simulates M on input x using the binary string as a guide.
- If any simulation leads to acceptance, N accepts; if none leads to acceptance, N rejects.

The simulator N witnesses that $L(M) \in$ DSPACE[$f(n)$]. Thus, we know NP $\subseteq$ PSPACE and NEXPTIME $\subseteq$ EXPSPACE.

In the proof of Savitch's theorem, we noted that if an NTM is $f(n)$ space-bounded, then its halting computation has a length of at most $c^{f(n)}$ for some constant $c > 0$. We can make a better argument as follows:

Let x be an input to M having a length of n. Let G be a graph whose vertices are the IDs of M on input x. The number of vertices of G is at most $c^{f(n)}$. In the graph G, we draw an edge from a node u to another node v if v is one of the possible next IDs of u. Then, M on x accepts if, and only if, there is a path from the initial ID to one of the accepting IDs (we can modify M so there is only one accepting ID). A TM can test the reachability by writing down the adjacency graph and then running a depth-first or breadth-first search to obtain a list of vertices reachable from the initial ID. There is a polynomial time algorithm for depth-first and breadth-first searches, and so the running time of the machine can be $O((c^{f(n)})^d)$ for some integer d. We can rewrite the running time as $O(2^{\alpha f(n)})$ for some constant α. Thus, NL $\subseteq$ P and PSPACE $\subseteq$ EXPSPACE.   □

Because of the hierarchy theorems, we know that in the aforementioned sequence of inclusions, there is a gap between NL and PSPACE, between PSPACE and

Table 10.1 The closure properties of the standard space complexity classes

Class	Intersection	Union	Concatenation	Complement	Kleene-star
L	Y	Y	Y	Y	?
NL	Y	Y	Y	Y	Y
PSPACE	Y	Y	Y	Y	Y
EXPSPACE	Y	Y	Y	Y	Y

EXPSPACE, and between P and EXPTIME. Is any inclusion from the aforementioned sequence proper? That is an open question.

For most of the above classes, we know which closure properties they have. Table 10.1 presents the list of these closure properties. The question mark in the table indicates that the field does not know whether or not the class has the property.

10.4   The Reachability Problem

A remarkable finding in computational complexity theory is that for all space-constructible functions, $f(n) = \Omega(\log n)$, NSPACE$[f(n)]$ is closed under complement. Specifically, since $\log n$ is a space-constructible function, we know NL $=$ coNL.

Theorem 10.7 (The Immerman-Szelepscényi Theorem) NL $=$ coNL.

> **Proof Overview**
> We can test the membership for a language in NL as the reachability in a directed graph, whose nodes represent the IDs of an NTM with a logarithmic space bound and whose directed edges represent the possible transitions of the machine. A polynomial of the input length bounds the size of the graph. We will develop a nondeterministic logarithmic-space algorithm for computing the number of vertices that are reachable from the vertex representing the initial ID. After learning the number, it is possible to use a nondeterministic algorithm to check the reachability. Our nondeterministic algorithm for the complement accepts if no accepting IDs are among the reachable vertices.

Proof Let L be a language in NL. Let M be an NTM that decides L and has a $c \log n$ as its space bound for some constant $c > 0$. We will develop a nondeterministic logarithmic space algorithm for deciding the membership in $\overline{L}$.

We may assume that M has only one work tape. Let Q be the state set of M and Γ be the work-tape alphabet of M. Let $\tilde{\Gamma}$ be the Γ with squiggle. Let us simplify the notation by equating $\log a$ and $\lceil \log a \rceil$ for all positive integers a. We aim to develop an NTM that decides $\overline{L}$ using $O(\log n)$ space. We call the target TM N, which has a constant number of tapes. Our design will ensure that N uses $O(\log n)$ cells on each tape, so the overall space requirement is $O(\log n)$.

Let x be an input for which we want to test whether or not $x \in \overline{L}$. For $x = \epsilon$, N can behave as a DFA and accept or reject according to the membership of ϵ it already knows, so we assume that $|x| \geq 1$.

Recall the binary path generation procedure from the proof of Theorem 6.6. A TM can generate an infinite series of binary numbers where the bits appear in the reverse order; that is, $1, 01, 11, 001, 101, 011, 111, 0001, 1001, \ldots$. A TM can count the occurrences of an event by executing an update each time it occurs. In particular, N can generate the binary representation of $|x| + 2$ with the bits in the reverse order. By applying updates to the binary number until the number takes the form $0^d 1$, N can generate $\log |x|$ in binary. Then, by copying the expression c times, N can mark a region having a length of exactly $c \log |x|$. Let us assume that N computes these binary representations immediately after marking the left end of each work tape.

Let κ be the length of the binary representation of $\|Q\|$. Let π be the length of the binary representation of $|x| + 2$. Let $V = \{0, 1\}^{\kappa + \pi} (\Gamma \cup \tilde{\Gamma})^{c \log(|x|)}$. Using a string in V, we can encode each ID of M on input x as follows:

- The first κ characters represent an index to an element in Q.
- The next π characters represent a position between 1 and $|x| + 2$.
- The next $c \log(|x|)$ characters represent the contents of the work tape of M.

Not all strings in V are valid, but N can check whether or not an element in V that appears on one work tape is a valid encoding, via referring to the strings it generated earlier in the computation. The validity is the conjunction of three conditions; the first component represents a value between 1 and $\|Q\|$, the second component represents a value between 1 and $|x| + 2$, and the third component has exactly one symbol from $\tilde{\Gamma}$. N can execute the iteration and check on a single tape using space:

$$\kappa + \xi + c \log |x| = O(\log |x|).$$

Thus, we treat all members of V as possible IDs. In addition, N can generate the possible next ID of any $u \in V$ in $O(\log |x|)$ space. For this generation, N extracts the input head position from u, moves the input head to that position, and reads the input character at that position. Since the content of the work tape, the position of the work-tape head, and the present state number are available in u, N can determine the next action to occur. After determining the action, N can compute, from u, the ID at the next step, which consists of the updated head positions, the updated work-tape content, and the updated state number. Finally, N can check whether or not an arbitrary two strings in V are identical. Thus, N has the capacity in the deterministic logarithmic space to:

- Produce the initial and the accept IDs
- Iterate all members of V

- Check the validity of any member of V
- Compute the next IDs of any member of V
- Check the equality of an arbitrary ID pair

For each i such that $0 \leq i \leq \|V\|$, we define $R(i)$ as follows:

$R(i) = $ the set of all elements in E that represent IDs of M on input x and reachable from the initial ID in at most i steps.

In addition, for each i such that $0 \leq i \leq \|V\|$, we define $\rho(i) = \|R(i)\|$. We inductively compute $\rho(i)$ for $i = 0, \ldots, \|V\|$. The basis is $R(0)$. The set consists only of the initial ID, so $\rho(0) = 1$.

We build the inductive computation on four nondeterministic algorithms:

- **Enumeration(i, r)** nondeterministically lists the elements of $R(i)$, assuming $r = \rho(i)$.
- **Reachability(u, i, r)** tests whether or not $u \in R(i)$, assuming $r = \rho(i)$.
- **Extended-Reachability(u, i, r)** tests whether or not $u \in R(i + 1)$, assuming $r = \rho(i)$.
- **Extended-Counting(i, r)** produces $\rho(i + 1)$, assuming $r = \rho(i)$.

All four require the knowledge of $\rho(i)$ and $O(\log(n))$ space and may produce "failure" as the output. While the computation may fail, we can guarantee that if $r = \rho(i)$, all four methods have a non-failing path, and for each non-failing path, the output is correct. We present them in Algorithms 10.2, 10.3, 10.4, and 10.5.

The way the algorithms work is as follows:

First, for the Enumeration program, for each $u \in V$, we examine whether or not $u \in R(i)$ by running M on x from the initial ID for i steps. For each u that is found to be in $R(i)$, we output u. We also count the number of elements in $R(i)$ we have found. When we have checked all members of V, we check if the count equals r. If they are equal, we have successfully enumerated all members of $R(i)$, so we output "success"; otherwise, we output "failure." The "success" and "failure" assertions do not appear until the end. If the count equals r, for each $u \in R(i)$, we found a path to u within i steps so that there is a successful computation path. Also, if the count is $< r$, the computation is unsuccessful, as there are unidentified IDs in $R(i)$.

The Reachability program runs the Enumeration program and checks if u appears in the enumeration, and the execution ends with "success." If both occur, we have found that $u \in R(i)$.

Algorithm 10.2 The enumeration algorithm

```
 1: procedure ENUMERATION(i, r)
 2:     c ← 0;
 3:     for each ID z ∈ E do
 4:         u ← the initial ID of M on x;
 5:         if u = z then
 6:             c ← c + 1;
 7:         else
 8:             for j ← 1, . . . , i do
 9:                 nondeterministically choose v from a pool of the next IDs of u;
10:                 if v = z then
11:                     append z to the list;
12:                     c ← c + 1;
13:                     terminate the check of z;
14:                 end if
15:             end for
16:         end if
17:     end for
18:     if c = r then
19:         append "success" to the list;
20:     else
21:         append "failure" to the list;
22:     end if
23: end procedure
```

Algorithm 10.3 The reachability testing algorithm

```
 1: procedure REACHABILITY(u, i, r)
 2:     f ← false;
 3:     run Enumeration(i, r);
 4:     for each ID z generated do
 5:         if u = z then
 6:             f ← true;
 7:         end if
 8:     end for
 9:     if the final output is "success" then
10:         if f = true then
11:             output "reachable";
12:         else
13:             output "unreachable";
14:         end if
15:     else
16:         output "failure";
17:     end if
18: end procedure
```

Algorithm 10.4 The extended reachability testing algorithm

 1: **procedure** EXTENDED-REACHABILITY(u, i, r)
 2:     $f \leftarrow false$;
 3:     run Enumeration(i, r);
 4:     **for** each ID z generated **do**
 5:         **if** $u = z$ or u is one of the next IDs of z **then**
 6:             $f \leftarrow true$;
 7:         **end if**
 8:     **end for**
 9:     **if** the final output "success" **then**
10:         **if** $f = true$ **then**
11:             output "reachable";
12:         **else**
13:             output "unreachable";
14:         **end if**
15:     **else**
16:         output "failure";
17:     **end if**
18: **end procedure**

Algorithm 10.5 An extended counting

 1: **procedure** EXTENDED-COUNTING(i, r)
 2:     $c \leftarrow 0$;
 3:     **for** each ID u **do**
 4:         run Extended-Reachability(u, i, r);
 5:         **if** the outcome is "failure" **then**
 6:             output "failure";
 7:         **else if** the output is "reachable" **then**
 8:             $c \leftarrow c + 1$;
 9:         **end if**
10:     **end for**
11:     output c;
12: **end procedure**

For Extended-Reachability, since each element in $R(i + 1) - R(i)$ is one computation step away from an element in $R(i)$, we run Enumeration to see if:

(a) u appears as a member of $R(i)$
(b) u follows from one of the elements of $R(i)$ in one step

Like before, we check that the Enumeration program ends with "success." For Extended-Counting, we execute Extended-Reachability for all $u \in V$.

The overall algorithm for $\overline{L}$ is Algorithm 10.6.

Algorithm 10.6 A non-reachability testing algorithm

```
 1: procedure NON-REACHABILITY(x)
 2:      r ← 1;
 3:      for i ← 1, . . . , ‖V‖ − 1 do r ← Extended-Counting(i, r);
 4:          if the execution is a failure then
 5:              output "failure";
 6:          end if
 7:      end for
 8:      u ← the accept ID;
 9:      f ← Reachability(u, ‖V‖, r);
10:      if the execution is a failure then
11:          output "failure";
12:      else if f is "reachable" then
13:          reject x;
14:      else
15:          accept x;
16:      end if
17: end procedure
```

This completes the proof. □

The NL = coNL proof is extendable to any space-constructible $\Omega(\log n)$ function. This is because the numbers of calculated IDs are proportional to the space the machine uses. We thus obtain the following result.

Corollary 10.3 *For all space-constructible functions $f(n)$ such that $f(n) = \Omega(\log n)$, NSPACE[$f(n)$] = co−NSPACE[$f(n)$].*

10.5 Examples of Space Complexity Classifications

We now explore some representative problems of space complexity classes.

By following an idea similar to the proof of Theorem 10.2, we can show that the validity testing of TM encodings requires only logarithmic space.

Proposition 10.2 *The language $\{\langle M \rangle \mid M$ is a TM$\}$ is in L.*

Proof Suppose we have a binary string, x, $|x| = n$, as an input and want to test its validity as a TM encoding. To simplify the test procedure, we can assume that the encoding has a prefix:

$$0^k 10^q 10^s 1.$$

Here, k is the number of tapes, q is the number of states, and s is the number of symbols. We assume that the states numbered 1, 2, and 3 are the initial, the accept, and the reject states, respectively. In addition, we assume that the first symbol is the blank symbol. After the prefix, the transition table appears. The table has $(q-2)s^k$

elements separated by 11 with each element taking the form:

$$0^{a_1} 10^{b_1} 1 \cdots 0^{a_k} 10^{b_k}.$$

Here, $a_1, \ldots, a_k \in \{1, \ldots, s\}$ and $b_1, \ldots, b_k \in \{1, 2, 3\}$ with 1, 2, and 3 indicating the head movements L, $-$, and R, respectively.

We will design a logarithmic space-bounded machine N that conducts the correctness of x's format. First, N marks $\log(n)$ cells on its work tapes to avoid using more than $\log(n)$ space. Next, using a DFA without using space at all, N checks whether the input x is in the correct format; i.e., x is a series of blocks of 0s with a block of 1 in between. If the input does not pass the check, the input is not a valid encoding, so N rejects x. If the input passes the test, N extracts k, q, and s in binary. Then, N confirms that x has $(q - 2)s^k$ entries in the transition table and that each entry is in the correct format. This is where ingenuity is required to execute in $\log(n)$. The main idea is to extract the components of each table entry on the work tape using the binary representations of the components and then verify that the components are in the required range; i.e., the symbol numbers are in $[1, s]$, and the head direction numbers are in $[1, 3]$. The encoding is invalid if the number of entries differs from $(q - 2)s^k$. Algorithm 10.7 describes how this is executed.   □

Using the same argument, we can show the following results:

Proposition 10.3 *The language*
$$\{\langle M, w \rangle \mid M \text{ is a TM, and } w \text{ is an input to } M\}$$
is in L.

Theorem 10.8 *The following four languages are in* NL:

1. $E_{\text{dist}} = \{\langle M, 0^k, 0^\ell \rangle \mid M$ *is a DFA, and the k-th and ℓ-th states of M are distinguishable*$\}$.
2. $E_{\text{indist}} = \{\langle M, 0^k, 0^\ell \rangle \mid M$ *is a DFA, and the k-th and ℓ-th states of M are indistinguishable*$\}$.
3. $E_{\text{unique}} = \{\langle M, 0^k \rangle \mid M$ *is a DFA, and the k-th state of M is distinguishable from all states of M with smaller indices*$\}$.
4. $E_{\text{final}} = \{\langle M, 0^k \rangle \mid M$ *is a DFA, and the k-th state of M is distinguishable from all states of M with smaller indices, and is a final state*$\}$.

Proof

(1) We already know that the encoding check of a TM is executable in the deterministic logarithmic space. Two states of M, p and q, are distinguishable if, and only if, there is a string a such that exactly one of $\delta(p, a)$ and $\delta(q, a)$ is a final state. If M has n states, the length of one such a can be no more than n. If exactly one of p and q is a final state, the value of a can be ϵ; otherwise, an NTM can execute a pair of concurrent nondeterministic walks, one from p and the other from q, for at most n steps. At each step, the machine nondeterministically selects a symbol α from the alphabet, updates the two states using the symbol,

---

Algorithm 10.7 A logarithmic-space validity test of a TM encoding

---

```
1: procedure VALIDITY-TEST(x)
2:     n ← |x|;
3:     mark log(n) cells on each work tape;
4:     check if the 1s appearing between 0s are valid punctuations;
5:     if the check fails then
6:         reject x;
7:     end if
8:     extract k, q, s, blank, q₀, q_acc, q_rej in binary;
9:     if the extraction requires more space than marked then
10:        reject x;
11:    end if
12:    secure space for counting up to (q − 2)sᵏ.
13:    if not enough space exists for counting then
14:        reject x;
15:    end if
16:    move the input head to the start of the table;
17:    c ← 0;
18:    while there remains a table entry do
19:        while moving the input head to the right, extract, in binary, the components of the
       entry;
20:            if the number of components is not 2k then
21:                reject x;
22:            end if
23:            if a symbol component is > s or a head direction component is > 3 then
24:                reject x;
25:            end if
26:            c ← c + 1;
27:            if c > (q − 2)sᵏ then
28:                reject x;
29:            end if
30:        end while
31:        if c < (q − 2)sᵏ then
32:            reject x;
33:        end if
34:        accept x;
35: end procedure
```

---

and then checks whether or not exactly one of the two is a final state. Thus, the distinguishability problem is in NL.

(2) Since $NL = coNL$, the indistinguishability is in NL as well.

(3) An NTM can use the algorithm from (1) to test the distinguishability of the k-th state from all the states with lower indices.

(4) An NTM can use the algorithm from (3) to test the distinguishability and then test if the k-th state is a final state.

□

Exercises

10.1 Show that if $t(n)$ is time-constructible, it is space-constructible as well.

10.2 Show that $\{\langle M, 0^i, 0^j\rangle \mid M$ is a DFA and the i-th state and j-th state are distinguishable$\}$ is in L.

10.3 Prove Theorem 10.1.

10.4 Show that for all integer constants $c \geq 1$, $(\log n)^c$ is space-constructible.

10.5 Show that for all rational constants $c > 1$, $\lceil n^c \rceil$ is space-constructible.

10.6 Show that 2^n is a space-constructible function.

10.7 Show that for all space-constructible functions $f(n)$ and $g(n)$, $f(n) + g(n)$ and $f(n) * g(n)$.

10.8 Show that for all space-constructible functions $f(n)$ and $g(n)$ such that $f(n) = \Omega(n)$, $f(g(n))$ is space-constructible.

10.9 Prove Proposition 10.1.

10.10 Prove Theorem 10.5.

10.11 Show that the following language is in L:
   $\{\langle M, 0^k, 0^\ell, 0^a\rangle \mid M$ is a DFA, k and ℓ are no more than the state number of M, and on the a-th symbol M transitions from the k-th state to the ℓ-th state$\}$.

10.12 Suppose a TM has two binary numbers, $a = a_1 \cdots a_m$ and $b = b_1 \cdots b_n$, on two separate work tapes. The numbers appear in the reverse order with a left-end marker $\vdash$ and $\sqcup$ as the right-end marker. In other words, the tapes' contents are $\vdash a_m \cdots a_1 \sqcup$ and $\vdash b_n \cdots b_1 \sqcup$. Show how to compute $a \times b$ in $O(m + n)$ space.

10.13 Recall that a **linear-bounded automaton** is a single-tape TM such that the input appears between left- and right-end markers, and the head does not move out of the region between the end markers. Prove that the language an LBA accepts is in DSPACE[n].

10.14 Show that $\{\langle M, N, i, j\rangle \mid M$ and N are square Boolean matrices having the same row and column numbers, and the (i, j) entry of $M \times N$ is $true\}$ is in L.

10.15 Prove Corollary 10.3.

10.16 Let $f(n) = \Omega(\log n)$. Show that if $f(n)$ is space-constructible, $f(n)$ is constructible in time $2^{cf(n)}$.

10.17 Let $f(n) = \Omega(\log n)$. Based on the previous question, show that for all positive integers c, both $2^{cf(n)}$ and $2^{cf(n)} f(n)$ are time-constructible.

10.18 Let $f(n) = \omega(\log n)$. Based on the previous questions, show that for some constant c, DSPACE[$f(n)$] $\subset$ DTIME[$2^{cf(n)} f(n)$].

10.19 Let $L \subseteq 1^*$ and is in DSPACE[$f(n)$] for some $f(n) = \Omega(\log n)$. Show that the set of binary integers t such that $1^t \in L$ is in DSPACE[$f(2^n)$].

10.20 Prove that NL is closed under Kleene-star.

10.21 Prove that NL is closed under union.

10.22 Prove that NL is closed under intersection.

Bibliographic Notes and Further Reading
Savitch's Theorem is by Savitch [2]. The Immerman-Szelepscényi Theorem is by
the independent work of Immerman [1] and Szelepscényi [3].

References

1. N. Immerman, Nondeterministic space is closed under complementation. SIAM J. Comput.
   17(5), 935–938 (1988)
2. W.J. Savitch, Relationships between nondeterministic and deterministic tape complexities. J.
   Comput. Syst. Sci. **4**(2), 177–192 (1970)
3. R. Szelepcsényi, The method of forced enumeration for nondeterministic automata. Acta
   Inform. **26**, 279–284 (1988)

Chapter 11
The Theory of NP-Completeness

11.1 The Polynomial-Time Many-One Reducibility

The original motivation for the NP-completeness was to obtain a mathematical characterization of NP and better understand the P vs. NP problem. Here, we introduce the polynomial-time many-one reducibility.

11.1.1 The Definition

First, we present the definition of polynomial-time many-one reducibility, which uses polynomial-time computable functions, as defined next.

Definition 11.1 (Polynomial-Time Computable Functions) Let Σ and Γ be (possibly identical) alphabets. Let f be a function from Σ^* to Γ^*. The function f is polynomial-time computable if a polynomial time-bounded multi-tape TM M with an output tape exists such that for all input x, M halts with $f(x)$ written on the output tape.

Definition 11.2 (Polynomial-Time Many-One Reductions) Let Σ and Γ be (possibly identical) alphabets. Let $A \subseteq \Sigma^*$ and $B \subseteq \Gamma^*$. A function f from Σ^* to Γ^* is a **polynomial-time many-one reduction from A to B** if:

(i) f is polynomial-time computable
(ii) For all $x \in \Sigma^*$, $x \in A \Leftrightarrow f(x) \in B$.

If a polynomial-time many-one reduction exists from A to B, we say A is **polynomial-time many-one reducible** to B and write $A \leq_{\mathrm{m}}^{p} B$.

© The Editor(s) (if applicable) and The Author(s), under exclusive license to
Springer Nature Switzerland AG 2025
M. Ogihara, *An Introduction to Theory of Computation*,
https://doi.org/10.1007/978-3-031-84740-0_11

When we speak of polynomial-time computability, we use the big-O notation, which can simplify the polynomial we use with one in the form $cx^c + c$, such that c is a natural number. The constant c in the polynomial cannot be 0 because a machine needs to run for at least one step, even on an empty input.

11.1.1.1   Examples of Polynomial-Time Many-One Reductions

We now present an example of polynomial-time many-one reductions.

A **Hamilton path** in a graph $G = (V, E)$ is an ordering of vertices $[u_1, \ldots, u_n]$ such that for each i between 1 and $n - 1$, $(u_i, u_{i+1}) \in E$. Put differently, a Hamilton path $[u_1, \ldots, u_n]$ in G visits every vertex exactly once. Figure 11.1 presents an example of a Hamilton path. The path appearing in thick lines connects the upper left corner of the graph and its lower left corner.

A **Hamilton cycle** in a graph $G = (V, E)$ is a sequence $[u_1, \ldots, u_n, u_1]$ such that $[u_1, \ldots, u_n]$ is a Hamilton path and (u_n, u_1) is another edge of the graph. Figure 11.2 presents an example of the Hamilton cycle. A graph having a Hamilton cycle is **Hamiltonian**.

The search for a Hamilton path or cycle, if any, occurs in many practical situations. We capture this search with decision problems.

Definition 11.3

1. HAMPATH $= \{\langle G, s, t\rangle \mid$ the graph G has a Hamilton path from s to $t\}$.
2. HAMCYCLE $= \{\langle G\rangle \mid$ the graph G has a Hamilton cycle$\}$.

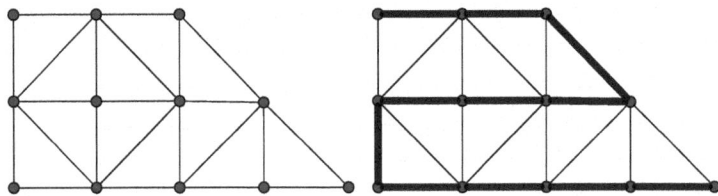

Fig. 11.1 A Hamilton path. The left panel: a given graph. The right panel: a Hamilton path between the vertex in the upper-left corner and the vertex in the lower-right corner. The thick lines represent the edges of the path

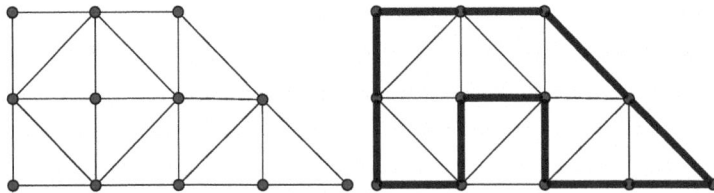

Fig. 11.2 A Hamilton cycle. The left panel: a given graph. The right panel: a Hamilton cycle. The path from Fig. 11.1 does not extend to a cycle because there is no edge between the paths' two ends

Suppose we map an arbitrary triple $\langle G, s, t \rangle$ for HAMPATH to a graph H constructed from G by adding a new vertex u and connecting u with s and t. Since u is connected to only s and t, H has a Hamilton cycle if, and only if, G has a Hamilton path from s and t. We augment the mapping by producing ϵ if the input is not a valid encoding. The mapping is computable in polynomial time. Thus, HAMPATH $\leq_m^p$ HAMCYCLE. Figure 11.3 shows the reduction.

Theorem 11.1 HAMPATH $\leq_m^p$ HAMCYCLE.

Using an idea similar to the reduction we have just constructed, we can build a reduction going in the other direction (see Exercise 11.8).

Theorem 11.2 HAMCYCLE $\leq_m^p$ HAMPATH.

11.1.2   The Definition of NP-Complete Languages

The polynomial-time many-one reducibility is transitive; if $A \leq_m^p B$ and $B \leq_m^p C$, then $A \leq_m^p C$. Thus, the polynomial-time many-one reducibility naturally induces a partial order among the languages in NP. The reducibility also induces equivalence classes. A surprising fact is that NP contains an equivalence class such that an arbitrary NP language is polynomial-time many-one reducible to an arbitrary member of the equivalence class. In other words, every sequence of NP languages ordered by $\leq_m^p$ reaches this equivalence class. We call this equivalence class **NP-complete**.

Definition 11.4 (NP-Complete) A language A is NP-complete if (a) $A \in$ NP and (b) every language in NP is polynomial-time many-one reducible to A.

We call a language satisfying (b) **NP-hard**.

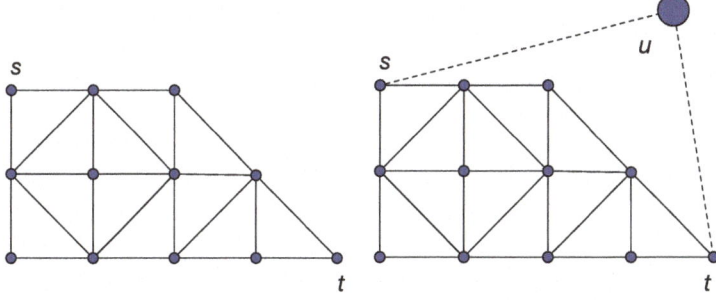

Fig. 11.3 A many-one reduction from the Hamilton path problem to the Hamilton cycle problem. On the right panel, the big circle is the new vertex u. The dashed lines are the connections between s and u and between t and u

Definition 11.5 (NP-Hard) A language A is NP-hard if every language in NP is polynomial-time many-one reducible to A.

Thus, we can restate the definition of NP-completeness as:

$$A \text{ language } A \text{ is NP-complete} \iff A \in \text{NP and NP-hard}.$$

Note that NP-hardness differs from NP-completeness. For example, $\text{ACCEPT}_{\text{NTM}}$, the NTM version of $\text{ACCEPT}_{\text{TM}}$, is NP-hard and undecidable. This means that $\text{ACCEPT}_{\text{NTM}}$ cannot be NP-complete.

A key property of NP-complete languages is that they rise and fall together, as we state next:

Proposition 11.1 *The following properties are equal:*

1. $P = NP$.
2. *Some NP-complete language is in* P.
3. *All NP-complete languages are in* P.

The NP-complete languages are closed under symmetric differences with any finite set.

Proposition 11.2 *Let A be an infinite NP-complete language and S be a finite set. Then $A \triangle S$ is NP-complete.*

11.1.3   A Canonical NP-Complete Language

We previously stated that $\text{ACCEPT}_{\text{NTM}}$ is NP-hard. The polynomial time-bounded version of $\text{ACCEPT}_{\text{NTM}}$ is NP-complete. Because it includes machine encoding, we call it a **canonical NP-complete language**.

Definition 11.6 $\text{NTMCANONICAL} = \{\langle M, w, 0^t\rangle \mid M$ is a multi-tape NTM, w is an input to M, $t \geq 1$, and M on w accepts in t steps for some computation path$\}$.

Theorem 11.3 NTMCANONICAL *is NP-complete.*

Proof To show $\text{NTMCANONICAL} \in \text{NP}$, think of a TM N that on input x, checks if $x = \langle M, w, 0^t\rangle$ for some M, w, and t, simulates M on w for at most t steps nondeterministically if the check passes, and accepts if, and only if, M accepts in the simulation; N rejects if the check fails. We already know there is a polynomial-time algorithm for the check. The simulation requires no more than $|x|$ steps, so N can be polynomial time-bounded.

To show that NTMCANONICAL is NP-hard, let A be an arbitrary language in NP and M be a polynomial time-bounded NTM that accepts A. Let $p(n)$ be a polynomial bounding the running time of M. Let f be a function that maps each

w to $\langle M, w, 0^{p(|w|)}\rangle$. For all w, $w \in A$ if, and only if, $f(w) \in$ NtmCanonical. Since M is fixed, f is polynomial-time computable. This proves the theorem.   □

11.1.4   Polynomial-Time Witness Schemes

From the canonical NP-complete problem, we draw a witness-based characterization of NP, the polynomial-time analog of the recursive witness scheme from Sect. 6.4.2.

Definition 11.7 Let $L \subseteq \Sigma^*$ be a language. A **polynomial-time witness scheme** is a pair $(p(n), A)$ such that $p(n)$ is a polynomial, $A \in$ P, and for all $x \in \Sigma^*$:

$$x \in L \iff (\exists y \in \Sigma^{\leq p(|x|)})[\langle x, y\rangle \in A].$$

We call A a **witness language** of L, and each string y satisfying the condition on the right-hand side for x a **witness for x's membership in L**.

Intuitively, if A is a witness language of L, then for any string $x \in \Sigma^*$, we can interpret the membership question of x in L as the question of whether or not there is a witness for $x \in L$.

Theorem 11.4 *A language L is in NP if, and only if, L has a polynomial-time witness scheme.*

Proof Let $L \subseteq \Sigma^*$ be a language in NP. Let M be a polynomial time-bounded single-tape NTM deciding L. Let $q(n)$ be a polynomial bounding the running time of M. We can assume that each ID of M has two possible IDs in the next step. Also, we can assume that once entering q_{acc}, M remains in the same ID indefinitely.

We define the language A as follows:

$A = \{\langle x, C_1\#\cdots\#C_{q(|x|)}\rangle \mid C_1, \ldots, C_{q(|x|)}$ are IDs covering $q(|x|)$ tape cells, C_1 is the initial configuration of M on x, $C_{q(|x|)}$ is an accepting ID of M, and for all i such that $2 \leq i \leq q(|x|)$, C_i is one of the possible next IDs of $C_{i-1}\}$.

Clearly, A is in P. There is a polynomial $p(n) = O(q(n)^2)$ such that the second part of the pair has a length of $\leq p(n)$. Thus, $(p(n), A)$ is a polynomial-time witness scheme for L.

Conversely, suppose a language L has a polynomial-time witness scheme $(p(n), A)$. In that case, we can construct an NTM that, on input x, nondeterministically selects y, $|y| \leq p(|x|)$, and accepts if $\langle x, y\rangle \in A$ (and rejects otherwise). The TM witnesses that $L \in$ NP.   □

11.2   The Satisfiability Problem (SAT)

The first known NP-complete problem is the satisfiability problem, which we can derive from the generic polynomial-time witness scheme from the previous section.

11.2.1   The NP-Completeness of SAT

Recall that a propositional formula with variables is satisfiable if a value assignment exists for the variables with which the formula's value is *true*. Let φ be a Boolean formula with variables $x_1, \ldots, x_n$. We encode φ using an alphabet having seven symbols: #, :, (), ¬, ∨, and ∧. In the encoding, we replace each occurrence of x_i with $\#^i$, surround the formula with a pair of parentheses, and attach $\#^n$; in the encoding. For example, we encode the formula:

$$\neg(\neg(x_1 \wedge (\neg x_2 \wedge x_3) \wedge (\neg x_1 \vee x_2 \vee x_3))) \wedge (x_1 \vee \neg x_2)$$

into the string:

$$\#\#\#; \ \neg((\neg(\# \wedge (\neg\#\# \wedge \#\#\#)) \wedge (\neg\# \vee \#\# \vee \#\#\#)) \wedge (\# \vee \neg\#\#)).$$

We can turn the seven-symbol encoding into a binary encoding by replacing each symbol with a unique three-bit number.

Definition 11.8 $\text{SAT} = \{\langle \varphi \rangle \mid \varphi \text{ is a satisfiable Boolean formula}\}$.

We prove:

Theorem 11.5   *SAT is NP-complete.*

Proof   Think of an NTM that, on input φ, nondeterministically generates a truth assignment to φ and accepts if the assignment satisfies the formula. The machine decides SAT and can run in polynomial time. Thus, $\text{SAT} \in \text{NP}$.

To prove that SAT is NP-hard, let $L \in \text{NP}$ and $(p(n), A)$ be the witness scheme from the proof of Theorem 11.4:

$A = \{\langle x, C_1\#\cdots\#C_{q(|x|)}\rangle \mid C_1, \ldots, C_{q(|x|)}$ are IDs covering $q(|x|)$ tape cells, C_1 is the initial configuration of M on x, $C_{q(|x|)}$ is an accepting ID of M, and for all i such that $2 \le i \le q(|x|)$, C_i is one of the next IDs of $C_{i-1}\}$.

We can assume that M does not move its head to the left when the head is on the leftmost cell.

Suppose we want to reduce the membership of x in L to a formula. Let $n = |x|$. We can encode each ID using $O(q(n))$ variables.

- $bra_{t,c}$, $1 \le t \le q(n) - 1$, and $c = 1, 2$: The variable indicates that the branch M has chosen at step t is c. For each t, exactly one of $bra_{t,1}$ and $bra_{t,2}$ must be *true*.

- $cel_{t,j,h}$, $1 \leq t \leq q(n)$, $1 \leq j \leq q(n)$, and $1 \leq h \leq \|\Gamma\|$: The variable indicates that the cell at position j at step t is the h-th symbol. For each combination of t and j, $cel_{t,j,h}$ is *true* for exactly one value of h.
- $sta_{t,h}$, $1 \leq t \leq q(n)$, and $1 \leq h \leq \|Q\|$: The variable indicates that M's state at step t is the h-th state. For each t, $sta_{t,h}$ is *true* for exactly one h.
- $pos_{t,j}$, $1 \leq t$, $j \leq q(n)$: The variable represents the head position of M. For each t, $pos_{t,j}$ is *true* for exactly one j.

φ is built from these variables and represents $\langle x, C_1\# \cdots \#C_{q(n)} \rangle \in A$. We build φ as follows:

First of all, for each variable group, we need to establish that exactly one variable in the group has the value *true*. We can express the uniqueness using a simple formula. For an arbitrary set of variables $y_1, \ldots, y_m$, $m \geq 2$, the condition that exactly one of the members is *true* can be expressed as:

$$(y_1 \vee \cdots \vee y_m) \wedge (\neg y_1 \vee \neg y_2) \wedge \cdots \wedge (\neg y_{m-1} \vee \neg y_m).$$

The number of literals in the formula is $m + m(m-1)/2 = m(m+1)/2$.

Next, we construct a formula representing that when $t = 1$, the variables represent the initial ID. $sta_{1,h} = true$ for the index h representing the initial state. For each j, $cel_{1,j,h} = true$ for the symbol appearing in cell j initially. Additionally, $pos_{1,1} = true$. The representation of the initial ID is the conjunction of all of these conditions. The number of literals here is $q(n) + 2$.

Next, we construct a formula representing that at step $t = q(n)$, the ID is accepting. The formula is single literal $sta_{q(n),h}$, where h is the index of q_{acc}. The number of literals here is 1.

Finally, we construct a formula representing that C_{t+1} is the next ID of C_t corresponding to the nondeterministic choice c at step t. If the head is on the j-th cell at step t, the symbol in the cell $j' \neq j$ is the same between steps t and $t+1$. This relation is expressible as:

$$pos_{t,j} \vee ((cel_{t,j,h} \vee \neg cel_{t+1,j,h}) \wedge (\neg cel_{t,j,h} \vee cel_{t+1,j,h}).$$

This is equivalent to:

$$\neg pos_{t,j} \rightarrow (cel_{t,j,h} = cel_{t+1,j,h}).$$

If $pos_{t,j} = true$, for each h such that $1 \leq h \leq \|\Gamma\|$, the value of $cel_{t+1,j,h}$ depends on bra_t, $cel_{t,j,h}$, and sta_t. We can express this relation as the conjunction of subformulas of the form:

If $pos_{t,j} = true$, $cel_{t,j,h} = true$, $bra_{t,c} = true$, and $sta_{t,r} = true$, then $cel_{t+1,j,h'}$.

This is equivalent to a five-literal disjunction:

$$\neg pos_{t,j} \vee \neg cel_{t,j,h} \vee \neg bra_{t,c} \vee \neg sta_{t,r} \vee cel_{t+1,j,h'}.$$

The combinations of h, c, r, and h' are taken from the transition function of M. There are $2\|Q\|\|\Gamma\|$ combinations for each t and j.

Similarly, we construct the state and head position formulas at step $t + 1$. The number of literals required for the expression is:

$$3 \cdot (q(n) - 1) \cdot q(n) \cdot (5 \cdot 2\|Q\|\|\Gamma\|) = O(q(n)^2).$$

Here, 3 represents the three distinct formula groups, $q(n) - 1$ represents the number of choices for t, $q(n)$ represents the number of choices for j, and 5 represents the size of the disjunction.

Thus, the entire formula has $O(q(n)^2)$ literals, so the formula is computable in polynomial time. Because of the construction design, the formula is satisfiable if, and only if, M accepts L.

This proves the theorem.   □

11.2.2   NP-Complete Variants of SAT

We now present variants of the satisfiability problem that are NP-complete.

11.2.2.1   The CNF Satisfiability

A well-known variant of the NP-complete satisfiability problem is the CNF satisfiability problem.

A Boolean formula is in the **conjunctive normal form** (for short, **CNF**) if it is a conjunction of disjunctions such that each disjunction unites variables or their negations. In CNF formulas, the negation appears only before a variable. We call the combination of a negation and a variable a **negative literal**. As opposed to this, we call a variable not accompanying a negation a **positive literal**. We then can say that a CNF formula is a conjunction of **disjunctive clauses**, in which each term is a literal.

For example, consider the formula:

$$x \wedge \neg y \wedge z \wedge (\neg x \vee y \vee z) \wedge (x \vee \neg y).$$

This is a CNF formula where the first three terms are disjunctions of single literals. By adding extra parentheses, the formula is equivalent to:

$$(x) \wedge (\neg y) \wedge (z) \wedge (\neg x \vee y \vee z) \wedge (x \vee \neg y).$$

Next, we define a special SAT, which restricts the formula to a CNF formula.

Definition 11.9 CNFSAT is the set of all satisfiable CNF formulas.

The formula we constructed in the proof of Theorem 11.5 is already in the conjunctive normal form. So, we have:

Theorem 11.6 CNFSAT *is* NP-*complete.*

11.2.2.2 3SAT

We can further restrict the format of the NP-complete formula. We call a CNFSAT where each disjunctive clause has at most three literals a **3CNF formula**.

Definition 11.10 $3\text{SAT} = \{\langle\varphi\rangle \mid \varphi$ is a satisfiable 3CNF formula$\}$.

It is possible to convert an arbitrary CNF formula into a 3CNF formula. For a clause $(u_1 \vee \cdots \vee u_k)$ such that $k \geq 4$, we introduce a new variable v and change the clause to a formula:

$$(v \vee u_3 \vee \cdots \vee u_k) \wedge (\neg v \vee u_1 \vee u_2) \wedge (\neg u_1 \vee v) \wedge (\neg u_2 \vee v).$$

We can satisfy this formula by satisfying $(u_1 \vee \cdots \vee u_k)$ and assigning the value of $u_1 \vee u_2$ to v. This change reduces the number of literals in the first clause from k to $k - 1$. By successively applying the modification, we can generate a 3CNF formula equivalent to the original. The modification requires $k - 3$ additional variables, $(k - 3)$ clauses with three literals, and $2(k - 3)$ clauses with two literals.

Once the number of literals becomes ≤ 3 for all clauses, we can adjust the number to exactly 3. For a clause with just one literal, (u), we can substitute the clause with a formula:

$$(u \vee v_1 \vee v_2) \wedge (u \vee v_1 \vee \neg v_2) \wedge (u \vee \neg v_1 \vee v_2) \wedge (u \vee \neg v_1 \vee \neg v_2).$$

Here, v_1 and v_2 are new variables. Satisfying this formula requires setting the value of u to *true*.

For a clause with just two literals, $(u \vee u')$, we can inflate the clause by replacing it by its copies, introducing a new variable, and inserting the variable positively into one and negatively into the other. If v is the new variable, the formula that replaces the clause is:

$$(u \vee u' \vee v) \wedge (u \vee u' \vee \neg v).$$

Satisfying this formula requires setting the value of $u \vee u'$ to *true*.

The conversion is easy to make, and it increases the size of the formula only by a constant factor. This means a polynomial-time many-one reduction exists from CNFSAT to 3SAT.

Thus, we have proven:

Theorem 11.7 3SAT *is* NP-*complete, even if the number of literals in each clause must be three.*

Note that the construction of a Boolean formula representing an accepting computation applies not only to single-tape TMs but to any multiple-tape TM. To extend the proof technique to a situation where the machine has multiple tapes, we introduce variables representing the contents and the head position for each additional tape. The set of subformulas describing the machine's permissible actions becomes more complex since each computation step handles all the tapes simultaneously.

11.2.2.3 NAE-SAT

An assignment for a CNF formula is a **not-all-equal assignment** (or an **NAE assignment**) if, for each clause, it satisfies one literal and fails to satisfy another. A variant of 3SAT is NAESAT, which asks if a 3CNF formula has a **not-all-equal assignment**.

Theorem 11.8 NAESAT *is* NP-*complete.*

Proof Showing NAESAT $\in$ NP is easy; we leave the task of proving the membership to the reader.

To show that NAESAT is NP-hard, let φ be an arbitrary 3CNF formula, where each clause has exactly three literals. We modify φ into a 4CNF formula φ' by turning each clause of the form $(\alpha \vee \beta \vee \gamma)$ into:

$$(\alpha \vee \beta \vee \gamma \vee \delta) \wedge (\overline{\alpha} \vee \overline{\beta} \vee \overline{\gamma} \vee \overline{\delta}).$$

We use the same δ for all the clauses.

We claim that φ' has an NAE assignment if, and only if, φ has a satisfying assignment. To prove this claim, suppose A is a satisfying assignment of φ. Suppose we extend A to A' by adding $w = false$. Then A' is an NAE assignment of φ'.

Conversely, if A' is an NAE assignment of φ' such that $A'(w) = false$, the remainder of A' becomes a satisfying assignment of φ. Additionally, if A' is an NAE assignment of φ' such that $A'(w) = true$, by switching between x and $\overline{x}$ for all variables x, we get to the same situation. Thus, the complementary assignment of A' is a satisfying assignment of φ.

Now, we construct a new formula φ'' by turning each 4-literal clause $(x \vee y \vee z \vee w)$ into:

$$(u \vee x \vee y) \wedge (\overline{u} \vee z \vee w).$$

Here, the variable u is not shared with other clauses. We can verify that from each NAE assignment to the 4-literal clause, we can construct an NAE assignment to the pair of 3-literal clauses (and vice versa) as follows:

- Suppose A is an NAE assignment to the four variables. If the assignment is *true* for both x and y in A. Then, the assignment to z or the assignment to w is *false*. We can assign *false* to u. Then the assignment to the two 3-literal clauses is an NAE assignment.
- Suppose A is an NAE assignment to the four variables. If the assignment is *true* for both z and w in A. Then, the assignment to x or the assignment to y is *false*. We can assign *true* to u. Then the assignment to the two 3-literal clauses is an NAE assignment.
- If B is an NAE assignment to the two 3-literal clauses. If $u = true$ in the assignment, then either x or y is *false*, and either z or w is *true*. Thus, the assignment to the four variables other than u is an NAE assignment to the 4-literal clause.
- If B is an NAE assignment to the two 3-literal clauses. If $u = false$ in the assignment, then either x or y is *true*, and either z or w is *false*. Thus, the assignment to the four variables other than u is an NAE assignment to the 4-literal clause.

receive *true* in

Our reduction outputs φ'' from φ. If φ has n variables and m clauses, φ'' has $n + m + 1$ variables and $4m$ clauses. We see that the construction can be carried out in polynomial time. Thus, NAESAT is NP-complete.   □

11.2.3   Some Complete Problems for coNP

Since coNP is the complementary class of NP, the unsatisfiability problem about Boolean logic is complete for coNP.

We define UNSAT as the set of all 3CNF formulas that are unsatisfiable.

Corollary 11.1 UNSAT *is* $\leq_{\mathrm{m}}^{p}$*-complete for* coNP.

Let φ be a Boolean formula. Let φ^c be the negation of the formula. φ^c can be a mirror image of φ, where:

- Every positive literal of φ appears as a negative literal
- Every negative literal of φ appears as a positive literal
- Every $\vee$ of φ appears as an $\wedge$
- Every $\wedge$ of φ appears as an $\vee$

For every truth assignment A of φ, A satisfies φ if, and only if, A fails to satisfy φ^c. Thus, the unsatisfiability problem is the question of whether or not all the truth assignments are satisfying. If every truth assignment is satisfying, the formula is a **tautology**.

We define TAUTOLOGY as the set of all 3CNF formulas that are unsatisfiable.

Corollary 11.2 TAUTOLOGY *is* $\leq_m^p$*-complete for* coNP.

We can develop another tautology problem. Let φ be a CNF formula. Then, φ^c, the negation of φ, is a disjunction of conjunctions. Every satisfying assignment of φ is a non-satisfying assignment of φ^c. The formula in this format is called a **disjunctive normal form** formula. Like 3CNF formulas, 3DNF formulas are DNF formulas where each clause has three literals.

We define DNFTAUT as the set of all DNF tautologies and 3DNFTAUT as the set of all 3DNF tautologies.

Corollary 11.3 DNFTAUT *and* 3DNFTAUT *are* $\leq_m^p$*-complete for* coNP.

In general, for a language A in a class C containing P, if every language in C is $\leq_m^p$-reducible to A, we call A C-**complete**.

11.3 Fundamental NP-Complete Problems

We have established a foundation for NP-completeness. We can now use this foundation to prove the NP-completeness for other problems.

11.3.1 The Clique Problem

The first problem we show to be NP-complete is the clique problem.

An undirected graph is a **clique** if an edge exists between every pair of vertices (see Fig. 11.4).

The clique problem asks whether an undirected graph contains a clique of a specific size.

Definition 11.11 CLIQUE $= \{\langle G, k \rangle \mid G$ has a k-clique$\}$.

We assume that the encoding of G and k takes the form:

$$0^n \# a_{11} \cdots a_{1n} \# \cdots \# a_{n1} \cdots a_{nn} \# 0^k.$$

Here, n is the number of vertices of the graph, and (a_{ij}) is the adjacency matrix of the graph G. In other words, for all i and j such that $i \neq j$, $a_{ij} = 1$ if an edge joins the i-th and j-th vertices; $a_{ij} = 0$ otherwise. Since the size of the largest possible

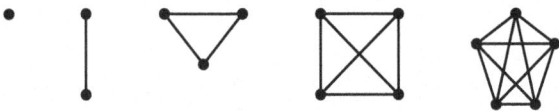

Fig. 11.4 Examples of cliques. From the left: a 1-clique, a 2-clique, a 3-clique, a 4-clique, and a 5-clique

clique of an n-vertex graph is n, regardless of the use of binary or unary encoding for k, the encoding length of $\langle G, k \rangle$ is $\Theta(n^2)$.

Now, we prove that the problem is NP-complete.

Theorem 11.9 CLIQUE *is NP-complete.*

Proof We prove the NP-completeness of CLIQUE in two steps. The first step is to show that CLIQUE is in NP. We do this by way of Algorithm 11.1. As we observed above, a TM can verify the validity of the input w and extract the graph G and the integer k in $O(|w|2)$ steps. Once this verification is complete, the machine can nondeterministically select vertices of G; see if k vertices have been selected and if every pair of vertices in the chosen set has an edge. If the set passes the test, the machine accepts it; if the set does not pass the test, the machine rejects it. The algorithm decides correctly and requires $O(n^2) = O(|w|^2)$ steps. Thus, CLIQUE $\in$ NP.

Algorithm 11.1 A TM that recognizes CLIQUE

```
 1: procedure CLIQUE(w)
 2:     check the validity of w as an encoding of a graph and an integer;
 3:     if w is valid then
 4:         extract the graph G = (V, E) and the integer k ≥ 1;
 5:     else
 6:         reject w;
 7:     end if
 8:     extract the number of vertices, n, of G;
 9:     for i ← 1, ..., n do
10:         nondeterministically select a Boolean value bᵢ;
11:     end for
12:     compute the number, c, of i such that bᵢ = true;
13:     if c < k then
14:         reject w;
15:     end if
16:     for i ← 1, ..., n do
17:         for j ← 1, ..., n do
18:             if i ≠ j and the adjacency matrix of G has 0 in row i and column j then
19:                 reject w;
20:             end if
21:         end for
22:     end for
23:     accept w;
24: end procedure
```

The second step is to show that CLIQUE is NP-hard. We only need to construct a $\leq_m^p$-reduction from an arbitrary known NP-hard language to CLIQUE. We select 3SAT for the purpose.

Suppose φ is a 3CNF formula of n variables and m clauses, each having three literals. We construct a graph G with $3m$ vertices. The $3m$ vertices match the $3m$ literals in φ. We then join every pair of vertices from two different clauses unless one literal complements the other (such as x and $\bar{x}$). The required size for a clique is m; that is, the output of the reduction is $\langle G, m \rangle$. Figure 11.5 shows an example

Fig. 11.5 An example of a
graph constructed for
reducing 3SAT to CLIQUE

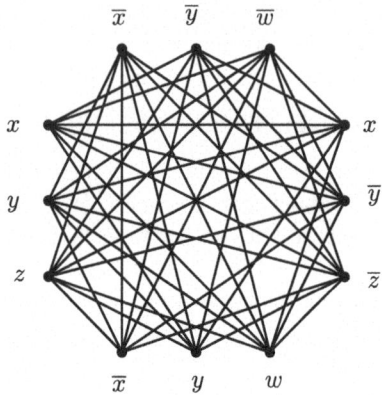

where the formula is:

$$(x \vee y \vee z) \wedge (x \vee \overline{y} \vee \overline{z}) \wedge (\overline{x} \vee \overline{y} \vee \overline{w}) \wedge (\overline{x} \vee \overline{y} \vee w).$$

We now show that G has an m-clique if, and only if, φ is satisfiable.

First, suppose the formula φ is satisfiable. We select one satisfying assignment of φ and then, from each clause, select one literal that this satisfying assignment satisfies. There are exactly m literals, so the number of nodes we choose is m. No two of the chosen vertices are complementary, so every pair is joined by an edge. This means that the m vertices we choose form an m-clique.

Next, suppose the graph has an m-clique. Since no edge joins vertices representing the same clause, the clique must pick one vertex from each clause. Since the edge cannot join two complementary vertices, for each variable x, at most one vertex in $\{x, \overline{x}\}$ appears in the clique. We construct an assignment A by selecting, for each variable x, $A(x) = true$ if a vertex representing x is in the clique, and $A(x) = false$ otherwise. The assignment A is an extension of what the clique represents, and it satisfies φ.

Constructing $\langle G, m \rangle$ from φ is straightforward and can be done in polynomial time. Thus, 3SAT $\leq_m^p$ CLIQUE.   □

11.3.2   The Vertex Cover Problem

Next, we study the problem VERTEXCOVER.

A **vertex cover** of an undirected graph $G = (V, E)$ is a set $S \subseteq V$ such that for all edges $(u, v) \in E$, u or v is in S. Figure 11.6 shows an example of a vertex cover.

The vertex cover problem asks whether or not a graph has a vertex cover of a specific size (or smaller).

Definition 11.12 VERTEXCOVER $= \{ \langle G, 0^k \rangle \mid G$ is an undirected graph, $k \leq n$ is an integer, and G has a vertex cover with cardinality of $\leq k \}$. Here, n is the number of vertices in G.

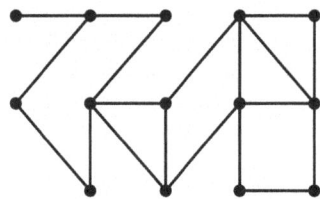 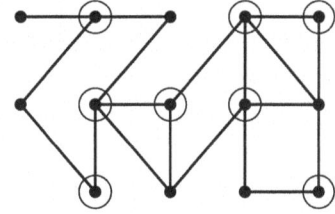

Fig. 11.6 A graph and one of its vertex covers. The right panel shows a vertex cover with eight graph vertices in the left panel. The double circles indicate the elements of the cover

We know that $k \leq n$ because the vertex set of a graph is a vertex cover.

Theorem 11.10 VERTEXCOVER *is* NP-*complete.*

Proof As with the proof for Theorem 11.9, this proof consists of showing that VERTEXCOVER $\in$ NP and showing VERTEXCOVER is NP-hard. For VERTEXCOVER $\in$ NP, we can use an algorithm similar to the one we used for CLIQUE.

Algorithm 11.2 A TM that recognizes VERTEXCOVER

1: **procedure** VERTEX-COVER(w)
2:      check the validity of w as an encoding of a graph and an integer;
3:      **if** w is valid **then**
4:          extract the graph $G = (V, E)$ and the integer $k \geq 1$;
5:      **else**
6:          reject w;
7:      **end if**
8:      extract the number of vertices, n, of G;
9:      **if** $k > n$ **then**
10:          reject w;
11:      **end if**
12:      **for** $i \leftarrow 1, \ldots, n$ **do**
13:          nondeterministically select a Boolean value b_i;
14:      **end for**
15:      compute the number, c, of i such that $b_i = true$;
16:      **if** $c \neq k$ **then**
17:          reject w;
18:      **end if**
19:      **for** $i \leftarrow 1, \ldots, n$ **do**
20:          **for** $j \leftarrow 1, \ldots, n$ **do**
21:              **if** $(i, j) \in E$ and both b_i and b_k are *false* **then**
22:                  reject w;
23:              **end if**
24:          **end for**
25:      **end for**
26:      accept w;
27: **end procedure**

Since $k \leq n$, if w is a valid encoding, its length is $\Theta(n^2)$. The double loop with which the machine conducts the verification requires $O(n^3)$ time, and so the running time of the algorithm is $O(n^3) = O(|w|^{1.5})$. Thus, the algorithm witnesses that VERTEXCOVER $\in$ NP.

To show that VERTEXCOVER is NP-hard, let φ be an instance of 3SAT with n variables $x_1, \ldots, x_n$ and m clauses, $C_j = (\lambda_{j,1} \vee \lambda_{j,2} \vee \lambda_{j,3}), 1 \leq j \leq m$. We construct a graph $G = (V, E)$ where $\|V\| = 2n + 3m$ and $e\| = n + 6m$ edges. In addition, we set $k = n + 2m$. The vertices of G are:

$$x_{i,1} \text{ and } x_{i,2} \text{ for each } i \text{ such that } 1 \leq i \leq n \text{ and}$$
$$a_{j,1}, a_{j,2}, \text{ and } a_{j,3} \text{ for each } j \text{ such that } 1 \leq j \leq m.$$

The edges of E have the following groups:

- $(x_{i,1}, x_{i,2})$ for each i such that $1 \leq i \leq n$
- $(a_{j,1}, a_{j,2}), (a_{j,2}, a_{j,3})$, and $(a_{j,3}, a_{j,1})$ for each j such that $1 \leq j \leq m$
- $(a_{j,h}, x_{i,1})$ for each i, j, and h such that $1 \leq i \leq n, 1 \leq j \leq m, 1 \leq h \leq 3$, and $\lambda_{j,h}$ is the literal x_i and
- $(a_{j,h}, x_{i,2})$ for each i, j, and h such that $1 \leq i \leq n, 1 \leq j \leq m, 1 \leq h \leq 3$, and $\lambda_{j,h}$ is the literal $\overline{x_i}$

Figure 11.7 shows an example of this. The formula is:

$$(x \vee y \vee z) \wedge (x \vee \overline{y} \vee \overline{z}) \wedge (\overline{x} \vee \overline{y} \vee \overline{w}) \wedge (\overline{x} \vee \overline{y} \vee w).$$

We claim the graph has a vertex cover with a cardinality of $n + 2m$ if, and only if, φ is a satisfiable formula.

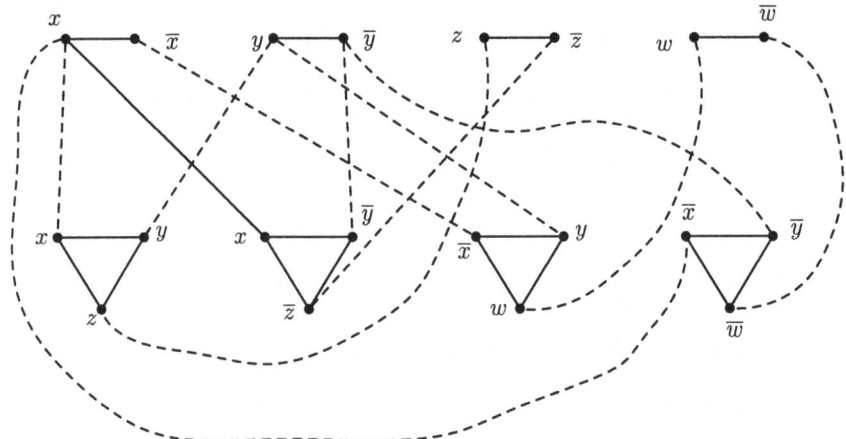

Fig. 11.7 A vertex cover instance. The top vertices correspond with the literals, and the bottom triangles correspond with the clauses. The dashed lines represent the connections between the literal vertices and their appearances

For each i, covering $(x_{i,1}, x_{i,2})$ requires placing one of $x_{i,1}$ and $x_{i,2}$ in the vertex cover. Covering the triangle among $a_{j,1}, a_{j,2}$, and $a_{j,3}$ requires minimally placing two in the vertex cover. Since the cardinality of the vertex cover must be at most $n + 2m$, we know that we must select exactly one from $x_{i,1}$ and $x_{i,2}$ for each i, and exactly two from $a_{j,1}, a_{j,2}$, and $a_{j,3}$ for each j. Each of the triangle vertices has one edge between an x vertex. Let us pick a triangle (a, a', a''). Let x, x', and x'' be the x vertices on the other end; i.e., we have edges (a, x), (a', x'), and (a'', x''). To cover all three edges under the maximum size constraint, we must place one of x, x', and x'' in the vertex cover (say, x) and place a' and a'' in the vertex cover. Figure 11.8 demonstrates this idea.

Suppose the vertex selection is possible in this manner. The chosen x vertices can be viewed as a truth assignment, and the edges from the triangle vertices connecting to the x vertices indicate the literals satisfied by the assignment. This means that the formula is satisfiable.

Next, suppose φ is satisfiable. Select one satisfying assignment A of φ. From A, we can construct a vertex cover. We choose vertices from the x vertex groups corresponding to the truth assignment. We exclude one satisfied literal from each triangle and select the remaining two. The cover has $n + 2m$ vertices.

It is not difficult to see that we can construct G from φ in time $O(|\varphi|^2)$ since $n + 2m = O(|\varphi|)$. Thus, VERTEXCOVER is NP-hard.   □

11.3.3 The 3-Coloring Problem

For an integer k, the k-coloring problem is the problem of deciding, given a graph G and a set of k colors C, if a color can be assigned to G's vertices so that for each edge (u, v) of the graph, u and v have different colors. 3-coloring is the k-coloring problem for $k = 3$.

We define 3COLOR as the language of all graphs having a 3-coloring.

Fig. 11.8 The local connection surrounding a triangle

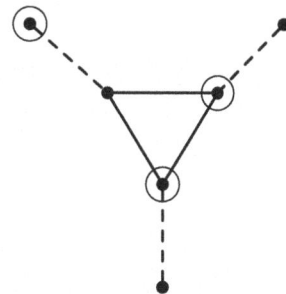

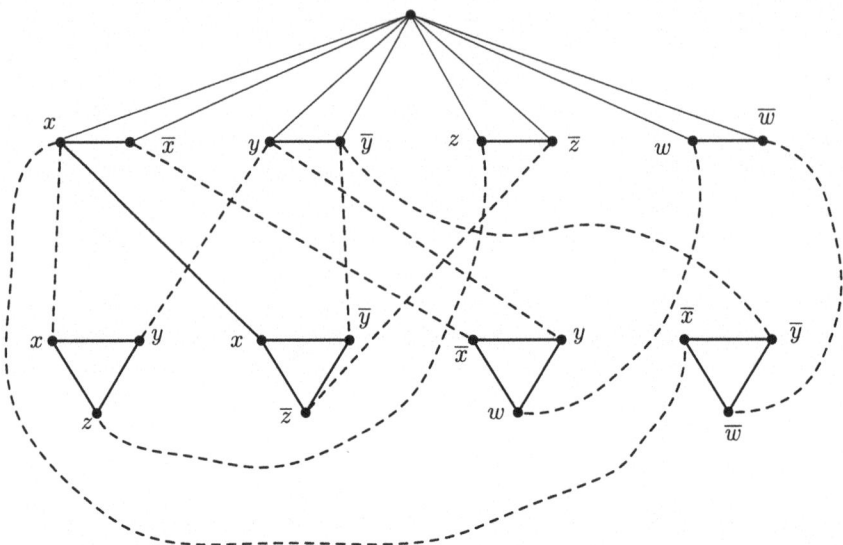

Fig. 11.9 A 3-coloring instance generated from an instance of NAESAT. The graph has one more vertex than the graph for VERTEXCOVER. The extra vertex appears at the top. The top vertex is adjacent to all assignment vertices

Theorem 11.11   3COLOR *is* NP-*complete.*

Here is a rough outline of the proof. Suppose we apply the reduction from 3SAT to VERTEXCOVER (as appearing in the proof of Theorem 11.10) to an instance of NAESAT. The reduction generates the same structure as in the VERTEXCOVER. We add one vertex to the graph and connect the new vertex to the assignment vertices for selecting between assignments in VERTEXCOVER. The resulting graph is Fig. 11.9. We can show that the graph has a 3-coloring if, and only if, the formula has an NAE truth assignment. We leave the rest of the proof to the reader (see Exercise 11.12).

11.3.4   The Hamilton Path Problem

Here, we prove that HAMPATH is NP-complete.

Consider the following nondeterministic algorithm to show that HAMPATH ∈ NP (Algorithm 11.3).

Algorithm 11.3 A TM that recognizes HAMPATH

1: **procedure** HAMILTONIAN-PATH(w)
2:    check the validity of w as an encoding of an instance of HAMPATH;
3:    **if** w is valid **then**
4:        extract the graph $G = (V, E)$, the start vertex s, and the end of t;
5:    **else**
6:        reject w;
7:    **end if**
8:    extract the number of vertices, n, of G;
9:    **for** $i \leftarrow 1, \ldots, n$ **do**
10:        nondeterministically select an integer u_i between 1 and n;
11:    **end for**
12:    **if** $u_1 \neq s$ or $u_n \neq t$ **then**
13:        reject w;
14:    **end if**
15:    **for** $i \leftarrow 1, \ldots, n$ **do**
16:        **for** $j \leftarrow 1, \ldots, n$ **do**
17:            **if** $u_j = i$ **then**
18:                break the internal loop;
19:            **end if**
20:        **end for**
21:        **if** the internal loop did not break **then**
22:            reject w;
23:        **end if**
24:    **end for**
25:    **for** $i \leftarrow 1, \ldots, n - 1$ **do**
26:        **if** (u_i, u_{i+1}) is not in E **then**
27:            reject w;
28:        **end if**
29:    **end for**
30:    accept w;
31: **end procedure**

Note that the algorithm verifies that the sequence $[u_1, \ldots, u_n]$ generated is one from s and t, visits each vertex at least once, and has an edge between each neighboring pair of vertices. If the sequence satisfies the criteria, then, since n is the number of vertices, the sequence visits each vertex exactly once and thus is a Hamilton path from s to t. The verification happens via rejecting any sequence that fails to satisfy any criterion.

To determine that HAMPATH is NP-hard, we use VERTEXCOVER. Let $\langle G, 0^k \rangle$ be an instance of VERTEXCOVER. Let $G = (V, E)$.

We create a 12-vertex graph for each edge $e = (u, v)$ in E. The 12-vertex graph consists of two parallel straight lines, with six vertices on each side. The sixth vertices are sequentially numbered from 1 to 6 on each side. Then, we connect the first on each side with the third on the other. We also connect the fourth on each side with the sixth on the other (see Fig. 11.10). In many NP-completeness proofs, we use a structure that forces a specific action, traversal, assignment, etc., under some constraints, and we call such a structure a **gadget**.

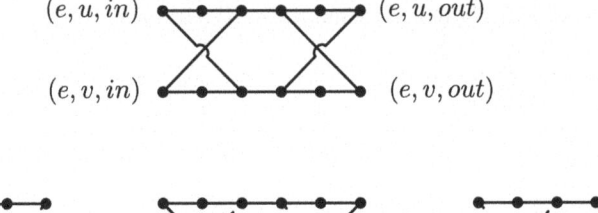

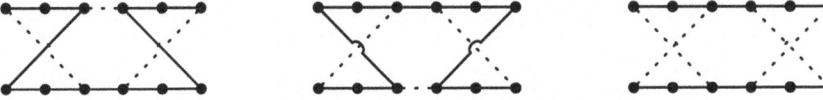

Fig. 11.10 The Hamilton path gadget and its three Hamilton-path traversals

In the figure, the top panel is the 12-vertex gadget. The two parallel series appear as the top and bottom six-vertex lines, with the ends on the left representing the entry points, and the ends on the right representing the exit points. In our construction, each gadget's middle eight points (the second through the fifth on both sides) have no other connections. This means that each Hamilton path that traverses the gadget must traverse it in one of the three possible ways, as the bottom panel of the figure shows. Let us consider the top line as the vertex u of the edge $e = (u, v)$ and the bottom line as the vertex v of the edge. The three traversals can be interpreted as placing only u in the vertex cover, placing only v in the vertex cover, and placing both u and v in the vertex cover, respectively.

We introduce vertices $s_1, \ldots, s_{k+1}$ additionally. For each $u \in V$, let $e_1, \ldots, e_m$ be an enumeration of all the edges one of whose endpoints is u. We then connect the m gadgets corresponding to the m edges by simply joining the exit vertex on the u side of e_i and the entry vertex on the u side of e_{i+1} with an edge for all i such that $1 \leq i \leq m - 1$. We also join s_j with the entry point of the u side of e_1 for all j such that $1 \leq j \leq k$ and the exit point of the u side of e_m for all j such that $2 \leq j \leq k + 1$.

This completes the construction. Let us call this graph H. We claim that H has a Hamilton path between s_1 and s_{k+1} if, and only if, G has a k-vertex cover.

We present how this instance of the Hamilton path problem looks like using a simple square with four vertices and four edges (see Fig. 11.11). By selecting two vertices diagonally opposite each other, we can construct a two-vertex cover. We thus set the value of k to 2.

As we have seen before, the Hamilton path problem is polynomial-time many-one reducible to the Hamilton cycle problem. By employing an algorithm very close to the one from Algorithm 11.3, we can show that the latter problem is in NP. The observations lead to the following result.

Corollary 11.4 HAMCYCLE *is NP-complete.*

Since HAMCYCLE $\leq_m^p$ HAMPATH (Theorem 11.2), we have the following result.

Corollary 11.5 HAMPATH *is NP-complete.*

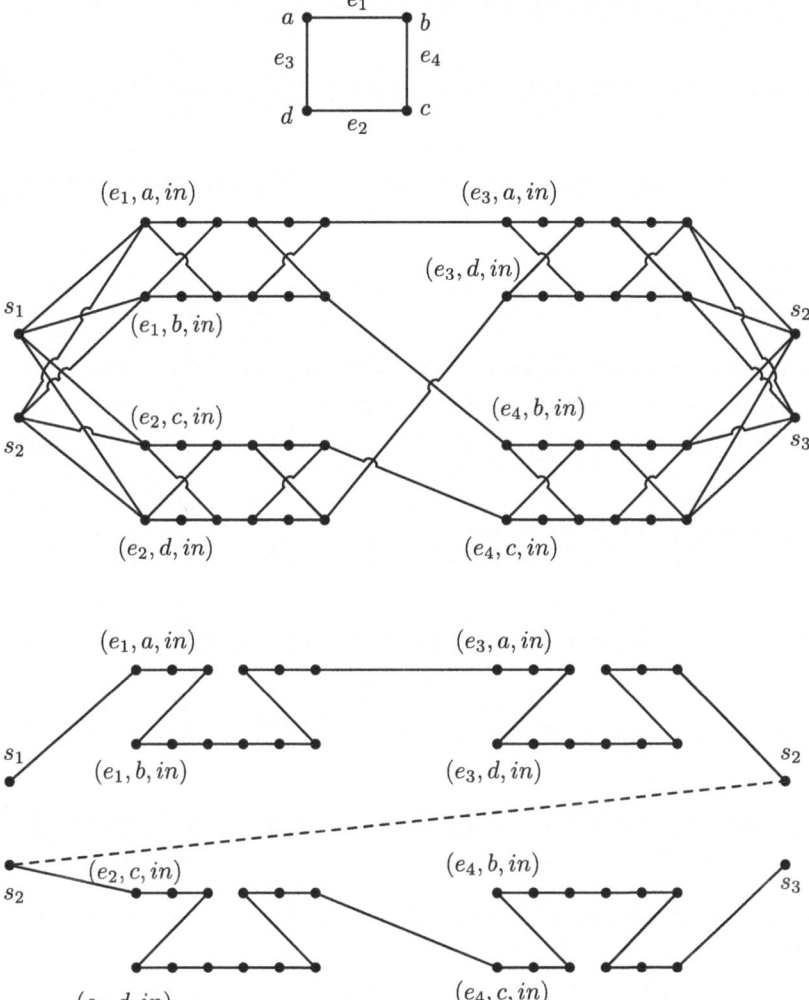

Fig. 11.11 Conversion to HAMPATH to VERTEXCOVER. The top panel is a graph for which we need to find a vertex cover. For this instance, the edges can be covered with two vertices. Two choices exist for the two vertices: a and d or b and c. The middle panel is the graph generated. The two vertices labeled s_2 (one on the left and the other on the right) are identical. The bottom panel is a Hamilton path representing a solution to the vertex cover problem, where the two end points of a required path are a and c. The dashed line represents the connection between the two identical nodes labeled s_2

11.3.5   NP-Completes Problems About Integers

Some NP-complete problems are concerned with organizing integers.

The **subset sum problem** is the problem of deciding, given a list of positive numbers $a_1, \ldots, a_m$ and a positive number T, whether or not there is a sublist from the list whose total is equal to T. As a set, the list $a_1, \ldots, a_m$ is a multi-set; any value can appear multiple times on the list. For example, given a list $[1, 2, 2, 7, 10, 25, 9]$, and a target of 14, the answer to the question of the problem is in the affirmative, since $2 + 2 + 10 = 14$; if the target becomes 6, the answer is in the negative.

We define SUBSETSUM as the set of all subset sum problem instances with affirmative answers. It is easy to see that the problem is in NP. Given an instance, consider nondeterministically deciding whether to use each number on the list in the sum and then testing whether the total of the chosen numbers is equal to the target. It is possible to implement the algorithm on an NTM so that it runs in polynomial time.

Let $\varphi = C_1 \wedge \cdots \wedge C_m$ be an instance of 3SAT with variables $x_1, \ldots, x_n$. We introduce four sets of quantities $a_1, \ldots, a_n, b_1, \ldots, b_n, c_1, \ldots, c_m,$ and $d_1, \ldots, d_m$ as follows:

- For each i such that $1 \leq i \leq n$, the value of a_i is 10^{m+i-1} plus the sum of $10^{j-1}, 1 \leq j \leq m$, such that the literal x_j appears in the clause C_j.
- For each i such that $1 \leq i \leq n$, the value of b_i is 10^{m+i-1} plus the sum of $10^{j-1}, 1 \leq j \leq m$, such that the literal $\neg x_j$ appears in the clause C_j.
- For each j such that $1 \leq j \leq m$, $c_j = 10^{j-1}$ and $d_j = 2 \cdot 10^{j-1}$.

We define $T = \sum_{i=m}^{m+n-1} 10^i + 4 \sum_{j=1}^{m} 10^{j-1}$.

We claim that φ is satisfiable if, and only if, the instance $a_1, \ldots, d_m$ (i.e., the list of the $2n + 2m$ numbers) with the target T is a positive instance of the subset sum problem. To see how the claim holds, we use the power-of-10 denominations and examine both the numbers on the list and the total. Every number in the $2n + 2m$ number list has a 0 or a 1 at each position. For each position i among the lowest m positions, exactly five numbers have a 1 at that position. Three of the five correspond to the literals of the clause. The remaining two come from c_i and d_i. For each of the remaining n positions, only two numbers have a 1 at that position. The total of the numbers is $2 \sum_{i=m}^{m+n-1} 10^i + 6 \sum_{j=1}^{m} 10^{j-1}$, and there is no chance for these numbers to produce a carry. Thus, the target T is achievable by selecting exactly one from a_i and b_i for each i and some c_js and d_js. We note that for each of the lowest m positions, there can be a maximum of two contributions using c_j and d_j. Thus, to achieve T, the combinations of a_i and b_i must be such that each of the lowest m positions has 1, 2, or 3. To raise 1, 2, and 3 to 4 at a position j is by adding $c_j + d_j$, d_j, and c_j, respectively. If the value at position j is 0, since $c_j + d_j$ has only 3 at the position, the value cannot go up to 4.

From these observations, we conclude that T is achievable if a truth assignment of φ satisfies at least one literal for each clause. We have thus proven the following theorem.

Theorem 11.12 SUBSETSUM *is NP-complete.*

Here is an example. Let

$$\varphi = (x_1 \vee x_2 \vee \overline{x_3}) \wedge (x_2 \vee x_3 \vee \overline{x_4}) \wedge (\overline{x_1} \vee x_2 \vee \overline{x_4}) \wedge (x_1 \vee \overline{x_2} \vee x_4) \wedge (\overline{x_1} \vee \overline{x_3} \vee x_4).$$

The formula has a few satisfying assignments. One of them is $x_1 = x_2 = x_3 = x_4 =$ *true*. Summing $a_1, a_2, a_3,$ and a_4 together yields the decimal 111112122. Adding c_5, $d_5, d_4, c_3, d_3, d_2,$ and d_1 to the partial sum yields the target 111144444 in decimal. (see Fig. 11.12).

11.3.5.1 The Partition Problem

Partition is the problem of computing, given a list of positive integers $a_1, \ldots, a_m$, a split of the m numbers into two groups so that the difference between the total of one part and the total of the other part is the smallest. We are interested in the computational complexity of decision problems so that we can cast the computation problem as a decision problem. PARTITION is the set of all integer lists $\langle a_1, \ldots, a_m \rangle$ having a split (I, J) of the indices $\{1, \ldots, m\}$ such that

$$\sum_{i \in I} a_i = \sum_{j \in J} a_j.$$

Theorem 11.13 PARTITION *is NP-complete.*

Fig. 11.12 The subset sum instance representing $\varphi = (x_1 \vee x_2 \vee \overline{x_3}) \wedge (x_2 \vee x_3 \vee \overline{x_4}) \wedge (\overline{x_1} \vee x_2 \vee \overline{x_4}) \wedge (x_1 \vee \overline{x_2} \vee x_4) \wedge (\overline{x_1} \vee \overline{x_3} \vee x_4)$

	x_4	x_3	x_2	x_1	C_5	C_4	C_3	C_2	C_1
a_1:	0	0	0	1	0	1	0	0	1
b_1:	0	0	0	1	1	0	1	0	0
a_2:	0	0	1	0	0	0	1	1	1
b_2:	0	0	1	0	0	1	0	0	0
a_3:	0	1	0	0	0	0	0	1	0
b_3:	0	1	0	0	1	0	0	0	1
a_4:	1	0	0	0	1	1	0	0	0
b_4:	1	0	0	0	0	0	1	1	0
c_1:	0	0	0	0	0	0	0	0	1
d_1:	0	0	0	0	0	0	0	0	2
c_2:	0	0	0	0	0	0	0	1	0
d_2:	0	0	0	0	0	0	0	2	0
c_3:	0	0	0	0	0	0	1	0	0
d_3:	0	0	0	0	0	0	2	0	0
c_4:	0	0	0	0	0	1	0	0	0
d_4:	0	0	0	0	0	2	0	0	0
c_5:	0	0	0	0	1	0	0	0	0
d_5:	0	0	0	0	2	0	0	0	0
t:	1	1	1	1	4	4	4	4	4

We can prove this theorem by reducing NAESAT to SUBSETSUM and removing all d_is. Alternatively, we can reduce SUBSETSUM to PARTITION by adding two integers U and V, where $U = V + D$ and D is the absolute value of the sum of all the integers on the list minus the target. We leave the task of proving this theorem to the reader (see Exercise 11.11).

11.3.5.2   The Knapsack Problem

Knapsack is the problem of packing items in a sack with a weight capacity so that the total weight of the items does not exceed the sack's capacity and that the total value of the sack is greater than or equal to an amount. Here, we use a pair of positive integers (w, v) to represent an item, where w is the weight and v is the item's value.

We define the language KNAPSACK as follows:

$$\text{KNAPSACK} = \{\langle w_1, v_1, \ldots, w_k, v_k, W, V \rangle \mid k \geq 1, w_1, v_1, \ldots, w_k, v_k, W, V \in \mathbb{N},$$
$$\text{and for some } I \subseteq \{1, \ldots, k\}, \sum_{i \in I} w_i \leq W \text{ and } \sum_{i \in I} v_i \geq V \}.$$

Theorem 11.14 KNAPSACK *is NP-complete.*

We can show the NP-hardness of KNAPSACK by reducing SUBSETSUM. We leave the proof to the reader (Exercise 11.14).

11.3.5.3   The Scheduling Problem

Scheduling (within intervals) is the following problem:

We have a list of tasks $t_1, \ldots, t_k$. For each i, the t_i has its release time r_i, deadline d_i, and length to complete l_i. All the quantities are integers. The task is to find out if we can assign an integer start time s_i to each task t_i so that the following conditions are met:

- Each task starts on or after its release time and is completed by its deadline; i.e., for all i such that $1 \leq i \leq k$, $r_i \leq s_i$ and $s_i + l_i \leq d_i$.
- No two tasks overlap (except for starting one at the time the other is complete); i.e., for all i and j such that $1 \leq i < j \leq k$, either $s_i + l_i \leq s_j$ or $s_j + l_j \leq s_i$.

Theorem 11.15 SCHEDULING *is NP-complete.*

We can show the NP-hardness of SCHEDULING with a $\leq_m^p$-reduction from PARTITION. Let $a_1, \ldots, a_m$ be an arbitrary instance of PARTITION. Let $B = a_1 + \cdots + a_m$. Then, B must be an even number for partitioning to be possible. Let $H = B/2$. The question for partitioning is whether or not there is a subset whose total is equal to H. The total of the remaining elements is necessarily $B - H = B - B/2 = B/2 = H$. We turn $a_1, \ldots, a_m$ to m tasks, where $r_i = 0$, $d_i = B + 1 (= 2H + 1)$, and $l_i = a_i$ for each i. We then add another task t_{m+1} such that $r_{m+1} = H, d_{m+1} = H + 1$, and $l_{m+1} = 1$. The start time, s_{m+1}, of t_{m+1} must be H. The other tasks start before H and are completed before H or after $H + 1$ and before B. We can show that the desired partitioning is possible if the other tasks can be scheduled. We leave the rest of the proof to the reader (Exercise 11.15).

11.3.6 NP-Complete Problems About Matching and Set Partitioning

Another NP-complete problem is about matching and dividing sets.

An instance of **three-dimensional matching** consists of three sets A, B, and C having the same size (i.e., $\|A\| = \|B\| = \|C\|$) and a set of triples $T \subseteq A \times B \times C$. Our question is whether or not a set $S \subseteq T$ exists so each element of A, B, and C appears exactly once in S. For example, suppose A, B, C, and T are given as follows:

$A = \{a_1, a_2, a_3, a_4\}$,

$B = \{b_1, b_2, b_3, b_4\}$,

$C = \{c_1, c_2, c_3, c_4\}$, and

$T = \{(a_1, b_2, c_3), (a_2, b_3, c_4), (a_3, b_4, c_4), (a_3, b_4, c_1), (a_4, b_1, c_2), (a_4, b_2, c_3)\}$.

Then, a matching is achievable with the following subset:

$$\{(a_1, b_2, c_3), (a_2, b_3, c_4), (a_3, b_4, c_1), (a_4, b_1, c_2)\}.$$

This problem-solving can be implemented in many practical situations. For example, think of a university having students meet counselors in offices. The number of students equals the number of counselors and the number of offices. Each counselor has some preferred offices for a meeting, and each student has some preferred counselors to meet with. Also, the meetings will occur concurrently in some places in the university, and the number of places available will equal the number of recruits. Joining these two sets of preferences provides triples of preferred combinations of a student, a counselor, and an office. We then ask if we can organize counseling sessions according to the triples of preferences.

Now, we define 3DM as the set of all positive instances for the three-dimensional matching problem.

It is not hard to show 3DM $\in$ NP. Given an input (A, B, C, T) of the problem, we can think of nondeterministically choosing whether or not to include each element of T in the subset S and then whether the subset S creates a matching of the components.

We prove the NP-hardness by reducing CNFSAT to the problem. Let $\varphi = D_1 \wedge \cdots \wedge D_m$ be a CNF formula of some n variables $x_1, \ldots, x_n$. Let $d_1, \ldots, d_m$ be the numbers of literals appearing in clauses $D_1, \ldots, D_m$, respectively. Let $d_0 =$

$d_1 + \cdots + d_m$. The total number of literals in φ is d_0. The elements in A have names a, e, and g; the elements in B have names b, f, and h; and the elements in C have names c and $\overline{c}$.

First, for each clause D_j, we introduce elements $a_{j1}, \ldots, a_{jn}$, $b_{j1}, \ldots, b_{jn}$, $c_{j1}, \ldots, c_{jn}$, and $\overline{c_{j1}} \ldots, \overline{c_{jn}}$.

In addition, for each clause D_j, and for each i such that $1 \le i \le n$, we introduce triples (a_{ji}, b_{ji}, c_{ji}) and $(a_{j,i+1}, b_{ji}, \overline{c_{ji}})$. Here, we will treat $a_{j,n+1}$ as a_{j1}.

We can visualize these elements and triangles as an alternating cycle as as and bs, $[a_{j1}, b_{j1}, a_{j2}, b_{j2}, \ldots, a_{jn}, b_{jn}, a_{j1}]$, where the neighboring pairs form triangles with $c_{j1}, \overline{c_{j1}}, c_{j2}, \overline{c_{j2}}, \ldots, c_{jn}, \overline{c_{jn}}$ (see Fig. 11.13). The elements as or bs occur in no other triples. Matching the as and bs thus needs these triples. Since the triples appear in a cycle so that each neighboring pair of triples shares one element in common, you must use exactly every other triple to cover all the as and bs. There are two ways to pick every other triple: starting with the first one and starting with the second one. The former covers all cs but leaves behind all $\overline{c}s$, and the latter covers all $\overline{c}s$ but leaves behind all cs. We view the selections for as and bs as representing the truth assignments to the variables of φ as follows. If $c_{ji}s$ remain for j, then the assignment to x_j is *true*, and if $\overline{c}_{ji}s$ remain for j, then the assignment to x_j is *false*.

Next, for each clause D_j, we introduce elements e_j and f_j and triples (e_j, f_j, c_{jk}) for each k such that x_k is a literal appearing in D_j and triples $(e_j, f_j, \overline{c_{jk}})$ for each k such that $\overline{x_k}$ is a literal appearing in D_j. The elements es and fs have no other occurrences in triples, so for each j, we need to select one triple having e_j and f_j. After making the choices for a and b, the choices for e and f must use the remaining ones. Covering es and fs requires selecting exactly one literal from each clause (see Fig. 11.14).

Finally, we introduce g_{jk} and h_{jk}, $1 \le j \le m$ and $1 \le k \le n-1$. Then, for each j such that $1 \le j \le m$, we introduce triangles (g_{ik}, h_{jk}, c_{ji}) and $(g_{ik}, h_{jk}, \overline{c_{ji}})$ for $1 \le k \le n-1$ and $1 \le i \le n$. For each j such that $1 \le j \le m$, to match the gs and hs, we need to pick $n-1$ elements from untouched cs or $\overline{c}$ from the corresponding index j. If the matching from the second step is successful, there are exactly $n-1$ elements in the cs and $\overline{c}s$ for j, so matching is possible.

Fig. 11.13 The variable assignment triples for 3DM. The triangles represent triples. The drawing shows the instance where there are only two variables (corresponding to the second indices i and 2). Because of the overlap among the vertices as and bs, any matching solution must select exactly one of the top-bottom and left-right triangle pairs

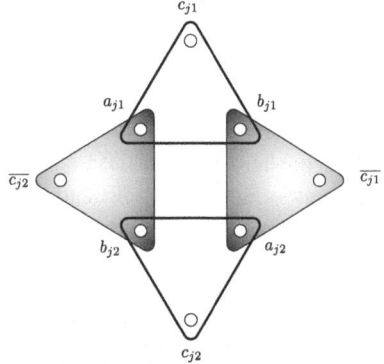

Fig. 11.14 The clause triples for 3DM. The triangles with dotted lines are those from Fig. 11.13. The clause has just two literals: x_1 and $\overline{x_2}$. The solid-line triangles represent the literals. Exactly one of the two is part of the matching

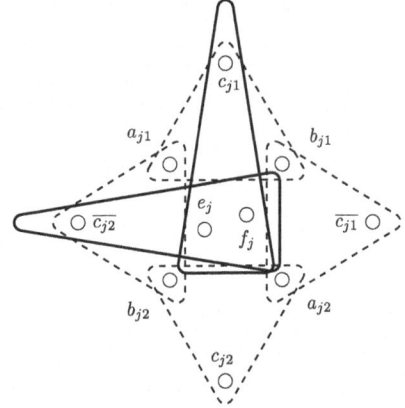

The ranges of indices i, j, and k are $\{1, \ldots, n\}$, $\{1, \ldots, m\}$, and $\{1, \ldots, n-1\}$, respectively. The number of elements in the three sets, A, B, and C, is as follows:

1. A has mn a_{ji}s, m e_js, and $m(n-1)$ g_{jk}s.
2. B has mn b_{ji}s, m f_js, and $m(n-1)$ h_{jk}s.
3. C has mn c_{ji}s and mn $\overline{c_{ji}}$s.

Each group has $2mn$ elements.

From how we constructed the elements and triples, it is clear that the instance has a matching, which is convertible to a satisfying assignment of φ. Also, it is easy to see that the instance's construction requires $O(mn)$ steps. Thus, the construction is a polynomial-time many-one reduction from CNFSAT to 3DM.

We have thus proven the following:

Theorem 11.16 3DM *is* NP-*complete.*

11.3.7 More Examples of NP-Complete Problems

Here are a few more examples of NP-complete languages. Their NP-completeness proofs are based on those from an earlier part of the section.

11.3.7.1 Exact Cover by Three Sets (X3C)

Exact cover by three sets (X3C) is the problem of deciding, given a universe U and a list of triples $T_1, \ldots, T_m \subset U$, if there is a partition of U into triples from the list. We define X3C as the language of all positive instances of X3C.

Theorem 11.17 X3C *is* NP-*complete.*

We leave the proof to the reader (Exercise 11.7).

11.3.7.2   The Independent Set Problem

Let $G = (V, E)$ be a graph and let $S \subseteq V$. We say that S is an **independent set** of G if G has no edge connecting any two vertices of S. We define INDEPENDENTSET as the language of all graph-integer pairs $\langle G, k \rangle$ such that G has an independent set having a size of $\geq k$.

Theorem 11.18 INDEPENDENTSET *is* NP-*complete.*

Again, we leave the proof to the reader (Exercise 11.10).

Exercises

11.1 Prove that the polynomial-time many-one reductions are transitive; that is, for all languages A, B, and C, if $A \leq_m^p B$ and $B \leq_m^p C$, then $A \leq_m^p C$.

11.2 Prove that the polynomial-time many-one reductions are reflexive; that is, for all languages A, $A \leq_m^p A$.

11.3 Prove Proposition 11.2.

11.4 Let $A \subseteq \Sigma^*$ be nontrivial; that is, A is neither $\emptyset$ nor Σ^*. Prove that A is polynomial-time many-one reducible to neither $\emptyset$ nor Σ^*.

11.5 Prove Proposition 11.1.

11.6 In the definition of polynomial-time witness schemes (Definition 11.7), $|y| \leq p(|x|)$. Show that the definition can be changed to $|y| = p(|x|)$.

11.7 Show that X3C is NP-complete.

Hint: You can prove the NP-hardness using the proof of Theorem 11.16. This time, you can collapse the three-dimensional Cartesian product $A \times B \times C$ to turn it into a set $A \cup B \cup C$.

11.8 Theorem 11.1 shows a reduction from the Hamilton path problem to the Hamilton cycle problem. Using a similar idea, give a polynomial-time many-one reduction from the Hamilton cycle problem to the Hamilton path problem.

11.9 Show that a vertex-set C is a vertex cover of a graph $G = (V, E)$ if, and only if, $V - C$ is an independent set of G.

11.10 Based upon the property you have proven in Exercise 11.9, show that INDEPENDENTSET is NP-complete.

11.11 Prove Theorem 11.13; i.e., PARTITION is NP-complete.

11.12 Complete the NP-completeness proof of 3COLOR by showing (a) 3COLOR is in NP and (b) the generated graph has a 3-coloring if, and only if, the formula has an NAE assignment.

11.13 Show that if the number of available colors is only two, the coloring problem is in P.

11.14 Show that KNAPSACK is NP-complete.

Hint: To prove NP-hardness for the problem, use the construction from 3SAT to SUBSETSUM. Try using the value of an element in SUBSETSUM item as both the weight and the value.

11.15 Complete the proof of Theorem 11.15.

11.16 An **edge-weighted graph** is a graph (V, E) with edge weight assignment $W : E \to \mathbb{N}$. The **traveling salesman problem** asks, given an edge-weighted graph G, a vertex s, and cost c, whether or not there is a Hamiltonian cycle from s whose total edge weight is at most c. Prove that the traveling salesman problem is NP-complete.

11.17 A **dominating set** of a directed graph $G = (V, E)$ is a set $D \subseteq V$ such that for all $u \in V - D$, there is an arc from some $v \in D$ to u. We define DOMINATINGSET as the set of all $\langle G, k \rangle$ such that G contains a dominating set with a size of $\leq k$. Prove that DOMINATINGSET is NP-complete.

Hint: Use the reduction from 3SAT to VERTEXCOVER and argue that the input formula with n variables and m clauses is satisfiable if, and only if, the graph has a dominating set with a size of $n + m$.

11.18 Prove that the following state minimization problem of a nondeterministic finite automaton is coNP-hard; given an NFA M and an integer k, test if there is an NFA equivalent to M whose number of states is $\leq k$.

Hint: Given an n-variable 3CNF formula φ, construct an NFA that accepts its input $w \in \{0, 1\}^*$ if $|w| < n$ or its n-character prefix is *not* a satisfying assignment.

11.19 Verify that from any NAE assignment to $(x \lor y \lor z \lor w)$, we can construct an NAE assignment to $(u \lor x \lor y) \land (\overline{u} \lor z \lor w)$, and vice versa.

11.20 1-IN-3-SAT is the language of all 3CNF formulas having a truth assignment that satisfies exactly one literal per clause. Show that 1-IN-3-SAT is NP-complete.

Hint: We can reduce 3SAT to 1-IN-3-SAT by constructing from each formula 3CNF formula $\varphi = C_1 \land \cdots \land C_m$ as follows:

For each clause $C = (\lambda_1 \lor \lambda_2 \lor \lambda_3)$ of φ, introduce eight new variables $a, b, c, d, e, f, g, \alpha, \beta$ and replace the clause with the formula:

$$(\lambda_1 \lor a \lor d) \land (\lambda_2 \lor b \lor d) \land (\lambda_3 \lor c \lor g) \land (a \lor b \lor e)$$

$$\land (c \lor d \lor f) \land (g \lor \alpha \lor \beta) \land (g \lor \overline{\alpha} \lor \overline{\beta}).$$

Show that the new formula has a 1-in-3 assignment if, and only if, φ is satisfiable.

11.21 Prove that **2SAT**, the CNF satisfiability in which the number of literals per clause is no more than 2, is in P.

11.22 Prove that the following problem is NP-complete:

Given a Boolean formula φ and a satisfying assignment α, decide whether or not φ has a satisfying assignment other than α.

11.23 Prove that the following problem called **LONGESTPATH** is NP-complete:

Given a graph G and an integer W, decide whether or not G has a simple path having a length of $\geq W$.

11.24 Prove that for each $k \geq 1$, the clique problem where the target clique size is fixed to k is in P.

Bibliographic Notes and Further Reading

The central driving force of computational complexity theory has been the P verus NP problem. Complexity theorists used to think that the problem emerged *after* the introduction of time-bounded TM computation (i.e., Hartmanis and Stearns' paper [4] in 1965). However, a surprising discovery was made at the end of the 1980s to show that the question had already been asked a decade earlier. The discovery is Kurt Gödel's letter to John von Neumann. In this letter, Gödel noted that there are problems solvable in deterministically quadratic time and asked von Neumann if a TM solving calculus in logic can be made to run in quadratic time (see [3, 8]). We can translate Gödel's question as whether or not PSPACE $\subseteq$ DTIME[n^2].

The concept of NP-completeness is by the independent work of Cook [1] and Levin [6]. While Levin's work shows that the problems searching for witnesses can be converted to SAT, Cook's work shows that the acceptance problem of a polynomial time-bounded NTM can be converted to TAUTOLOGY.

Karp [5] formalized Cook's approach into the notion of the polynomial-time many-one reductions. In this paper, Karp demonstrated the importance of NP-completeness by presenting 21 complete problems that are practically important. HAMPATH, HAMCYCLE, SUBSETSUM, 3SAT, VERTEXCOVER, INDEPENDENTSET, 3COLOR, KNAPSACK, and CLIQUE were among these 21 problems. The polynomial-time many-one reduction is often called the polynomial-time Karp reduction.

In contrast with Karp's approach, Cook's approach has a property that the answer obtained from TAUTOLOGY is negatively interpreted; the answer about satisfiability is positive if, and only if, the answer about TAUTOLOGY is negative. The next chapter of this book introduces a more flexible reduction. In this method, the membership of an input string may be determined using not just a single membership question but a dynamically generated series of questions. This flexible type of reduction is generally called the polynomial-time Turing reduction but is also often called the Cook-Levin reduction (or simply Cook reduction).

The polynomial-time witness preserving reduction is by Garey and Johnson [2]. The reduction is called the "strong" NP-completeness in Garey and Johnson's work. Numerous papers have presented newly found NP-complete problems. There is no exact count of problems that have been shown to be NP-complete in the literature, but the number could be way over 10,000. The book by Garey and Johnson is the standard reference for NP-complete problems; this book lists about 700 problems as NP-complete. Their book also categorizes the techniques for proving NP-completeness.

The NP-completeness of NaeSat and 1-in-3-Sat is by Schaefer [7]. In the paper, Schaefer studied the logical templates for defining the value of clauses when the clauses are conjunctively connected and showed that for each template, the satisfiability problem is either polynomial-time decidable or NP-complete.

References

1. S.A. Cook, The complexity of theorem proving procedures, in *Proceedings of the Third Annual ACM Symposium on Theory of computing* (Association for Computing Machinery, New York, 1971), pp. 151–158
2. M.R. Garey, D.S. Johnson, *Computers and intractability*, vol. 174 (Freeman San Francisco, 1979)
3. J. Hartmanis, Gödel, von Neumann and the P=?NP problem, in *Current Trends in Theoretical Computer Science: Essays and Tutorials* (World Scientific, Singapore, 1993), pp. 445–450
4. J. Hartmanis, R.E. Stearns, On the computational complexity of algorithms. T Am. Math. Soc. **117**, 285–306 (1965)
5. R.M. Karp, Reducibility among combinatorial problems, in *Complexity of Computer Computations*, ed. by R.E. Miller, J.W. Thatcher (Plenum, New York, 1972), pp. 85–103
6. L.A. Levin, Universal sequential search problems (in Russian). Problemy Peredachi Informatsii **9**(3), 115–116 (1973)
7. T.J. Schaefer, The complexity of satisfiability problems, in *Proceedings of the Tenth Annual ACM Symposium on Theory of Computing* (1978), pp. 216–226
8. A. Urquhart, Von Neumann, Gödel, and complexity theory. Bull Symbol Logic **16**(4), 516–530 (2010)

Chapter 12
Beyond NP-Completeness

12.1 The Complexity of Finding a Witness

In the previous chapter, we saw that the languages in NP are characterized using a polynomial-time witness scheme. How difficult is finding a witness given an instance for a language in NP? In this section, we study the problem of finding an optimal witness. Here, we give a linear order among witnesses and compute the largest or smallest witness among them if a witness exists. The key concept in finding an optimal witness is the **polynomial-time Turing reducibility**.

Recall from Definition 11.9 that CNFSAT is the problem of deciding whether or not a CNF formula is satisfiable. We used the oracle TM model in Sect. 8.5 and defined the arithmetical hierarchy. Recall that a language oracle A is a unit-cost black box that provides the membership of an arbitrary string in A. With CNFSAT as the oracle, we can compute a satisfying assignment of any satisfiable CNF formula in polynomial time. Let φ be a CNF formula with n variables $x_1, \ldots, x_n$. We use Algorithm 12.1 to find, if one exists, a satisfying assignment to the formula φ.

Does the algorithm correctly compute a satisfying assignment when φ is satisfiable? Since the oracle correctly answers the question about the satisfiability of CNFSAT, the algorithm proceeds to Line 6. We thus know that φ_0 is a satisfiable CNF formula. Then, using induction on i from $i = 1$ to $i = n$, we can prove that φ_i is a satisfiable CNF formula and that the assignment Λ at the end of round i reduces φ to φ_i. Suppose the two properties hold for j such that $0 \leq j \leq n - 1$ and $i = j + 1$. The algorithm generates ψ_0 and ψ_1 by setting the value of x_i to *false* and *true*, respectively. Since by assumption, we know that φ_j is satisfiable and Λ reduces φ_0 to φ_j, we know that ψ_0 or ψ_1 is satisfiable. The way the algorithm selects φ_i from ψ_0 and ψ_1 thus ensures that φ_i is satisfiable, and the new list Λ reduces φ_0 to φ_i. Note that ψ_0 and ψ_1 are computable from φ_j by setting the value of x_i to *false* and *true*, respectively. We will simplify the formula after the value assignment to x_i. For ψ_0, every clause containing the literal $\overline{x_i}$ is satisfied, so we will remove the clause

---

Algorithm 12.1 An algorithm for finding a satisfying assignment using an oracle

---

```
 1: procedure FIND-SATISFYIING-ASSIGNMENT(φ)
 2:     φ is a CNF formula;
 3:     ask the oracle if φ is satisfiable;
 4:     if the oracle returns "no" then
 5:         assert that φ is not satisfiable;
 6:     end if
 7:     Λ ← [];
 8:     φ₀ ← φ;
 9:     for i ← 1, . . . , n do
10:         construct ψ₀ from φᵢ₋₁ by setting xᵢ = false;
11:         construct ψ₁ from φᵢ₋₁ by setting xᵢ = true;
12:         ask the oracle if ψ₀ is satisfiable;
13:         if the oracle answers "yes" then
14:             append xᵢ = false to Λ;
15:             φᵢ ← ψ₀;
16:         else
17:             append xᵢ = true to Λ;
18:             φᵢ ← ψ₁;
19:         end if
20:     end for
21:     report Λ as a satisfying assignment;
22: end procedure
```

---

entirely from the formula; in addition, we will remove all remaining occurrences of x_i. For ψ_1, every clause containing the literal x_i is satisfied, so we will remove the clause from the formula; in addition, we will remove all remaining occurrences of $\overline{x_i}$. The simplification process ensures that the resulting formulas are CNF formulas.

Note that the simplification process may empty a clause. Such a clause is unsatisfiable; thus, any formula containing an empty clause is unsatisfiable. Fortunately, since φ_{i-1} is satisfiable, such an empty clause will appear in at most one of ψ_0 and ψ_1.

Here is an example. Let

$$\varphi = (x_1 \vee x_2 \vee \overline{x_3}) \wedge (x_2 \vee x_3 \vee \overline{x_4}) \wedge (\overline{x_1} \vee x_2 \vee \overline{x_4}) \wedge (x_1 \vee \overline{x_2} \vee x_4) \wedge (\overline{x_1} \vee \overline{x_3} \vee x_4).$$

The formula is satisfiable, with several satisfying assignments. So, given φ as input, the algorithm proceeds to Line 6. For $i = 1$, $\psi_0 = (x_2 \vee \overline{x_3}) \wedge (x_2 \vee x_3 \vee \overline{x_4}) \wedge (\overline{x_2} \vee x_4)$ and $\psi_1 = (x_2 \vee x_3 \vee \overline{x_4}) \wedge (x_2 \vee \overline{x_4}) \wedge (\overline{x_3} \vee x_4)$. Both formulas are satisfiable, so the algorithm chooses ϕ_0 with $x_1 = false$ and adds it to Λ.

For $i = 2$, $\psi_0 = (\overline{x_3}) \wedge (x_3 \vee \overline{x_4})$ and $\psi_1 = (x_4)$. Both formulas are satisfiable, so the algorithm chooses ϕ_0 with $x_2 = false$ as an addition to Λ.

For $i = 3$, $\psi_0 = (\overline{x_4})$ and $\psi_1 = ()$. Only ψ_0 is satisfiable. The algorithm chooses ϕ_0 with $x_3 = false$ as an addition to Λ.

For $i = 4$, $\psi_0 = true$ and $\psi_1 = ()$. Only ψ_0 is satisfiable. The algorithm chooses ϕ_0 with $x_4 = false$ as an addition to Λ. Thus, in the end, the algorithm reports that $x_1 = x_2 = x_3 = x_4 = false$ is the satisfying assignment it has found.

Note the task at hand is to compute a satisfying assignment, so the order in which ψ_0 and ψ_1 become queries can be arbitrary. Note that a fixed polynomial also serves as an upper bound of the algorithm's actions for each i in n. Thus, the algorithm runs in polynomial time.

Definition 12.1 Let L be an NP-language and $(p(n), A)$ be a polynomial-time witness scheme for L. Suppose that the scheme $(p(n), A)$ has the property that for each member of L, a witness is computable in polynomial time using L as the oracle. Then, we say that the **search reduces in polynomial time to the decision** for L.

The above phenomenon for CNFSAT now can be stated as:

Theorem 12.1 *The search reduces in polynomial time to the decision for CNFSAT.*

Using a similar idea, we can show an algorithm for solving the subset sum problem (see Sect. 11.3.5). We say that an instance $I = [a_1, \ldots, a_m, T]$ is trivial if T is 0, since the sum of 0 is always achievable.

Algorithm 12.2 Finding a solution to the subset sum problem

```
 1: procedure SOLVING-SUBSETSETSUM(I)
 2:     receive I = ⟨a₁, ..., aₘ, T⟩ as the input
 3:     ask the oracle if I is a positive instance;
 4:     if the oracle returns "no" then
 5:         assert T is not achievable;
 6:     end if
 7:     Λ ← [];
 8:     while I is not trivial do
 9:         a ← I's first element;
10:         construct from I a new instance I' by removing a;
11:         ask the oracle if I' is a positive instance;
12:         if the oracle answers "no" then
13:             update I by removing a and subtracting a from T;
14:             add a to Λ;
15:         else
16:             update I by removing a;
17:         end if
18:     end while
19:     report Λ as a solution;
20: end procedure
```

In Line 9, the algorithm asks whether the element x must be used to achieve the total. If x must be used, removing x from the list makes it impossible to achieve the total. Thus, we add x to the list Λ, and then, since x is an essential member, we subtract x from T, accounting for the contribution from x. Otherwise, x is not essential; T is achievable without using x. So, we remove x from the list without changing T. This algorithm will check, for each element, whether or not the element must be used, and then, depending on the answer received, update Λ, I, and T. When T becomes 0, we have found a solution: the list Λ.

Theorem 12.2 *The search reduces in polynomial time to the decision for* SUBSETSUM.

12.2   The Polynomial-Time Turing Reducibility

We can generalize the concept of "search reduces in polynomial time to the decision" and define polynomial-time Turing reductions.

By extending Definition 8.9, we define oracle TMs deciding languages in polynomial time.

Definition 12.2 Let A be a language. The class P^A is the collection of all languages L satisfying the following condition:

- There is a deterministic oracle TM M such that $L = L(M^A)$, and M is polynomial time-bounded regardless of its oracle.

Definition 12.3 A language L is polynomial-time Turing-reducible to a language A if $L \in P^A$. We write $L \leq_T^p A$ to mean that L is polynomial-time Turing reducible to A.

We often call the polynomial-time Turing reducibility **Cook-reduciblity** and the polynomial-time many-one reducibility **Karp-reducibility**. The above definition guarantees that the reduction runs in polynomial time regardless of its oracle. As shown next, the polynomial-time Turing reducibility in which the oracle TM is polynomial time-bounded regardless of its oracle is as powerful as the polynomial-time Turing reducibility in which the oracle TM may not be polynomial time-bounded if the oracle is not A.

Proposition 12.1 *Let A be a language. The class P^A is the collection of all languages L for which there exists some deterministic oracle TM M such that $L = L(M^A)$ and for all oracles X, and M is polynomial time-bounded when A is the oracle.*

Proof Suppose L is a language in P^A with M as the oracle TM. Let $p(n) = kn^k + k$ be a polynomial bounding the running time of M with oracle A. We define D as a multiple-tape oracle TM with one work tape added to M. On input x, D computes $1^{p(|x|)}$ on one tape and moves the head on the tape to the leftmost 1. D then simulates M on x. At each step in the simulation, D moves the head on $1^{p(|x|)}$ by one cell to the right. If the head reaches the cell immediately following $1^{p(|x|)}$, D stops the simulation and rejects x. If the simulation completes while the head is on $1^{p(|x|)}$, D accepts or rejects accordingly.

Constructing the unary representation of $p(|x|)$ requires $O(p(|x|))$ steps. Since the simulation has a hard stop at step $p(|x|)$, D runs in time $O(p(|x|))$ for all inputs regardless of its oracle. Since the computation of D is by simulation of M and early termination results in rejection, for all oracle X, $L(D^X) \subseteq L(M^X)$. Since early termination does not occur when the oracle is A, $L(D^A) = L(M^X)$. This proves the proposition.   □

We can normalize the computation of the oracle TM by requiring it to make the same number of queries regardless of its oracle.

Proposition 12.2 *Let A be a language. The class P^A is the collection of all languages L for which there exists some deterministic oracle TM M such that $L = L(M^A)$ and for all oracles X, M is polynomial time-bounded. In addition, for each input x, M asks the same number of queries regardless of its oracle.*

Proof Let $L \in P^A$. Recall the construction of D in the proof of Proposition 12.1. We define E as a new TM, with yet another tape to count the queries M makes. E runs the program for D, but using the string $1^{p(|x|)}$ prepared at the start on the new tape. E counts the queries made to the oracle. When the simulation is about to halt, E queries the oracle further and inflates the number to $p(|x|)$. E ignores the answers to the additional queries. The empty string can serve as the additional query string. The running time of E is at most $p(|x|)$ plus the running time of D. Thus, E is polynomial time-bounded, accepts the same language as D for each oracle, and makes $p(|x|)$ queries.   □

Definition 12.4 Let C be a language class. The class P^C is $\bigcup_{A \in C} P^A$.

12.2.1   The Problem of Finding the Least Satisfying Assignment

In this section, we study P^{NP}, the class of all languages that polynomial time-bounded oracle TMs with some oracle in NP. We will show that the class P^{NP} has a $\leq_m^p$-complete language.

Let φ be a Boolean formula of some n variables. We represent a truth assignment to φ by an n-bit sequence $b = b_1 \cdots b_n$, where for each i such that $1 \leq i \leq n$, $b_i = 0$ and $b_i = 1$, respectively, mean that the assignment b assigns the value of *false* and *true* to x_i. The bit representation of truth assignments naturally induces the complete order among the truth assignments for each formula.

We define ODDMAXSAT as the language of all CNF formulas φ whose lexicographically maximum satisfying assignment is odd.

Theorem 12.3 ODDMAXSAT *is P^{NP}-complete.*

Proof Overview
We define an NTM that simulates the action of an oracle TM with a language in NP as the oracle. An NTM can guess the answers that the oracle TM would receive from the oracle and guess the accept/reject decision that the oracle TM makes. Then, the oracle TM verifies all the "yes" answers and outcomes by simulating the NTM that decides the oracle language. We encode the computation of the NTM as a CNF formula as we did for the proof for the NP-completeness of the satisfiability problem. The ordering of the variables is such that the guesses for the oracle answers come first, and the guess about the decision by the oracle TM comes last. The construction forces the satisfying assignments of the formula to encode the path matching the computation of the oracle TM, with the last variable representing the final decision the oracle TM makes.

Proof Let L be a language in P^{NP}. By Proposition 12.2, there exists a polynomial time-bounded oracle TM E and a language A in NP such that (i) L is the language that E decides with A as its oracle and (ii) there is a polynomial $p(n)$ such that E makes $p(|x|)$ queries for each input x regardless of its oracle.

Let N be a polynomial time-bounded NTM that decides A. Let $q(n)$ be a polynomial that bounds the running time of N. For simplicity, let x be a string having length ℓ that E has its input. The machine E will make $p(\ell)$ queries regardless of the oracle and then accept or reject. Think of simulating E on x with a $(p(\ell) + 1)$-bit string $b = b_1 \cdots b_{p(\ell)} b_{p(\ell)+1}$ as a "guide" as follows:

For each i such that $1 \leq i \leq p(\ell)$, we assume that the oracle's answer is "yes" if, and only if, $b_i = 1$. The last bit of b, $b_{p(\ell)+1}$, represents the simulation result; the bit is 1 if, and only if, E accepted in the simulation.

For each i such that $1 \leq i \leq p(\ell)$, let $Q(b, i)$ be the i-th query E on x with b as the guide. We define W as the set of all $(p(\ell) + 1)$-bit strings b such that:

- (**query consistency**) For all i and j such that $1 \leq i < j \leq p(\ell)$, if $Q(b, i) = Q(b, j)$, then $b_i = b_j$.
- (**positive correctness** For each i such that $1 \leq i \leq p(\ell)$ and $b_i = 1$, $Q(b, i) \in A$.

- (**decision consistency**) The value of $b_{p(\ell)+1}$ equals the outcome of E on x with b as the guide.

We can use an NTM, S, to test the membership of an arbitrary $(p(\ell) + 1)$-bit string b in W as follows, where the TM has x and b as the input:

- S simulates E on x using b as the guide and obtains $Q(b, 1), \ldots, Q(b, p(\ell))$.
- S checks the query and decision consistencies. If either fails to hold, S rejects.
- S checks the positive correctness by nondeterministically simulating N on $Q(b, i)$ for each i such that $1 \leq i \leq p(\ell)$. The simulation occurs sequentially

for the qualifying values of i. If N accepts in all the simulations, S accepts; otherwise, S rejects.

The set W contains the guide, $\hat{b}$, matching E's computation on input x with A as the oracle. For all i such that $1 \leq i \leq p(\ell)$, $Q(\hat{b}, i) = 1 \iff Q(\hat{b}, i) \in A$, and the $(p(\ell) + 1)$-th bit of $\hat{b}$ is 1 if, and only if, E on x accepts with A as the oracle. Let b be an arbitrary $(p(\ell) + 1)$-bit string strictly greater than $\hat{b}$. Let i be the first position at which b and $\hat{b}$ disagree. Suppose $i \leq p(\ell)$. We have (a) for all j such that $1 \leq j \leq i$, $Q(b, j) = Q(\hat{b}, j)$, (b) the i-th bit of b is 1, and (c) the i-th bit of $\hat{b}$ is 0. The property (a) means $Q(b, i) = Q(\hat{b}, i)$. The property (b) means b assumes that $Q(b, i)$ is in A. The property (c) means $Q(\hat{b}, i) \notin A$, so $Q(b, i) \notin A$. Since the i-th bit of b is 1, b fails the positive correctness test. Suppose $i = p(\ell + 1)$; then b and $\hat{b}$ are different only at the result of simulation, which is "accept" for b and "reject" for $\hat{b}$. Since $\hat{b}$ is the correct guide, E must reject x, so b fails the decision consistency test. Thus, $\hat{b}$ is the largest string in W.

Consider an NTM T that, on input x (now we are talking about an arbitrary input x), generates a $(p(|x|) + 1)$-bit string b nondeterministically, simulates S on the pair x and b, and accepts if S accepts and rejects if S rejects. The queries T generates are at most $p(|x|)$ in length, and there will be $p(|x|)$ queries. Since N is $q(n)$ time-bounded, we know that T is $O(p(n) + p(n) \cdot q(p(n)))$ time-bounded.

We now construct the satisfiability formula that represents an accepting computation of T on x according to the proof from Chap. 11. We identify the time, t_0, at which the machine T completes its generation of b, and identify the $p(|x|) + 1$ variables $y_1, \ldots, y_{p(|x|)+1}$ that represent whether or not the $p(|x|) + 1$ bits of b are 1, respectively. We then perform the CNF conversion to the formula. After that, we renumber the variables so that $y_1, \ldots, y_{p(|x|)}$ are the first $p(|x|)$ variables of the formula in this order and $y_{p(|x|)+1}$ is the last variable. The satisfying assignments of this CNF formula represent accepting computation paths of T and thus also represent the members of W. The way that we renumbered the variables guarantees that the lexicographically maximum satisfying assignment of the CNF formula represents $\hat{b}$. Hence, the CNF formula's maximum satisfying assignment is odd if, and only if, the last bit of $\hat{b}$ is odd. The latter condition equals whether or not E accepts x with A as its oracle.

This proves the theorem.   □

We now modify the construction we have seen thus far by recalling the proof of Theorem 11.7. In the proof of Theorem 11.7, we converted CNF formulas to 3CNF formulas using a polynomial-time many-one reduction.

Let φ be a CNF formula and ψ be the 3CNF formula that the reduction generates from φ. Suppose φ has n variables $x_1, \ldots, x_n$ and ψ has m variables. The m variables in ψ consist of those in φ and those representing the values of partial clauses of φ. The construction preserves the satisfying assignments of φ so that each satisfying assignment of φ has a unique representation among the satisfying assignments of ψ, which has the same assignments to $x_1, \ldots, x_n$. Also, there is no additional satisfying assignment of ψ that does not represent a satisfying assignment of φ.

Definition 12.5 Let f be a polynomial-time many-one reduction from an NP-language L_1 to an NP-language L_2, where languages $A_1 \in P$ and $A_2 \in P$ serve as the witness scheme languages. We say that f is "witness-preserving" if there is a pair of polynomial-time computable functions $g(\cdot, \cdot)$ and $h(\cdot, \cdot)$ such that for all x and y, if $f(x) = y$, then the following properties hold:

- $x \in L_1$ if, and only if, $y \in L_2$ (because f is a many-one reduction from L_1 to L_2).
- If $x \in L_1$ and w is a witness for $x \in L_1$ with respect to A_1, then $g(x, w)$ is a witness for $y \in L_2$ with respect to A_2; that is, $\langle y, g(x, w) \rangle \in A_2$.
- If $y \in L_2$ and z is a witness for $y \in L_2$ with respect to A_2, $h(y, z)$ is a witness for $x \in L_1$ with respect to A_1; that is, $\langle x, h(y, z) \rangle \in A_1$.
- For $x \in L_1$, then for all witnesses w for $x \in L_1$ with respect to A_1, $h(y, g(x, w)) = w$, where $y = f(x)$.

We write $L_1 \leq^p_{\text{wit}} L_2$ to mean that L_1 is polynomial-time witness-preserving reducible to L_2.

Returning to the reduction from CNFSAT to 3SAT, the reduction preserves the variables appearing in the input formula. In the case where the input CNF formula is satisfiable, each satisfying assignment of the input formula becomes a satisfying assignment of the output 3CNF formula, where the values of the additional variables are uniquely determined from the values of the variables in the input formula. Calculating the values of the additional variables serves as the function g. To go back from a satisfying assignment of the output 3CNF formula to a satisfying assignment of the input CNF formula, we only need to remove the values corresponding to the additional variables. The removal action serves as the function h.

Proposition 12.3 CNFSAT $\leq^p_{\text{wit}}$ 3SAT.

Noting that the witness-preserving reduction from CNFSAT to 3SAT preserves the lexicographic order among the satisfying assignments, we obtain the following result.

Corollary 12.1 *The 3CNF version of* ODDMAXSAT *is* P^{NP}*-complete.*

When we return to the proof of Theorem 11.12, we notice that for each instance of SUBSETSUM that the reduction generates from an instance of 3SAT, there is a one-to-one correspondence between a satisfying assignment and a subset that achieves the target sum. More specifically, the choice between a_i and b_i represents the choice between the two truth assignments of the i-th variable, and the choice from the three combinations c_j, d_j, and $c_j + d_j$ represents the number of literals that the assignment satisfies in the j-th clause. Thus, we can easily convert a satisfying assignment to a subset that achieves the target total by supplementing it with cs and ds. Similarly, we can convert a subset that achieves the target to a satisfying assignment by eliminating cs and ds.

We define ODDMAXSUM as the problem of deciding, given an instance $\langle L, T \rangle$ for SUBSETSUM, whether or not the largest of all the subsets achieving the target has the last element of the list L. Based on the above discussion, we have the following:

Corollary 12.2 *The reduction from* 3SAT *to* SUBSETSUM *appearing in the proof of Theorem 11.12 is a witness-preserving reduction.*

Corollary 12.3 ODDMAXSUM *is* P^{NP}-*complete.*

12.3 The Polynomial Hierarchy (PH)

In this section, we study the **polynomial hierarchy**, the polynomial-time analog of the arithmetical hierarchy from Sect. 8.5.

12.3.1 The Definition

As we did for the class P with an oracle, we similarly define the classes NP and coNP with an oracle.

Definition 12.6 Let A be a language. The class NP^A is the collection of all languages L for which there exists some nondeterministic oracle TM M such that $L = L(M^A)$ and with A as the oracle, and M is polynomial time-bounded regardless of its oracle.

Definition 12.7 Let C be a class of languages. The class NP^C is $\cup_{A \in C} NP^A$.

Definition 12.8 Let A be a language. The class $coNP^A$ is the collection of all languages L for which there exists some nondeterministic oracle TM M such that $L = \overline{L(M^A)}$ and with A as the oracle, and M is polynomial time-bounded regardless of its oracle.

Definition 12.9 Let C be a class of languages. The class $coNP^C$ is $\cup_{A \in C} coNP^A$.

We define the polynomial hierarchy PH as the following:

Definition 12.10 We define $\{\Delta_k^p\}_{k \geq 0}$, $\{\Sigma_k^p\}_{k \geq 0}$, and $\{\Pi_k^p\}_{k \geq 0}$ as follows:

1. $\Delta_0^p = \Sigma_0^p = \Pi_0^p = P$.
2. For all $k \geq 1$, $\Delta_k^p = P^{\Sigma_{k-1}^p}$, $\Sigma_k^p = NP^{\Sigma_{k-1}^p}$, and $\Pi_k^p = coNP^{\Sigma_{k-1}^p}$.
3. $PH = \cup_{k \geq 0} \Sigma_k^p$.

The following inclusions easily follow from the definition.

Fig. 12.1 The polynomial
hierarchy. The figure shows
within each class up to level
3. Each class contains all the
classes that appear at lower
positions

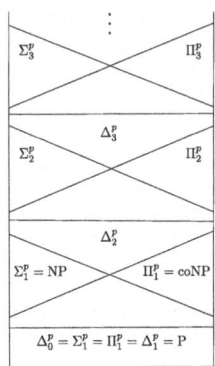

Proposition 12.4 *The following properties hold:*

1. For all $k \geq 1$, $(\Sigma_{k-1}^p \cup \Pi_{k-1}^p) \subseteq \Delta_k^p \subseteq (\Sigma_k^p \cap \Pi_k^p)$.
2. For all $k \geq 0$, $\mathrm{co-}\Sigma_k^p = \Pi_k^p$ and $\mathrm{co-}\Pi_k^p = \Sigma_k^p$.

Figure 12.1 shows the inclusions among the classes up to level 3.

12.3.2   Logical Characterizations of PH

Next, we obtain logical characterizations of Σ_k^p and Π_k^p for $k \geq 1$.

A **quantified Boolean formula (QBF)** is a formula constructed with $\vee, \wedge, \neg, ()$,
$\exists$, and $\forall$. Here, $\exists x$ with a Boolean variable x means "for a Boolean value assigned
to x," and $\forall x$ with a Boolean variable x means "for both Boolean values assigned to
x." In a quantified Boolean formula, a quantified variable may occur only after its
quantifier. For example, a formula:

$$x \vee (\forall x)(\exists y)[(x \vee y) \wedge (\overline{x} \vee \overline{y})]$$

is invalid because the first term x precedes the quantification of x. If we replace the
first x with a different variable w, we get a valid formula:

$$F_0 = w \vee (\forall x)(\exists y)[(x \vee y) \wedge (\overline{x} \vee \overline{y})].$$

We can evaluate the part after $w\vee$:

$$F_1 = (\forall x)(\exists y)[(x \vee y) \wedge (\overline{x} \vee \overline{y})].$$

Let F_2 be the formula inside the []. If $x = true$, $y = false$ makes $F_2 = true$, and
if $x = false$, $y = true$ makes $F_2 = true$. This means $F_1 = true$. Hence, F_0 is
equivalent to w.

A formula is **fully quantified** if, for each variable appearing in it, its first occurrence is preceded by a quantifier. In the example, F_1 is fully quantified while F_0 is not. A fully quantified formula is equivalent to a Boolean constant.

Definition 12.11 A QBF is in the **prenex normal form (PNF)** if all of its quantifiers appear before the appearance of any variable.

F_1 is a PNF formula, but F_0 is not. Suppose we rewrite F_0 as:

$$(\forall x)(\exists y)[((x \vee y) \wedge (\overline{x} \vee \overline{y})) \vee w].$$

Then, F_0 is a PNF formula.

We use PNF formulas to obtain local characterizations of Σ_k^p and Π_k^p. In the characterizations, we show that extensions of the satisfiability problem with alternating quantities are complete for Σ_k^p and Π_k^p.

Before getting to the statement and proof of the characterizations, we make simple observations about the NP and coNP computations with an oracle.

Definition 12.12 A language $A \subseteq \Sigma^*$ is **polynomial-time conjunctive truth-table reducible** to a language B, denoted $A \leq_{\text{ctt}}^p B$, if there exists a polynomial-time computable function f such that for each $x \in \Sigma^*$, $f(x)$ is a list of strings $y_1, \ldots, y_m$, and $x \in A$ if, and only if, $y_1, \ldots, y_m \in B$.

Definition 12.13 A language $A \subseteq \Sigma^*$ is **polynomial-time disjunctive truth-table reducible** to a language B, denoted $A \leq_{\text{dtt}}^p B$, if there exists a polynomial-time computable function f such that for each $x \in \Sigma^*$, $f(x)$ is a list of strings $y_1, \ldots, y_m$, and $x \in A$ if, and only if, for some i such that $1 \leq i \leq m$, $y_i \in B$.

Proposition 12.5 *For all language A, NP^A and coNP^A are closed under $\leq_{\text{ctt}}^p$ and $\leq_{\text{dtt}}^p$ reductions.*

We leave the proof of the proposition to the reader.

For a set of Boolean variables X, let $A(X)$ denote the set of all possible truth assignments to X.

Theorem 12.4 *The following properties hold:*

1. For all $k \geq 1$, a language L is in Σ_k^p if, and only if, there exists a polynomial $r(n)$ and a language $A \in \text{P}$ such that for all x:

$$(\exists a_1 \in \Sigma^{\leq r(|x|)})(\forall a_2 \in \Sigma^{\leq r(|x|)}) \cdots (Q_k a_k \in \Sigma^{\leq r(|x|)})$$

$$[\langle x, a_1, a_2, \cdots, a_k \rangle \in A].$$

Here, for each j such that $1 \leq j \leq k$, $Q_j = \exists$ if j is odd, and $\forall$ otherwise.

2. *For all $k \geq 1$, a language L is in Π_k^p if, and only if, there exists a polynomial $r(n)$ and a language $A \in P$ such that for all x:*

$$(\forall a_1 \in \Sigma^{r(|x|)})(\exists a_2 \in \Sigma^{r(|x|)}) \cdots (Q_k a_k \in \Sigma^{r(|x|)})$$

$$[\langle x, a_1, a_2, \cdots, a_k \rangle \in A].$$

Here, for each j such that $1 \leq j \leq k$, $Q_j = \exists$ if j is even, and $\forall$ otherwise.

Proof Overview
The proof is by induction on k. Because of the complementarity between Σ_k^p and Π_k^p, we only need to prove the statement for Σ_k^p or Π_k^p. In the induction step, where $k \geq 2$, we can assume that the nondeterministic oracle TM queries to the complete language for Σ_{k-1}^p. We use templates to specify possible queries of the machine. We encode the oracle TM's computation using a quantified Boolean formula specifying the configuration of the templates, the query outcomes, and the overall computation. We substitute the queries with the templates and conform the formula to the required format.

Proof The proof is by induction on k. For the base case, let $k = 1$. Due to Theorem 11.4, for each $L \in NP$, a polynomial $p(n)$ and a language $A \in P$ exists such that for all x, $x \in L$ if, and only if, for some y such that $|y| \leq p(|x|)$, $\langle x, y \rangle \in A$. By taking the complement of the property, we get that for each $L' \in coNP$, a polynomial $p(n)$ and a language $A' \in P$ exists such that for all x, $x \in L'$ if, and only if, for all y such that $|y| \leq p(|x|)$, $\langle x, y \rangle \in A'$. These two characterizations match the statements of the theorem. Thus, the base case holds.

For the induction step, suppose $k \geq 2$ and the characterizations hold for all smaller values of k. Let L be a language in Σ_k^p. Let M be an oracle TM and $B \in \Sigma_{k-1}^p$ such that M accepts L with B as the oracle. Suppose $p(n)$ is a polynomial bounding the running time of M with B as the oracle. We can make $p(n)$ large enough so that $p(n)$ is time-constructible, and for all oracles X, M^X is $p(n)$ time-bounded. We can also assume M has at most two nondeterministic choices at each step. We define the following witness language for L:

$C = \{\langle x, y \rangle \mid |y| \leq p(|x|)$, y encodes an accepting computation path of M on x for some oracle, (a) all the positively answered queries on the path are in B, and (b) all the negatively answered queries on the path are in $\overline{B}\}$.

Then, for all x, $x \in L$ if, and only if, for some y such that $|y| \leq p(|x|)$, $\langle x, y \rangle \in C$. We define the following supersets of C.

$C_1 = \{\langle x, y \rangle \mid |y| \leq p(|x|)$, y encodes an accepting computation path of M on x for some oracle, all the positively answered queries on the path are in $B\}$.

$C_2 = \{\langle x, y \rangle \mid |y| \le p(|x|),\ y$ encodes an accepting computation path of M on x
   for some oracle, all the negatively answered queries on the path are in $\overline{B}\}$.
Then, for all x,

$$x \in L \iff (\exists y : |y| \le p(|x|))[\langle x, y \rangle \in C_1 \cap C_2]. \tag{12.1}$$

The condition that y encodes an accepting computation is in P. Since $\mathrm{P} \subseteq \Sigma_{k-1}^p$
and $\mathrm{P} \subseteq \Pi_{k-1}^p$, C_1 is $\le_{ctt}^p$-reducible to some language in Σ_{k-1}^p and C_2 is $\le_{ctt}^p$-
reducible to some language in Π_{k-1}^p. Because both $\sigma k - 1$ and Π_{k-1}^p are closed
under $\le_{ctt}^p$-reductions (Proposition 12.5), $C_1 \in \Sigma_{k-1}^p$ and $C_2 \in \Pi_{k-1}^p$. By the
induction hypothesis, C_1 is characterized with a polynomial $q_1(n)$ and a language
$D_1 \in \mathrm{P}$ such that for all z:

$$z \in C_1 \iff (\exists u_1 : |u_1| \le q_1(|z|))(\forall u_2 : |u_2| \le q_1(|z|))$$
$$\cdots (Q_{k-1} u_{k-1} : |u_{k-1}| \le q_1(|z|))$$
$$[\langle z, u_1, \ldots, u_{k-1} \rangle \in D_1].$$

Here, $Q_{k-1} = \exists$ if $k - 1$ is odd, and $\forall$ otherwise. Similarly, C_2 is characterized with
a polynomial $q_2(n)$ and a language $D_2 \in \mathrm{P}$ such that for all z:

$$z \in C_2 \iff (\forall v_1 : |v_1| \le q_2(|z|))(\exists v_2 : |v_2| \le q_2(|z|))$$
$$\cdots (R_{k-1} v_{k-1} : |v_{k-1}| \le q_2(|z|))$$
$$[\langle z, v_1, \ldots, v_{k-1} \rangle \in D_2].$$

Here, $R_{k-1} = \exists$ if $k - 1$ is even, and $\forall$ otherwise.

In Eq. 12.1, we replace the membership conditions in C_1 and C_2 with the characterizations of C_1 and C_2. Since the two characterizations use two independent series
of quantified strings, $u_1, \ldots, u_{k-1}$ and $v_1, \ldots, v_{k-1}$, we can list the elements of the
two quantifier sequences in an alternating order: $u_1, v_1, u_2, v_2, \ldots, u_{k-1}, v_{k-1}$. The
resulting formula is:

$$x \in L$$
$$\iff (\exists y : |y| \le p(|x|))(\exists u_1 : |u_1| \le q_1(|y|))(\forall v_1 : |v_1| \le q_2(|y|))$$
$$(\forall u_2 : |u_2| \le q_1(|y|))(\exists v_2 : |v_2| \le q_2(|y|)) \cdots$$
$$(Q_{k-1} u_{k-1} : |u_{k-1}| \le q_1(|y|))(R_{k-1} v_{k-1} : |v_{k-1}| \le q_2(|y|))$$
$$[\langle \langle x, y \rangle, u_1, \ldots, u_{k-1} \rangle \in D_1 \wedge \langle \langle x, y \rangle, v_1, \ldots, v_{k-1} \rangle \in D_2]. \tag{12.2}$$

Since D_1 and D_2 are in P, the last condition is in P.

For two arbitrary binary strings s and t, let $s\#t$ denote the string constructed
from s and t by encoding each character b appearing in s and t as the two-character

string $b0$ and connecting the elongated strings with 11 between them. The length of $s\#t$ is $2(|s| + |t| + 1)$. We can extract s and t from $s\#t$ by splitting it into the parts before and after the first occurrence of 11 and then collecting the characters at even-numbered positions. By joining the neighboring string pairs having the same quantifies, we get:

$$w_1 = y_1 \# u_1, \; w_2 = v_1 \# u_2, \ldots, \; w_{k-1} = v_{k-2} \# u_{k-1}, \; w_k = v_{k-1}.$$

The quantifiers attached to them alternate starting with $\exists$. Before joining, the parts of each pair have a length of at most $q(p(|y|))$. Thus, there is a polynomial $r(n)$ such that $|w_1|, \ldots, |w_k| \leq r(|x|)$.

We define a language A as the set of all $\langle x, w_1, \ldots, w_k \rangle$ satisfying the last part of Eq. 12.2:

$$\langle\langle x, y \rangle, u_1, \ldots, u_{k-1} \rangle \in D_1 \wedge \langle\langle x, y \rangle, v_1, \ldots, v_{k-1} \rangle \in D_2].$$

Here, $y, u_1, \ldots, u_{k-1}, v_1, \ldots, v_{k-1}$ are extracted from $x, w_1, \ldots, w_k$. Since D_1 and D_2 are in P, $A \in$ P. Thus, for all x,

$$x \in A \iff (\exists w_1 : |w_1| \leq q(|x|))(\forall w_2 : |w_2| \leq q(|x|))$$

$$\cdots (S_k w_k : |w_k| \leq q(|z|))$$

$$\langle x, w_1, \ldots, w_k \rangle \in A. \tag{12.3}$$

Here, $S_k = \exists$ if k is odd, and $\forall$ otherwise. Thus, the claim holds for k.

Since Π_k^p is the complement of Σ_k^p, by taking the complement of the characterization, we obtain the characterization for Π_k^p.   □

The membership condition in Eq. 12.3 is in P. Since P $\subseteq$ NP $\cap$ coNP, the condition is expressible as $(\exists h_1)[\varphi_1(x, w_1, \ldots, w_k, h_1)$ such that φ_1 is a 3CNF formula and $(\forall h_2)[\varphi_2(x, w_1, \ldots, w_k, h_2)$ such that φ_2 is a 3DNF formula. By choosing the former when $S_k = \exists$ and the latter when $S_k = \forall$, we obtain characterizations where the base formula is a 3CNF or a 3DNF.

Corollary 12.4 *The following properties hold:*

1. For all $k \geq 1$, a language L is in Σ_k^p if, and only if, there exists a polynomial $r(n)$ and a Boolean formula φ such that for all x:

$$(\exists a_1 \in \Sigma^{\leq r(|x|)})(\forall a_2 \in \Sigma^{\leq r(|x|)}) \cdots (Q_k a_k \in \Sigma^{\leq r(|x|)})$$

$$[\varphi(x, a_1, a_2, \cdots, a_k) = true].$$

Here, for each j such that $1 \leq j \leq k$, $Q_j = \exists$ if j is odd, and $\forall$ otherwise; φ is a 3CNF formula if k is odd, and a 3DNF formula otherwise.

2. *For all $k \geq 1$, a language L is in Π_k^p if, and only if, there exists a polynomial $r(n)$ and a Boolean formula φ such that for all x:*

$$(\forall a_1 \in \Sigma^{\leq r(|x|)})(\exists a_2 \in \Sigma^{\leq r(|x|)}) \cdots (Q_k a_k \in \Sigma^{\leq r(|x|)})$$

$$[\varphi(x, a_1, a_2, \cdots, a_k) = true].$$

Here, for each j such that $1 \leq j \leq k$, $Q_j = \exists$ if j is even, and $\exists$ otherwise; φ is a 3CNF formula if k is even and a 3DNF formula otherwise.

Theorem 12.5 *For each $k \geq 1$, the following statements are equivalent:*

1. $\text{PH} = \Sigma_k^p$.
2. $\text{PH} = \Pi_k^p$.
3. $\Sigma_k^p = \Pi_k^p$.
4. $\Pi_k^p \subseteq \Sigma_k^p$.
5. $\Sigma_k^p \subseteq \Pi_k^p$.

Proof We prove the theorem by showing that (1)–(4) are equivalent to (5). Evidently, (3) is equivalent to (5) due to the complementary between Σ_k^p and Π_k^p. By taking the complement, we know that (1) is equivalent to (2) and (4) is equivalent to (5). Since $\Sigma_k^p \subseteq \Delta_{k+1}^p$, (4) implies (4). Also, since $\Delta_{k+1}^p \subseteq \text{PH}$, (1) implies (5). Similarly, (2) implies (5).

We are now left to show (5) implies (1). To show this, assume (5) is true. We consider an arbitrary formula, say φ, which is in the shape for S_{k+1}; φ has $k + 1$ alternating quantifiers starting with $\exists$. If we remove the first quantifier from φ, the shape of the formula matches the shape of the formulas for P_k. Because of this match, the P_k formula is $\leq_m^p$-reducible to an S_k formula by our assumption. We then substitute in φ the part matching the shape for P_k with the formula obtained by executing the reduction. Then, the new formula has two consecutive $\exists$ quantifiers at the start. These two consecutive quantifiers can be collapsed into one $\exists$ quantifier. After the collapse, the formula matches the shape for S_k.   □

12.4 Between P and NP-Complete

Here, we look at the area between P and NP. We know that if P $\neq$ NP, NP − P contains all NP-complete languages. Does the area contain anything other than NP-complete? The answer is yes, as we prove next.

Theorem 12.6 *If P $\neq$ NP, then there is a language in NP that is neither NP-complete nor in P.*

Proof Overview
Assume P $\neq$ NP. We select an arbitrary NP-complete language S. We construct a non-decreasing function $t : \mathbb{N} \to \mathbb{N}$. The range of t is $\mathbb{N}$ or $[0, q]$ for some q. While constructing t, we construct a language A using two alternating sequences of diagonalization. One sequence ensures that $A \notin$ P, and the other ensures that S is not $\leq_m^p$-reducible to A. We design the construction so that the range of t is finite if, and only if, one of the diagonalization sequences stops advancing. The latter condition implies $S \in$ P.

Proof Assume P $\neq$ NP. We will construct a language $A \in$ NP $-$ P that is not NP-complete. Let $\Sigma = \{0, 1\}$. Let $S \subseteq \Sigma^*$ be an arbitrary NP-complete language. Since P $\neq$ NP and S is NP-complete, $S \notin$ P. Since $S \notin$ P, we have $S \notin \{\emptyset, \Sigma^*\}$. We select $y_0 \in \overline{S}$. Let D_S be an arbitrary deterministic TM that decides S. We are not concerned with the running time of D_S.

Along with A, we construct a polynomial time-bounded TM T that receives an input in $\{0\}^*$ and produces an output in $\{0\}^*$. We define $t(n)$ as the length of the output that T produces on input 0^n. Using $t(n)$ and S, we define A as follows:

$$A = \{x \mid x \in S \text{ and } t(|x|) \text{ is even}\}.$$

In other words, for all $n \geq 0$ such that $t(n)$ is even, the length-n portion of A is identical to the length-n portion of S, and for all $n \geq 0$ such that $t(n)$ is odd, the length-n portion of A is empty. Consider the following f:

For all x:

$$f(x) = \begin{cases} x & \text{if } t(|x|) \text{ is even,} \\ y_0 & \text{otherwise.} \end{cases}$$

Since t is polynomial-time computable, f is polynomial-time computable. Because of the definition of A and the choice of y_0, for all x, $x \in A \iff f(x) \in S$. Thus, f is a polynomial-time many-one reduction from A to S. This implies that $A \in$ NP. $\square$

12.4.1 Two Enumerations of TMs

We use two enumerations of TMs: TM deciders $M_1, M_2, \ldots$ and TM transducers $R_1, R_2, \ldots$. All the machines have Σ as the input alphabet, and the transducers $R_1, R_2, \ldots$ have Σ as the output alphabet.

For both enumerations, for all $i \geq 1$, the i-th machine in the enumeration is the i-th member of Σ^* in lexicographic order. We employ an encoding scheme that permits trailing 0s, as we did in the proof of Theorem 9.5. Due to the trailing 0s, each TM appears infinitely many times in its respective enumeration. Because of the trailing-0 attachment, many strings in Σ^* disqualify as an encoding of a TM. We assume that all trivial deciders reject all inputs and outputs ϵ. As we have seen many times in this book, checking the validity of an encoding is decidable. Specifically, due to Theorem 10.2, the extraction of the TM from its binary encoding is in L, so it is doable in polynomial time.

The machine T imposes a clock on the machines it simulates. For all $i \geq 1$, the simulation of the i-th machine runs with $i \cdot n^i + i$ as the maximum number of steps, the input is rejected for M_i, and the output is ϵ for R_i. Despite the hard stop, because we attach trailing 0s, every machine reappears with more 0s and thus with more computation time.

12.4.2 T's Program

We define $t(0) = 0$ and $t(1) = 1$. The machine T must output ϵ on input ϵ and 0 on input 0. The production of these inputs requires $n + 1$ steps for $n = 0, 1$. We set $p(n) = n + 1$ and set the running time of T to something greater than $p(n)$.

For $n \geq 2$, the action of T on input 0^n goes as follows:

Phase 1: Obtain $p(n)$ in unary T computes $0^{p(n)}$ on one tape.

Phase 2: Recomputation   In $p(n)$ steps, T executes its program and tries to recompute $t(n')$ for as many possible values for $n' = 1, 2, \ldots, n - 1$. The $0^{p(n)}$ from Phase 1 is used to limit the number of steps for the recalculation to at most $p(n)$.

Phase 3: Preparation for the next stage   Let h be the maximum value of n' for which T could recompute $t(n')$ in the allocated $p(n)$ steps. Set $m = t(h)$ and $j = \lceil (m+1)/2 \rceil$. T will output 0^m or 0^{m+1} and will use Phase 5 for determining which.

Phase 4: Machine decoding   If m is even, extract the machine M_j from the j-th smallest binary string; if m is odd, extract the machine R_j from the j-th smallest binary string.

Phase 5: Simulation   1. If m is even, execute the following:

   a. Using no more than $p(n)$ steps, try to test the following condition for as many x as possible:

   $$M_j \text{ on } x \text{ accepts if, and only if, } x \in A.$$

   Here, the lexicographic order is used to generate the candidates for x.
   Testing the membership in A may require running T's program and executing S's decider, D_S.

    b. If the result is positive for all the tests, the output is 0^m; otherwise (i.e., the result is negative for at least one test), the output is 0^{m+1}.

2. If m is odd, do the following:

    a. Using no more than $p(n)$ steps, for as many strings x in Σ^* as possible, check the condition:

$$x \in S \text{ if, and only if, the output of } R_j \text{ on } x \text{ ix in } A.$$

    Testing the condition may require recomputing T and simulating the decider D_S.

    b. If the result is positive for all the tests, the output is 0^m; otherwise (i.e., the result is negative for at least one test), the output is 0^{m+1}.

This completes the description of the algorithm.

Overall, T executes the following:

- Obtain h, $1 \leq h \leq n - 1$, $m = t(h)$, and index j.
- Using $p(n)$ as the time limit, check if there is evidence that M_j does not act as a decider for A or R_j does not act as a $\leq_m^p$-reduction from A to S. If no evidence is found, output m; otherwise, output $m + 1$.

The program uses the value of m to determine which machine to test the condition in Phase 5.

12.4.3 T's Running Time

Let us analyze the running time of T. The running time is $O(p(n))$ for Phases 1, 2, 3, and 5. The time required for extracting the machine in Phase 4 is $O(n)$ because T only must remove the trailing 0s. Thus, the total running time of T is $O(p(n))$. This means that T is polynomial time-bounded, and thus t is polynomial-time computable.

12.4.4 t's Range and Its Non-decreasing Property

Now, let us examine the output of T. In Phase 5, T may output 0^{m+1} if, and only if, T produces 0^m on some smaller input. This means that the range of t is consecutive, i.e., the interval $[0, q]$ for some integer q or the entire set of nonnegative integers.

We claim that t is non-decreasing. The proof is by induction on n. The base case is when $n = 0$. We know that $t(0) = 0 \leq t(1) = 1 = t(0) + 1$. Thus, the claim holds for $n = 0$. For the induction step, let $n \geq 1$ and suppose that the claim holds for all smaller values of n. Let us compare the actions of T on input 0^n and input

0^{n+1}. Let h_n, m_n, and j_n be the values of h, m, and j on input 0^n, respectively. Let h_{n+1}, m_{n+1}, and j_{n+1} be the values of h, m, and j on input 0^{n+1}, respectively. Since T has only one extra step in the simulation, $h_n \leq h_{n+1} \leq h_n + 1$. Since T must recompute t from $t(0)$, $h_n < n - 1$ and $h_{n+1} < (n + 1) - 1 = n$. So, by the induction hypothesis, the strict non-decreasing property holds for both $t(h_n)$ and $t(h_{n+1})$, which are m_n and m_{n+1}, respectively.

We consider two cases: $m_n = m_{n+1}$ and $m_n \neq m_{n+1}$. Suppose $m_n = m_{n+1}$. The machine T simulates on input 0^n is identical to the machine T simulates on input 0^{n+1}. Since T has more time to use in simulation, if it finds a counterexample on input 0^n, it finds a counterexample on input 0^{n+1}. Thus, the possible value pairs for $(t(n), t(n+1))$ are (m_n, m_n), $(m_n, m_n + 1)$, and $(m_n + 1, m_n + 1)$. Hence, the claim holds. Next, suppose $m_n \neq m_{n+1}$. By our induction hypothesis, $m_n < m_{n+1}$. Since $t(n) \leq m_n + 1 \leq t(n + 1)$ and $t(n + 1) \geq m_{n+1}$, we have $t(n) \leq t(n + 1)$, so the claim holds.

Since t is non-decreasing without a gap, for all $n \geq 0$, $t(n) \leq t(n + 1) \leq t(n)$ (see Exercise 12.11).

12.4.5 t's Unboundedness

We claim that for each q, there is some n such that $t(n) \geq q$. The proof is by contradiction. Assume, by contradiction, that a value n_0 exists such that $t(n) = q$ for all $n \geq n_0$. For all sufficiently large n, T arrives at h such that $t(h) = q$ and $j = \lceil (q + 1)/2 \rceil$ and finds no counterexamples in the equivalence tests; otherwise, $t(n)$ would be $q + 1$. Suppose q is an odd number. Then, M_j passes the equivalence test for all inputs, so M_j decides S. Since M_j's running time is $j \cdot n^j + j$, we get $S \in P$. This is a contradiction.

On the other hand, suppose q is an even number. Then, R_j passes the equivalence test for all inputs, so R_j reduces S to A. Since R_j's running time is $j \cdot n^j + j$ and S is NP-complete, we get that A is NP-complete. However, $h(n) = q$ for all $n \geq n_0$ and q is odd. Since A consists of all $w \in S$ such that $t(|w|)$ is even, every member of A has a length of $< n_0$. This means that A is finite. Since finite sets are in P, this implies P = NP. This is a contradiction. Hence, t is unbounded.

12.4.6 The Final Touch

Since the value of h_n increases by at most 1 and j_n is one-half of m_n, the equivalence tests are conducted for all M_js and R_js. The unboundedness of $t(n)$ guarantees that T finds a counterexample for all of them. Thus, $A \notin P$ and S is $\leq^P_m$-reducible to A.

This completes the proof of the theorem.

12.5 PSPACE-Complete Problems

In this section, we explore complete problems for PSPACE.

12.5.1 Quantified Boolean Formulas (QBF)

We define a canonical complete problem with quantified Boolean formulas.

Definition 12.14 We define PSPCANONICAL $= \{\langle M, x, 1^s \rangle \mid M$ is a deterministic offline TM and accepts x using no more than s tape cells$\}$.

The completeness of PSPCANONICAL, stated next, is easy to prove. We leave the proof to the reader (Exercises 12.18 and 12.19).

Proposition 12.6 PSPCANONICAL *is* PSPACE-*complete under* $\leq_m^p$-*reductions.*

The canonical complete problem does not help find problems complete for PSPACE. Therefore, we obtain a logical characterization.

Recall that we defined the polynomial hierarchy, specifically the Σ_k^p classes, using a stack of nondeterministic oracle TMs. Also recall that we characterized the Σ_k^p classes using alternating quantifiers (Theorem 12.4). In the characterization, we guessed a prospective accepting computation path and verified its correctness with queries to languages in Σ_{k-1}^p and Π_{k-1}^p. We apply an idea similar to the characterization here in this proof. The idea comes from the proof for Savitch's theorem (Theorem 10.4). The level in the polynomial hierarchy corresponds to the exponent in the reachability distance.

Definition 12.15 TQBF is the problem of determining the value of fully quantified Boolean formulas.

Theorem 12.7 TQBF *is* $\leq_m^p$-*complete for* PSPACE.

Proof Let L be a language in PSPACE and M be a polynomial space-bounded deterministic TM M that decides L. We may assume that M is a single-tape machine. Additionally, we may assume that M has a unique accepting ID $q_{acc}\sqcup^*$ (see Exercise 12.20) In other words, all the tape cells are blank, and the head is on the leftmost cell of the tape in the ID. Because M is polynomial space-bounded, a polynomial $p(n)$ exists such that for all x, we can encode each possible ID during the execution of M on x as a $p(|x|)$-bit string, thus as $p(|x|)$ variables.

Let us fix an input x having a length of n. Let $\mathcal{W}$ be the variables representing the ID of M and $\mathcal{A}$ be the set of all truth assignments to $\mathcal{W}$. A unique truth assignment in $\mathcal{A}$ represents the initial ID of M on x. In addition, a unique truth assignment in $\mathcal{A}$ represents the accepting ID of M. Let A_{ini} and A_{acc} be the unique initial and accepting IDs, respectively. We can identify $\mathcal{A}$ as $\{0, 1\}^{p(n)}$. For each $X, Y \in \mathcal{A}$ and $d \geq 0$, we define $R(X, Y, d)$ as the tertiary relation Y is reachable from X in at most 2^d steps. As with the proof for Savitch's theorem (Theorem 10.2), we use the following recursion on the value of d where $d \geq 1$:

$R(X, Y, d)$

$\Leftrightarrow (X = Y) \vee$

$\quad (\exists Z)(\forall U, V)[((U = X \wedge V = Z) \vee (U = Z \wedge V = Y)) \Rightarrow R(U, V, d - 1)]$.

We can express the condition as a formula without the implication:

$R(X, Y, d)$

$\Leftrightarrow (X = Y) \vee$

$\quad (\exists Z)(\forall U, V)[((U \neq X \vee V \neq Z) \wedge (U \neq Z \vee V \neq Y)) \vee R(U, V, d - 1)]$.

For $d = 0$, instead of the recursion, we have the following property:

$$R(X, Y, 0) \iff (X = Y) \vee Y \text{ is the next ID of } X.$$

In proving SAT's completeness, we introduced a propositional formula representing the "next ID" relation. We use the same formula here. The "next ID" is expressible as a propositional formula. We recursively substitute the R predicate with a smaller d until $d = 0$. Here we attach the subscript d to U, V, and Z at level d. The recursive substitution produces the following:

$$R(X, Y, d) \iff (\exists Z_d)(\forall U_d, V_d)(\exists Z_{d-1})(\forall U_{d-1}, V_{d-1}) \cdots (\exists Z_1)(\forall U_1, V_1)[\phi].$$

Here, ϕ consists of the equality testing for all levels and the "next ID" test. By quantifying X and Y with $\exists$ and adding the conditions representing $X = A_{\text{ini}}$ and $Y = A_{\text{accept}}$ conjunctively, we get the formula for M's acceptance of x:

$$\psi = (\exists X, Y, Z_d)(\forall U_d, V_d)(\exists Z_{d-1})(\forall U_{d-1}, V_{d-1}) \cdots (\exists Z_0)(\forall U_0, V_0)$$

$$[X = A_{\text{ini}} \wedge Y = A_{\text{accept}} \wedge \phi]. \tag{12.4}$$

This is a TQBF formula. Since $\|\mathcal{A}\| = 2^{p(n)}$, if M accepts x, then it does so in $2^{p(n)}$ steps. Thus, we can set $d = p(n)$. This proves the theorem. $\qquad \square$

We can turn a TQBF formula into a normalized form. First, since Eq. 12.4 is a propositional formula, we can change it to a 3CNF formula with additional variables. This change raises the complexity of the equation from P to NP, but the overall complexity of ψ is unchanged. Next, we insert irrelevant variables to the formula so that the quantifiers alternate between $\exists$ and $\forall$ variable after variable, starting and ending with $\exists$. The resulting formula is in the format:

$$(\exists x_1)(\forall x_2)(\exists x_3) \cdots (Q_{k-1} x_{k-1})(\exists x_k) \phi(x_1, \ldots, x_k).$$

Here, k is odd, and ϕ is a 3CNF formula.

Corollary 12.5 *The* TQBF *problem is* PSPACE-*complete, where the number of variables is odd, the base formula is 3CNF, the quantifiers alternate variable after variable, and the starting and ending quantifiers are* $\exists$.

12.5.2 Games and Winning Strategies

From the characterization in Corollary 12.5, we obtain game-based complete problems.

The first complete problem is the following two-player **logic game**. In this game, the players receive a Boolean formula $\phi(x_1, \ldots, x_{2n})$ and assign values to the variables in $2n$ rounds. In an odd-numbered round r, Player 1 selects the value for x_r; in an even-numbered round r, Player 2 selects the value for x_r. After $2n$ rounds, they evaluate the formula with the chosen variables. Player 1 wins if the formula is *true*; Player 2 wins otherwise.

Definition 12.16 FORMULAGAME $= \{\langle \phi \rangle \mid \phi$ has some $2n$ variables, and Player 1 has a winning strategy in the game$\}$.

Theorem 12.8 FORMULAGAME *is* PSPACE-*complete*.

Proof To show that FORMULAGAME is in PSPACE, let $\phi(x_1, \ldots, x_{2n})$ be a $2n$-variable Boolean formula. For each $b, c \in \{0, 1\}$, let ϕ_{bc} be the formula constructed from ϕ by assigning b to x_1 and c to x_2. Then:

$$\phi \in \text{FORMULAGAME} \iff (\exists b)(\forall c)[\phi_{bc} \in \text{FORMULAGAME}].$$

We think of a TM that uses recursive calls and evaluates the membership of ϕ in FORMULAGAME. The machine then determines the membership using four possible assignments to the variable pair (b, c) with four recursive calls. If the results are positive for $(0, 0)$ and $(0, 1)$ or positive for $(1, 0)$ and $(1, 1)$, the machine accepts ϕ; otherwise, the machine rejects ϕ. Each of the four calls has two fewer variables. The depth of the recursive algorithm is thus n, so the space required for the recursive evaluation is $O(n \cdot |\phi|)$. Thus, FORMULAGAME $\in$ PSPACE.

To show the $\leq_m^p$-hardness of FORMULAGAME, we use Corollary 12.8, where the complete problem demands alternating quantifiers. Suppose we are given the following PNF formula with alternating quantifiers:

$$\psi = (Q_1 x_1)(Q_2 x_2) \cdots (Q_k x_k)[\phi(x_1, \ldots, x_k)].$$

Here, $Q_1, \ldots, Q_k$ alternate between $\exists$ and $\forall$. We make two possible modifications to ψ so the quantification sequence starts with $\exists$ and ends with $\forall$. First, if Q_1 is $\forall$, we insert a new starting quantification $(\exists x_0)$ with a new variable x_0 not appearing in ϕ. Second, if Q_k is $\exists$, we insert a new ending quantification $(\forall x_{k+1})$ with a variable x_{k+1} not appearing in ϕ. Neither modification alters the value of the formula. The addition of the two variables does not alter the value of the QBF. Now, the truth value of the QBF can be obtained from the membership of the formula in FORMULAGAME. □

Algorithm 12.3 Recursive algorithm for FORMULAGAME

```
 1: procedure FORMULA-GAME(φ)
 2:     if φ has no free variables then
 3:         return the value of the formula;
 4:     end if
 5:     construct formulas φ₀₀, φ₀₁, φ₁₀, φ₁₁;
 6:     make recursive calls and obtain the membership of
 7:     the four sub-formulas in FORMULAGAME;
 8:     if φ₀₀ = φ₀₁ = true then
 9:         return 1;
10:     else if φ₁₀ = φ₁₁ = true then
11:         return true;
12:     else
13:         return false;
14:     end if
15: end procedure
```

12.5.3 The Geography Game

The PSPACE-complete problem is Geography.

Geography is reminiscent of the Japanese word game "Shiritori." In Shiritori, the players take turns stating a word. Before playing the game, the players agree on the word category (e.g., animals, vegetables, and country names). The first player is free to choose the initial word. After that, the players must state a word whose first syllable is identical to the previous player's last syllable. The vocabulary is imaginary, and other players must endorse each word. If the word is not endorsed, the player must select another word. Since the Japanese language does not have words starting with the syllable "N," a player must not use a word ending with "N." The player who cannot make the connection loses the game. For example, if animals are chosen as the category, the words may connect like:

"ne-ko" (the cat), "ko-ji-ka" (the fawn), "ka-mo-no-ha-shi" (the duck-bill), "shi-ma-u-ma" (the zebra), "ma-n-gu-u-su" (the mongoose), "su-zu-me" (the sparrow).

We generalize the game as Geography, where the players agree on vocabulary.

In Geography, the problem is represented as a directed graph with multiple edges. The graph's vertices are the syllables, and the edges are the words connecting syllables. When a player selects an edge, the vertex of origin moves along the edge, and the edge is removed from the graph. We bound the number of edges by some polynomial in the number of vertices. To achieve this, we use an edge list. We may consider an adjacency matrix with integer entries to encode the problem, but such a graph may have an exponential number of edges. We also restrict the number of players to two, and the player having no available edges loses the game. Since there are two players, the opponent of the losing player is the winner.

Definition 12.17 GEOGRAPHY $= \{\langle G, s\rangle \mid G$ is a multiple-edge directed graph, s is a vertex in G, and Player 1 has a winning strategy$\}$.

We again reduce TQBF to prove the following:

Theorem 12.9 GEOGRAPHY *is* PSPACE-*complete.*

Proof We use a recursive algorithm to show GEOGRAPHY $\in$ PSPACE. In the recursive algorithm for FORMULAGAME, the recursion keeps Player 1 in the initial question as the first player in the recursive calls. Here, we reverse the order of the players in each recursive call. By symmetry, for all i such that $1 \leq i \leq k$,

Player 1 has a winning strategy in $\langle G, s\rangle \iff$ Player 2 has no winning strategy in
$$\langle G_i, u_i\rangle \text{ for some } i.$$

The algorithm uses this fact. At each recursive call, the graph loses one edge. Since the number of edges is no more than the length of the input, the recursion depth is linear. Thus, the program runs in polynomial space.

We use the variable-wise quantifier-alternating version of TQBF from Corollary 12.5. Suppose the following ψ is an instance of TQBF:

$$(\exists x_1)(\forall x_2)\cdots(\forall x_{2k})(\exists x_{2k+1})[\phi(x_1,\ldots,x_{2k+1})].$$

Here, ϕ is a 3CNF formula. Let m be the number of clauses in ϕ. We construct a Geography game from ψ such that $\psi = true \iff$ Player 1 has a winning strategy.

A key ingredient in the construction is the gadget in Fig. 12.2. Suppose a player must choose an edge from the top vertex. There are only two ways to go from top to bottom: to the left and right. Both require three steps, meaning the same player picks the branch at the bottom and follows the last edge. If there are no other outgoing edges from the middle vertices, the selection eliminates the use of the child that the first player chooses.

Fig. 12.2 The variable
selection gadget in the
reduction to GEOGRAPHY

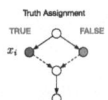

We connect $2k + 1$ copies of the five-vertex gadget in a sequence by identifying the bottom vertex of a gadget with the top vertex of the next gadget. We locate the game's starting point to the top vertex of the gadget sequence. Since the top and last players inside each gadget are identical, and the number of gadgets is odd, the first and last players in the gadget series are the same.

After constructing the sequence, we connect the bottom edge of the last gadget to a vertex with m outgoing edges, connecting to m vertices representing the clauses. Each clause-representing vertex has three children, representing the literals in the clause. We identify the literal vertices with corresponding assignments in the five-vertex gadget sequence (see Fig. 12.3).

Multiple choices are available at the start of each gadget, at the clause selection, and at the literal selection. The multiple choices Player 1 receives are at the odd-numbered five-vertex gadgets and the literal choice. The multiple choices Player 2 receives are at the even-numbered five-vertex gadgets and the clause choice. For the multiple choices available at the five-vertex gadgets, Player 1 receives all the assignment selections for the existentially quantified variables. In contrast, Player 2 receives all the assignment selections for the universally quantified variables. At literal selection, if the selection matches the truth assignment, there is no edge to traverse from there. If the literal selection disagrees with the truth assignment, there is an arrow that Player 2 can follow; following this arrow, the players arrive at a vertex with no more outgoing edges. Thus, after arriving at the clause selection, Player 1 wins the game if, and only if, the clause Player 2 chooses is satisfiable. Thus, Player 1 has a winning strategy if, and only if, $\psi = true$.

The construction of the graph can be carried out in time polynomial in $|F|$, so the reduction is a $\leq_m^p$ reduction. This proves the theorem. □

Fig. 12.3 The construction for reducing TQBF to GEOGRAPHY

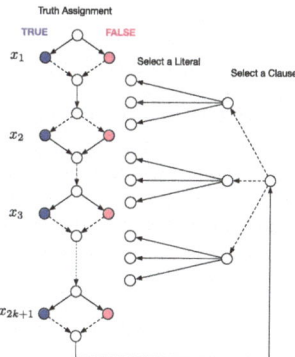

Algorithm 12.4 Recursive algorithm for GEOGRAPHY

1: **procedure** GEOGRAPHY(G, s)
2:     **if** s has no outgoing edges **then**
3:         return *false*;
4:     **end if**
5:     obtain the list of all out-going edges of s as $e_1 = (s, u_1), \ldots, e_k = (s, u_k)$;
6:     **for** $i \leftarrow 1, \ldots, k$ **do**
7:         construct G_i by removing e_i from G;
8:         make a recursive call about $\langle G_i, u_i \rangle$ and obtain the result r_i;
9:         **if** r_i is *false* **then**
10:             return *true*;
11:         **end if**
12:     **end for**
13:     return *false*;
14: **end procedure**

Exercises

12.1 Suppose C is a complexity class. Prove that $P^C = P^{\text{co}-C}$, $NP^C = NP^{\text{co}-C}$, and $\text{coNP}^C = \text{coNP}^{\text{co}-C}$.

12.2 Suppose C is a complexity class with a $\leq_m^p$-complete set A. Prove that $P^C = P^A$, $NP^C = NP^A$, and $\text{coNP}^C = \text{coNP}^A$.

12.3 Prove that NP^A for every language A, NP^A is closed under $\leq_{\text{ctt}}^p$.

12.4 Prove that for every language A, coNP^A is closed under $\leq_{\text{dtt}}^p$.

12.5 Prove that the polynomial-time Turing reducibility is reflexive and transitive.

12.6 Prove that the search reduces in polynomial time to the decision for VERTEXCOVER.
   Hint: Using a greedy algorithm, we can eliminate vertices that do not contribute to a vertex cover of the required size.

12.7 Prove that the search reduces in polynomial time to the decision for CLIQUE.
   Hint: Using a greedy algorithm, we can eliminate edges that do not contribute to a clique of the required size.

12.8 Prove that the search reduces in polynomial time to the decision for PARTITION.
   Hint: We can increase the value of a pair of elements with the same amount to check if they are in different parts.

12.9 Prove that the search reduces in polynomial time to the decision for 3DM.

12.10 The proof of Theorem 12.4 converts a 3DNF to a 3CNF with the variables existentially quantified. Suppose the DNF ϕ has m clauses in the form:

$$\phi = (\ell_{1,1} \wedge \ell_{1,2} \wedge \ell_{1,3}) \vee \cdots \vee (\ell_{m,1} \wedge \ell_{m,2} \wedge \ell_{m,3}).$$

We refer to the i-th clause as D_i. Construct a full CNF formula for $(\exists i : 1 \leq i \leq m)[D_i]$ by introducing two sets of variables. The first set is a_i such that $1 \leq i \leq m$, indicating which D_i is *true*. The second set is b_i such that $2 \leq i \leq m$, representing $a_1 \vee \cdots \vee a_i$.

12.11 In the proof of Theorem 12.6, we used the property $t(n+1) \in \{t(n), t(n)+1\}$ for all $n \geq 0$. Prove this property by combining the two properties of t; t's range is contiguous, and t is non-decreasing.

12.12 Recall that INDEPENDENTSET is the set of $\langle G, k \rangle$ such that G has an independent set of size k. Give an algorithm for computing one maximum independent set of a graph G using INDEPENDENTSET as the oracle.

12.13 Recall that HAMPATH is the set of $\langle G, s, t \rangle$ such that G has a Hamiltonian path from s to t. Show that the search reduces in polynomial time to the decision for HAMPATH.

12.14 Recall that HAMCYCLE is the set of graphs $\langle G \rangle$ such that G has a Hamiltonian cycle3. Show that the search reduces in polynomial time to the decision for HAMCYCLE.

12.15 Let A be an arbitrary language in NP $\cap$ coNP. Show that $NP^A = NP$.

12.16 Let A be an arbitrary language in NP $\cap$ coNP. Show that $P^A \subseteq NP \cap coNP$, and so $NP \cap coNP = P^{NP \cap coNP}$.

12.17 Let M be a polynomial time-bounding NTM such that for all inputs x, M on x makes at most $c \log |x|$ nondeterministic choices on every computation path. Show that the language M accepts is in P.

12.18 Prove that the canonical complete problem in Proposition 12.6 is in PSPACE.

12.19 Prove that the canonical complete problem in Proposition 12.6 is PSPACE-hard under the polynomial-time many-one reductions.

12.20 Prove that single-tape TMs can be normalized so that the format of their accepting IDs is $q_{acc}\sqcup^*$.

Bibliographic Notes and Further Reading
The definition of oracle TMs is by Turing [6]. The completeness of ODDMAXSAT for P^{NP} (Theorem 12.3) is by Krentel [1]. The polynomial hierarchy was first studied by Meyer and Stockmeyer [3, 5]. The logical characterization of PH (Theorem 12.4) is from the work of Stockmeyer [5]. Theorem 12.6 is by Ladner [2].

The completeness of FORMULAGAME and GG is by Schaefer [4].

References

1. M.W. Krentel, The complexity of optimization problems, in *Proceedings of the Eighteenth Annual ACM symposium on Theory of computing* (ACM, New York, 1986), pp. 69–76
2. R.E. Ladner, On the structure of polynomial time reducibility. J. ACM **22**(1), 155–171 (1975)
3. A.R. Meyer, L.J. Stockmeyer, The equivalence problem for regular expressions with squaring requires exponential space, in *Proceedings of the Thirteenth Annual IEEE Symposium on Switching and Automata Theory*, vol. 72 (1972), pp. 125–129
4. T.J. Schaefer, On the complexity of some two-person perfect-information games. J. Comput. Syst. Sci. **16**(2), 185–225 (1978)
5. L.J. Stockmeyer, The polynomial-time hierarchy. Theor. Comput. Sci. **3**(1), 1–22 (1976)
6. A.M. Turing, Systems of logic based on ordinals. Proc. Lond. Math. Soc. Ser. 2 **45**, 161–228 (1939)

Part V
Advanced Topics in Computational Complexity Theory

Chapter 13
The Probabilistic Polynomial-Time Classes

13.1 The Probabilistic Turing Machine Model

This section introduces the probabilistic TM model and the classes defined with this model.

13.1.1 The Definition

Let us begin with the definition of the probabilistic TM model.

A probabilistic TM has access to a random bit generated with a probability of $1/2$ at each step. The random bits are mutually independent, so their values have no correlations with their previous values. Put differently, the transition function of a probabilistic TM has one or two values for each state-symbol combination. At each step, if the transition function has only one value, the machine chooses the action; if the function has two values, the machine picks one of the two possibilities with a probability of $1/2$.

There are two ways to measure the computation time of a probabilistic TM. One way is to use the maximum computation time among all possible computation paths, and the other is to use the expected computation. When we use the expected computation time measurement, a probabilistic TM may run for a very long time. The time bounds in this chapter use the maximum computation time.

Definition 13.1 Let $t(n)$ be a function from $\mathbb{N}$ to $\mathbb{N}$. A probabilistic TM M is $t(n)$ time-bounded if, for all inputs x, M on input x terminates within $t(|x|)$ steps regardless of M's probabilistic choices.

© The Editor(s) (if applicable) and The Author(s), under exclusive license to
Springer Nature Switzerland AG 2025
M. Ogihara, *An Introduction to Theory of Computation*,
https://doi.org/10.1007/978-3-031-84740-0_13

Given a time-bounded probabilistic TM M, an input x, two IDs I and I', and an integer $s \geq 0$, we can assess the probability that M transitions from I to I' in s steps. The assessment can be inductive in the following manner:

- If $s = 0$, the probability is 1 if $I = I'$, and 0 otherwise.
- If $s > 0$, let I_1 and I_2 be the two possible next IDs of I, where I_1 may be identical to I_2. Let p_1 and p_2 be the probability of reaching I' in $s - 1$ steps from I_1 and I_2, respectively. The probability in question is:

$$\frac{1}{2} \cdot p_1 + \frac{1}{2} \cdot p_2 = \frac{p_1 + p_2}{2}.$$

Using the transition probability between IDs, we define our first probabilistic complexity class, BPP, as the class having **bounded-error polynomial-time randomized algorithms**.

Definition 13.2 BPP is a class of languages L for which there exists a polynomial time-bounded TM M such that for all x,

1. If $x \in L$, the probability that M on x accepts is $\geq 1/2 + \epsilon$
2. If $x \notin L$, the probability that M on x rejects $\geq 1/2 + \epsilon$

Here, ϵ is a positive constant.

We say that M's computation is **successful** if its definition is consistent with the input's membership (i.e., accepting for a member and non-accepting for a nonmember). Using this notion, we can state that a language L is in BPP if there is a polynomial time-bounded probabilistic TM whose success probability is $1/2 + \epsilon$. We also define M's **error probability** as 1 minus the success probability. Thus, BPP is the class of languages with a probabilistic polynomial-time decider whose error probability is $\leq 1/2 - \epsilon$.

The following result can be easily derived from the definition.

Proposition 13.1 BPP $=$ co$-$BPP.

Proof Let M be a probabilistic TM witnessing $L \in$ BPP. Let M' be the TM that runs the program of M and accepts/rejects its input if, and only if, M rejects/accepts. The bound on the error probability is the same between the members and nonmembers. Since M is polynomial time-bounded, M' is polynomial time-bounded. Thus, M' witnesses that $\bar{L} \in$ BPP.   □

Three subclasses of BPP exist:

- RP is the subclass of BPP where the error probability for nonmembers is 0.
- coRP is the subclass of BPP where the error probability for members is 0.
- ZPP $=$ RP $\cap$ coRP.

We often refer to BPP as "bounded-error probabilistic polynomial time," RP as "one-side bounded-error probabilistic polynomial time," and ZPP as "zero-error probabilistic polynomial time."

Proposition 13.2 RP $\subseteq$ NP, coRP $\subseteq$ coNP, *and* ZPP $\subseteq$ NP $\cap$ coNP.

The constant error bound of BPP seems too large. We can reduce the error probability of BPP languages to $2^{-r(n)}$ for an arbitrary polynomial $r(n)$. The reduction is achieved using the following Chernoff-Hoeffding bound.

Lemma 13.1 (The Chernoff-Hoeffding Bound) *Let* $X_1, \ldots, X_n$ *be independent random variables whose values are from* $\{0, 1\}$. *Let* $S = X_1 + \cdots + X_n$ *and* E *be* S's *expectation. Then, for all* $t > 0$,

$$\Pr[S \geq E + t] \leq \exp\left(-\frac{2t^2}{n}\right).$$

An intuitive description of the Chernoff-Hoeffding bound is that the sum of independent Boolean variables is unlikely to be away from its expectation. With multiple executions of a bounded-error decision algorithm, we can widen the gap between the expected number of accepts when the input is a member and the expected number of accepts when the input is a nonmember.

Lemma 13.2 *Let* M *be a probabilistic TM that accepts a language* L *with a success probability of* $1/2 + \epsilon$ *for some positive* ϵ. *Let* $p(n)$ *be an arbitrary polynomial and* $c \geq \frac{1}{2\epsilon^2}$ *be an integer. Let* M' *be a probabilistic TM that, given an input* x, *simulates* M *on* x $cp(|x|)$ *times independently and accepts if, and only if, at least one-half of the simulations accept. Then, for all* x, *the following properties hold:*

1. *If* $x \in L$, *the probability that* M' *on* x *accepts is* $\geq 1 - 2^{-p(|x|)}$.
2. *If* $x \notin L$, *the probability that* M *on* x *rejects* $\geq 1 - 2^{-p(|x|)}$.

Proof Let L, M, M', p, and c be as in the hypothesis of the lemma. Let x be an input to M' and $n = |x|$. Let X_i be the variable indicating the success/failure of the i-th simulation, where $1 \leq i \leq cp(n)$; i.e., $X_i = 1$ if the i-th simulation is successful, and 0 otherwise. We know $\Pr[X_i = 1] \geq 1/2 + \epsilon$ independently for each i. We define S and E as with Lemma 13.2. Then, $E \geq (1/2 + \epsilon)(cp(n))$. Since M' takes the majority vote, it makes an error when $S < cp(n)/2$. Since $E \geq (1/2+\epsilon)(cp(n))$, an error occurs when:

$$E - S \geq \epsilon cp(n).$$

Let $t = \epsilon cp(n)$. According to Lemma 13.1, the probability that the deviation, $E - S$, is $\geq t$ is at most:

$$\exp\left(-\frac{2(\epsilon cp(n))^2}{cp(n)}\right) = \exp(-2\epsilon^2 cp(n)).$$

Since $c \geq 1/(2\epsilon^2)$, the right-hand side is at most:

$$\exp(-p(n)) < 2^{-p(n)}.$$

Thus, M' has an error probability of $< 2^{-p(n)}$.   □

13.2   Primality Testing Algorithms

The most famous problem in BPP is primality testing: a problem of testing if an integer given in binary is a prime number.

13.2.1   Number Theory Basics

We begin with a review of relevant concepts and results in number theory.

An integer m **divides** n (or m is a **divisor** of n) if the remainder of n divided by m, $n \bmod n$, is 0. In other words, m divides n if $n = dm$ for some integer d. We write $m \mid n$ to mean that m divides n. A **trivial divisor** of n is 1 and n. A **nontrivial divisor** of n is a divisor between 2 and $n - 1$. A natural number $n \geq 2$ is a **prime number** if, for all b, $2 \leq b \leq n - 1$, the remainder of n divided by b is not 0 (i.e., no integer between 2 and $n - 1$ is n's divisor). A natural number $n \geq 2$ is a **composite** number if it is not a prime number.

The list of the prime numbers <100 are:

$$2, 3, 5, 7, 11, 13, 17, 19, 23, 29, 31, 37,$$

$$43, 47, 53, 59, 61, 67, 71, 73, 79, 83, 89, 93, 97.$$

The following proposition states that each positive integer is uniquely expressed as the product of prime numbers. The proof is left to the reader (see Exercise 13.9).

Proposition 13.3 *Each integer $n \geq 1$ is uniquely decomposed as the product of distinct prime powers. In other words, for each integer $n \geq 1$, there exists exactly one combination of positive integers $k, p_1, \ldots, p_k, e_1, \ldots e_k$ such that*

$$n = (p_1)^{e_1} \cdots (p_k)^{e_k}.$$

Here, $p_1 < \cdots < p_k$ are prime numbers.

We call this decomposition the **prime factorization** of n.

Given integers m and n such that m or n is nonzero, the **greatest common divisor** (**GCD**) of m and n, denoted by $\gcd(m, n)$, is the largest positive integer d such that d is a divisor of m and n. Also, integers m and n are **relatively prime** to each other if $\gcd(m, n) = 1$. A concept related to the greatest common divisor is the **least common multiple** of nonzero integers m and n, $\mathrm{lcm}(m, n)$, which is the smallest positive integer d such that m and n divide d. For two strictly positive integers m and n, $\mathrm{lcm}(m, n)$ is given as

$$\mathrm{lcm}(m, n) = \frac{m \cdot n}{\gcd(m, n)} .$$

Both these two quantities extend to more than two numbers.

There is an efficient method for computing the GCD of two integers. The results in this chapter do not depend on the algorithm, but we present this method in Algorithm 13.1 for completeness. In the algorithm, $m \bmod n$ is the remainder of m divided by n. The algorithm computes $\gcd(m, n)$ and integers a and b such that $am + bn = \gcd(m, n)$. In the algorithm, $am + bn = g$ is an invariant condition of the loop; i.e., it is a condition that is maintained before and after executing the loop's body. Another invariant is e, which is the number of exchanges that occurred between m and n.

Algorithm 13.1 A recursive method for computing $\gcd(m, n)$

```
 1: procedure GCD(m, n)
 2:     m ≥ 1 and n ≥ 1;
 3:     a ← 0; b ← 1; g ← n;                          ▷ am + bn = g
 4:     e ← 0;
 5:     while m > 0 do
 6:         if m < n then
 7:             exchange values between m and n;
 8:             exchange values between a and b;
 9:             e ← e + 1;
10:         else
11:             r ← m mod n;
12:             d ← (m − r)/n;
13:             a ← 1 − d · a;
14:             b ← −d · b;
15:             g ← r;
16:         end if
17:     end while
18:     if e is even then
19:         return (a, b, g);
20:     else
21:         return (b, a, g);
22:     end if
23: end procedure
```

In primality testing, **congruence classes** play a crucial role.

Let $n \geq 2$ be an integer. We say an integer a is **congruent** to another integer b **modulo** n if n divides the difference $a - b$ and write $a \equiv b \pmod{n}$. With Z_n, we denote the set of numbers reduced using the congruence modulo n. There are n

congruence classes in Z_n. We denote the class equivalent to a with $[a]_n$. The typical representatives are $0, \ldots, n-1$, but -1 also serves as a representative for $[n-1]$. If the modulus n is evident from the context, we write $[a]$, or simply a, to mean the modulo-n congruence class, including a.

The set Z_n is an n-element **commutative ring** since it has the following properties:

- Z_n is an additive group.

    - Z_n is closed under addition with $[0]$ as the identity element.
    - Each element $[a]$ has the negative element $[-a]$.
    - The addition admits the associative law; i.e., for all a, b, and c:

$$([a] + [b]) + [c] = [a] + ([b] + [c]).$$

    - The addition admits the commutative law; i.e., for all a and b:

$$[a] + [b] = [b] + [a].$$

- Z_n is a multiplicative monoid.

    - Z_n is closed under multiplication with the identity element $[1]$.
    - The multiplication admits the associative law; i.e., for all a, b, and c:

$$([a] \cdot [b]) \cdot [c] = [a] \cdot ([b] \cdot [c]).$$

    - The multiplication admits the commutative law; i.e., for all a and b:

$$[a] \cdot [b] = [b] \cdot [a].$$

- The combination of multiplication and addition admits the distributive laws; i.e., for all a, b, and c:

$$([a] + [b]) \cdot [c] = [a] \cdot [c] + [b] \cdot [c] \text{ and}$$
$$[c] \cdot ([a] + [b]) = [c] \cdot [a] + [c] \cdot [b].$$

In addition to Z_n, we consider Z_n^*. Z_n^* is the set of congruence classes of n that are relatively prime to n (i.e., each member $[a]$ satisfies $\gcd(a, n) = 1$). Z_n^* is a commutative multiplicative group with $[1]$ as the identity element. When n is a prime number, Z_n^* consists of all the $n-1$ congruence classes other than 0. When n is a composite number, the size of Z_n^* is less than $n-1$. For example, Z_5^* consists of four classes, $[1]_5$, $[2]_5$, $[3]_5$, and $[4]_5$, while Z_6^* consists of just two congruence classes, $[1]_6$ and $[5]_6$.

13.2.1.1   Fermat's Little Theorem

The main idea of the primality testing algorithm is the following **Fermat's little theorem**.

Theorem 13.1 (Fermat's Little Theorem) *For all odd prime numbers p and all nonzero $a \in Z_n^*$, $a^{p-1} \equiv 1 \pmod{p}$.*

Proof Let p be an odd prime number. Let a be an integer, $1 \leq a \leq p - 1$. Think of $p - 1$ multiples of a as follows:

$$1 \cdot a, 2 \cdot a, \ldots, (p - 1) \cdot a.$$

Since p is a prime number, none of the products are multiples of p. Also, none of the two different multiples of $p - 1$ are equal. Thus, as congruence classes, we have:

$$[1 \cdot a] \cdot [2 \cdot a] \cdots [(p - 1) \cdot a] = [1] \cdots [p - 1].$$

The left-hand side is equal to:

$$([1] \cdots [p - 1]) \cdot [a]^{p-1}.$$

The product $[1] \cdots \cdots [p - 1]$ is not 0, so can simply the equation by dividing both sides by its inverse. This produces:

$$[a]^{p-1} = [1].$$

By removing the $[\cdot]$ notation, we get $a^{p-1} \equiv 1 \pmod{p}$. $\qquad \qquad \square$

The theorem raises hopes that we can test the primality of an odd integer $n \geq 3$ by checking if for some a such that $1 \leq a \leq n - 1$, n fails to satisfy $a^{n-1} \equiv 1 \bmod n$. Unfortunately, satisfying $a^{n-1} \equiv 1 \pmod{n}$ for all a such that $\gcd(a, n) = 1$ does not guarantee the primality. There are composite numbers n such that for all a relatively prime to n, $a^{n-1} \equiv 1 \pmod{n}$. We call such numbers the **Carmichael numbers**. There are infinitely many Carmichael numbers, and their existence makes it impossible to use Fermat's little theorem to detect compositeness. As we will see later in this chapter, we can test the primality of n by examining how the series $a, a^2, \ldots, a^{n-1}$ approaches 1 for a random a.

13.2.1.2   The Chinese Remainder Theorem

We build the test using the following theorem, called the **Chinese Remainder Theorem**.

Theorem 13.2 (The Chinese Remainder Theorem) *Let $k \geq 2$. Let $n_1, \ldots, n_k$ be positive integers that are relatively prime to each other. Let $N = n_1 \cdots n_k$. Let $r_1, \ldots, r_k$ be integers such that for all i, $0 \leq r_i \leq n_i$. There exists exactly one $R, 0 \leq R \leq N - 1$, such that $R \equiv r_i \pmod{n_i}$ for all i.*

Proof We can prove the theorem by induction on k. The base case is $k = 2$. We claim that integers m_1 and m_2 exist such that

$$m_1 n_1 + m_2 n_2 = 1.$$

We prove the existence by contradiction. Assume that the smallest positive integer you can construct as $m_1 n_1 + m_2 n_2$ is $d > 1$. Since n_1 and n_2 are relatively prime to each other, d is relatively prime to n_1 or n_2. Suppose d is relatively prime to n_1. Let $n_1 = sd + t$, where s is the quotient of n_1 divided by d and t the remainder. Then:

$$s(m_1 n_1 + m_2 n_2) = sd = n_1 - t,$$

so:

$$t = n_1 - s(m_1 n_1 + m_2 n_2) = (1 - s m_1) n_1 - s m_2 n_2.$$

The same can be done for n_2 if n_2 is relatively prime to d. In both cases, $1 \leq t < d$. This contradicts the minimality of d. Thus, the desired m_1 and m_2 exist.

Now we define $R = m_2 n_2 r_1 + m_1 n_1 r_2 + \ell n_1 n_2$. Here, we choose ℓ so that R falls between 0 and $n_1 n_2 - 1$. We have:

$$
\begin{aligned}
R &= m_1 n_1 r_2 + m_2 n_2 r_1 + \ell n_1 n_2 \\
  &= \ell n_1 n_2 + m_1 n_1 r_2 - m_1 n_1 r_1 + m_1 n_1 r_1 + m_2 n_2 r_1 \\
  &= \ell n_1 n_2 + m_1 n_1 (r_2 - r_1) + (m_1 n_1 + m_2 n_2) r_1 \\
  &= \ell n_1 n_2 + m_1 n_1 (r_2 - r_1) + r_1 \\
  &= (\ell n_2 + m_1 (r_2 - r_1)) n_1 + r_1.
\end{aligned}
$$

Thus, $R \equiv r_1 \pmod{n_1}$. Additionally:

$$
\begin{aligned}
R &= m_2 n_2 r_1 + m_1 n_1 r_2 + \ell n_1 n_2 \\
  &= \ell n_1 n_2 + m_2 n_2 r_1 - m_2 n_2 r_2 + m_2 n_2 r_2 + m_1 n_1 r_2 \\
  &= \ell n_1 n_2 + m_2 n_2 (r_1 - r_2) + (m_1 n_1 + m_2 n_2) r_2 \\
  &= \ell n_1 n_2 + m_2 n_2 (r_1 - r_2) + r_2 \\
  &= (\ell n_1 + m_2 (r_1 - r_2)) n_2 + r_2.
\end{aligned}
$$

Thus, $R \equiv r_2 \pmod{n_2}$, and the claim holds for $k = 2$.

For the induction step, suppose $k \geq 3$, and the claim holds for all smaller values of k. Let $N_0 = n_1 \cdots n_{k-1}$ and $R_0, 0 \leq R_0 \leq N_0 - 1$, be such that for all i such that $1 \leq i \leq k - 1$, $R_0 \equiv r_i \pmod{n_i}$. We apply the base case to the pair N_0 and n_k to find m_1 and m_2 such that

$$m_1' N_0 + m_2' n_k = 1.$$

We then define:

$$R = m_2' n_k R_0 + m_1' N_0 r_k + \ell' N_0 n_k.$$

Here, ℓ' puts R between 0 and $N_0 n_t - 1$. We have:

$$
\begin{aligned}
R &= \ell' N_0 n_t + (m_2' n_t R_0 - m_2' n_t r_t) + (m_2' n_t r_t + m_1' N_0 r_t) \\
&= \ell' N_0 n_t + m_2' n_t (R_0 - r_t) + (m_2' n_t + m_1' N_0) r_t \\
&\equiv r_t \pmod{n_t},
\end{aligned}
$$

and similarly:

$$R \equiv R_0 \pmod{N_0}.$$

Because of the definition of R_0, the last congruence gives $R \equiv r_i \pmod{n_i}$ for all i such that $1 \leq i \leq k - 1$. Thus, the claim holds for k.

Hence, the claim holds for all k, so the induction is complete. The proof of R's uniqueness is left to the reader (see Exercise 13.13). $\square$

The following result immediately follows from the Chinese Remainder Theorem. We leave the proof to the reader (see Exercise 13.14).

Corollary 13.1 *Let $k \geq 2$. Let $n_1, \ldots, n_k$ be positive integers that are relatively prime to each other. Let $N = n_1 \cdots n_k$. Then, for all integers r, $r \equiv 1 \pmod{N}$ if, and only if, $r \equiv 1 \pmod{n_i}$ for all i. Additionally, for all integers r, $r \equiv -1 \pmod{N}$ if, and only if, $r \equiv -1 \pmod{n_i}$ for all i.*

13.2.1.3 Generators

Since Z_n^* is a multiplicative group, for each $a \in Z_n^*$, a positive integer k exists such that $a^k \equiv 1 \pmod{n}$ (see Exercise 13.11). The smallest positive integer d is the **order** of a in Z_n^*. We denote it with $\mathrm{ord}_n(a)$. By convention, if $a \notin Z_n^*$, the order of a is ∞.

Fermat's little theorem states that for all prime numbers p and integers a not divisible by p, the order of a is a divisor of $p - 1$. Is there an integer a whose order is $p-1$? If an element a has order $p-1$, then $a, a^2, \ldots, a^{p-1}$ are different elements and thus cover the entire Z_p^*. We call an element with an order $p-1$ a **generator** for Z_n^*.

For each power of a prime number p^e such that p is a prime number and e is a positive integer, $\varphi(p^e) = p^{e-1}(p-1)$. $\varphi(p^e)$ is the cardinality of the multiplicative group $Z_{p^e}^*$. The proof of the following theorem is complex. We give only the statement of the theorem.

Theorem 13.3 *For every odd prime number p and a positive integer e, $(Z_{p^e})^*$ has a generator. The order of the generators is $\varphi(p^e) = p^{e-1}(p-1)$.*

We can say more about the existence of generators. We leave the proof of the following proposition to the reader (see Exercise 13.15).

Proposition 13.4 *If Z_n^* has a generator, Z_n^* has $\varphi(\varphi(n))$ generators.*

We also have the following result. Again, we leave the proof to the reader (see Exercise 13.16).

Proposition 13.5 *If g is a generator in Z_n^* and e is a positive integer, $\mathrm{ord}_n(g^e) = \varphi(n)/(\gcd(\varphi(n), e))$.*

13.2.2 The Miller-Rabin Test

Now, we state our probabilistic primality testing algorithm. Primality testing is vital in modern cryptography, specifically in the celebrated Rivest-Shamir-Adleman security (hereby RSA). The RSA cryptography uses the following simple property:

If an integer triple (n, e, d) satisfies $ed \equiv 1 \pmod{\varphi(n)}$, then for all $m \in Z_n$,
$$(m^e)^d \equiv m.$$

RSA's participants independently select their own triple (n, e, d) and publish (n, e). To send a secret message to a recipient whose published key is (n, e), the sender converts the message as a series of numbers in Z_n, raises each number to the power of e in modulo n, and sends the sequence of powers to the recipient. The recipient raises the received numbers to the power of d modulo n and recovers the message.

Traditional cryptosystems required $M(M-1)/2$ sets of keys to serve M people for their pairwise secret communications. The public-key system was revolutionary in that the system with M people needs only M sets of keys because communications to a receiver use the same set of keys.

The security of the system comes from the difficulty of computing $\varphi(n)$ without knowing n's prime factors. A typical choice for n is the product of two large primes, say p and q, where $\varphi(n) = (p-1)(q-1)/\gcd(p-1, q-1)$. For each selection of e that is relatively prime to $\varphi(n)$, d can be easily computed using the process of computing $\gcd(e, \varphi(n))$. Assuming that factoring large integers is a practically impossible problem, an eavesdropper cannot compute d from n and e without knowing the prime factors p and q.

If we take the difficulty of factoring integers for granted, a crucial question is finding large prime numbers. The **prime number theorem** states that the proportion of prime numbers below X is $\Omega(1/\log(X))$. Thus, you can expect to encounter a prime number by selecting $\log X$ candidates below X. But how do you test if a number is a prime number? This question leads us to whether or not we can effectively test the primality of any given number. Formally, we consider the following two decision problems in Definition 13.3.

Definition 13.3 PRIMES $= \{n \mid n$ is a prime number$\}$ and COMPOSITES $= \{n \mid n \geq 2$ is a composite number$\}$.

In this section, we prove the following:

Theorem 13.4 PRIMES *is in* coRP, *and so it is in* BPP.

Proof We use the so-called **Miller-Rabin test** to show PRIMES $\in$ coRP. Here is a brief description of the algorithm. After eliminating nontrivial cases, we decompose $n - 1$ as an integer product $b2^d$ where b is an odd integer. Then, we select $a \in Z_n$ uniformly at random and compute, in modulo n, the following series:

$$a^b, a^{b \cdot 2}, a^{b \cdot 4}, \ldots, a^{b \cdot 2^d}.$$

If n is a prime number, the final quantity is 1, and if the series does not start with 1, the last value before 1 is -1. So, if the final value is not 1 or the last value before 1 is not -1, n is a composite number. We will show that if n is a composite number, the probability of selecting an a witnessing the compositeness is $\geq 1/2$.

The algorithm relies on the ability to select a uniformly at random from $\{0, \ldots, n-1\}$. It is tempting to assume a universal random number generator for the purpose. However, our TM model permits at most two possible moves for each state-symbol combination, and the selection between the two occurs with a probability of $1/2$. So, assuming the ability to produce a random a for an arbitrary n may be unrealistic. This leads to the question of whether or not selecting a for a fixed number of branches is possible. Indeed, we can do that with an exponentially small probability of failure.

The selection of a goes as follows:

We choose an integer ℓ greater than the bit length of n and a positive integer k. We let $N = 2^{k\ell}$, $r = N \bmod n$, and $s = N - r$. We then pick ℓ independent bits and compute x as the ℓ-bit integer these independent bits collectively represent. The range of x is $[0, N-1]$ and each x appears with a probability $1/N$. We then check if $x < s$. If $x < x$, we set $a = x \bmod n$. Otherwise, we assert that the random number generation was unsuccessful. Assume that $\ell = k\lceil \log n \rceil$. Then, the probability of failure is:

$$\frac{r}{N} \leq \frac{n-1}{N} < \frac{n}{N} \leq \frac{n}{n^k} = \frac{1}{n^{k-1}}.$$

We call the algorithm the "primitive random number generator" (see Algorithm 13.2).

Algorithm 13.2 An algorithm for primitive random number generation

---
1: **procedure** RANDOM-NUMBER(n, k)
2:     $\ell \leftarrow k \lceil \log n \rceil$;
3:     $N \leftarrow 2^{\ell}$;
4:     $r \leftarrow N \bmod n$;
5:     $s \leftarrow N - r$;
6:     generate ℓ independent random bits $\beta_1, \ldots, \beta_\ell$ and form $x, 0 \leq x \leq N - 1$;
7:     **if** $a \geq s$ **then**
8:         return -1, indicating a failure;
9:     **else**
10:        return $x \bmod n$;
11:    **end if**
12: **end procedure**

We also recall the binary exponentiation algorithm (Algorithm 13.4) for computing $a^b \bmod n$ for any positive $a, b,$ and n.

Algorithm 13.3 A binary exponentiation algorithm

1: **procedure** BINARY-EXPONENTIATION(a, b, n)
2:     $denom \leftarrow a$;
3:     $prod \leftarrow 1$;
4:     **for** $i \leftarrow 1, \ldots, q$ **do**
5:         **if** $b_i = 1$ **then**
6:             $prod \leftarrow prod * denom \bmod n$;
7:         **end if**
8:     **end for**
9:     return $prod$;
10: **end procedure**

Now, we present the Miller-Rabin test in Algorithm 13.4.

Algorithm 13.4 A probabilistic primality testing

1: **procedure** PROBABILISTIC-PRIMALITY-TESTING(n)
2:   **if** $n = 2, 3$ **then**
3:     assert that n is a prime number and stop;
4:   **else if** n is even **then**
5:     assert that n is a composite number and stop;
6:   **end if**
7:   decompose $n - 1$ into $b2^d$ where b is an odd integer;
8:   $\ell \leftarrow 2\lceil \log n \rceil$;
9:   **for** $\ell + 1$ times **do**
10:     call Random-Number(n, 2) to obtain a random integer a, $0 \le a \le n - 1$;
11:     **if** the generation fails or $a = 0$ **then**
12:       advance to the next round;
13:     **end if**
14:     using Binary-Exponentiation to compute $c_0 = a^b \bmod n$;
15:     **for** $j \leftarrow 1, \ldots, d$ **do**
16:       compute $c_i = c_{i-1}^2 \bmod n$ using repeated squaring;
17:     **end for**
18:     **if** $c_d \ne 1$ **then**
19:       assert that n is a composite number and stop;
20:     **else if** for some j such that $0 \le d - 1$, $c_{j+1} = 1$ and $c_j \ne 1, n - 1$ **then**
21:       assert that n is a composite number and stop;
22:     **end if**
23:   **end for**
24:   assert that n is a prime number and stop;
25: **end procedure**

Algorithm 13.4 works correctly for $n = 3$ and all even n. Suppose $n \ge 5$ is an odd integer. Let $\rho = 2^{2\ell} \bmod n$ and $\sigma = \lfloor 2^\ell \rfloor$, i.e., the remainder and quotient of $2^{2\ell}$ divided by n. The algorithm fails if the random number generation fails or $a = 0$ is generated. Let ρ be the probability that the random number generation fails. Then, the probability of a round not making an assertion is:

$$\rho + (1 - \rho)\frac{1}{n} \le \frac{1}{n} + \frac{1}{n} = \frac{2}{n}.$$

Thus, the algorithm advances further with a probability of $\ge \frac{n-2}{n}$.

If the algorithm advances further and n is a prime number, by Fermat's little theorem, $a^{n-1} \equiv 1 \pmod{n}$. Since n is a prime number n, 1 and -1 are the only solutions for $x^2 \equiv 1 \pmod{n}$. So, $c_d = 1$ and if $c_i = 1$ and $c_{i-1} \ne 1, c_{i-1} = n - 1$. Thus, n passes the test.

If the algorithm advances further and n is a composite number, we analyze the probability that the algorithm asserts that n is prime as follows:

Suppose $\gcd(a, n) = 2$. Then, $c_0, \ldots, c_d$ are all multiples of $\gcd(a, n)$, which is ≥ 2, and so the test fails. Suppose $\gcd(a, n) = 1$. Let the following be the prime factorization of n:

$$n = p_1^{e_1} \cdots p_k^{e_k}.$$

Here, $p_1, \ldots, p_k$ are odd prime numbers in the increasing order, $e_1, \ldots, e_k$ are strictly positive, and if $k = 1$, $e_1 \geq 2$.

For each i, let $n_i = p_i^{e_i}$ and g_i be an arbitrary generator of $Z_{n_i}^*$. Since $n_1, \ldots, n_k$ are relatively prime to each other, the Chinese Remainder Theorem states that a's congruence class in $Z_{n_i}^*$. Let $r_1, \ldots, r_k$ be a's congruence classes in $Z_{n_1}^*, \ldots, Z_{n_k}^*$, respectively. If $r_i^{n-1} \not\equiv 1 \pmod{n_i}$ for some n_i, the Chinese Remainder Theorem gives that $a^{n-1} \not\equiv 1 \pmod{n}$. Since we are assuming that $a^{n-1} \equiv 1 \pmod{n}$, $r_i^{n-1} \equiv 1 \pmod{n_i}$ for all i. Because we are assuming a is relatively prime to n, the selection of r_i is equivalent to selecting u_i uniformly from $[0, \varphi(n_i) - 1]$ and then setting $r_i = g_i^{u_i}$.

Since b and d are fixed throughout the execution of the algorithm, and the calculation starts with powering a to a^b, we can view that the generator g_i is already raised to the power of b. More specifically, let $h_i = g_i^b \bmod n_i$ and $\mu_i = \mathrm{ord}_{n_i}(h_i)$. We can view the selection process as follows:

- We select t_i from $0, \ldots, \mu_i - 1$ uniformly, with each having the probability of μ_i to be selected.
- We then compute $r_i = (h_i)^{t_i} \bmod n_i$ and integrate the r_is into a.

Since b is an odd number and the generator's order is a multiple of 2, we see that μ_i is an even number. The test we are conducting is the occurrence of -1 as the value immediately before the first occurrence of 1, so the value we choose for t_i has a property that $\mu_i / \gcd(\mu_i, t_i)$ is a power of 2.

We consider two cases: $k = 1$ and $k \geq 2$. First, suppose $k = 1$. Then, $n - 1 = (p_1)^{e_1} - 1$. The quantity is not a multiple of p_1, so b is not a multiple of p_1. Since $\varphi(n_1)$ is a multiple of p_1, μ_1 is a multiple of p_1. This means the probability that the r_1's order is a power of 2 is at most $1/p_1 < 1/2$.

Next, suppose $k \geq 2$. For each i, $\mu_i / \gcd(\mu_i, t_i)$ is a power of 2, and at least two possibilities exist for the power. The possibilities are as follows:

- t_i is odd.
- t_i is divisible by 2 but not 4.
- t_i is divisible by 4 but not 8.
- etc.

Since we make a uniform choice for t_i, none of these cases occur with a probability $> 1/2$. We translate these possibilities into the value of c_js. We see that the translated events are as follows:

- $c_0 \equiv 1 \pmod{n_i}$.
- $c_0 \equiv -1 \pmod{n_i}$.
- $c_1 \equiv -1 \pmod{n_i}$.
- etc.

In addition, these events occur with a probability $\leq 1/2$. For n to pass the test, the event must be equal for all i. Since $k \geq 2$, and at least two choices exist for the event, the probability that n passes the test is at most $2(1/2)^k = 1/2$.

Summarizing the analysis above, if we make the algorithm assert n as a prime number if the random number generation fails, a composite number n passes one round of test with a probability of:

$$\frac{2}{n} + \left(1 - \frac{2}{n}\right) \cdot \frac{1}{2} = \frac{1}{2} + \frac{1}{n} = \frac{1}{2}\left(1 + \frac{1}{2n}\right).$$

Since we execute the test for $\ell + 1$ times independently, the probability that a composite number n passes all the tests is at most:

$$\left(\frac{1}{2}\left(1 + \frac{1}{2n}\right)\right)^{\ell+1} \leq \frac{1}{2} \cdot \left(\frac{1}{2}\right)^{\log n} \left(1 + \frac{1}{2n}\right)^{2n \cdot \frac{\ell+1}{2n}} \leq \frac{1}{2n} e^{\frac{1}{2}} \leq \frac{1}{n}.$$

This means the following:

- If n is a prime number, the algorithm asserts that with probability 1.
- If n is a composite number, the algorithm asserts that n is a prime number with probability at most $1/n$.

What is the algorithm's running time? The addition and subtraction in Z_n are executable in $O(\log n)$. The multiplication in Z_n is executable in $O((\log n)^2)$. Computing b and d requires $O(\log n)$. Using the binary exponentiation, computing the powers $c_0, \ldots, c_d$ for each a requires $O(\log n)$ multiplication, so it requires $O((\log n)^3)$ steps. The number of repetitions is $O(\log n)$, so the total computation time is $O((\log n)^4)$.

We have thus proven the theorem. $\square$

13.2.2.1   Miller's Algorithm

Algorithm 13.4 relies on the high probability of selecting a favorable witness a whenever n is a composite number. There is a formal term for the favorable a; for a composite number n and an integer a such that $1 \leq a \leq n - 1$, we say that n is **pseudoprime to the base** n if the test passes when the algorithm picks a as the base. If we use a deterministic method for generating the values for a, how many as do we need to get to one for which n is not a pseudoprime? Specifically, if we select a from the increasing sequence $2, 3, 4, 5, \cdots$, when do we get to a favorable a? A mathematical conjecture finds the smallest favorable a is $O(\log n)$. One round of algorithm execution requires $O((\log n)^3)$ steps. Based on the conjecture, the deterministic version runs in time $O((\log n)^4)$. The correctness of the conjecture is yet to be verified, but experimentally, most odd composite numbers have a witness

≤ 5. The Miller test is a special case of the Miller-Rabin test where the deterministic selection is used to pick a from the increasing sequence $2, 3, 4, \cdots$.

While the Miller-Rabin test puts PRIMES in coRP, and thus, also in coNP, we wonder if PRIMES $\in$ RP. Although we do not present the proof, it is known that PRIMES $\in$ RP, so the problem is in ZPP.

Theorem 13.5 PRIMES, COMPOSITES $\in$ ZPP.

Recall that the algorithm's action is deterministic after choosing the value for a. If we use an increasing sequence of values $2, 3, 4, \ldots$ for a, at which value of a do we find a is a composite number? Research has found that n up to $1, 373, 653$, either 2 or 3 for a works.

It is now known that PRIMES is P.

Theorem 13.6 PRIMES $\in$ P.

13.2.3   The Polynomial Zero-Testing Problem

Another example of a polynomial-time randomized algorithm is the **zero-testing of multivariate polynomials** over a finite field.

Let S be a finite field whose additive identity is 0. Let $p(x_1, \ldots, x_n)$ be a polynomial over the variables $x_1, \ldots, x_n$. Each term of the polynomial takes the form $\alpha x_1^{e_1} \cdots x_n^{e_n}$ with $\alpha \in S - \{0\}$ and $e_1, \ldots, e_n \geq 0$. The **total degree** of a term $\alpha x_1^{e_1} \cdots x_n^{e_n}$ is $e_1 + \cdots + e_n$. The **total degree** of p is the maximum total degree of its terms. The polynomial $p(x_1, \ldots, x_n)$ is a **0-polynomial** if for all $(a_1, \ldots, a_n) \in S^n$, $p(a_1, \ldots, a_n) = 0$.

Definition 13.4 The **zero-polynomial testing problem** over a finite field S is the problem of deciding, given a polynomial $p(x_1, \ldots, x_n)$ having a total degree of d, whether or not p is a 0-polynomial.

Proposition 13.6 *Let p be an n-variate polynomial over a finite field S with a total degree d. If p is not a 0-polynomial, p has no more than $d \|S\|^{n-1}$ roots.*

Proof We prove the proposition by induction on n. Let S be a finite field. Let $d \geq 1$. Suppose $p(x_1, \ldots, x_n)$ is a non-0, n-variate polynomial over a finite field S with a total degree d.

The base case is $n = 1$. Since S is a field, no pair of elements in $S - \{0\}$ produces 0 as the product. Thus, the number of roots is at most d.

For the induction step, suppose $n \geq 2$, and the claim holds for all smaller values of n. Since the total degree is at most d, we can express p as:

$$\sum_{j=0}^{d} x_1^j p_j(x_2, \ldots, x_n).$$

Here, $p_j(x_2, \ldots, x_n)$ is a polynomial over $x_2, \ldots, x_n$. Let e be the largest j such that $p_j(x_2, \ldots, x_n)$ is not a 0-polynomial. The total degree of p_j is at most $d - e$. Due to the inductive hypothesis, the number of choices for $x_2, \ldots, x_n$ to make $p_e = 0$ is $(d - e)\|S\|^{n-2}$. If the choices for $x_2, \ldots x_n$ do not reduce p_e to 0, they reduce p to a polynomial over the variable x_1 with a degree at most e. The polynomial has at most e roots. Thus, the number of choices for $x_1, \ldots, x_n$ that turn p into 0 is at most:

$$\|S\| \cdot (d - e)\|S\|^{n-2} + e \cdot \|S\|^{n-1} = d\|S\|^{n-1}.$$

Thus, the property holds for n. $\qquad\qquad\qquad\qquad\qquad\qquad\qquad\qquad\square$

Theorem 13.7 *Assuming the total degree is at most $\|S\|/2$, the zero-polynomial testing problem is in* BPP.

Proof Suppose we select $x_1, \ldots, x_n$ uniformly at random. Like with the algorithm for primality testing, we may assert that the test is inclusive with a small probability. Otherwise, we evaluate the polynomial at the chosen $x_1, \ldots, x_n$ and assert the polynomial to be a non-0 polynomial if, and only if, the value is not 0. $\qquad\square$

The BPP-membership of the zero-polynomial testing problem has many applications, which this book does not cover.

13.3 Relations Between BPP and PH

What is the relationship between BPP and NP? From the definition, we know that RP $\subseteq$ NP and coRP $\subseteq$ coNP. Whether NP $\subseteq$ BPP or BPP $\subseteq$ NP is unknown, but we can show that BPP $\subseteq \Sigma_2^p$.

Theorem 13.8 BPP $\subseteq \Sigma_2^p$.

Proof Overview
Let $L \in$ BPP. Lemma 13.2 gives a probabilistic TM M whose running time is $q(n)$, and success probability (accepting when the input is a member and rejecting when the input is a nonmember) is $1 - 2^{-n}$. We define an easy-to-compute bijection from the set of all computation paths to itself. The bijection uses each computation path as its seed, so the number of bijections is $2^{q(n)}$. For $x \in L$, there is a small set of seeds such that every computation path of M on x is an accepting path after applying the bijection to the path with one of the seeds; there is no such set if $x \notin L$. The existence of such a set of seeds is testable in Σ_2^p.

Proof Let L be a language in BPP. Because of Lemma 13.2, a machine M exists with an error probability less than 2^{-n}. Let $q(n)$ be a polynomial bounding the running time of M.

Let x be an arbitrary input of M and $n = |x|$. Let $m = q(n)$ and $S = \Sigma^m$. S is the set of all computation paths of M on x. For all u and $y \in S$, we define $u \oplus y$ as the bit-wise exclusive-or of u and y. The operation $\oplus$ is symmetric. For all y and $z \in S$, there exists exactly one $u \in S$ such that $u \oplus y = z$. We define $Q(u, y)$ as a condition stating that $u \oplus y$ is an accepting computation path of M on x.

For each u, let $W(u)$ be the set of all y such that $Q(u, y)$ holds. We have the following properties:

1. If $x \in L$, $\|S\| - \|W(u)\| < 2^{-n}\|S\|$.
2. If $x \notin L$, $\|W(u)\| < 2^{-n}\|S\|$.

We claim:

$$x \in L \iff (\exists(u_1, \ldots, u_m) \in S^m)[W(u_1) \cup \cdots \cup W(u_m) = S].$$

In other words,

$$x \in L \text{ if, and only if, we can pick } u_1, \ldots, u_m \text{ from } S \text{ so that for all}$$
$$y \in S, y \in W(u_i) \text{ for some } i.$$

Let's prove the claim. First, suppose $x \in L$. For each $y \in S$, the proportion of $u \in S$ such that $y \notin W(u)$ is $< 2^{-n}$, so the proportion of $u_1, \ldots, u_m$ such that $y \notin W(u_i)$ for every i, is $(2^{-n})^m = 2^{-nm}$. We consider the proportion of $(u_1, \ldots, u_m) \in S^m$ such that for some $y \in S$, $y \notin W(u_i)$ for all i. There are 2^m possible choices of y, so the proportion is at most $2^m \cdot 2^{-nm} < 1$. This implies that there exists $(u_1, \ldots, u_m) \in S^m$, $S = W(u_1) \cup \cdots \cup W(u_m)$.

On the other hand, suppose $x \notin L$. Since $\|W(u)\|/\|S\| < 2^{-n}$, for all $u_1, \ldots, u_m$, $\|W(u_1) \cup \cdots \cup W(u_m)\|/\|S\| < n2^{-n} < 1$. Thus, for all $(u_1, \ldots, u_m) \in S^m$, there exists some y such that $y \notin W(u_1) \cup \cdots \cup W(u_m)$.

The claim holds.

For all $u, y, z \in S$, if $z = u \oplus y$, then $y = z \oplus u$. The condition $W(u_1) \cup \cdots \cup W(u_m) = S$ is equivalent to the condition:

$$\text{for all } z \in S, \text{ one of } Q(u_1 \oplus z), \ldots, Q(u_m \oplus z) \text{ holds.}$$

The condition is in Π_2^p because Q evaluates the computation of M on one path. Thus, L's membership condition above is in Σ_2^p.

The membership $L \in \Pi_2^p$ holds because BPP = co$-$BPP. $\square$

13.4 The Class PP

Each language in BPP has a polynomial time-bounded probabilistic TM that correctly decides the membership with a $1/2 + \epsilon$ probability. The constant ϵ is the probabilistic machine's advantage over a random membership guess. We now introduce the probabilistic polynomial-time class PP, whose advantage is negligible.

Definition 13.5 A language $L \in$ PP if a probabilistic polynomial-time TM M exists such that for all inputs x, $x \in L$ if, and only if, M on x accepts with probability at least $1/2$.

We can easily see that BPP and NP are subclasses of PP.

Proposition 13.7 BPP $\subseteq$ PP.

Proposition 13.8 NP $\subseteq$ PP.

Additionally, we have:

Proposition 13.9 PP $=$ co$-$PP.

We know that BPP $\subseteq \Sigma_2^p$. Does a similar containment hold for PP, i.e., PP $\subseteq \Sigma_k^p$ for some k? The answer is no, unless the polynomial hierarchy is finite, due to the following **Toda's theorem**, which we state without a proof.

Theorem 13.9 (Toda's Theorem) PH $\subseteq$ P^{PP}.

Exercises

13.1 An alternate definition of a probabilistic TM uses a read-only one-way infinite random-bit tape on which an infinitely long binary string appears at the start. The bit at each position is chosen independently with probability $1/2$. Prove this model is equivalent to the one given in this chapter.

13.2 An alternate definition of BPP uses $1/3$ as the threshold instead of $1/2 + \epsilon$. Prove that the two definitions are equal.

13.3 Let $p(n)$ be a polynomial. Let M be a probabilistic TM with a property that if M on input x accepts, then M accepts in $\le p(|x|)$ steps. Show that a probabilistic TM N and a polynomial $q(n)$ exist such that for all inputs x, N on x halts in $\le q(|x|)$ steps and the probability of M on x accepts equals the likelihood of N on x accepts.

13.4 We use the majority vote on the outcomes derived from multiple executions of a probabilistic TM to amplify the success probability. Prove that, for languages in RP, we can replace the majority vote with the condition "the machine accepts on at least one execution" for amplifying the success probability. Assuming that the success probability is $1/2 + \epsilon$, analyze how many executions will be necessary to increase the likelihood to $1 - (1/2)^n$ for inputs with a length of n.

13.5 Prove that $P^{BPP} = BPP$.

Hint: Think of a polynomial time-bounded deterministic oracle TM M that accepts a language in P^{BPP} with $A \in BPP$ as the oracle. Let N be a probabilistic TM with which $A \in BPP$. We can assume that N's probability of failure is exponentially small. We can simulate M by handling each query with a simulation of N.

13.6 Prove Proposition 13.2.

13.7 Prove if $NP \subseteq BPP$, $NP = RP$.

Hint: Assuming a BPP-algorithm for SAT, you can find the maximum satisfying assignment and verify the correctness of the assignment.

13.8 Combine known results to prove $NP \subseteq BPP \Rightarrow \Sigma_2^p = \Pi_2^p$.

13.9 Prove Proposition 13.3; i.e., each integer $n \geq 1$ is uniquely expressible as the product of distinct prime powers.

13.10 With the GCD algorithm presented in Algorithm 13.1, if $m > 0$, the value of n will become $\leq n/2$ in one or two executions of the loop-body. Prove this property. Then, prove that the running time of the algorithm is $O((\log(m + n))^3)$.

13.11 Prove that for all integers $n \geq 2$ and $a \in Z_n^*$, a positive integer k exists such that $a^k \equiv 1 \pmod{n}$.

13.12 Prove if p is an odd prime number, and $e \geq 1$ is an integer, then the equation $x^2 \equiv 1 \pmod{p^e}$ has only ± 1 as its solution.

Hint: Examine the coefficients of $\alpha p \pm 1 \pmod{p^e}$.

13.13 Prove that the R in the Chinese Remainder Theorem (Theorem 13.2) is unique.

13.14 Prove Corollary 13.1.

13.15 Prove Proposition 13.4.

13.16 Prove Proposition 13.5.

13.17 Prove that $BPP \subseteq PP$.

13.18 Prove that $NP \subseteq PP$.

13.19 Prove that $PP = co{-}PP$.

13.20 Based on Toda's theorem, show that if $PP \subseteq \Sigma_k^p$, then $PH = \Delta_{k+1}^p$.

Bibliographic Notes and Further Reading

Probabilistic TM models and the classes BPP, RP, coRP, ZPP, and PP were introduced by Gill [6]. The results about BPP appearing in Exercises 13.5 and 13.7 are by Ko [8]. Simon's independent work introduced and studied the class PP (under a different name of CP, meaning the "counting polynomial time"). Simon also considered the class $C_=P$, a superclass of coNP, and a subclass of PP. Toda's theorem [18] is by Toda. Related to this, Toda and the author of this textbook showed that an analog of Toda's theorem, $NP^{C_=P}$, holds for $C_=P$ [19].

The inclusion of BPP in the polynomial hierarchy theorem 13.8 is due to the independent work of Lautemann [9] and Sipser [16].

The Chernoff-Hoeffding bound integrates independent but related results by Chernoff [4] and Hoeffding [7].

Many accessible elementary number theory books exist. The reader may consult with [3]. Miller's test is by Miller [10]. Miller's conjecture about the minimum base serving as a witness for compositeness is based on the generalized Riemann hypothesis. Rabin's primality testing algorithm is fully probabilistic and appears in [13]. While the Miller-Rabin test puts PRIMES in coRP, and thus, in coNP, it was unknown if PRIMES ∈ RP. The result about the smallest bases with which pseudoprimes can be detect is by Pomerance, Selfridge, and Wagstaff [11].

Theorem 13.5 is by Adleman and Huang [1]. Its proof is more than 100 pages in length. Before the resolution, the only known result was PRIMES ∈ NP by Pratt [12]. Theorem 13.6 is by Agrawal, Kayal, and Saxena [2]. The RSA cryptography is by Rivest, Shamir, and Adleman [14]. Although not covered in this chapter, Solovay and Strassen [17] proposed a primality testing algorithm that uses Euler's primality criterion based on the Jacobi symbol. Compared with PRIMES ∈ coRP, showing PRIMES ∈ RP was more challenging.

The zero-polynomial testing algorithm was discovered independently by Demillo and Lipton [5], Zippel [20], and Schwartz [15].

References

1. L.M. Adleman, M.-D.A. Huang, *Primality Testing and Abelian Varieties Over Finite Fields* (Springer, Berlin, 2006)
2. M. Agrawal, N. Kayal, N. Saxena, PRIMES is in P. Ann. Math. **160**(2), 781–793 (2004)
3. J.A. Anderson, J.M. Bell, *Number Theory with Applications*, 1st edn. (Prentice-Hall, Upper Saddle River, 1997).
4. H. Chernoff, A measure of asymptotic efficiency for tests of a hypothesis based on the sum of observations. Ann. Math. Stat. **23**(4), 493–507 (1952)
5. R.A. Demillo, R.J. Lipton, A probabilistic remark on algebraic program testing. Inform. Process. Lett. **7**(4), 193–195 (1978)
6. J. Gill, Computational complexity of probabilistic Turing machines. SIAM J. Comput. **6**(4), 675–695 (1977)
7. W. Hoeffding, Probability inequalities for sums of bounded random variables. J. Am. Stat. Assoc. **58**(301), 13–30 (1963)
8. K.-I. Ko, Some observations on the probabilistic algorithms and NP-hard problems. Inform. Process. Lett. **14**(1), 39–43 (1982)
9. C. Lautemann, BPP and the polynomial hierarchy. Inform. Process. Lett. **17**(4), 215–217 (1983)
10. G.L. Miller, Riemann's hypothesis and tests for primality. J. Comp. Syst. Sci. **13**(3), 300–317 (1976)
11. C. Pomerance, J.L. Selfridge, S.S. Wagstaff, The pseudoprimes to $24 \cdot 10^9$. Math. Comp. **35**, 1003–1026 (1980)
12. V.R. Pratt, Every prime has a succinct certificate. SIAM J. Comput. **4**(3), 214–220 (1975)
13. M.O. Rabin, Probabilistic algorithm for testing primality. J. Number Theory **12**(1), 128–138 (1980)

14. R.L. Rivest, A. Shamir, L.M. Adleman, A method for obtaining digital signatures and public-key cryptosystems. Commun. ACM **21**(2), 120–126 (1978)
15. J.T. Schwartz, Fast probabilistic algorithms for verification of polynomial identities. J. ACM **27**(4), 701–717 (1980)
16. M.J. Sipser, A complexity theoretic approach to randomness, in *Proceedings of the Fifteenth Annual ACM Symposium on Theory of Computing, STOC '83* (1983), pp. 330–335
17. R. Solovay, V. Strassen, A fast Monte-Carlo test for primality. SIAM J. Comput. **6**(1), 84–85 (1977)
18. S. Toda, PP is as hard as the polynomial-time hierarchy. SIAM J. Comput. **20**(5), 865–877 (1991)
19. S. Toda, M. Ogiwara, Counting classes are at least as hard as the polynomial-time hierarchy. SIAM J. Comput. **21**(2), 316–328 (1992)
20. R. Zippel, Probabilistic algorithms for sparse polynomials, in *Symbolic and Algebraic Computation*, ed. by E.W. Ng (Springer, Berlin, Heidelberg, 1979), pp. 216–226

Chapter 14
Circuit Complexity and Unambiguity

14.1 The Circuit Computation Models

In this section, we study the circuit model and the class of languages recognized by a series of polynomial-size circuits.

14.1.1 The Boolean Circuit Model

The primary circuit model is the **Boolean circuit model**, which operates on Boolean values. A Boolean circuit is a vertex-labeled acyclic directed graph, whose vertices are called the **gates** and are expected to compute Boolean functions. The vertex labels are the Boolean functions they compute. We call the edges connecting between gates the **wires**. The source vertices of the circuit are for receiving the circuit's input and are called the **input gates**. The value at each input gate is fixed before the computation according to the input received. The value a gate computes is transmitted along its outgoing edges to each destination vertex. Each non-input vertex computes its function according to the input values it receives. The circuit's sink vertices serve as the **output gates**. We can envision Boolean signals traveling from the input and output gates. We sometimes call Boolean circuits **feed-forward Boolean circuits** to reflect upon this idea. The number of source vertices is the **input size**, and the number of sink vertices is the **output size**. Each non-input vertex has a Boolean function as its label, and it computes the Boolean function of the values calculated at its source gates. The in-degree of the gate matches the argument number of the Boolean function.

Two quantities exist for measuring a circuit's resource requirements: the **size** and **depth**. The size of a circuit is the number of vertices in the network, and the depth is the length of the longest source-to-sink path in the network. For a circuit C,

© The Editor(s) (if applicable) and The Author(s), under exclusive license to
Springer Nature Switzerland AG 2025
M. Ogihara, *An Introduction to Theory of Computation*,
https://doi.org/10.1007/978-3-031-84740-0_14

size(C) and depth(C) represent the size and the depth of **C**, respectively. Note that depth(C) $\leq$ size(C).

Given a circuit C and its input x, we denote its output with $C(x)$. Since a circuit is acyclic, we determine $C(x)$ by stratifying the gates into levels according to the distance from the input gates, where the input gates are at level 0, and the output gates are at level depth(C). The level of a non-input gate is 1 plus the maximum level of the gates from which the gate receives the input signals.

We classify circuits according to the **basis**, the set of functions that can appear at the gates. Any complete Boolean basis can be used to compute any Boolean function using a circuit. The most typical basis is $\{\vee, \wedge, \neg\}$; $\{\vee, \wedge\}$ can be used instead. A circuit with $\{\vee, \wedge\}$ as the basis is a **monotone** circuit. For a monotone circuit, we augment its input by adding the negation of each input value, which doubles the number of source vertices in the graph.

We classify circuits by the maximum number of inputs we can feed to the basis functions. When the in-degree is 2 for both types, a circuit is a **bounded fan-in circuit**. When the in-degree has no upper bounds, a circuit is an **unbounded fan-in circuit**. When the in-degree is at most two for only one type, a circuit is a **semi-unbounded fan-in circuit**.

When drawing a circuit, we often place the input gates at the bottom and the output gates at the top. Figure 14.1 shows an example.

Since a Boolean circuit has a fixed input size, we require a circuit for each input size n. Unlike the computation models we previously studied, circuit models thus require a family of circuits indexed by the input size, where the indices start from 1. The lack of input values for size-0 inputs justifies the exclusion of input size 0.

Definition 14.1 Let $C = \{C_n\}_{n\geq 1}$ be a circuit family. We say that C **decides** a language $L \subseteq \{0, 1\}^*$ if for all n and x, $|x| = n$, $x \in L$ if, and only if, $C_n(x) = 1$.

Since the circuit-based decision of languages requires an infinite sequence of circuits for all input sizes, we consider how to obtain the circuit for each length. We say that a circuit family C is **uniform** if there is a TM that, for every n, produces C_n from n. An input to the machine is the single-letter encoding, 1^n, of n. The encoding of a Boolean circuit can be the adjacency matrix of a vertex-labeled directed graph. We can assume that the first n vertices in the matrix are the input gates, and the

Fig. 14.1 A four-input Boolean circuit that tests whether or not bits 1 and 2 are equal, and bits 3 and 4 are equal. The size of the circuit is 13, and the depth is 4

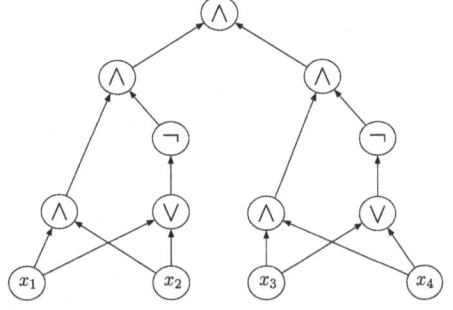

last vertex is the output gate. In the case of a model in which the negation of the input is readily available, the n vertices after the input are the negation of the input. Along with the connectivity, a bit sequence representing the gate types is part of the encoding. For example, we can use two bits each with 00 for the input, 01 for $\vee$, 10 for $\wedge$, and 11 for $\neg$. A family without the specification of the uniform circuit production is a **nonuniform** circuit family.

There are multiple **uniformity** types in use. Among them, the most typical are **logspace uniformity** and **P uniformity**. The former requires the circuit that produces the TM to use space $O(\log n)$, and the latter requires that the machine runs in polynomial time. In this section, we use P-uniformity, but the results also hold for logspace uniformity.

We now define some circuit complexity classes.

Definition 14.2 For each $k \geq 0$, AC^k is the class of languages decidable by a P-uniform family of polynomial-size, $O((\log n)^k)$-depth unbounded-fan-in circuits.
We define $AC = \cup_{k \geq 0} AC^k$.

Definition 14.3 For each $k \geq 0$, NC^k is the class of languages decidable by a P-uniform family of polynomial-size, $O((\log n)^k)$-depth bounded-fan-in circuits.
We define $NC = \cup_{k \geq 0} NC^k$.

Definition 14.4 For each $k \geq 0$, SAC^k is the class of languages decidable by a P-uniform family of polynomial-size, $O((\log n)^k)$-depth semi-bounded-fan-in circuits.
We define $SAC = \cup_{k \geq 0} SAC^k$.

Definition 14.5 PSIZE is the class of languages decidable by a P-uniform family of polynomial-size circuits.

Among NC, SAC, and AC, the fan-in is the most restrictive in NC and the most flexible in AC. So, we immediately have the following proposition.

Proposition 14.1 *For all $k \geq 0$, $NC^k \subseteq SAC^k \subseteq AC^k$.*

For each m, the $\vee$ of m inputs can be computed by a bounded fan-in circuit of 2-fan-in $\vee$ gates having a size of $m - 1$ and a depth of $\lceil \log m \rceil$. The same holds for $\wedge$. Suppose we substitute each gate with its bounded-fan-in version, given an unbounded-fan-in circuit having a size of s and a depth of d. Since each gate in the original circuit has at most s inputs, the substitution increases the size to $O(s^2)$. Also, since the longest path in the original is d, the substitution increases the depth to $O(d \log s)$. Suppose we apply the substitution to all members in an AC circuit family whose size is $O(p(n))$ and depth is $O((\log n)^k)$. The resulting circuit family still accepts the same language and has size $O((p(n))^2)$ and depth $((\log n)^k \log(p(n)))$. Since $p(n)$ is polynomial, the size of the resulting circuit is still bounded by some polynomial, and the depth is $O((\log n)^{k+1})$. This observation gives the following proposition:

Proposition 14.2 $AC^k \subseteq NC^{k+1}$.

Thus, we have a hierarchy of circuit classes.

$$NC^0 \subseteq SAC^0 \subseteq AC^0 \subseteq NC^1 \subseteq SAC^1 \subseteq AC^1 \subseteq \cdots \subseteq PSIZE.$$

It is unknown which containments in the sequence are proper, except for the following two.

Proposition 14.3 $NC^0 \subset SAC^0$; i.e., NC^0 is properly contained in SAC^0.

Theorem 14.1 $AC^0 \subset NC^1$; i.e., AC^0 is properly contained in NC^1.

The first one is easy to prove since constant-depth bounded-fan-in circuits can examine only a constant number of input bits. We leave the task of proving the proposition to the reader.

Proving the second proper containment is elaborate. The proof uses the so-called random restriction technique, which selects some input bits and selects their values according to a probability distribution.

Both containment results hold regardless of the uniformity condition.

14.1.2 Relations Between Boolean Circuit-Based Classes and TM-Based Classes

Comparing TM-based and circuit-based complexity classes requires the conversion of an arbitrary alphabet to a binary alphabet. Given an alphabet size of m, we encode the alphabet's symbols using unique m-bit strings with exactly one bit set to 1. The position at which the sole bit 1 appears gives the symbol's index, which can be quickly recovered from the s-bit string. The binary encoding increases the input length from n to nm. From this point on, we consider only languages of binary strings.

The following result, whose proof is left to the reader, connects polynomial-time Turing-machine computation and polynomial-size circuit computation.

Proposition 14.4 $P = PSIZE$.

This proposition raises the question of whether or not subclasses of P have relations with subclasses of PSIZE. The following proposition makes such a connection.

Theorem 14.2 $NL \subseteq SAC^1$.

Proof Let L be a language in NL. Let $M = (Q, \{0, 1\}, \Gamma, \delta, q_0, q_{acc}, q_{rej})$ be a one work tape offline nondeterminic TM that accepts L. In the proof of Theorem 10.7, we analyzed the reachability of a directed graph connecting between IDs of a machine. In that graph, for each pair of IDs I and J, we drew an edge from I to J

if M could transition from I to J in one step. Any ID of a TM consists of its state, head positions, and tape contents. Because M is $O(\log n)$ space-bounded, for each input having a length of n, the encoding of ID has a length of $c \log n$) in binary, and a polynomial $p(n) = 2^{c \log n}$. Let $I_1, \ldots, I_{p(n)}$ be an enumeration of all $(c \log n)$-bit strings. All the possible IDs of M on inputs having a length of n are among them. We build a reachability graph with these IDs as the vertices as follows:

- A unique ID corresponds to the initial ID.
- A unique ID corresponds to a unique accepting ID.
- The indices of the initial and accepting IDs are the same for all inputs having a length of n.
- If $s = t$, the self-loop (I_s, I_t) exists.
- For other prospective edges $e = (I_s, I_t)$ such that $s \neq t$, there are four possibilities:

  - e is absent regardless of the input.
  - e is present regardless of the input.
  - e is present if a bit x_k of the input is 0 for some k.
  - e is present if a bit x_k is 1 for some k.

We can use $(p(n))^2$ bits to encode the reachability graph's adjacency matrix, G, on input x. The matrix is computable from the input by examining at most one input bit for entry. Let $H = G^{p(n)}$ with $\{\vee, \wedge\}$ as the basis. We can compute H using $2\lceil \log(p(n)) \rceil$ matrix multiplications. Each entry in the matrix product is the inner product of a row vector and a column vector having a dimension of $p(n)$ with a $p(n)$-fan-in $\vee$ and $p(n)$i two-fan-in $\wedge$s. In other words, given two matrices $A = (a_{ij})$ and $B = (b_{ij})$, the a_{ij} of the product AB is:

$$a_{i1} \cdot b_{1j} + a_{i2} \cdot b_{2j} + \cdots + a_{i,p(n)} \cdot b_{p(n),j}.$$

Here, $(a_{i1}, \ldots, a_{i,p(n)})$ is the i-th row vector of A, and $(b_{1j}, \ldots, b_{p(n),j})$ is the j-th column vector of B. Thus, the computation of single matrix multiplication can be carried out with a depth-2 semi-unbounded-fan-in circuit. Since the computation of H requires a sequence of $O(\log(p(n))) = O(\log n)$ matrix multiplications, an $O(\log n)$-depth semi-unbounded circuit is sufficient for computing H. After computing H, we can check if M accepts x by examining H's entry corresponding to the edge from the initial ID to the accepting ID.

As we observed, the bit of the matrix is 0, 1, x_k for some k, or $\neg x_k$ for some k. Assuming that the input is augmented by its negation, 0 is producible with an $\wedge$ of x_1 and $\neg x_1$, and 1 is producible with an $\vee$ of x_1 and $\neg x_1$. Thus, the depth of the circuit is $O(\log n)$. The size of the circuit is:

$$2 + (p(n))^2 (p(n) + 1)(2 \log(p(n))) = O(p(n)^3 \log n).$$

Thus, the circuit is a polynomial-size circuit. This proves the theorem.   □

14.1.3   The Arithmetic Circuit Model

An extension of the Boolean circuit model is the **arithmetic circuit model** that operates in a finite field F (such as Z_p for some prime number p). In this model, a circuit receives a series of elements from a field F and processes the input through field operations $(+, -, \text{and} *)$. Since the operations are binary and unary, we only consider bounded fan-in circuits as viable models.

Definition 14.6 Let F be a finite field. For each k, NC_F^k is the class of problems computable using polynomial-size, $O((\log n)^k)$-depth bounded-fan-in arithmetic circuits over F.

A wide variety of problems in linear algebra over F are known to be in NC_F^k, including the following result, which we state without proof:

Theorem 14.3 *For every finite field F, the determinant of a matrix over F is in the logspace-uniform NC_F^2.*

Given the logspace-uniform NC^2 computability of the determinant in the field F, several circuit complexity results follow.

14.2   The Class P/poly

P/poly is the nonuniform version of the polynomial-size circuit complexity class.

Definition 14.7 P/poly is the class of languages decidable by a nonuniform family of polynomial-size circuits.

Proposition 14.4 states the equality between P and PSIZE. We have the following result since P/poly is the nonuniform version.

Proposition 14.5 $P \subseteq P/\text{poly}$.

P/poly has an alternate definition that employs languages in P.

A sequence $\{w_n\}_{n \geq 1}$ is **polynomial length-bounded** if there is a polynomial $p(n)$ such that for all $n \geq 1$, $|w_n| \leq p(n)$.

Definition 14.8 A language L is in P/poly if a polynomial length-bounded sequence $W = \{w_i\}_{i \geq 1}$ and a language $A \in P$ exists such that for all x:

$$x \in L \iff \langle x, w_{|x|} \rangle \in A.$$

We call the string sequence W the **advice**, and call A the witness language. The equality of the two definitions is easy to prove (see Exercise 14.6).

How large is the class P/poly? We know $\text{BPP} \subseteq P/\text{poly}$.

Theorem 14.4 $\text{BPP} \subseteq P/\text{poly}$.

Proof Suppose $L \in$ BPP. As with the proof for Proposition 14.4, we consider the binary input alphabet. By Lemma 13.2, a polynomial-time probabilistic TM M exists such that M's error probability is less than 2^{-2n}. Let $p(n)$ be a polynomial bounding the running time of M. Let n be an integer. We consider all computation paths, in $\{0, 1\}^{p(n)}$, for all inputs having a length of n. Since there are 2^n inputs having a length of n and the error probability is less than 2^{-2n}, the aggregate total of the error probability values is < 1. This means that there is a computation path producing an error for no inputs. We select such a path and appoint it as the advice for length n. The witness language is the set of pairs $\langle x, y \rangle$ such that M accepts x using y as the computation path. This circuit has its size bounded by $O(p(n)^2)$ and correctly decides the membership of all inputs having a length of n. $\qquad\square$

Does the containment in P/poly hold for other classes? A natural candidate for this containment is NP. We do not have a definitive answer, but we know NP $\subseteq$ BPP implies the collapse of the polynomial hierarchy.

Theorem 14.5 *If* NP $\subseteq$ P/poly, *then* $\Pi_2^p \subseteq \Sigma_2^p$.

Proof Overview
Let L be an arbitrary language in Π_2^p. Due to Theorem 12.4, L has a "universal" witness scheme in NP; a string $x \in L$ if, and only if, for all $y, |y| \leq q(|x|)$, $f(x, y)$ is satisfiable, where f is a polynomial-time computable function that maps an arbitrary pair of strings to a 3CNF formula. There is a polynomial $r(n)$ bounding the length of the formula f produced from x with any $y, |y| \leq q(|x|)$, as the input. Every nontrivial 3CNF formula has the **disjunctive self-reducibility** as we observed in Sect. 12.1; a 3CNF formula φ is satisfiable if, and only if, φ_0 or φ_1 is satisfiable, where φ_0 and φ_1 are constructed from φ by assigning *false* and *true* to the first variable φ, respectively.

Assume NP $\subseteq$ P/poly. A pair of polynomial $p(n)$ bounding the length of advice and a polynomial-time witness language A puts 3SAT in P/poly. Let x be a string we want to test if $x \in L$. Suppose we nondeterministically guess $r(|x|)$ advice strings $w_1, \ldots, w_{r(|x|)}$ and conduct the following test for all nontrivial formulas φ having a length $\leq r(|x|)$:

(i) We generate φ_0 and φ_1 from φ by assigning the value of *false* and *true* to the first variable of φ, respectively.
(ii) We use A and the guessed advice strings to compute the satisfiability of the three formulas, φ, φ_0, and φ_1.
(iii) We check if the three values we computed in (ii) are consistent with the self-reducibility of 3SAT; i.e., φ is satisfiable if, and only if, φ_0 or φ_1 is satisfiable.

(continued)

By the assumption that 3SAT is in P/poly, a sequence of advice strings passes the test. Once we have such a sequence, we can determine the membership of x in L by checking if, for all y, $f(x, y)$ produces a 3CNF formula that satisfies the advice sequence and A. The correctness verification of the advice sequence is in coNP. The membership test for x is in coNP for each fixed advice sequence. Thus, we have $\Pi_2^p \subseteq \Sigma_2^p$.

Proof Assume NP $\subseteq$ P/poly. Then a polynomial advice scheme exists for the NP-complete 3SAT; there exists a language $A \in$ P and a polynomial length-bounded advice sequence $\{w_n\}_{n \geq 1}$ such that for all 3CNF formulas φ, $\varphi \in$ 3SAT if, and only if, $\langle \varphi, w_{|\varphi|} \rangle \in A$. Let $p(n)$ be a polynomial such that for all n, $|w_n| \leq p(n)$.

Let L be an arbitrary language in Π_2^p. There exists a polynomial $q(n)$ and a language $B \in$ NP such that for all x, $x \in L$ if, and only if, for all z such that $|z| = q(|x|)$, $\langle x, z \rangle \in B$. Let f be a $\leq_m^p$-reduction from B to 3SAT. Then, we have a characterization of L; for all x, $x \in L$ if, and only if, for all z such that $|z| = q(|x|)$, $f(x, z) \in$ 3SAT. Because f is polynomial-time computable, there exists a polynomial $r(n)$, such that for all x such that $|x| = n$, and for all z such that $|z| = q(n)$, $|f(x, z)| \leq r(n)$.

Let $s(n) = p(r(n))$. By combining the two characterizations, for all x, $x \in L$ if, and only if, there exists a sequence of advice $W = [w_1, \ldots, w_{s(|x|)}]$ satisfying the following conditions:

(i) W's elements serve as correct advice strings for all formulas whose length is at most $r(|x|)$ with A as the witness language.
(ii) For all z such that $|z| = q(|x|)$, $f(x, z)$ is satisfiable according to W and A.

We use the following **disjunctive self-reducibility** of SAT, which 3SAT also possesses, to test (i):

A nontrivial formula φ is satisfiable if, and only if, φ_0 or φ_1 is satisfiable, where φ_b is the formula obtained from φ by assigning the value b to its first variable.

Test for (i) is this for all formulas φ:

*   If φ has only one variable, $\varphi \in$ 3SAT $\iff \langle \varphi, W_{|\varphi|} \rangle \in A$.
*   If φ has more than one variable, $\varphi \in$ 3SAT $\iff \langle \varphi_0, W_{|\varphi_0|} \rangle \in A \vee \langle \varphi_1, W_{|\varphi_1|} \rangle \in A$.

Using induction on the number of variables, we can show that if W satisfies the two conditions, W serves as a correct advice sequence for all formulas φ whose length is at most $s(n)$ (see Exercise 14.7).

Since $A \in$ P, the tests for (i) and (ii) are in coNP. Thus, L is the set of all x for which a sequence W passes the coNP tests for (i) and (ii). This implies that $L \in \Sigma_2^p$.

This proves the theorem.   □

The concept of P/poly with polynomial length-bounded advice and a witness language in P naturally extends to other witness language classes.

Definition 14.9 Let C be a language class. A language L is in C/poly if there exists a polynomial $p(n)$, a language $A \in C$, and a sequence of strings $\{W_n\}_{n \geq 1}$ such that:

1. For each $n \geq 1$, $|W_n| \leq p(n)$
2. For all x, $x \in L \iff \langle x, W_{|x|} \rangle \in A$

14.3 Unambiguous Accepting Computation Paths of NTMs

We now look into the question of ambiguity in NTM computation.

Previously, we referred to the multiple possibilities in leftmost production trees as ambiguity. Suppose we have a CNF grammar G. Think of an NTM M for testing the membership in $L(G)$. Suppose M's algorithm is to start from the start variable, apply $2|w| - 1$ times any applicable production rule to the leftmost variable, and check if w emerges. The TM places $L(G) \in \text{NTIME}[n]$. Also, if G is unambiguous, then M has only one accepting computation path for each member of $L(G)$. We call such a TM unambiguous. We define a subclass UP of NP as follows:

Definition 14.10 UP is the class of languages a polynomial-time ambiguous NTM accepts.

The class UP resides in is between P and NP; i.e., $\text{P} \subseteq \text{UP} \subseteq \text{NP}$. It is still being determined whether or not either inclusion is proper. Also unknown is if $\text{UP} = \text{NP}$ implies the collapse of the polynomial hierarchy.

A problem similar to UP is the problem of testing if a 3CNF formula has exactly one satisfying assignment. We refer to this problem as USAT. The uniqueness in USAT differs from that in UP. USAT asks if the number of satisfying assignments is exactly 1, where each candidate formula may have any number of satisfying assignments. In contrast, if we encode the computation of a TM witnessing a language in UP, the formula is guaranteed to have 0 or 1 satisfying assignment(s). In addition, coNP is a subclass of USAT.

The following result, which we can prove using the isolation lemma, connects NP and USAT.

Theorem 14.6 *A randomized polynomial-time algorithm for* SAT *exists such that for each input formula* φ, *the algorithm generates a polynomial number of formulas* $\psi_1, \ldots, \psi_m$, *with the following properties:*

- *If* φ *is not satisfiable, none of* $\psi_1, \ldots, \psi_m$ *is satisfiable.*
- *If* φ *is satisfiable, the probability that one of* $\psi_1, \ldots, \psi_m$ *has exactly one satisfying assignment is* $\geq 1/$.

Put differently, SAT *is randomized polynomial-time disjunctively truth-table reducible to* USAT.

We postpone the proof of Theorem 14.6 to the Exercises section.

A logarithmic-space analog of UP is the unambiguous NL, denoted as UL.

Definition 14.11 UL is the class of languages a logarithmic space-bounded ambiguous NTM accepts.

Interestingly, as stated next, we know the equality UL $=$ NL if polynomial length-bounded advice is available.

Theorem 14.7 NL/poly $=$ UL/poly.

Proof Overview
The proof of NL $=$ coNL (Theorem 10.7) employed an inductive counting method for the reachability problem in a directed graph representing the computation of a nondeterministic logarithmic space-bounded machine. We augment the proof in four ways.

1. We consider assigning random weights to each edge. We show that with probability $\geq 1/2$, the weight assignment induces a unique minimum-weight path between any vertex pair (s, t) such that t is reachable from s.
2. We show that when there are some polynomial number of independent weight assignments, one of the weight assignments induces a unique minimum-weight path.
3. Using an argument similar to BPP $\subseteq$ P/poly (Theorem 14.4), we show that a sequence of weight functions works for all n-vertex graphs.
4. We show that the inductive counting method is extensible to the case where minimum-weight paths are unique.

Proof Let M be a logarithmic space-bounded nondeterministic single-tape offline TM. Let $L = L(M)$. The ID of an offline TM comprises the tape content, the head positions, and the state. As with the proof from earlier in this chapter, let $p(n)$ be a polynomial that bounds the number of IDs of M. We can assume that each graph we consider has exactly $p(n)$ vertices for some n, and Vertices 1 and $p(n)$ are the initial ID and the accepting ID, respectively. Since our interest is in reachability, we can safely remove all the self-loops.

We will show that there is a reachability algorithm in UL/poly. Then, we can construct an algorithm for L in UL/poly. The algorithm dynamically generates the instance of the reachability problem from its input and runs the UL/poly algorithm on the graph.

Let $G = (V, E)$ be an m-vertex graph and t be a vertex pair. Let $v_1, \ldots, v_m$ be an enumeration of G's vertices. We want to test whether or not v_m is reachable from v_1. Let W be a random edge-weight function, where each prospective edge receives an integer weight chosen independently and uniformly at random from the interval

$[1, 4m^3]$. Let u and e be such that u is a vertex, e is an edge, u is reachable from v_1, and e appears on some path from v_1 to u. We say that e's weight is *singular* for u if there are two minimum-weight paths from v_1 to u, where one passes through e, and the other avoids e. If e is singular for u, increasing e's weight turns all the paths containing e into non-minimal ones, and decreasing e's weight turns all the paths avoiding e into non-minimal ones. We extend the definition of singularity to the weight assignment W. We say that W is singular if, for some u and e, e's edge in W is singular for u. Each e has at most one singular weight for each u. There are m possibilities for u, so the proportion of e's singular weight choices for some u is at most m out of $4m^3$. The proportion equals 1 out of $4m^2$. There are $2m^2$ possibilities for e. The proportion of singular Ws is maximized where each singular W gives the singularity of one edge e. Thus, the proportion of singular W is $\leq (1/4m^2)(2m^2) = 1/2$.

Suppose $Y = \langle W_1, \ldots, W_{m^2} \rangle$ is a sequence of weight assignments. We say that Y is singular if all its weight assignments are singular. If the weight assignments are independently chosen, the probability that Y is singular is at most $1/2^{m^2}$. There are $m(m-1)$ possible directed edges in an m-vertex directed graph without self-loops, so there are $2^{m(m-1)}$ possible m-vertex directed graphs. This means that the proportion of singular Y is $\leq (1/2^{m^2})(2^{m(m-1)}) = 1/2^m$, so some Y is singular for no graphs. Let us choose one such Y as the advice for all m-vertex graphs.

We will now show that for each graph G and a weight assignment W, there is a UL-type algorithm for testing W's singularity; the algorithm runs nondeterministically in logarithmic space and asserts W is singular/non-singular in exactly one computation path. The algorithm aborts the computation without a conclusion in the other computation paths.

From G and W, we construct a graph G_W by replacing an edge $e = (u, v)$ having a weight w to a path $[u_0, \ldots, u_w]$ by introducing new vertices $u_1, \ldots, u_{w-1}$, where $u_0 = u$ and $u_w = v$. The new vertices are not shared with other such paths. The graph G_W has $\leq m(4m^3)$ vertices. Since G_W represents each weighted edge as a path, W is non-singular if, and only if, every vertex reachable from v_1 has a unique shortest path from v_1. Also, the shortest path from v_1 to v_m in G_W, if any, has a path length of at most $m \cdot (4m^3) = 4m^4$.

For each d such that $0 \leq d \leq 4m^4$, let ρ_d be the number of vertices in G_W reachable from v_1 in at most d steps, and σ_d be the sum of the shortest path length from 1 to the vertices in ρ_d. For all d, $\rho_d \leq 4m^4$ and $\sigma_d \leq (4m^4)^2 = 16m^8$. Also, $\rho_d = 1$ (i.e., only v_1 is reachable from v_1 with a distance of 0), and $\sigma_0 = 0$.

We show that ρ_d and σ_d are computable from ρ_{d-1} and σ_{d-1} in UL in the following manner:

We initialize two counts R and S to 0. Then, for each vertex v in G_w, we nondeterministically follow a path from v_1 having a length of $1, \ldots, d-1$ in this order to see if the path leads to v. If we find such a path, we add 1 to R and the path length to S. When the examination is complete for all vertices, the following properties hold:

- $R > \rho_{d-1}$ never occurs.
- If $R < \rho_{d-1}$, the search missed a vertex reachable in $\leq d - 1$ steps, so we abort the computation.
- If $R = \rho_{d-1}$ and $S > \sigma_{d-1}$, the search found a non-minimal path, so we abort the computation.
- If $R = \rho_{d-1}$, $S < \sigma_{d-1}$ never occurs.
- If $R = \rho_{d-1}$ and $S = \sigma_{d-1}$, assuming that G_W is non-singular for all the vertices reachable in $\leq d - 1$ steps, there is only one computation path that finds $R = \rho_{d-1}$ and $S = \sigma_{d-1}$.

Now, using the verification procedure of R and S, we compute $\delta = \rho_d - \rho_{d-1}$. We initialize δ with 0. We then repeatedly run the verification procedure to check, for each vertex u, if it satisfies the following sequence of conditions:

- If the distance of u from v_1 is $\leq d - 1$, no further action for u.
- If the distance of u from v_1 is $\geq d$, count the vertices u' whose distance from v_1 is exactly $d - 1$, and there is an edge (u', u).
- If this count is ≥ 2, W is singular, so abort the computation.
- If the count is 1, add 1 to δ.

After the checks are complete for all u, we add δ to ρ and $\delta \cdot d$ to σ.

We rerun the verification after computing ρ_{4m^4}. We accept if the target vertex is among the vertices at a distance $\leq 4m^4$ and reject otherwise.

The proof is complete.   □

Exercises

14.1 Prove $NC^0 \subset SAC^0$.

14.2 Prove $P = PSIZE$.

14.3 We can prove something more substantial than the equality from the previous question; for each language in P, there is a logspace-uniform family of polynomial-size circuits accepting it. Prove this inclusion.

14.4 Theorem 14.3 states that the determinant of a matrix over a field F can be computed in NC_F^2. Based on this theorem, show that NC_F^2 circuits can solve the system of linear equations over F, $Ax = b$, where A is a square matrix of dimension n, b is an n-dimensional vector, and x is a vector of n indeterminates.

14.5 Prove that P/poly contains a non-recursive language.

Hint: Construct a language in $\{0\}^*$. A polynomial size-circuit family can recognize the language (the size can be linear in the length of the input). The construction can be based on $HALT_{TM}$ or any non-recursive language.

14.6 Prove that the circuit-based and the advice-based definitions of P/poly are equivalent.

14.7 In the proof of Theorem 14.5, we stated that the candidate advice sequence W serves as a correct advice sequence if it satisfies the disjunctive self-reducibility condition. Prove this property using induction on the number of variables.

14.8 Show that SUBSETSUM is disjunctive self-reducible.

14.9 Show that 3DM is disjunctive self-reducible.

14.10 A sequence $\{w_n\}_{n \geq 1}$ is **logarithmic length-bounded** if there is a constant c such that for all $n \geq 1$, $|w_n| \leq c \log n$. Let P/log be a version of P/poly where the advice sequence is logarithmic length-bounded. Show that if NP $\subseteq$ P/log, then NP = coNP.

Hint: Think of the version of SAT, $\text{SAT}' = \{w01^t \mid w \in \text{SAT}\}$. Assuming NP $\subseteq$ P/log, we can try all possible advice strings to find the correct advice and then use it to determine the satisfiability.

14.11 Show that NL/poly = coNL/poly = UL/poly.

14.12 We define CIRCUITSAT as the problem of deciding if a Boolean circuit outputs 1 for some input. Show that CIRCUITSAT is NP-complete.

14.13 Show that $P^{P/poly} = P/poly$.

14.14 Show that the reachability circuit in the proof of Theorem 14.2 is producible in $O(\log n)$ space, and so NL is in the logspace-uniform SAC^1.

14.15 Show that TAUTOLOGY is $\leq_m^p$-reducible to USAT.

14.16 We can prove Theorem 14.6 using a weight assignment scheme similar to the one we used in the proof of Theorem 14.7. Let φ be a 3CNF formula with n variables. Suppose we assign independent integer weights from $[1, 2n]$ uniformly at random to the n variables. We define each truth assignment's weight as the total weights of the variables that receive *true* as the assignment. Show that the probability that the minimum-weight satisfying assignment is unique is $\geq 1/2$.

14.17 Let φ be a formula with n variables, $x_1, \ldots, x_n$, and $W = [w_1, \ldots, w_n]$ be a weight assignment to φ's variables where each weight is from $\{1, \ldots, 2n\}$. Show that for each integer t between 1 and $2n^2$, a formula φ_t with additional variables such that in every satisfying assignment φ_t, if any, the total weight of x_i that receives *true* is exactly t.

14.18 Complete the proof of Theorem 14.6 based on the answers to the previous two questions.

14.19 Show that the parity function is computable in NC^1.

14.20 Sorting is the problem of, given a sequence of bits $a_1, \ldots, a_n$, reordering the bits so that any 0 appears before any 1. For example, sorting $[0, 1, 0, 0, 1, 0]$ results in $[0, 0, 0, 0, 1, 1]$. Show that a depth-1 bounded-fan-in circuit can sort two bits.

14.21 Continuing the previous question, MERGESORT sorts numbers by recursively splitting the input numbers into halves, sorting each half, and then merging the sorted halves to generate a global sorted sequence. Show that merging two sorted halves of 2^m elements can be accomplished by a depth-$O(m)$ bounded-fan-in circuit.

Hint: Connecting the result from the second half in the reverse order gives a pattern $0^i 1^j 0^k$. Sorting is complete by shifting the 1s to the right.

14.22 Continuing the previous questions, show that sorting is in NC^2 by a circuit that employs MERGESORT.

14.23 An important Boolean function is the threshold function, which receives some n input bits and a parameter t in the form $0^{n-t} 1^t$ and answers whether or not the number of 1s in the input is greater than or equal to t. Show that an NC^0 circuit placed on top of a sorting network can compute the threshold function.

Bibliographic Notes and Further Reading

The inclusion of NL in SAC^1 (Theorem 14.2) is by Sudborough [17]. Proposition 14.2 is by Ruzzo [15]. The naming NC ("Nick's Class") was suggested by Cook [7] to honor Nick Pippenger, who extensively studied the model [13]. The separation between AC^0 and NC^1 is by the independent work of Furst, Saxe, and Sipser [8] and Ajtai [2], who showed that AC^0 cannot compute the parity function (the function that answers whether or not the number of 1s in the input is odd).

Theorem 14.3 is by Chistov [6]. An excellent exposition of circuit-based solutions to the determinant and other problems in linear algebra was given by von zur Gathen's article [19].

An NC^1 sorting network is known to exist via Ajtai, Komlós, and Szemerédi [3]. The construction is very intricate and goes beyond the coverage of this book. Paterson [12] offers a simplified construction.

Karp and Lipton [10] proved the collapse of the polynomial hierarchy with the assumption of $NP \subseteq P/poly$ (Theorem 14.5).

Theorem 14.4 is a generalization of Adleman's earlier observation that $RP \subseteq P/poly$ [1] and appears in Bennett and Gill [5] and Schöning [16]. The bound appears in many probability textbooks, including one by Alon and Spencer [4].

Valiant and Vazirani [18] showed Theorem 14.6 using a series of random vectors to filter the satisfying assignments by applying the inner product. Using weight assignments to generate unique minimal weight paths is by Mulmuley, Vazirani, and Vazirani [11]. Both filtering techniques are referred to as **isolation techniques**. Theorem 14.7 is by Reinhardt and Allender [14]. The proof of Theorem 14.6 here adapts the isolation technique by Mulmuley, Vazirani, and Vazirani [11], as appearing in Hemaspaandra and Ogihara [9]. The former technique played a significant role in the proof of Toda's theorem (Theorem 13.9).

References

1. L.M. Adleman, Two theorems on random polynomial time, in *Proceedings of the 19th Annual Symposium on Foundations of Computer Science, Ann Arbor, Michigan, USA, 16–18 October 1978*, STOC '78 (IEEE Computer Society, 1978), pp. 75–83
2. M. Ajtai, Σ_1^1-formulae on finite structures. Ann. Pure Appl. Logic **24**(1), 1–48 (1983)
3. M. Ajtai, J. Komlós, E. Szemerédi, An $o(n \log n)$ sorting network, in *Proceedings of the Fifteenth Annual ACM Symposium on Theory of Computing* (1983), pp. 1–9
4. N. Alon, J.H. Spencer, *The Probabilistic Method*. Wiley Series in Discrete Mathematics and Optimization (Wiley, New York, 2015)
5. C.H. Bennett, J. Gill, Relative to a random oracle A, $P^A \neq NP^A \neq coNP^A$ with probability 1. SIAM J. Comput. **10**(1), 96–113 (1981)
6. A.L. Chistov, Fast parallel calculation of the rank of matrices over a field of arbitrary characteristic, in *International Conference on Fundamentals of Computation Theory* (Springer, Berlin, 1985), pp. 63–69
7. S.A. Cook, A taxonomy of problems with fast parallel algorithms. Inform. Control **64**(1–3), 2–22 (1985)
8. M.L. Furst, J.B. Saxe, M.J. Sipser, Parity, circuits, and the polynomial-time hierarchy. Math. Syst. Theory **17**(1), 13–27 (1984)
9. L.A. Hemaspaandra, M. Ogihara, *The Complexity Theory Companion* (Springer, Berlin, 2013)
10. R.M. Karp, R.J. Lipton, Some connections between nonuniform and uniform complexity classes, in *Proceedings of the Twelfth Annual ACM Symposium on Theory of Computing*, STOC '80 (Association for Computing Machinery, New York, 1980), pp. 302–309
11. K. Mulmuley, U. Vazirani, V. Vazirani, Matching is as easy as matrix inversion. Combinatorica **7**, 105–113 (1987)
12. M.S. Paterson, Improved sorting networks with $o(\log N)$ depth. Algorithmica **5**(1), 75–92 (1990)
13. N. Pippenger, On simultaneous resource bounds, in *Proceedings of the Twentieth Annual Symposium on Foundations of Computer Science*, FOCS '79 (IEEE, Piscataway, 1979), pp. 307–311
14. K. Reinhardt, E.W. Allender, Making nondeterminism unambiguous. SIAM J. Comput. **29**(4), 1118–1131 (2000)
15. W.L. Ruzzo, Tree-size bounded alternation (extended abstract), in *Proceedings of the Eleventh Annual ACM Symposium on Theory of Computing*, STOC '79 (Association for Computing Machinery, New York, 1979), pp. 352–359
16. U. Schöning, *Complexity and Structure* (Springer, Berlin, 1986)
17. I.H. Sudborough, On the tape complexity of deterministic context-free languages. J. ACM **25**(3), 405–414 (1978)
18. L.G. Valiant, V.V. Vazirani, NP is as easy as detection unique solution. Theor. Comput. Sci. **47**, 85–93 (1986)
19. J. von zur Gathen, Parallel linear algebra, in *Synthesis of Parallel Algorithms*, ed. by J. Reif (Morgan Kaufmann, Los Altos, 1993), pp. 574–615

Appendix A
A List of Major Results

A.1   Characterizations of Language Classes

- $\Pi_k^p, \Sigma_k^p, k \geq 1$

    - $\Pi_k^p =$ the languages in P with k preceding quantifiers that start with $\forall$ and alternate (Theorem 12.4); 3CNF formulas in place of the languages in P if k is odd; 3DNF formulas if k is even (Corollary 12.4).
    - $\Sigma_k^p =$ the languages in P with k preceding quantifiers that start with $\exists$ and alternate (Theorem 12.4); 3CNF formulas in place of the languages in P if k is even; 3DNF formulas if k is odd (Corollary 12.4).

- CFL

    - CFL $=$ the languages with a CNF grammar (Theorem 4.2).
    - CFL $=$ the languages with a GNF grammar (Theorem 4.3).

- P

    - P $=$ the languages accepted by polynomial time-bounded nondeterministic TM making $O(\log(n))$ nondeterministic choices (Exercise 12.17).

- NP

    - NP $=$ the languages having a polynomial-time witness scheme (Theorem 11.4).

- R

    - R $=$ the languages decidable by a multi-tape TM (Theorem 6.1).
    - R $=$ the languages decidable by an NTM (Theorem 6.6).

- RE

    - RE $=$ the languages accepted by a multi-tape TM (Theorem 6.2).

- RE = the languages accepted by an NTM (Theorem 6.5).
  - RE = the languages having an enumerator (Theorem 6.7).
  - RE = the languages having a witness language in R (Theorem 6.8).

- REG

  - REG = the languages NFAs accept (Theorem 2.1).
  - REG = the languages with regular expressions (Theorem 2.3).
  - REG = the languages with a finite number of equivalence classes (the Myhill-Nerode theorem) (Theorem 3.1).

A.2   Relations Between Language Classes

- $\Delta_k, \Pi_k, \Delta_k$

  - $\Delta_k = \Sigma_k \cap \Pi_k$ for all $k \geq 1$ (Theorem 8.10).
  - $\Sigma_k \cup \Pi_k \subset \Delta_{k+1}$ for all $k \geq 1$ (Theorem 8.11).
  - Σ_k and Π_k are incomparable for all $k \geq 1$ (Theorem 8.11).

- AC, NC, SAC

  - $AC^0 \subset NC^1$ (Theorem 14.1).
  - $NC^0 \subset SAC^0$ (Proposition 14.3).
  - $NC^k \subseteq SAC^k \subseteq AC^k$ for all $k \geq 0$ (Proposition 14.1); $AC^k \subseteq NC^{k+1}$ for all $k \geq 0$ (Proposition 14.2).

- BPP, RP, zpp

  - BPP $\subseteq$ PP (Theorem 13.7); BPP $\subseteq$ P/poly (Theorem 14.4); BPP $\subseteq \Sigma_2^p$ (Theorem 13.8).
  - NP $\subseteq$ RP^{USAT} (Theorem 14.6).
  - P^{BPP} = BPP (Exercise 13.5).
  - RP $\subseteq$ NP, coRP $\subseteq$ coNP, ZPP $\subseteq$ NP $\cap$ coNP (Proposition 13.2).

- CFL

  - CFL $\subseteq$ P (Theorem 9.9).

- L

  - L $\subseteq$ NL $\subseteq$ P $\subseteq$ NP $\subseteq$ PSPACE $\subseteq$ EXPTIME $\subseteq$ NEXPTIME $\subseteq$ EXPSPACE (Theorem 10.6).

- NL

  - NL = coNL (Theorem 10.7).

- NP

  - NP $\subseteq$ P/poly $\Rightarrow \Pi_2^p \subseteq \Sigma_2^p$ (Theorem 14.5).

- NP $\subseteq$ BPP $\Rightarrow$ NP $=$ RP (Exercise 13.7).
- NP$^{\text{NP}\cap\text{coNP}}$ $=$ NP (Exercise 12.15); P$^{\text{NP}\cap\text{coNP}}$ $=$ NP$\cap$coNP (Exercise 12.16).

- **NSPACE**

  - NSPACE$[f(n)]$ $=$ co-NSPACE$[f(n)]$ for all space-constructible functions $f(n) = \Omega(\log(n))$ (Corollary 10.3).

- **P**

  - P $\subseteq$ NP $\cap$ coNP $\subseteq$ NP $\cup$ coNP $\subseteq$ EXPTIME $\subseteq$ NEXPTIME $\cap$ coNEXPTIME $\subseteq$ NEXPTIME $\cup$ coNEXPTIME (Proposition 9.2).
  - P $\subseteq$ P/poly (Proposition 14.5).
  - P $=$ PSIZE (Proposition 14.4).

- **PH**

  - PH $= \Sigma_k^p \iff$ PH $= \Pi_k^p \iff \Sigma_k^p = \Pi_k^p \iff \Sigma_k^p \subseteq \Pi_k^p \iff \Pi_k^p \subseteq \Sigma_k^p$ (Theorem 12.5).
  - PH $\subseteq$ P^{PP} (Theorem 13.9).

- **R**

  - P/poly $\not\subseteq$ R (Exercise 14.5).
  - R $=$ RE $\cap$ coRE (Theorem 6.3).

- **REG**

  - REG $\subset$ CFL (Exercise 4.1).
  - REG $\subset$ DCFL $\subset$ CFL (Corollary 5.1).

A.3   Closure Properties of Language Classes

- Π_k, Σ_k, for all $k \geq 0$, are closed under:

  - $\cup, \cap$, the marked union (Theorem 8.10).

- CFL is closed under:

  - ^{R} (Exercise 4.23); $\cup, \cdot, ^*$ (Proposition 4.2); $\cap$ with REG (Theorem 5.3).
  - PREFIX$(\cdot)$ (Exercise 4.25); the proper prefix (Exercise 5.19).

- DCFL is closed under:

  - ^{c} (Theorem 5.4).
  - The "marked" concatenation (Exercise 5.23).
  - The prefix-free homomorphisms (Exercise 5.11); the prefix-free inverse homomorphisms (Exercise 5.12).

- NL is closed under:

    - ^{c} (Theorem 10.7);
    - * (Exercise 10.20);
    - ∪ (Exercise 10.21);
    - ∩ (Exercise 10.22).

- NP is closed under:

    - * (Exercise 9.20);
    - ∪ (Exercise 9.21);
    - ∩ (Exercise 9.22).
    - $\leq_{\text{ctt}}^{p}$ and $\leq_{\text{dtt}}^{p}$ even if NP has an oracle (Exercise 12.5).

- NP-complete is closed under:

    - △ with a finite set (Proposition 11.2).

- R is closed under:

    - ∪, ∩, ^{c} (Exercise 6.21); the marked union (Exercise 6.25); * (Exercise 6.22).

- RE is closed under:

    - ∪, ∩ (Exercise 6.23); the marked union (Exercise 6.26); * (Exercise 6.24).

- REG is closed under:

    - ^{c}, ∪, ∩, ·, * (Theorem 2.2).
    - CYCLE(·) (Exercise 3.15).
    - HALF(·) (Exercise 3.13).
    - Homomorphisms and inverse homomorphisms (Exercise 3.9).
    - PREFIX$_{1/k}$(·) (Exercise 3.14).
    - MID3(·) (Exercise 3.19).
    - NOMID3(·) if the alphabet size is 1 (Exercise 3.21).
    - The right quotient (Exercise 3.22); the left quotient (Exercise 3.23).

A.4   Non-closure Properties of Language Classes

- CFL is not closed under ^{c}, ∩ (Theorem 4.1); NOMID3(·) (Exercise 5.21).
- DCFL is not closed under union (Exercise 5.24); intersection (Exercise 5.25).
- REG is not closed under the "no middle third" operation (Exercise 3.20).

A.5   Classifications of Specific Languages

- CFL

- The Dyck language (Exercise 4.10); The k-th Dyck language (Exercise 4.11).

- coNP-complete

  - TAUTOLOGY (Corollary 11.2); DNFTAUT, 3DNFTAUT (Corollary 11.3).

- L

  - Deterministic TMs encoded in binary (Proposition 10.2).
  - Deterministic TMs with an input, encoded in binary (Proposition 10.3).

- NP-complete

  - 3DM (Theorem 11.16).
  - CLIQUE (Theorem 11.9).
  - HAMCYCLE (Corollary 11.4); HAMPATH (Corollary 11.5).
  - INDEPENDENTSET (Theorem 11.18).
  - NTMCANONICAL (Theorem 11.3).
  - SAT (Theorem 11.5); CNFSAT (Theorem 11.6); 3SAT (Theorem 11.7); UNSAT (Corollary 11.1); NAESAT (Theorem 11.8); 1-IN-3-SAT (Exercise 11.20).
  - SUBSETSUM (Theorem 11.12); KNAPSACK (Theorem 11.14); PARTITION (Exercise 11.11); SCHEDULING (Theorem 11.15).
  - VERTEXCOVER (Theorem 11.10); 3COLOR (Theorem 11.11); DOMINATINGSET (Exercise 11.17).
  - X3C (Exercise 11.7).

- P

  - TMs encoded in binary (Proposition 9.3).
  - TMs with an input, encoded in binary (Proposition 9.4).
  - FAs whose state-set size is reducible to a given number (Proposition 9.5).

- P^{NP}-complete

  - ODDMAXSAT (Theorem 12.3); the 3CNF-version (Corollary 12.1).
  - ODDMAXSUM (Corollary 12.3).

- PSPACE-complete

  - FORMULAGAME (Theorem 12.8).
  - GEOGRAPHY (Theorem 12.9).
  - PSPCANONICAL (Proposition 12.6).
  - TQBF (Theorem 12.7); with a 3CNF as the base, alternating quantiers starting with $\exists$ (Corollary 12.5).

- R

  - ACCEPT$_{FA}$ (Theorem 7.1); EMPTY$_{FA}$ (Theorem 7.2); INFINITE$_{FA}$ (Theorem 7.3); TOTAL$_{FA}$ (Theorem 7.4); SUBSET$_{FA}$ (Theorem 7.5); EQUAL$_{FA}$ (Theorem 7.6).
  - ACCEPT$_{NFA}$, EMPTY$_{NFA}$, EQUAL$_{NFA}$, TOTAL$_{NFA}$, SUBSET$_{NFA}$ (Corollary 7.1).

- ACCEPT$_{REX}$, EMPTY$_{REX}$, EQUAL$_{REX}$, TOTAL$_{REX}$, SUBSET$_{REX}$ (Corollary 7.2).
- ACCEPT$_{CFG}$ (Theorem 7.7); EMPTY$_{CFG}$ (Exercise 7.9); INFINITE$_{CFG}$ (Exercise 7.11).
- ACCEPT$_{DPDA}$, EMPTY$_{DPDA}$, TOTAL$_{DPDA}$, INFINITE$_{DPDA}$ (Corollary 7.3); EQUAL$_{DPDA}$ (Theorem 7.8).
- FAs whose state-set size is reducible to a given number (Exercise 7.8).
- PCP over a single-letter alphabet (Exercise 8.19).

• RE

- NONTOTAL$_{CFG}$ (Theorem 8.6).
- One-tape TMs not making left moves (Exercise 7.5).

• Undecidable

- ACCEPT$_{TM}$ (Theorem 8.2); HALT$_{TM}$ (Theorem 8.3); EMPTY$_{TM}$, INFINITE$_{TM}$, TOTAL$_{TM}$ (Corollary 8.2); SUBSET$_{TM}$ and EQUAL$_{TM}$ (Corollary 8.3).
- TOTAL$_{CFG}$ (Theorem 8.5); EQUAL$_{CFG}$ (Corollary 8.4); SUBSET$_{CFG}$ (Corollary 8.5). REGULAR$_{TM}$ (Exercise 8.12); FINITE$_{TM}$ (Exercise 8.13); EMPTY$_{TM}$ (Exercise 8.14).
- TMs encoded in unary not accepting themselves (Theorem 8.1).
- TMs accepting themselves (Corollary 8.1).
- SUBSET$_{DPDA}$ (Theorem 8.7).
- PCP (Theorem 8.9); MPCP (Theorem 8.8); PCP over a binary alphabet (Exercise 8.20).
- Rice's Theorem: every nontrivial property about TMs (Theorem 8.4).

• Other classification results

- PRIMES $\in$ coRP (Theorem 13.4); COMPOSITES $\in$ RP (Theorem 13.4).
- PRIMES $\in$ RP (Theorem 13.5); COMPOSITES $\in$ coRP (Theorem 13.5).
- PRIMES $\in$ P (Theorem 13.6).
- Zero-Polynomial Testing is in BPP if the total degree is $\leq \|S\|/2$ (Theorem 13.7).

A.6   Polynomial-Time Many-One and Witness Reductions

• $\leq_m$ is reflexive and transitive (Proposition 8.3); not symmetric (Proposition 8.4).
• $\leq_m^p$ is transitive (Proposition 11.1); reflexive (Proposition 11.2).
• 3SAT $\leq_{wit}^p$ SUBSETSUM (Corollary 12.2).
• $A \leq_m B \wedge B \in R \Rightarrow B \in R$, for all A, B (Proposition 8.2).
• CNFSAT $\leq_{wit}^p$ 3SAT (Proposition 12.3).
• HAMPATH $\leq_m^p$ HAMCYCLE (Theorem 11.1); HAMCYCLE $\leq_m^p$ HAMPATH (Theorem 11.2).

- P = NP $\iff$ all NP-complete languages are in P (Proposition 11.1).
- P $\neq$ NP $\Rightarrow$ ($\exists A \in$ NP $-$ P)[A is not NP-complete] (Theorem 12.6).
- Search reduces in polynomial time to decision for CNFSAT (Proposition 12.1).
- Search reduces in polynomial time to decision for SUBSETSUM (Proposition 12.2).

A.7   Pumping Lemmas

- REG:

  - For all $L \in$ REG, there exists $p \geq 1$ such that ($\forall w \in L : |w| \geq p$)($\exists u, v, x$)[$w = uvx, |uv| \leq p, |u| \geq 1$, and ($\forall i \geq 0$)[$uv^i x \in L$]] (Lemma 3.3).
  - For all $L \in$ REG, there exists $p \geq 1$ such that ($\forall w = a_1 \cdots a_p b \in L : |a_1|, \ldots, |a_p| \geq 1$)($\exists s, t : 1 \leq s < t \leq p$)($\forall i \geq 0$)[$a_1 \cdots a_{s-1}(a_s \cdots a_t)^i a_{t+1} \cdots a_p b \in L$] (an extended version) (Lemma 3.5).

- CFL:

  - For all $L \in$ CFL, there exists $p \geq 1$ such that ($\forall w \in L : |w| \geq p$)($\exists u, v, x, y, z$)[$w = uvxyz, |vxy| \leq p, |vy| \geq 1$, and ($\forall i \geq 0$)[$uv^i x y^i z \in L$]] (the pumping lemma) (Lemma 5.1).
  - For all $L \in$ CFL, there exists $p \geq 1$ such that ($\forall w \in L : |w| \geq p$)($\forall S \subseteq \{1, \ldots, |w|\}, \|S\| \geq p$)($\exists u, v, x, y, z$)[$w = uvxyz, x$ covers ≥ 1 index in S, vxy covers $\leq p$ indices in S, either both u and v cover ≥ 1 in S or both y and z cover ≥ 1 index in S, and ($\forall i \geq 0$)[$uv^i x y^i z \in L$] (Ogden's lemma) (Lemma 5.2).
  - For all $L \in$ CFL, there exists $p \geq 1$ such that ($\forall w \in L, |w| \geq p$)($\forall S \subseteq \{1, \ldots, |w|\}, \|S\| \geq p$)($\exists u, v, x, y, z$)[$w = uvxyz, vy$ covers ≥ 1 index in S, vxy covers $\leq p$ indices in S, and ($\forall i \geq 0$)[$uv^i x y^i z \in L$] (a simpler Ogden's lemma) (Lemma 5.3).

A.8   Normalization and Behavior of Computing Objects

- BPP's error probability can be exponentially decreased (Lemma 13.2).
- CNF grammars need $2n - 1$ rule applications for producing strings having a length of n (Proposition 4.3).
- DPDAs can be normalized so they increase or decrease the stack height by 1 at each step (Exercise 5.7).
- Inherently ambiguous CFL languages exist (Theorem 5.5).
- NFAs with k states can accept x in $\leq k|x| + 1$ steps (Proposition 2.1).

- Single-tape TMs can be normalized so that their accepting ID is $q_{acc}\sqcup^*$ (Exercise 12.20).
- PDAs can be normalized so that they increase or decrease the stack height by 1 at each step (Exercise 5.6).
- Two-stack PDAs can simulate TMs (Exercise 6.17).

A.9   Time and Space Constructibility

- Let $f(n)$ be a time-bounding function. Then:

  - DTIME$[f(n)] \subseteq$ DTIME$[n + cf(n)]$ for all c such that $0 < c < 1$ (the linear speedup theorem (Theorem 9.1).
  - DTIME$[f(n)] \subseteq$ DTIME$[f(n)^2]$ by one-tape simulators (Theorem 9.2).
  - DTIME$[f(n)] \subseteq$ DTIME$[f(n)\log(f(n))]$ by two-tape simulators (Theorem 9.3).
  - DTIME$[f(n)] \subset$ DTIME$[g(n)]$ for all time-constructible $g(n) = \omega(f(n)\log(f(n)))$ (the Time Hierarchy Theorem) (Theorem 9.5).
  - DTIME$[f(n)] =$ DTIME$[cf(n)]$ for all $c > 0$ and $f(n)$ such that $(\exists \alpha > 0)(\forall^\infty n \geq 1)[f(n) \geq (1 + \alpha)n]$ (Corollary 9.1).
  - DTIME$[f(n)] \subseteq$ NTIME$[f(n)]$ (Proposition 9.1).
  - NTIME$[f(n)] \subseteq$ NTIME$[n + cf(n)]$ for all c such that $0 < c < 1$ (the nondeterministic speedup theorem) (Theorem 9.7).
  - NTIME$[f(n)] =$ NTIME$[cf(n)]$ for all $c > 0$ and $f(n)$ such that $(\exists \alpha > 0)(\forall^\infty n \geq 1)[f(n) \geq (1 + \alpha)n]$ (Corollary 9.3).
  - NTIME$[f(n)] \subseteq \cup_{c \geq 1}$DTIME$[2^{cf(n)}]$ (Proposition 9.8).

- Let $f(n)$ be a space-bounding function. Then:

  - DSPACE$[f(n)] \subseteq$ DSPACE$[cf(n)]$ for all c such that $0 < c < 1$ (the space compression theorem) (Theorem 10.1).
  - DSPACE$[f(n)] \subset$ DSPACE$[cf(n)]$ for all $c > 1$ (the space hierarchy theorem) (Theorem 10.2).
  - DSPACE$[n^d] \subset$ DSPACE$[n^c]$ for all c, d such that $c > d \geq 1$ (Corollary 10.1).
  - DSPACE$[(\log(n))^d] \subset$ DSPACE$[(\log(n))^c]$ for all $c, d \in \mathbb{Q}$ such that $c > d \geq 1$ (Corollary 10.2).
  - NSPACE$[f(n)] \subseteq$ NSPACE$[cf(n)]$ for all c such that $0 < c < 1$ (the nondeterministic space compression theorem) (Theorem 10.3).
  - NSPACE$[f(n)] \subseteq$ DSPACE$[f(n)^2]$ (Savitch's theorem) (Theorem 10.4).
  - NSPACE$[f(n)] \subseteq$ NSPACE$[g(n)]$ for all space-constructible $g(n) = \omega(f(n)^2)$ (the nondeterministic space hierarchy theorem) (Theorem 10.4).

- $f(n)$ is time-constructible $\iff$ a TM exists that for all inputs 1^n, produces $1^{t(n)}$ in $O(t(n))$ steps (Theorem 9.4).
- $(\log(n))^c$ is space-constructible for all $c \geq 1$ (Exercise 10.4).

- $\lceil n^c \rceil$ is space-constructible for all rational numbers $c > 1$ (Exercise 10.5).
- 2^n is space-constructible (Exercise 10.6).
- The space-constructible functions are closed under addition and multiplication (Exercise 10.7).
- The time-constructible functions are closed under addition, multiplication, and composition (Exercise 9.7).
- If $f(n)$ and $g(n)$ are space-constructible and $f(n) = \Omega(n)$, $f(g(n))$ is space-constructible (Exercise 10.8).

A.10   Number and Probability Theories

- Let $S = X_1 + \cdots + X_n$ where $X_1, \ldots, x_n$ are independent random variables in $\{0, 1\}$. Let E be S' expectation. Then, $(\forall t > 0) \left[\Pr[S \geq E + t] \leq \exp\left(-\frac{2t^2}{n}\right) \right]$ (the Chernoff-Hoeffding bound) (Lemma 13.1).
- For all $n_1, \ldots, n_k \in \mathbb{Z}$ that are pairwise relatively prime and $a_1 \in \mathbb{Z}_{n_1}, \ldots, a_k \in \mathbb{Z}_{n_k}$, there is exactly one integer $b, 0 \leq b < n_1 \cdots n_k$ such that $b \equiv a_i \pmod{n_i}$ for all i (the Chinese Remainder Theorem) (Theorem 13.2).
- For all odd prime numbers p and for all $a \in \mathbb{Z}_p^*$, $a^{p-1} \equiv 1 \pmod{p}$ (Fermat's Little Theorem) (Theorem 13.1).

Index

Symbols
$^+$ (Kleene-plus), 11
$*$ (Kleene-star), 10
Σ_ϵ, 31, 77
∞ (infinity), 4
$\cap$ (set intersection), 4
$||\cdot||$ (cardinality), 4
$\lceil\cdot\rceil$, 253
$^-$ (set complement), 4
^{c} (set complement), 4
$[\cdot]$ (congruence class), 330
$\cup$ (set union), 4
$\dashv$ (right-end marker), 245
$\emptyset$ (empty set), 3
ϵ (empty string), 10
$\exists$ (existential quantifier), 8, 304
$\forall$ (universal quantifier), 8, 304
$\forall^\infty$ (almost all), 9
$\in$ (is contained), 3
$\wedge$ (logical AND), 5
$\leq_T^p$ (polynomial-time Turing reduction), 298
$\leq_{ctt}^p$ (polynomial-time conjunctive truth-table reduction), 305
$\leq_{dtt}^p$ (polynomial-time disjunctive truth-table reduction), 305
$\leq_{wit}^p$ (polynomial-time witness-preserving reduction), 302
$\leq_m$ (many-one reduction), 189
$\vee$ (logical OR), 5
$\ni$ (contains), 3
$\langle\cdot\rangle$ (encoding function), 172
$\leq_m^p$ (polynomial-time many-one reduction), 263
$\overset{G,*}{\Longrightarrow}$ (multi-step production), 74

$\overset{G}{\Longrightarrow}$ (production), 74
$\{\cdots\}$ (set), 3
$\setminus$ (set difference), 4
$\sqcup$ (blank symbol), 136
$\subset$ (proper subset), 3
$\subseteq$ (subset), 3
$\supset$ (proper superset), 3
$\supseteq$ (superset), 3
$\triangle$ (symmetric difference), 4
$\vdash$ (left-end marker), 245
Δ_k^p, 303
$\mathbb{N}$, 4
$O(\cdot)$, 9
$\Omega(\cdot)$, 9
$\mathcal{P}(\cdot)$, 4
Π_k^p, 303, 353
$\mathbb{Q}$, 4
$\mathbb{R}$, 4
$\Sigma^{\leq n}$, 10
$\Sigma^{<n}$, 10
Σ^n, 10
Σ^*, 10
Σ_k^p, 303, 341, 353
$\mathbb{Z}$, 4
$\aleph_0$, 4, 186
$\aleph_1$, 4, 186
co-, 11
$dom(\cdot)$, 9
gcd, 329
lcm, 329
$o(\cdot)$, 9
$\Omega(\cdot)$, 9, 230
$range(\cdot)$, 9
$\Theta(\cdot)$, 9

© The Editor(s) (if applicable) and The Author(s), under exclusive license to
Springer Nature Switzerland AG 2025
M. Ogihara, *An Introduction to Theory of Computation*,
https://doi.org/10.1007/978-3-031-84740-0

1-IN-3-SAT, 291
2SAT, 291
3CNF formula, (*see* Boolean formula,
      3-conjunctive normal form)
3COLOR, 279
3-dimensional matching, (*see* 3DM)
3DM, 287, 320
3DNFTAUT, 274
3SAT, 271, 353

A
AC, 349
ACCEPT$_{CFG}$, 181, 191
ACCEPT$_{DPDA}$, 181
ACCEPT$_{FA}$, 175
ACCEPT$_{NFA}$, 180
ACCEPT$_{NTM}$, 266
ACCEPT$_{REG}$, 173
ACCEPT$_{REX}$, 180
ACCEPT$_{TM}$, 186
Accepting
    by a finite automaton, 25
    by a nondeterministic finite automaton, 31
    by a nondeterministic Turing machine, 136,
       158
    by a pushdown automaton, 97
Additive group, 330
Adjacency, 13
Adleman, L.M., 345, 360
Agrawal, M., 345
Aho, A.V., 56
Ajtai, M., 360
Algorithm
    bounded-error, 326
    divide and conquer, 249
    greedy, 18, 83, 320
    inductive, 18, 239, 356
    randomized, 326
    recursive, 249
Allender, E.W., 360
Alon, N., 360
Alphabet, 10, 24
    augmented, 96
    input, 96, 136, 175
    marked, 143
    stack, 96
    tape, 135
Ambiguity
    inherent, 114
    of accepting computation paths, 355
    of a context-free grammar, 79, 355
Amortized analysis, 230
Arc, (*see* Edge, directed)

Arithmetical hierarchy, 204, 295, 303
Assignment, 8
    not-all-equal, 272
    one-in-three satisfying, 291
    satisfying, 272
    truth, 8
Associative law, 330

B
Bar-Hillel, Y., 72, 131
Bennett, C.H., 360
Bijection, (*see* Function, bijective)
Boasson, L., 131
Boolean algebra, 5
Boolean formula, 6
    3-conjunctive normal form, 271
    conjunctive normal form, 270
    disjunctive normal form, 274
    fully quantified, 305
    prenex normal form, 305
    quantified, 304
    satisfiable, 8, 268
    unsatisfiable, 8, 273
Boolean logic, 5, 6
Boolean operation, 5
    conjunction, 5
    disjunction, 5
    logical AND, 5
    logical OR, 5
    negation, 5
Bounceback, 135
BPP, 326, 341, 352
Brzozowski, J.A., 72

C
C$_=$P, 344
Cantor, D.G., 93
Carmichael number, 331
Cartesian product, (*see* Sets, Cartesian product
      of)
Cartor, G., 185
Cell, 135
Cell block, 217
CFG, (*see* Context-free grammar (CFG))
CFL, 74
Character, 10
Chernoff, H., 345
Chernoff-Hoeffding Bound, 327
Chinese Remainder Theorem, 331, 338
Chistov, A.L., 360
Chomsky, N., 93, 131
Church, A., 169

Church-Turing Thesis, 165
Circuit
  arithmetic, 352
  basis, 348
  Boolean, 347
  bounded fan-in, 348
  constant-depth, 350
  depth, 348
  feed-forward, 347
  input size, 347
  monotone, 348
  non-uniform, 348, 352
  output size, 347
  semi-unbounded fan-in, 348
  size, 348
  unbounded fan-in, 348
  uniform, 348
CIRCUITSAT, 359
Class, 11
  complementary, 11
  deterministic space complexity, 245
  deterministic time complexity, 215
  language, 11
  nondeterministic space complexity, 248
  nondeterministic time complexity, 233
  probabilistic time complexity, 326
CLIQUE, 274, 320
Clique, 14, 274
Clock, 311
Closure
  of context-free languages under
    complement, 117
    concatenation, 117
Closure property, 40, 68
  of context-free languages under
    intersection, 79
    intersection with a regular language,
      107
    Kleene-star, 79
    union, 79
  of NL under
    intersection, 261
    Kleene-star, 260
    union, 261
  of NP^A under
    $\leq_{ctt}^{p}$, 305
    $\leq_{dtt}^{p}$, 305
  of NP under
    intersection, 242
    Kleene-star, 242
    union, 242
  of regular languages under
    complement, 41
    concatenation, 43

cycle, 71
first-half, 70
intersection, 43
Kleene-star, 41, 53
left-quotient, 71
middle-third, 71
right-quotient, 71
union, 42
CNF formula, (*see* Boolean formula,
      conjunctive normal form)
CNF grammar, (*see* Grammar, Chomsky
      normal form)
CNFSAT, 270, 295
Cobham, A., 243
Cocke, J., 183
Co-decidable, 137
Commutative group, 330
Commutative law, 330
Commutative ring, 330
Completeness, 274
Complexity
  time, 216
Composite number, 328
COMPOSITES, 335
Computational complexity theory, 215
Configuration, 142, 151
coNEXPTIME, 235
Congruence class, 329, 338
Congruent, 329
coNL, 250
Connected component, 13
  strongly, 13
coNP, 235, 273
$coNP^A$, 303
$coNP^C$, 303
Context-free grammar (CFG), 73
  ambiguous, 209
Context-free language (CFL), 74, 95, 239
  deterministic, 109, 193
Contrapositive, 67
Cook, S.A., 292, 360
Corasick, M.J., 56
coRE, 138
Co-recursive, 137
Co-recursively enumerable, 137, 156
coRP, 327, 335
Countable, 185
CP, 344
Cycle, 12
  simple, 12

D
Davis, M., 169

DCFL, (*see* Context-free language, deterministic)
Decidable, 137, 175
Decider, 165
Deciding
  by a deterministic Turing machine, 137
  by a nondeterministic Turing machine, 158
Demillo, R.A., 345
DeMorgan's Laws, 118
Derivation, (*see* Production)
Derivation rule, (*see* Production rule)
Derivation sequence, (*see* Production, sequence)
Derivation tree, (*see* Production tree)
Determinant, 352
DFA, (*see* Finite automaton, deterministic)
Diagonal argument, 185
Diagram
  transition, 26
Digraph, (*see* Graph, directed)
Distinguishability, (*see* State, distinguishability)
Distributive laws, 330
Divisor, 328
  nontrivial, 328
  trivial, 328
DNF formula, (*see* Boolean formula, disjunctive normal form)
DNFTAUT, 274
DOMINATINGSET, 291
Dominating set, 291
Domino tile, 195
  clean-up, 198
  computation, 197
  start, 196, 197
DPDA, (*see* Pushdown automaton, deterministic)
DSPACE, 246

E
Edge
  directed, 11
  incoming, 11
  outgoing, 11
Edmonds, J., 243
EMPTY$_{CFG}$, 183
EMPTY$_{DPDA}$, 181
EMPTY$_{FA}$, 177
EMPTY$_{NFA}$, 180
EMPTY$_{REX}$, 180
EMPTY$_{TM}$, 188
Encoding
  multi-cell, 152

  scheme, 171
  validation, 171
Enumeration, 47, 310
  equivalence class, 63
  ID, 254
  member, 164, 185
  of TM deciders, 310
  of TM transducers, 310
  rule, 116
  state, 35
Enumerator, 162
EQUAL$_{DPDA}$, 182
EQUAL$_{FA}$, 180
EQUAL$_{NFA}$, 180
EQUAL$_{REX}$, 180
EQUAL$_{TM}$, 188
Equivalence class, 62, 265, 330
  maximal, 62
Euler's criterion, 345
Evey, R.J., 131
Exact Cover by Three Sets, (*see* X3C)
Exponential Space (EXPSPACE), 250
Exponential Time (EXPTIME), 235, 250

F
FA, (*see* Finite automaton (FA))
False, 5
Fermat's Little Theorem, 331
Finite automaton (FA), 24
  deterministic, 24, 108
  nondeterministic, 30, 108, 180
    equivalent to FA, 34
  pseudo-nondeterministic, 35
Finite control, 135
Finite field, 340, 352
Fischer, M.J., 243
Floyd, R.W., 93
Forest, 14
FORMULAGAME, 316
Function, 8
  bijective, 9
  domain of, 9
  inverse, 9
  non-decreasing, 215, 245
  one-to-one, 9
  onto, 9
  partial, 9
  polynomial-time computable, 263
  range of, 9, 30
  semantic encoding, 172
  space-bounding, 245
  space-constructible, 246
  time-constructible, 230

total, 9
transition, 24, 30, 136
Furst, M.L., 360

G
Gadget, 281
Game, 316
    turning, 23
Garey, M.R., 292
Gasarch, W., 72
Gate, 347
    input, 347
    output, 347
GCD, (*see* Greatest common divisor (GCD))
Generalized Riemann Hypothesis, 345
Generator, 333
GEOGRAPHY, 317
Gill, J., 344, 360
Ginsburg, S., 72, 93, 131
GNF grammar, (*see* Grammar, Greibach
        normal form)
Gödel, K., 292
Grammar
    ambiguous, 79
    Chomsky normal form, 80, 101, 119, 181,
        183, 240
    CNF, 112
    context-free, 181, 239
    Greibach normal form, 87, 183
    unambiguous, 79, 81
Graph, 11
    acyclic, 12
    complete, (*see* Clique)
    cycle-free, 12
    directed, 11
    edge-weighted, 291
    undirected, 13
Greatest common divisor (GCD), 328
Greibach, S., 131
Greibach, S.A., 93
Gross, M., 93
Grzegorczyk, A., 243

H
Haines, L.G., 131
HALT$_{TM}$, 187
Halting Problem, 174, 187
HAMCYCLE, 264, 282, 321
Hamilton cycle, 264
Hamiltonian, 264
Hamilton path, 264

HAMPATH, 264, 280, 321
Hartmanis, J., 242
Head, 135
    reading by, 135
    writing by, 135
Head move
    left, 135
    right, 135
    stationary, 135
Hemaspaandra, L.A., 360
Hennie, F.C., 243
Hoeffding, W., 345
Homomorphism, 171
Huang, M.-D.A., 345
Huffman, D.A., 55

I
ID, (*see* Instantaneous description (ID))
Identity, 330
Immerman, N., 261
Immerman-Szelepscényi Theorem, 252
Indistinguishability, (*see* State,
        distinguishability)
INDEPENDENTSET, 290, 321
INFINITE$_{CFG}$, 183
INFINITE$_{DPDA}$, 181
INFINITE$_{FA}$, 178
INFINITE$_{TM}$, 188
Instantaneous description (ID), 97, 142, 151
    accepting, 97, 192
    initial, 97, 192
Isolation technique, 360

J
Jacobi symbol, 345
Johnson, D.S., 292

K
Karp, R.M., 292, 360
Kasami, T., 183
Kayal, N., 345
Kleene-plus, (*see* ++Kleene-plus)
Kleene, S.C., 72, 169
Kleene-star, (*see* *)
KNAPSACK, 286
Knuth, D.E., 56
Kobayashi, K., 243
Ko, K.-I., 344
Komlós, J., 360
Krentel, M.W., 321

L

L, 250
Ladner, R.E., 321
Lall, A., viii
Language, 10
    diagonal, 231
    non-context-free, 117
Lautemann, C., 345
Laws
    associative, 6
    commutative, 6
    De Morgan's, 5
    distributive, 6
L_{diag}, 186
Least common multiple (LCM), 329
Length-bounded
    logarithmic, 359
    polynomial, 352
Levin, L.A., 292
Linear bounded automaton, 183
Linear Speed-up Theorem, 216, 234
Lin, R., viii
Lipton, R.J., 345, 360
Literal, 6
    negative, 6, 270
    positive, 6, 270
Logic, 6
    contraposition, 6
    contrapositive, 6
    equivalence, 6
    implication, 6
    relation, 6
Logic game, 316
LONGESTPATH, 292
Loop invariant, 329
L_{self}, 186

M

Ma, K., viii
Mapping, (*see* Function)
Marker, 160
    left-end, 149, 160, 216, 245
    right-end, 149, 245
Matrix multiplication, 12, 351
McCulloch, W.S., 55, 72
McNaughton, R., 72
Mealy, G.H., 55
MERGESORT, 359
Meyer, A.R., 243, 321
Miller, G.L., 345
Miller-Rabin test, 335
Miller test, 340
mod, 329

Moore, E.F., 55
Morris, J.H., 56
MPCP, (*see* Post's Correspondence Problem,
    Marked)
Mulmuley, K., 360
Multiplicative monoid, 330
Myhill, J., 72
Myhill-Nerode Theorem, 62, 64

N

NAE assignment, (*see* Assignment,
    not-all-equal)
NAESAT, 272
Nerode, A., 72
Nick's Circuit Class (NC), 349
Node, 11
Nondeterministic exponential time
    (NEXPTIME), 235, 250
Nondeterministic finite automaton (NFA), 30
Nondeterministic logspace (NL), 250, 350
Nondeterministic polynomial space
    (NSPACE), 248
Nondeterministic polynomial time (NP), 235,
    250
Nondeterministic Space Hierarchy Theorem,
    250
Non-terminal, (*see* variables)
NONTOTAL$_{CFG}$, 191
Nontrivial property, 190
NP^A, 303
NP^C, 303
NP-complete, 265
NP-hard, 265
NTIME, 233
NTM, (*see* Turing machine, nondeterministic)
NTMCANONICAL, 266
Numbers, 4
    integer, 4
    natural, 4
    positive rational, 4
    positive real, 4
    rational, 4
    real, 4

O

Occam's Razor, 57
ODDMAXSAT, 299
ODDMAXSUM, 303
Oettinger, A.G., 131
Ogden's Lemma, 118
Ogden, W.F., 131
Ogihara, E., viii

Ogihara, M., 344, 360
Oracle, 203
    positive correctness, 300
    query consistency, 300

P
P, 234, 250
P/log, 359
P/poly, 352
P^A, 298
P^C, 299
Palindrome, 67, 99, 143, 193
Parikh, R.J., 93
Partial order, 265
PARTITION, 285, 320
Paterson, M.S., 360
Path, 12, 119
    computation, 106
    destination of, 12
    source of, 12
    straight, 112, 119
PDA, (see Pushdown automaton (PDA))
    equivance to CFL, 101
Perles, M., 72, 131
Pigeon-hole principle, 66, 111, 112, 119, 124,
        125, 127, 128
Pippenger, N., 360
Pitts, W.A., 55, 72
PNF, (see Boolean formula, prenex normal
        form)
P^{NP}, 299
P vs. NP Problem, 235, 263
Polynomial, 234
    multivariate, 340
Polynomial hierarchy (PH), 303, 343
    characterization of, 306
Post's Correspondence Problem (PCP),
        195
    Marked, 196
Post, E.L., 169
Powering, 338
Pratt, V., 345
Pratt, V.R., 56
Predicate, 7
    binary, 7
    domain, 7
    ternary, 7
    unary, 7
Primality testing, 328
Prime factorization, 328
Prime number, 328
Prime Number Theorem, 335

PRIMES, 335
Probabilistic polynomial time (PP), 343
Probability
    error, 326
    success, 326
Problem
    acceptance, 173, 175
    computation, 285
    containment, 173, 179
    decision, 285
    emptiness, 173, 177
    equality, 173, 180
    infiniteness, 173, 178
    totality, 173, 179, 191
Production, 73
    leftmost, 79
    rightmost, 79
    sequence, 74
Production rule, 73
    component of, 74
    length of, 74
Production tree, 77, 112, 119
Promerance, C., 345
Proof, 15
    by contradiction, 15, 80, 313
    by counterexample, 15
    by induction, 16, 306, 332, 340
    by inference, 15
    by pigeon-hole principle ((see Proof, by
            piegeon-hole principle))
Pseudoprime, 339
PSIZE, 349
PSPACE, 250
PSPACE-complete, 314
PSPCANONICAL, 314
Pumping Lemma
    for CFL, 111
    for REG, 66
Pushdown automaton (PDA), 95, 181
    deterministic, 108

Q
q_0, 136
q_{acc}, 136
q_{no}, 203
q_{query}, 203
q_{rej}, 136
Quantified Boolean formula (QBF), 304
Quantifier, 8
    existential, 8
    universal, 8
q_{yes}, 203

R
R, 138
Rabin, M.O., 55, 56, 345
Random bit, 325
Random number generator, 336
Random polynomial time (RP), 327, 355
Reachability, 12, 17, 249, 252, 356
Recipient, 334
Recognizing
    by a nondeterministic Turing machine, 158
Recursive, 137
Recursively enumerable, 137, 156, 158, 162,
    203
Recursively enumerable languages (RE), 138
Reducibility
    Cook, 292, 298
    Cook-Levin, 292
    Karp, 292, 298
    many-one, 189
    polynomial-time conjunctive truth-table,
      305
    polynomial-time disjunctive truth-table,
      305
    polynomial-time many-one, 263
    polynomial-time Turing, 292, 295, 298
    witness-preserving, 301
Regular expression, 44, 180, 238
    equivalent to FA, 45
    inductive construction, 44
    visualizing construction of, 50
Regular language (REG), 26
Reinhardt, K., 360
Rejecting
    by a nondeterministic Turing machine, 136
Relation, 7
    binary, 7
    equivalence, 7, 58, 59, 62
    reflexive, 7, 59, 189, 290, 320
    symmetric, 7, 58, 59, 189
    transitive, 7, 59, 189, 265, 290, 320
Relatively prime, 329
Reverse, 67
Rice's Theorem, 188, 190
Rives, H., viii
Rivest, R.L., 345
Rogers, Jr., H., 169
Root, 14
Rose, G.F., 72
Rosenberg, B., viii
Rosenkrantz, D.J., 93
RSA cryptography, 334
Rule
    ϵ, 82
    long, 82

    mixed, 82
    terminal-only, 82
    unit, 82
    variable only, 82
Ruzzo, W.L., 360

S
Satisfiability Problem, SAT, 268
Satisfiability Problem, (SAT), 268
Savitch's Theorem, 248, 250, 314
Savitch, W.L., 261
Saxena, N., 345
Saxe, J.B., 360
Schaefer, T.J., 293, 321
SCHEDULING, 286
Schöning, U., 360
Schützenberger, M.P., 93, 131
Schwartz, J.T., 183, 345
Scott, D., 55, 56
Search
    depth-first, 250
    exhaustive, 17
Search reduces to the decision, 297, 320
    CNFSAT, 297
    SUBSETSUM, 298
Seiferas, J.I., 243
Self-loop, 13
Self-reducibility, 359
Selfridge, J.L., 345
Semi-unbounded alternate circuits class (SAC),
    349, 350
Sender, 334
Sénizergues, G., 183
Sets, **3**
    cardinality of, 4
    Cartesian product of, 5, 43
    complement of, 4
    difference of, 4
    disjoint, 4
    element of, 3
    empty, 3
    finite, 4
    infinite, 4
    intersection of, 4
    join of, 4
    meet of, 4
    member of, 3
    membership, 3
    power, 4, 31
    size of, 4
    specification of, 3
    symmetric difference of, 4, 266
    union of, 4

Shamir, A., 345
Shamir, E., 72, 131
Simon, J., 344
Simulation
    of an NP-oracle, 301
    single-tape, 220
    two-tape, 220, 221
Single-tape Simulation Theorem,
        220
Sipser, M.J., 345, 360
Solovay, R., 345
Space, 215
Space Compression Theorem, 246
Space Hierarchy Theorem, 246
Spanier, E.H., 72
Spencer, J.H., 360
Squiggle, 143
Stack, 95
    popping from, 95
    pushing onto, 95, 96
Star, (see *)
State, 24, 135
    accepting, 136
    distinguishability, 57
    final, 24, 96
    initial, 24, 96, 136
    minimization, 57, 291
    of a pushdown automaton, 96
    rejecting, 136
State set, 24, 135
Stearns, R.E., 242, 243
Stirling, C., 183
Stockmeyer, L.J., 321
Strassen, V., 345
String, 10
    concatenation, 10
    empty, 10
    prefix of, 10
    proper prefix of, 10
    proper suffix of, 10
    suffix of, 10
Subgraph, 13
    edge-induced, 13
    proper, 13
    vertex-induced, 13
Subset, 3
    proper, 3
SUBSET$_{\text{CFG}}$, 193
SUBSET$_{\text{DPDA}}$, 193
SUBSET$_{\text{FA}}$, 179
SUBSET$_{\text{NFA}}$, 180
SUBSET$_{\text{REX}}$, 180
SUBSETSUM, 284
SUBSET$_{\text{TM}}$, 188

Substring, 10
    proper, 10
Subword, 10
    proper ((see Substring, proper))
Sudborough, I.H., 360
Superset, 3
    proper, 3
Symbol, 10
    blank, 136
    bottom, 95
    initial, 95, 96
Szelepscényi, R., 261
Szemerédi, E., 360

T
Tape, 135
    finite, 135
    infinite, 135
    input, 245
    one-way infinite, 135
    oracle, 203
    output, 162
    read-only, 245
    tracks, 152
    two-way infinite, 135, 222
    work, 245
    write-only, 203, 245
TAUTOLOGY, 273, 359
Tautology, 8, 273
Terminal, 73
Time, 215
$time_M$, 215
Time complexity, 215
Time Hierarchy Theorem, 230, 233
TM, (see Turing machine (TM))
    nondeterministic, 233
    normalization of, 299, 321
    oracle, 295
    probabilistic, 325
    single-tape, 321
    time-bounded, 215, 233
Toda, S., 344, 360
Toda's Theorem, 343
TOTAL$_{\text{CFG}}$, 191, 193
TOTAL$_{\text{DPDA}}$, 181
TOTAL$_{\text{FA}}$, 179
TOTAL$_{\text{NFA}}$, 180
TOTAL$_{\text{REX}}$, 180
TOTAL$_{\text{TM}}$, 188
TQBF, 314
Track, 222
Tractable, 234
Transducer, 165

Transition
    diagram ((*see* Diagram, transition))
    ϵ, 30
    table, 25
Transition function, (*see* Function, transition)
Traveling Salesman Problem, 291
Tree, 11, 14
    binary, 14
    height of, 14
True, 5
Turing, A.M., 169, 183
Turing machine (TM), 135
    k-tape, 149
    deterministic, 157
    halting, 158
    multi-tape, 149, 175
    nondeterministic, 157
    offline, 149, 245
    oracle, 203
    recognition by, 137
    simulation of, 152
    single-tape, 149
    space-bounded, 245, 247
    universal, 172

U
Ullian, J., 93
Unambiguous Logspace (UL), 356
Uncountable, 185
Uniformity, 349
    logspace, 349
    P, 349
Universe, 4
UNSAT, 273
UP, 355
USAT, 355

V
Valiant, L.G., 360
Variable, 73
    nullable, 82
    start, 73
    useless, 92

Vazirani, U., 360
Vazirani, V.V., 360
Vertex cover, 276
VERTEXCOVER, 276, 320
Vertices, 11
    depth of, 14
    destination, 11
    distance from, 14
    leaf, 14
    parent of, 14
    sink, 12
    source, 11, 12
Von Neumann, J., 292
Von zur Gathen, J., 360

W
Wagstaff, S.S., 345
Winning strategy, 316, 318, 319
Wire, 347
Witness, 165, 267, 295
Witness language, 267
Witness scheme, 165, 295, 353
    polynomial-time, 267
Word, (*see* String)
Worst-case complexity, 216

X
X3C, 289
Xia, M., viii

Y
Yamada, H., 72
Younger, D.H., 183

Z
Zero-polynomial testing, 340
Zippel, R., 345
Z_n, 329
Z_n^*, 330
ZPP, 327

The manufacturer's authorised representative in the EU is Springer
Nature Customer Service Centre GmbH, Europaplatz 3, 69115 Heidelberg,
Germany. If you have any concerns regarding our products, please
contact ProductSafety@springernature.com

Printed and bound by CPI Group (UK) Ltd, Croydon, CR0 4YY
29/04/2026
02099543-0003